# THE ART OF ANGLO-SAXON ENGLAND

BOYDELL STUDIES IN MEDIEVAL ART AND ARCHITECTURE

ISSN 2045–4902

Series Editors
Dr Julian Luxford
Professor Asa Simon Mittman

This series aims to provide a forum for debate on the art and architecture of the Middle Ages. It will cover all media, from manuscript illuminations to maps, tapestries, carvings, wall-paintings and stained glass, and all periods and regions, including Byzantine art. Both traditional and more theoretical approaches to the subject are welcome.

Proposals or queries should be sent in the first instance to the editors or to the publisher, at the addresses given below.

Dr Julian Luxford, School of Art History, University of St Andrews, 79 North Street, St Andrews, Fife, KY16 9AL, UK

Professor Asa Simon Mittman, Department of Art and Art History, California State University at Chico, Chico, CA 95929–0820, USA

Boydell & Brewer, PO Box 9, Woodbridge, Suffolk, IP12 3DF, UK

Previously published titles in the series are listed at the back of this volume.

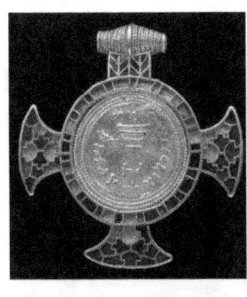
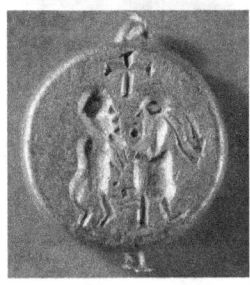
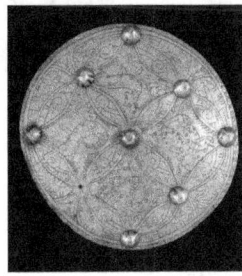
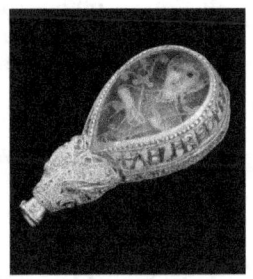

# THE ART OF ANGLO-SAXON ENGLAND

Catherine E. Karkov

THE BOYDELL PRESS

© Catherine E. Karkov 2011

*All Rights Reserved.* Except as permitted under current legislation
no part of this work may be photocopied, stored in a retrieval system,
published, performed in public, adapted, broadcast,
transmitted, recorded or reproduced in any form or by any means,
without the prior permission of the copyright owner

The right of Catherine E. Karkov to be identified as
the author of this work has been asserted in accordance with
sections 77 and 78 of the Copyright, Designs and Patents Act 1988

First published 2011
The Boydell Press, Woodbridge
Paperback edition 2016

ISBN 978 1 84383 628 5 hardback
ISBN 978 1 78327 095 8 paperback

The Boydell Press is an imprint of Boydell & Brewer Ltd
PO Box 9, Woodbridge, Suffolk, IP12 3DF, UK
and of Boydell & Brewer Inc.
668 Mt Hope Avenue, Rochester, NY 14620–2731, USA
website: www.boydellandbrewer.com

The publisher has no responsibility for the continued existence or accuracy
of URLs for external or third-party internet websites referred to in this
book, and does not guarantee that any content on such websites is, or will
remain, accurate or appropriate

A CIP catalogue record for this book is available
from the British Library

# CONTENTS

*List of Illustrations*   vi
*Abbreviations*   xi
*Acknowledgements*   xiii

    INTRODUCTION   1

1. THE ART OF ORIGINS   11
2. SACRED SPACE   43
3. ART, STATUS AND AUTHORITY   96
4. OBJECT AND VOICE   135
5. BOOKS, WORDS AND BODIES   179
6. ART AND CONQUEST   247

*Bibliography*   293
*Index*   315

# ILLUSTRATIONS

**Colour plates (between pp. 178 and 179)**

Plate 1   Shoulder clasps from Sutton Hoo Mound 1 (by permission of the British Museum)
Plate 2   Sarre brooch and necklace (by permission of the British Museum)
Plate 3   Lichfield angel with colour digitally restored (courtesy of Lichfield Cathedral)
Plate 4   Salisbury Psalter, fol. 122 (by permission of Salisbury Cathedral; photo: R. J. L. Smith of Much Wenlock)
Plate 5   Portrait of the scribe Eadwine, Eadwine Psalter. Cambridge, Trinity College Library, MS R.17.1, fol. 283v (by permission of the Master and Fellows, Trinity College, Cambridge)
Plate 6   Page with crosses, Stockholm Codex Aureus. Stockholm, Royal Library, MS A.135, fol. 11 (by permission of the Royal Library, Stockholm)
Plate 7   Portrait of Eadwig from the Eadwig Psalter. London, BL, MS Arundel 155, fol. 133 (copyright The British Library Board, all rights reserved)
Plate 8   Dedication of a church, Benedictional of Æthelwold. London, BL, MS Add. 49598, fol. 118v (copyright The British Library Board, all rights reserved)
Plate 9   St Swithun, Benedictional of Æthelwold. London, BL, MS Add. 49598, fol. 90v (copyright The British Library Board, all rights reserved)
Plate 10  Ascension of Christ, Sacramentary of Robert of Jumièges. Rouen, Bibl. Mun. MS Y 6, fol. 81v (by permission of the Bibliothèque Municipale, Rouen)
Plate 11  Harrowing of Hell, the Tiberius Psalter. London, BL, MS Cotton Tiberius C.vi, fol. 14 (copyright The British Library Board, all rights reserved)
Plate 12  Emma and Cnut present a cross to the New Minster Winchester, New Minster Liber Vitae. London, BL, MS Stowe 944, fol. 6 (copyright The British Library Board, all rights reserved)

ILLUSTRATIONS

## Black and white figures

| | | |
|---|---|---|
| Fig. 1 | Fifth-century belt buckle from Mucking (by permission of the British Museum) | 12 |
| Fig. 2 | Plan of early Anglo-Saxon Canterbury (after Gameson, *St Augustine and the Conversion of England*, pl. 2) | 14 |
| Fig. 3 | St Martin's Canterbury (photo, Helen Gittos). | 15 |
| Fig. 4 | Large hanging bowl from Sutton Hoo Mound 1 (by permission of the British Museum). | 22 |
| Fig. 5 | Detail of figure 4 (by permission of the British Museum) | 23 |
| Fig. 6 | Wilton cross pendant (by permission of the British Museum) | 28 |
| Fig. 7 | Carpet page, Lindisfarne Gospels. London, BL, MS Cotton Nero D.iv, fol. 26v (copyright The British Library Board, all rights reserved) | 30 |
| Fig. 8 | Portrait of St Matthew, Lindisfarne Gospels. London, BL, MS Cotton Nero D.iv, fol. 25v (copyright The British Library Board, all rights reserved) | 37 |
| Fig. 9 | Copenhagen Gospels, portrait of St Matthew. Copenhagen, Kongelige Bibliotek, MS Gl. Kgl. Sml 10, 2º, fol. 17v (by permission of the Kongelige Bibliotek) | 40 |
| Fig. 10 | Plan of Wearmouth, phase 1 (after Cramp, *Wearmouth and Jarrow Monastic Sites*, vol. 1, p. 96) | 46 |
| Fig. 11 | Door jamb, porch of St Peter's Wearmouth (author) | 48 |
| Fig. 12 | Herebericht stone, St Peter's Wearmouth (courtesy of CASSS; photo T. Middlemass) | 51 |
| Fig. 13 | Plan of church and monastic buildings, Jarrow (after Cramp, *Wearmouth and Jarrow Monastic Sites*, vol. 1, p. 149) | 53 |
| Fig. 14 | Fragment with vinescroll, St Paul's Jarrow (courtesy of CASSS; photo T. Middlemas) | 56 |
| Fig. 15 | Hexham Abbey, crypt (after Taylor and Taylor, *Anglo-Saxon Architecture*, vol. 3, p. 1016) | 60 |
| Fig. 16 | Fragment with vinescroll, Hexham (courtesy of CASSS; photo T. Middlemass) | 62 |
| Fig. 17 | Fragment with vinescroll, Hexham (photo author, by permission of the Dean and Chapter, Durham Cathedral) | 63 |
| Fig. 18 | Panel with rosette decoration, Hexham (photo author) | 64 |
| Fig. 19 | Acca's Cross, Hexham (courtesy of CASSS; photo T. Middlemass) | 65 |
| Fig. 20 | Bewcastle Cross, west side (photo author) | 70 |
| Fig. 21 | Bewcastle Cross, south side (photo author) | 71 |
| Fig. 22 | Ruthwell Cross, Annunciation (courtesy of CASSS; photo T. Middlemass) | 80 |
| Fig. 23 | Breedon-on-the-Hill angel (photo author) | 81 |
| Fig. 24 | Winterbourne Steepleton angel (courtesy CASSS; photo D. Craig) | 82 |

| | | |
|---|---|---|
| Fig. 25 | Inglesham Virgin and Child (courtesy CASSS; photo K. Jukes and D. Craig) | 84 |
| Fig. 26 | Reliquary cross (by permission of the Victoria and Albert Museum) | 87 |
| Fig. 27 | Virgin and Child panel from the coffin of St Cuthbert | 92 |
| Fig. 28 | Osgyth name stone, Lindisfarne | 93 |
| Fig. 29 | Hackness Cross (courtesy of CASSS; photo T. Middlemass) | 94 |
| Fig. 30 | Desborough necklace (by permission of the British Museum) | 98 |
| Fig. 31 | Plan of Yeavering (author) | 100 |
| Fig. 32 | The Repton Stone (author) | 103 |
| Fig. 33 | Imitation dinar of Offa (by permission of the British Museum) | 105 |
| Fig. 34 | Ivory panel from Larling (by permission of the Castle Museum and Art Gallery, Norwich) | 107 |
| Fig. 35 | Baldhild ring, reverse (by permission of the Castle Museum and Art Gallery, Norwich) | 123 |
| Fig. 36 | Rings of Æthelwulf and Æthelswith (by permission of the British Museum) | 125 |
| Fig. 37 | Coin of Cynethryth (by permission of the British Museum) | 127 |
| Fig. 38 | Godwine seal (by permission of the British Museum) | 130 |
| Fig. 39 a and b. | Ruthwell Cross, vinescroll and runic inscription (courtesy of CASSS; photo T. Middlemass) | 136 |
| Fig. 40 | Ruthwell Cross, original east side (photo author) | 139 |
| Fig. 41 a and b. | Franks Casket, front and back panels (by permission of the British Museum) | 146 |
| Fig. 42 | Coppergate helmet (by permission of the Castle Museum, York) | 154 |
| Fig. 43 | St Ninian's Isle chape (by permission of the National Museum of Scotland) | 156 |
| Fig. 44 a and b. | Sutton, Isle of Ely, brooch (by permission of the British Museum) | 157 |
| Fig. 45 | The Brussels Reliquary Cross (by permission of the Cathedral of St Michael and St Gudule; photo Christopher R. Fee and James Rutkowski, Gettysburg College [http://public.gettysburg.edu/~cfee/MedievalNorthAtlantic/] | 159 |
| Fig. 46 | Durham Gospels, Crucifixion (by permission of the Dean and Chapter, Durham Cathedral) | 166 |
| Fig. 47 | Portrait of Dunstan with Christ, St Dunstan's Classbook. Oxford, Bodl. Lib. Auct. F.4.32, fol. 1 (by permission of the Bodleian Library) | 168 |
| Fig. 48 | Christ Judge. Cambridge, Trinity College Library, MS .15.34, fol. 1 (by permission of the Master and Fellows, Trinity College, Cambridge) | 172 |
| Fig. 49 | Bury Psalter Creation, Vatican, Biblioteca Apostolica, Reg. lat. 12, fol. 68v (by permission of the Biblioteca Apostolica) | 180 |

ILLUSTRATIONS

| | | |
|---|---|---|
| Fig. 50 | Incipit to Matthew, Lindisfarne Gospels, London, BL, MS Cotton Nero D.iv, fol. 27 (copyright The British Library Board, all rights reserved) | 183 |
| Fig. 51 | Chi-rho page, Stockholm Codex Aureus. Stockholm, Royal Library, MS A.135, fol. 161 (by permission of the Royal Library, Stockholm) | 184 |
| Fig. 52 | St Luke, Reims Gospels. Reims, Bibl. Mun., MS 9, fol. 88 (by permission of the Bibliothèque Municipale, Reims) | 192 |
| Fig. 53 | St Matthew, The Book of Cerne. Cambridge, University Library, Ll.1.10, fol. 2v (by permission of the University Library, Cambridge) | 194 |
| Fig. 54 | St John, The Book of Cerne, Cambridge, University Library, Ll.1.10, fol. 31v (by permission of the University Library, Cambridge) | 195 |
| Fig. 55 | Crucifixion, the Ramsey Psalter. London, British Library, MS Harley 2904, fol. 3v (copyright The British Library Board, all rights reserved) | 196 |
| Fig. 56 | Ancestors of Christ, Boulogne Gospels. Boulogne, Bibl. Mun. MS 11, fol. 11v (by permission of the Bibliothèque Municipale, Boulogne) | 200 |
| Fig. 57 | Annunciation and Nativity, Boulogne Gospels. Boulogne, Bibl. Mun. MS 11, fol. 12 (by permission of the Bibliothèque Municipale, Boulogne) | 201 |
| Fig. 58 | St John, Arenberg Gospels. New York, Pierpont Morgan Library, M. 869, fol. 126v (by permission of the Pierpont Morgan Library) | 204 |
| Fig. 59 | Canon Table, Hereford Gospels. Cambridge, Pembroke College MS 302, fol. 5v (by permission of the Master and Fellows, Pembroke College, Cambridge) | 210 |
| Fig. 60 | Canon Table, Hereford Gospels. Cambridge, Pembroke College, MS 302, fol. 6 (by permission of the Master and Fellows, Pembroke College, Cambridge) | 211 |
| Fig. 61 | The Alfred Jewel (by permission of the Ashmolean Museum, Oxford) | 215 |
| Fig. 62 | The Bowleaze Cove Jewel (by permission of the British Museum) | 218 |
| Fig. 63 | Ivory pen box (by permission of the British Museum) | 219 |
| Fig. 64 | St. Æthelthryth, Benedictional of Æthelwold, London, BL, MS Add. 49598, fol. 97v (copyright The British Library Board, all rights reserved) | 226 |
| Fig. 65 | The nuns of Barking receive their book from Aldhelm, *De Virginitate*. London, Lambeth Palace Library MS 200, fol. 68v (by permission of Lambeth Palace Library) | 229 |
| Fig. 66 | Death and Coronation of the Virgin, Benedictional of Archbishop Robert. Rouen, Bibl. Mun. MS Y. 7, fol. 54v (by permission of the Bibliothèque Municipale, Rouen) | 232 |

| Fig. 67 | Satan sends his messenger to tempt Adam and Eve. Oxford, Bodl. Lib., MS Junius 11, p. 20 (by permission of the Bodleian Library) | 241 |
| Fig. 68 | Detail of Satan. Oxford, Bodl. Lib., MS Junius 11, p. 20 (by permission of the Bodleian Library). | 242 |
| Fig. 69 | Bowl from the Halton Moor hoard (by permission of the British Museum) | 250 |
| Fig. 70 | Pentney brooches (by permission of the British Museum) | 251 |
| Fig. 71 | Three of the Brompton hogbacks (courtesy of CASSS; photo T. Middlemass). | 253 |
| Fig. 72 | The Gosforth Cross (courtesy of CASSS; photo T. Middlemass) | 255 |
| Fig. 73 | The Kirkdale sundial (courtesy of CASSS; photo T. Middlemass) | 259 |
| Fig. 74 | Cross head, Durham Cathedral (courtesy of CASSS; photo T. Middlemass) | 261 |
| Fig. 75 | Agnus Dei penny (by permission of the British Museum) | 262 |
| Fig. 76 | Emma Enthroned, *Encomium Emmae*. London, BL, MS Add. 33241, fol. 1v (copyright The British Library Board, all rights reserved) | 268 |
| Fig. 77 | St Matthew, St Margaret's Gospel. Oxford, Bodl. Lib., MS Lat. Liturg. F.5, fol. 3v (by permission of the Bodleian Library) | 272 |
| Fig. 78 | Discovery of Cuthbert's incorrupt body, Life of Cuthbert. Oxford, University College MS 165, p. 118 (by permission of the Master and Fellows, University College, Oxford) | 279 |
| Fig. 79 | Durham Cathedral (photo Richard Morris) | 282 |
| Fig. 80 | Cnut Enthroned, Life and Miracles of Edmund. New York, Pierpont Morgan Library, M 736, fol. 41v (by permission of the Pierpont Morgan Library) | 284 |
| Fig. 81 | Gregory the Great, Dialogues of Gregory. Oxford, Bodl. Lib., MS Tanner 3, fol. 1 (by permission of the Bodleian Library) | 286 |
| Fig. 82 | Cotton Mappamundi. London, BL, MS Cotton Tiberius B.v, fol. 56v (copyright The British Library Board, all rights reserved) | 288 |

# ABBREVIATIONS

| | |
|---|---|
| ASC | Anglo-Saxon Chronicle |
| *ASE* | *Anglo-Saxon England* |
| *ASSAH* | *Anglo-Saxon Studies in History and Archaeology* |
| BAR | British Archaeological Reports |
| BL | British Library |
| Bodl. Lib. | Bodleian Library |
| CASSS | Corpus of Anglo-Saxon Stone Sculpture |
| CCCC | Corpus Christi College, Cambridge |
| CCCM | Corpus Christianorum Continuatio Mediaevalis |
| CCSL | Corpus Christianorum, Series Latina |
| CSEL | Corpus Scriptorum Ecclesiasticorum Latinorum |
| EEMF | Early English Manuscripts in Facsimile |
| EETS | Early English Text Society |
| *EHR* | *English Historical Review* |
| *FS* | *Frühmittelalterliche Studien* |
| HE | *Bede's Ecclesiastical History of the English People*, ed. Bertram Colgrave and R. A. B. Mynors (Oxford, 1991, rev. edn) |
| *JBAA* | *Journal of the British Archaeological Association* |
| *JEGP* | *Journal of English and Germanic Philology* |
| *JMEMS* | *Journal of Medieval and Early Modern Studies* |
| *JWCI* | *Journal of the Warburg and Courtauld Institute* |
| Ker | N. R. Ker, *Catalogue of Manuscripts Containing Anglo-Saxon* (Oxford, 1957) |
| *MÆ* | *Medium Aevum* |
| MGH | Monumenta Germaniae Historica |
| n.s. | new series |
| o.s. | original series |
| *PL* | *Patrologiae cursus completus, Series Latina*, ed. J-P. Migne. Paris, 1844–82 |
| S | P. H. Sawyer, ed., *Anglo-Saxon Charters: an Annotated List and Bibliography* (London, 1968) |
| *s.a.* | *sub anno* |
| s.s. | supplementary series |

# ACKNOWLEDGEMENTS

I would like to thank the following for help and advice of various kinds during the writing of this book: Fred Orton, Ian Wood, Clare Lees, Barbara Engh, Pat Conner, Elaine Treharne, Chris Jones, Helen Damico, Roy Liuzza, Michael Hare, Hal Momma, Mary Swan, Lara Eggleton, Alex Hannay, Nancy Wicker, Karen Overbey, Michelle Brown, Jane Rosenthal, Martin Foys, Rosemary Cramp, Éamonn Ó Carragáin, the late Nick Howe, Richard Morris, Simon Keynes, Anna Gannon, Tony Abramson, Sarah Larratt Keefer, Karen Jolly, Eva Frojmovic and the participants in our AHRC Network *Postcolonising the Medieval Image*. I would also like to express my gratitude to Caroline Palmer for her infinite patience, and to the British Academy for a grant towards the purchase of illustrations. Finally, a special thanks to Boris and Natasha for their editorial expertise. Any errors that remain are of course my own.

# INTRODUCTION

The subject of this book is the art of Anglo-Saxon England, that is, the art produced in England or by English artists between roughly the sixth and the twelfth centuries. It is not intended as a conventional survey in that it does not present a linear history of 'styles', 'iconographies' and 'influences', and it is not encyclopaedic. Nevertheless it does provide coverage of the broad range of art produced in Anglo-Saxon England, its major patrons and its primary audiences. My intention is threefold. Firstly, I want to provide a discussion of the different types of images and monuments, their meanings and their functions, that make the art of this particular time and place unique. Secondly, I am particularly interested in the ways in which Anglo-Saxon art works to create and narrate the processes of becoming a culture or a nation, and to map its changing identities. Thirdly, I hope to provide some sense of just what it is that makes Anglo-Saxon art 'art' rather than a series of historical or archaeological artefacts. Art and material culture in general played a significant role in the making of England and English identity, and were every bit as active a force in the political and cultural discourse of the time as were texts. However 'art' by definition has an aesthetic and emotional value and a visual language of its own. In fact, these two qualities, art as active force and art as aesthetic vehicle, are integral to each other; they allow us to talk about what makes something a work of art, but also to talk about the work that art does in the creation of a people, a culture or a nation.

This book is then a study of the art produced in England during the centuries in which England was itself coming into being; that is during the period in which it was transformed from sub-Roman Britain to Anglo-Saxon England, to Anglo Scandinavian England, to Anglo-Norman England. The variety of names by which the same basic geographic area is known, and the hyphenation of all of them, are indicative of the waves of conquerors and settlers who came to the island during the 600 or so years with which this book is concerned. While cultures never exist in total isolation, and are always formed in response to contacts with other cultures, the repeated arrival of new peoples to the nascent England makes this process of encounter and tranformation manifest exceptionally clearly in the visual (and textual) record. For all these reasons, a postcolonial approach to Anglo-Saxon art, the approach taken in this book, is particularly appropriate.

Anglo-Saxonists in other fields (mainly literature) have already demonstrated the value of postcolonial theory both in understanding and in asking new questions about Anglo-Saxon England. Both Kathleen Davis and Nicholas Howe, amongst others, have explored the role that language, text and writing played in constructing England as a place with a national and cultural identity both real and imagined.[1] In many ways this is to be expected, as language is at the core of postcolonial theory, most especially in its focus on the ways in which the languages of colonized and colonizer transform the construction and perception of identity, whether personal, national or cultural.[2] Art history, however, is a conservative discipline, at least when it comes to the study of medieval art and, even though most would agree that art has a visual language, art historians have been slow to accept contemporary critical theory of any sort.[3] In the conventional language of the art historian, art 'reflects' influences, 'copies' models and 'illustrates' texts or ideas. It has meaning, but that meaning is often understood solely in religious terms, and rarely is early medieval art of any type understood as actively producing cultural or political meaning in its own right. The art historical terminology (influences, copies, models) also implies that the development of art is a straightforward, passive and rather unidirectional phenomenon. Discussions of the influence of Rome or the Carolingians on Anglo-Saxon art, for example, usually assume that the art of a culture more advanced in certain ways (a more classical figure style, the ability to construct monumental stone architecture) has a positive impact on the development of the more 'primitive' art of a culture that is in one way or another perceived as less accomplished. Alternatively, the more 'primitive' culture, Celtic Britain for example, can have a 'negative' influence on the art of the more sophisticated culture, in this case that of the Roman conquerors, leading to the latter's degradation as it comes into contact with 'mere pattern'.[4] Such scenarios construct a cultural hierarchy in which the art of one culture colonizes that of the other, although they are rarely discussed in these terms. From a postcolonial point of view, however, British and Roman art are actually in negotiation with each other, with neither culture, nor the art of that culture, established as more

---

[1] Kathleen Davis, 'National Writing in the Ninth Century: A Reminder for Postcolonial Thinking about the North', *JMEMS* 28.3 (1998), 61–37; Nicholas Howe, *Writing the Map of Anglo-Saxon England: Essays in Cultural Geography* (New Haven, CT, 2008).
[2] See, for example, Homi K. Bhabha, *Nation and Narration* (London, 1990); Bhabha, *The Location of Culture* (London, 1994).
[3] See, e.g., the recent conservative critique by Herbert R. Broderick III: 'Meta-textuality, Sexuality and Intervisuality in MS Junius 11', *Word and Image* 25.4 (2009), 384–401.
[4] Martin Henig, *The Art of Roman Britain* (London, 1995), ch. 1.

sophisticated than the other. The result of such encounters is a series of shifting hybrid identities, each of the original cultures leaving its mark on the other in a way that allows for the emergence of a third space, in the particular case at hand, Romano-Britain.[5] From the Romano-British encounter with the Germanic peoples who settled in Britain in the fifth and sixth centuries comes the third space of Anglo-Saxon England, and so forth.

The concept of hybridity does itself need some interrogation. Hybridity has multiple meanings and the word cannot be used the same way in all contexts. On the simplest level it can refer to the fact that no culture is pure, cultures always show the evidence of contact with other cultures that leads to changes (hybridities) within both cultures. The Lindisfarne Gospels (figs. 7, 8, 50), for example, could be called the hybrid product of the encounter of Anglo-Saxon culture with the cultures of the Irish and Mediterranean worlds. On another level, hybridity is the product of a process of translation and counter-translation between cultures. Translation in postcolonial studies is often limited to language and literature,[6] but we can see similar processes at work in the translation of the visual language of Romano-British art into Anglo-Saxon art, and the counter-translation of the language of Anglo-Saxon art into Romano-British contexts at Hexham Abbey (figs. 15, 16, 17, 19), or in the Anglo-Norman 'tracing' of an Anglo-Saxon image of the Roman Pope Gregory the Great (fig. 81). On yet a third level, hybridity is a new space (the 'third space') that locates itself between cultures or displaces the cultures from which it is born. Anglo-Scandinavian art in northern England demonstrates just such a hybridity. It emerges from Anglo-Saxon art and Scandinavian art, but it displaces both, establishing something that both references yet is very different from the art of either pre-existing culture. Hybridity can also be the result of mimicry, the desire to appear 'authentic', a desire that it is possible to see at work in the production of the very Italianate Codex Amiatinus at Wearmouth-Jarrow,[7] or in the Anglo-Saxon identities created by and for Emma and Cnut.[8]

Exile, migrancy, haunting and the return of the repressed are also key parts of both Anglo-Saxon culture and the postcolonial experience. All are states that produce a curious sort of division and doubling of experience – the self divided between two cultures, the doubling of another place

---

[5] See further Homi K. Bhabha, 'The Third Space: Interview with Homi K. Bhabha', in *Identity: Community, Culture, Difference*, ed. Jonathan Rutherford (London, 1990), 207-21.
[6] On translation see Ananya Jahanara Kabir and Deanne Williams, eds. *Postcolonial Approaches to the European Middle Ages: Translating Cultures* (Cambridge, 2005); and with less specific reference to the medieval, Harish Trivedi and Susan Bassnett, eds. *Post-Colonial Translation: Theory and Practice* (London, 1999).
[7] So successful were its creators that when their original dedication was crossed out and a new one added in Italy, the manuscript was accepted as Italian until 1888.
[8] See below p. 264. Mimicry can also be a form of threat or mockery, though it is rarely, if ever, manifested as such in Anglo-Saxon art.

or time in a present that is elsewhere. This type of experience has been characterized as 'uncanny'.⁹ The term is borrowed from Freud's essay of the same name, but means something rather different. For Freud, the uncanny is the emergence of the repressed in a way that makes the familiar foreign or the foreign familiar.¹⁰ For Bhabha, however, the term can also be used to describe the 'unhomely' experience of the exile, the repetition that can never actually be a repetition of the experiences of a past or a life elsewhere in a new time and place.¹¹ A specific example of the 'unhomely' experience as played out in the art historical record is again provided by the art of Anglo-Scandinavian England, where styles and motifs from the homeland (e.g., the Borre Style) are repeated but in a completely new form. The past, the other place of the homeland, is kept alive in the present of the new country, but it is also not and can never be the same as it was; it is divided from what it used to be at the same time that it doubles it. On the one hand, this recreated life is very familiar, but on the other, completely strange and foreign.

A related form of division and doubling, of uncanniness or unhomeliness, is evident in the recurring yet ever-changing origin stories of the Anglo-Saxons: their appropriation of the Exodus myth, of the story of the fall of the rebel angels, and their persistent and nostalgic looking back to, in some instances even mourning, a lost (and ever-changing) golden age that never really existed – at least not as it is imagined to have existed. All three represent a form of looking back to an unattainable homeland or time that keeps changing each time the story is retold. The stories are familiar to us from the textual record of the Anglo-Saxons, but they were also narrated in the art and architecture of the Anglo-Saxons and across the Anglo-Saxon landscape – the repetition of migrancy or exile in the journey of the Cuthbert community across the north of England and the monuments they erected as part of that journey, for example. There must also have been something uncanny in the Anglo-Saxons' encounter with the ruined landscapes and cityscapes of Romano-Britain, and this is expressed in both their wonder at the beauty of the monuments and their meditations on their ruin.

But who were the 'Anglo-Saxon' people, and what was 'Anglo-Saxon' England? The term itself tells us nothing about the ethnicity, gender or social status of artists or patrons, nor about the religious, political or cultural circumstances of artistic production and reception. Similarly,

---

⁹ Homi K. Bhabha, 'The World and the Home', *Social Text* 10.31–32 (1992), 141–53; see also Edward Said, 'Reflections on Exile', in *Reflections on Exile and Other Literary and Cultural Essays* (London, 2000), 173–86; Iain Chambers, *Migrancy, Culture, Identity* (London, 1994).
¹⁰ Sigmund Freud, 'The "Uncanny"', in *The Standard Edition of the Complete Psychological Works of Sigmund Freud*, ed. James Strachey, vol. 17: *An Infantile Neurosis and Other Works* (London, 2001), 219–56.
¹¹ Bhabha, 'The World and the Home'.

how does one identify England in this period, a period in which England was in the process of being formed, its boundaries shifting and changing shape, and its peoples subject to settlement and colonization by a number of different foreign peoples? There is also the problem of dates. When does Anglo-Saxon art first appear? With the arrival in Britain of the Angles, Saxons and Jutes? Is the art they produced in the immediate wake of the migrations markedly different from that produced by the inhabitants of sub-Roman Britain? What is the relationship between the art produced in the area we now call England and that produced in places like Wales, Cornwall or Scotland? Does one need to have a sense of Anglo-Saxon identity in order to have an Anglo-Saxon art? And does Anglo-Saxon art end in any meaningful sense with the arrival of the Normans in 1066? It is easy to use dates that have historical significance in order to define cultural eras, but historical events and dates often have no bearing on the styles, techniques or motifs used by artists and architects, nor on the ways in which art was received and interpreted by the men and women living in a given era. It has become increasingly clear that Anglo-Saxon language and literature continued long after the Norman Conquest,[12] and many elements of Anglo-Saxon art did as well.[13] That is not to say that it did not change, simply that it did not disappear. Whatever term we use to describe the art of this place and period, it is important to remember that that art was constantly being defined and redefined in terms of its relationship to that of other peoples, places and times: the Roman past, the Viking incursions of the present, the political desires of the future.

As a means of avoiding some of these problems, art historians frequently use terms such as 'Hiberno-Saxon' or 'Insular'. The former refers to the art of Ireland, Wales, southern Scotland and the north of England produced during the seventh, eighth and first half of the ninth centuries. The art of these areas shares certain stylistic and iconographic features such as intricate lacertine (animal interlace) or birds' head spirals. The Lindisfarne Gospels would be considered a characteristic example of Hiberno-Saxon art from the north of England – although it can also be considered Anglo-Saxon or Insular. While the term Hiberno-Saxon has the advantage of placing art produced in northern England in a broad (and hybrid) cultural context that highlights the role played by cultural encounter in the development of a particular style of art, it has the disadvantage of imposing chronological and geographical divisions on the material that can be too rigid. Hiberno-Saxon style does not end in the ninth century in Ireland, for example. Within England the term separates the art produced prior to the Viking invasions from that produced after them, and the art produced in the north of England from that in the south.

---

[12] See Mary Swan and Elaine M. Treharne, eds. *Rewriting Old English in the Twelfth Century* (Cambridge, 2000), see also http://www.le.ac.uk/ee/em1060to1220.
[13] See, for example, the discussion of the Eadwine Psalter, below pp. 175–8.

'Insular' art is generally understood simply as the art of early medieval Ireland and the British Isles, though it is often taken to be synonymous with Hiberno-Saxon art. It is a convenient term to use when speaking generally of styles, monument types, or a broad geographic area, but it elides even more variables and differences than does the term Anglo-Saxon. Art historians and archaeologists have been wrestling with the problem of dates and terminology for generations, and there are still no clear solutions. While this book will use the conventional terminology 'Anglo-Saxon', and will remain largely within the conventional dates, it will not ignore the issues they create; rather it will deal directly with problems of labelling, terminology and classification in order to highlight the dynamic, politically active, indeed hybrid nature of Anglo-Saxon art; the sometimes tension-filled ways in which it came into being, and the equally tension-filled ways that it has been dealt with by art historians, archaeologists and others. One of its central concerns is the work that art does in the production of meaning for its audiences within and between cultures, rather than the ways in which it may or may not conform to a particular set of formal, stylistic or iconographic criteria. The art of early medieval England, especially at the beginning of the period of Anglo-Saxon hegemony, is a postcolonial art, an art that maps the flux of cultural encounters in a myriad of different ways.

Finally, problems with terminology extend to the word 'art' and the way in which that word is often used to refer to the material culture of the Anglo-Saxons in a not particularly art-historical way. What are the implications of calling images, objects and monuments created during the Anglo-Saxon period art, a term that some argue is applicable only to the art of the Renaissance and later? The titles of books such as David Wilson's *Anglo-Saxon Art from the Seventh Century to the Norman Conquest* (London, 1984), or C. R. Dodwell's *Anglo-Saxon Art: A New Perspective* (Manchester 1982) give the impression that there is general agreement that what the Anglo-Saxons produced can in fact be called art. It is fair to say, however, that both books actually take an archaeological rather than an art-historical approach, treating their material primarily as artefacts rather than as art. Wilson was concerned above all with establishing the dates, origins and provenance of the works included in his book. He described and classified objects, iconographies and styles, but only rarely did he address the ways in which the viewer, whether Anglo-Saxon or modern, might appreciate the works on an aesthetic or emotional level.[14] For Wilson, art did make cultural statements, but these were almost exclusively statements having to do with religious ritual or function – whether Christian or pagan. Dodwell, on the other hand, was concerned with what the Anglo-Saxons themselves had to say about their art. His

---

[14] There are exceptions to this general format however – for example the discussion of the use of line in the Lindisfarne Gospels on p. 40.

book is an archaeology of the written sources broken down by medium – painting, textiles, jewellery and so forth. Most of the book is focused on what we can learn about lost works of art and what the sources reveal about artists, patrons and the display of art. However he does include a chapter (chapter 2) on 'Anglo-Saxon taste', which documents such things as the Anglo-Saxon love of glittering surfaces, reddish tones and light reflections. In terms of the meaning of Anglo-Saxon art, the book is again concerned entirely with iconography and the religious meaning and use of art.

One of the great contributions of Dodwell's book was that it showed just how much the Anglo-Saxons really were interested in art. They wrote about it a lot in all manner of texts from wills and charters to poetry. Lines such as *Maxim II*'s 'wrætlic weallstana geweorc' (beautifully worked stonewalls' 3a), or *The Ruin*'s 'wrætlic is þes wealstan' (beautifully made is the stonewall' 1a) in which the poets linger over the beauty of monumental stone architecture, indicate an appreciation for the aesthetic qualities of buildings, not just their size.[15] Patrons could also make their tastes known. Bishop Æthelwold, for example, was clearly aware of the power of form, style and colour when he commissioned his Benedictional (London, BL, Add. 49598; plates 8, 9; fig. 64). In addition to wanting a book that would serve his religious and political agenda, he also desired it to have 'many arches well adorned and filled with various figures decorated with manifold beautiful colours and with gold'.[16] The Anglo-Saxons' love of art was not unique in medieval Europe, but it did set them apart from, for example, the Carolingians, who were deeply involved in the debate over religious art that grew out of Byzantine iconoclasm, but were far less interested in the aesthetic qualities of art.[17] The Anglo-Saxons by contrast never became involved in the debate over iconoclasm.

The use of the word 'art' in reference to medieval images of all eras and genres was problematized by the publication of Hans Belting's *Bild und Kult: eine Geschichte des Bildes vor dem Zeitalter der Kunst* in 1990.[18] Belting argued that holy images should be treated as devotional objects rather than works of art, and that images reveal their meaning most effectively through their use or function. Most Anglo-Saxon art, like most medieval art, does have a religious meaning and function, and art

---

[15] Nicholas Howe, 'Anglo-Saxon England and the Postcolonial Void', in *Postcolonial Approaches to the European Middle Ages: Translating Cultures*, ed. Kabir and Williams, 25–47, at 31–3; Seth Lerer, '"On fagne flor": The Postcolonial *Beowulf*, from Heorot to Heaney', in ibid., 77–102, at 82.
[16] G. F. Warren and H. A. Wilson, eds, *The Benedictional of St Æthelwold, Bishop of Winchester 963–984* (Oxford, 1910); quoted in Andrew Prescott, *The Benedictional of St Æthelwold: A Masterpiece of Anglo-Saxon Art* (London, 2002), 5.
[17] See further Thomas F. X. Noble, *Images, Iconoclasm, and the Carolingians* (Philadelphia, PA, 2009).
[18] It appeared in English as *Likeness and Presence: A History of the Image before Art*, trans. Edmund Jephcott (Chicago, 1994).

historical studies of Anglo-Saxon art have for the most part focused on its religious rather than its social meaning and function. Nevertheless, the meaning and function of Anglo-Saxon religious images are very different from those of the images that Belting surveys. The vast majority of them are not icons in the narrow sense of the word, that is images used exclusively for devotional purposes, and images that made a clear distinction between portrait and portrayed. An icon is never a portrait in the sense of a representation of a historical or living human being; an icon is an image of a form that acts as a pointer towards (or index of) a spiritual truth.[19] Belting himself may have recognized the difference of Anglo-Saxon art as the only Anglo-Saxon images to be mentioned in his book are the icons brought back from Rome to Wearmouth by Benedict Biscop and the coffin of St Cuthbert (fig. 27), the decoration of which may have referenced the Wearmouth icons. Indeed, despite all their visits to Rome, the Anglo-Saxons, Biscop and his community aside, do not seem to have taken to icons, even if they did adopt iconic compositions.[20] Unlike icons, at least unlike pre-eleventh-century icons, Anglo-Saxon art is full of movement, drama, narrativity and pattern. It confronts and interacts with the viewer, and it usually cannot be confined to an exclusively, even primarily, religious function.

Like Wilson and Dodwell, Belting's methodology was that of the iconographer. 'Iconography' (literally picture writing) remains the most common method used to analyse and interpret medieval art.[21] It is concerned with subject matter – what is represented and what does it mean. In order to determine that meaning it relies on religious or historical contexts, texts and the archive of earlier images and monuments. For this reason, the iconographic approach is both text-bound and backward-looking, always searching for the source of an image or the development of a theme in pre-existing documents or works of art.[22] Clearly this has a value in providing certain historical information about a work of art, but it

---

[19] On icons see especially Henry Maguire, *The Icons of Their Bodies: Saints and Their Images in Byzantium* (Princeton, NJ, 1996); A. Eastmond and Liz James, eds. *Icon and Word: The Power of Images in Byzantium* (Aldershot, 2003).

[20] The individual panels on the main faces of the Ruthwell Cross (fig. 22), for example, are iconic in that they focus on one non-narrative figure or pair of figures set against a timeless blank background. However they are also part of a very complex metonymic narrative, see below, p. 139.

[21] For an excellent critique of the terms 'iconography' and 'iconology' see Georges Didi-Huberman, *Devant l'image: Questions posées aux fins d'une histoire de l'art* (Paris, 1990); Didi-Huberman, *Devant le temps: Histoire de l'art et anachronisme des images* (Paris, 2000); Didi-Huberman, *Confronting Images: Questioning the Ends of a Certain Art History*, trans. John Goodman (University Park, PA, 2005); Didi-Huberman et al., eds., *Relire Panofsky* (Paris, 2008).

[22] It should be stressed that this was not actually the purpose of the iconographic method as originally developed by Panofsky. On the tension between iconographic theory and practice see Michael Ann Holly, *Panofsky and the Foundations of Art History* (Ithaca, NY, 1984); Didi-Huberman, *Confronting Images*.

also has serious limitations. It is of little use in dealing with non-narrative subjects and nonrepresentational art, and it has little to tell us about issues of audience reception, of class or of gender. Moreover, it also keeps works bound within the past in that they become little more than end-points in a linear development of form, image, theme or object.

Even if they have not made the distinction between image and art that Belting makes, historians of Anglo-Saxon art have implicitly denied the 'art' of Anglo-Saxon art by understanding it solely within the context of the period in which it was produced. Anglo-Saxon art is not simply the result of a chronological progression of style and iconography, it is still with us, we still view it, interact with it and interpret it. The meaning of the Lindisfarne Gospels, for example, did not suddenly end in the eighth century, or in the eleventh; the manuscript is still being copied in the form of ever more technically advanced facsimiles, and its meaning is still being made. In some ways our understanding of Anglo-Saxon art is probably not far removed from that of its original audience. We still understand an evangelist portrait as an author portrait, for example, and we still make the same connection between the authors of the original gospels and the scribes and artists of specific gospel books made by Aldred in the colophon he added to the Lindisfarne Gospels.[23] The Ruthwell Cross still directs our viewing of the monument (as long as we are literate in its languages and images) in the same way that it did that of the community that erected it. But we also have a modern perspective that is no less valid even though it might not necessarily have been shared, or perhaps not shared consciously, by an Anglo-Scandinavian audience, and the fact that we are able to ask new questions of the monuments and see new meanings in their styles, forms and images is one of the things that tells us most clearly that this is art and not simply a collection of artefacts to be catalogued and described. To elucidate these meanings is not ahistorical. It is abundantly clear that the Anglo-Saxons themselves viewed works of art as existing within a continuing process of creation, recreation and changing meanings. The Nunburnholme Cross, for example, began as an Anglian monument, was recarved into an Anglo-Saxon monument, and recarved again into a Norman monument.[24] Each campaign of carving altered its meaning and function, not simply its visual appearance. It is also clear from Aldred's colophon that those who added to a work of art were considered to be as much its creator (artist or author) as the man or woman who first brought the work into being. To represent, reproduce, restore or reuse was never simply to copy or make do, it was to add new layers of meaning. On a most basic level the meanings of Anglo-Saxon

---

[23] See below p. 34.
[24] For a good general discussion of the monument see Martin K. Foys, *Virtually Anglo-Saxon: Old Media, New Media, and Early Medieval Studies in the Late Age of Print* (Gainesville, FL, 2007), ch. 5.

art are determined by the historical and cultural contexts in which that art was first produced and in which it first circulated; but, as Derrida put it, while 'no meaning can be determined out of context ... no context permits saturation'.[25]

---

[25] Jacques Derrida, 'Living On: Borderlines', in *Deconstruction and Criticism*, ed. L. H. Bloom *et al.* (New York, 1979), 81.

# THE ART OF ORIGINS  1

England did not experience one period of colonization and conversion, but many. The period with which this book is concerned saw the departure of the Romans (the first to engage in both colonization and conversion on a large scale), and the arrival of the Angles and the Saxons, the Vikings, and finally the Normans. Each group left its mark on the landscape, on society and on culture. Moreover, while there was no full-scale conversion to a religion other than Christianity, the process of christianization was gradual, and even once established its practices and its monuments were adapted to suit the requirements of new settlers, new political and religious reforms and local or individual ideologies.

The transformation of Roman Britain to Anglo-Saxon England was also a gradual one. Long before the departure of the Romans there were Saxons (as well as Irish) in Britain in the form of military recruits, some of whom stayed on as settlers. As early as 367 a major attack against the Romans was launched by a united group of Saxons, Picts and Irish, and most of the fifth century witnessed a violent struggle between the Saxons and the British for control of southern Britain. These peoples have left their traces in the material record at sites such as Mucking, on the Thames estuary in Essex, one of the earliest of the Anglo-Saxon settlements.[1] A fifth-century buckle from grave 117 at Mucking, decorated in the quoit-brooch style (fig. 1), is typical of those worn by Saxon recruits, and as such it marks both an end and a beginning. It is cast bronze inlaid with silver, and was probably made in Britain. Its geometric patterns look forward to those of the more elaborate and more famous patterns of the Sutton Hoo (plate 1) or Staffordshire hoard metalwork, as well as those of early Insular manuscripts (fig. 7), though this does not imply that they necessarily carry the same meaning. Multiple crosses are embedded within the designs of spirals and key pattern, but they cannot be taken as unequivocal signs of Christian content. Pairs of sea-creatures flank stylized masks in the

---

[1] On the site and its excavation see Helena Hamerow, *Mucking*, vol. 2: *The Anglo-Saxon Settlement* (London, 1993).

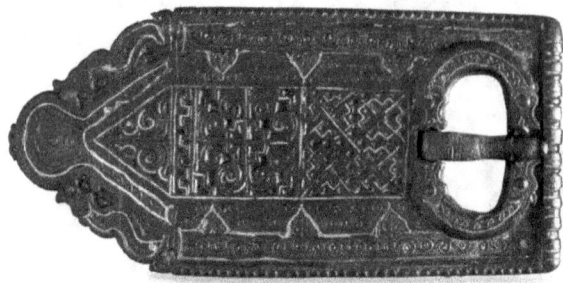
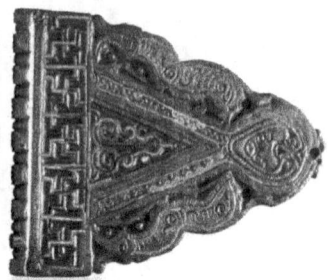

FIG. 1.
FIFTH-CENTURY
BELT BUCKLE
FROM MUCKING

triangular ends of the buckle, a motif that will be echoed in the men flanked by beasts on the Sutton Hoo purse lid and later depictions of Daniel flanked by lions, or Christ flanked by animals, but these creatures are certainly not linked directly to either of those iconographies. Nor can we say that there is any direct connection between such seemingly related images and patterns. While there are continuities between Romano-Britain and Anglo-Saxon England, there are also gaps and losses. Moreover, images and patterns can be revised, revived, transformed and given new meanings to fit new social or economic contexts. Nevertheless, it is possible that some of the motifs that decorated the belt are related in function to the later imagery. The cross was ubiquitous in antiquity and an important image in many religions in forms such as the ankh or the swastika. It could be a protective sign long before it became the ultimate protective image for any Christian on whom it was placed.[2] It also became a sign of Christian militancy from the age of Constantine onwards. Beast ornament, such as the double-headed creatures that form the loop of the buckle, also had an apotropaic function within sub-Roman art across the Germanic world that made an easy transition into the art of Christianity.[3] Thus, whether the ornament is to be interpreted as Christian or as pagan, this was a belt designed to protect but also to impress. Indeed, it is entirely possible that the piece was valued more for its seemingly sophisticated combination of ornament than for any religious meaning or protective function it might have carried. Of equal interest are the

[2] On the variety of forms the cross could take in Anglo-Saxon England see Catherine E. Karkov, Karen L. Jolly and Sarah Larratt Keefer, eds, *The Place of the Cross in Anglo-Saxon England* (Woodbridge, 2006); Karen L. Jolly, Sarah Larratt Keefer and Catherine E. Karkov, eds, *The Sign of the Cross in Anglo-Saxon England* (Morgantown, WV, 2007); Sarah Larrat Keefer, Catherine E. Karkov and Karen L. Jolly, eds, *Cross and Cruciform in the Anglo-Saxon World: Studies to Honor the Memory of Timothy Reuter* (Morgantown, WV, 2010).

[3] The term 'Germanic' is even more problematic than 'Anglo-Saxon' as it reduces a variety of different peoples with their own distinctive cultures into one enormous monolithic 'tradition'. It is nevertheless retained here as unravelling what we have come to identify as the Germanic tradition would require a book in itself.

design elements that were to continue as a feature of Anglo-Saxon art in a variety of media. The depth of the casting and the use of silver inlay, for example, create a spatial play between figure and ground that will appear again in works such as the Lindisfarne Gospel carpet pages (fig. 7); while the ambiguity between centre and margin (what exactly is the central or the most important image on this buckle?) will remain crucial to works as diverse in time, purpose and medium as the Ruthwell monument (figs. 22, 39, 40) and the Bayeux Tapestry. It is not enough however to say simply that there is a spatial play between image and ground, centre and margin; the relationship between these different fields is dynamic and shifting, and forces us to question hierarchies of motif and composition. Admittedly, the Mucking buckle is a fairly mundane and utilitarian object compared to something like the Bewcastle Cross or the Lindisfarne Gospels, but as is the case with these later and grander monuments, the designers of the buckle have used ambiguity and movement to add a temporal element to our understanding of the piece. The beasts wriggle, patterns change in the light, the eye traces the lines of the inlaid silver. We can see, not interpret or read, but see this buckle as both a product and a representation in miniature of a microcosm of the shifting cultural relationships, the shifting centres and peripheries, that effected the transition from Roman Britain to Anglo-Saxon England on a grand scale. It speaks in miniature of arrivals and departures on a much grander scale, of exiles and migrations that would be repeated over and over by different peoples across the next six centuries.

Once departed, the Romans left behind them a country covered with the objects and monuments, traces and memories, of their world, and one has to wonder how those left behind as well as those moving into the country reacted to the landscape they found around them. Poetry indicates that the Anglo-Saxons found the remains of buildings, mosaics, sculptures, fountains, even roads, impressive and indeed beautiful in terms of their scale, building techniques and style, but also that they were very aware of the loss and decay of culture that they represented, lying in ruin and in fragments in certain areas, the more so as time went on. Seth Lerer has suggested that the 'fagne flor' of Heorot in *Beowulf* describes a Romano-British mosaic floor and was used precisely because it was both familiar from the floor mosaics that would have survived across the country and because it represented memory, 'something old, rich, artistic, and alien'.[4] The Anglo-Saxon encounter with the ruins of the Romano-British world must have been an uncanny experience in the contrasts it embodied – order and disorder, careful construction and unstoppable decay, flourishing empire and desolate emptiness – but also in the many ways in which these ruins would be used to construct new structures and

---

[4] Lerer, "'On fagne flor'", 84.

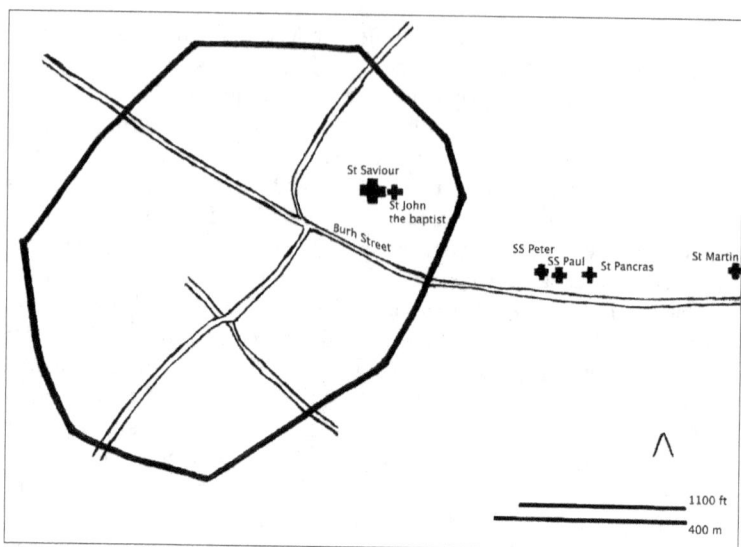

FIG. 2.
PLAN OF EARLY
ANGLO-SAXON
CANTERBURY

new cities. With the coming of Christianity, the Roman church would become a crucial centre for the Anglo-Saxons, and *romanitas* would become a potent political tool in the hands of King Alfred, but there must also have been a certain amount of ambivalence. In the post-Roman era this was a landscape that spoke of death, destruction, abandonment and absence, the almost complete collapse of any form of order. There is evidence of a certain ambivalence towards the Romans that will be discussed more fully below, yet however complex the Anglo-Saxon experience of the post-Roman landscape was, it became something to be built on, and something that would become very much a part of the way in which Anglo-Saxon England defined itself. Interestingly, while the geographical frontiers the Romans had established helped to shape the political and cultural borders of the country, language would become the primary defining feature of the new peoples within it – British or Celtic languages in Wales, south-west England and Scotland, and Old English in the areas settled by the Angles, Saxons, Jutes and their successors. Latin, the language of the church, would exist alongside English, but it can never really be said to have dominated it, no matter how much it might have been perceived as the language of authority. Similar to the designs on the Mucking buckle, Latin and Old English were to exist in a dynamic and shifting power relationship for centuries to come.[5] Perhaps this is one of

---

[5] On the relationship between the two languages see especially Uppinder Mehan and David Townsend, '"Nation" and the Gaze of the Other in Eighth-Century Northumbria', *Comparative Literature* 53.1 (2001), 1–26, and the discussion of language on the Ruthwell Cross below (p. 144).

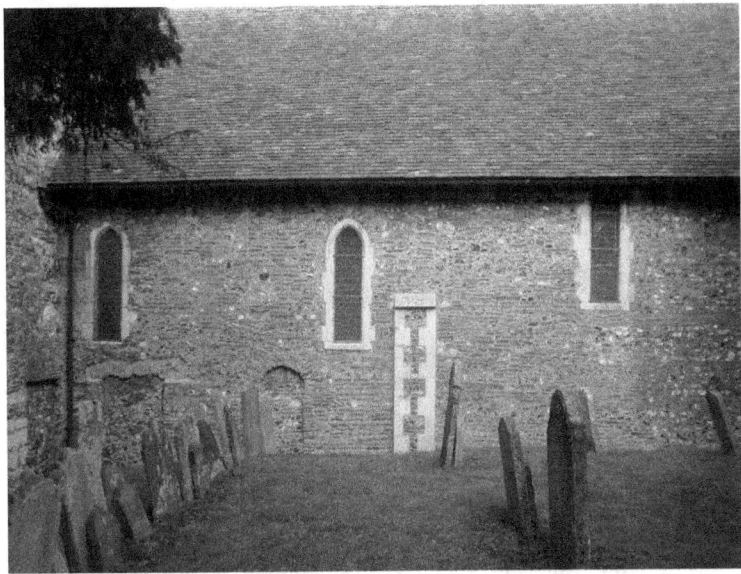

FIG. 3.
ST MARTIN'S
CANTERBURY

the reasons that language would go on to become such a feature of the art of early medieval England.

When Augustine arrived from Rome in 597, he found a land that was very much a mixture of cultures, languages and religions. It was also a country in which temporality and geography mattered, and would continue to do so. Bertha, the Frankish queen of King Æthelberht of Kent, was already a practising Christian with her own bishop, Liudhard, and they had been given an old Romano-British building just outside the Roman walls of Canterbury in which to practise their faith (figs. 2, 3).[6] It was renovated and dedicated to St Martin of Tours, a dedication which would have evoked home for Bertha in a very particular way: Tours was within her father's kingdom and, according to Gregory of Tours, her half-sister was a nun in a convent founded in the forecourt of St Martin's church in that city.[7] Given Bertha's origins and the lack of stone masons in England, it seems likely that Gallic builders and craftsmen would have been brought over to restore the building in a style which also would have been familiar to Bertha from her homeland. However significant use was also made of the Romano-British past. Parts of the original elevation survive within the present structure, and indicate that both the original building and the sixth- to seventh-century renovations were of Roman brick and that the

---

[6] *HE* i.26. There is some debate about whether it was in fact a Roman church, or some other type of structure. For details of the argument see Richard Morris, *Churches in the Landscape* (London, 1989), 17–23.
[7] Gregory of Tours, *The History of the Franks*, trans. Lewis Thorpe (Harmondsworth, 1974), 518. See also below pp. 269–73 on women and memory.

church had a rectangular nave and chancel. Fragments of a Roman style opus signinum floor have also been recovered.[8] It was in the vicinity of this church that the Liudhard metalet, a coin reused as a pendant and inscribed with the name Liudhard, was discovered in 1844 along with five coin pendants and other objects from one or more female graves during excavations in the nineteenth century.[9] These finds, along with the fact that Bertha and Liudhard worshipped regularly in this church, suggest that the royal court must have been located nearby. No matter how foreign many aspects of his new home might have been, the Christian community at court, along with the material traces of the old Roman Empire that surrounded them, provided Augustine and his followers with the material signs of an earlier Christian past and an evocation of both Rome and the journey they had just completed, a recurring trajectory traced across time and space. Fragments and ruins, the signs of absence and abandonment, but also of homeland and Roman culture, provided material to be built into something new and enduring.

From the start there was close co-operation between the court and the missionaries. Æthelberht himself did not convert to Christianity until some time after Augustine's arrival, but Pope Gregory the Great would later write to the king and queen comparing them to Constantine and Helena, thus putting the foundation of the English church in direct historical parallel to the beginnings of Christian Rome and Constantinople (an oft forgotten third spoke to the England–Rome axis), as well as reinscribing the king and queen into the Romano-British past.[10] At first the missionaries worshipped in the queen's church of St Martin,[11] whose dedication would have had a meaning almost as special for Augustine as it had for Bertha. Tours was one of the places he had visited on his way north, and Martin, like Augustine, had been an exile, a missionary and monastic founder in a foreign land. Yet a new statement was also necessary, and with royal support they soon set about building an ecclesiastical landscape that

---

[8] *Opus signinum* is a mosaic technique in which a variety of stones or other materials are laid either in simple patterns or without any pattern at all.
[9] See Leslie Webster and Janet Backhouse, eds., *The Making of England: Anglo-Saxon Art and Culture AD 600–900* (London, 1991), cat. no. 5; P. Grierson, 'The Canterbury (St Martin's) Hoard of Frankish and Anglo-Saxon Coin Ornaments', *British Numismatic Journal* 27 (1952–4), 39–51. The first published account of the 'hoard' identifies the find spot as St Augustine's, however the two churches are relatively near to each other; C. Roach-Smith, 'Merovingian Coins, etc. Discovered at St Martin's, near Canterbury', *Numismatic Chronicle* 7 (1845), 187–91.
[10] The comparison is particularly interesting for the somewhat ambivalent position in which it places the king and queen. On the one hand, it can be understood as bestowing on them an imperial grandeur that goes back not just to the foundation of Christian Rome, but also back to Roman Britain, Constantine's homeland. On the other hand it might be understood as an appropriation of English identity by the Roman church. Moreover, any comparison emphasizes difference at the same time that it establishes similarity. Æthelberht and Bertha are like, but they are not Constantine and Helena.
[11] *HE* i.26.

looked to that of Rome and, eventually, to an Italian building tradition. According to Bede,[12] Augustine restored a Roman church within the city walls for his cathedral, dedicating it to St Saviour,[13] a dedication that echoed that of the papal cathedral in Rome (later St John Lateran). Bede may have been a bit keener on establishing a direct line of continuity with a Romano-British Christian past than was Augustine, or perhaps the true history of the building had been forgotten by the time he wrote. Excavations have shown that the church was not in fact a rebuilt Roman structure but a new purpose-built church constructed of reused Roman bricks. Its walls would thus have been similar in appearance to those of St Martin's, something that Tim Eaton has suggested may have been an attempt by Augustine to 'assimilate' his church into Canterbury's past.[14] Bede's mistake may indeed be a sign of his success in doing just that, but Eaton's comment is a reminder that it is unlikely that a contemporary audience would have mistaken these buildings for Roman. They may have been built using Roman materials, and they may have referenced Continental structures in certain details of their plans, elevations or decoration, but they were new Anglo-Saxon churches that would have looked very different from the contemporary churches of Rome or Gaul. Outside the city walls, near St Martin's, Augustine founded a monastery dedicated to SS Peter and Paul, the remains of which are still visible within the ruins of St Augustine's abbey. The dedication mirrored that of the two great Roman churches, as well as the very foundations of the Christian church, in the apostles to whom they were dedicated. Its plan declared its difference from the earlier Canterbury churches, although aspects of its design – the buttressed doorway of the narthex, for example – may still have looked to Gaul.[15] It had a western narthex, *porticus* along both the north and south walls, and possibly a polygonal or semicircular apse at the east end.[16] The church was intended to house the bodies of the archbishops of Canterbury and the kings of Kent, its position outside the city walls reflecting the Roman tradition of extramural burial. The tombs of Augustine and other early archbishops were located in and around the *porticus* on the north side of the nave, and those of Æthelberht, Bertha and Liudhard were contained in the *porticus* to the south.[17] The church

---

[12] *HE* i.33.
[13] It would later become known as Christ Church.
[14] Tim Eaton, *Plundering the Past. Roman Stonework in Medieval Britain* (Stroud, 2000), 130.
[15] Eric Cambridge, 'The Architecture of the Augustine Mission', in *St Augustine and the Conversion of England*, ed. Richard Gameson (Stroud, 1999), 202–36, at 223.
[16] See Eric Fernie, *The Architecture of the Anglo-Saxons* (London, 1983), 37–8. Richard Gem, 'Reconstructions of St Augustine's Abbey, Canterbury, in the Anglo-Saxon Period', in *St Dunstan, His Life, Times and Cult*, ed. Nigel Ramsay, Margaret Sparks and Tim Tatton-Brown (Woodbridge, 1992), 57–73; Cambridge, 'The Architecture of the Augustine Mission', 205–7.
[17] In 760 archepiscopal burial was moved inside the city walls to the cathedral.

was not completed until after Augustine's death, and was dedicated some time between 604 and 619.

The second generation of Canterbury churches, St Pancras,[18] St Mary[19] and the martyrium church of the Four Crowned Martyrs (*c.* 620), again evoked Rome in their dedications, but followed the churches of Ravenna in aspects of their plans and structures. Cambridge has suggested quite plausibly that the reason for this was a decline of the building industry in Ravenna and the north of Italy at the end of the sixth century, an event which provided a ready pool of skilled labour for the church in Kent.[20] Purely practical considerations may have taken precedence over symbolic statements, but it is worth remembering how significant the city of Ravenna was as a point of contact between Rome in the west and Byzantium in the east, and how important it would become to the architecture of the Carolingian world.

The remains of St Pancras show two phases of building, the first possibly of Roman date.[21] Too little of the east end survives to establish the exact shape of the apse, but it was clearly stilted, inset from the nave, and separated from it by a triple arcade, a feature of Ravennate churches.[22] The only architectural evidence for the church of St Mary is the western wall of the nave. Goscelin, writing in the eleventh century, refers to *porticus*, but it is impossible to ascertain whether these were original features or later additions.[23] Both St Mary's and St Pancras were constructed of reused Roman brick, and both were built in a linear alignment between SS Peter and Paul's and St Martin's – St Mary's approximately 5 metres to the east of SS Peter and Paul's,[24] and St Pancras approximately 30 metres east of that. This linear alignment of churches had its sources both in Gaul (especially the Paris region, Bertha's homeland) and in the arrangement of pre-Christian high-status British complexes such as Yeavering (fig. 31),[25] and would be repeated with some variation at other early Anglo-Saxon monastic sites such as Wearmouth-Jarrow and Lindisfarne. It is a reminder to us now that one of the most important features of these early sites

[18] Some debate over the date of this church remains. See Cambridge, 'The Architecture of the Augustine Mission', 212–14.
[19] Built 616–24 and sponsored by Æthelberht's son, Eadbald.
[20] Cambridge, 'The Architecture of the Augustine Mission', 223–6.
[21] See F. Jenkins, 'Preliminary Report on Excavations at the Church of St Pancras, Canterbury', *Canterbury Archaeology* (1975–6), 4–5.
[22] Cambridge, 'The Architecture of the Augustine Mission', 213–15.
[23] Gem, 'Reconstructions of St Augustine's Abbey', 61.
[24] The two churches were linked by an octagon constructed during the abbacy of Wulfric in the eleventh century.
[25] See further John Blair, *The Church in Anglo-Saxon Society* (Oxford, 2005), 199–202; John Blair, 'Anglo-Saxon Minsters: A Topographical Review', in *Pastoral Care before the Parish*, ed. John Blair and Richard Sharpe (Leicester, 1992), 226–66; Helen Gittos, 'Sacred Space in Anglo-Saxon England: Liturgy, Architecture and Place', Unpublished D.Phil thesis, Oxford University, 2002; Rosemary Cramp, 'Monastic Sites', in *The Archaeology of Anglo-Saxon England*, ed. David M. Wilson (London, 1976), 201–52, 453–7.

would have been the movement through the spaces between churches in addition to the movement through the architectural spaces of the individual structures.

Within twenty-five years of their arrival in England, Augustine and his followers had created an ecclesiastical topography akin to that of Rome and other Continental cities, with a series of churches stretching out from the eastern walls of Canterbury.[26] At the same time they had created something new, something built on and of the fragments of the Romano-British past that transformed that past forever, providing it with a new Christian meaning. It was not just a reuse of the past, but an active intervention in the material of the past that gave to the history it represented a new meaning and a new life in the present. Indeed, it has been interpreted as a key element in Anglo-Saxon ethnogenesis, and one that would continue to define the Anglo-Saxons' positioning of themselves in relation to history.[27] Already the reuse of the past had begun to spread out to other areas. The churches at Rochester and Reculver were built on old Roman sites, and the reuse of Roman sites, materials and objects quickly became common across England, although the reasons for that reuse could vary enormously.[28] While it undoubtedly made economic sense to reuse Roman structures and their stonework, there has been a great deal of disagreement about whether or not this was the Anglo-Saxons' only motive. While the incorporation of Roman work into new Anglo-Saxon buildings used to be understood as simple quarrying, it has become far more popular to see reuse as a form of appropriation.[29] Yet poems such as *The Ruin* and *Maxims II* reveal that the Anglo-Saxons were very clear both about what these buildings represented and about their beauty.[30] They translated them into words that meditated on the trope of beauty and decay. They also translated them into buildings, buildings which, like the poems, were new works, works that repeated (in the sense of rebuilding) the past at the same time as they changed it.

---

[26] Morris, *Churches in the Landscape*, 1, 26.
[27] Nicholas Brooks, 'Canterbury, Rome and the Construction of English Identity', in *Early Medieval Rome and the Christian West, Essays in Honour of Donald Bullough*, ed. Julia M. H. Smith (Leiden, 2000), 221–47.
[28] On this topic see Eaton, *Plundering the Past*; David Stocker, 'Rubbish Recycled: A Study of the Re-use of Stone in Lincolnshire', in *Stone Quarrying and Building in England AD 43–1525*, ed. David Parsons (London, 1990), 83–101; Jane Hawkes, '*Iuxta Morem Romanorum*: Stone and Sculpture in Anglo-Saxon England', in *Anglo-Saxon Styles*, ed. Catherine E. Karkov and George Hardin Brown (Albany, NY, 2003), 69–99; Martin Henig, 'Remaining Roman in Britain AD 300–700: The Evidence of Portable Art', in *Debating Late Antiquity in Britain AD 300–700*, ed. Rob Collins and James Gerrard, BAR Brit. Ser. 365 (Oxford, 2004), 13–23; on the amuletic reuse of Roman objects being linked to women and children see below, p. 27.
[29] E.g., Eaton, *Plundering the Past*; Howe, 'Anglo-Saxon England and the Postcolonial Void'.
[30] See above p. 7.

According to Bede, Æthelberht had delayed his own conversion because of his reluctance to abandon the beliefs and traditions of his ancestors.[31] Once baptized, however, he became active in the conversion of his neighbours, convincing both his nephew, Sæbert of Essex (d. 616-17), and Rædwald, king of East Anglia (r. 616-27) to be baptized. The latter, however, remained only semi-convinced in the long term, famously maintaining altars to both the Christian and pagan gods, and carving out for himself a space between religions. Little evidence for what pagan Anglo-Saxon altars or temples might have looked like survives. Traces of enclosed square-plan wooden structures have been located at a number of pre-Christian sites, including Yeavering, and several are located on or near earlier prehistoric structures. Place-name evidence indicates that some structures were also located near burial mounds, and shrines may also have been placed over certain burials.[32] Gregory had advised Augustine that pagan idols were to be destroyed, and that pagan temples should be destroyed or converted to Christian use, so that much, though by no means all, of the pagan past disappeared in and beneath the new Christian landscape. Architecture and stone, as we have seen, were reused.

Significantly, burial with grave goods, a practice that the Anglo-Saxons brought with them from the Continent, was never condemned, so we can also surmise something of pagan practices and the conversion to Christianity from burial practices. Because graves were all about memory as well as remembrance, they reveal quite a lot about social memory in addition to whatever they might reveal about the memory of the individual dead.[33] Tombs are inherently about the past but also about the persistence of that past in the present memories of those by and for whom they were made. They were part of spectacles that often involved smells and sounds and community participation. For us, they provide information on how groups produced images of themselves and their pasts that remain in memory down to the present day, not only as they constitute objects of history, but also as they continue to produce images in the form of reconstructions, heritage centres, as well as surviving more ephemerally in our persistent desire to tie them to texts, to solve the riddles they pose – for example, our desire to tie Sutton Hoo Mound 1, or the site of Lejre (Denmark) with its burial ground to *Beowulf*,[34] or to put a name and a face to the mound's absent body. Objects within graves also speak

---

[31] *HE* i.25.
[32] David Wilson, *Anglo-Saxon Paganism* (London, 1992), 10-13, 48-50.
[33] In general see now Howard Williams, *Death and Memory in Early Medieval Britain* (Cambridge, 2006); Howard Williams, 'Death Warmed Up: The Agency of Bodies and Bones in Early Anglo-Saxon Cremation Rites', *Journal of Material Culture* 9 (2004), 263-91.
[34] On Sutton Hoo see especially Roberta Frank, '*Beowulf* and Sutton Hoo: The Odd Couple', in *Voyage to the Other World: The Legacy of Sutton Hoo*, ed. Calvin B. Kendall and Peter S. Wells (Minneapolis, 1992), 47-64; on Lejre and modern scholarship on the site see John D. Niles and Marijane Osborn, eds., *Beowulf and Lejre* (Tempe, AZ, 2007).

to memory. Many items chosen for inclusion in burials were heirlooms of some sort, often (like the Sutton Hoo hanging bowls) showing signs of use and repair. Others (like the Prittlewell gold belt buckle) appear to have been hastily made objects of display designed specifically for the individual funeral spectacle.

The location of some of the most famous pagan cemeteries, such as Snape or Sutton Hoo, and the presence of ship burials at both locations, indicate that a prominent landscape setting and a symbolic journey over water were important parts of at least some beliefs. So also, it seems, was a sense of continuity or association with the pagan past, as some burials were located in or near ancestral cemeteries. It is difficult to make any general inferences about these or other burial sites, however, as burial practices were varied and in a constant state of flux throughout the sixth and seventh centuries.[35] Particularly relevant are the 'Final Phase' cemeteries of the seventh century, the cemeteries in which we can see the transition from pagan to Christian burial practices made manifest. Yet Christianity was not the only factor in the changes taking place; there were also social, political and economic forces at work that complicate the picture.[36] Objects recovered from graves of this period may carry multiple messages. They may tell us about religious belief, status, personal or communal identity, even the consumption and destruction of material resources. Specific meanings and messages are often difficult if not impossible to pin down, but we can be certain that people were buried with objects that spoke about who they were and how they were perceived and remembered by those who buried them. This is perhaps most easily seen in the famous 'princely' burials at Prittlewell and Mound 1 Sutton Hoo (figs. 4, 5, plate 1), both dating from the early seventh century. The dates, location and combination of Christian and pagan objects in both burials have led to their being identified as the graves of Sæbert and Rædwald respectively, though there is no particularly compelling reason to link them with either man. All that can really be said about the men buried in these graves is that they were both clearly wealthy and important figures, yet the two burials do not portray them as equals. They also convey very different ideas about the tomb and the afterlife.

At Prittlewell, the less grand of the two burials, the grave was within a pre-existing cemetery and consisted of a wooden chamber in which the body and accompanying grave goods were laid out. The body had been placed in or on a wooden structure (a coffin or a bed?) towards the centre

---

[35] See further Williams, *Death and Memory*; Sally Crawford, 'Votive Deposition, Religion and the Anglo-Saxon Furnished Burial Ritual', *World Archaeology* 36 (2004), 87–102.

[36] See further Williams, *Death and Memory*; Helen Geake, *The Use of Grave Goods in Conversion-Period England, c. 600–c. 850*, BAR Brit. Ser. 261 (Oxford, 1997); Dawn Hadley, 'Equality, Humility and Non materialism? Christianity and Anglo-Saxon Burial Practices', *Archaeological Review from Cambridge* 17 (2000), 149–78.

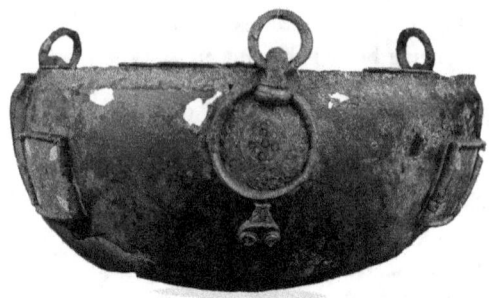

FIG. 4. LARGE HANGING BOWL FROM SUTTON HOO MOUND 1

of the chamber and facing east. The grave goods, which included personal items such as jewellery, along with weapons and objects used for feasting and entertainment, were neatly arranged on the body and around the walls of the chamber. All in all, the grave seems to have been perceived as a dwelling within a community of the dead.[37] The grave goods included clearly Christian items: two small gold foil crosses were placed on or near the head, and a cross-inscribed silver spoon was found in a box in the corner of the chamber.[38] The overall assemblage spoke of exceptional rank and status, but was nowhere near the lavish and ostentatious display of wealth of Mound 1 Sutton Hoo, and it is tempting to take this relative austerity as a sign of the Christianity of the deceased or those who buried him.

At Mound 1 Sutton Hoo, the body was also laid out on a bed or in a coffin within a chamber with the grave goods carefully arranged around it; but this chamber was constructed near the centre of a ship and, as noted above, was thus part of a vehicle for a symbolic journey of some sort. As at Prittlewell, the burial was part of a larger royal cemetery adjacent to an earlier sixth-century burial ground. Amongst the grave goods were Byzantine silver bowls and a pair of inscribed silver spoons, all of which were Christian objects, but nothing else in the burial was positively indicative of a Christian context. Mound 1 seems to have been a clearly pagan burial, though whether it was meant specifically as a statement of defiance of or opposition to Christianity is another question.[39] In addition to Byzantium, the cultural affiliations of the objects in Mound 1 included Rome, Francia, Celtic Britain and Scandinavia. This was a sophisticated statement of dominance over and appropriation of, or at the very least contact with, the cultural and political powers of the early medieval world, however fictional that statement might have been.

A group of three bronze hanging bowls is believed to have come from northern Britain, both because of the object type and because of the style of their decoration. Much scholarship has been devoted to their provenance

---

[37] John Hines, 'No Place like Home? The Anglo-Saxon Social Landscape from Within and Without', in *Anglo-Saxon England and the Continent*, ed. Hans Sauer and Jo Story, Anglo-Saxon Studies 3 (Tempe, AZ, forthcoming). I am grateful to John Hines for letting me read a copy of his paper prior to publication.

[38] On the contents of the burial see Museum of London Archaeology Service, *The Prittlewell Prince. The Discovery of a Rich Anglo-Saxon Burial in Essex* (London, 2004); Hines, 'No Place like Home?'

[39] On Mound 1 in general see Martin Carver, *Sutton Hoo: A Seventh-Century Burial Ground and Its Context* (London, 2005); Rupert Bruce-Mitford, *The Sutton Hoo Ship Burial*, 3 vols (London, 1978–83).

and possible function – they held liquid of some sort, probably water – but relatively little attention has been paid to how they function as works of art. Despite their fragmentary and repaired status, the bowls were thoughtfully designed. The largest of the bowls (fig. 4) is decorated with alternating circular escutcheons and square enamel and millefiori glass mounts that create an up-and-down rhythmical movement around the bowl's exterior, which helps to move the eye around the object. The sense of movement is continued inside the bowl, where a tinned-bronze fish swivels on a pedestal at its centre. Decoration and function were thus closely related.[40] The mounts and escutcheons are of differing designs, but each design is focused on a central square or circle surrounded by running spirals. The spiral patterns of the mounts and escutcheons also convey a sense of movement. The circular escutcheons (fig. 5) are especially suited to this particular object. Within the outer band of red enamel is a ring of bird's-head spirals that encloses a pattern of circles within circles inset with tiny pieces of millefiori glass. The design has an organic, kinetic quality quite distinct from the more compartmentalized designs of the Roman world, which serves not only to enliven the surface of the bowl but also to echo its overall shape. The pattern of circles within circles, on the other hand, suggests containment, again neatly mirroring the function of the bowl. Abstract beast snouts are positioned beneath the escutcheons, and biting beast heads rise from their tops to hold in place the rings from which the bowl would have been suspended. Together the three pieces – snout, escutcheon and beast head – articulate the upward curve of the bowl; but further than that, they turn the object into a miniature world over, around and in which creatures circle and swim. It is impossible to know now what the individual motifs and animals might have meant to the Anglo-Saxons, but their cumulative effect is to bring the object to life visually.

A similar effect is achieved on the far more lavish pair of shoulder clasps made of gold and set with garnet, blue and millefiori glass (plate 1). Here, Style II animal interlace surrounds each of the central rectangular panels,[41] an overlapping pair of boars caps each of the four ends, and a

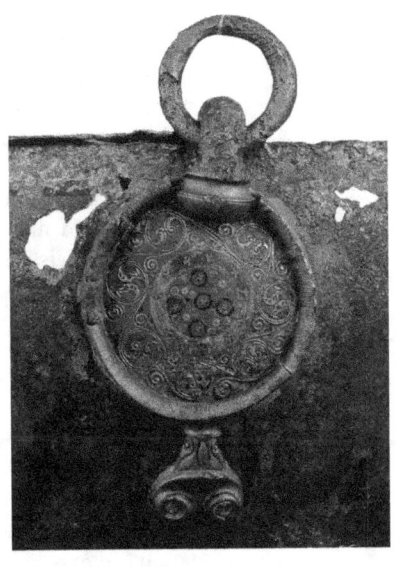

FIG. 5. DETAIL OF FIGURE 4

---

[40] The same would have been true of the now lost Witham bowl with its central water-creature.
[41] The quoit-brooch style of the Mucking buckle was succeeded by 'Style I' animal ornament in which the bodies of the animals were fragmented and formed into patterns. Style I was in turn succeeded by 'Style II' in which the ribbon-like bodies of the animals

serpent-headed pin, its body formed by the attached chain, locks each clasp in place. Tiny filigree birds and snakes composed of individual gold granules fill the spaces between the legs of the boars.[42] As with the hanging bowl mounts and escutcheons, geometric patterns are formed by images of animals in rhythmic motion. In this case, the artistry of the design has long been recognized[43] and adds weight to the notion that the beautiful balance between object and decoration on the hanging bowl discussed above is indeed more likely to have been deliberate than accidental. In the central panels, the stepped shape of the cloisons and the horizontal and vertical lines of the overall composition are picked up in the millefiori chequer boards. Gold foils stamped with a grid pattern reflect light out from beneath the garnets[44] and also highlight the diagonal arrangement of the cloisons. The strict rectilinearity of the panels is relieved by the curving movements of the interlaced beasts that surround them, and by the interlocking arches of the boars' backs. The bright blue of the millefiori patterns balances the red of the garnets, an effect that would have been even more pronounced had the blue glass that originally filled the eyes of the interlaced beasts survived. Again, ornament serves to articulate function. Interlocking boars and serpentine creatures, knotted filigree beasts and a serpent-headed pin all decorate an object whose purpose is to lock together sections of the military garment to which it was once attached. The animals chosen are also appropriate as both serpents and boars were symbolic of power and aggression, and serpentine interlace is seen as having an apotropaic function in Germanic art in general.[45] Yet these images would have been relatively difficult to make out for someone looking at the clasp as originally worn.

The use of light in the shoulder clasps merits further consideration. The light reflected out by the patterned gold foils beneath the garnets gives depth to what would otherwise be a basically flat visual field, but once again it infuses the pieces with an element of temporality, the time

are interlaced across the surfaces of the objects they decorate. See further Bernhard Salin, *Die altgermanische Thierornamentik* (Stockholm, 1904).

[42] The use of granules, as opposed to beaded wire, is relatively rare in Anglo-Saxon art. See Elizabeth Coatsworth and Michael Pindar, *The Art of the Anglo-Saxon Goldsmith* (Woodbridge, 2002), 128-9.

[43] See in particular Webster and Backhouse, *The Making of England*, 29-30.

[44] On garnets see B. Arrhenius, *Merovingian Garnet Jewellery: Emergence and Social Implications* (Stockholm, 1985). On the Frankish connections of the burial see especially Ian N. Wood 'The Franks and Sutton Hoo', in *People and Places in Northern Europe, 500-1600: Essays in Honour of Peter Hayes Sawyer*, ed. Ian N. Wood and Niels Lund (Woodbridge, 1991), 1-14; Carver, *Sutton Hoo*, 312-13, 499-502.

[45] On the meaning of animal ornament see N. Åberg, *The Anglo-Saxons in England during the Early Centuries after the Invasion* (Uppsala, 1926); F. Klingender, *Animals in Art and Thought to the End of the Middle Ages* (London, 1971); George Speake, *Anglo-Saxon Animal Art and its Germanic Background* (Oxford, 1980); Carola Hicks, *Animals in Early Medieval Art* (Edinburgh, 1993). On boars in particular see Roberta Frank, 'The Boar on the Helmet', in *Aedificia Nova: Studies in Honor of Rosemary Cramp*, ed. Catherine E. Karkov and Helen Damico (Kalamazoo, MI, 2008), 76-88.

traced by the path of the light through the stone and back out again, a path that is followed by the eye of the viewer. It also creates a sense of ambiguity between ground and motif that complicates our perception of depth. The opaque colours of the millefiori form flat planes of colour that stop the eye at the surface of the piece, and they thus appear to float against the background of red and gold. Yet the depth of the cloisons and the prominent linear patterns of the clasps cause the millefiori cells to recede against the flickering light of the field of garnets. Time and visual ambiguity are also manifested in the movement of the animals and the time it takes our eyes to unravel their visual riddles, as well as the difficulty of working out exactly what is going on between the legs of the boars. The little granulated creatures stand out visually when light hits the piece, but their tiny size makes it extremely difficult to determine exactly what they represent. These shoulder clasps were clearly prestige objects whose materials, artistry and imagery were all indexes of wealth and power, but they also present us with puzzles whose meanings are less apparent, and which require some time and effort to unravel. As such they problematize the all too frequent modern association of the riddle with texts and with Christian literacy.[46] The riddle between image and the purpose or function of the object/image would go on to become a prominent feature of Anglo-Saxon art in general. The purpose of the clasps was to lock and to unlock, and their ornament addresses that purpose every bit as effectively as do the images and texts of the Ruthwell Cross (figs. 22, 39, 40) or the Franks Casket (fig. 41). In sum, the clasps require us to think about meaning and how it is conveyed. Michael King has recently raised the possibility that the clasps might contain an even more complex and explicitly Christian riddle. He points out that the front legs of the boars rest on stepped bases that support central pine-cone shapes This central motif, he suggests might be intended to represent the fountain of life, with the boars and the creatures between their legs either bowing down or reaching up to drink its waters.[47] This reading of the clasps' iconography is possible, although in order to unravel it the viewer would have to contemplate the design literally holding the pieces in his or her hand. There are certainly, however, many other pieces of jewellery that carried concealed meanings or messages known only to the wearer. Ultimately, whether accepted or not, King's close study of the boar panels

---

[46] For an important exception to the linking of visual riddles with texts see Leslie Webster, 'Encrypted Visions: Style and Sense in the Anglo-Saxon Minor Arts AD 400–900', in *Anglo-Saxon Styles*, ed. Karkov and Brown, 11–30. See also Jane Hawkes, 'Symbolic Lives: The Visual Evidence', in *The Anglo-Saxons from the Migration Period to the Eighth Century: An Ethnographic Perspective*, ed. John Hines (Woodbridge, 1997), 311–38.

[47] Michael King, 'Besette swinlicum: Sources for the Iconography of the Sutton Hoo Shoulder-clasps', in *The Anglo-Saxons in Their World*, ed. Gale Owen-Crocker (forthcoming).

on the clasps reveals a subtle play between two- and three-dimensional form that is entirely in keeping with the rest of the decoration.

There is no reason to believe that the Sutton Hoo clasps are not of East Anglian manufacture, although their prototypes lie in the Roman world.[48] Clearly they would have leant to the wearer an air of imperial authority, yet they also serve to unite, to lock together, histories and cultures. The decoration brings together styles (interlace), motifs (the boar), even media (the millefiori) that signalled combined British, Germanic and Roman traditions on an object that was of both the Romano-British past and the Anglo-Saxon present. There is also an aesthetic harmony evident in all of the jewellery from Mound 1 that has been taken to indicate that the Anglo-Saxon elite desired a unified look that conveyed a consistent message, and this desire for a co-ordinated look has been reinforced by the unified style of the objects in the discovered in 2009 Staffordshire hoard.[49]

Women too received high-status burial, and their grave assemblages were just as politically or culturally symbolic as those of their male counterparts, though generally on a much smaller scale. Evidence for Christianity became increasingly apparent in female burials as the seventh century progressed.[50] One example several notches down the scale of wealth from the princely burials discussed above is a female burial discovered in 1860 at Sarre, Kent. Amongst the grave goods were a gilt bronze cloisonné disc brooch inlaid with garnets and white shell, and a bead necklace hung with four gold coin pendants and a reused millefiori glass roundel (plate 2). The garnets and shell on the brooch are arranged to form a large cross at its centre, and the coin pendants are all from the issues of Christian emperors. In other words, these are undoubtedly Christian objects, even though that does not guarantee that the woman with whom they were buried was herself a Christian; other factors, fashion for example, may have been involved in their selection.[51] Like the Sutton Hoo shoulder clasps, the brooch is derived ultimately from Mediterranean models, but worked in what by this time had become typically Anglo-Saxon techniques. The metalworking techniques used on the Sarre brooch are just as accomplished as those of the shoulder clasps,[52] but the materials are not as lavish as those used for either the Sutton Hoo or Prittlewell jewellery. This is likely due not simply to the lesser status of

---

[48] See Webster and Backhouse, *Making of England*, 29–30.
[49] See below p. 102.
[50] Crawford, 'Votive Deposition'.
[51] On the use of grave goods in the conversion period see Geake, *The Use of Grave Goods in Conversion-Period England*; Helen Geake, 'Invisible Kingdoms: The Use of Grave-goods in Seventh-Century England', *ASSAH* 10 (1999), 203–15. On the Kentish disc brooches see R. Avent, *Anglo-Saxon Inlaid Disc and Composite Brooches*, BAR Brit. Ser. 11, 2 vols (Oxford, 1975); Crawford, 'Votive Deposition'.
[52] Coatsworth and Pindar, *The Art of the Anglo-Saxon Goldsmith*, 244.

the patron or burial, but also to the increasing scarcity of both gold and garnets. The garnets are also much simpler in shape than those of the Sutton Hoo jewellery, a trend that would continue with garnets becoming even simpler later in the century.[53] And, rather than being worked of solid gold, this brooch is cast bronze with silver and gilt. The back plate is silver, while the pin that it supports has garnet inlay collars around its head and a catchplate formed of animals and birds' heads.[54] On this brooch, the old Germanic animal ornament has been moved to the back of the brooch, leaving the cross as the main focus of the primary visual field. But the Sarre brooch does still present us with a visual puzzle. There are in fact three crosses on its face: the cross formed by the garnet and shell bosses, the cross formed by the gilt panels with their filigree ornament, and the cross formed by the gilt silver strips supporting the large central cabochon garnet. The five bosses that form the primary cross may have been understood as a symbolic crucifixion, with the bosses themselves (or perhaps the five circular garnets at their centres) standing for the five wounds of Christ.[55]

The use of coins as pendants amongst the Anglo-Saxons was a fashion of the late sixth and first half of the seventh century, and a number of examples survive from women's graves in Kent. It is also the case that both reused Roman objects and Scandinavian bracteates are found predominantly in the graves of women,[56] although quite why this should be the case is now a matter of debate. Coins, medallions and bracteates are all objects worn or used in life primarily by men in the early Middle Ages. It may be that they were given to women and ended up in their burials once they no longer had political or cultural currency, or it may be that their use by the living of both genders was more complex than we currently understand it to have been.

The coins on the Sarre necklace consist of quasi-imperial gold solidi of Maurice Tiberius, and Heraclius, and a solidus of Chlotar II, all struck at Arles or Marseilles. When worn together, the crosses on the reverses of the coins would have furthered the Christian message of the brooch, while the diademed busts on the obverses are clear signs of royal, if not imperial grandeur. We cannot know whether it mattered that these were

---

[53] See, for example, the late seventh-century Boss Hall brooch illustrated in Webster and Backhouse, *The Making of England*, 52. See also David A. Hinton, *Gold and Gilt, Pots and Pins. Possessions and People in Medieval Britain* (Oxford, 2005), 67.
[54] For an illustration of the back see Speake, *Anglo-Saxon Animal Art*, pl. 10a.
[55] See below note 64.
[56] A bracteate is a thin gold circular pendant with decoration stamped on one side only. On gender and grave goods see especially Nancy L. Wicker, *Goldsmiths, Patrons, and Women: Typology, Chronology, and the Social Life of Early Medieval Scandinavian Jewelry*, forthcoming; see also Natasha Dodwell, Sam Lucy and Jess Tipper, 'Anglo-Saxons on the Cambridge Backs: The Criminology Site Settlement and King's Garden Hostel Cemetery', *Proceedings of the Cambridge Antiquarian Society* 93 (2004), 95–124; Bettina Arnold and Nancy L. Wicker, eds., *Gender and the Archaeology of Death* (Walnut Creek, CA, 2001).

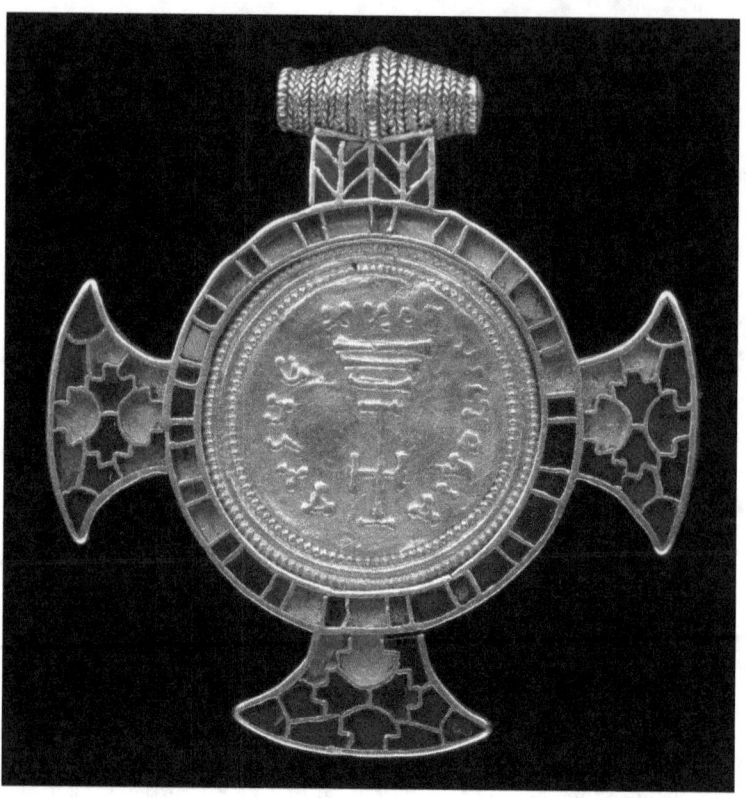

FIG. 6. WILTON CROSS PENDANT

Roman coins, or whether they were valued simply because they were elite gold objects, although the fact that so many Roman objects come from women's graves suggests that their Roman origin may indeed have been important. Similarly, we cannot know whether the two objects were produced as a set or intended to be worn together. They are indeed made of different materials; however the circular shapes of the coins are echoed by those of the brooch and its bosses, and the red, white and gold colours of the brooch are repeated in the pendants and some of the beads of the necklace. This suggests that, even several steps down the social scale from the princely occupants of the Mound 1 and Prittlewell burials, those who wore jewellery may have desired a visually consistent aesthetic.

The Wilton cross pendant (fig. 6) is syntactically similar in type to the Sarre necklace, but in terms of workmanship it is of much higher quality; indeed, it has been attributed to the Sutton Hoo workshop.[57] The Wilton cross was a stray find, so there is no way of knowing whether

---

[57] See e.g., the entry for the pendant in Webster and Backhouse, *The Making of England*, 28.

it was worn by a man or a woman. At the centre of the pendant is a solidus of 613–30 depicting Heraclius with Heraclius Constantine on the unseen obverse. On the reverse, struck upside down to the design on the obverse, is a cross on steps. Clearly when the coin was made into a pendant the cross became the primary motif as it was the one chosen for display,[58] though it is unclear why the cross has been set upside down. One theory is that the artist did not want to invert the human faces on the other side, even though they were not visible; another is that the cross was intended to be seen from the wearer's perspective. With its flat upper bar and stepped base, this type of cross has been identified with the True Cross of the Crucifixion; as such it provides yet another example of Anglo-Saxon *romanitas*, and perhaps also establishes a parallel between the origins of the Church and the church of the Anglo-Saxons. The garnets in the expanded arms of the cloisonné mount have been cut and arranged so that additional crosses are formed by the pairs of stepped and mushroom-shaped stones at their centres. Each arm is also divided into twelve cells, a number that often signified the twelve apostles, as well as the idea that the apostles preached the trinity to the four corners of the earth – a message particularly appropriate within any conversion context. The complex and symbolic designs of the Wilton cross and similar cross-ornamented pendants and brooches from the seventh century are important precedents for the even more complex design and symbolism of the cross carpet pages of the Lindisfarne Gospels (fig. 7) and other early Insular manuscripts, and indeed they were designed using the same simple grid and compass tools that were used for the later manuscripts.[59]

Colour is as important on the Sarre brooch and Wilton cross as it was on the Sutton Hoo shoulder clasps, although on these objects it most probably has a symbolic as well as an aesthetic function. The red and gold colour combination seen on both has its origins in the gold and garnet jewellery in favour in Francia and adopted by the Anglo-Saxons, yet by this point it had very likely become symbolic of the interrelated images of the blood-covered cross of the Crucifixion and the apocalyptic *crux gemmata*.[60] Red stones were associated with the blood of Christ and the martyrs in exegesis,[61] and gold shone with the light of heaven.

---

[58] The back of the pendant is sheet gold, and the coin has been set so that the busts of the rulers are still visible, but the arms of the mount in which it is set are undecorated.
[59] Coatsworth and Pindar, *The Art of the Anglo-Saxon Goldsmith*, 164.
[60] On the background to the True Cross and the *crux gemmata* and their reception in Anglo-Saxon England see Ian N. Wood, 'Constantinian Crosses in Northumbria', in *The Place of the Cross in Anglo-Saxon England*, ed. Karkov, Keefer and Jolly, 3–13.
[61] 'Qui ex integro sanguinei coloris est, martyrum gloriam significat ... merito sexto loco positus, cum dominus noster et sexta aetate saeculi incarnatus, et sexta feria sit pro totius mundi salute crucifixus' (which is wholly blood-red in colour, signifies the glory of martyrs ... and is put in the sixth place accordingly, because our Lord was incarnate in the sixth period of the age, and was crucified on the sixth day of the week [for the salvation of the whole world]): Bede, *Bedae Presbyteri Expositio Apocalypseos*,

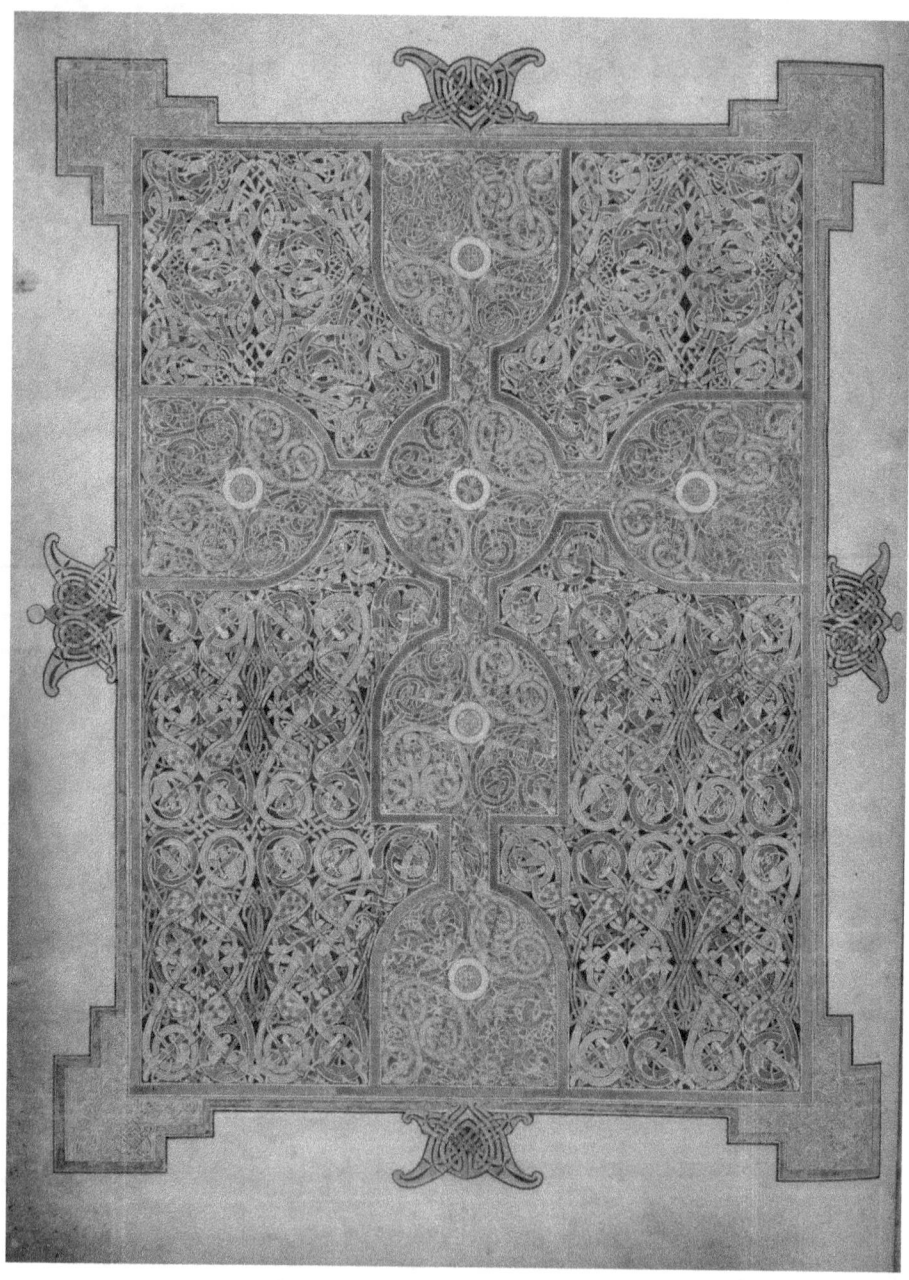

FIG. 7. CARPET PAGE,
LINDISFARNE GOSPELS.
LONDON, BL, MS COTTON
NERO D.IV, FOL. 26V

The Old English poem *The Dream of the Rood*, preserved in the c. 1000 Vercelli Book, though perhaps composed at (or reflecting, quoting or incorporating a poem of) a much earlier date, describes a great visionary cross that is at once covered with the blood of Christ and gleaming with gold and jewels, the struggle and the blood discernable through the gold.

> Þuhte me þæt ic gesawe    syllicre treow
> on lyft lædan,    leohte bewunden,
> beama beorhtost.    Eall þæt beacen wæs
> begoten mid golde;    gimmas stodon
> fægere æt foldan sceatum;    swylce þær fife wæron
> uppe on þam eaxlegespanne.    Beheoldon þær engel Dryhtnes ealle,
> fægere þurh forðgesceaft.    Ne wæs ðær huru fracodes gealga.
> Ac hine þær beheoldon    halige gastas,
> men ofer moldan    ond eall þeos mære gesceaft.
>     Syllic wæs se sigebeam,    ond ic synnum fah,
> forwunded mid wommum.    Geseah ic wuldres treow,
> wædum geweorðode,    wynnum scinan,
> gegyred mid golde;    gimmas hæfdon
> bewrigene weorðlice    wealdes treow.
> Hwæðre ic þurh þæt gold    ongytan meahte
> earmra ærgewin,    þæt hit ærest ongan
> swætan on þa swiðran healfe.    Eall ic wæs mid s[o]rgum gedrefed.
> Forht ic wæs for þære fægran gesyhðe.    Geseah ic þæt fuse beacen
> wendan wædum ond bleom;    hwilum hit wæs mid wætan bestemed,
> beswyled mit swates gange,    hwilum mid since gegyrwed.
> Hwæðre ic þær licgende    lange hwile
> beheold hreowcearig    Hælendes treow,
> oððæt ic gehyrde þæt hit hleoðrode.[62] [5–26]

I thought that I saw a wondrous tree rising in the air surrounded by light, brightest of beams. All that beacon was covered with gold; gems stood fair at its earthen base; there were also five on its shoulder-span. I beheld there the angel of the Lord, fair through eternity. On the gallows there was not an evil criminal, but he there beheld by holy spirits, men on earth and all this

---

ed. R. Gryson, CCSL 121A (Turnhout, 2001), 543. On colour symbolism in Anglo-Saxon England in general see Peter Kitson, 'Lapidary Traditions in Anglo-Saxon England I: The Background: The Old English Lapidary', *ASE* 7 (1978), 9–60; Peter Kitson, 'Lapidary Traditions in Anglo-Saxon England II: Bede's *Expositio Apocalypseos* and Related Works', *ASE* 12 (1983), 72–123.

[62] Text based on Michael J. Swanton, ed., *The Dream of the Rood*, rev edn (Exeter, 1987); translation my own.

> glorious creation. Wondrous was that victory-tree, and I stained with sins, wounded with wrongs. There I saw that glorious wood adorned with beautiful shining garments, dressed with gold, gems splendidly covered the Lord's tree. Nevertheless through that gold I could make out the wretched ancient struggle, when it first began to bleed on its right side. I was all consumed with sorrows. I was afraid for that fair vision. I saw that shining beacon change coverings and colours; sometimes it was soaked with moisture, covered with flowing blood, sometimes covered with treasure. Nevertheless I lay there a long while and beheld sorrowfully the Saviour's tree, until I dreamt that it spoke.

The cross of the poem is simultaneously gleaming with gold and jewels and drenched in blood,[63] a visionary combination that evokes not only the materials of the brooch and pendant but also the way in which the stamped gold foils shine through the blood-red of the garnets. While the written version of the poem is later than any of the jewellery discussed above, the five gems of the visionary cross also recall the five jewelled bosses of the Sarre brooch.[64] The connection between the wounds of Christ and gemstones is made explicit in the tenth-century Blickling homily 'Annunciato S Mariae',[65] but the association between blood and red stones is much earlier than that, as Bede's *Expositio Apocalypseos* makes clear. Near the end of *The Dream of the Rood* the cross tells the dreamer that no one who carries the sign of the cross in his breast need be afraid of judgement.[66] It is a salvific sign, just as the cross decorated brooches and pendants worn on the breasts of Anglo-Saxon men and women from the sixth and seventh centuries onward were (or at least could be) signs of their hoped-for salvation.

---

[63] Although the dreamer says that it was sometimes covered with blood and sometimes covered with treasure, he (or she) seems to be able to envisage both images at the same time. Moreover, the 'ancient struggle' and the bleeding cross can be seen through the gold. On vision in the poem see Thomas N. Hall, 'Prophetic Vision in *The Dream of the Rood*', in *Poetry, Place and Gender: Studies in Medieval Culture in Honor of Helen Damico*, ed. Catherine E. Karkov (Kalamazoo, MI, 2009), 60–74.

[64] The pattern of five bosses placed in and around the centre of a cross would survive to become a form of symbolic crucifixion in stone sculpture of a slightly later date. On the more general relationship between the poem and art see Barbara C. Raw, '*The Dream of the Rood* and its Connections with Early Christian Art', MAe 39 (1970), 239–56.

[65] R. Morris, ed., *The Blickling Homilies of the Tenth Century*, EETS 58, 63, 73 (London, 1980), 8–11. 'he sealde his þone readan gim, þæt wæs his þæt halige blod, mid þon he us gedyde dæl-nimende þæs heofonlican rices' (he gave that red gem, that was his holy blood, and in doing so made us participators in the heavenly kingdom).

[66] 'Ne þearf ðær þonne ænig unforht wesan / þe him ær in breostum bereð beacna selest' (117–18).

## THE ORIGINS OF THE ANGLO-SAXON ILLUMINATED BOOK

Colonization, conversion and the transformation of cultures are also about translation, and this too can take many forms.[67] Traditions and practices from the homeland may be translated into a new cultural and geographic setting, or pagan may be translated into Christian, as we have seen happen with Anglo-Saxon burial practices and grave goods of the sixth and seventh centuries. There is also translation between languages. In this book, translation between Latin and Old English will be our major concern, but there was also translation between Latin, Old English and the Celtic languages.[68] In addition, Anglo-Saxon art provides abundant evidence for translation between objects and media, and here I am talking about much more than a simple commonality of style or aesthetic. One of the most important instances of this last form of translation in conversion period England may be seen in the translation of motifs, styles and iconographies from traditional art forms such as metalworking into new media and types of object such as the book. The Lindisfarne Gospels (London, BL, Cotton Nero D.iv) may not be the earliest manuscript produced in Anglo-Saxon England, but it is an excellent example of this type of translation involving media, form and language. It is also a book that would remain a crucial touchstone of Anglo-Saxon and, later, English identity down to the present day.

The Lindisfarne Gospels was most probably produced at the island monastery of Lindisfarne in the late seventh or early eighth century,[69] and is believed to have accompanied the community when it fled the island following Viking attacks.[70] The first solid evidence for its possession by the community of St Cuthbert is the Old English colophon and gloss on the Latin text added to the manuscript in the third quarter of the tenth century by the priest Aldred at Chester-le-Street. Aldred's colophon names Lindisfarne as the site of the manuscript's production, and also names the men involved in its creation and the motivation for their work. The colophon is important in its own right, and while I will be returning to it in more detail in a later chapter, it is worth quoting here in full. It begins with an inscription in Latin written to the right of the explicit to John's gospel: '+Lit(er)a me pandat sermonis fida ministra. Omnes alme meos fratres voce salvta' (+May the letter, faithful servant of the word, speak

---

[67] On translation as a point of intersection between the medieval and the postcolonial, see especially Kabir and Williams, *Postcolonial Approaches to the European Middle Ages*.
[68] The interaction of Celtic languages with Anglo-Saxon culture is especially apparent in the art of south-western England. See especially Rosemary Cramp, *South-West England*, CASSS 7 (Oxford, 2006), ch. 8 and appendix H.
[69] For a complete discussion of the manuscript see Michelle P. Brown, *The Lindisfarne Gospels: Society, Spirituality and the Scribe* (London, 2003).
[70] See below p. 000.

for me. Greet all my brothers with a kindly voice).[71] Then follows a text known as the 'Five Sentences' written in alternating lines of Old English and Latin.

> ðe ðrifalde 7 ðe anfalde god ðis godspell / aer vorvlda gisette
> +Trinus et unus d(eu)s evangelium hoc ante / saecula con stituit
> ærist avrat of mvðe crist(es)
> +Matheus ex ore c(h)r(ist)i scripsit
> of mvðe petres avrat
> +Marcus ex ore Petri scrips(it)
> of mvðe paules avrat
> +Lvcas de ore Pauli ap' scrips(it)
> in deigilnisi ł i(n) f(ore)esaga siðða rocgetede ł gisprant
> +Ioh(annes) in prochemio deinde eructavit
> word mið gode gisalde 7 halges gastes 'ł mið godes geafa | 7 halges gastes
> verbum d(e)o donante et sp(irit)v s(an)c(t)o scrips(it) |mæht avrát ioh(annes)[72]

> +God, three in one, these gospels have since [the dawn of] the age consisted of:
> +Matthew who wrote what he heard from Christ, / +Mark who wrote what he heard from Peter, / +Luke who wrote what he heard from the apostle Paul, / +John who willingly thereupon proclaimed and wrote the Word given by God through the Holy Spirit.

Then follows Aldred's account of this book.

> +eadfrið bisco[p/b] lindisfearnensis æcclesiæ
> he ðis boc avrát æt frvma gode 7 s(an)c(t)e
> cvðberhte 7 allvm ðæm halgvm. ða 'gimænelice' ðe
> in eolonde sint. 7 eðilvald lindisfearneolondinga 'bisc(op)'
> hit vta giðryde 7 gibélde sva hé vel cuðę.
> 7 billfrið se oncrę he gismioðade ða
> gihríno ða ðe vtan ón sint 7 hit gi<->
> hrínade mið golde 7 mið gimmvm ęc
> mið svlfre' of(er)gylded faconleas feh:
> 7 [ic] Aldred p(res)'s'b(yte)r indignus 7 misserim(us)[73]
> mið godes fvltv(m)mę 7 s(an)c(t)i cvðberhtes

---

[71] The transcription of the colophon is based on that in Jane Roberts, 'Aldred Signs Off from Glossing the Lindisfarne Gospels', in *Writing and Texts in Anglo-Saxon England*, ed. Alexander R. Rumble (Woodbridge, 2006), 28–43; see also Brown, *The Lindisfarne Gospels*, 102–3. For further discussion of the colophon see Lawrence Nees, 'Reading Aldred's Colophon for the Lindisfarne Gospels', *Speculum* 78 (2003), 333–77.

[72] Text and translation Brown, *The Lindisfarne Gospels*, 102–3.

[73] In the margin next to this line is written 'Ælfredi natvs aldredvs uocar bonæ mvlieris filivs eximvs loquor' (Aldred son of Alfred is my name, the son of a good woman, I speak).

# THE ART OF ORIGINS

hit of(er)glóesade ón englisc 7 hine gihamadi
mið ðæm ðríim dælv(m). Mathevs dǽl
gode 7 s(an)c(t)e cvðberhti. Marc(vs) dǽl.
ðæm bisc(ope). 7 lvcas dæl ðæm hiorode
7 æht 'v' ora s[eo \'v']lfres mið tó inláde.:-
7 sci ioh(annes) dæl f(ore) hine seolfne /'i(d est) f(or)e his savle'/
7 feover óra
s[eo]'v'lfres mið gode 7 s(an)c(t)i cvðberhti. Þ(æt)te he
hæbbe ondfong ðerh godes miltsæ on heofnv(m).
séel 7 sibb on eorðo forðgeong 7 giðyngo
visdóm 7 snyttro ðerh s(an)c(t)i cvðberhtes earnvnga:,
+eadfrið, oeðilvald, billfrið, Aldred. hoc evange(lium) d(e)o 7
Cuðberhto constrvxer(vn)t (ve)l ornavervunt.

+Eadfrith, bishop of the Lindisfarne church, first wrote this book for God and St Cuthbert, and all the saints whose relics are in the island. And Eðilwald, bishop of the Lindisfarne islanders, pressed it and covered it on the outside as well he knew how to do. And Billfrið the anchorite made the metal ornaments that are on the outside, and decorated it with gold and with gems and also with gilded over silver – pure treasure. And [I] Aldred, unworthy and most miserable priest, glossed it in English with the help of God and St Cuthbert, and made a home for himself with these three sections: the section of Matthew was for God and St Cuthbert, the section of Mark for the bishop, the section of Luke for the members of the community together with eight ores of silver for his induction, and the section of John for himself, i.e. for his soul, together with four ores of silver for God and St Cuthbert so that, through the mercy of God, he may gain acceptance into heaven, happiness and peace on earth, success and progress, wisdom and knowledge through the reward of St Cuthbert.
+Eadfrið, Oeðilwald, Billfrið and Aldred made this gospel book for God and St Cuthbert

While the colophon is a later addition to the manuscript, embedded in it is a verse passage that may have been adapted from an earlier source, perhaps an inscription on the original cover of the gospels.[74] Jane Roberts has reconstructed the verse as:

+Eadfrið biscop   ðis boc avrat
allvm ðæm halgvm   ðe in eolonde sint.
Eðilvald biscob   hit vta giðryde,
gibelde sva he vel cuðę.   Billfrið se oncrę

---

[74] Brown, *The Lindisfarne Gospels*, 95–6, 210–12.

> gigyrede hit mið golde  7 mið gimmvm ęc
> mið svlfre of(er)gylde,  faconleas feh.⁷⁵

As well as possibly recording the true origins of the book, the colophon reveals something of the way in which the book was perceived within the community. It was not just an object but a labour for God, Cuthbert, the saints and the community, and one which brought its makers (including Aldred) spiritual rewards. The colophon also places Eadfrið, Eðilwald, Billfrið and Aldred in a direct line of scribal descent from the four evangelists, the authors of the original gospels. Their work was a continuation, not a mere copying, translating or glossing of that of the evangelists.⁷⁶ However, if this is indeed a trace of an earlier inscription, it indicates that Aldred did not fabricate the origins of the book and the names of its first three makers simply so that he could situate himself in the position of John.

Admittedly the colophon is not itself part of the art of the Lindisfarne Gospels, but it provides a rare example of the Anglo-Saxons' own perception of their artists. The men who made the book's cover and its decoration were considered 'authors' of the book along with its scribe and glossator. Aldred also names Eadfrið as the scribe of the manuscript, but does not name an illuminator, which suggests that Eadfrið both wrote and illuminated the book. This is supported by the unity of the text and artwork in the book itself, exemplified here by the three-page opening sequence to Matthew. The sequence starts with the portrait of the writing evangelist Matthew (fig. 8). This is first of all a type of author portrait that has its sources in the art of late antiquity, and this in and of itself indexes the origins of the illuminated gospel book in the Mediterranean world. Michelle Brown has identified the Lindisfarne Gospels as containing the earliest representations of the evangelist scribes to survive from northern Europe.⁷⁷ Significantly the bright colours and linear patterns of the figures and objects depicted translate them into enamel- or jewel-like forms that float against the flat surface of the background rather than appearing to occupy any three-dimensional or architectural space. Above Matthew's head is his trumpeting symbol, representing the divine inspiration that lies behind the written word of the human evangelist. The symbol is labelled in Latin half-uncials 'imago hominis' (image of a man), while the evangelist is labelled in transliterated Greek 'Hagios Mattheus' (St Matthew) written in Latin lettering with runic elements. The combination of language and scripts, the trumpeting symbol and the writing man, work together to convey the process of the transmission and translation of texts. The reception of texts is suggested further by the book-holding figure,

---

[75] Roberts, 'Aldred Signs Off', 40. Roberts has emended 'gihrinade' to 'gigyrede' because it makes better metrical sense, but the verse stands without the emendation.
[76] See further chapter five.
[77] Brown, *The Lindisfarne Gospels*, 349.

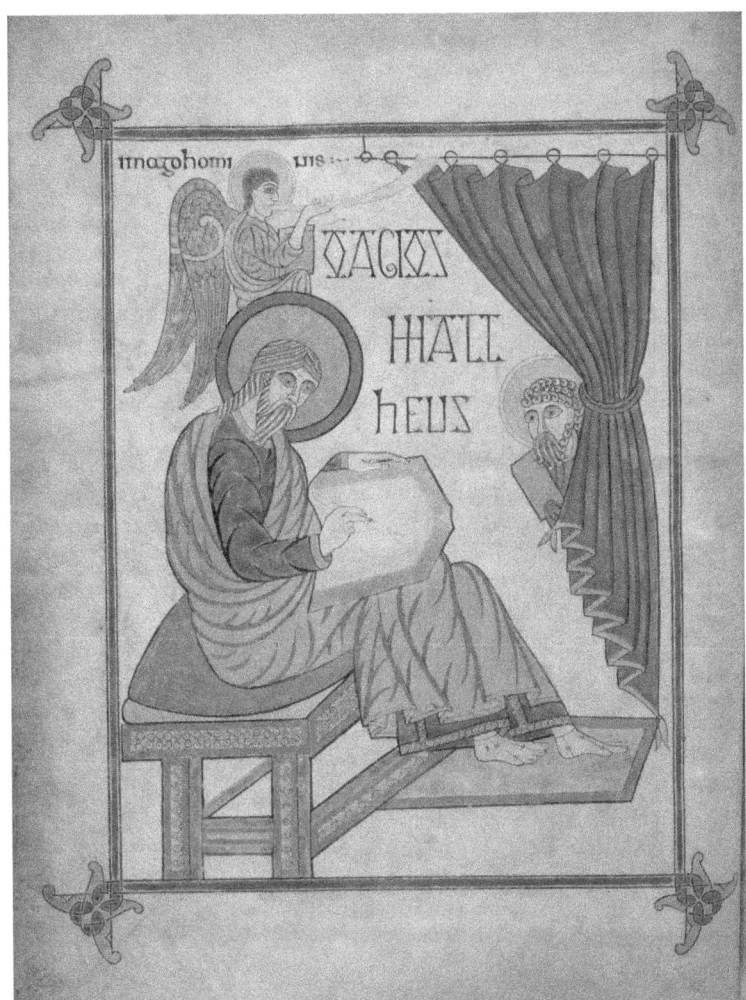

FIG. 8.
PORTRAIT OF
ST MATTHEW,
LINDISFARNE
GOSPELS. LONDON,
BL, MS COTTON
NERO D.IV, FOL. 25V

whoever he may be, who peers from behind the curtain.[78] His grey hair and beard, purple robe and green book mirror those of the evangelist, while his pose and wide staring eyes direct our attention back to Matthew and his act of writing.

Each of the Lindisfarne evangelist portraits is on a verso page facing a blank recto, an arrangement which furthers the iconic focus on the writing figures of the evangelists and the books they either write or

---

[78] He has been identified variously as Christ, Moses or St Cuthbert.

display.⁷⁹ Turning the page, a cross-carpet page on the verso serves as a painted version of a jewelled book cover for the incipit of the gospel on the recto.⁸⁰ Both are alive with the same form of animal ornament, play between foreground and background, and visual riddles that characterize Anglo-Saxon metalwork, here again translated onto the painted page. The white circles at the centre of each of the chalice-shaped sections of the cross at the centre of the carpet page make a particularly apt comparison with the bosses of the Sarre brooch. On the incipit page (fig. 50) the opening lines of Matthew's gospel, 'Liber generationis ...' are written in letters that sprout tails and beast heads – the Word truly brought to life. Above the border that frames the incipit proper is written in gold '+ihs̄ xp̄s Mattheus homo', words that refer us back to the evangelist portrait. Here, in Latin, words from the two separate inscriptions on the portrait page, the name of Matthew from his inscription, and the 'homo' from that of his symbol, are combined to show that the written text is the product of both the earthly author and the divine inspiration that entered into him when he wrote – the divine and unknowable translated into human script and language. Aldred's Old English gloss is visible above the text and in the right margin of the page.

Quotation as well as translation is also an important part of this particular set of images. The Matthew portrait quotes the roughly contemporary Ezra portrait from the Codex Amiatinus, produced at Wearmouth-Jarrow in the early eighth century, and is in turn quoted by the late tenth- or early eleventh-century Matthew portrait in the Copenhagen Gospels (Copenhagen, Royal Library, Gl. Kgl. Sml 10, 2°, fol. 17v; fig. 9).⁸¹ Let's look first at the relationship between the Lindisfarne

---

[79] Matthew, Mark and Luke write, while John displays his text. Depicting John in a pose different from that of the other three evangelists was a typical way of indicating the special nature of John and his gospel.

[80] Brown has suggested that the carpet pages may also serve as symbolic crucifixions or be signs of prayer-mats, labyrinths or maps of Jerusalem: *Lindisfarne Gospels*, 320–6.

[81] The exact date and provenance of the manuscript are disputed. Some believe it to have been begun at Winchester in the late tenth century and finished elsewhere – possibly at Peterborough or Christ Church Canterbury – in the early eleventh century. See T. A. M. Bishop, 'The Copenhagen Gospel Book', *Nordisk Tidsckrift for Bok-och Biblioteksväsen* 54 (1967), 33–41; Elżbieta Temple, *Anglo-Saxon Manuscripts 900–1066* (London, 1976), no. 47; D. H. Turner, 'The Copenhagen Gospels', in *The Golden Age of Anglo-Saxon Art 966–1066*, ed. Janet Backhouse, D. H. Turner and Leslie Webster (London, 1984), no. 48; Brown, *Lindisfarne Gospels*, 354; Carol A. Farr, 'Style in Late Anglo-Saxon England: Questions of Learning and Education', in *Anglo-Saxon Styles*, ed. Karkov and Brown, 117–20. Heslop believes that the entire manuscript was produced in one campaign *c.* 1020 by scribes from two separate fenland centres: Peterborough and possibly Thorney (T. A. Heslop, 'The Production of *de luxe* Manuscripts and the Patronage of King Cnut and Queen Emma', *ASE* 19 (1990), 151–95, at 165–9, 191–5. Recently, Thomas Rydén has suggested that the manuscript was written and illustrated *c.* 970–75 at Winchester; Thomas Rydén, *Det anglosaksiska köpenhamnsevangeliariet, Det Kongelige Bibliotek Gl. Kongl. Saml. 10 2o* (Lund, 2001).

and Amiatinus portraits.[82] The Amiatinus image has been discussed as a portrait of the Old Testament scribe Ezra and as an image of Cassiodorus himself adapted to make reference to Ezra,[83] but Michelle Brown makes the point that it may also be read as 'a homage to the continued process of rediscovery and emendation of sacred text continually inspired by the Holy Spirit'.[84] The nine volumes in the bookcase behind the seated scribe bear the names of patristic authors such as Origen and Jerome on their spines, but they also signify Cassiodorus's own nine-volume Codex Grandior. The Codex Amiatinus was one of the three great pandects (one-volume bibles) produced at Wearmouth-Jarrow under the direction of Abbot Ceolfrid. Its text is based on that of Cassiodorus's Codex Grandior, but it is not a copy, as Brown notes further; rather it is 'an active, dynamic work of scholarly compilation and emendation', possibly with reference to the process through which Jerome went in compiling and editing his three translations of the Bible.[85] The Ezra portrait thus points to a lengthy historical scribal genealogy and series of translations that bring the viewer from the origins of the Bible in the Old Testament to eighth-century Northumbria. It suggests a movement across time, space and culture, and would have taken its Anglo-Saxon audience back to the Old Testament world and the story of Exodus from which they derived one of their most fundamental myths of origin.[86] But this book was also intended as a gift for the pope in Rome, and would thus have returned something of Anglo-Saxon England to the Roman church (and Mediterranean world), which had been so influential on the beginnings of the church in England.

The monks of Lindisfarne were in close, very close if Michelle Brown is correct,[87] contact with events at Wearmouth-Jarrow at the time that both the Codex Amiatinus and the Lindisfarne Gospels were produced. There is no doubt that the Lindisfarne portrait of Matthew draws from the iconography of the Amiatinus Ezra. The pose of the two men, the benches on which they sit, and the arrangement of their feet are all very

---

[82] See Paul Meyvaert, 'The Date of Bede's *In Ezram* and His Image of Ezra in the Codex Amiatinus', *Speculum* 80.4 (2005), 1087–133; Richard Marsden, 'Job in His Place: The Ezra Miniature in the Codex Amiatinus', *Scriptorium* 49.1 (1995), 3–15; Scott Degregorio, 'Bede's *In Ezram et Neemiam* and the Reform of the Northumbrian Church', *Speculum* 79.1 (2004), 1–25. On the textual relationship between Amiatinus and Lindisfarne see Brown, *The Lindisfarne Gospels*, 153–61.
[83] Jennifer O'Reilly, 'The Library of Scripture: Views from the Vivarium and Wearmouth-Jarrow', in *New Offerings, Ancient Treasures: Essays in Medieval Art for George Henderson*, ed. Paul Binski and William G. Noel (Stroud, 2001), 3–39.
[84] Brown, *The Lindisfarne Gospels*, 195.
[85] Brown, *The Lindisfarne Gospels*, 156; see also Celia Chazelle, 'Christ and the Vision of God: The Biblical Diagrams of the Codex Amiatinus', in *The Mind's Eye: Art and Theological Argument in the Middle Ages*, ed. Jeffrey Hamburger and Anne-Marie Bouché (Princeton, NJ, 2006), 84–111.
[86] On which see Nicholas Howe, *Migration and Mythmaking in Anglo-Saxon England* (New Haven, CT, 1989).
[87] Michelle P. Brown, *In the Beginning Was the Word: Books and Faith in the Age of Bede*, Jarrow Lecture (Jarrow, 2000).

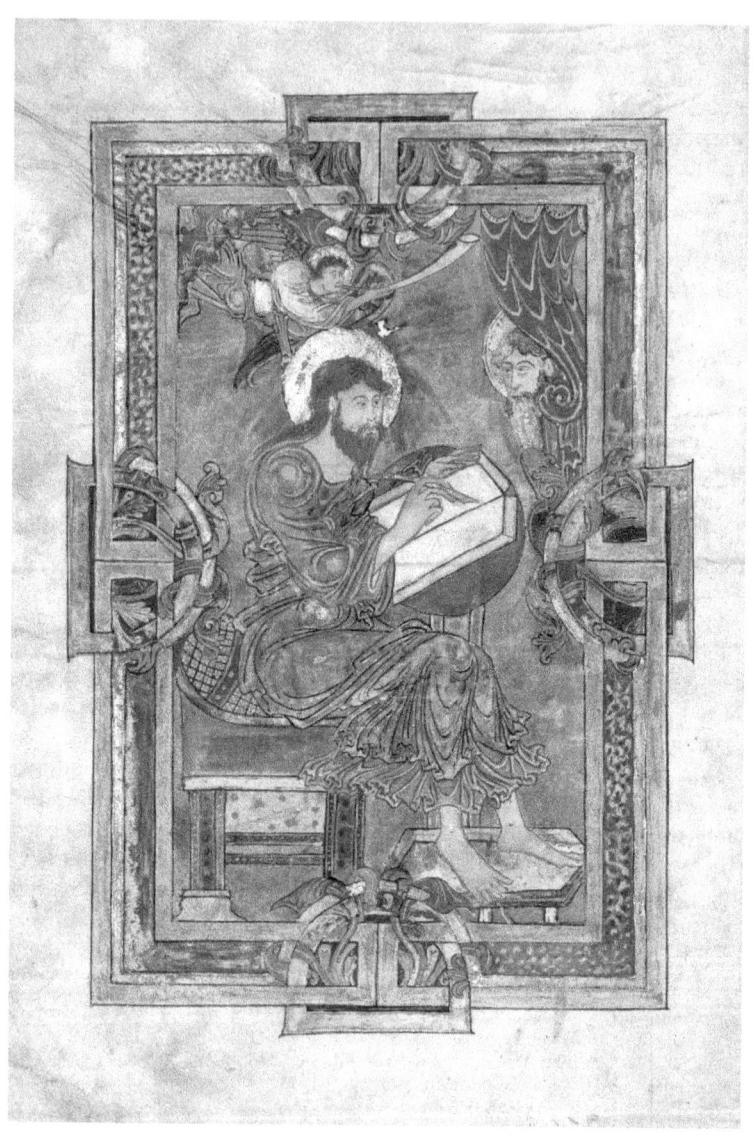

FIG. 9.
COPENHAGEN
GOSPELS, PORTRAIT
OF ST MATTHEW.
COPENHAGEN,
KONGELIGE
BIBLIOTEK, MS GL.
KGL. SML 10, 2º,
FOL. 17V

similar, but they are not identical. Nor should we think of the Lindisfarne portrait, with its odd perspective and curiously drawn sandals, as simply 'derivative' or as a misunderstood copy of the Amiatinus image. Rather it forms yet another link in the chain of authors and translations. Matthew is also positioned at the point at which the vertical and horizontal axes of the composition meet. There is a vertical axis formed by Matthew and his symbol that traces the origin of the written text from its divine inspiration downwards to the writing evangelist; the horizontal axis then follows the text outward, past the book that is being written to the book-holding figure behind the curtain (and beyond that to the text itself when one turns the page). Indeed, it might be that the book-holding figure who peers from behind the curtain is meant to emphasize this very process. These figures are located not in a closed room (as is the Amiatinus Ezra), but against the flat space of the page, suggesting the eternal, ongoing nature of their actions, the words of the gospel spreading out through both divine inspiration (the trumpeting symbol) and the written book. Despite having been painted over 200 years before Aldred's gloss and colophon were written, it also provides a perfect visual preface to the history of authors and authorial inspiration of which he writes.

The Copenhagen Gospels miniature (fig. 9) stands in a similar relationship to Lindisfarne as does Lindisfarne to Amiatinus. It includes the essential pictorial elements of the earlier miniature, the writing evangelist, the trumpeting symbol and the book-holding figure behind the curtain, but the relationship of these figures to each other, as well as important details of both the figures and the overall composition, have been transformed. The image is, first of all, less iconic and more narrative than the Lindisfarne miniature. The angel swoops in from above, and Matthew's eyes are no longer on his book but on the figure behind the curtain. The fluttering 'Winchester style' drapery and foliage add motion to the page, which furthers the sense of narrative motion created by the figures. The inscriptions identifying the evangelist and his symbol, a prominent part of the Lindisfarne page, are not present in the Copenhagen portrait. The complex textuality of Lindisfarne is therefore lost, but it has been replaced by a sense of oral transmission between the figures represented, possibly meant to illustrate the tradition that Matthew wrote what he heard from Christ – as recorded in the 'Five Sentences' of Aldred's colophon. The transmission and translation of texts are again at the heart of the miniature, but its seeming emphasis on the centrality of the spoken word adds a layer of living oral transmission to the textual semiosis of Lindisfarne and Amiatinus. It has been suggested that the Copenhagen Gospels portrait was not copied directly from the Lindisfarne Matthew, but that both are derived from a common model. However Michelle Brown points out that the chalice-shaped designs of the border are most likely derived from the similarly shaped terminals of the cross on the Matthew carpet page.[88] (Interestingly, the composition places the writing evangelist at the centre of the cross he defines, furthering the

---

[88] Brown, *The Lindisfarne Gospels*, 355. See also Farr, 'Style in Late Anglo-Saxon England', 118–19 for a discussion of the transfer process evidenced by indentations made by a stylus, and the implications of this process.

connection between his act of writing and Christ the Word.[89]) If the image and inscription in the Lindisfarne miniature were used to embed it with a sense of a shared classical past, possibly even an imagined ecumenical community in which the Cuthbert community could participate, at least through their book, the Copenhagen Gospels image repositions that past and that community within England itself.

The models of transmission from Amiatinus to the Lindisfarne Gospels to the Copenhagen Gospels sketched briefly here bring us to a slightly different understanding of the art of origins that has formed the subject of this chapter; yet in their reference to or use of each other, they provide a fitting example in microcosm of at least one important facet of the Anglo-Saxon approach to art. Roland Barthes wrote that the writer of a text was merely the orchestrator of the 'already-written' rather than its originator,[90] and though the works surveyed in this book were produced centuries before Barthes and modern theories of the death of the author, the concept of artistic creation that lies behind them has distinct similarities with this definition of authorship. Origins for the Anglo-Saxons were something that were always present in the earlier object, text, culture or historical moment, but existed in a permanent state of transformation and renewal. Practically speaking, the physical world (and hence artistic creation) did have an ultimate origin in Creation itself, but even before that, as manuscript illumination will demonstrate to us again and again, there was the Word. Visual complexity and riddling had been a part of Anglo-Saxon art before the coming of Christianity to England and before the book, but it was within the sacred space of ecclesiastical art that it would be exploited to the full, and it is to the sacred space in which that art developed that we will now turn.

---

[89] This type of composition is common in earlier Insular manuscripts. See, for example, folio 31r and the portrait of the Virgin and Child in the Book of Kells (Dublin, Trinity College Library, MS 58), where text and figures respectively become part of a larger cruciform composition with terminals of similar shape.

[90] Roland Barthes, S/Z (London, 1974), 21.

# SACRED SPACE 2

Where the sacred began and ended for the Anglo-Saxons is a hard thing to pin down, both in terms of physical space, especially when it comes to landscape, and in terms of the spiritual space of devotion. Communities, both monastic and lay, had their saints and relics whose protective power was not limited to the space of the church, although the church did serve as a focus for it. The landscapes of both settlement (early Canterbury, for example, or the area of Bamburgh/Lindisfarne) and monastic retreat (Bewcastle might be an example, Cuthbert's cell on Farne Island certainly is) were filled with religious observances from prayers to processions, with crosses and other forms of sculpture, and with the memories of the dead. At the centre of it all was the church. As building and as institution the church was literally a centre of life for the surrounding community, but it was also very much a centre from which the ordering of land and society radiated out in multiple forms, from liturgical processions to the production of documents such as histories and charters, to the quarrying of stone and the construction (in some cases reconstruction) of stone architecture.

## ART AND THE EARLY CHURCH

As the church spread throughout England its use of the architecture and landscape of the past continued to develop, though not on any single model. Each church and each monastery constructed its unique space, architecture and relation to its social and landscape setting. In the north of England Christianity had been reintroduced from Iona by the Irish Aidan (d. 651), who founded the monastery of Lindisfarne in 635, and the Columban tradition and Irish connections that he brought with him remained strong, even after it was decided at the 664 Synod of Whitby that the Northumbrian church would follow Roman rather than Irish practices. The earliest architecture of Lindisfarne (and many other communities) was of wood, and relatively little is known about the appearance of the monastery or the individual structures within it during its earliest phases, although excavations at Iona and other early sites have shown that wooden buildings could well have been elaborately decorated.[1] The location of the monastery is important. Lindisfarne, or 'Holy Island', is cut off from the mainland twice a day by the tide, and it is overlooked by the Bernician royal fortress of Bamburgh castle. Indeed, it was King Oswald (himself converted to Christianity while in exile amongst the Irish) who had requested that Aidan come to Northumbria to help in the conversion of his people, and had given him the island on which to found his monastery and episcopal seat. The combination of the desire for separation from the world, if not solitude via seclusion in the monastic desert, with the need for continued involvement with the doings of king and court, represented by the location of the monastery, is crucial. It made visible in the landscape the mutual support and, when necessary, censure that the two institutions enjoyed. Although not all monasteries would be located in such close proximity to royal strongholds, the church and court would remain closely integrated centres of power from the time of conversion on.

Monasteries also created and retained close links with each other, both through the creation of dependent houses – Hackness was a daughter house of Whitby, for example[2] – and through the establishment of intellectual or economic ties, as existed between Lindisfarne and Whitby or Lindisfarne and Bede's monastery of Wearmouth-Jarrow. Unique in the Anglo-Saxon historical record is the foundation of Wearmouth-Jarrow as one monastery in two places. Thanks to both the writings of Bede and modern excavations we also know more about this twin foundation than we do about most other early Anglo-Saxon monasteries. Wearmouth was founded in 673, and Jarrow in 681 by Benedict Biscop (d. 689), both on land donated by King Ecgfrith. By the eighth century the two together housed over 600 monks, an enormous number especially at such an early date, and a sign of the monastery's popularity and its power. For his rule, Benedict selected what he considered to be the best elements from the rules of seventeen different Continental monasteries,[3] a good indication of how unlikely it was that any one monastery would simply follow the practices of any other. Indeed, despite their union and many similarities, Wearmouth and Jarrow would come to be quite distinct even from each other. Their eclectic natures might be at least partially attributable to Benedict's own background. Originally named Biscop Baducing, the abbot was the son of a noble Northumbrian family and was raised at the court

---

[1] Peter Hill, *Whithorn and St Ninian: The Excavation of a Monastic Town 1984–91* (Stroud, 1997), 67–182; Catherine E. Karkov, 'The Decoration of Early Wooden Architecture in Ireland and Northumbria', in *Studies in Insular Art and Archaeology*, ed. Catherine E. Karkov and Robert T. Farrell (Oxford, OH, 1991), 27–48.
[2] See below p. 93.
[3] Bede, *Venerabilis Baedae opera historica*, ed. Charles Plummer, vol. 1 (Oxford, 1986), 364–82, 388.

of King Oswiu. Between 652 and 664 he made two journeys to Rome, the first with Wilfrid, before eventually becoming a monk at Lerins and adopting the name Benedict. In 668 he was again in Rome and travelled from there to England with Theodore, the newly consecrated Archbishop of Canterbury, to become temporary abbot of SS Peter and Paul. He returned to the Continent in 671/2 to procure books and relics from Rome and Vienne.[4] Shortly after his return to England, Benedict went back to his native Northumbria and so impressed Ecgfrith with his assembled books and relics that the king gave him land from the royal estates on which to found his monastery.[5] Given this background, it is not surprising that his twin monastery should be dedicated to St Peter (Wearmouth) and St Paul (Jarrow), nor that it should look both to the Continent, especially Rome, and to native Northumbrian traditions for architectural and artistic inspiration. Like Canterbury, Wearmouth-Jarrow would soon transform itself into a cosmopolitan centre.

Bede records that Wearmouth (fig. 10) was established 'in the Roman manner', and that Benedict turned to Gaul for both masons and glaziers who could not only construct his church but also instruct the English in their crafts. Further books, icons, and no doubt vestments and liturgical vessels were brought from Rome to fill the new church, which was dedicated in 675/6. The church was built of limestone rubble, a type of fabric also known from local Roman structures.[6] It was a simple cellular nave and chancel church with a length–width ratio of 3:1 (19.5 x 6 metres externally), and a height of 9 metres, possibly incorporating a second storey. It is likely that the church had *porticus* to north and south, but a *prothesis* and *diaconicon* at the east end of the church are equally possible. If the latter suggestion is correct, the church could have been T-shaped in plan, perhaps an intentional reference to the plan of Old St Peter's itself and/or to the plans of earlier Kentish churches. The latter may have come to be seen as hybrid Roman–Anglo-Saxon structures – which, strictly speaking, they were.[7] Alternatively, Ian Wood has suggested that in proportions and some architectural details, such as the baluster shafts and narrow windows, the church may have been modelled on the biblical Temple of Solomon.[8] The Temple of Solomon was enormously influential

---

[4] *Historia abbatum auctore Beda*, in Bede, *Venerabilis Baedae opera historica*, ed. Plummer, i.4, 6.
[5] See Bede, *Venerabilis Baedae opera historica*, ed. Plummer. The original grant was either fifty hides (Anonymous Life of Ceolfrid, *Historia abbatum auctore anonymo*, 7) or seventy hides (*Historia abbatum auctore Beda*, 1.4). Jarrow was founded with a similar grant of forty hides.
[6] Rosemary Cramp, *Wearmouth and Jarrow Monastic Sites*, vol. 1 (Swindon, 2005), 352. The information that follows is deeply indebted to that contained in Cramp's excavation report, which should be consulted for a more in-depth description and analysis of the monastery, as well as detailed plans and illustrations.
[7] See Cramp, *Wearmouth and Jarrow Monastic Sites*, vol. 1, 68 for alternative plans.
[8] Ian N. Wood, *The Most Holy Abbot Ceolfrid*, Jarrow Lecture (Jarrow, 1995), 15.

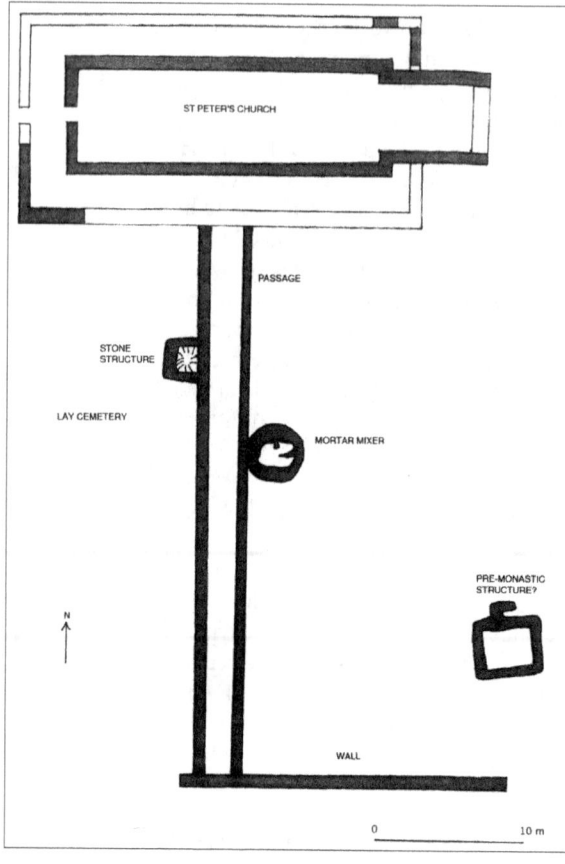

FIG. 10. PLAN OF WEARMOUTH, PHASE 1

on both art and architecture throughout the Middle Ages.[9] It was, for example, one of the sources for Anicia Juliana's church of St Polyeuktos built in Constantinople in the early sixth century,[10] and is represented schematically on folios 2v–3r of the late seventh-century Codex Amiatinus (Florence, Biblioteca Mediccea Laurenziana MS Amiatinus i), a product of Wearmouth-Jarrow. It is certainly possible that multiple architectural references were intended. If Benedict could select aspects of seventeen different monastic rules for his monastery, there is no reason to suppose that he could not have been equally selective when designing its architecture. At his death, Benedict Biscop was interred in a funerary *porticus* to the east of the high altar,[11] but its plan and structure are uncertain – it may have been integral with the first church, or it may have been a later extension. The sanctuary may have been slightly raised, and the lion armrests recovered at the site suggest that there was a *synthronon* (clergy bench) for the abbot and senior monks.

The original church had some form of western annexe, but by 716 a two-storey porch with a steep gable roof was added and later extended upwards into the tower that survives today.[12] The east end may also have

---

[9] Joseph Gutmann, ed., *The Temple of Solomon: Archaeological Fact and Medieval Tradition in Christian, Islamic and Jewish Art* (Missoula, MT, 1976).
[10] R. M. Harrison, *A Temple for Byzantium: The Discovery and Excavation of Anicia Juliana's Palace Church in Istanbul* (London, 1989).
[11] In Book IV of his *Gesta Pontificum Anglorum*, William of Malmesbury records that Bishop Æthelwold 'purchased the body for a great price' when he refounded Thorney Abbey c. 964. See William of Malmesbury, *Gesta Pontificum Anglorum*, ed. N. E. S. A. Hamilton (London, 1870), 329.
[12] It is uncertain whether the tower is pre- or post-Conquest, but it is definitely eleventh-century. Abbot Eosterwine's bones (d. 685) were removed from beneath the porch in 716.

been extended, and perhaps further divided spatially at this date. Two single splayed windows high in the west wall of the church are part of the original build and suggest that the nave walls of the church may have had windows of similar form. The number of lathe-turned balusters found at Wearmouth may be the remains of multiple windows or openings of other types. The western porch and west wall of the nave are now all that survives above ground of the original fabric. The upper floor of the porch has an arched opening (originally a window) into the nave, which possibly opened into a western gallery. Its monolithic jambs and round head carved from a single block of stone are original. A second window looked out into what might have been a western courtyard or atrium. The function of the porch's upper chamber is a matter of conjecture:

> certainly its east window could have been used to gain a view of the main body of the church, and since the chamber could be entered from outside the church it could have allowed participation in services by persons who were not members of the community. It could also have allowed anyone observing the liturgy from inside to communicate with people outside in the western courtyard through the west window.[13]

While different in structure, and perhaps also in function, this upper chamber puts one in mind of the upper chapels of Carolingian structures such as Charlemagne's palace chapel at Aachen (begun 792) or the *c.* 800 gatehouse at Lorsch. Clearly we cannot be certain about the function of this space, but it does raise questions about the originality of the structure. Anglo-Saxon architecture is generally viewed as almost entirely derivative of Continental buildings, especially those of Rome and Francia, but the increasing evidence for early multi-storey structures in Anglo-Saxon England suggests a degree of innovation only just beginning to be recognized.

The interior of the church would from the start have been plastered and painted and elaborately fitted out, and apparently in a very Roman manner. In 679–80 Benedict Biscop made his fourth journey to Rome, this time bringing back wooden panels painted with biblical scenes. These are universally understood to have been icons used as a focus for prayer and devotion. They were hung across the chancel of the church with scenes from the Apocalypse on the north wall (an especially appropriate location, perhaps, as by tradition hell was believed to lie to the north), scenes from the gospels on the south wall, and images of Mary and the twelve apostles arranged on a *tabulatum*, a boarding, that spanned the opening of the chancel from wall to wall. The *tabulatum* has reasonably been understood

---

[13] Cramp, *Wearmouth and Jarrow Monastic Sites*, vol. 1, 70.

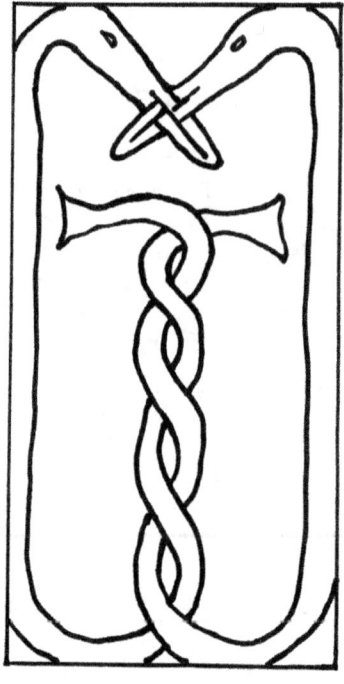

FIG. 11. DOOR JAMB, PORCH OF ST PETER'S WEARMOUTH

as a form of iconostasis.[14] On his next journey to Rome Benedict brought back similar panels painted with scenes from the life of Christ (*dominicae historiae picturas*),[15] which he hung around the interior of the now lost church or chapel of St Mary. In addition to the painted panels we must also imagine the church ablaze with the coloured light created by the stained glass windows and golden and jewelled objects – reliquaries, lamps and candlesticks, liturgical vessels, books in precious bindings, and so forth – of the type discussed below.[16]

Sculptural decoration also embellished both the church and probably its surroundings, as evidenced by the significant corpus of sculptural fragments found at the site. Most of the sculpture would have been painted with red and black and perhaps other colours on a white background. In terms of style, motif and even carving techniques, the sculpture evinces a unique combination of Insular and Roman traditions. Panels carved with interlace and animal ornament of an Insular or Germanic type sat side-by-side with classicizing forms such as the lion armrests of the *synthronon*, or the monumental figure (possibly meant to represent Christ or St Peter) carved in high relief on the west wall of the tower.[17] Indeed, the tower provides a microcosm of the range of architectural sculpture that once filled the church: stringcourses, friezes, and panels bearing relief carvings of crosses, animals and figural motifs, as well as decorated jambs and

---

[14] R. D. H. Gem, 'Documentary References to Anglo-Saxon Painted Architecture', in *Early Medieval Wall Painting and Painted Sculpture in England*, ed. S. Cather, D. Park and P. Williamson, BAR Brit. Ser. 216 (Oxford, 1990), 1–16, at 2–3; see also Cramp, *Wearmouth and Jarrow Monastic Sites*, vol. 1, 69.
[15] *Historia abbatum auctore Beda*, in Bede, *Venerabilis Baedae opera historica*, ed. Plummer, 9.
[16] For the stained glass see Rosemary Cramp, *Wearmouth and Jarrow Monastic Sites*, vol. 2 (Swindon, 2006), ch. 27.
[17] Rosemary Cramp, *County Durham and Northumberland*, CASSS 1 (Oxford, 1984), pt 1, 127, pt 2, 116; Cramp, *Wearmouth and Jarrow Monastic Sites*, vol. 2, 175, 176. The figure has been cut away from the wall but part of the head remains and the shape of the body can still be traced.

balusters. Perhaps the best known of the architectural sculptures are the jambs of the western door of the entrance porch (fig. 11). Each jamb is carved with a symmetrical pair of serpent-like creatures with interlocking beak-like jaws and intertwining tails. While their origins lie ultimately in metalwork of the type found at Sutton Hoo, it is possible that similar sorts of carvings would have been familiar from earlier Insular timber architecture.[18] They have been interpreted convincingly as apotropaic figures keeping watch over the building at its most vulnerable point, the entrance.[19] It is no doubt significant in this regard that their beaks and tails come together to form two crosses, one in the shape of the Greek letter chi and the other in the shape of the letter tau.[20] They should perhaps also be thought of in combination with the figural sculpture from the second storey of the tower which may also have had a protective function. If this was indeed the case, images of power and protection from the twin native and Roman traditions stood watch over the doorway and perhaps helped to proclaim visually the larger monastic agenda of conformity to Roman practices, but the conversion of those practices to fit the needs of a new Anglo-Saxon church and order. These carvings also look forward to the vastly expanded sculptural programmes surrounding the doorways of Romanesque pilgrimage churches such as the eleventh-century pilgrimage church of Moissac (Tarn-et-Garonne, France), where the entrance is watched over by sculptures of St Benedict and the monastery's abbot on the outer wall of the porch and three pairs of crossed lions on the trumeau of the doorway.

In addition to the architectural sculpture and furniture, fragments of monumental and funerary sculpture also survive. Two fragments (Monkwearmouth 1 and 2 in the Corpus of Anglo-Saxon Stone Sculpture) may have come from freestanding stone crosses, although this type of monument certainly does not seem to have been as popular at Wearmouth as it was at Jarrow.[21] There is, however, an interesting range of grave markers. The pyramidal tenth-century 'Tidfrið stone' has the masculine name Tidfrið carved in runes on its main face. Below the inscription two figures hold a rectangular object over a cross. Their short tunics suggest that they are members of the laity, but who specifically they might have represented and what exactly they are doing remain a puzzle. On the reverse of the stone an equally curious figure with elongated arms

---

[18] Karkov, 'The Decoration of Early Wooden Architecture in Ireland and Northumbria'.
[19] Ernst Kitzinger, 'Interlace and Icons: Form and Function in Early Insular Art', in *The Age of Migrating Ideas: Early Medieval Art in Northern Britain and Ireland*, ed. R. Michael Spearman and John Higgitt (Edinburgh, 1993), 3–15, at 4.
[20] X and T crosses were symbols of the New and Old Testament respectively. Richard N. Bailey sees only the tails as forming a cross, and suggests that the composition may be a symbolic representation of Christ between two beasts based on the Canticle of Habakkuk (*England's Earliest Sculptors* (Toronto, 1996), 38).
[21] Cramp, *County Durham and Northumberland*, pt 1, 122–3, pt 2, pl. 107.

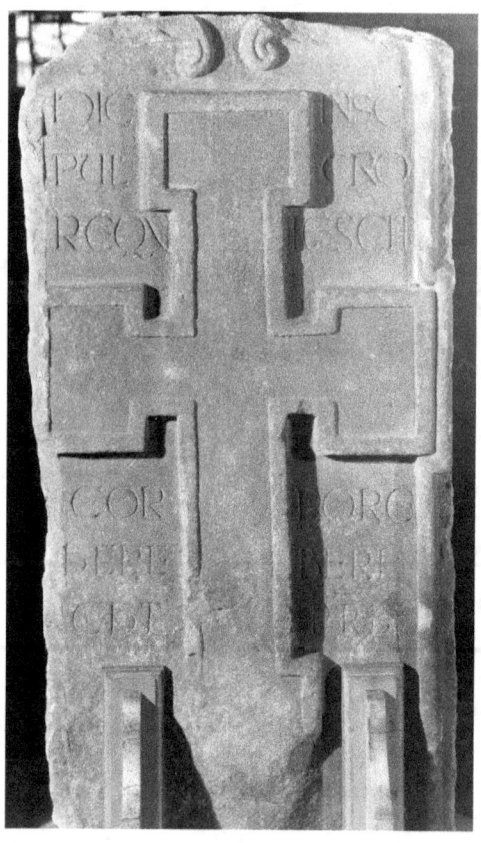

FIG. 12.
HEREBERICHT
STONE, ST PETER'S
WEARMOUTH

is shown walking to the right. One fragment of a late seventh- or early eighth-century name-stone (a type of monument common at Irish foundations such as Clonmacnoise and, in England, at monasteries such as Lindisfarne (fig. 28) or Hartlepool which followed the Irish church up until the Synod of Whitby, but otherwise unattested at either Wearmouth or Jarrow) has a fragmentary runic inscription (eo) in its upper left quadrant and an inscription in Anglo-Saxon capitals (ĂID) in its lower left quadrant. The different names are generally believed to be those used by the individual commemorated before and after entry into the religious life, with the act of conversion and the cultural translation that was a part of that process further signified by the two different alphabets. The simple square-ended cross at its centre is characteristic of the type of cross preferred at Wearmouth-Jarrow. Monasteries did often favour particular forms of the cross, just as they favoured particular styles of carving or inscription and, when similar shapes recur often on funerary or memorial sculpture, the idea may have been to suggest equality and monastic allegiance amongst the dead.[22] The dead, like the living, were perceived as being part of the monastic and social community, and a tangible link to their history and origins.

The Wearmouth name-stone is tiny (the surviving fragment is only 4 x 2¼ inches), but a similar square-ended cross of more monumental proportions is carved in high relief at the centre of the famous Herebericht stone from the first quarter of the eighth century (fig. 12). The Latin inscription is again divided into quadrants, though this time it is written entirely in Anglo-Saxon capitals. It reads 'HIC IN SEPULCRO REQUIESCIT CORPORE HEREBERICHT PR(ES)B(YTER)' (Here in the tomb rests the body Herebericht the priest). Directly above the cross the beaks of two birds meet. Their heads originally protruded from the roll

---

[22] At Whitby, for example, dozens of fragments of undecorated cross slabs of similar shape have survived. See James T. Lang, *Northern Yorkshire*, CASSS 6 (Oxford, 2001), 231–66.

moulding which once framed the slab.²³ The decoration of the stone shows the same fusion of Roman and Insular traditions seen in the sculptural decoration of the porch and tower, and the overall composition of the piece can be related to that of the beast-decorated jambs discussed above. The slab was discovered above a coffin buried beneath the west porch during excavations in September of 1866.²⁴ Sculpturally it is of extremely high quality. The difference in the layout and script of the last two lines of the inscription indicates that it has been reused. The original surface was rubbed down and Herebericht's name and title inserted, which raises the question of whether this was done because the slab had some special associations for Herebericht or those who buried him or as a matter of simple necessity.²⁵ The location of the Herebericht burial, however, indicates it was of a special nature and suggests that the stone was more likely to have been carefully chosen.

Most of the community would have been buried in the main cemetery located to the south of the church. The cemetery included both monastic and lay burials, and the burials of women as well as men. Yet here too there seems to have been a social hierarchy. Rosemary Cramp has suggested that an area close to the church may have been considered special, and may have been used for important members of the laity. She notes, for example, that the only remains of gold thread found in the cemetery came from this area.²⁶

The cemetery was bisected in the Anglo-Saxon period by an elaborately decorated covered passageway that ran from about midway down the south wall of the church to a pair of two-storey buildings thought to have housed the refectory and dormitory and a multipurpose hall respectively. All three of these structures have provided evidence of painted decoration in the form of red stripes and other geometric shapes on a white plaster background.²⁷ There would also have been workshops, barns and agricultural buildings, as well as a library and scriptorium.

The monastery is known to have included churches or chapels dedicated to St Mary and, in the monks' dormitory, St Lawrence,²⁸ along with other oratories, but none of these structures has been located archaeologically. It is likely that their arrangement, or at least their use, was based on

---

²³ For a reconstruction see Richard N. Bailey, 'Sutton Hoo and Seventh-Century Art', in *Sutton Hoo: Fifty Years After*, ed. Robert T. Farrell and Carol Neuman de Vegvar (Oxford, OH, 1992), 31–41, at 35.
²⁴ See further Cramp, *County Durham and Northumberland*, pt 1, 124, pt 2, pl. 110; Cramp, *Wearmouth and Jarrow Monastic Sites*, vol. 2, 193.
²⁵ The reuse and recarving of sculpture, including coffins and sarcophagi, was not at all uncommon in Anglo-Saxon England.
²⁶ Cramp, *Wearmouth and Jarrow Monastic Sites*, vol. 1, 88; see the cemetery plan at p. 89.
²⁷ Cramp, *Wearmouth and Jarrow Monastic Sites*, vol. 1, 6–8, 16–17.
²⁸ *Vita Ceolfridi*, ch. 25.

the stational system of Rome.[29] One must imagine liturgical processions making use of all these spaces, and try to envisage the spectacle that would have been created: chanting monks, swinging censers, flickering candles, the gleam of processional crosses and other liturgical objects. Some sense of what such a procession would have entailed is provided by the account of Abbot Ceolfrid's departure from Wearmouth described in the anonymous *Vita Ceolfridi* and Bede's *Historia Abbatum*.[30] There was a mass at daybreak in St Peter's at which the abbot prayed with all his monks, followed by a second mass in St Mary's. Ceolfrid carried a censer as he kissed his monks farewell on the altar steps of St Peter's and proceeded to the chapel of St Lawrence, singing songs and antiphons. He was still singing as he crossed the river flanked by deacons holding a cross and candles. Once on the other side of the river he expressed his devotion to the cross and departed. The ceremony served as an enactment in miniature of the pilgrimage to Rome on which he was setting out.[31] With him he also carried the Codex Amiatinus, written in an uncial script developed at Wearmouth-Jarrow and based on the script of Gregory the Great's Italy, for presentation to the pope. Both the ceremony and the manuscript are indicative of the unique and uncanny cultural doubling that seems to have existed at Wearmouth-Jarrow. One journey, one exile (and pilgrimage was a form of exile) and one landscape are repeated and inscribed in a different place and time. The book, which mimicked the world of Rome to the extent that it 'copied' Cassiodorus's Codex Grandior, both repeated the journey of the Codex Grandior from Italy to Northumbria in reverse and gave back to Rome a little bit of itself, at the same time as its sister pandects retained some of Rome for Northumbria.

The cultural hybridity of Wearmouth extended to its very plan and location. Although neither the exact layout nor limits of the monastery are known, all evidence points to its having been carefully and symbolically planned. It may have been located in relation to the site of an earlier Anglo-Saxon settlement,[32] but its layout seems to have been designed to evoke the plans of the late antique villas with which Benedict would certainly have been familiar. Benedict's use of the past is referenced today in the design of the museum building at Bede's World, Jarrow, which is based on the same Roman and early medieval architectural styles from which Benedict and his masons would have drawn – though it is in no way intended as an exact copy.

Both Benedict and Ceolfrid, the first abbot of Jarrow, stressed repeatedly that their houses were one monastery in two places (and indeed there

---

[29] Éamonn Ó Carragáin, *The City of Rome and the World of Bede*, Jarrow Lecture (Jarrow, 1994), 12.
[30] In Bede, *Venerabilis Baedae opera historica*, ed. Plummer, 381–2, 396–8.
[31] Ó Carragáin, *The City of Rome and the World of Bede*, 12–14.
[32] Cramp, *Wearmouth and Jarrow Monastic Sites*, vol. 1, 111.

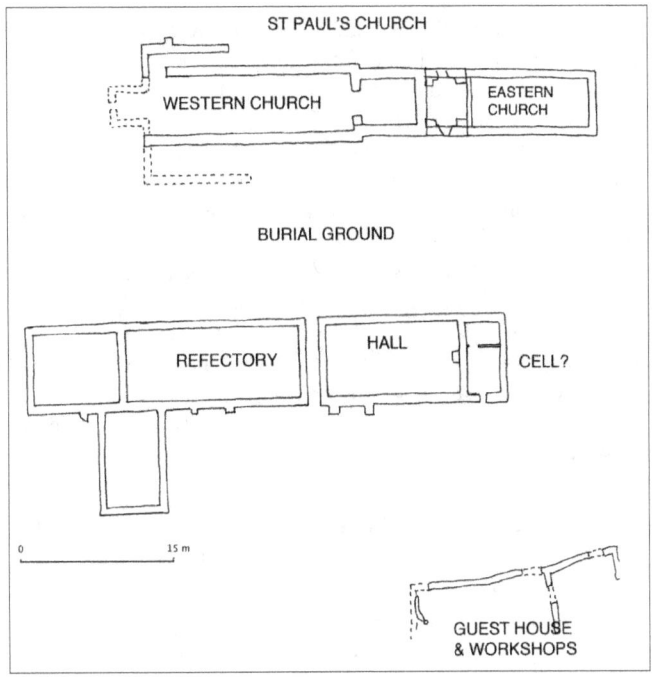

FIG. 13. PLAN OF CHURCH AND MONASTIC BUILDINGS, JARROW

is something uncanny in that very concept), but this means that it is sometimes hard to know how activities such as manuscript production, with all its associated resources, would have been divided between the two. In addition to the Codex Amiatinus, two other pandects were produced, one to be housed at Wearmouth and one at Jarrow, so there certainly must have been two libraries. Fragments of other early manuscripts including gospel books and a copy of Gregory's *Moralia* also survive, and it has been suggested that the St Cuthbert (or Stonyhurst) Gospel of St John (London, BL, Loan MS 74) may also have come from the monastery.[33] In addition there were the many writings of Bede. Amiatinus and its sister pandects alone would have required the skins of 1,545 calves,[34] some, though not necessarily all, of which must have come from the monastic herds.

Despite their many similarities the twin monasteries of Wearmouth and Jarrow would have been very different in appearance, and that

---

[33] See Malcolm Parkes, *The Scriptorium of Wearmouth-Jarrow*, Jarrow Lecture (Jarrow, 1982); Brown, *Lindisfarne Gospels*, 76, 97–8, 118, 255, 256, 316, 402–3. Other manuscripts have also been attributed to the monastery over the years, but scholarly desire to attribute manuscripts to known centres of production runs the danger of leading us to favour houses like Wearmouth-Jarrow (or Lindisfarne or Canterbury) over less well-known centres.

[34] Rupert Bruce-Mitford, *The Art of the Codex Amiatinus*, Jarrow Lecture (Jarrow, 1967), 2.

combination of similarity and difference must have been deliberate. At Jarrow, from at least the eighth century, if not from its foundation in the 680s, there were two churches on axis, the major western church of St Paul's and the smaller church of St Mary to its east (fig. 13). Both were built of neatly cut and coursed ashlar blocks, much of it reused Roman masonry. It is possible that the smaller church of St Mary was built first for use by the community while the larger basilica was being constructed, but this is only a supposition. It is equally possible that the two churches were contemporary and that St Mary's was built as an eastern funerary chapel with lay access.[35] Its dimensions were approximately 12 x 4.7 metres. It was 18 feet high to the springing of the roof and lit by small windows. Rosemary Cramp notes that it is possible that the church was built over a 'pre-monastic feature on the headland such as a mortuary chapel'.[36] Two damaged fragments of a Roman military memorial were found inside the walls of St Peter's. They read:

> DIVORVM OMNIVM FILIVS IMP CAESAR TRAIANVS HADRIANVS AVGVSTVS IMPOSITA NECESSITATE IMPERII INTRA FINES CONSERVATI DIVINI PRAECEPTO ... COS III ...
>
> DIFFVSIS BARBARIS ET PROVINCIA RECIPERATA BRITANNIA ADDIDIT LIMITEM INTER VTRVMQVE OCEANQVE LITVS PER M P LXXX EXERCITVS PROVINCIAE OPVS VALLI FECIT SVB CVRA A PLATORI NEPOTIS LEG AVG PR PR[37]
>
> (Son of all the deified emperors, the Emperor Caesar Trajan Hadrian Augustus, after the necessity of keeping the empire within its limits had been laid upon him by divine precept ... thrice consul ...
>
> After the barbarians had been dispersed and the province of Britain had been recovered, he added a frontier-line between either shore of the Ocean for 80 miles. The army of the province built this defence-work under the charge of Aulus Platorius Nepos, emperor's propraetorian legate.)[38]

While the original purpose of the stone was to record Roman triumph and the construction of defences against the barbarians, its message is also perfectly appropriate to the kingdom's new defensive structure, the church, and its advance westward along the same lines of the wall.

The earliest phase of the western church was a cellular nave and chancel

---

[35] Cramp, *Wearmouth and Jarrow Monastic Sites*, vol. 1, 147–68. Again, much of the information that follows is drawn from the two-volume report on the site.
[36] Cramp, *Wearmouth and Jarrow Monastic Sites*, vol. 1, 167.
[37] http://www.roman-britain.org/epigraphy/rib_borders.htm
[38] The reconstructed translation is taken from Eaton, *Plundering the Past*, 128.

structure flanked by a narrow northern aisle or passage which returned around the front of the church and had its eastern end at the junction of the nave and chancel. A similar aisle may have existed to the south, and it is possible that there was a western porch. It is also possible that the north and south (if it existed) aisles were *porticus*, but it is more likely that they were remodelled as *porticus* in a secondary phase of construction. The east end of the chancel was flat rather than apsidal (the same may have been true at Wearmouth), an arrangement that would remain popular in England into the late Middle Ages. The church was pulled down in 1782 so little more can be said about its original dimensions or appearance. Ian Wood has speculated that, like St Peter's Wearmouth, St Paul's Jarrow was based on the biblical description of the Temple of Solomon, noting that it too featured baluster shafts and narrow windows, and that Bede may have had these features in mind when he wrote his detailed description of its architectural features in *De Templo*.[39] The dedication slab from the original basilica is preserved and is set above the chancel of the present church. It is the oldest English church dedication to survive. The slab is made up of two stones carrying an eight-line Latin inscription in Anglo-Saxon capitals. It begins with the chi-rho monogram and continues:

> DEDICATIO BASILICAE S(AN)C(T)I PAVLI VIIII K(A)
> L(ENDAS MAI(AS) ANNO XV ECFRIDI REG(IS) CEOLFRIDI
> ABB(ATIS) EIVSDEMQ(UE) ECCLES(IAE) D(E)O AVCTORE
> CONDITORIS ANNO IIII
>
> (The dedication of the basilica of St Paul on the ninth day before the Kalends of May in the fifteenth year of King Ecfrid and in the fourth year of Abbot Ceolfrid founder by the guidance of God, of the same church.)[40]

Like so much else at Jarrow, the slab is thoroughly Roman in character. The two stones that have now been placed together may originally have been divided and perhaps set either side of a sculptural panel,[41] as it is notable that the inscription on the first stone ends with the name and title of the king, and that of the second stone begins with those of the abbot, publicly proclaiming the joint power behind the monastery.

At some point, possibly in the last decade of the eighth century, the two churches were united by a two-storey annexe constructed in the space between the chancel of St Paul's and the west wall of St Mary's, and possibly surmounted by a small tower. It is only the first two storeys of the tower that are definitely pre-Conquest. The reasons for the joining of the two buildings and the function of the spaces within the junction building are

---

[39] Wood, *The Most Holy Abbot Ceolfrid*, 15; Seán Connolly, ed., *Bede: On the Temple* (Liverpool, 1995), 25–6; and see above p. 45.
[40] Cramp, *County Durham and Northumberland*, pt 1, 113.
[41] Cramp, *County Durham and Northumberland*, pt 1, 114.

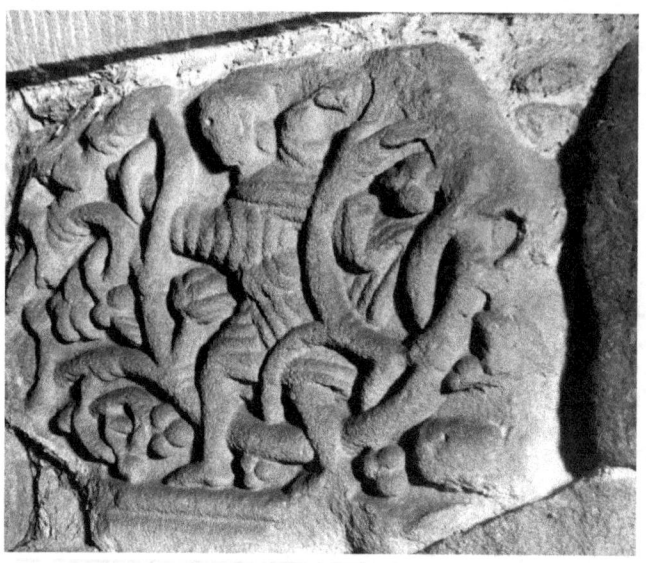

FIG. 14.
FRAGMENT WITH
VINESCROLL, ST
PAUL'S JARROW

unclear. Large arched openings joined the tower with the western and eastern churches at ground level, and there were also doors in the north and south walls. The upper storey may have been used for teaching or storage, or perhaps as a choir loft or for access into a higher bell tower.[42] Whatever the reasons for the joining of the two churches, the result was that St Mary's became an eastern chapel contiguous with St Paul's. It thus looks forward to the arrangement of the Lady Chapels of the English Gothic.

The interior of the churches at Jarrow would have been as ornate and colourful as those at Wearmouth. The structures at both monasteries are known to have been glazed, and at Jarrow some of the fragments of stained glass recovered during excavations have been reconstructed in the windows of the chancel (the original church of St Mary). The reconstructions are conjectural, but do serve to give an idea of what the light inside the original buildings would have been like. The shapes of some of the fragments of glass used to reconstruct the famous figural window do suggest that while the overall reconstruction might not be entirely accurate, the pieces were originally part of a figural composition of some variety.[43]

An even larger corpus of sculpture survives at Jarrow than does at Wearmouth, almost all of it from the eighth century or later. The Jarrow sculptures are executed in a very classicizing style, generally in high relief, and show little interest in Insular ornament of the type found at Wearmouth.[44] There is no surviving architectural sculpture in the former eastern church, and since the western church has been demolished it is impossible to determine its original scheme of decoration. Window heads and balusters are much like those recovered at Wearmouth, but the fragments of architectural friezes and decorative panels are quite different,

---

[42] Cramp, *Wearmouth and Jarrow Monastic Sites*, vol. 1, 168.
[43] See further Cramp, *Wearmouth and Jarrow Monastic Sites*, vol. 2, ch. 27.
[44] Cramp, *Wearmouth and Jarrow Monastic Sites*, vol. 2, 165–6.

and include friezes decorated with baluster ornament and finely carved inhabited vinescrolls (fig. 14). In the panel illustrated, a running figure confronts a beast which gnaws at the branches of the scroll in the upper corner. The head of a second figure lies on the ground by his left foot. In both subject matter and style the panel has its origins in the art of Rome, although the execution is thoroughly Anglo-Saxon, a point that will be discussed further below in connection with similar fragments from Hexham. The meaning of the piece may relate to the battle between good and evil or the salvation of the human soul – both were common Christian reinterpretations of pagan Roman hunting scenes. A second fragment, possibly from the same frieze, is decorated with birds pecking at the fruit of the True Vine, in whose tendrils a serpent coils.

A different but no less classical type of plant ornament interspersed with interlace patterns covers a column from Building A. The function of this building is uncertain, as is the function of the column. It may have been an architectural feature, or it may have supported a lectern – which would add weight to the interpretation of the building, or part of it, as a refectory.[45] Lessons were commonly read during monastic meals throughout the medieval period. A number of fragments of shafts (possibly cross shafts) and cross heads were recovered from the walls and foundations of the church, as well as from other locations within the monastery. Some are decorated with variations of plantscroll ornament borrowed from the repertoire of cloisonné metalwork, and may have been embellished with glass or metal fittings, others are carved with interlace panels, and still others have been left plain, as at Whitby.[46] It may be that the different decorative motifs and shapes of the monuments signalled differences in function, patronage or location. Like Irish monasteries, Jarrow is arranged into different zones of occupation, although they are linear zones rather than the concentric ones favoured in Ireland, and crosses may have been used, as they were in Irish monasteries, to mark the boundaries of different spaces, especially that of the most sacred space surrounding the church; however, without further evidence all such suggestions must remain in the realm of speculation.

As at Wearmouth, crosses with square terminals are favoured on slabs and grave markers.[47] There are no runic inscriptions found to date at Jarrow, nor any use of name-stones of the Lindisfarne/Hartlepool type. One cross slab in particular merits special attention. It is a reused Roman stone that was inscribed and carved with a cross in high relief at some point in the late seventh or early eighth century. The inscription, in classically inspired seriffed Anglo-Saxon capitals, flanks the lower shaft of the cross.

---

[45] Cramp, *Wearmouth and Jarrow Monastic Sites*, vol. 1, 193–6; vol. 2, 176–9.
[46] On Whitby see Lang, *Northern Yorkshire*, 897–915.
[47] It should be noted that it remains uncertain whether some slabs were funerary or architectural.

It reads: 'IN HOC SINGULARI SIGNO VITA REDDITUR MUNDO' (In this unique sign life is returned to the world).[48] Originally thought to have been set up after the plague known to have decimated the monastery in the late seventh century,[49] the stone is more likely associated with the cult of the cross, and may have been part of a chapel dedicated to the Holy Cross.[50] In 1943 Levison suggested that the first part of the inscription derives from Rufinus's translation of Eusebius's account of Constantine's dream before his victory at the Battle of the Milvian Bridge in 312. Such a reference would be especially appropriate given both Jarrow's insistent *romanitas* and Ceolfrid's documented devotion to the cross discussed above. The slab's reference to an imperial victory and conversion may also have resonated with the Northumbrian court and the memory of Oswald's raising of the vexillum of the cross before his victory at the Battle of Heavenfield in 634 and the ensuing reintroduction of Christianity into Northumbria.[51] Such an interpretation should not, however, entirely rule out the possibility of a connection with the plague. Sickness and other natural disasters were understood to be signs of divine wrath or trial, and thus battles in which sin or evil had to be defeated.

A bit more is known about the overall arrangement of the monastery at Jarrow even though, as at Wearmouth, excavation of the site has been only partial. The two churches and cemetery were located on the top of a slope with the western church forming the centre-point of the monastery. Two large communal buildings, perhaps the refectory/dormitory and a multipurpose hall, stood on a platform further down the slope with a garden beneath them,[52] and alongside the banks of the river was a guest house and, by the ninth century, an area of workshops.

Contemporary with Benedict's foundation of Wearmouth-Jarrow was Bishop Wilfrid's foundation of a monastery at Hexham on land granted to him by Queen Æthelthryth before she entered the monastic life. It was but one of an extensive *paruchia* of monasteries associated with the bishop whose sphere of influence extended into Mercia, Kent and Sussex. Indeed, his biographer, Stephen of Ripon, described him as presiding over a kingdom of churches (*regnum ecclesiarum*).[53] Like Benedict and Ceolfrid, Wilfrid looked to Rome and the Continent for his architectural and sculptural models, but he did so with a sense of grandeur unmatched by either abbot. In addition to being highly educated, he was charismatic,

[48] Cramp, *County Durham and Northumberland*, vol. 1, 113.
[49] J. Brand, *The History and Antiquities ... of Newcastle upon Tyne*, vol. 2 (London, 1789), 62–4.
[50] Cramp, *Wearmouth and Jarrow Monastic Sites*, vol. 2, 199; Cramp, *Wearmouth and Jarrow Monastic Sites*, vol. 1, ch. 13.
[51] *HE*, iii.2. See also Levison, 'The Inscription on the Jarrow Cross' *Archaeologia Aeliana* 21 (1943), 121–6.
[52] Cramp, *Wearmouth and Jarrow Monastic Sites*, vol. 1, 359.
[53] Stephen, *The Life of Wilfrid by Eddius Stephanus*, ed. Bertram Colgrave (Cambridge, 1927), 42.

evangelical and extremely political, making a vivid impression – for better or worse – wherever he went. The architecture of Hexham was equally impressive. As at Jarrow, there were originally two churches in alignment, the larger nave and chancel church of St Andrew, and the smaller apsidal church of St Mary directly to its east. Stephen expressed his awe of St Andrew's as follows:

> Cuius profunditatem in terra cum domibus mire politis lapidibus fundatem et super terram multiplicem domum columnis variis et porticibus multis suffultam mirabileque longitudine et altitudine murorum ornatam et liniarum variis anfractibus viarum, aliquando sursam, aliquando deorsum per cocleas circumductam, non est meae parvitatis hoc sermone explicare, quod sanctus pontifex noster, a spiritu Dei doctus, opera facere excogitavit, necque enim ullam domum aliam citra Alpes montes talem aedificatam audivimus.

> (My feeble tongue will not permit me to enlarge here upon the depth of the foundations in the earth, and its crypts of wonderfully dressed stone, and the manifold building above ground supported by various columns and many side aisles, and adorned with walls of notable length and height, surrounded by various winding passages with spiral stairs leading up and down; for our holy bishop being taught by the Spirit of God, thought out how to construct these buildings; nor have we heard of any other house on this side of the Alps built on such a scale.)[54]

William of Malmesbury, writing several hundred years later, stated that 'those who have visited Italy allege that at Hexham they see the glories of Rome once again'.[55] The crypt beneath the east end of the present church (fig. 15) is all that survives of the fabric of the St Andrew's about which they wrote. In plan and structure it is similar to the slightly earlier crypt at Wilfrid's other major Northumbrian monastery, Ripon. Both are built of reused Roman stone and both consist of a rectangular vaulted main chamber (which would have been plastered and painted) and a smaller rectangular antechamber, both rooms lit by lamps set in niches. At Ripon, two passages allowed entrance and exit from the crypt, but at Hexham that was increased to three to allow for a smoother flow of traffic. One staircase leads down from the nave of the church, while the other two passages flank the crypt to the north and south. While it would have been possible to enter or exit from any direction, it is most likely that pilgrims were intended to enter through the long dark northern passage into the light of the crypt, mirroring the journey of the Christian from the darkness of

---

[54] Stephen, *The Life of Wilfrid*, text and translation, 46–7.
[55] William of Malmesbury, *Gesta Pontificum*, ed. Hamilton, 255.

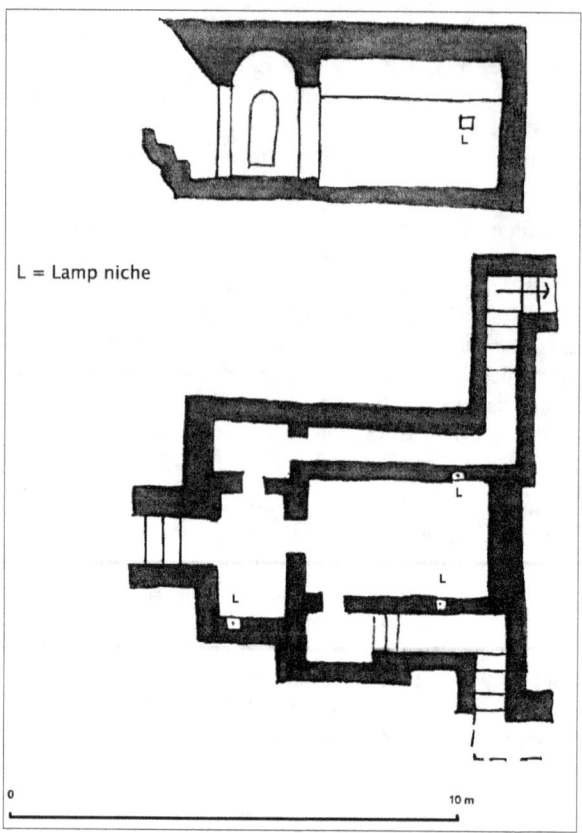

FIG. 15.
HEXHAM ABBEY,
CRYPT

this world into the light of the next. The arrangement of the passages also meant that pilgrims could gain access to the relics housed in the crypt without disrupting activities taking place in the church above. There is no exact parallel for the design of either the Hexham or Ripon crypts, and it may be that Wilfrid (like Benedict Biscop) was borrowing specific elements from a variety of sites either visited personally in his extensive travels or known from literary descriptions, such as the catacombs, the crypt of Old St Peter's or the tomb of the Holy Sepulchre.[56] John Crook has noted that the plan is very like that of the cubicula of the Roman catacombs, burial chambers that, when they contained the relics of the saints, were simply adopted as crypts in order to avoid disturbing the bodies of the dead, and thus could be somewhat awkwardly integrated with the architecture of the church built above them. At Hexham and Ripon, however, the 'catacomb'

---

[56] See further Richard N. Bailey, 'St Wilfrid, Ripon and Hexham', in *Studies in Insular Art and Archaeology*, ed. Karkov and Farrell, 3–25; Harold M. Taylor and Joan Taylor, *Anglo-Saxon Architecture*, 3 vols (Cambridge, 1965), vol. 1, 297–312; vol. 2, 516–18.

was created artificially and was of a type long out of fashion in Rome.[57] But contemporary Roman fashions in crypt building may have been less important to Wilfrid than the symbolic reference to the resting places of the Roman saints.

Hexham has long been understood to have been a straightforward statement of *romanitas*, in part because of the amount of Romano-British stonework that was incorporated into its fabric. John Blair, for example, has suggested that Wilfrid's 'systematic robbing of the carved and inscribed stones of Corbridge' should be interpreted as a 'symbolic relocation of the Roman town to Hexham'.[58] But just how Roman it was needs to be questioned. Stephen was in wonder at its scale and the details of its architecture, and William of Malmesbury noted the uncanny experience of visitors who encountered a building that evoked the glories of Rome, but neither author stated that it was or could be mistaken for Roman work. Wilfrid and his successors certainly made abundant use of the past and of Romano-British materials but, as with the crypt, it is likely to have been the specific historical, geographical and cultural references that were most important. For example, Wilfrid's reuse of stone from Corbridge should be understood in the context of Hexham's location near Hadrian's Wall and its reworking of that particular landscape. The wall was a testament to Roman power, but it was also built on what was now Anglo-Saxon land, and the stone from which it was made was a part of that land. Moreover, the area was important not just for the wall, but also for the 634 Battle of Heavenfield, an event which brought together the Roman and the Anglo-Saxon in a mutually affective dialogue that was played out in part through stone, as will be discussed further below.

Both the Hexham crypt and the apparent grandeur of the apostolic church provide evidence of a rather different sort of monastery than Wearmouth-Jarrow. The presence of the crypt suggests a much greater interest in attracting and accommodating pilgrims from outside the monastic community, while Stephen's description of the church suggests grandeur on a quasi-imperial scale which Wilfrid would no doubt have considered appropriate to his status. It is of course possible that Stephen's description of the church was embellished for literary effect, but the range and quality of architectural and monumental sculpture from Hexham are exceptional, so it is easy to believe that the architecture would have been as well. Much of the sculpture has been discussed in terms of its Roman influences or sources. Some fragments are indeed Roman and were reused in the walls of Wilfrid's Hexham, though we cannot be sure exactly how, but others might not be Roman at all. Fragments carved with inhabited vinescroll (figs. 16, 17) are so classical in style that it has been questioned

---

[57] John Crook, *The Architectural Setting of the Cult of Saints in the Early Christian West c. 300–c1200* (Oxford, 2000), 92–3.
[58] Blair, *The Church in Anglo-Saxon Society*, 190–1.

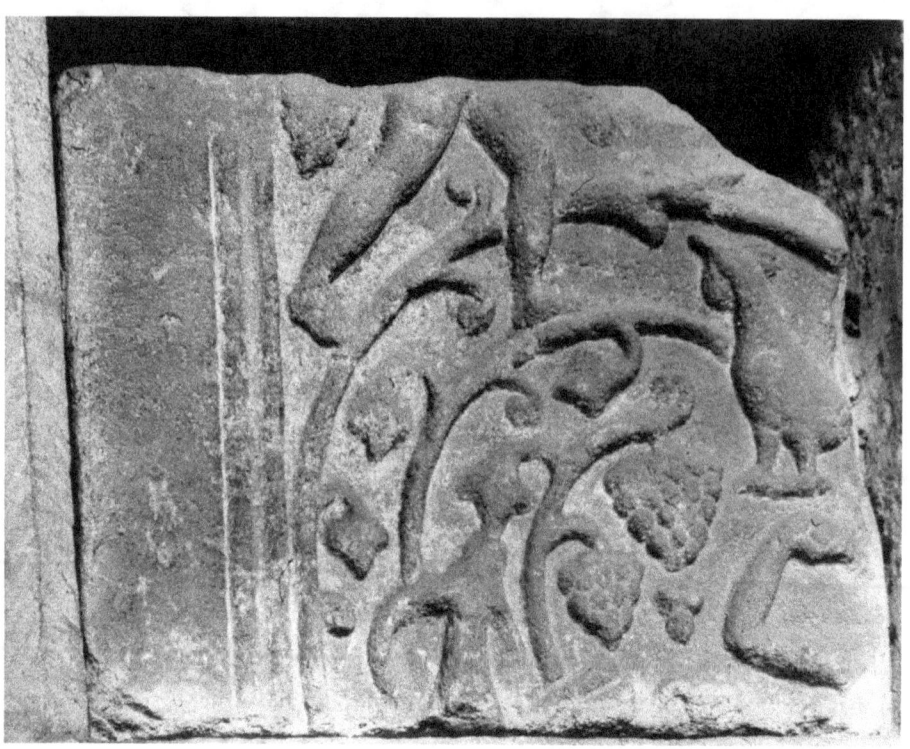

FIG. 16.
FRAGMENT WITH
VINESCROLL,
HEXHAM

whether they might not be Roman, sub-Roman, or Continental rather than Anglo-Saxon.[59] The naked human figures they contain are rare in Anglo-Saxon sculpture (although naked figures appear at both Breedon and Rothbury), and they are similar in style to figures found in the Romano-British sculpture of Corbridge.[60] More telling perhaps is the heaviness of Anglo-Saxon vinescrolls in comparison to these two fragments, as can be seen in the Jarrow vinescroll discussed above. However, close examination of the two Hexham fragments reveals some significant differences between them. The carving of the leaves and the musculature of the legs and arms in figure 17 appear less detailed and less accomplished than those of the two fragmented forms in figure 16. The thickness of the

[59] Cramp, *County Durham and Northumberland*, pt 1, 185–6, pt 2, pl. 179. It has been thought possible that these two panels are from a single composition. They were first drawn and mentioned in the late nineteenth century. Both have been dated either Roman or last quarter of the seventh century. Rosemary Cramp, in her 'Early Northumbrian Sculpture at Hexham', in *St Wilfrid at Hexham*, ed. D. P. Kirby (Newcastle, 1974), 115–40, 172–9, considers the fragments to be Roman, despite earlier thinking they were Anglo-Saxon. She notes that Anglo-Saxon vinescrolls do not contain naked putti, and that the plant forms seem to have had no influence on those seen on the crosses of the Hexham School (p. 125).

[60] Cramp, *County Durham and Northumberland*, pt 1, 185–6.

tendrils in which the figure is caught up is less regular, and the leaf shapes are treated differently. The little cockerel in figure 16 also compares well with birds in surviving sculpture at Corbridge and other Roman sites, but has no convincing parallels in Anglo-Saxon sculpture.[61] It is possible that these two panels map a movement away from the Roman, the one mimicking the other in style and motif at the same time as it was in the process of transforming them into something new. If we look again at the Jarrow vinescroll (fig. 14), a movement even further away from the Roman becomes apparent. This is now definitely an Anglo-Saxon vinescroll, and even the meaning seems to have shifted from a subject set in a paradise landscape of abundance to something more suggestive of danger, a threat to body and soul.

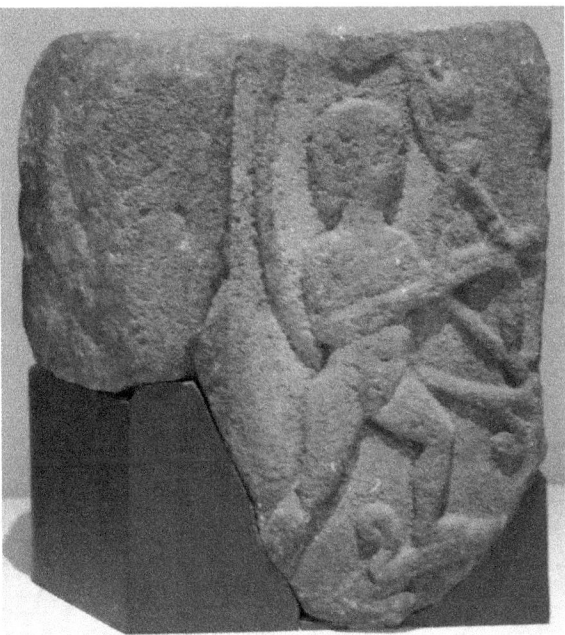

FIG. 17.
FRAGMENT WITH VINESCROLL, HEXHAM

Similar questions have been raised with regard to an architectural panel with a compass-drawn rosette or marigold carved in relief (fig. 18). It is included in the corpus of Romano-British sculpture with a note of caution[62] but it is also included in the Corpus of Anglo-Saxon Stone Sculpture.[63] Richard Bailey felt that the plaque is closest in design to sculpture from contemporary Poitiers, and that many of the other Hexham fragments have parallels at seventh- or eighth-century sites such as Cividale and S. Juan de Baños.[64] This particular stone, however, is now firmly believed to be Roman.[65]

Bailey believes that the style used here and at Jarrow, may have been more a statement about the unity of the church than the imitation of any single site.[66] While there can be no doubt that the unity of Christian

---

[61] See, e.g., the cockerel beneath the naked figure of Mercury on a second- or third-century relief carving from Corbridge in E. J. Phillips, *Corpus signorum imperii romani*, vol. 1, fascicle 1 (Oxford, 1977).
[62] Phillips, *Corpus signorum imperii romani*, vol. 1, fascicle 1, 55–6.
[63] Cramp, *County Durham and Northumberland*, pt 1, 186.
[64] Bailey, *England's Earliest Sculptors*, 31–3.
[65] Martin Henig, pers. comm.
[66] Bailey, *England's Earliest Sculptors*, 37.

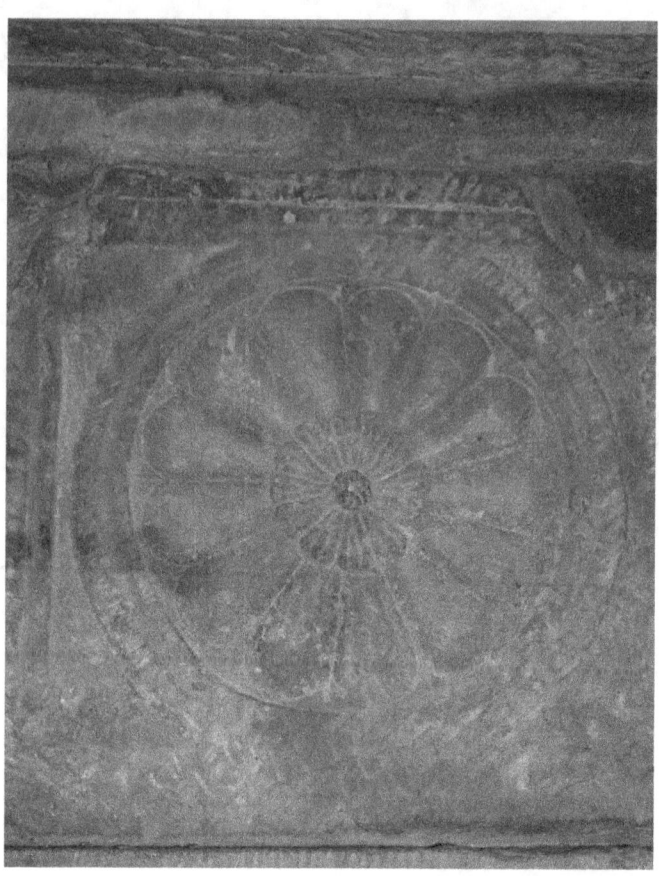

FIG. 18. PANEL WITH ROSETTE DECORATION, HEXHAM

practice and belief would have been central to the message of all Anglo-Saxon churches, unity with each other might have been a less certain, or at least a more nuanced, matter. Despite the reuse of Roman objects and the mimicking of Roman and Continental styles at both Hexham and Jarrow, one has to question how effective such a statement of unity, if intended, would have been. The sculpture at both monasteries may display similar motifs – vinescroll in particular – but details of these motifs, as well as the style of the carvings at the two foundations, are quite distinctive. Style and motif may have been used at Hexham in order to declare both allegiance and difference, perhaps a more cosmopolitan approach to what constituted an Anglo-Saxon church, or perhaps a more imperial attitude appropriate to Wilfrid's metropolitan ambitions. Certainly Wilfrid's primary support came not from his Northumbrian colleagues, amongst whom he was an often divisive and controversial figure, but from the pope in Rome. Hexham's Romanness then was profound, but it was also a very Anglo-Saxon Romanness, built as it was on the ruins of Romano-Britain.

One of the most distinctive of the Hexham sculptures is Acca's Cross (fig. 19), wrongly identified by antiquaries as the cross described by Symeon of Durham as standing over the grave of Wilfrid's successor, Bishop Acca (d. 740). The cross is believed to date from the second quarter of the eighth century, but fragments of a number of stone crosses survive at Hexham, and there is nothing to associate this one with the grave of Acca. One side of the cross bears the remains of an inscription that may once have extended over the entire face. Still partially visible are the words *unigenito filio dei* (the only begotten son of the Lord) from the Nicene Creed.[67] The other three sides are decorated with exquisitely carved continuous vinescrolls, so finely carved that the Jarrow sculptures still appear clumsy in comparison. A fragment of the lower arm of the cross head remains at the top of the shaft and indicates that the head was originally decorated with a cross surrounded by a pelleted border.[68] The lack of figural ornament on this and other Hexham sculptures has led to the suggestion of iconoclastic tendencies at Hexham, but it is unclear why this is believed to have been the case at Hexham yet not at other sites where

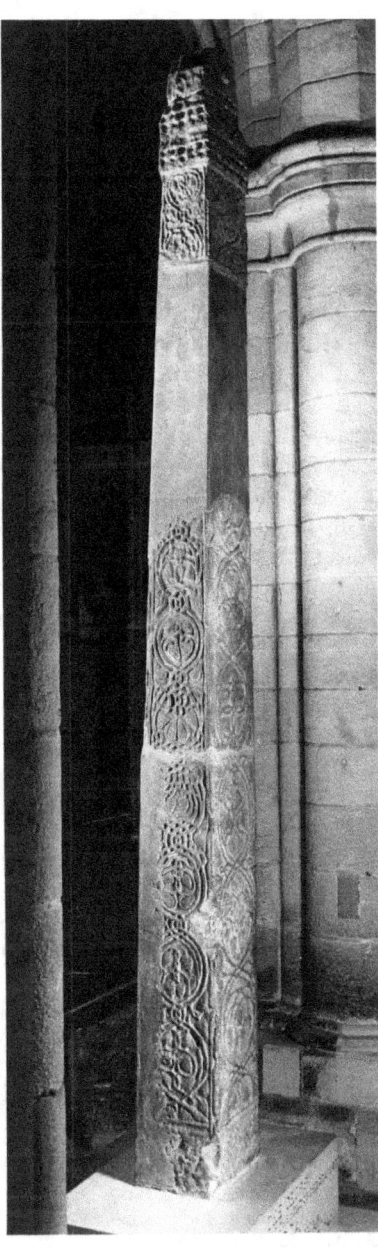

FIG. 19. ACCA'S CROSS, HEXHAM

[67] Identified by Michael J. Swanton, 'Bishop Acca and the Cross at Hexham', *Archaeologia Aeliana*, ser. 4, 48 (1970), 157–68, at 161–3; see also Bailey, *England's Earliest Sculptors*, 44. Cramp, *County Durham and Northumberland*, pt 1, 175, states that not enough of the inscription survives to be certain of this reading.
[68] See Bailey, *England's Earliest Sculptors*, fig. 67.

non-figural ornament is also found in significant numbers. The presence of the naked figures in the vinescroll discussed above, whether Roman or Anglo-Saxon, also argues against it.

The vinescrolls on Acca's Cross are very different from those of the two fragments discussed above. Most obviously, they are not inhabited. The pelleted ornament of the cross head has its origins in the beaded borders of metalwork and one of the closest Anglo-Saxon parallels for the vinescroll ornament of the shaft is provided by the late eighth-century Rupertus cross in Bischofshofn, Austria.[69] Further afield, Islamic parallels in the mosaics of the Dome of the Rock in Jerusalem and the Great Mosque of Damascus have been cited,[70] but it should be remembered that the decoration of both these buildings is heavily indebted to late antique and Byzantine art. It is most likely that Byzantine art, perhaps mediated through Rome or Ravenna, was the ultimate source of the vinescroll ornament on Acca's Cross. When painted, as it was originally, the cross would have appeared to be a monumental gold and jewelled cross translated into stone. Some idea of the effect the monument was intended to convey may be provided by the cross depicted in the apse mosaic of S. Pudenziana, one of Rome's earliest churches. In the background of the mosaic is a city which may be intended to represent both Jerusalem and the heavenly Jerusalem with the 'Constantinian' cross on the hill of Golgotha at its centre.[71] The Nicene Creed from which at least part of the Hexham inscription is assumed to have been taken was adopted at the First Council of Nicaea in 325 as an expression of the unity of Christian belief and the unity of the Christian church under Constantine. Such an identification with the imperial foundations of the church in Rome is likely to have served the imperial pretensions of Wilfrid and his successors well. After Wilfrid's power was divided and he was driven from his see in 678, it was in 'the Constantiniana' (the papal cathedral of St Saviour) that Pope Agatho received Wilfrid and decreed that he be restored to power.[72]

Hexham was also an early centre of that most Constantinian of Anglo-Saxon saints' cults, the cult of St Oswald. The story of Oswald's raising of the cross before his victory at the Battle of Heavenfield (a mere four miles from Hexham) has been outlined briefly above. Bede records that the Hexham community celebrated the vigil of the feast of St Oswald first by singing psalms beside the cross at Heavenfield, and later in a church built

---

[69] As noted in Cramp, *County Durham and Northumberland*, pt 1, 176; and Bailey, *England's Earliest Sculptors*, 121–2.
[70] Cramp, *County Durham and Northumberland*, pt 1, 176; Bailey, *England's Earliest Sculptors*, 53.
[71] The presence of the cross in the mosaic suggests that the city is meant to represent Jerusalem, but the presence of the four symbols of the evangelists in the sky above suggests the heavenly Jerusalem. While believed for much of the Middle Ages to have been erected by Constantine, the Golgotha cross was actually put up by the Emperor Theodosius. See Wood, 'Constantinian Crosses in Northumbria', 9–11.
[72] Stephen, *The Life of Wilfrid*, 56.

on the site to accommodate the increasing numbers of pilgrims wishing to visit it. Fragments of Oswald's cross, like fragments of the True Cross, worked miracles and were in great demand, especially for their ability to cure sick men and beasts. Alan Thacker has speculated on the possible political motivations for Hexham's support of the cult. In 703 Wilfrid had again been driven from power and deprived of most of his possessions by Berhtwald, archbishop of Canterbury, and the Northumbrian King Aldfrith. Once again he turned to the pope. Wilfrid was reconciled with Berhtwald and the new king, Aldfrith's son Osred, and his power and possessions were restored at the Synod of Nidd in 705. It may have been at this point that Hexham began to eclipse Bamburgh as the centre of Oswald's cult.

> It is tempting to suppose that in their time of trial the family and adherents of Aldfrith's son made their vow to Wilfrid before Oswald's imperishable arm and that one of the fruits of the reconciliation was a fresh promoting of their dynastic cult. Quite possibly the annual pilgrimage to Heavenfield was then inaugurated or at least upgraded as a sign of the new concord between Bamburgh and Hexham; certainly it was after that date that the site was honoured with a church.[73]

It is also possible that it was at about this time that the monks of Lindisfarne began promoting the cult of their own saint, Cuthbert, in what might be interpreted as a battle for cult power with Hexham.[74] In this regard it is useful to consider Uppinder Mehan and David Townsend's analysis of the ways in which the notion of 'metropole', as it has been articulated in postcolonial studies, is complicated in the relationship established between Rome and Anglo-Saxon England at this time. Bede's description of Heavenfield is one of their most telling examples of that complication. Bede writes:

> Vocatur locus ille lingua Anglorum Hefenfeld, quod dici potest latine Caelestis Campus, quod certo utique praesagio futurorum antiquitus nomen accepit; significans nimirum quod ibidem caeleste erigendum tropeum, caelestis inchoanda uictoria caelestia usque hodie forent miracula celebranda.
>
> (This place is called in English Heavenfield, and in Latin *Caelestis Campus*, a name which it certainly received in days of old as an omen of future happenings; it signified that a heavenly sign was

---

[73] Alan Thacker, '*Membra Disjecta*: The Division of the Body and the Diffusion of the Cult', in *Oswald: Northumbrian King to European Saint*, ed. Clare Stancliffe and Eric Cambridge (Stamford, 1995), 97–127, at 110.
[74] Eric Cambridge, 'Archaeology and the Cult of St Oswald in Pre-Conquest Northumbria', in *Oswald: Northumbrian King to European Saint*, ed. Stancliffe and Cambridge, 128–63, at 158.

to be erected there, a heavenly victory won, and that heavenly miracles were to take place there continuing to this day.)[75]

Mehan and Townsend's focus is on the glossing of the place-name. For Townsend,

> One could choose to read the gloss ... as a reduction of English specificity to the object of metropolitan scrutiny. But the reader can plausibly see the relation of Englisc [sic] to Latin as more contestatory ... By invoking the prophetic aptness of the vernacular place-name, Bede ascribes to Englisc the capacity to signify spiritual truths independently of their transposition into Latin.[76]

He concludes by noting the simultaneous inability of the Latin ever to be adequate to English experience, and the transformation by the English of the language imposed by the Roman church into their own mother tongue. It is possible to understand Wilfrid's strategy at Hexham as working in a similar way. The victory won at Heavenfield was not just Oswald's but also that of Wilfrid and Hexham. If Latin was the written and spoken language of a metropolitan Roman church, then the stones cut and carved by the Romans were its material language, but one that spoke now from within an English landscape and built environment. At Heavenfield a Roman altar decorated with Roman vinescroll was transformed into an Anglo-Saxon cross base, and Anglo-Saxon vinescroll was added to the Roman decoration,[77] creating a hybrid monument which embedded the Anglo-Saxon within the Roman and vice versa in a way that left neither culture untouched. We can in fact see the same contestatory relationship that Mehan and Townsend see in Bede's use of Latin and English language played out materially in the hybrid Roman/Anglo-Saxon stonework and sculpture of Hexham. It is tempting then to see the desire of Wilfrid and the monks of Hexham as working towards the establishment of a new metropolitan centre within England itself.

## TIME, MEMORY AND THE SPIRITUAL LANDSCAPE

The monasteries discussed so far were all large coenobitic foundations under the rule of a professed, educated and theologically trained abbot (or abbess in the case of Whitby and Hackness). In the early years of the eighth century a new type of monastery appeared, the aristocratic or family monastery, about which Bede complained so vigorously in

---

[75] *HE*, iii.2.
[76] Mehan and Townsend, '"Nation" and the Gaze of the Other in Eighth-Century Northumbria', 12.
[77] Cramp, *County Durham and Northumberland*, pt 1, 222.

his letter to Bishop Ecgberht of York in 734.[78] Aristocratic monasteries were founded by lay men and women and, at least in some cases, were probably little different from the great monasteries established under the regular control of the church. According to Bede, however, they were very different in nature, houses of sin and greed run by inexperienced and uneducated lay abbots and abbesses, and housing disreputable monks and nuns in addition to the founder's family members. The real issue was less one of morals than one of land. Land was traditionally granted by the king to his nobles on a lifetime basis and thus could not be passed on, but land granted to the church was granted in perpetuity, the transaction formalized and recorded for posterity by charter. For the laity, founding a monastery thus became a way of maintaining control over land and establishing the right to preserve both land and wealth within families.[79] Certainly some monasteries may have been as problematic as Bede claimed, but others may have been virtually indistinguishable in function and piety from the more acceptable foundations. Moreover, rule of monasteries such as Whitby or Wearmouth was also passed down within families, at least in the decades immediately following their foundation, so that they too could be considered family monasteries.

Bewcastle (Cumbria) has often been considered the site of such an aristocratic monastery, though there is absolutely no proof one way or the other that this was the case. The reason for the identification is the apparently aristocratic context and exclusively vernacular inscriptions of the memorial monument that survives in the churchyard (figs. 20, 21). It is not even certain that there was a monastery at Bewcastle, though the fact that it has such a monumental and elegant piece of sculpture makes it likely. Whatever its origin, Bewcastle is certainly a very different sort of place from either Wearmouth-Jarrow or Hexham. It is, however, no less consciously built on a Romano-British past, and no less the locus of a complex layering of time and place. The monument, almost certainly originally a cross, is located on what would have been the terrace of the old Roman fort of Fanum Cocidii just north of Hadrian's Wall, but it is not, as were the major Northumbrian monasteries, on or close to major roads or rivers, nor is it near a major royal centre as was Lindisfarne.

There has been debate in recent years as to whether the Bewcastle monument was originally a cross, became a cross secondarily, or was a column from the outset.[80] There is a mortise in the top of the shaft, so the monument did continue upwards, but when that upper stone was

---

[78] Bede, *Epistola ad Ecgbertum episcopum*, in *Venerabilis Baedae opera historica*, ed. Plummer, 2.
[79] For an excellent summary see Blair, *The Church in Anglo-Saxon Society*, 100–8.
[80] For the major arguments see Fred Orton and Ian Wood with Clare A. Lees, *Fragments of History: Rethinking the Ruthwell and Bewcastle Monuments* (Manchester, 2007); Éamonn Ó Carragáin, *Ritual and the Rood: Liturgical Images and the Old English Poems of the Dream of the Rood Tradition* (London, 2005).

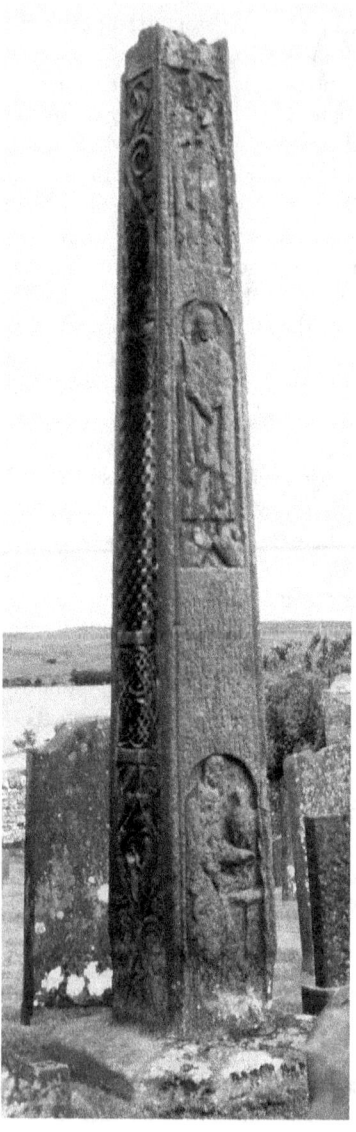

FIG. 20.
BEWCASTLE
CROSS,
WEST SIDE

added and what form it took cannot now be proven with any certainty. A cross head was found at Bewcastle, but that does not mean that it was originally attached to this cross. Nevertheless, the word 'segbecn' in the inscription quoted in full below is a word used for the cross, and a visual riddling on the cross is very much a part of the monument's non-figural ornament and no doubt also its larger meaning; it will therefore be accepted here as a cross.

The Bewcastle monument is first of all a memorial monument. In the lowest panel of the west face is a man in secular aristocratic dress holding a falcon. Above him is a panel of roughly equal size that bears a now largely illegible runic inscription which could be read as '+þis sigbecn [...] setton Hwætred [...] þgær ... æft [.]lcfri[.]' (This victory beacon Hwætred ... thgær and .. set up in memory of (after) .lcfri). The next to last line may contain a form of *gebiddan*, meaning 'to pray'. The inscription tells us that the monument was set up by Hwætred and someone else as a 'victory beacon', or memorial, for someone whose name contains the letters 'lcfri', and possibly requested prayers for his soul.[81] In the panel over the inscription is the figure of Christ over the beasts with his name carved in runes above: '[+] g[e]ssus kristtus'. It is significant that the lower parts of the panels that carry inscriptions form arches over the figures of Christ and the falconer,

---

[81] Other names have been inscribed in the borders between the panels on the monument's north and south faces. The only one now legible is the female name kynbur*g̃ inscribed just above the lowest panel of plantscroll on the north face.

containing them as if within an architectural setting, and making it clear to the viewer that the inscribed words relate to the figure below. A simple rectangular panel encloses the figure of John the Baptist with the Agnus Dei at the top of the shaft. There is a difference in the space this figure inhabits and possibly also in the way he is meant to be perceived. John with the Agnus Dei is an eschatological image, referring to the future, the second coming of Christ and the heavenly Jerusalem. The designers of the monument may have wished to suggest that in death the man commemorated was united with Christ, as he is united with Christ on the monument by the similarity of settings, but that the time and space of ultimate salvation, the time at which all shall dwell with the lamb of God, has not yet been realized. The arched panels containing the figures may be modelled after those of Roman funerary monuments such as the Murrell Hill tombstone, and thus the rectangular shape of the John the Baptist panel may have indicated closure at the top of the monument's figural panels.[82] This is possible, but it should be noted that figures within arched settings are relatively common in early Anglo-Saxon sculpture, so there need not be any direct connection with Roman funerary monuments, though by the same token it should not be ruled out altogether. The figural panels

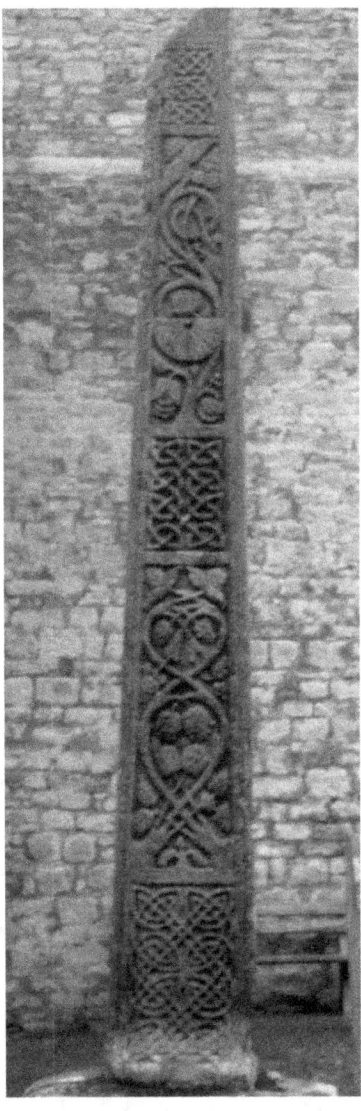

FIG. 21.
BEWCASTLE
CROSS, SOUTH
SIDE

---

[82] See further, Martin Henig, '*Murum civitatis, et fontem in ea a Romanis mire olim constructum*: The Arts of Rome in Carlisle and the Civitatis of the Carvetti and Their Influence', in *Carlisle and Cumbria: Roman and Medieval Architecture, Art and Archaeology*, ed. Mike McCarthy and David Weston, JBAA 27 (Leeds, 2004), 11–28; Orton and Wood with Lees, *Fragments of History*, 9.

and vinescroll on the east face of the cross have fascinated scholars for centuries, but less well studied is the monument's geometric and interlace ornament.

One of the things that makes the study of nonrepresentational ornament so difficult is that, if it carries meaning, it is not meaning that can be understood using the traditional art historical iconographic approach. There is no narrative or text to which it can be linked with any certainty. There have been attempts to make such identifications, for example in manuscript illumination, where references to prayer mats, labyrinths and Crucifixion scenes have been read into the decoration of carpet pages.[83] Ernst Kitzinger, on the other hand, argued in 1993 that 'very strict limits must be imposed if floodgates are not to be opened to wild and reckless interpretations of every bit of knotwork or zoomorphic interlace in Insular art',[84] a view that clearly stifles any attempt to find meaning in the abstract patterns of early medieval art. The tendency of many scholars has been to concur with Kitzinger's view that the 'aesthetic effect' of the knot was an end in itself.[85] If we turn to the art of other areas of the medieval world, however, pattern and abstraction do carry meaning at the same time as they also carry aesthetic importance. The layers of ornament that cover the walls of the Alhambra in Granada, for example, have been shown to carry cultural and political significance,[86] as have the patterns that cover the art and architecture of eighth- through thirteenth-century India.[87] Such specific connections cannot be made for most Anglo-Saxon sculptures as we know so little about their history.[88] It is possible to say, however, that knots do take time to design, to create and to unravel, and as such become traces of labour, time and the act of deciphering the image. They are also often self-referential in their construction, without apparent beginning or end, and can in fact draw the viewer deeper into contemplation of the work of art. Indeed, in some cases the knot might be described as standing metaphorically for the work of art itself, in that the monument is a knot that binds together time, place and viewer across the centuries.

The Bewcastle Cross, as noted above, is a memorial or commemorative monument erected by Hwætred (about whom we know nothing) and someone else in memory of someone possibly named Alcfriþ. As it

---

[83] Brown, *Lindisfarne Gospels*, 320–6. See above, p. 38.
[84] Kitzinger, 'Interlace and Icons', 3.
[85] Kitzinger, 'Interlace and Icons', 4.
[86] Lara Eggleton, 'Crumbling Empires, Nostalgia, and the Politics of Ornament in Islamic Spain', unpublished paper delivered at the International Medieval Congress, Leeds, July 2009.
[87] Finbarr B. Flood, *Objects of Translation: Material Culture and Medieval 'Hindu-Muslim' Encounter* (Princeton, NJ, 2009). For connections between the Anglo-Saxons and the Islamic world see Katharine Scarfe Beckett, *Anglo-Saxon Perceptions of the Islamic World* (Cambridge, 2003).
[88] Like the Islamic and Indian monuments, Bewcastle's patterns would originally have been picked out with paint, and some were embellished with glass or metal fittings.

survives, Bewcastle has five panels of geometric interlace ornament, two on its north side and three on its south side (fig. 21), and there are also knots formed by the twisting stems of the plantscrolls in the panels – two on the north and two on the south – that alternate with the panels of interlace. In all of these panels one can find crosses formed by the strands of interlace, the spaces between them and the shapes of the plants, so clearly they were intended at the very least to focus the eye and the mind on the form and meaning of the cross, the larger monument, but that does not mean we have to see this as their only function. Similarly, we can't be certain that the desire to present 'hidden symbols' is a likely explanation for the general popularity of knots and interlace in Anglo-Saxon art.[89] The two most obvious crosses at Bewcastle, those embedded in the lowermost panel of interlace on the south side and the uppermost panel of interlace on the north side, help spur us on to a close looking that brings into focus similar forms in the other panels. They reveal a recognizable image, a sign of figuration, at the centre of the ordered design, yet at the same time they stop short of collapsing the visible into the legible, demanding meditation rather than providing instant recognition or ease of reading.[90] And of course these hidden crosses are embedded within the larger Christian order created by and within the monument as a whole. Order is important. When the north and south sides are viewed together, there is a harmonic balance created between the symmetrical and the asymmetrical (one moreover that extends to the cross as a whole), as well as a diversity built up out of variation on what is at heart two basic looped patterns.[91] The designs in each panel are also made up of multiple strands, although each gives the appearance of being formed by a single seamless looped or knotted strand without beginning or end. Above all, it is in the knots and segmented lines of the interlace patterns that the viewer becomes aware of measure and number and their regulation of form. All these patterns are constructed from regular discrete units of measure. As such, they are a visual complement to the sundial on the south side of the cross which, with its thirteen lines and twelve divisions, makes clear the intersection of linear time and measure with the cycle of cosmic time, while simultaneously imposing geometric and linear order on the natural world of the plantscroll.

In *The Reckoning of Time* Bede wrote that there was no measurement of hours before the fourth day of Creation, the day on which the sun, moon and stars were created:

---

[89] Hawkes, 'Symbolic Lives: The Visual Evidence', 332.
[90] There is an ease of reading about the legible that is not operative with this type of ornament.
[91] See further the description of the interlace in Richard N. Bailey and Rosemary Cramp, *Cumberland, Westmorland and Lancashire North of the Sands*, CASSS 2 (Oxford, 1988), 61–72.

> ibi namque temporis initium statuit, qui luminaribus conditis dinit: Ut sint in signa, et tempora, et dies, et annos … et quarto demum mane sol a medio procedens Orientis, horis umbratim suas per lineus currentibus, aequinoctium quod annuatim servaretur inchavit.[92]

> (For He decreed the beginning of time at the point when, upon creating the luminaries, He said, Let them be for signs, and for seasons, and for days and for years … Not until the fourth morning did the Sun, rising from the mid-point of the east, with the hours running through their lines by the shadow, inaugurate the equinox, which has been maintained every year.)[93]

As Faith Wallis notes, in this passage Bede imagines the creation of a natural sundial coterminous with the creation of the sun, 'an interesting indication of how deeply Bede's concept of time was bound up with the notion of the measurable'.[94] But as Fred Orton has stressed, this does not mean that Bede himself used a sundial for the measurement of time,[95] only that he was familiar with what sundials were used for, and the ways in which they made visible the connections between divine and natural order.

Bede introduces his explanation of the 'Three ways of reckoning time' with the oft-quoted statement:

> Tempora igitura temperando nomen accipiunt, sive quod unumquodque illorum spatium separatim temperatum sit: seu quod momentis, horis, diebus, mensibus, annis, saeculisque et aetatibus omnia mortalis.'[96]

> (Times (*tempora*) take their name from 'measure' (*temperamentum*) either because every unit of time is separately measured (*temperatum*), or because all the courses of mortal life are measured (*temperentur*) in moments, hours, days, months, years, ages and epochs.)[97]

The composition of the passage sets up a rhythm through its repetition of the cognate terms for time and measure that is itself reflective of measure. The content of the passage reveals time as both division and regulation, something that is also made clear in the biblical account of the fourth day

---

[92] *PL* 90, col. 317A.
[93] Bede, *Bede: The Reckoning of Time*, ed. and trans. Faith Wallis (Liverpool, 1999), 24.
[94] Bede. *The Reckoning of Time*, ed. Wallis, n. 31.
[95] Orton and Wood with Lees, *Fragments of History*, 140–1.
[96] *PL* 90, col. 298B.
[97] Bede, *The Reckoning of Time*, ed. Wallis, 13.

of Creation with its division of light from darkness and its regulation of the day and the night by the sun and the moon.[98]

The processes of division, measurement and regulation that lie behind time and its creation were understood to be mirrored in artistic creation in general, but perhaps nowhere are they more evident to mortal eyes than in the production of interlace which – when done well as it is at Bewcastle – consists of exact units of measure that both divide a pattern into linear segments and multiply those regular units of measure into a larger, ordered repeating whole – as years, ages and epochs are constituted by moments, hours and days. I am not saying here that interlace is a symbol of time, but rather that interlace both reflects and takes place in time, and that it does so differently from figural representation. We recognize a man, for example a man standing over two beasts (fig. 20), and it may take us some time to make the conventional iconographic connections back to the multiple textual sources to which it refers, but we unravel or decipher interlace differently, through form itself. Without recourse to textual sources, it makes the eye aware of line and shape and their regulated movement and repetition through time and across the surface of the monument.

The monument itself is also a knot of a sort, a point at which production and interpretation (or making and deciphering), the past and the present, Bewcastle as it has changed through time (both physically and in terms of what it represents or how it is understood) all converge, bound together by the materiality of the cross. Bewcastle was the site of Fanum Cocidii, a large Roman fort constructed as a defensive outpost in the wild country just to the north of Hadrian's Wall. Like the other forts along the line of the wall, it was built at the regular interval of 7⅓ Roman miles (6.8 statute miles) from its nearest neighbouring fort – in this case Birdoswald. As such it was part of an ordered pattern of linear wall and enclosed fortification that divided Roman Britain from the lands and peoples to the north, that imposed a colonial structure and order on both land and human activity, and that regulated life in the area. It brought what was seen as order to disorder, civilization to the barbarians, and all the new religious and political practices that went along with Roman governance. The fort was also, of course, a postcolonial monument – the name Fanum Cocidii commemorates the Celtic deity Cocidius[99] – and there is

---

[98] Genesis 1:14–18: 'And God said: Let there be lights made in the firmament of heaven, to divide the day and the night, and let them be for signs, and for seasons, and for days and years: 15 To shine in the firmament of heaven, and to give light upon the earth. And it was so done. 16 and God made two great lights: a greater light to rule the day; and a lesser light to rule the night: and the stars. 17 And he set them in the firmament of heaven to shine upon the earth. 18 And to rule the day and the night, and to divide the light and the darkness. And God saw that it was good.'

[99] See further Kenneth J. Fairless, 'Three Religious Cults from the Northern Frontier Region', in *Between and Beyond the Walls: Essays on the Prehistory and History of North*

a certain hybridity or statement of appropriation about the place and its past, although it cannot be shown that the monument itself consciously references anything further back in time than the Romans. The cross stands on what was once a terrace just inside the southern gate, aligned with the *via principalis* and directly in front of the bath house of the fort, at least parts of which were likely to have still been standing at the time the cross was erected.[100] Its form and location suggest reappropriation of site, if not of form – the form of a Roman obelisk or of a Jupiter column, for example.[101] Certainly, Bewcastle's preoccupation with time signals its involvement with its Roman past. The sundial came to Anglo-Saxon England from the Roman world and is part of the monument's Romanness (as is the plantscroll of which it is part). However three of the dial's lines terminate in crosses, and it is itself part of a cross, a clear Christianization of classical ways of telling time, just as the crosses at the centre of two of the interlace panels may be read as a Christianization of a typically Insular type of ornament that also goes back to a pre-Christian past. Christian time was part of yet another rule, order and division. The sundial would not have functioned to mark the hours of the day, despite its division into twelve, but it could have been used to mark the liturgical hours at which a monastic community (or a devout lay person) would have been expected to stop for prayer. This was, as has been noted, a very different sort of time from the 'mainly natural time' of rural agricultural Northumbria[102] and it would have separated whoever made and used the monument from other inhabitants of the area; it would have created an 'us' and a 'them' as effectively as the Roman wall and fort of Bewcastle – though perhaps in a more subtle manner. As Kathleen Davis has emphasized, monastic time, especially for Bede, was neither ahistorical nor apolitical.[103] Its importance to the Bewcastle community and its prominent materiality on the monument are equally clear statements of a historical perspective and political order at Bewcastle.

But monastic and historical time are not the only sorts of time we experience. There is a time that is 'an essentially human, interior phenomenon'[104] which takes place in, but is separate from the cycles

---

*Britain in Honour of George Joby*, ed. Roger Miket and Colin Burgess (Edinburgh, 1984), 228–35.

[100] See further Orton and Wood with Lees, *Fragments of History*, chs 2 and 5.

[101] On the latter see John Mitchell, 'The High Cross and Monastic Strategies in Eighth-Century Northumbria', in *New Offerings, Ancient Treasures: Studies in Medieval Art for George Henderson*, ed. Paul Binski and William Noel (Stroud, 2001), 88–114; Henig, 'Murum civitatis', 20–1.

[102] Orton and Wood with Lees, *Fragments of History*, 134, 137.

[103] Kathleen Davis, *Periodization and Sovereignty: How Ideas of Feudalism and Secularization Govern the Politics of Time* (Philadelphia, PA, 2008), esp. 1–2, 123–30.

[104] Giorgio Agamben, *Infancy and History: On the Destruction of Experience* (London, 1993), 104. See also, St Augustine, *Confessions*, trans. R. S. Pine-Coffin (Harmondsworth, 1961), xi.15, p. 265: 'we are gifted with the ability to *feel* and measure time'.

of heaven and earth. In his *Confessions*, St Augustine wrestled with the distinction between, and experience and visualization of, the two: the 'intricate puzzle' as he described it, of past, present and future.

> Audivi a quodam homine docto, quod solis et lunae ac siderum motus, ipsa sint tempora, et nil annui. Cur enim non potius omnium corporum motus sint tempora? An vero si cessarent coeli lumina, et moveretur rota figuli, non esset tempus quo metiremur eos gyros et diceremus aut aequalibus morulis agi: aut si alias tardius, alias velocius moveretur alios magis diuturnos esse, alias minus ... Nemo ergo mihi dicat coelestium corporum motus esse tempora ... Video igitur tempus quamdam esse distentionem sed video, an videre mihi videor?[105]

> (I once heard a learned man say that there is nothing but the movement of the sun and the moon and the stars, but I do not agree. Would it not be more likely that time was the movement, not only of heavenly bodies, but of all other bodies as well? If all the lights of the sky ceased to move but the potter's wheel continued to turn, would there not still be time by which we could measure its rotations? Should we no longer be able to say that it turned with a regular rhythm or that its speed varied, or that some turns took more and others less time ... I cannot accept the suggestion that time is constituted by the movement of the heavenly bodies ... I see time therefore as an extension of some sort. But do I see this or only seem to see it?)[106]

And again:

> Duo ergo illa tempora, praetesritum et futurum quomodo sunt, quando et praeteritum jam non est, et futurum nondum est? Praesens autem si semper esset praesens, nec in praeteritum transiret; jam non esset tempus, sed aeternitas. Si ergo praesens, ut tempus sit, ideo fit quia in praeteritum transit; quomodo et hoc esse dicimus, cui causa ut sit illa est?[107]

> (Of these three divisions of time [past, present and future], then, how can two, the past and the future, be, when the past no longer is and the future is not yet? As for the present, if it were always present and never moved on to become the past, it would not be time but eternity. If therefore the present is time only by reason of the fact that it moves on to become the past, how can we say that even the present is?)[108]

The Bewcastle sundial allows you to tell the time, a particular time of day,

---

[105] *PL* 32, cols 820–1.
[106] St Augustine, *Confessions*, trans. Pine-Coffin, xi.23, pp. 271–2.
[107] *PL* 32, col. 816.
[108] St Augustine, *Confessions*, trans. Pine-Coffin, xi.14, pp. 264–5.

but it does not visualize time itself. Neither do the figural panels, which depict moments in a narrative; we know what comes before and what comes after, but we see those moments only with the mind's eye. The plantscrolls represent life and growth, the forward movement of linear time, but one frozen at a particular moment in the life cycle. It is only in the interlace panels that time as both linear movement and eternal cycle is made visible – not through its being symbolized or represented but through its being experienced visually. As our eyes follow the lines and make out the patterns and puzzles, we are aware of movement from point to point, from a still visible point of origin to a visible point in the future. In so doing we also become aware of the panels' creation in time by a sculptor (or sculptors) who traced these same patterns, and of the process of design that lies behind them. As such, it might be possible to understand the panels within the context of the sort of 'iconology' proposed by Hans Belting, one in which the image serves as a bridge between past and present rather than simply as a bridge between an artwork and a text or established tradition of representation although, at least as deployed by Belting, the methodology remains tied to the figurative.[109]

To be sure, the interlace panels with their patterns of knots and lines exist in relation to the other carvings on the cross and to their recording and representation of the movement of the heavens, the liturgical hours of the day and the biblical narratives of the past. The purpose of the knot is to fasten together, and the monument too is thus a knot, though a knot of a different sort, one in which different moments are bound up together. Although we cannot see the movement, the passing of time from one to another, we are aware of its workings. The Bewcastle we see now has its Roman strand, its several Anglo-Saxon strands, and the further strands of history and heritage, memory and perception. It brings into perception, in the words of St Augustine, 'praesens de praeteritis, praesens de praesentibus contuitus, praesens de futuris exspectatio'[110] (a present of past things, a present of present things, and a present of future things),[111] all knotted together in the monument and our experience of it. It also exists in time, a time which is continuous and not divided into minutes or days or years or eras or linear measured sections, and which moves, as the orientation and memorial function of the monument remind us, ever forwards towards death. The monument as a whole has been oriented so that the sun rises behind the figural panels on its west face, an orientation generally used in Christian art to symbolize rebirth and the coming of Christ, just as the setting sun in the evening would have illuminated the

---

[109] See further Hans Belting, 'Image, Medium, Body: A New Approach to Iconology', *Critical Inquiry* 31.2 (2005), 302–19, esp. 303–6.
[110] *PL* 32 col. 819.
[111] St Augustine, *Confessions*, trans. Pine-Coffin, xi.20, p. 269.

portrait of the dead man and the memorial inscription, along with the salvific figures of Christ and John the Baptist.

While we know very little about what type of community existed at Bewcastle in the eighth century, the monument tells us that it was wealthy enough to employ top-quality artists. We know too that life, death, time and memory were important here, and important enough to be made visible in and on the landscape. One wonders whether the cross might not have been part of an attempt to create a dynastic cult centre at Bewcastle. The monument has some interesting similarities to, but also differences from, known or possible cult monuments at sites such as Lindisfarne, Whitby and Hackness, which will be discussed further below. Certainly it is an aristocratic sculpture, and the site may well have been one of Bede's family monasteries, but if so, the community at Bewcastle seems to have been highly educated and well versed in the practices and traditions of the more orthodox monasteries.

## THE INDIVIDUAL AND THE SACRED

Outside the liturgical ceremonies of the church, individual access to the holy and the sacred was mediated largely through objects and images – manuscripts such as psalters or gospel books, reliquaries with their relics, painted icons like those of Wearmouth-Jarrow, and sculpture like the Bewcastle Cross. Unfortunately the Wearmouth-Jarrow painted icons no longer survive, but iconic compositions and devotional images have been preserved from across the Anglo-Saxon period. One of the most popular and enduring figures in such images was the angel. The Lichfield angel (plate 3), discovered in the summer of 2003 in a sunken chamber at the east end of the present cathedral of St Peter, is believed to have been part of the shrine of St Chad (d. 672) constructed in the eighth century. Bede describes Chad's coffin as being both wooden and house-shaped, and as having a hole in one side through which visitors could insert their hands and remove some of the dust which was known to work miracles.[112] The angel is thought to have formed one half of an Annunciation group on the gable end of a stone shrine that may have covered (or perhaps replicated) the wooden coffin,[113] although it could also have come from a wall of the church. It has been dated to the late eighth or early ninth century and, if part of a shrine, has general parallels with the c. 800 St Andrew's sarcophagus and the similarly dated Hedda stone in Peterborough Cathedral. Much of the angel's original polychromy has

[112] *HE*, 3 iv.3.
[113] Warwick Rodwell, Jane Hawkes, Emily Howe and Rosemary Cramp, 'The Lichfield Angel: A Spectacular Anglo-Saxon Painted Sculpture', *Antiquaries Journal* 88 (2008), 48–108. Analysis of the shape of the stone has shown that it would have fitted over rather than contained an object (ibid., 64), but Bede's use of the term 'covered' does not necessarily imply that the coffin was covered by a shrine (*pace* Rodwell *et al.*, 55).

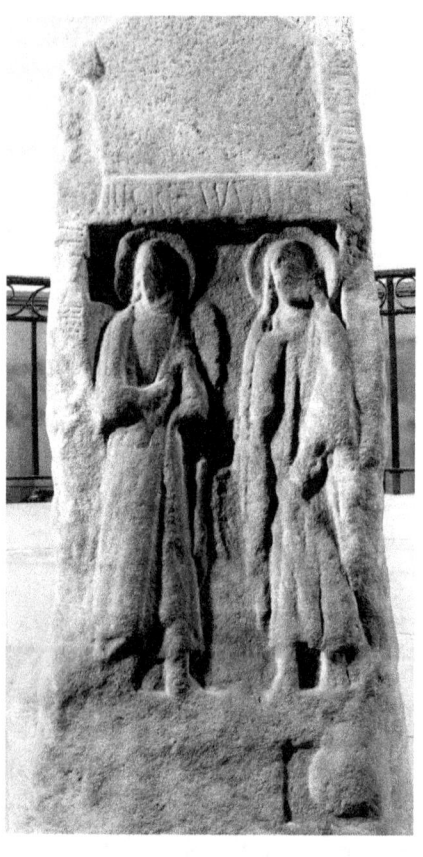

FIG. 22.
RUTHWELL CROSS, ANNUNCIATION

been preserved, and has allowed its original appearance to be reconstructed. Michelle Brown cited the combination of colours, and particularly the use of purple, as unusual for sculpture, but paralleled in manuscript painting by the mid-eighth-century Lichfield Gospels, which is now displayed alongside the angel in Lichfield Cathedral, and the Book of Cerne (Cambridge, University Library, MS Ll.I.10), both likely to have been made for Lichfield.[114] Analysis of the pigments has, however, shown that purple was not used, and that the original colours were white, red, yellow, black and flesh pink.[115]

The angel itself is depicted in motion, as if just entering into earthly space. One foot rests on the ground while the other is just in the process of stepping off a plant probably intended as a symbol of paradise. A similar sense of motion is conveyed by the angel of the Annunciation on the Ruthwell Cross, Dumfries (fig. 22), and especially by the angel now set into the western tower of the church at Breedon-on-the-Hill (fig. 23). Breedon, like Lichfield, was part of the kingdom of Mercia, and the Breedon angel is especially close to that of Lichfield in terms of pose, the detailed carving of the feathers of the wings, and the inclusion of a paradise plant – in this case a pomegranate. An early ninth-century date has been proposed for the Breedon angel, though there is still some disagreement on the matter. In general, angels have their origins in the winged victory figures of the classical world, as explored most notably by Aby Warburg.[116] Models for the Lichfield and other Anglo-Saxon angels have been cited in the art of early Christian Rome and Constantinople,[117] but inspiration from sculpture much closer to home is also possible. A Victory figure originally from the Roman fort at Stanwix and now in the Great North Museum, Newcastle upon Tyne, provides a particularly provocative comparison.[118]

[114] See further Michelle P. Brown, 'The Lichfield Angel: Lichfield as a Centre of Insular Art', *JBAA* 160.1 (2007), 8–19.
[115] Rodwell *et al.*, 'The Lichfield Angel', 63–4.
[116] Aby Warburg, *The Renewal of Pagan Antiquity*, ed. Kurt W. Forster, trans David Britt (Los Angeles, 1999), 89–156.
[117] Brown, 'Lichfield Angel', 15.
[118] See J. C. Coulston and E. J. Phillips, *Corpus signorum imperii romanii*, vol. 1, fasc. 6

One thing that unites all three of the Anglo-Saxon angels (and also the Stanwix Victory) is the dramatic yet peaceful sense of motion that the sculptors have been able to capture. In Warburg's terms, the pose of all three angels exemplifies the *Nachleben* or afterlife of the ecstatic figures of classical nymphs and maenads. By *Nachleben* Warburg did not mean the direct source of the iconographers. There were gaps and fissures between the appearance of an image in one place and time and its appearance in another place or at a later date, but such images could be related on a psychological level. The pose, no matter what the context or meaning of the individual figure, signified joy, and of course the Annunciation is a moment of great joy. It is also a moment of great sorrow in that it foreshadows the sorrow of the Crucifixion, and all three sculptors have managed to capture that duality in the combination of active stance and fluttering draperies with the monumentality of the angels' bodies and (at least at Lichfield and Breedon) the calm yet serious expression of their faces. These sculptures appeal as much to the emotions of viewers as they do to the eye.

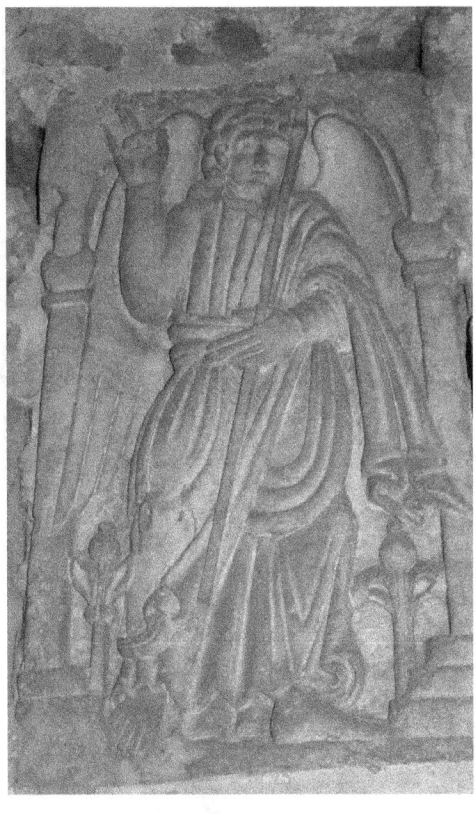

FIG. 23.
BREEDON-ON-THE-HILL ANGEL

Angels appear in a number of different types of scenes from Creation to Last Judgement, and their meaning thus changes according to context. In Anglo-Saxon England the Annunciation also occurs on early funerary or memorial monuments, such as the Wirksworth or Hovingham slabs, both originally part of stone shrines or sarcophagi.[119] The connotations of birth and rebirth inherent in the episode, as well as the coming together of the divine and the human that it represents, no doubt made it particularly appropriate for this type of monument; however, there might also have been special reasons for its depiction on a monument associated with St Chad. The church founded by the saint at Lichfield was dedicated to Mary,

---

(Oxford, 1988), no. 272, p. 108; Catherine E. Karkov, *Between Languages/Between Styles: The Afterlife of Images and the Origins of England*, forthcoming.
[119] Jane Hawkes, 'The Wirksworth Slab: An Iconography of *Humilitas*', *Peritia* 9 (1995), 246–89; Jane Hawkes, 'Mary and the Cycle of Resurrection: The Iconography of the Hovingham Panel', in *The Age of Migrating Ideas*, ed. Spearman and Higgitt, 254–60.

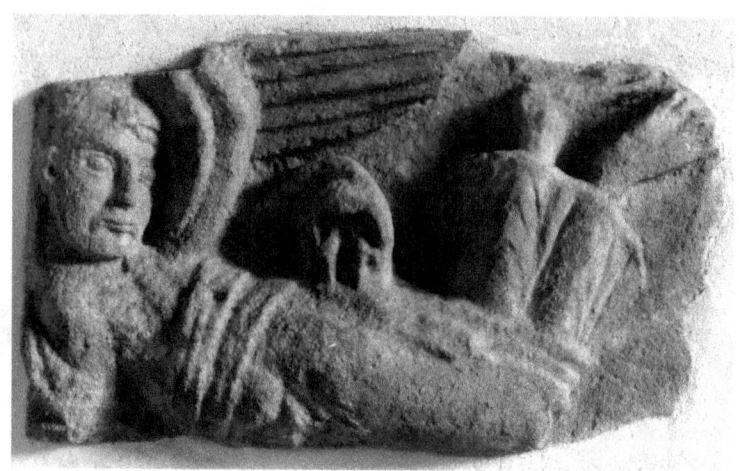

FIG. 24.
WINTERBOURNE
STEEPLETON
ANGEL

and it was outside this church that Chad was originally buried. Moreover, according to Bede, angels were said to have been seen descending from the sky to carry Chad's soul up to heaven.[120] If the hole in the wooden shrine described by Bede could still be accessed when it was either replaced, covered or replicated by the stone shrine, one wonders if it might have been positioned at the centre of the Annunciation between the figures of Gabriel and the Virgin, that point at which the divine and the human came together. Clearly this is now purely conjectural, and we cannot be absolutely certain that the Lichfield angel actually was part of an Annunciation scene, or even that it was ever associated with St Chad – though both seem likely – but it is worth noting that a cavity, possibly a relic cavity, has been hollowed out at the centre of the Ruthwell Annunciation panel, and that in later medieval churches the figures of Gabriel and Mary were often depicted in the spandrels to either side of the chancel arch so that the meeting of the divine and human that took place between them was positioned over the altar below.

Given its similarities with the Lichfield angel, the Breedon angel is also likely to have been part of an Annunciation group; however the frequent comparison of it with the Byzantine ivory depicting the archangel Michael demonstrates that the two archangels cannot always be clearly distinguished from one another.[121] A veiled book-holding figure, usually interpreted as an image of Mary, survives at Breedon, but as the Virgin, if it is she, is carved in three-quarter length and faces out at us, and as both she and the arch under which she is depicted are treated differently

---

[120] *HE*, 3 iv.3.
[121] Brown, 'Lichfield Angel'; Richard Jewell, 'Classicism of Southumbrian Sculpture', in *Mercia: An Anglo-Saxon Kingdom in Europe*, ed. Michelle P. Brown and Carol A. Farr (Leicester, 2001), 246–82.

from the figure and setting of the angel panel, she is unlikely to be have been paired with the angel.

Not all angels are alike, and their depiction does vary both chronologically and geographically. The Winterbourne Steepleton angel (fig. 24) is an altogether different sort of image. The sculpture dates from the late tenth or eleventh century, and depicts a somewhat cramped and distorted flying figure. It may originally have been part of a Crucifixion group, and has often been compared with the angels from Bradford-on-Avon (Wiltshire) which originally flanked a rood. However, as has been pointed out, this angel does not face forwards as if attending on Christ, but backwards; hence it is more likely that it supported a figure within a mandorla, as do the angels in the late tenth- or early eleventh-century wall-painting at Nether Wallop.[122]

While still deeply carved and showing a classicizing attention to the forms of the body beneath the drapery, the style of the Winterbourne Steepleton angel is very different and does very different work from that of the Lichfield and Breedon angels. There is a sense of motion here, just as there is in the earlier images, but it is the motion of struggle rather than that of a figure calmly stepping into earthly space. The contortion of the angel's body reflects its supporting function, as if a weight is actually bearing down on its shoulders. The right arm of the angel is bent backwards as if pushing against the weight of the mandorla. The left arm has been described as missing,[123] but it is quite possible that what has been understood as the curve of the wing is actually the arm thrown back over the angel's head to support the weight pressing down on him. If so, the figure looks forward to those of the angels that support Christ in the Last Judgement tympanum at the early twelfth-century cathedral of St Lazare at Autun. There is again an appeal to the emotions. The twisted pose and sharp diagonals of the angel's body add to the drama of the scene and to the sense that this is not everyday space or time. Both the style and content of the scene are symptomatic of the sombre nature of much post-reform period art, with its turn to the pathos and torment of the Crucifixion (evident in the contorted body of Christ on the Breamore rood or the smaller of the two roods at Langford),[124] the sorrow of Mary, the enormity of the Second Coming, and even the turmoil of human suffering and emotion (fig. 68). As Richard Bailey has observed, architectural sculpture of the tenth and eleventh centuries is a southern phenomenon, and some of the most noteworthy examples, such as the great sculpted roods, cluster around the city of Winchester, capital of the reform. It should be

---

[122] Cramp, *South-West England*, 125–6; R. D. H. Gem and Pamela Tudor-Craig, 'A Winchester School Wall Painting at Nether Wallop, Hampshire', *ASE* 9 (1981), 71–110.
[123] Cramp, *South-West England*, 125.
[124] See Dominic Tweddle, Martin Biddle and Birthe Kjølbye-Biddle, *South-East England*, CASSS 4 (Oxford, 1995); Bailey, *England's Earliest Sculptors*, 98–103.

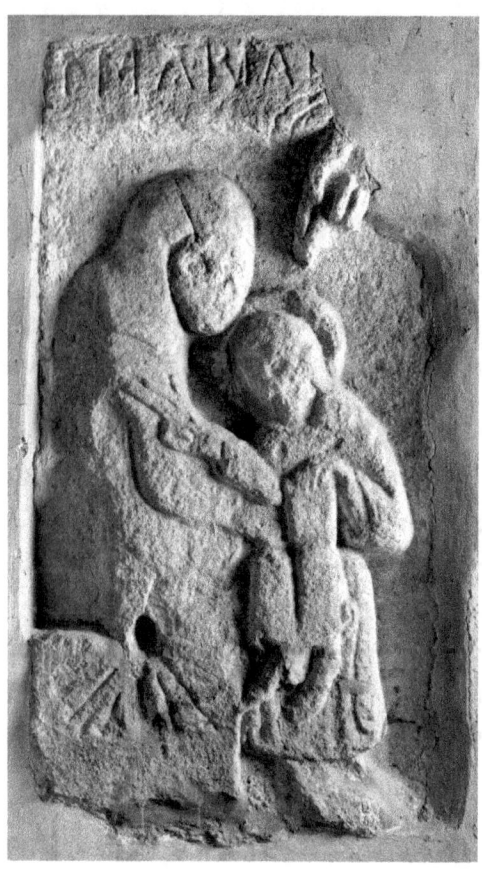

FIG. 25.
INGLESHAM
VIRGIN AND
CHILD

noted further that late Anglo-Saxon art preserves decorative motifs that add to the sense of motion and drama yet might also be understood as distracting from the darker tenor of the message – for example, the loop of drapery that flares up above the left hip of the Winterbourne Steepleton angel, a feature associated with the stylistic innovations of reform-period manuscript illumination, but one that also connects this image back to the Lichfield, Breedon and Ruthwell angels with their fluttering draperies.

A similar change in the tone of late Anglo-Saxon art is evident in the tenth- or eleventh-century Virgin and Child panel now set in the wall of the south aisle of the church of St John the Baptist at Inglesham (fig. 25). The basic composition of the panel is close to that of the Virgin and Child on the coffin of St Cuthbert (fig. 27), but the emphasis on the divinity of Christ and his role as judge is new. Even though the cult of Mary grew substantially during the reform period, at least in and around Winchester, she appears here as a small, haloless,[125] very human-looking mother. The Child, on the other hand, is quite large by comparison and has a prominent halo. The book he displays is a reference to his eternal existence as the Word, but it is also a reference to the book of judgement and his Second Coming as the divine judge rather than the human child of the incarnation. His divine nature is further stressed by the prominent hand of God in the upper right corner. The sundial at lower left is a secondary feature, but also an appropriate sign of the movement across time and the interrelatedness of the two events. Additionally it indicates that at some point in its history the panel was set in an exterior position.

No matter what the subject depicted, architectural sculptures like the Winterbourne Steepleton angel and the Inglesham Virgin and Child would almost certainly have had a liturgical or synactic meaning or

---

[125] The halo may have been painted in (Cramp, *South-West England*, 219), although there is no material evidence for this. Moreover, why Mary's halo would have been painted in while Christ's is carved is unclear.

function, and might thus be understood in connection with the developing interest in liturgical drama associated with Winchester and the reformed church.[126] Even if not part of liturgical ceremonies proper, such images would have had a popular appeal, perhaps encouraging their audience to a full emotional as well as physical participation in the liturgy, and aiding identification with the drama enacted or depicted. Yet they would also have been on permanent display in and on the church, and thus have had an existence and meaning outside liturgical performance. On a day-to-day level, they may have functioned more generally as a focus for private contemplation, prayer and devotion, and as a reminder of coming judgement.

Baptismal fonts, objects which, like the images discussed above, served as points of contact between the individual Christian and the larger community of the church, were introduced to the English church in the immediate pre-Conquest period. Again, surviving examples are all from the south of England: Little Billing (Northants.) Deerhurst (Glouc.), Potterne (Wilts.), Wells (Som.). It has recently been suggested that the eleventh-century font at Melbury Bubb (Dorset) should be added to this group.[127] There are problems with this identification. It is possible that the object, now upside down, was originally part of a column or cross shaft rather than a font, although its iconography is derived from the bestiary tradition and thus has a well-established baptismal significance. There are additional questions about the style of the carving as well as the date of the font. Rosemary Cramp points out that although the style is not distinctively Anglo-Saxon (or pre-Conquest), neither is it distinctively Romanesque (or post-Conquest). It is mentioned here as an example of the uncertainty that still surrounds so much Anglo-Saxon, indeed so much early medieval, art and that problematizes our attempts to define the Anglo-Saxon period. Nevertheless, it is becoming increasingly evident that many of what have been seen as the innovations of Romanesque art – visual narrative, drama, emotion – were actually already features of late Anglo-Saxon art, as the Winterbourne Steepleton angel illustrates. Whatever the date of the Melbury Bubb font, however, it is an example of a monument type that was beginning to be familiar to late Anglo-Saxon churchgoers.

Also at the intersection between public space, liturgical performance and individual piety were objects such as reliquaries. The Lichfield angel discussed above seems likely to have been part of a monumental shrine containing the relics of St Chad, and reliquaries of many different shapes,

---

[126] On the development of liturgical drama see M. Bradford Bedingfield, *The Dramatic Liturgy of the Late Anglo-Saxon Church* (Woodbridge, 2002); Joyce Hill, 'Rending the Garment and Reading by the Rood: *Regularis Concordia* Rituals for Men and Women', in *The Liturgy of the Late Anglo-Saxon Church*, ed. Helen Gittos and M. Bradford Bedingfield (Woodbridge, 2005), 53–64.
[127] Cramp, *South-West England*, 38, 104–6.

sizes and media would have filled Anglo-Saxon churches of all dates and regions. Most of the best-known reliquaries are made of precious materials; however, the mid-eleventh-century Uttoxeter Casket (most likely a reliquary) is a rare survival of wood carving, a medium which would have been extremely common across medieval Europe.[128] It is made of boxwood and carved with scenes from the life of Christ. On the four sides of the base are the Nativity, Baptism of Christ, Entry into Jerusalem and Ascension; and on the lid the Crucifixion and Christ in majesty on front and back respectively, with a scroll carrying angels in each of the two gables. While one can never be certain of the function of an empty box, its subject matter and quality would suggest that it was intended to house a relic or relics. This is an extremely complex piece whose scenes may be read as forming a linear narrative around the base of the casket – from Nativity through Ascension – and also as symbolically and theologically related to each other in different ways. The Nativity with Christ lying in the manger looks forward to the Crucifixion with Christ's body on the cross. The Crucifixion is also the moment of transformation from the human Christ who is born and dies, to the divine Christ who ascends and reigns in heaven. If the box was a reliquary, the way in which the figure of Christ appears centrally in each of the scenes on the base and the front and back of the lid suggests that it may have held a relic from one of the events of Christ's life. As the box is made of wood, a piece of the True Cross would have been especially appropriate. While many of the surviving reliquaries of the True Cross are cruciform in shape, there is not always a correspondence between the shape of the reliquary and the object it contained. Moreover, boxes such as this could contain multiple relics and even smaller reliquaries of varying shapes and materials. Queen Emma is known to have given a 'Greek shrine' containing multiple relics to the New Minster, Winchester, which, while likely to have been larger than the Uttoxeter Casket, provides a general parallel.[129]

Far more splendid in materials, though similar in function, is the c. 1000 crucifix reliquary now in the Victoria and Albert Museum (fig. 26). This was a form of reliquary that became quite popular across Europe during the tenth century. One wonders whether some of the standing stone crosses of early Anglo-Saxon England might not also have acted as reliquaries, though admittedly they were hardly portable. It has, for example, been suggested that the holes in the lower panels at both Ruthwell and Bewcastle may have been relic cavities, although other explanations are certainly possible. Like other crosses of its type, the Victoria and Albert cross is composed of a wooden core covered with gold sheeting. The sheet on the back of the cross has been reused from a similar object of slightly different size, and may be of German manufacture. In roundels at the

---

[128] Wilson, *Anglo-Saxon Art from the Seventh Century to the Norman Conquest*, 193.
[129] See below p. 266.

end of each of the arms are half-length symbols of the evangelists, while at the centre is a roundel enclosing the Agnus Dei flanked by crosses. A gold sheet around the edges of the cross contains a badly damaged inscription in which can still be read the name of Christ (HIS XPS) and the word *ligni* (of wood). The front of the cross is covered with gold sheeting decorated with an all-over abstract pattern of foliage worked in filigree. Enamel roundels in each of the arms again contain symbols of the evangelists, and a pair of enamel plaques at the top of the cross reads 'IHS Nasa/RENUS' (Jesus of Nasareth). What really sets this cross apart from others of the Anglo-Saxon group, however, is that it still bears the ivory figure of Christ on its front. The energetic lines of the carving and the sad yet calm expression of his face link the figure with contemporary manuscript illumination, and it is often compared with the Christ of the Ramsey Psalter Crucifixion (London, BL, MS Harley 2904; fig. 55). As was the case with the late Anglo-Saxon stone sculpture discussed above, it is representative of the interest in emotion, especially pathos, that became so much a feature of late Anglo-Saxon art. And, like the Uttoxeter Casket, it presents us with the two bodies of Christ, the human redemptive body of the Crucifixion, and the divine and apocalyptic Agnus Dei.

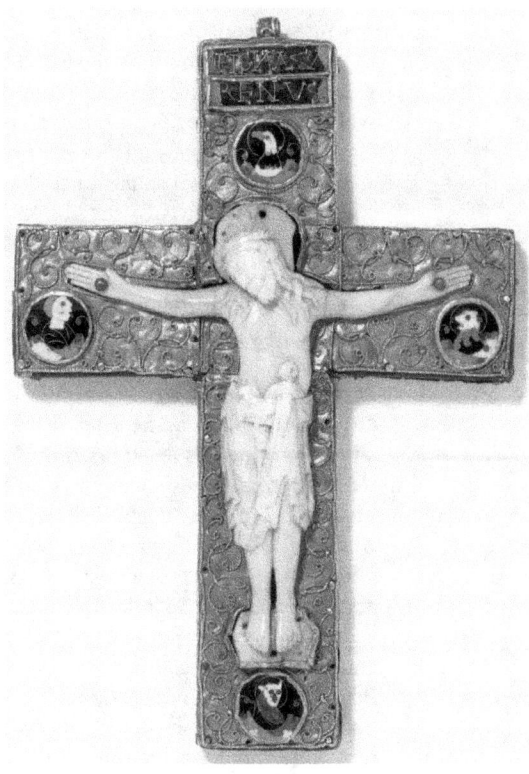

FIG. 26. RELIQUARY CROSS

A cavity beneath the body of Christ was found to contain the relic of a human finger when the corpus was removed in 1926. While the shape of the reliquary need not resemble the relic it contains, given the inscription, it is most likely that the primary function of this object was to hold a fragment of wood from the True Cross. Relics of the True Cross were believed to have the ability to turn the wood of the reliquaries that contained them into the wood of the Cross itself, so the Victoria and Albert reliquary would have maintained its original function even if the original relic had been lost. It is also possible that the gold sheeting on the back of the cross was seen as a relic of sorts. It is most unusual to have the evangelist symbols depicted on both sides of a cross, and it was not uncommon for particularly valued objects or materials to be reused in such a way. It could be the case that the reuse was simply for practical purposes, but it is becoming more and more clear that, as was the case with the reuse of stone in the churches discussed at the beginning of this chapter, reuse could and did have its own meaning. A suspension loop at the top of the cross indicates that the reliquary originally hung from something, possibly suspended over or behind an altar.

Manuscript illumination preserves some idea of what the interiors of tenth- and eleventh-century churches would have looked like. A miniature of St Erhard celebrating the mass on folio 4r of the c. 1025 Uta Codex (Munich, Bavarian State Library, Clm 13601) shows the saint before an altar covered with a richly decorated altar cloth on which sit a chalice, paten, liturgical book and ciborium. Above the altar hang oil lamps and votive crowns. The ciborium depicted in the miniature, the Arnulf Ciborium, still survives in the Residenzmuseum in Munich.[130] Nothing quite so detailed remains from Anglo-Saxon England, however the c. 970 Benedictional of Æthelwold does contain a miniature showing a bishop, presumably Æthelwold, dedicating a church which may be intended to represent the Old Minster, Winchester (plate 8). A golden chalice and paten rest on an altar covered with a cloth of gold and silver, while the bishop reads from a book that is surely intended to represent the Benedictional itself. The church and congregation are represented in outline drawing, not because the miniature is unfinished, but as a way of signalling the importance of the bishop for whom the book was made, and as a way of making clear his connection with the miniature of St Swithun in the same manuscript (plate 9). The drawing includes a number of believable details, such as the bell rope, and appears to indicate that the church had towers at both ends, possibly reflecting the increasing elaboration of the west end of the building that culminated in the dedication of a westwork in 980. The architectural development of the west end of the Old Minster was part of Æthelwold's promotion of the cult of St Swithun, a previously obscure former bishop of the church, who was translated once in 971 and again in 974, as part of Æthelwold's consolidation of the monastic reform. As a pre-reform figure, Swithun provided continuity with the minster's past, as well as a suitable figure around which to build a cult. Virtually nothing is known of Swithun prior to his discovery during the period in which Æthelwold was abbot,[131] but he did provide Æthelwold with both the historical reference point and a blank slate with which to create a cult that responded to his specific needs. It is more than likely that Æthelwold also had an eye on the

---

[130] See further Adam Cohen, *The Uta Codex: Art, Philosophy, and Reform in Eleventh-Century Germany* (University Park, PA, 2000), 77–96.
[131] See further Michael Lapidge and Michael Winterbottom, eds., *The Life of St Æthelwold* (Oxford, 1981); Michael Lapidge, ed., *The Cult of St Swithun*, Winchester Studies 4/2 (Oxford, 2003).

future promotion of his own cult. Architectural expansion and reform art at the Old Minster became firmly linked with the two names and figures of Æthelwold and Swithun, and it is perhaps for these reasons that they are paired in the Benedictional, which was produced for Æthelwold's personal use. Swithun, like Æthelwold, stands beneath an arch, holds a golden book in one hand and makes a sign of blessing with the other. His robes are the same colour as those of Æthelwold, although in the case of the saint the gold takes precedence over the blue. In the miniature, Swithun's body is made to negotiate the space between the historical human figure that he was and the architectural feature that he became. His feet balance on the base of a column, suggesting that he is both a literal and figurative support for the church that contains him, while the upper part of his body turns naturalistically to gaze at the opening of the benediction for his feast day on the opposite page.[132]

Æthelwold was equally inventive with the cult of St Æthelthryth at Ely, discovering her shrine and body which had never really been lost but which had been neglected – or so it was claimed – by the secular canons who occupied the abbey prior to its reform. With the help of his new abbot, Byrhtnoth, Æthelwold began a programme of restoration and decoration of the church that would eventually see the altar surrounded by the shrines of St Æthelthryth and her 'sisters', as well as by statues of the women covered in gold and silver and studded with gems. Later a life-sized enthroned Madonna and Child, and a Crucifixion group, all in gold and silver, were added.[133] Virginity was heavily promoted by the reformers, and Æthelthryth provided Æthelwold with a saint who was both a virgin and royal. While the images of both Æthelthryth and Swithun will be discussed at greater length in chapter 5, it is important to note here that the reformers were not interested in the promotion or development of prominent women's houses. Ely, like many other early monasteries, had been a double house, home to a community of both nuns and monks under the rule of an abbess, but it was reformed in the tenth century as a house for men only. It is perhaps for his reason that Æthelthryth appears as an 'image' or artefact in Æthelwold's Benedictional (fig. 64). She is even more golden than Swithun and stands isolated against the plain vellum background of the page.[134]

Although the reform period did not favour women's foundations, women in the early Anglo-Saxon church were as adept at promoting and manipulating cults through their use of sacred space as were men. One

---

[132] On Swithun's shrine see John Crook, 'King Edgar's Reliquary of St Swithun', *ASE* 21 (1992), 177–202.
[133] See Simon Keynes, 'Ely Abbey 672–1109', in *A History of Ely Cathedral*, ed. P. Meadows and Nigel Ramsay (Woodbridge, 2003), 3–58.
[134] See further Catherine E. Karkov, 'The Body of St Æthelthryth: Desire, Conversion and Reform in Anglo-Saxon England', in *The Cross Goes North: Processes of Conversion in Northern Europe AD 300–1300*, ed. Martin Carver (York, 2003), 397–411.

has only to think of the abbess Ælfflæd's promotion of a dynastic cult at Whitby in the latter part of the seventh century.[135] More unusual was the shrine created by abbess Hildelith at Barking. Pressed for space, she had the bones of the monks and nuns exhumed from the cemetery and reinterred together within the church, where they began to work miracles. It may be significant to the story that the church was dedicated to 'the blessed mother of God',[136] so that the bones were in effect encased within the body of their spiritual mother, a symbolism that has never been attributed to the shrine of St Swithun. Bede's account of the plague that struck Barking provides some evidence of the division of space within the monastery. The men and women lived in different parts of the monastery, separated by enough of a distance that 'the men had begun to die in large numbers before any of the women showed signs of the disease'.[137] The two groups also met separately and were buried separately until Hildelith had their bones dug up and united within the church.

## DEATH AND BURIAL

In addition to being shrines, the monuments discussed above are also simply forms of burial, albeit ones that makes visible the special nature of the saintly dead. The enclosure of multiple bodies within one container, whether it be the church at Barking or the coffin of St Cuthbert,[138] is relatively unusual but, even before the conversion, there do seem to have been instances of the remains of multiple individuals being buried together – though obviously for rather different purposes. At the early Anglo-Saxon cemetery of Spong Hill (Norfolk), for example, some of the urns that held the ashes of the dead were found to contain the remains of multiple individuals (or parts of individuals), as well as animals. While translation of the saints regularly involved an affirmation of bodily integrity – the case of St Cuthbert being a particularly striking example – the rituals surrounding the cremation and burial of ordinary people involved an affirmation of the removal of the body from the world of the living or its complete physical destruction. They were, however, no less public or performative. In early Anglo-Saxon England, as Howard Williams notes,

> From the washing and preparation of the body, through its placement upon the pyre together with sacrificed animals and artefacts, cremation focused primarily on the public transformation of the dead body. This would have been

---

[135] See Catherine E. Karkov, 'Whitby, Jarrow and the Commemoration of Death', in *Northumbria's Golden Age*, ed. Jane Hawkes and Susan Mills (Stroud, 1999), 126–35.
[136] *HE*, iv.10.
[137] *HE*, iv.7.
[138] See below p. 92.

followed by the visible destruction of the body's integrity and surfaces and its transformation into heat, flame, smoke, steam, ash and bone ... this process would have been a public experience witnessed by mourners, participants and onlookers. The corporeal interaction of the living and the dead did not end there; it would have continued once the pyre had cooled and the ashes were searched for the remains of the dead. The selection of artefacts and bone from the ashes and their placement in an urn would have involved an intimate engagement between the bodies of the dead and the living. Finally, after a procession to the burial site, the interment of the ashes and the cinerary urn would have been the final connection between the living and the dead.[139]

While we tend to think of the burials of pagans as different from those of Christians, or the burial of ordinary men and women as different from the burial and translation of the saints, the lines are blurred, at least in relation to ritual. Although cremation gave way to inhumation with the coming of Christianity, the process was a slow one. Moreover, both sets of ritual involved the washing and preparation of the body and a very public burial, translation or elevation.[140] Christians were meant to leave the materiality of this world behind at death, but various types of what are basically grave goods could also be included in Christian burial, especially in the early period. The tombs and shrines of the saints could also include or acquire an impressive display of objects. The burial and translations of St Cuthbert again provide what is perhaps the most famous example of this process. At his death in 687 Cuthbert's body was brought from his hermitage on Farne Island to Lindisfarne where it was met by the community all singing psalms. It was washed, dressed in bishop's robes and wrapped in cloth before being placed in a stone coffin on the right side of the altar in the church of St Peter – presumably beneath the floor of the church. Eleven years later it was translated to a new tomb placed on the pavement above the old grave, and Bishop Eadbert, Cuthbert's successor, was buried in the original grave. As part of the original burial and several ensuing translations, Cuthbert's coffin came to house a significant collection of material, including a gospel book, portable altar, chalice, paten, the famous pectoral cross, luxury silks, the head of King Oswald and the bones of Bede.[141]

St Cuthbert's wooden coffin is believed to have been produced for

---

[139] Williams, *Death and Memory in Early Medieval Britain*, 86–7.
[140] Executions too were very public events that made visible the destruction of the body in different ways. See Andrew Reynolds, *Anglo-Saxon Deviant Burial Customs* (Oxford, 2009).
[141] See further below p. 281.

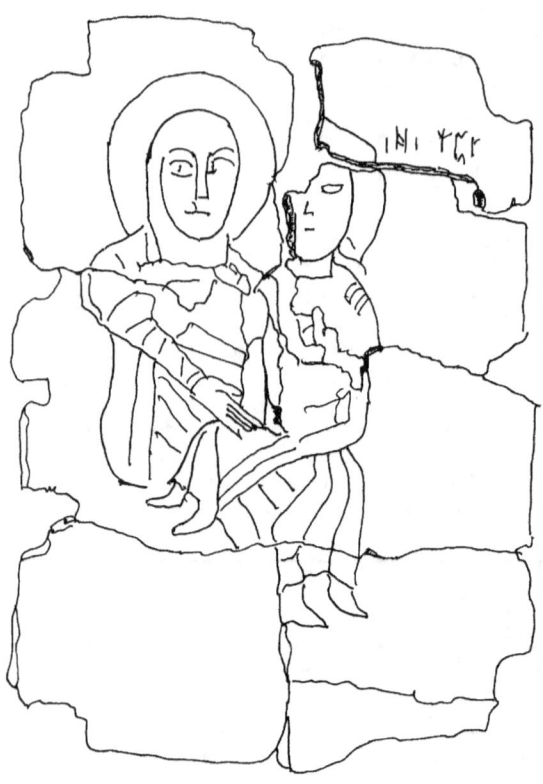

FIG. 27. VIRGIN AND CHILD PANEL FROM THE COFFIN OF ST CUTHBERT

the saint's first translation in 698. It is made from oakwood and was the innermost of three coffins that contained the saint's body when the grave (in Durham since 995) was opened in 1827. It had become a relic as well as reliquary of St Cuthbert. It is incised on the lid and four sides with a sophisticated iconographic programme: on the outer lid is the apocalyptic image of Christ surrounded by the four symbols of the evangelists, on the inner lid is a cross of a type most common amongst the funerary monuments of Whitby, on the two long sides are the twelve apostles and five archangels respectively, at the head two more archangels, and at the foot the Virgin and Child (fig. 27). The source of the imagery is Mediterranean, although its linearity is wholly Insular – compare the portrait of Matthew from the Lindisfarne Gospels (fig. 8), a book produced at least in part in memory of St Cuthbert. The arrangement of the scenes is interesting. The apocalyptic image of the salvific sign of the cross on the two faces of the lid face heaven and earth respectively, while the imagery of the two short and two long sides provides a balance of, and perhaps transition between, the earthly and the heavenly: on one long side the human twelve apostles, on the other the five celestial archangels; on one end the human Virgin and Christ incarnate, on the other end the heavenly archangels. There is also a balance between the runic and Latin alphabets in the inscriptions that identify the figures on all four sides of the coffin, although it is an uneven one. The names of Mary and of all the archangels and apostles are in Latin with the exception of Matthew, Mark and John, which are in runes. The monogram of Christ is also in runes. Why runes were used at all is not clear. It is possible that there is no meaning or pattern to the combination of alphabets, although it should be remembered that runes are used on the Bewcastle Cross, a commemorative monument, for the poem about the death of Christ on the cross inscribed around the narrow sides of the Ruthwell Cross, and on a variety of other funerary or commemorative monuments. It may be that they had a particular association with death or memory in the early Anglo-Saxon world that is now lost to us.

The Osgyth stone (fig. 28), one of a group of so-called 'name-stones' from the monasteries of Lindisfarne and Hartlepool, provides another example of this combination of alphabets. The Old English feminine name Osgyth appears twice on the stone, once in runes in the upper quadrants of the stone, and a second time in Roman letters in the lower quadrants. In this case it has been suggested that the different alphabets may have been used to differentiate Osgyth's identity before and after entering the monastic life, though a distinction between the living and dead woman is also possible. Others, but by no means all, of the name-stones follow the same pattern – some are inscribed with a single name only and others display two different names. The stones are generally identified as 'grave markers' as some have been found in close proximity to graves; however it is now unclear whether they were originally placed over the graves or contained within them – their relatively good condition would suggest the latter. Elizabeth Okasha has recently put forward the hypothesis that the Lindisfarne series had nothing to do with burial, and may have served as a sort of *liber vitae* in stone on the interior of the church.[142] If true, the arrangement would provide a symbolic parallel to that of the Barking shrine, with the names of the dead rather than their bodies contained within the protective vessel of the church. As the church was dedicated to St Peter, it might also have provided a model here on earth of the hoped-for union in the kingdom of heaven to which Peter held the keys.

On the Hackness 1 monument (fig. 29) inscriptions seem to have played an 'unusually important' role, but again the reasons for the use of multiple alphabets are far from clear, and what remains is very badly damaged.[143] The monument commemorates a woman named Oedilburga

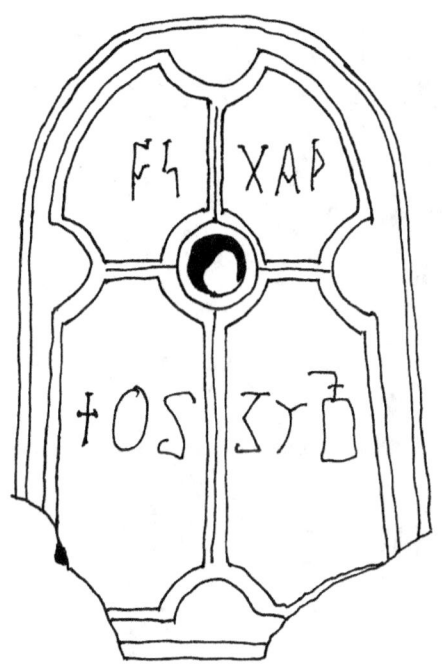

FIG. 28. OSGYTH NAME STONE, LINDISFARNE

---

[142] Elizabeth Okasha, 'Memorial Stones or Grave-Stones?' in *The Christian Tradition in Anglo-Saxon England: Approaches to Current Scholarship and Teaching*, ed. Paul Cavill (Woodbridge, 2004), 841–6.
[143] The numbering and quotation are from James T. Lang, *York and Eastern Yorkshire*, CASSS 3 (Oxford, 1991), 136–7, and the description and translations that follow are based on those of the Corpus description. See also Catherine E. Karkov, 'Naming and

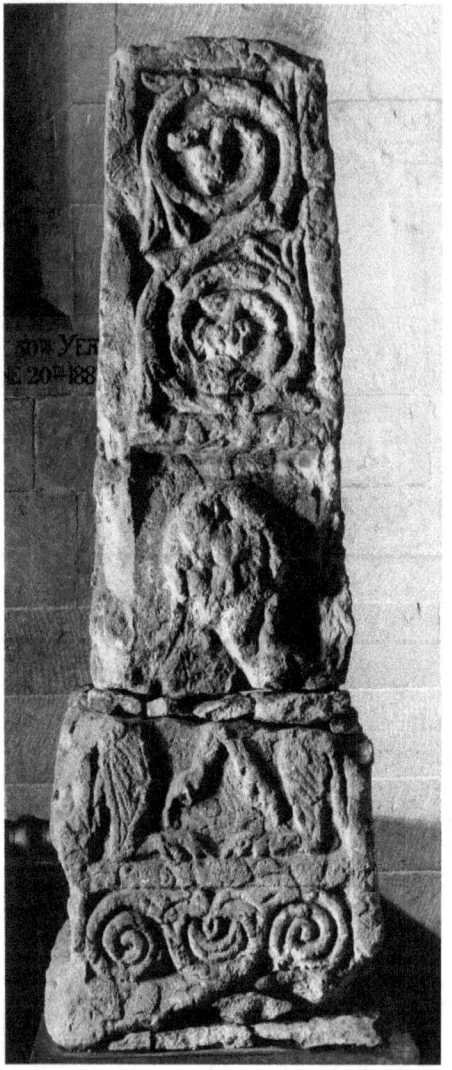

FIG. 29.
HACKNESS CROSS

who is described as 'blessed forever' (*beata ad semper*). A second inscription is written in cryptic Ogham-like characters and remains untranslated. A third inscription has been partially reconstructed as reading 'semper memores ... mater amantissima', meaning something along the lines of 'forever mindful ... most loving mother'. A fourth inscription is in a combination of runic letters and is too badly damaged to be reconstructed with any certainty. It ends with the Latin capitals 'ORA', likely to be a part of some form of the Latin word *orare* (to pray). The final surviving inscription appears to contain the word abbess (*abbatissa*), the name Oedilburga and other names now lost to us. If the present arrangement of the stones is correct, the inscriptions have been placed in a balanced composition across three of the four sides of the shaft and base. The multiple forms of runes indicate that there is more going on with this monument than the relationship between the Latin and Old English languages, or the past and the present. Were the different inscriptions meant to evoke different times or different stages in the progress from this world to the next? Were they intended to be readable only by certain audiences – a different kind of us-and-them relationship from those created by the Bewcastle and Ruthwell monuments?[144]

The imagery of the monument is equally enigmatic. As at Bewcastle, foliate and interlace ornament, suggesting the ideas of growth and time, is contained within discrete panels. Perhaps, as has been suggested for both Bewcastle and the Lindisfarne name-stones, it

Renaming: The Inscription of Gender in Anglo-Saxon England', in *Theorizing Anglo-Saxon Stone Sculpture*, ed. Catherine E. Karkov and Fred Orton (Morgantown, WV, 2003), 31–64; Carol A. Farr, 'Questioning the Monuments: Approaches to Anglo-Saxon Sculpture through Gender Studies', in *The Archaeology of Anglo-Saxon England: Basic Readings*, ed. Catherine E. Karkov (Albany, NY, 1999), 375–402.
[144] On Ruthwell see below p. 140.

was conceived of as a sort of *liber vitae* in stone.[145] The 'primary' face of the shaft carries the bust of a figure with long hair. If female, as it is usually assumed to be, it might be intended as a portrait of Oedilburga. Beneath the bust is a panel containing a much-damaged depiction of two confronted beasts with crossed paws. While these are different in form and composition, they bring to mind the beasts with crossed paws at Bewcastle and Ruthwell. Could this face of the monument have been carved with a scene of Christ over the beasts? Christ at both Ruthwell and Bewcastle has long hair, similar to that of the Hackness bust. True, there is no halo, but that could have been painted in. Alternatively, if the portrait is that of a woman (perhaps Oedilburga), might the designers of the monument have been elevating her in status by suggesting the reverence or prayer of the creatures below? (Confronted beasts with crossed paws are not very common in Anglo-Saxon sculpture.) Ultimately we cannot be at all certain about what was represented, or what meaning the images might have carried, especially because we have no way of telling how much of the monument has been lost. James Lang believed that a substantial part of the shaft is missing,[146] but that assumes a gradual taper, as at Bewcastle. It is also possible that the taper was less gradual and that the monument was somewhat short and squat, as is the case with the lower stone at Ruthwell, and therefore that relatively little has been lost.

One thing that burial and commemoration, whether of the saints or of the ordinary dead, makes clear is that our comprehension of sacred space can never be limited to architecture and objects. For the Anglo-Saxons, sacred space was alive with the miracle-working bodies of the saints and the memories of the dead, and the very colourful and impressive rituals associated with both. It was not ordinary space, but it was a space in which ordinary men and women could encounter the wonder that the sacred made manifest in the world.

---

[145] Éamonn Ó Carragáin, 'A Liturgical Interpretation of the Bewcastle Cross', in *Medieval Literature and Antiquities: Studies in Honour of Basil Cottle*, ed. Myra Stokes and T. L. Burton (Cambridge, 1987), 15–42; Okasha, 'Memorial Stones or Grave-Stones?'
[146] Lang, *York and Eastern Yorkshire*, 139.

# 3 ART, STATUS AND AUTHORITY

Bede wrote his *Ecclesiastical History of the English Church and People* for a king, Ceolwulf of Northumbria, and in it he documented the coming together of church and courts in the forging of the kingdoms and sub-kingdoms that would go on to become England. The interdependence of church and court was also manifested materially in art and architecture, most particularly in works produced by and for the secular elite. Throughout the period kings and queens continued to use books produced for them by the men and women of the church as a way of expressing both identity and authority within the expanding nation. From Yeavering and Bamburgh Castle to tenth- and eleventh-century Winchester, courts sat side by side with politically important monasteries. Perhaps the greatest testament to the joint power of the two was Edward the Confessor's Westminster Abbey. It may have been a religious complex, but it was above all a statement of the power and authority of the king and his new regime. The lives and visions of those with lesser social status and authority, however, are much harder to detect in the art historical record – in part because their interaction with the canonical works of art and architecture was less clear, but also because their lives and stories were of little importance to the men and women for whom those works were made.

## EVERYDAY LIFE IN THE SECULAR WORLD

As far as the objects one would have encountered and used in everyday life are concerned, it may be virtually impossible to distinguish the secular from the monastic – the tools, utensils, simple types of jewellery (pins for example) used or worn by both groups would have been very much the same. It is also very difficult in some cases to distinguish a secular site from a monastic one as both would have included houses, craft buildings, areas for agriculture and animal husbandry, churches and cemeteries. As the story of Cædmon, as well as the excavation of monastic cemeteries, demonstrate, monastic communities also housed secular workers although they have left little trace in the art historical record as art is produced by and large for the elite whether of church or court. Similarly, images that at first glance seem to us today to depict the realities of life and to have nothing to do with the church would not have been understood that way by the Anglo-Saxons. Calendar illustrations provide a glimpse of the sorts of activities that would have been undertaken by the men of the labouring classes, but they can hardly be described as representing reality. Anglo-Saxon calendar illustrations, like virtually all medieval calendar illustrations, present us with an idealized world in which the land is always fertile, free from droughts, floods and other natural disasters, and workers always appear healthy, adequately dressed and fed, and not unduly strained by their lot. That the Anglo-Saxons were the first to depict the 'labours of the months', that is the actual work undertaken throughout the year as opposed to just a landscape image or allegorical figure, may say as much about their interest in mapping and control of the land as it does about any value placed on labour per se. Even though the labourers depicted may be laymen, calendars themselves had a religious function in that they were primarily a record of the feasts and festivals of the liturgical year, and any labour performed in the service of God was valuable. Moreover, as calendars were produced by and for a learned elite (we cannot be certain whether clerical or secular), their images of productive land and workers served also to reinforce a certain social and ideological status quo.[1]

The actual landscape and its archaeological record can be equally ambiguous. Brandon, a high-status Middle Saxon (late seventh- to mid-ninth-century) site on an island in the River Ouse in Suffolk, is thought to have been monastic, but we cannot be certain of this. As Brandon was rebuilt and the site of occupation extended in at least three phases, it is also conceivable that the nature of the settlement changed over time. Excavation has revealed the remains of thirty-five buildings, a church, two cemeteries, an area for clothworking and a range of objects suggesting the presence of highly skilled craft-workers. Styli and inscriptions from the site also indicate literacy, although the limited number and nature of the finds should be borne in mind. While Brandon has not been completely excavated, only three styli have been found at the site compared to seventeen from Brandon's sister site at Flixborough, suggesting that literacy may have been limited to a small proportion of the population.[2] In any event, while literacy and education may be associated predominantly with monastic sites, they were not exclusive to

---

[1] Catherine E. Karkov, 'Calendar Illustration in Anglo-Saxon England: Realities and Fictions of the Anglo-Saxon Landscape', in *The Landscape of Anglo-Saxon England*, ed. Nicholas Higham (Woodbridge, 2010).
[2] On Brandon and Flixborough in general see Blair, *The Church in Anglo-Saxon Society*, 206–11.

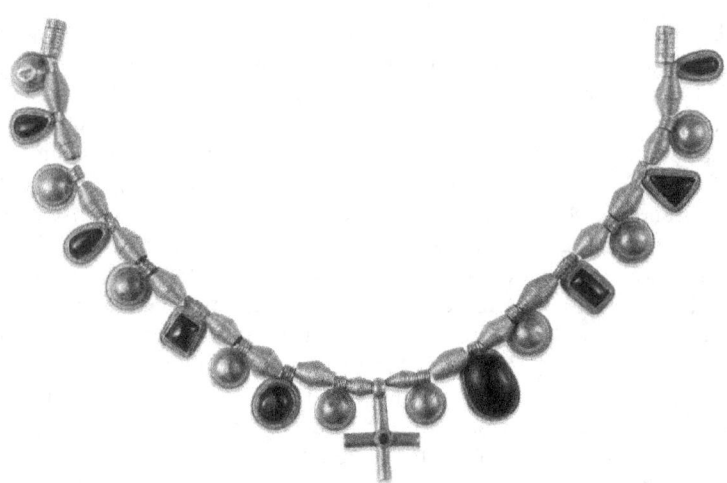

FIG. 30.
DESBOROUGH
NECKLACE

them. The nature of other objects found at Brandon is equally ambiguous. An extremely high-quality plaque incised with a Latin inscription and a symbol of John the evangelist holding a book and pen is likely to have come from a book cover, altar cross or perhaps shrine – again objects associated with, but not exclusive to, monastic churches. Two objects bear runic inscriptions: a pair of tweezers inscribed with the name 'Aldred', and a late eighth- or early ninth-century silver-gilt disc-headed pin, the back of which is inscribed with the first sixteen letters of the futhorc (fuþorcjwhnij+pxs). On everyday objects such as these, runic has often been associated with informal secular inscriptions, in contrast to the use of Latin for formal Christian texts, but the distinction is not absolute. The front of the pin is decorated with an elegant design of two confronted animals with their legs and wings interlaced, pecking at a plant. David Hinton has read the design as a reference to Psalm 104 'the fowls of the air have their habitations, which sing among the branches',[3] though a more general reference to paradise is equally possible. In contrast, one of the Brandon strap-ends bears the image of a naked man and would theoretically have been out of place in a monastic setting, although naked figures do appear in the Hexham vinescrolls discussed in the previous chapter, so theory and practice may have been two different things. It is of course also possible that the strap-end was lost by a visitor to the site and thus has nothing to tell us about Brandon's permanent inhabitants.

Grave goods and personal objects, while revealing of status, are less revealing of religious affiliation or identity. The gold and garnet Desborough necklace (fig. 30), which dates from the second half of the

---

[3] Hinton, *Gold and Gilt, Pots and Pins*, 298 n. 118.

eighth century and was discovered in one of a group of sixty graves in 1876, is several notches up the scale from the Brandon finds in both the quality of its workmanship and its material value, although it certainly cannot compare in fineness with the objects from Sutton Hoo or the Staffordshire hoard. The cross at its centre indicates that it was made to be worn by a Christian woman, though again that does not necessarily mean that the occupant of the grave in which it was found was a Christian. All jewellery was an indication of social and economic status, but for women, necklaces have an intriguing double value in the gendered economy of church and state. In both the material and literary records golden jewelled necklaces are signs of aristocratic women. Hild's mother, for example, had a prophetic dream just before her daughter's birth in which she discovered a necklace hidden within the folds of her dress; Iurminburg, Ecgfrith's queen, scandalized Wilfrid by wearing the reliquary she took from him as an ornament, presumably around her neck; while Æthelthryth saw the painful tumour on her neck as a just punishment for the gold and jewels she had worn in her youth, a punishment that remained marked on her body after her death by the red line of her scar, all that remained of her miraculously healed wound.[4] (On the other hand, Edith of Wilton, a nun from birth, refused to give up her royal finery even when chastized by Bishop Æthelwold.[5]) The motif of the wound as jewel can be traced back to early Christian hagiography, but the Anglo-Saxons fondness for the combination of gold and garnets, as on the Desborough necklace, renders it particularly appropriate within this cultural context.

## ART AND THE COURTS

The works discussed in the previous section are all high-status objects, though not royal, or not necessarily royal in the case of the Desborough necklace. Admittedly, it is often impossible to distinguish the royal from the simply high-status without some sort of identifying feature or discovery of an object at a known court centre.

The earliest known royal site is Yeavering, Northumberland (fig. 31).[6] The site incorporates far more than just the Anglo-Saxon royal residence and, as with Canterbury and other of the locations discussed in the last

---

[4] Bede, *HE*, iv.23, p. 410; Stephen, *Life of Wilfrid*, 71; *HE*, iv.19, pp. 394–6. See below p. 000 for Æthelthryth's contemporary, Balthild, and the motif of the necklace.
[5] A. Wilmart, 'La Légende de Ste Édith en prose et vers par le moine Goscelin', *Analecta Bollandiana* 56 (1938), 5–101 and 265–307, at 70–1; Michael Wright and Kathleen Loncar, 'Vita of Edith', in *Writing the Wilton Women: Goscelin's Legend of Edith and Liber confortatorius*, ed. Stephanie Hollis, with W. R. Barnes (Turnhout, 2004), 23–67, at 38, 42–3, 67.
[6] See Brian Hope-Taylor, *Yeavering: An Anglo-British Centre of Early Northumbria* (London, 1977); R. Bradley, 'Time Regained: The Creation of Continuity', *JBAA* 140–1 (1987–8), 1–17; Christopher Scull, 'Post-Roman Phase 1 at Yeavering: A Reconstruction', *Medieval Archaeology* 35 (1991), 51–63.

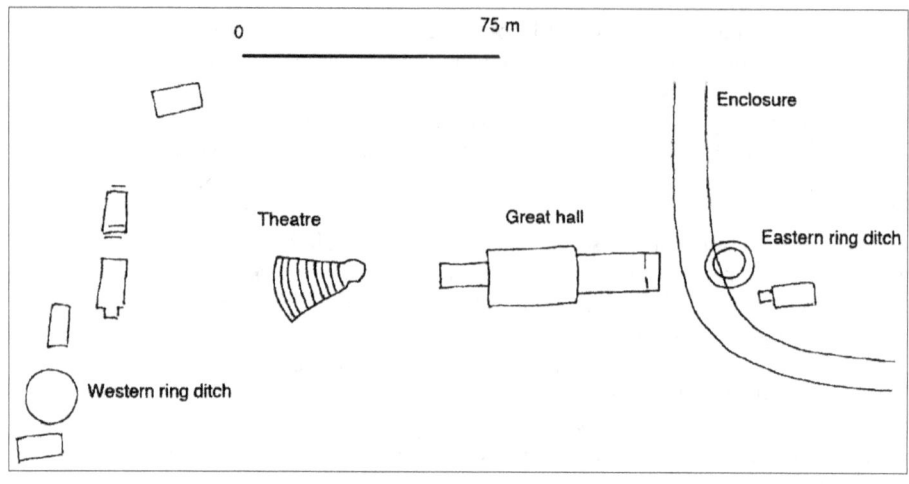

FIG. 31. PLAN OF YEAVERING

chapter, it is an example of the continuity and conversion of important centres from the past. Bede refers to the site as 'Ad Gefrin' (Hill of Goats), the name given to the impressive Iron Age hill-fort that overlooks the Anglo-Saxon settlement on the banks of the River Glenn in the valley below. There is also a prehistoric round-barrow and a stone circle (the focus of a prehistoric cemetery) to the east and west of the site respectively. Although the sequence and dating of structures at Yeavering are not always clear, the earliest part of the site used by the Anglo-Saxons may have been the large palisaded enclosure thought to have been used for cattle, though it is possible that this is in fact a Romano-British structure. Just to the west of the enclosure a series of increasingly large halls was constructed, the most impressive being 25 metres x 12 metres and built of massive timbers. The halls would have had internal decoration and would have been used for feasts and other gatherings, as described in the flight of the sparrow speech made by one of King Edwin's thegns during the conversion of the Bernician court.[7] It was at Yeavering that Edwin and his court were baptized by Paulinus in 626. To the west of the halls was a wooden theatre based ultimately on Roman stone models that could have been used for assemblies of various types. The linear arrangement of the Anglo-Saxon structures is similar to the arrangement of the churches within the monastic sites discussed in the previous chapter, but at Yeavering the arrangement has been extended to include prehistoric features and a pair of freestanding posts of uncertain (possibly totemic) significance. There were also two cemeteries, an area of workshops that provided evidence of metalworking and, to the south-west, a structure believed to have been a church. Even though some of the elements may look back to a Roman or

[7] Bede, *HE*, ii.13.

Romano-British past, there are British prehistoric elements at Yeavering that make it unique and remind us that the Anglo-Saxons were heirs to more than simply the Roman tradition. For example, new burials were added to the prehistoric cemetery during the seventh century, and these reveal a mixture of Anglo-Saxon and British burial practices indicative of a mixed population of some variety. There is no evidence that the site was in use beyond the mid- to late seventh century, and the lack of significant levels of settlement debris suggests that it was inhabited only intermittently for some time before its abandonment. Richard Bradley was the first to argue that the reuse of monuments at Yeavering and other sites was the result of a deliberate strategy to connect the present with the past rather than the result of continuous use or habitation.[8] Such reuse created a sense of communal and temporal connection that could be read in the landscape. Others have suggested that reuse, specifically as regards burial, legitimized or created claims to territory, history or genealogy.[9] Clearly one explanation does not fit all circumstances, and we must allow for a variety of motivations behind the reuse of monuments and the consequent reshaping of the past, but Yeavering, like Hexham was an important political and religious centre and the location of the conversion of a people. As such, the conversion of a past landscape to a new use, an act that both linked present to past and rewrote that past in terms of the present, became a particularly potent act. Edwin (586–632) was the son of King Ælle of Deira (d. 588), the pagan king in whose name Gregory the Great had identified an inherent pre-conversion Christianity in his play on Ælle/alleluia.[10] He had married Æthelburh, daughter of Æthelberht and Bertha of Kent, on the condition that he and his court convert to Christianity, and the layering of the landscape of Yeavering that created a postcolonial hybrid landscape may thus be understood in relation to that of the court at Canterbury in which Æthelburg had been raised.

Like most Anglo-Saxon kings, Edwin was a warrior as well as a king, dying in 632 at the battle of Hatfield Chase. Our understanding of the look, if not the life, of the early Anglo-Saxon warrior elite has been enhanced by the discovery in July 2009 of the Staffordshire hoard of more than 1,600 objects, most of which had been carefully removed from weapons or military gear. The hoard stands out not only for the quantity but also for the quality of its objects, with the finest being at least the equal of those from the Sutton Hoo burial. It included eighty-six sword pommels of different shapes and dates (but broadly seventh- and eighth-century), many showing signs of wear, numerous helmet fragments, and the mounts

---

[8] Bradley, 'Time Regained'.
[9] See e.g., Williams, *Death and Memory in Medieval Britain*, 181–5; Sam Lucy, *The Anglo-Saxon Way of Death* (Stroud, 2000).
[10] Bertram Colgrave, ed., *The Earliest Life of Gregory the Great* (Cambridge, 1985), 94–7; HE, ii.1.

(including mysterious gold snakes) from what could have been any number of objects (saddles, shields, purses, book covers). A large number of the pieces display garnet or filigree work of the highest quality, with sets of objects being decorated in apparently single styles.[11]

While the objects in the hoard can be broadly dated, the date of its deposition cannot, and its origins remain elusive. Its Mercian find spot may give material substance to the historic wealth and power of the kingdom, but the individual pieces are likely to have been assembled selectively over time. Neither the dates of its contents nor the location of its burial suggest that it can be related to any known battle or other historic event. It is also as interesting for what it excludes as what it includes. There are no objects that can be associated with women, no coins and no vessel fragments. There are the remains of three gold crosses, objects perhaps not normally associated with battle, but ones that equally would not have been out of place in battle either. The best known of these is the folded cross, originally set with five garnets, which has been reconstructed as an altar or processional cross. It could just as easily have led warriors into battle (as did the Cathach of Columba)[12] as monks in a liturgical procession. Also believed to be the arm of a cross is the strip inscribed with words from Numbers 10.35 and Psalm 67.1-2: 'Surge domine et dissipentur inimici tui et fugiant qui oderunt te a facie tua' ('Rise up, O Lord, and may thine enemies be dispersed and those who hate thee be driven from thy face'). While the words may refer generally to the everyday spiritual battles of men (and women), they would clearly be equally appropriate and comforting to a warrior or army marching into physical battle.

There are no portraits of the early Anglo-Saxon kings (or queens) who were associated with such battles, or who inhabited Yeavering or other of the early royal sites, but we can get a sense of the image of office, or power, they wished to project through assemblages such as those of the Staffordshire hoard and the Sutton Hoo or Prittlewell burials, as well as through the formulaic 'official' representations found on coins and perhaps too on the Repton Stone, a fragmentary sculpture discovered in a pit outside the church of St Wystan, Repton in 1979 (fig. 32). The location of its discovery, as well as its iconography, have led to its identification as a memorial monument for one of the early Anglo-Saxon kings known to have been buried at Repton. Style, iconography and the assumption that the fragment that remains must have been part of a cross shaft have led to its identification as a 'portrait' of King Æthelbald of Mercia (d. 757).[13] There are problems with virtually every aspect of this identification. The image of the mounted warrior on one of the broad faces of the

---

[11] See further Kevin Leahy and Roger Bland, *The Staffordshire Hoard* (London, 2009).
[12] See below p. 181.
[13] Martin Biddle and Birthe Kjølbye-Biddle, 'The Repton Stone', *ASE* 14 (1985), 233–92, at 289–90.

stone is derived from a classical formula used both for *adventus* scenes depicting triumphant emperors and for funerary monuments such as the gravestone of Flavinus now in Hexham Abbey – likely to have been one of the Corbridge stones reused by Wilfrid in the construction of his church. Certainly the image is in line with Æthelbald's imperial pretensions as recorded by Bede (*HE*, v.23) and as evidenced by his styling himself 'king of Britain' in the Ismere charter (S 89), but it was also an iconography adopted for warrior saints, and while the Repton rider has a diadem rather than a halo, identification as a saint (perhaps Wigstan or Guthlac)[14] or a more generalized *miles Christi* figure, or even Christ, cannot be ruled out altogether. Such an interpretation would be supported by the hell-scene on one of the narrow sides of the stone, and the possible Crucifixion on the second broad side, and would call into question the view that the stone commemorates a secular king.

A second problem is that the stone has been reconstructed as the upper stone of a hypothetical cross 3–4 metres in height.[15] A hole in the top of the stone indicates that it probably did support some sort of upward extension, but to assume that this was a cross head, and to project a standing stone cross of such height from a fragment less than a metre high is risky in the extreme, especially when references to other types of monuments such as the Glastonbury pyramids survive.[16] Moreover, the assumption that the monument was once a cross has led to the developmental sequence of the standing stone cross being used to

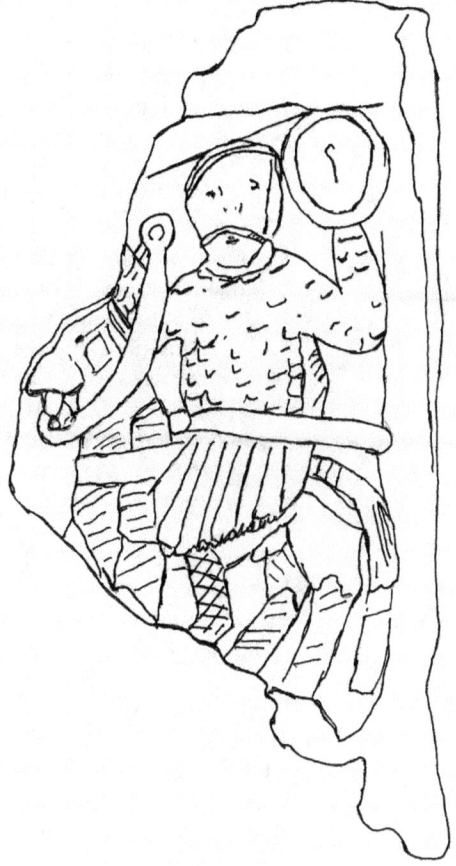

FIG. 32 THE REPTON STONE

---

[14] Biddle and Kjølbye-Biddle, 'The Repton Stone', 272–3, state that the lack of nimbus makes it unlikely that the figure could be a major saint, but it should be noted that even major saints do appear without nimbus – Mary in the scene of the Visitation on the Ruthwell Cross, for example.
[15] Biddle and Kjølbye-Biddle, 'The Repton Stone', 240.
[16] William of Malmesbury, *De Gestis Regum Anglorum*, ed. W. Stubbs, 2 vols., Rolls Series (London, 1887–9), i.25–6. Biddle and Kjølbye-Biddle, 'The Repton Stone', 283 silently turn the Glastonbury pyramids themselves into crosses without any further explanation.

support an eighth-century context for the monument,[17] clearly something of a circular argument. Style is of little help in either dating the stone or attempting to identify the rider, both because the stylistic chronology of Mercian sculpture is notoriously difficult to pin down,[18] and because style is an ideological tool that can be manipulated for any number of reasons – as has been shown to have been the case with the sculptural styles used at Hexham, Wearmouth and Jarrow.[19]

Even if the Repton rider eludes identification he is depicted as a victorious warrior, an iconography used for both kings and saints, but one that has its sources in depictions of secular power. As David Hinton has noted, if the sculpture does indeed represent one of the Anglo-Saxon kings, 'it is indicative of their increasing authority and position at the top of the administrative hierarchy'.[20] However, Repton was both a pilgrimage centre for the cult of St Wigstan and the site of a royal mausoleum, and the stone could fit easily into either context: an image of power that unites the religious and the secular by depicting victory in this world (the rider) and the next (the rider read together with the hell mouth on the narrow side). As such, it becomes not a portrait but a representation of spiritual victory, the type of victory won by Edwin when he led his people to baptism at Yeavering in 626, or the type of victory won by Guthlac over the demons that tormented him.[21]

Equally general in their imagery although easier to associate with individuals, at least from the mid- eighth century on, are the portraits that survive on coins. Amongst the largest, earliest and most finely executed of these are the coins of Offa, king of the Mercians (757–96), which introduce to England a new type of penny, modelled on Carolingian coinage. Offa's pennies display both the king's name and (usually) title along with a portrait bust. Offa was an ambitious and militant ruler, adept at creating real or imagined links between himself and his kingdom and powerful emperors and empires past and present. He attempted to unite his dynasty in marriage with that of Charlemagne and maintained political connections and trading links with the Mediterranean world. He was also a great monastic patron – whether out of genuine piety or as a means of maintaining control of church and land. While he never wielded the power of Charlemagne or the Byzantine emperors, he did succeed in rebuilding the Mercian kingdom and in maintaining and projecting the image of a strong military and administrative leader, and this is reflected in the careful design and execution of the bulk of his coinage. While

[17] Biddle and Kjølbye-Biddle, 'The Repton Stone', 283.
[18] Jewell, 'Classicism of Southumbrian Sculpture'.
[19] See further the essays in *Anglo-Saxon Styles*, ed. Karkov and Brown, and more generally Meyer Schapiro, 'Style' in his *Theory and Philosophy of Art: Style, Artist, and Society* (New York, 1994), 51–102.
[20] Hinton, *Gold and Gilt, Pots and Pins*, 106.
[21] Felix, *Felix's Life of Saint Guthlac*, ed. Bertram Colgrave (Cambridge, 1956).

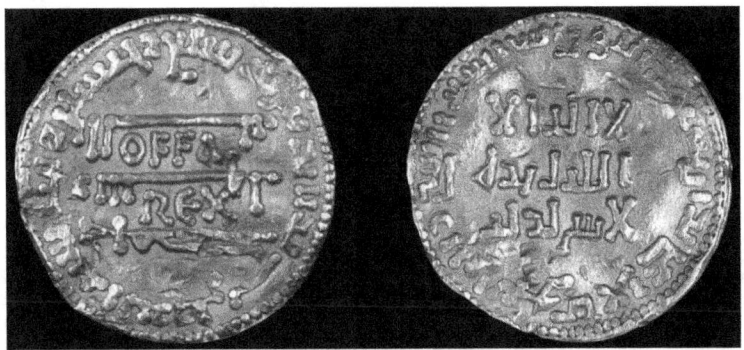

FIG. 33
IMITATION
DINAR OF OFFA

they are very much of a type, a profile bust facing right surrounded by the king's name and title (Offa Rex, or Offa Rex Merciorum), there is also variation that may or may not carry meaning. On the majority of coins, for example, Offa is shown bareheaded and usually with a curly hairstyle,[22] though he is also depicted with straight hair, wearing a diadem or other form of headdress, and 'haloed'. The models for the portraits are ultimately classical or Byzantine, though filtered through Anglo-Saxon and Continental intermediaries. The message is undeniably one of power and authority expressed both through the imperial associations of the image and attributes of clothing and regalia and through the modelled profile and upward gaze of the face. There is a notable balance maintained between the profile bust and the inscription that frames or surrounds it, with the king often depicted gazing at, and thus drawing the viewer's attention to, his own name or title.

Unique in the corpus is a gold imitation dinar of the Abbasid caliph al-Mansur minted 773–74 (fig. 33).[23] The coin itself dates from the period 773–96 and was found in Rome. It is inscribed on one side with a flawed Arabic inscription reading 'there is no god but Allah', and on the other with Offa's name and title positioned upside down in relation to the Arabic inscription. Despite the lack of imagery, the same artistic balance between centre and border, inscription/design and background is evident. The function of the coin is debated however. Some believe that its purpose was to mimic (in the sense of to 'pass' for) the Islamic original as part of Mercian trading networks in the Mediterranean. Others believe that it may have been part of the annual payment made by Offa to the pope, largely because of its find site. The inscription may be inappropriate in this context

---

[22] Anna Gannon, *The Iconography of Early Anglo-Saxon Coinage* (Oxford, 2003), 31–3 offers one interpretation of the hairstyle, suggesting it was meant to liken Offa to the biblical King David.
[23] C. E. Blunt, 'The Coinage of Offa', in *Anglo-Saxon Coins: Studies Presented to F. M. Stenton on the Occasion of his 80th Birthday*, ed. R. H. M. Dolley (London, 1961), 39–62, at 50–1.

but that alone is insufficient reason to rule out such a scenario. Arabic inscriptions along with inscriptions in other 'exotic' scripts, were often copied for their artistic value, with little concern shown for the meaning of the words themselves. Islamic patterns and pseudo-Kufic lettering are a feature of Ottonian manuscript illumination, while the door of the north chapel of the cathedral of Notre-Dame at Le Puy-en-Velay (Auvergne) carries an equally 'inappropriate' inscription in praise of Allah.[24] On the other hand, it is not beyond the realm of possibility that the coin mimics its original as a way of subtly subverting its message and power, especially as the Arabic inscription is upside down in relation to the name and title of the king on the obverse, the coin's main side. Whatever its specific economic function might have been, its use of Islamic sources may be understood as extending Offa's language of power beyond the usual realms of Rome and Byzantium to incorporate that of a new and growing empire.

Although styles and motifs that have their origin in Islamic art can arguably be seen in some of the plant and animal designs favoured by the Anglo-Saxons,[25] never again was Islamic culture to be mimicked quite so literally. The shadow of the Roman world would remain dominant and produce some of the richest examples of connections between coins and art in other media. Æthelberht, a local ruler in East Anglia, was executed at Offa's command in 794 because of his attempts to establish political independence from Mercia, in part through his independent minting of coinage and perhaps also because of its blatantly political message. A cult of the 'martyred' king developed after his assassination; its exact origins and history are obscure, but it merited the writing of no fewer than three lives.[26] A penny engraved with a profile bust of Æthelberht on the obverse, and an image of Romulus and Remus suckled by the she-wolf on the reverse, and the inscription 'Æthelberht Rex', may not be quite as classicizing in style as the portrait bust coins of Offa, but its message of power and empire building is every bit as clear. As has been noted previously, the model for the coin is likely to have been Constantinian rather than Anglo-Saxon, and the motif of the wolf and twins, an image synonymous with the founding of Rome, was also a well known symbol of the church nourishing the faithful, although it could also be a play on the name of the Wuffingas dynasty.[27] A late eighth-century whalebone panel from Larling (Norfolk) is carved with the same motif (fig. 34) and, it

---

[24] A similar inscription has been read in the sculpted arch of the Romanesque church of San Juan de Busa in Spain.
[25] See e.g., Gannon, *Iconography of Early Anglo-Saxon Coinage*, 95–7.
[26] See M. R. James, 'Two Lives of Ethelbert, King and Martyr', *EHR* 32 (1917), 214–44; Alan Thacker, 'Kings, Saints and Monasteries in Pre-Viking Mercia', *Midland History* 10 (1985), 1–25, at 16–18; Sheila Sharp, 'Æthelberht, King and Martyr: The Development of a Legend', in *Æthelbald and Offa: Two Eighth-Century Kings of Mercia*, ed. David Hill and Margaret Worthington, BAR Brit. Ser. 383 (Oxford, 2005), 59–63.
[27] Gannon, *Iconography of Early Anglo-Saxon Coinage*, 147; Hicks, *Animals in Early Medieval Art*.

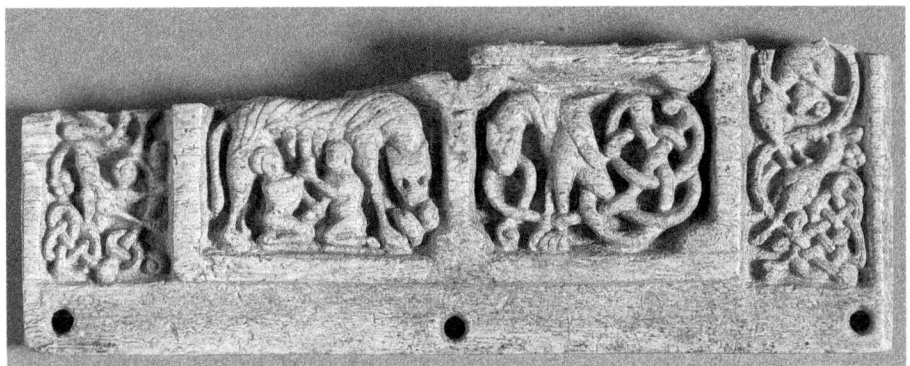

FIG. 34. IVORY PANEL FROM LARLING

should be noted, worked in an equally classicizing style. It was found near the church dedicated to St Æthelberht and is thus generally associated with the king's cult if not his political agenda. The cross motif at the centre of the panel certainly implies a religious interpretation, and suggests it may have come from an object with a religious or devotional significance. The panel is thought to have been part of a book cover, but it could also have been part of a shrine. In either case, if it is indeed to be interpreted in the context of the cult of a martyred king, it would be unwise to attempt to separate the religious from the political too rigidly and, if indeed it is connected with Æthelberht, it may well have carried the same range of meanings as has been attributed to his coins.

Certainly a message of strong union between court and church is apparent in the more famous and extensively studied coinage of King Alfred (871–99). And like that of his predecessors in Mercia and East Anglia, the imagery of Alfred's coins was designed to evoke empires past, in this case Rome above all others, in the forging of a new kingdom and dynasty in Wessex. Unlike his predecessors, Alfred had more diverse and plentiful sources of wealth and a more stringent programme of currency management.[28] Alfred introduced three new coins based explicitly on Roman designs: the Two Emperors type, the Cross-and-Lozenge type and the London Monogram type. The Two Emperors coin is a close copy of a fourth-century gold solidus, and has a profile bust of the diademed king and the inscription 'ÆLFRED REX ANGLO[RUM]' on the obverse, and an angel whose wings cover two seated figures with a cross, or crossed arms, and an orb between them on the reverse.[29] The origins of the designs on both sides of the coin are to be found in imperial Rome, so the issue is unmistakably a projection of political power. The seated figures have

---

[28] See further David Pratt, *The Political Thought of King Alfred the Great* (Cambridge, 2007), ch. 2.
[29] For a picture and extended discussion of the Two Emperors coins see Catherine E. Karkov, *The Ruler Portraits of Anglo-Saxon England* (Woodbridge, 2004), 25–8.

been interpreted as signifying the temporary alliance between Alfred and Ceolwulf of Mercia[30] or, less plausibly, the coronation of Alfred and his queen Ealhswith.[31] The picture is complicated, however, by the fact that the Roman Two Emperors coins had been copied earlier, c. 650–75, on gold shillings minted in Kent. It must therefore be asked if Alfred was consciously referring back to both imperial Rome and the origins of a Christianized England. We cannot, of course, know now whether or not Alfred knew of the earlier Kentish coins, but they were as common as their Roman models, and if Roman coins were known or turning up in ninth-century Wessex, there is no reason why the seventh-century Kentish coins should not have been turning up as well. If not deliberate, it is certainly fortuitous that the earlier Two Emperors coins date from precisely the 'happy times' of the seventh century and the foundation of the English church in Kent for which Alfred was nostalgically yearning in his preface to the *Regula Pastoralis*.[32] It is true that the ninth-century coins copy the Roman originals rather than the seventh-century Anglo-Saxon issue, but that can be explained by the simple fact that the Roman coins are of much higher quality and are much closer in size to the Alfredian coins than are the Kentish ones. On the other hand, the halo-like ringing of the heads and the shape of the cross between the kings on the Alfredian coins is closer to the Kentish shillings than to their Roman prototypes. That Alfred was fully capable of adopting and adapting particular aspects of earlier coinages to suit contemporary circumstances is further suggested by the likely influence of certain of Offa's coins on Alfred's Cross-and-Lozenge type,[33] and the possible commemoration of Ecgberht's *Lundonium* signature type (a type issued after Ecgberht had conquered Mercia and established a mint in London) in the London Monogram series issued after Alfred had regained control of the city.[34] It is with Alfred that a truly consistent and identifiable dynastic court culture can be said to begin in Anglo-Saxon England, and Alfred would go on to become a model of empire-building for later Anglo-Saxon kings and, beginning in the nineteenth century, a pre-figurer of modern British imperial rulers.[35]

---

[30] Two coins of the same series struck for Ceolwulf of Mercia survive.
[31] Janet L. Nelson, '"A King across the Sea": Alfred the Great in a Continental Perspective', *Transactions of the Royal Historical Society* 5th ser., 36 (1986), 45–68, at 60.
[32] See Simon Keynes and Michael Lapidge, eds. *Alfred the Great: Asser's Life of King Alfred and Other Contemporary Sources* (Harmondsworth, 1983), 25, 33, 124 and 294 n. 2.
[33] Mark Blackburn and Simon Keynes, 'A Corpus of the *Cross-and-Lozenge* and Related Coinages of Alfred, Ceolwulf II and Archbishop Æthelred', in *Kings, Currency and Alliances*, ed. Mark Blackburn and David N. Dumville (Woodbridge, 1998), 125–50, at 134.
[34] R. H. M. Dolly and C. E. Blunt, 'The Chronology of the Coins of Alfred the Great', in *Anglo-Saxon Coins: Studies Presented to F. M. Stenton*, ed. R. H. M. Dolly (London, 1961), 77–94, at 83. Dolly and Blunt date the coin c. 886 rather than c. 880, but on the earlier dating see Blackburn and Keynes, 'A Corpus of the *Cross-and-Lozenge* and Related Coinages', 121.
[35] See further Barbara Yorke, 'The "Old North" from the Saxon South in Nineteenth-

In the art-historical record, however, it was only during the reign of Alfred's grandson Edgar (959–75) that a consistent visual image of king and court was to become apparent. Like Alfred, Edgar seems to have been keenly aware of a Romano-British past distinct from but complementary to the Roman origins of the church. His second consecration in 973 took place in the imperial Romano-British centre of Bath. The event was followed by a sort of *adventus* ceremony in which Edgar led a large naval force to Chester, 'the city of Legions', to receive the allegiance of a group of six to eight 'British' rulers, probably including the kings of the Welsh and the Scots. Like Alfred, Edgar was also set on reform. Early in his reign Edgar is known to have copied certain of the coins of his predecessors, including Alfred and Edward the Elder,[36] and in 973 he instituted his famous monetary reform which centralized die-cutting at Winchester and restored the weight and fineness of coins to Alfredian standards. The coins displayed a diademed portrait bust that also looked to the past but was, more importantly, a sign of Edgar's authority and imperial aspirations.

Edgar is, of course, best known for the prominent part he played in the monastic reform which, although under way prior to Edgar's accession to the throne, can be said to begin in earnest with his promotion of Æthelwold to bishop of Winchester in 963 and the expulsion of the secular canons from the New Minster in 964. The refoundation of the reformed abbey was commemorated by the production in 966 of the New Minster Charter (London, BL, Cotton Vespasian A.viii) with its famous frontispiece,[37] and consolidated in the *Regularis Concordia* composed by Æthelwold in the early 970s. The *Regularis Concordia* is a consuetudinary, the purpose of which was to establish a uniform observance for English monks and nuns. It could also be described as a charter for the revival of religious life in tenth-century England.[38] It was augmented with a lengthy prologue extolling the role of King Edgar and Queen Ælfthryth in the reform, and an epilogue repeating the virtues of King Edgar, both written in Æthelwold's characteristic hermeneutic style. British Library, MS Cotton Tiberius A.iii, produced at Christ Church Canterbury around the middle of the eleventh century, preserves a frontispiece (fol. 2v) depicting Edgar enthroned between two figures generally identified as Bishop Æthelwold and Archbishop Dunstan[39] which is believed to be a copy of a reform period

Century Britain', in *Anglo-Saxons and the North. Essays Reflecting the Theme of the Tenth Meeting of the International Society of Anglo-Saxonists in Helsinki, August 2001*, ed. Matti Kilpio, Leena Kahlas-Tarkka, Jane Roberts and Olga Timofeeva (Tempe, AZ, 2009), 131–49.
[36] See Karkov, *Ruler Portraits*, 102–3. For the coinage of Edward the Elder see below.
[37] Karkov, *Ruler Portraits*, ch. 3; Catherine E. Karkov, 'The Frontispiece to the New Minster Charter and the King's Two Bodies', in *Edgar, King of the English 959–975: New Interpretations*, ed. Donald Scragg (Woodbridge, 2008), 224–41.
[38] D. H. Turner in *The Golden Age of Anglo-Saxon Art 966–1066*, ed. Janet Backhouse, D. H. Turner and Leslie Webster (London, 1984), cat. no. 28, p. 47.
[39] The image is reproduced in Temple, *Anglo-Saxon Manuscripts*, pl. 313, and is also

original,[40] possibly designed by Æthelwold himself.[41] As originally bound, the manuscript opened with a copy of the Benedictine Rule prefaced by a miniature depicting the enthroned Benedict being presented with a copy of his rule (now folio 117v). This was followed by a set of texts associated with the court of Louis the Pious,[42] and the *Regularis Concordia* with its frontispiece. Both codicologically and in the repetition of an enthroned figure above a genuflecting scroll-holding monk, the manuscript made it clear that the Carolingian reform was both the source and model for the Anglo-Saxon reform, that Edgar mirrored Louis the Pious in his role as king and reformer,[43] and that Æthelwold and Dunstan were the heirs of Benedict. The emphasis in both miniatures is on 'authorship' and the transmission of texts, but the frontispiece to the *Regularis Concordia* is also important, perhaps groundbreaking, for the image of kingship that it projects.

In the upper register of the miniature, Edgar, Æthelwold and Dunstan sit beneath three arches on what appears to be a single continuous throne, a clear reference to both the Trinity and the unity of the church and state in promulgating monastic and secular rule. In their hands the three men grasp a single uninscribed scroll, an unambiguous representation of the three as joint authors of the text that follows. As it was apparently Edgar who convened the council that drew up the document, Dunstan who inspired it and Æthelwold who wrote it,[44] the image can be described as a true author portrait in every sense of the word, depicting in a single

available through British Library images online (image 014491). See Benjamin Withers, 'Interaction of Word and Image in Anglo-Saxon Art, II: Scrolls and Codex in the Frontispiece to the *Regularis Concordia*', *Old English Newsletter* 31.1 (1997), 38–40, for an alternative reading of the miniature. The identification of the three as Edgar, Æthelwold and Dunstan is accepted here because it harmonizes well with the text of the prologue that the frontispiece prefaces, as well as with the later historical record. The only other surviving illustrated Anglo-Saxon copy of the *Regularis Concordia* (Durham, Cathedral Library, MS B.111.32), also from Christ Church Canterbury, and also dated *c*. 1050, is prefaced by a miniature depicting only Æthelwold and Dunstan synthronoi.

[40] J. J. G. Alexander, 'The Benedictional of St Æthelwold and Anglo-Saxon Illumination in the Reform Period', in *Tenth Century Studies: Essays in the Commemoration of the Millennium of the Council of Winchester and Regularis Concordia*, ed. David Parsons (London and Chichester, 1975), 169–83 at 183; Robert Deshman, '*Benedictus Monarcha et Monachus*: Early Medieval Ruler Theology and the Anglo-Saxon Reform', *FS* 22 (1988), 204–40, at 207–10 and 219.

[41] Deshman '*Benedictus Monarcha et Monachus*', 210.

[42] The texts are: (1) the final part of *Memoriale qualiter* (a supplement to the Beneditine Rule), (2) the thirty-sixth article of the Mainz council of 813, (3) an Aachen capitulary of 818-19. For the relationship of these texts to the *Regularis Concordia* see Deshman, '*Benedictus Monarcha et Monachus*', 229.

[43] Deshman, '*Benedictus Monarcha et Monachus*', 229. On the Continental sources and inspirations for the text of the *Regularis Concordia* see most especially Patrick Wormald, 'Æthelwold and his Continental Counterparts: Contact, Comparison, Contrast', in *Bishop Æthelwold: His Career and Influence*, ed. Barbara Yorke (Woodbridge, 1988), 13–42.

[44] Prologue to the *Regularis Concordia*, chs. 4 and 7 (T. Symons, ed., *Regularis Concordia Anglicae Nationis Monachorum Sanctimonialiumque* (New York, 1953), 2, 4); E. O. Blake, ed., *Liber Eliensis* (London, 1962), vol. 2, ch. 37, p. 111.

frame the 'author functions' of patron, writer and muse. Benjamin Withers has made a good case for the scroll, with its sinuous contrast to the rectangular codex in which it is contained, representing not just the Rule, but the process of production itself,[45] an interpretation supported by the way in which the two clerics turn towards Edgar as if intent on the judgements and decrees they will receive from him. Below the three authors is a monk who has done just what the text of the Benedictine Rule advises and girded his loins with the 'faith and good works' to which he is also extolled by the *Regularis Concordia*.[46] It is reasonable to assume that this part of the image was intended to represent active reception, paralleling the process of active production depicted in the upper register, and visualizing the promulgation of legal texts as both written record and oral performance (the Rule being a system of governance akin to a law code).[47] The monk's dynamic pose of genuflection suggests the gratitude of the monastic community and provides a formal contrast to the static, timeless image of authority above him. His eyes, as well as those of Dunstan and Æthelwold, focus our attention on Edgar, who stares fixedly out at us like Christ in majesty, or like the impressively imperial portraits of the Ottonian emperor Otto III.

While the motif of the scroll is used to unite the three men to each other, to the text and to the monk below them, it is also significant that it separates Edgar's head, shoulders and the palm branch he holds from his body. The arrangement, as I have noted elsewhere, has similarities with the portrait of Otto III on folio 16r of the *c*. 996 Aachen (or Liuthar) Gospels (Aachen, Cathedral Treasury), where a scroll carried by the symbols of the four evangelists divides the emperor's head from his body.[48] In his discussion of the Aachen Gospels portrait, Ernst Kantorowicz suggested that the way the scroll crosses the king's body was part of the visualization of the idea of the king's two bodies: the body itself representing the mortal king, and the staring frontal head crowned by God his eternal and divinely granted authority – the body politic, so to speak – which Kantorowicz went on to relate to the process of state formation.[49] The separation of head from body in the portrait of Edgar is likely to have carried a similar meaning, especially given the repeated references made in the literary sources to the sacral nature of Edgar's kingship. Kantorowicz's theories,

---

[45] Withers, 'Interaction of Word and Image'. Withers goes further and suggests that the scroll is a sign of oral rather than written production (p. 39).
[46] Deshman, '*Benedictus Monarcha et Monachus*', 205.
[47] On law as performance see Patrick Wormald, *Legal Culture in the Early Medieval West: Law as Text, Image and Experience* (London, 1999).
[48] Karkov, *Ruler Portraits*, 95–6.
[49] Ernst Kantorowicz, *The King's Two Bodies: A Study in Medieval Political Theology* (Princeton, NJ, 1997), 61–78. See also Henry Mayr-Harting, *Ottonian Book Illumination: An Historical Survey*, 2 vols (London and New York, 1991), vol. 1, 60–1. This interpretation has also been questioned: see F. Mütherich, 'Zur Datierung des Aachener ottonischen Evangeliars', *Aachener Kunstblatter* 32 (1966), 66–9, at 66.

including his interpretation of the Aachen Gospels portrait, have been much criticized, and a complete rereading of his work has become popular in recent years.[50] But what Kantorowicz had to say about the portrait of Otto III is relevant to Edgar's portrait, as the various documents surviving from Edgar's reign make clear. Edgar *was* portrayed both visually and textually as a type of Christ. He *was* concerned with the relationship of the royal body to the national body, and he *was* portrayed, especially in the manuscript portraits that survive of him, as straddling the line between mortal life and blessed eternity.[51] In both these portraits he stands or sits firmly on the ground but the upper part of his body reaches into another sphere. In the New Minster charter image, angels reach down to unite him in a circle with Christ, while in the *Regularis Concordia* image, the haloed head above the scroll signifies the enduring authority of kingship. 'The king is dead, long live the king.' The king's authority in both images might be eternal, but Edgar's claim to eternal authority was manifested through the lasting power of the written word here on earth. It was in the text that the 'two bodies' of the Anglo-Saxon king came together. The book might also be understood as a metaphor for the king himself as it too was an earthly material body, while the Rule it contained was enduring law which had its origins in Christ's eternal law. Because it was the product of a united court and church, the *Regularis Concordia* was also literally a union of the temporal and the spiritual, an expression of *regum et sacerdotum*. By the time the *Regularis Concordia* portrait was made, Edgar had been dead for approximately seventy-five years and the image had therefore taken on additional layers of meaning. Edgar's kingship did now have both a historical and an eternal or spiritual dimension,[52] and the palm that he holds indicates quite literally that he is now amongst the saints in heaven. It also suggests that the intercessory prayers of the monastic community signified by Æthelwold, Dunstan and the nameless monk beneath them, had succeeded in bringing about his ascent into heaven.

The co-enthronement of the three figures might relate further to actual architectural developments at Winchester. The westwork added to the Old Minster between 974 and 980 would certainly have been in the planning stages by 973, and could well have been contemporary with the design of the *Regularis Concordia* frontispiece. If the Biddles are correct in suggesting that it would have housed a royal throne (as was the case with many of its possible Continental models such as Corvey or Aachen), then we might imagine the paired figures of the king enthroned in the west end of the church and the bishop enthroned in the east end. Archaeological

---

[50] See especially *Representations* 106 (2009), a special issue of the journal devoted entirely to *The King's Two Bodies*.
[51] Karkov, 'The Frontispiece to the New Minster Charter'.
[52] The haloes, presumably not a part of the Æthelwoldian original, suggest the same for the two clerics.

evidence reveals that the westwork would have been impressive indeed: 23 metres square and more than 35 metres high.[53] While there can be no certainty in the matter, a royal chapel within the Old Minster would have been particularly appropriate as the royal palace is thought to have been immediately opposite the west end of the church, and the cemetery over which the westwork was constructed was known to have housed a number of royal burials.[54] Real architectural space, or at least the balance of authority symbolized by that space, may thus have been referenced in the manuscript drawing.

So far I have accepted the theory that the miniature is a copy of a lost original and have concentrated on what the image might have meant within a tenth-century context, but it must be remembered that the date of the manuscript is *c.* 1050, and whether the image is based on a tenth-century original or not, it would have meant something rather different to the eleventh-century community. In addition to its function as an authorial portrait, it would also have been an image or sign of historical memory and the origins of the reformed community. Robert Deshman was of the opinion that it was in Tiberius A.iii that the texts and frontispieces of the Benedictine Rule and *Regularis Concordia* were first united.[55] If this was indeed the case, the combination of texts and images also took on new historicizing and nostalgic functions. As Richard Gameson suggested in his study of manuscript illumination at Canterbury in the mid-eleventh century, the manuscript may have been the product of a 'resurgence of interest shortly before the Conquest in the golden age of reformed monasticism, its heroes and what they stood for',[56] a scenario that repeats, yet repeats differently, Alfred's look back to the seventh century. In this context, both the portrait of Benedict and the frontispiece to the *Regularis Concordia* may have been more important for what they were able to say about the history and development of monasticism in Anglo-Saxon England in general, and at Canterbury in particular, than for what they revealed about the individual men depicted. These men and their texts represented the foundations on which late Anglo-Saxon monasticism had been built, but their images have also been worked into a programme that alludes to the reception and production of texts at Christ Church. There is no doubt that the overall compositions of the two frontispieces were meant to mirror one another. The portrait of Benedict, however, was also intended to mirror the miniature of Benedict presenting his Rule to a group of monks in the Arundel Psalter (London, BL, MS Arundel

---

[53] Martin Biddle, '*Felix Urbs Winthonia*: Winchester in the Age of Monastic Reform', in *Tenth Century Studies: Essays in the Commemoration of the Millennium of the Council of Winchester and Regularis Concordia*, ed. Parsons, 123–44.
[54] Biddle, '*Felix Urbs Winthonia*', 138.
[55] Deshman, '*Benedictus Monarcha et Monachus*'.
[56] Richard Gameson, 'English Manuscript Art in the Mid-Eleventh Century: The Decorative Tradition', *The Antiquaries Journal* 71 (1991), 64–122, at 77.

155, fol. 133), painted (or at least thought to have been painted) at Christ Church between 1012 and 1023 by the famous Canterbury scribe Eadwig Basan (pl. 7).[57] If Tiberius A.iii was produced around the time of Eadwig's death, it may have been compiled in part to commemorate him. Tiberius A.iii was a private monastic manuscript, and it has been suggested that Eadwig may have been its original owner, perhaps even the compiler of the manuscript, though naturally we cannot be certain of this.[58] Within the chain of 'authors', the difference between the frozen frontal portrayal of Edgar and the active poses of the ecclesiastical figures again becomes important. Edgar appears as the historical authority behind the reform and its texts, a king whose authority is itself authorized by Christ, and whose person is part of the writing of monastic history, but he is not literally a scribe or author in the mode of Æthelwold, Dunstan or Eadwig, no matter how close his involvement with the production of texts might have been.

Along with the rise of Wessex came the development of permanent court centres at Winchester and London that, much like the image of the king, proclaimed publically the united power of church and state. In Winchester the Old Minster, began as the church of SS Peter and Paul, a small cruciform building constructed by King Cenwalh in 648, and possibly intended from the outset as a palace chapel. The royal palace was located just to its west, though it is not clear precisely when this arrangement first took shape. Alfred's predecessors had favoured Sherborne, but in the later years of his reign Winchester was clearly an administrative centre of some importance, and it is likely that this coincided with its transformation into a royal centre. Under Alfred and his successors the city was transformed by a series of campaigns of building and rebuilding. The New Minster and Nunnaminster were both begun under Alfred and finished by his son Edward the Elder. The former was located just to the north of the Old Minster and the latter to the east of the Old Minster on the grounds of an estate that had belonged to Alfred's queen, Ealhswith, suggesting that she rather than Alfred may have been the real founder.[59] The record of Ealhswith's donation was written in a blank space on folio 40v of the Book

---

[57] See further Karkov, *Ruler Portraits*, 98–9.
[58] Richard W. Pfaff, ('Eadui Basan: Scriptorum Princeps'? in *England in the Eleventh Century: Proceedings of the 1990 Harlaxton Symposium*, ed. Carola Hicks [Stamford, 1992], 267–83, at 280) following Ker (no. 186, p. 240) notes that a late eleventh-century marginal inscription on fol. 164 of the manuscript reads *Eadui m[...]me ah*, with *munuc* being the illegible word. 'The presumption is that the writer of these words thought that an "Eadui" either possessed the book or had obtained the book, or was the author ("owner") of the Benedict of Aniane treatise on the Rule or even the maker of the collection of largely monastic documents that comprise the codex' (p. 281). Unfortunately, we cannot now determine whether this 'Eadui' was indeed Eadwig Basan, or whether the late eleventh-century writer might not have associated the book with Eadwig *because* of its pictorial referencing of the Arundel Psalter.
[59] See ASC s.a. 903; Simon Keynes, ed., *The Liber Vitae of the New Minster and Hyde Abbey, Winchester: British Library Stowe 944: Together with Leaves from British Library*

of Nunnaminster (London, BL, Harley MS 2965), a ninth-century Mercian prayerbook that may have belonged to Ealhswith herself.[60] The charter through which Edward the Elder acquired the land on which to build the New Minster survives in later manuscripts,[61] and Rumble has quite rightly described the abbey's foundation as an overtly political act 'underlining the king's power in the borough as against that of the bishop who had previously been the most powerful figure in the area'.[62] According to the charter, Edward acquired the new land in order to build a church for the salvation of his soul and that of his venerable father Alfred. A second charter of the same year calls for prayers of intercession to be said daily for Edward, Alfred and their ancestors.[63] The New Minster very quickly became a dynastic mausoleum with the translation of Alfred's body into the new church shortly after its construction[64] and the subsequent burial there of Ealhswith in 902, Æthelweard in the early 920s and Edward and his son Ælfweard in 924. Eadwig (d. 959), Edgar's brother, was the last of the West Saxon kings to be buried there. Although Edgar, like his father Edmund, was buried at Glastonbury, the New Minster was clearly by Edgar's day a church associated with the bodies of the West Saxon royal family that it housed, and during his life Edgar certainly threw his royal support behind the combined reform/rebuilding of it, the Old Minster and the Nunnaminster. The expansion and elaboration of the city's churches in the third quarter of the tenth century were thus as much a part of court as ecclesiastic or monastic culture.

The Old Minster was enlarged in conjunction with the translations of St Swithun, which took place in 971 and 974, culminating in the construction of the massive westwork (dedicated 980) which publically proclaimed the bond between the body of the saint and the architecture and power of

---

*Cotton Vespasian A. VIII and British Library Cotton Titus D. XXVII* (Copenhagen, 1996), 31–2, 81–2.

[60] For the text see Alexander R. Rumble, *Property and Piety in Early Medieval Winchester: Documents Relating to the Topography of the Anglo-Saxon and Norman City and Its Minsters*, Winchester Studies 4.iii (Oxford, 2002), pp. 45–8. See also Michelle P. Brown, *The Book of Cerne: Prayer, Patronage and Power in Ninth-Century England* (London, 1996), 168–71 and fig. 13; Michelle P. Brown, 'Female Book Ownership and Production in Anglo-Saxon England: The Evidence of the Ninth-Century Prayerbooks', in *Lexis and Texts in Early English: Studies Presented to Jane Roberts*, ed. Christian J. Kay and Louise M. Sylvester (Amsterdam, 2001), 45–67, at 51–6. For the later history of the abbey see Sarah Foot, *Veiled Women: Female Religious Communities in England, 871–1066*, 2 vols (Aldershot, 2000), vol. 2, 244.

[61] S 1443; Sean Miller, ed., *Charters of the New Minster, Winchester*, Anglo-Saxon Charters IX (London, 2001), no. 2. An incomplete copy is preserved on fol. 57v of the New Minster Charter (BL, Stowe 944); Rumble, *Property and Piety in Early Medieval Winchester*, 50–6; Karkov, 'Frontispiece to the New Minster Charter', 236.

[62] Rumble, *Property and Piety in Early Medieval Winchester*, p. 30.i.

[63] S 365; Miller, *Charters of the New Minster, Winchester*, no. 4.

[64] As Miller points out (*Charters of the New Minster*, no. 4), S 365 implies that Alfred's body might already have been buried in the earlier ruined 'wind-church' that stood on the land acquired by Edward.

the church. The New Minster was, from the start, much larger and more spacious than the Old Minster. In the 980s, under the patronage of King Æthelred II, it was augmented with a tower of six storeys, each floor dedicated to, in ascending order, Mary and her virgins, the Holy Trinity, the Holy Cross, all saints, the archangel Michael and the heavenly powers, and the four evangelists. There is some debate as to whether the different levels were decorated with sculpture and the ways in which that sculpture, if it existed, might have made reference to the individual dedications of each storey. Barbara Raw has described what such sculptural embellishment might have looked like:

> The ground floor was appropriately dedicated to Mary because she was the source of Christ's human nature ... The carving of the Trinity, placed above that of Mary, showed Christ's divine origin; the carving of the cross recalled the redemption which came through his incarnation, made possible by the assent of the human mother. The carving of all saints portrayed those people redeemed by Christ who had already reached their home in heaven; that of St Michael and all angels reminded the viewer of the powerful forces who protected him. Finally the figures of the four evangelists symbolised the spreading of the message of redemption throughout the world.[65]

It was during the reform period that the bishop's palace was constructed at Wolvesey in the south-eastern corner of the city, separated from both the Old and New Minsters. From this point on, a shift away from the secular world and towards the power of the church became increasingly evident in the city's topography.

Before royal presence there began to decline in earnest, however, the city was re-established as a royal centre during the reign of Cnut and his queen Ælfgifu/Emma, and both the king and queen maintained houses within the city. The royal palace, presumably home to Cnut's court, was, as noted above, located across from the west end of the Old Minster. Further west, and to the north of the ecclesiastical complex and royal palace was the house granted to Emma by her first husband Æthelred II, on what is now the High Street.[66] There is no evidence to suggest that she did not maintain the property. What is particularly interesting about this specific property arrangement is that it locates the king to the south of the New Minster and the queen to the north, a topography that may be reflected in

---

[65] Barbara C. Raw, *Anglo-Saxon Crucifixion Iconography and the Art of the Monastic Revival* (Cambridge, 1990), 20–1. For a possible reconstruction of the tower see Birthe Kjølbye-Biddle, 'Old Minster, St Swithun's Day 1093', in *Winchester Cathedral: Nine Hundred Years, 1093-1993*, ed. John Crook (Chichester, 1993), 13–20, at 15. Richard Gem has questioned whether such sculptural decoration would have been present: R. D. H. Gem, 'Towards an Iconography of Anglo-Saxon Architecture', *JWCI* 46 (1983), 1–18.
[66] S 925; Rumble, *Property and Piety in Early Medieval Winchester*, 215–19.

their unusual depiction in the frontispiece to the New Minster Liber Vitae (London, BL, Stowe 944; plate 12). The miniature is discussed in more detail in the final chapter of this book, and it is sufficient to note here only that the traditional hierarchical iconography of the donor portrait is reversed in the drawing. The queen stands in the place of honour to Christ's right, and the king in the lesser position to his left. There are a number of reasons why the traditional formulae may have been reversed in this instance,[67] but the possibility that their positions were intended to reflect the position of their respective seats of power relative to the church in which the manuscript would have been displayed should not be overlooked. Looking west from the high altar in the east end of the New Minster, Emma's residence would have been to the right of Christ and Cnut's to the left. Their portraits in this manuscript, which records so many donations to the church, along with the portrait of Edgar in the New Minster Charter of refoundation (London, BL, MS Cotton Vespasian A.viii, fol. 2v) would have been displayed side by side on the high altar, reminding the community as a whole of the royal support that had made the city such a powerful ecclesiastical centre.

In London, Westminster was also developed as a joint royal and religious centre. Its origins are somewhat problematic, with a number of legends having been attributed to the site. According to a later Westminster tradition, the church was 'restored' or 'refounded' by Offa, a late seventh-century sub-king of the East Saxons, who may have had his royal palace at Aldermanbury inside the city of London.[68] Early Westminster may have been a satellite of London's primary cathedral, St Paul's. What happened to the ecclesiastical site during the Viking invasions is not at all clear, but some form of religious life may have continued. By the tenth century, however, the area was in West Saxon hands, and c. 959 it was 'refounded' by Dunstan and Edgar. Cnut is credited with being one of the abbey's patrons and, according to some sources, it was from London that he had Emma 'fetched' to become his queen.[69] It is possible that he also began work on a new royal palace beside the abbey church,[70] however it is usually Edward the Confessor who is credited with the construction of the palace, and it was certainly Edward who had the abbey rebuilt in a style which combined traditional Anglo-Saxon elements with aspects of the new Romanesque style of architecture that was becoming popular on the Continent. His motives are uncertain. According to the *Vita Edwardi*, he had the church rebuilt out of pious devotion to St Peter because of its

---

[67] See further Karkov, *Ruler Portraits*, 121–40.
[68] On the early history of the site see Emma Mason, *Westminster Abbey and Its People, c. 1050–c. 1216* (Woodbridge, 1996), ch. 1.
[69] Alistair Campbell and Simon Keynes, eds., *Encomium Emmae Reginae* (Cambridge, 1998), xxiii–xxiv.
[70] Mason, *Westminster Abbey*, 11; see also C. Morton and H. Muntz, eds., *The Carmen de Hastingae Proelio of Guy, Bishop of Amiens* (Oxford, 1972), xli and 42–3.

favourable position near to both London and the Thames, and because it would make a fitting place for his own burial, while the later *De Constructione Westmonasterii*, written by the monk Sulcard, claims that he restored the monastery in lieu of making a pilgrimage to Rome.[71]

While the abbey is primarily an ecclesiastical rather than a royal structure, it has rightly been said that Edward's primary concern in rebuilding Westminster was the contribution it would make to his image and authority as king rather than its monastic function.[72] Indeed it could be said that as an earthly king Edward's reputation rests more on his image than on his authority. The portraits of Edward known from his coinage and his seal place a new stress on the attributes of power – orb, sceptre, throne, sword – but the individual elements of the imagery had all appeared in portraits of earlier Anglo-Saxon kings and queens.[73] The fact that they are combined in new ways in Edward's portraits may reflect his desire to achieve a break from the old regime of Cnut and Emma, while still maintaining a connection to the Anglo-Saxon past, a motivation which is also likely to have been behind his rebuilding of Westminster and his possible commissioning of a new crown.[74] The documentary evidence for Edward as both ætheling and king is full of gaps and often inconsistent, even contradictory. In most of the English sources Edward actually does very little. The description provided by the earliest surviving source, the *Encomium Emmae*, is most notable for its presentation of Edward as repeatedly not coming to the aid of his brother or mother, though the Chronicle of William of Jumièges (begun in the 1050s) suggests otherwise.[75]

In the *Vita Edwardi*, the account of Edward's reign commissioned by his queen, Edith, shortly before his death, Edward does little other than preside over his court in the luxurious garments with which Edith provided him.

> hec a principio sue coniunctionis talibus eum ex suo ipsius opere uel studio redimiuit ornamentis, ut uix ipse Salomon in omni gloria sua ita indutus putari posset. In quibus ornandis

---

[71] R. D. H. Gem, 'The Romanesque Rebuilding of Westminster Abbey', in *Proceedings of the Battle Conference on Anglo-Norman Studies, III, 1980*, ed. R. Allen Brown (Woodbridge, 1981), 33–60, at 33; Frank Barlow, ed., *The Life of King Edward who Rests at Westminster, Attributed to a Monk of Saint-Bertin*, rev. edn (Oxford, 1992), 60–1.
[72] Mason, *Westminster Abbey*, 16.
[73] See Karkov, *Ruler Portraits*, 157–9.
[74] Spearhavoc, abbot of Abingdon and bishop elect of London, is recorded as having been commissioned by Edward to make him a new crown. See . J. Stevenson, ed., *Chronicon Monasterii Abingdon*, vol. 1 of *Rerum Britannicarum Mediiævi Scriptores or Chronicles and Memorials of Great Britain and Ireland* (London, 1858), 463; Frank Barlow, *Edward the Confessor* (Berkeley, CA, 1970), 106, 115; Karkov, *Ruler Portraits*, 159.
[75] For an assessment of the documentary evidence see Richard Mortimer, 'Edward the Confessor: The Man and the Legend', in *Edward the Confessor: The Man and the Legend*, ed. Richard Mortimer (Woodbridge, 2009), 1–40.

non estimabatur quanto preciosi lapides et rare gemme atque uniones candidi pararentur; in clamidibus et tunicis, caligis quoque et calciamentis nulla auri quantitas in uarietate florum multipliciter se effundencium pensabatur. Sedes ubique nitebat parata palliis acu operante auro intextis; loca subpedanea tegebantur preciosioribus Hispanie tapetis. Baculus eius ad cotidianum incessum auro et gemmis operiebatur. Sella et phalera eius bestiolis et auiculis auro paratis ipsa fabrile opus dictante, appendebantur.

([Edith] from the very beginning of her marriage, clad him in raiments either embroidered by herself or of her choice, and of such a kind that it could not be thought that even Solomon in all his glory was ever thus arrayed. In the ornamentation of these no count was made of the cost of the precious stones, rare gems and shining pearls that were used. As regards mantles, tunics, boots and shoes, the amount of gold which flowed in the various complicated floral designs was not weighed. The throne, adorned with coverings embroidered with gold, gleamed in every part; the floors were strewn with precious carpets from Spain. Edward's staff, for everyday use when walking, was encrusted with gold and gems. His saddle and horse-trappings were hung with little beasts and birds made from gold by smiths under her direction.)[76]

In this passage the living king disappears beneath the layers of gold and jewels by which he is covered, giving the description very much the impression of that of a saintly relic encased within a reliquary. It is in fact very similar to the description of Westminster Abbey and the magnificent possessions with which Edward had provided it at the time of its consecration.

Cumulatur uariis basilica beati principis apostolorum sufficienter ornamentis, sacrorumque uasorum instauratur utensilibus preciosis. Que cotidiano in ecclesia dei congruant ministerio, queque magnifica resplendeant in die festo, liberalis munificentia regis ad copiam contulit, et domum domini larga uenustate sollempniter decorauit. In auro et preciosis lapidibus nescitur modus, et qui in rebus temporalibus modum non excesserat, in regalibus donatiuis mensurum non seruat. Adiecit et his in diuersarum prouinciarum territoriis ditia regalium fiscorum predia, opulentisque dotibus noua dei sponsa refloruit, et sicut intus in moribus, sic extra in facultatibus, uberius coruscauit. Quot prata, quot pascua, quot siluas, quot aquas, quot rura, quot sata contulit ecclesie! ... Magna uero et iocunda sollempnitas, qua regina Saba in uestibus deauratis a dextris

---

[76] Barlow, *The Life of King Edward*, rev. edn, 24–5.

astitit ueri Salomonis, ineffabile tripudium contulisset patrie, si non esset prepeditum grauante regis infirmitate.

(The basilica of the blessed Prince of the apostles was amply heaped with ornaments of all kinds, and stocked with all the precious vessels and sacred utensils. The king's liberal bounty gave an abundance both of those that would be suitable for daily service in God's church and the sumptuous things that would shine gloriously on festive days, and religiously adorned the house of the Lord with much beauty. Measure was not observed with the gold and precious stones, and he who in temporal affairs had not transgressed due measure, in his royal gifts gave no heed to amount. And to these he added rich estates situated in the territories of various provinces and pertaining to the royal treasury. With these rich dowry gifts the new bride of God bloomed again, and, as much internally in conduct as externally in possessions, shone out more fruitfully. What gifts of meadowland, pasture, woodland, waters, farms, and crops he made to the church! ... This great and joyful occasion, when on the right hand of the true Solomon did stand the queen of Sheba in clothing of wrought gold, would have conveyed ineffable joy to the country, had it not been checked by the sickness oppressing the king.)[77]

Westminster Abbey was dedicated on 28 December 1065 but Edward was too ill to attend the ceremony. He died on 5 January and his body was carried in procession from the palace at Westminster to the abbey and buried in front of the altar, the rebuilt church with its gold and jewels becoming not just a royally funded abbey, but a royal shrine and the consecration church of the future kings and queens of England.

The exact chronology of the building is hard to establish, but the *Vita Edwardi* describes an impressive if unfinished structure:

> Principalis arę domus altissimis erecta fornicibus quadrato opere parique commissura circumuoluitur; ambitus autem ipsius edis dupplici lapidum arcu ex utroque latere hinc et inde fortiter solidata operis compage clauditur. Porro crux templi quę medium canentium deo chorum ambiret, et sui gemina hinc et inde sustentatione medię turris celsum apicem fulciret, humili primum et robusta fornice simpliciter surgit, cocleis multipliciter ex arte ascendentibus plurimis tumescit, deinde uero simplici muro usque ad tectum ligneum plumbo diligenter tectum peruenit. Subter uero et supra disposite educuntur domicilia, memoriis apostolorum, martyrum, confessorum, ac uirginum consecranda per sua altaria. Hec autem multiplicitas tam uasti operis tanto spatio ab oriente ordita est ueteris templi,

---

[77] Barlow, *The Life of King Edward*, rev. edn, 114–15.

ne scilicet interim inibi commorantes fratres uacarent a seruitio Christi, ut etiam aliqua pars spatiose subiret interiaciendi uestibuli.⁷⁸

(The house of the principal altar, raised up with very high arches [*or* vaults], is surrounded with squared work and even jointing; moreover, the periphery of the building itself is enclosed on either side by a double arch of stones, strongly consolidated with a joining together of work from different directions. Further on is the crossing of the temple; which might surround the central quire of those singing to God, and with its twin abutment from different directions might support the lofty apex of the central tower; it rises simply, at first, with a low and strong vault [*or* arch]; grows, multiple in art, with very many ascending spiral stairs; then, indeed, reaches with a plain wall right up to the wooden roof, carefully roofed with lead: indeed, disposed below and above, lead out chapels, fit to be consecrated by means of their altars to the memories of the apostles, martyrs, confessors and virgins. Moreover, this multiplicity of so vast a work is set out so great a space from the East [end] of the old temple that, of course, in the meantime the brethren staying therein might not cease from the service of Christ; and furthermore so that some part of the nave to be placed between might advance.)⁷⁹

Archaeological excavations have established that the actual church differed in many ways from the literary description, but that it would have been every bit as impressive as the description implies.⁸⁰ With an internal length of around 98 metres, its scale alone signalled a striking departure from its Anglo-Saxon predecessors, and was rivalled only by the great Ottonian imperial churches of Speyer (99 metres) and Mainz (71 metres excluding the length of its sanctuary and western transept).⁸¹ It had an extended sanctuary ending in a pronounced transept, and a nave with twelve bays. The design of the nave with its alternating square and cruciform supports, the transept with tribunes, and details such as the half-columnar wall shafts and double-scotia bases are most closely paralleled in Norman churches, especially Jumièges,⁸² making it at once

---

⁷⁸ Frank Barlow, ed., *The Life of King Edward the Confessor who Rests at Westminster, Attributed to a Monk of Saint-Bertin* (London, 1962), 45–6.
⁷⁹ Translation by Gem in 'Romanesque Rebuilding of Westminster Abbey', 36; and see 48–9 for a reconstruction by W. T. Ball.
⁸⁰ For a detailed discussion see Eric Fernie, 'Edward the Confessor's Westminster Abbey', in *Edward the Confessor: The Man and the Legend*, ed. Mortimer, 139–15; Warwick Rodwell, 'New Glimpses of Edward the Confessor's Abbey at Westminster', in ibid., 151–67.
⁸¹ Gem, 'Romanesque Rebuilding of Westminster Abbey', 46.
⁸² Gem, 'Romanesque Rebuilding of Westminster Abbey', 46–7; see also 53–5 for a discussion of the difficult chronologies of both Westminster and Jumièges. The design of Westminster may have priority, but that does not make it any more Anglo-Saxon.

an allusion to Edward's Norman roots and Norman support, as well as a statement of a brand new political order.[83] Its glittering interior and colourful painted and tiled surfaces, however, were entirely in the Anglo-Saxon tradition. Continental comparisons were probably not the only thing on Edward's mind however; Edward was also in an architectural competition with his queen who managed to complete her rebuilding of the church at Wilton before the completion of Westminster, and we do not know how closely the two churches might have resembled each other. Whatever the case, Edward died before the church was completed, and building continued into the 1070s.

## WOMEN, ART AND AUTHORITY

The courts of Cnut and Emma, Edward and Edith, stand out in that they provide us with clear-cut examples of powerful women manipulating the material and documentary record for their own ends. Emma certainly used her position as patron of numerous churches, most especially the New Minster, Winchester as a means of securing her own power base.[84] She is, for example, given pride of place in the New Minster Liber Vitae (plate 12). It is her name and her image that come first in a book that is devoted to the memory of the community's special dead. During the struggle for power that followed the death of Cnut she commissioned the *Encomium Emmae* in a much less successful attempt to retain a position of power during the reigns of her sons Harthacnut and Edward the Confessor. Edith's model of queenship was both based on and a reaction against that of her mother-in-law. Emma was a great patron of the church, but Edith was no such thing, indeed rather the opposite, even though she did rebuild the church at Wilton Abbey, one of the wealthiest of the West Saxon women's houses, at the same time that Edward was rebuilding Westminster.[85] She commissioned the *Vita Edwardi*, a text which responds in many ways to the *Encomium Emmae*, as a slightly more successful means of maintaining her own position and providing her own vision of Edward's reign and her family history at the time of the Norman Conquest.

We may not know as much about women and art of the earlier courts, but there is certainly evidence that royal and aristocratic women were

---

[83] Robert, abbot of Jumièges, accompanied Edward on his return to England. He was made bishop of London in 1044 and archbishop of Canterbury in 1051, returning to Jumièges in 1052. While Robert may provide a link between the two buildings, the date at which Westminster was begun remains uncertain.
[84] On the imperial aspects of Emma's patronage see Lynn Jones, 'Emma's Greek *Scrine*', in *Early Medieval Studies in Memory of Patrick Wormald*, ed. Stephen Baxter, Catherine E. Karkov, Janet L. Nelson and David Pelteret (Farnham, 2009), 499–507.
[85] Catherine E. Karkov, 'Pictured in the Heart: The Ediths at Wilton', in *Intertexts: Studies in Anglo-Saxon Culture Presented to Paul E. Szarmach*, ed. Virginia Blanton and Helene Scheck (Tempe, AZ, 2008), 273–85; Karkov, *Ruler Portraits*, 164–5.

active as patrons and recipients of books and other objects, and they were also portrayed in the same sort of official portraits as were men, albeit less frequently. An early example of such a portrait is a double-sided seal from a seal ring found at Postwick, Norfolk (fig. 35). The ring was made in northern France c. 658–80 and likely found its way to England as a gift. One side of the ring bears the portrait of a woman with what could be either long flowing hair or possibly a crude rendering of the triple pendants of a Byzantine-style diadem.[86] The surrounding inscription reads '+BALDEHILDIS', leading to its identification as the ring of Balthild, a member of the East Anglian royal court who married the Frankish king Clovis II in 648, even though the name on the ring is not an exact match for that of the queen. Clovis died in 657 and Balthild served as regent for her three sons until they came of age to rule. In 664/5 she retired to the convent of Chelles, which she had refounded and enlarged, and died there in 680.[87] Although she had a reputation for murder and treachery,[88] the late seventh-century *Vita Sanctae Balthildis*, probably written by a nun of Chelles, describes her as a great patron of churches such as Chelles, Corbie, Jouarre, Jumièges, Luxeuil and St Denis, all royal ecclesiastical centres, although it also recounts that she was not immediately accepted by the nuns of Chelles who were suspicious of her motivation for entering the community.[89] Whatever the truth of her character, she went on to become a popular saint. It was very likely her presence at Chelles that led to its being a haven for Anglo-Saxon women entering the monastic life.[90]

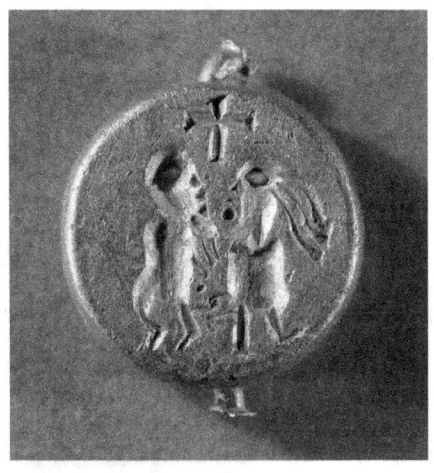

FIG. 35. BALDHILD RING, REVERSE

---

[86] See, for example, the sixth- or early seventh-century Lombardic or Ostrogothic Gumedruta seal-ring in the British Museum (reg. no. PY 1920, 1028.2)
[87] On Balthild's history and status see Paul Fouracre and Richard Gerberding, *Late Merovingian France: History and Hagiography 640–720* (Manchester, 1996), 121; Janet L. Nelson, 'Gendering Courts in the Early Medieval West', in *Gender in the Early Medieval World East and West, 300–900*, ed. Leslie Brubaker and Julia M. H. Smith (Cambridge, 2004), 185–97.
[88] See also Stephen, *Life of Wilfrid*, ch. 6.
[89] Jo Ann McNamara and John E. Halborg, with E. Gordon Whatley, eds, *Sainted Women of the Dark Ages* (Durham, NC, 1992), 274.
[90] Joanna Story, *Carolingian Connections: Anglo-Saxon England and Carolingian France, c. 750–870* (Aldershot, 2003), 38; Rosamond McKitterick, 'The Diffusion of Insular Culture in Neustria between 650 and 850: The Implications of the Manuscript Evidence', in *La Neustrie*, ed. H. Atsma and K.-F. Werner (Sigmaringen, 1989), 395–432, at 408–9; Janet L. Nelson, 'Queens as Jezebels: The Careers of Brunhild and Balthild in Merovingian History', in *Medieval Women: Essays Presented to Rosalind Hill*, ed. D. Baker (Oxford, 1978), 31–77, at 32.

As is the case with so many female saints, clothing and jewellery loom large both in the story and amongst the relics of the saint. She donated her royal girdle to Curbior (Saint-Laumer-de-Moutier),[91] and her chemise is still a relic at Chelles. The latter is a simple linen garment, but the neckline is embroidered with coloured silk thread in a motif of three jewelled necklaces. The embroidery may have served as a sign of the real jewels she presumably either gave away or abandoned on entering the religious life,[92] yet it functions simultaneously as a sign of the royal status which she never fully abandoned. As such it blurs the line between Balthild's royal and monastic (or saintly) identities, as does the seal ring. The frontal portrait on the front of the ring is an image that underscores authority by presenting the face of the queen as one who addresses or confronts us directly, rather than as a more passive profile which presents the sitter for our examination. On the other hand, the woman is crowned not with a crown or diadem but with the cross of Christ. The scene on the back of the ring has been interpreted as representing marital union, though its precise nature has been questioned, largely because what exactly the two figures are doing is not clear. It could be a scene of sexual union, with an emphasis presumably on the fertility of the marriage and hopes for dynasty. The prominent cross above the couple would, however, suggest a less worldly meaning, and it may be that the couple is meant to be shown simply holding hands – an imagery that goes back to late antique gold glasses made for the celebration of marriages, as well as one that appears on contemporary Anglo-Saxon coinage where it has been taken to symbolize peace or concord.[93] The union is, in other words, a union in Christ. It should also be noted that the male figure is placed in the position of honour. There is no indication that rings were a part of the ceremonies surrounding marriage at such an early date, though they could have been part of the various gifts exchanged between the couple, and there is nothing to indicate that this couple is royal other than the fact that such an object could only have been owned by a woman with a high level of status and authority. Such seals were used for impressing the wax that sealed letters. It is possible that this seal reached England accompanying one such letter, that it was a gift in its own right, or indeed that it had become a secondary relic of the saint – if the ring did indeed belong to Queen Balthild.

---

[91] McNamara, and Halborg *Sainted Women of the Dark Ages*, 272.
[92] See above p. 99 for the motif of the necklace in the Anglo-Saxon sources. The metaphor of the jewel, particularly the necklace, as wound goes back to the early Christian period; see especially Virginia Burrus, 'Macrina's Tattoo', *JMEMS* 33.3 (2003), 403–17. The metaphor is also used for the wounds of Christ as, for example, on the folding cross from the Staffordshire hoard, on which five garnets – one at the centre and one in the terminals of each of the cross arms – symbolize his five wounds.
[93] Gannon, *Iconography of Early Anglo-Saxon Coinage*, 63–4.

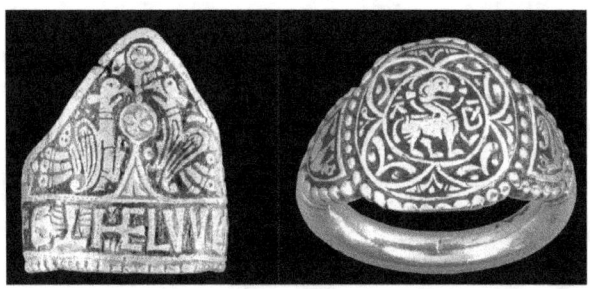

FIG. 36. RINGS OF ÆTHELWULF AND ÆTHELSWITH

The later gold and niello rings of Æthelwulf, king of Wessex (839–58) and his daughter Æthelswith, queen of Mercia (853–74) are decorated with symbolic imagery rather than figural portraits, but are identified by their inscriptions: '+ETHELWULF REX' and '+EAÐELSWIÐ REG[I]na' respectively (fig. 36).[94] Both are too big to have been worn except on a thumb or over a glove, practices for which no evidence survives from the Anglo-Saxon period.[95] While unquestionably the work of different craftsmen, both could have functioned as seals accompanying royal messages, both could have been produced in association with royal marriages (Æthelswith married Burgred of Mercia in 853, while Æthelwulf married Judith, daughter of Charles the Bald in 856), or both could be baptismal. The motifs decorating the rings have both royal and baptismal associations. Æthelwulf's ring is decorated with a motif that can be interpreted either as two peacocks flanking a tree of life, an image that has its sources in early Christian art, or as two peacocks flanking the fountain of life. Leslie Webster has identified Carolingian sources for the latter interpretation in manuscripts such as the Godescalc Evangelistry (Paris, BN, n.a. lat. 1203, fol. 3v) commissioned by Charlemagne c. 780[96] although, if Michael King's interpretation of the Sutton Hoo shoulder clasps is correct, it was already an image associated with royalty in England in the early seventh century.[97] The Agnus Dei of Æthelswith's ring is rare in Anglo-Saxon art prior to the tenth century, but does appear in Carolingian manuscripts such as the Gospels of Saint-Medard of Soissons (Paris, BN, lat. 8850, fol. 1v) also produced for Charlemagne c. 800. Both the manuscript parallels are the products of Charlemagne's Court School, and it is possible that the two Anglo-Saxon rings were also commissioned as part of a West Saxon attempt at establishing a similar pattern of royal patronage, if not a royal centre of production, along with, perhaps,

---

[94] On Æthelswith's ring the title REGINA has been abbreviated to REG and the last two letters appear to be later additions.
[95] Hinton, *Gold and Gilt, Pots and Pins*, 108–9.
[96] Leslie Webster, 'Ædificia Nova: Treasures of Alfred's Reign', in *Alfred the Great*, ed. Timothy Reuter (Aldershot, 2003), 79–103, at 91.
[97] See above p. 25.

associated royal imagery. Æthelwulf was known for his lavish gift-giving, especially of precious metalwork,[98] and royal gift-giving would continue to grow during the reigns of his successors. I have argued elsewhere that particular styles and motifs may be associated with royal patronage. It is suggestive, for example, that the Agnus Dei at the centre of the quatrefoil bordered by floral or foliate sprigs appears again at the centre of the stole commissioned for Frithestan, bishop of Winchester (909–31), and later donated to the shrine of St Cuthbert.[99]

One interesting difference between the two rings is the location of their respective inscriptions. The king's name and title are part of the primary design of the ring. The motif of birds and fountain (or tree) is centred neatly above the king's name, while the name itself is surrounded by cross motifs: two form part of the fountain, a cross begins the inscription and a cross formed by the abbreviated 'REX' ends it. Further cruciform designs flank the inscribed panel. Whoever saw or received the ring could not have failed to understand its message that Æthelwulf was a devout and blessed king. The inscription on Æthelswith's ring, by contrast, is located beneath the bezel and would not have been immediately apparent to the viewer or recipient. It is possible that the inscription is secondary, but it is also possible that such a lengthy inscription could not have been incorporated successfully into the design of the ring's exterior, a design which, it must be said, is far more accomplished that that of the Æthelwulf ring.

Queens and royal wives seem to have had a consistently higher profile at the Mercian court than anywhere else in Anglo-Saxon England during the period spanned by the reigns of Offa in Mercia (757–96) and Edward the Elder in Wessex (899–924).[100] The foundation on which this power rested was laid by Offa and his queen Cynethryth,[101] although just how much political power (if any) Cynethryth exercised is questionable. The evidence provided by charters and coins, however, makes it clear that Cynethryth did play an important role during the reign of her husband,[102] and she is the only queen to have coins minted in her own name. All were minted in Canterbury beginning at some time in the 780s by the moneyer Eoba. It may be that Offa had granted her the rights to the income from a single moneyer, and perhaps that the move was a calculated attempt to usurp minting rights held by the archbishop of Canterbury.[103] Stafford suggests

---

[98] Webster, 'Aedificia Nova', 91–4.
[99] See further Karkov, Ruler Portraits, 74–6.
[100] As noted by Pauline Stafford, 'Political Women in Mercia: Eighth to early Tenth Century', in Mercia: An Anglo-Saxon Kingdom in Europe, ed. Brown and Farr, 35–49; see also Keynes and Lapidge, Alfred the Great, 71–2, 235.
[101] Stafford, 'Political Women', 37.
[102] On the charter evidence see Stafford, 'Political Women', 36–42.
[103] Gareth Williams, 'Mercian Coinage and Authority', in Mercia: An Anglo-Saxon Kingdom in Europe, ed. Brown and Farr, 211–28, at 216–17.

ART, STATUS AND AUTHORITY

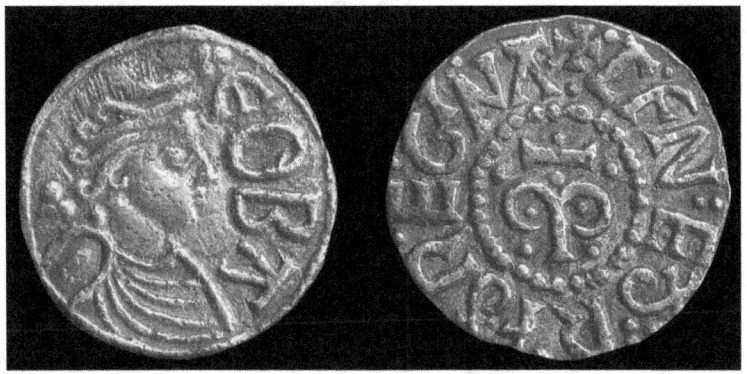

FIG. 37. COIN OF CYNETHRYTH

further that the coins may have been part of Offa's very public emphasis on the legitimacy of his marriage and thus the legitimacy of his heirs.[104] Whatever the reasons for the issue, the message of the coins was entirely imperial, modelled on the late Roman practice of coins issued in the names of emperors' wives.[105] The design too was based on Roman prototypes, with the majority of the coins displaying a profile bust of the queen on the obverse and her name and title on the reverse (fig. 37). A distinctly Mercian addition is the abbreviated M for *Merciorum* at the centre of the reverse. While the hairstyles differ, all depict the queen with elaborately styled hair and classical attire based on Roman and eastern Mediterranean models. On most she is crowned with a diadem. The positioning of the bust and upward gaze of the queen on the example illustrated are similar in design to the portrait busts of Offa on his own coinage. Some of the coins are 'mules', carrying Offa's portrait on the obverse but Cynethryth's name on the reverse. Gannon believes that, being the product of an administration as efficient and closely regulated as Offa's, the coins are not accidents but rather reflect 'significant production requirements', and perhaps also the idea that it might have been the name of the queen that mattered more than the conventionalized portrait bust.[106] One could go further and suggest that the combination of the image of the king and the name of the queen might have carried its own significance, projecting a message of joint authority, even if the authority exercised by the queen was more symbolic than actual. These 'mules' might, then, prefigure the much later double portrait of Emma and Cnut (plate 12).

Such an interpretation of the Cynethryth/Offa coinage could also be seen as providing a background for the unusual Mercian issues of coinage during the reign of Edward the Elder when his sister Æthelflæd was

---

[104] Stafford, 'Political Women', 37–8.
[105] Williams, 'Mercian Coinage', 216; Blunt, 'The Coinage of Offa', 46–7.
[106] Gannon, *Iconography of Early Anglo-Saxon Coinage*, 41.

'Lady' of the Mercians.[107] Although not a queen by title,[108] Æthelflæd was effectively ruler of the sub-kingdom from shortly before the death of her husband Æthelred in 911 until her own death in 918. There is no doubt that she acknowledged her brother Edward as overlord, but there is also no doubt that the two worked together militarily as well as administratively, and Edward's son Æthelstan was fostered at Æthelflæd's court. Could a similar sharing of power be evident in coinage? There is a group of coins with exceptional designs on the reverse, all minted in West Mercia during the period in which Æthelflæd was ruling Mercia and assisting Edward in driving the Danes from the eastern part of the kingdom. It has been suggested that the coins might have been Æthelflæd's way of 'distinguishing the output of her mints from that of her brother's',[109] but there may in fact have been more to it. Some of the designs on these coins may have been seen as carrying a specifically Mercian meaning and identity. Some of the coins display a foliate or floral motif with fronds curled in the shape of the Mercian M that appeared on Offa's coinage.[110] Another recurring design is that of a gate or tower, the design of which may have been copied from Constantinian bronze coins.[111] The main source of the Tower type was Chester,[112] and it is possible that it was adapted from late Roman sources because of its relevance to the Roman origins of the burh, or because of its relevance to events in the city and perhaps elsewhere. Two significant events occurred at gateways during the period in which Æthelflæd was governing Mercia.[113] The Mercian Register records the death of four of her 'dear thegns' within the gate of Derby in 917,[114] while the Fragmentary Annals of Ireland record that Chester was attacked by the Vikings in 907,

[107] On Æthelflæd in general see F. T. Wainwright, 'Æthelflæd, Lady of the Mercians', in *Scandinavian England: Collected Papers of F. T. Wainwright*, ed. H. P. R. Finberg (Chichester, 1975), 305–24; and Stafford, 'Political Women'.
[108] Æthelflæd's mother, Ealhswith, Alfred's queen in all but title, was commemorated as 'the true and beloved Lady of the English' ('uera domina Anglorum Ealhswythe cara') (Simon Keynes, 'King Alfred and the Mercians', in *Kings, Currency and Alliances*, ed. Blackburn and Dumville, 1–45, at 10. Æthelflæd is referred to as a queen (*regina*) in Annales Cambriae s.a. 917 and as a famous queen (*famosissima regina saxonum*) in the Annals of Ulster s.a. 918. She is given a title (*vrenhines*) equal to that of Alfred (*venhin*) in the *Brut y Tywysogion* s.a. 918 (s.a. 898 for Alfred). See J. Williams ab Ithal, ed., *Annales Cambriae* (London, 1860); S. Mac Airt and G. Mac Niocaill, eds. *The Annals of Ulster (to AD 1131)* (Dublin, 1983); T. Jones, ed., *Brut y Tywysogion of the Chronicle of the Princes, Red Book of Hengest Versim* (Cardiff, 1955).
[109] C. E. Blunt, B. H. I. H. Stewart and C. S. S. Lyon, *Coinage in Tenth-Century England from Edward the Elder to Edgar's Reform* (Oxford, 1989), 42; see further ibid., 22–3, 35–43.
[110] Blunt et al., *Coinage in Tenth-Century England*, pls. 4.8–10.
[111] Blunt et al., *Coinage in Tenth-Century England*, 36.
[112] Blunt et al., *Coinage in Tenth-Century England*, 38.
[113] Catherine E. Karkov, 'Æthelflæd's Exceptional Coins'? *Old English Newsletter* 28.3 (1996), 41.
[114] Katherine O'Brien O'Keeffe, ed., *The Anglo-Saxon Chronicle. A Collaborative Edition*, vol. 5, MS C (Cambridge, 2001); 'Her Æthelflæd Myrcna hlafdige Gode fultum gendum foran to Hlafmæsson begeat þa burh mid eallum þam ðe þærto hyrde þe ys hatan

the same year in which Æthelflæd had fortified the city. In response to the attack Æthelflæd and Æthelred, who was on the verge of death, ordered their troops to lure the enemy army into the city gates where it could be (and was) ambushed and slaughtered. The fact that Chester was the main source of the Tower coins makes it likely that the image of the tower was associated with the new fortifications and the battle at the city gates.[115] The image would also likely have become a sign of victory when the Vikings of York submitted to her shortly before her death in 918.

Mercian identification with at least certain of the exceptional designs, and especially with the designs as associated with Æthelflæd, would explain the reversion to Edward's Horizontal type of coinage around the time of Æthelflæd's death.[116] The change in coinage along with the sudden and most likely violent removal of Æthelflæd's daughter Ælfwyn from power in Mercia may both have been part of Edward's attempts to discourage any form of Mercian separatism, and to bring the sub-kingdom firmly and permanently under West Saxon control. In contrast, Æthelstan's use of a building on coins issued after the death of Sitric of York commemorates his conquest of the north, and may have been designed to continue the triumphant message of his aunt's coinage.[117]

While minting in Anglo-Saxon England was limited to kings, the occasional queen, and powerful ecclesiastics, seals were produced for and used by a wider cross-section of aristocratic women and men. The seals of two monastic women survive and demonstrate that, as with so many other aspects of 'portraiture', the images of their owners are very much a generic statement of status and lifestyle. The seal of Edith of Wilton, Edgar's illegitimate daughter, shows the veiled Edith with one hand raised before her and the other holding a book, a standard formula for depicting nuns and saints that can be paralleled in the portraits of Æthelthryth in the Benedictional of Æthelwold (London, BL, Add. 49598; fig. 64), or the slightly later figure of Mary on the dedication page of the New Minster Liber Vitae (London, BL, MS Stow 944; plate 12). The inscription identifies Edith as *regalis adelpha* (royal sister), a phrase which could refer both to her status as a nun and to the fact that she was the half-sister of Edgar's legitimate sons Edward and Æthelred. The acanthus decoration of the handle of the matrix, which was also intended to leave an impression in the wax, similarly parallels both the acanthus ornament of royal objects like the

---

Deoraby. Þæt wæron eac ofslegene hyre þegna fewner ðe hire besorge wæron binnan þam gatum.'
[115] See P. Grierson and Mark Blackburn, *The Early Middle Ages (5th–10th centuries), Medieval European Coinage, with a Catalogue of the Coins in the Fitzwilliam Museum, Cambridge*, 1 (Cambridge, 1986), 609 for parallels in contemporary architecture and manuscript illumination.
[116] Blunt et al., *Coinage in Tenth-Century England*, 43.
[117] Gareth Williams, unpublished paper delivered at the University of Leeds, 24 November 2009. On Æthelstan's coinage, the building is usually identified as a church; see Blunt et al. *Coinage in Tenth-Century England*, 267, pl. 7.24.

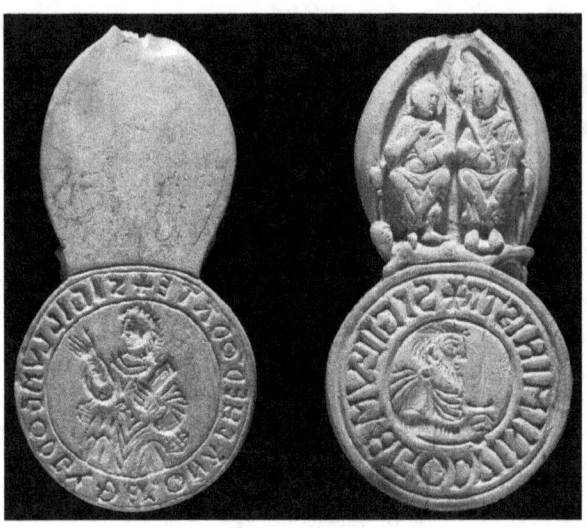

FIG. 38.
GODWINE SEAL

Alfred Jewel (fig. 61) and the lush acanthus of the borders of such manuscripts as the New Minster Charter and Æthelwold's Benedictional. Even though she had been part of the Wilton community since infancy, Edith may have preferred the ambivalence of both image and title as a way of expressing the dual aspects of her life at a time when they may perhaps have been seen to be in conflict. In his late eleventh-century Life of Edith, Goscelin strains at times to reconcile Edith's royal status and habits with her monastic life. Edith was not a professed nun, she dressed luxuriously, maintained her interaction with court life, kept a private zoo, and did little to help the abbey in times of hardship.[118]

The increasing number of seals that either survive or are mentioned in the documentary sources (e.g., the seal of Cnut) from the tenth century onward is indicative of the increasing need for written records of business and property transactions, and perhaps also of rising literacy. A late tenth- or early eleventh-century walrus-ivory seal matrix from Wallingford, Oxfordshire (fig. 38) is carved on both sides and may have been the seal of an aristocratic man and his widow (or perhaps daughter). On the primary side is the portrait of a man holding a sword surrounded by the inscription '+SIGILLUM GODÞINI MINISTRI' (the seal of Godwin the thane). This part of the matrix is a statement of secular power, but in the handle above is the Trinity with the Father and Son making a footstool of an enemy. The reference is to Psalm 109:1: 'The Lord said to my Lord: Sit thou at my right hand: Until I make thy enemies thy footstool.' As David Hinton has noted, this part of the seal can be read as an image of judgement 'appropriate for the seal of someone likely to have had a role in the shire and hundred courts'.[119] Read together with the portrait of Godwin, however, the second verse of the psalm also becomes relevant: 'The Lord will send forth the sceptre of thy power out of Sion: rule thou

---

[118] See Hollis et al., *Writing the Wilton Women*, 224, 226; Wilmart, 'La Légende de Ste Édith', 61-2, 266-9, 297-9; Wright and Loncar, 'Life of Edith', 37-8; Wright and Loncar, '*Translatio* of Edith', in *Writing the Wilton Women*, ed. Hollis et al., 69-71, 89-90; Karkov, 'Pictured in the Heart'.
[119] Hinton, *Gold and Gilt, Pots and Pins*, 146.

in the midst of thy enemies.' The two images thus conjure up the biblical authority behind secular law and judgement, and should be compared with the written formulae of contemporary charters in which a proem articulating increasingly severe forms of biblical judgement prefaces the dispositive section, which details the specifics of day-to-day property transactions in the here and now.

The reverse of the matrix displays at its centre the image of a woman dressed and posed much like Edith of Wilton. The surrounding inscription reads '+SIGILLUM GODGYÐE MONACHE DODATE' (the seal of Godgyða a nun given to God). A plausible explanation for the seal's reverse is that Godwin's widow (or daughter) had it recarved after his death when she would have needed to conduct business in her own name – even if she had entered a convent,[120] though other explanations, including the simple need to conserve resources, are possible. It is tempting to link the matrix to Earl Godwin, father of Edward the Confessor's queen Edith, and his wife Gytha, but the connection seems unlikely for a number of reasons.[121]

A number of manuscripts also provide evidence of reuse and reworking by women, usually in the form of alterations to the text in order to change masculine readings to feminine ones. One such manuscript is the Shaftesbury Psalter (Salisbury, Cathedral Library, MS 150; plate 4), in which the masculine phrase 'famulum tuum' in the prayer 'Omnipotens et misericors deus …' following Psalm 151 has been altered to the feminine 'famulam tuam' in a hand that is not that of the scribe. Two feminine names added to the obits some time before 1100 – Hisbel (9 August) and Seflet (23 October) – also suggest that the manuscript was being used in a nunnery,[122] even if it had not originally been made for one. The psalter was produced c. 969–87 and has traditionally been attributed to Shaftesbury (Dorset), a nunnery which Asser tells us was founded by King Alfred, and which was subsequently patronized by the West Saxon royal family, but Sherborne, Amesbury and Wilton have also been suggested. Daphne Stroud has surveyed the evidence for all four houses and concluded that the evidence for Shaftesbury and Wilton is strongest, though problematic in both cases.[123] Shaftesbury received the body of King Edward the Martyr in 981. His name, preceded by a cross, has been entered in the calendar by a later hand, however the feasts for his *adventus* (18–20 February) and translations (13 February and 20 June), as well as the feast of St Aelgiva, are absent, and one would expect them to appear in a Shaftesbury manuscript.[124]

---

[120] Hinton, *Gold and Gilt, Pots and Pins*, 147.
[121] Hinton, *Gold and Gilt, Pots and Pins*, 146–7, n. 32.
[122] Daphne Stroud, 'The Provenance of the Shaftesbury Psalter', *Library*, 6 ser. 1 (1979), 225–35, at 226.
[123] Stroud, 'Provenance of the Shaftesbury Psalter'.
[124] Stroud, 'Provenance of the Shaftesbury Psalter', 228.

The case for Wilton may be slightly stronger, but again it is largely circumstantial, and rests on additions to the calendar which may be related to St Edith of Wilton.[125] The feast of the Invention of the Holy Nails has been entered on 7 May. This is a rare feast, but Goscelin's Life of Edith records that the saint's mother, Wulfthryth, had acquired a small relic of the nails for the abbey.[126] Edith is also known to have had a special interest in St Denis, to whom she dedicated her famous wooden chapel,[127] and entries relating to Denis have been entered on 8 February, 27 February, 22 April, 14 July and 9 October. The feast of Edith herself has been entered on 16 September.[128] The manuscript contains the Gallicanum text of the psalter and is therefore believed to show Continental influence. In addition, the calendar includes entries for a large number of saints from Lorraine, possibly via Edith's teacher Benno of Trier and his associates.[129] Stroud notes that the entries relating to Edith herself are later in date, and that the feast of her translation (3 November) is absent.[130] This need not, however, be inconsistent with a Wilton provenance. The nuns of Wilton seem to have maintained a certain ambivalence towards Edith, and it is only with the writing of Goscelin's two versions of her life in the last twenty years or so of the eleventh century that we find any real evidence for a sustained cult.[131]

There is nothing about the style or imagery of the psalter that would help to link it to any particular house. It has survived in a badly mutilated state, missing pages and with many of its initials as well as the full-page miniatures that prefaced Psalms 1, 51, 101 and 109 all cut out or otherwise lost. From what survives, however, it is evident that the initials and text are the work of a single scribe.[132] The page illustrated introduces Psalm 119: 'Ad Dominum cum tribularer clamavi et exaudivit me' ('In my trouble I cried to the Lord: and he heard me'). Christ stands atop a beast mask with wide staring eyes which crowns an initial A made up entirely of biting dragons or dragon-like creatures. The two dragons that fly out from the top of the letter suggest a connection with the image of Christ over the beasts (Psalm 90:13), a scene that was frequently depicted in Anglo-Saxon art. Both psalms speak of the protection of the Lord, and the general imagery of the page is likely meant to invoke the protection of the Lord as a 'shield of faith' against evil, temptation and the demonic, as signified by the hellish beasts of the initial letter and the bestial mask

---

[125] Stroud, 'Provenance of the Shaftesbury Psalter', 233.
[126] Wright and Loncar, 'Life of Edith', 45.
[127] Wilmart, La Légende de Ste Édith, 86–7; Wright and Loncar, 'Life of Edith', 53.
[128] An entry on 2 September for the same feast has been erased.
[129] Stroud, 'Provenance of the Shaftesbury Psalter', 233.
[130] Stroud, 'Provenance of the Shaftesbury Psalter', 233.
[131] See above p. 130.
[132] With the exception of the Athanasian Creed, the Old English gloss is by a later hand.

that meets the viewer's gaze.[133] One of the more interesting aspects of the page is the way in which image and text interact with each other, simultaneously suggesting a unified harmony and the threat of order being pulled apart. Beneath Christ's feet the words 'clamavi et exaudivit me' have been inserted so that the page reads literally 'I cried to the Lord and he heard me. To the Lord in my trouble I cried and he heard me.' At the same time, the addition of the phrase creates a visual division between Christ and the letter on which he stands, and a horizontal line that parallels the horizontal of the dragons who attempt to escape from the confines of the letter.

The Shaftesbury Psalter raises interesting questions concerning our assumptions about the gender of both artists and audiences in Anglo-Saxon England, indeed in the early Middle Ages in general. It is usually assumed, unless there is concrete evidence to the contrary, that the producers and users of manuscripts were male, but this is not necessarily the case.[134] While the changes to the wording of the prayer following Psalm 151 indicate that this part of the book was altered to accommodate the needs of a later reader, they do not eliminate the possibility that the manuscript was intended for use within a female community or by a female patron from the start. Ælfwine's Prayerbook (London, British Library MS Cotton Titus D. xxvii and xxvi) written for Ælfwine c. 1020 while he was dean of the New Minster, Winchester, contains prayers with feminine endings, even though the manuscript was written for a man.[135] It is not until later in the Middle Ages that standard types of manuscripts such as psalters and books of hours would be routinely written to accommodate different types of reader and different voices. The same is true of images. Are, for example, the highly unusual prominence and signs of status given to the female descendants of Adam and Eve in the Junius 11 *Genesis* (Oxford, Bodleian Library, MS Junius 11, pp. 47, 51, 53, 54, 56, 57) signs that aristocratic women who might have seen themselves reflected in the manuscript's images were amongst the intended audience for these images?[136] Or do the images function more generally to identify the secular aristocracy of both genders as the daughters and sons of Eve and Adam, marked by the

---

[133] On this theme see further Herbert L. Kessler, 'Evil Eye(ing) Romanesque Art as a Shield of Faith', in *Romanesque Art and Thought in the Twelfth Century*, ed Colum Hourihane (Princeton, NJ, 2008), 107–35.
[134] See Brown, 'Female Book Ownership and Production in Anglo Saxon England', 47–8; Clare A. Lees and Gillian R. Overing, 'Before History, Before Difference: Bodies, Metaphor, and the Church in Anglo-Saxon England', *Yale Journal of Criticism* 11.2 (1998), 315–34.
[135] Beate Günzel, ed., *Ælfwine's Prayerbook* (London, 1993), 4.
[136] Catherine E. Karkov, *Text and Picture in Anglo-Saxon England: Narrative Strategies in the Junius 11 Manuscript* (Cambridge, 2001), 81–8; Catherine E. Karkov, 'The Anglo-Saxon Genesis: Text, Illustration and Audience', in *The Old English Hexateuch: Aspects and Approaches*, ed. Benjamin C. Withers and Rebecca Barnhouse (Kalamzoo, MI, 2000), 187–223.

signs of sexuality and pride? Either way, they raise questions about the role and status of the viewer/reader that cannot be ignored.

It is in the late tenth and eleventh centuries, the period in which both the Shaftesbury Psalter and Junius 11 manuscripts were produced, that we have sustained evidence for both secular and religious women as patrons, recipients and readers of books, many of which still survive. Emma is prominent as both a patron of books and a presence within them.[137] Her daughter-in-law, Edith Godwinson, followed in her footsteps as patron of the *Vita Edwardi*, and while no miniatures of her survive, she does appear in the scene of Edward's death in the Bayeux Tapestry, her image, like that of her mother-in-law, modelled on that of Mary. Judith of Flanders, wife of Edith's brother Earl Tostig, owned four great illuminated gospels,[138] no doubt amongst other books. Queen Margaret of Scotland was also a great reader and book collector.[139] Whether this represents an actual change in court life from the early Anglo-Saxon period or simply a change in the number of sources that survive is debatable. Bertha, the first Christian queen in Anglo-Saxon England, exchanged letters with Gregory the Great, and both she and her daughter, Æthelburh, the first Christian queen of Northumbria, were clearly literate readers. And there is of course the famous story of the young Alfred, inspired to literacy by the beauty of his mother's illuminated book,[140] a story that would become crucial both to the Anglo-Saxon sense of political identity and to the creation, centuries later, of a specifically English Empire.[141]

---

[137] Heslop, 'The Production of *de luxe* Manuscripts'; Karkov, *Ruler Portraits*, 119–33, 146–55.
[138] Jane Rosenthal, 'An Unprecedented Image of Love and Devotion: The Crucifixion in Judith of Flanders's Gospel Book', in *Tributes to Lucy Freeman Sandler*, ed. K.-A. Smith and C. Krinsky (Turnhout and London, 2008), 21–36; Jane Rosenthal with Patrick McGurk, 'Author, Symbol and Word: The Inspired Evangelists in Judith of Flanders's Anglo-Saxon Gospel Books', in *Tributes to Jonathan J. G. Alexander*, ed. Susan l'Engle and Gerald B. Guest (Turnhout and London, 2006), 185–202; Patrick McGurk, with Jane Rosenthal, 'The Anglo-Saxon Gospel Books of Judith, Countess of Flanders: Their Text, Make-up and Function', *ASE* 24 (1995), 251–308.
[139] See below pp. 271–7.
[140] Keynes and Lapidge, eds., *Alfred the Great*, 75; see below p. 213.
[141] See further Yorke, 'The "Old North" from the Saxon South in Nineteenth-Century Britain'.

# OBJECT AND VOICE 4

The Anglo-Saxons were surrounded by texts, not only by manuscripts, but also by inscribed objects, and a large number of those inscriptions gave voice to the objects on which they appeared. While speaking objects may have been common, the ways in which these objects spoke and continue to speak, what they have to say, and to whom their messages are addressed vary a great deal. Some inscriptions translate between languages or cultures, or between language and object. Sometimes objects speak of their own origins, sometimes they are meant to invoke the authority of an absent owner or patron, or sometimes they function to unite the viewer/reader with the work of art. In all cases they provide us with provocative questions not only about Anglo-Saxon literacy but also, even more provocatively, about Anglo-Saxon notions of self and identity, both individually and as a people. While most of the inscriptions discussed in this chapter were designed to be read by individuals or small groups, there is some evidence for more public inscriptions that gave voice to buildings rather than just objects. One such inscription survives at the late, perhaps 970–1020, church of St Mary's, Breamore, in Hampshire.[1] In the arch over the entrance from the nave to the south *porticus*, perhaps originally a baptistery or chapel, are the words 'HER SƷUTELAÐ SEO GECƷYDRÆNES ÐE' ('Here is made manifest the Covenant to you'). The reference is to God's covenant with Noah in Genesis 9.8–17, and the inscription looks back to one of the great origin myths of the Anglo-Saxons', their understanding of themselves as the chosen people, their migration mirrored in the stories of Noah and of Exodus.[2] Richard Gameson comments on the fact that the inscription is in a part of the church used by the clergy, yet it is in the vernacular rather than Latin, and this he takes

---

[1] For a discussion of the date of the church see Fernie, *The Architecture of the Anglo-Saxons*, 113–14.
[2] Daniel Anlezark, *Water and Fire: The Myth of the Flood in Anglo-Saxon England* (Manchester, 2006); Howe, *Migration and Mythmaking in Anglo-Saxon England*.

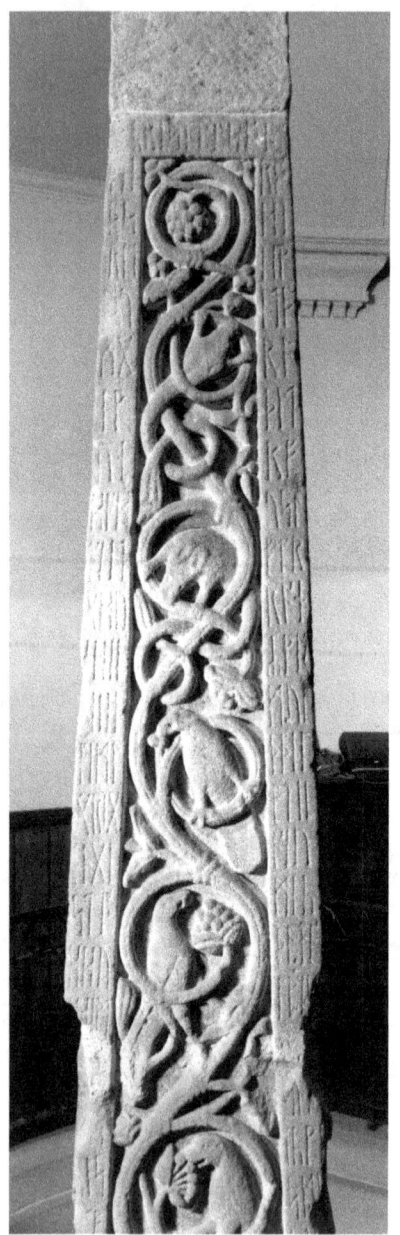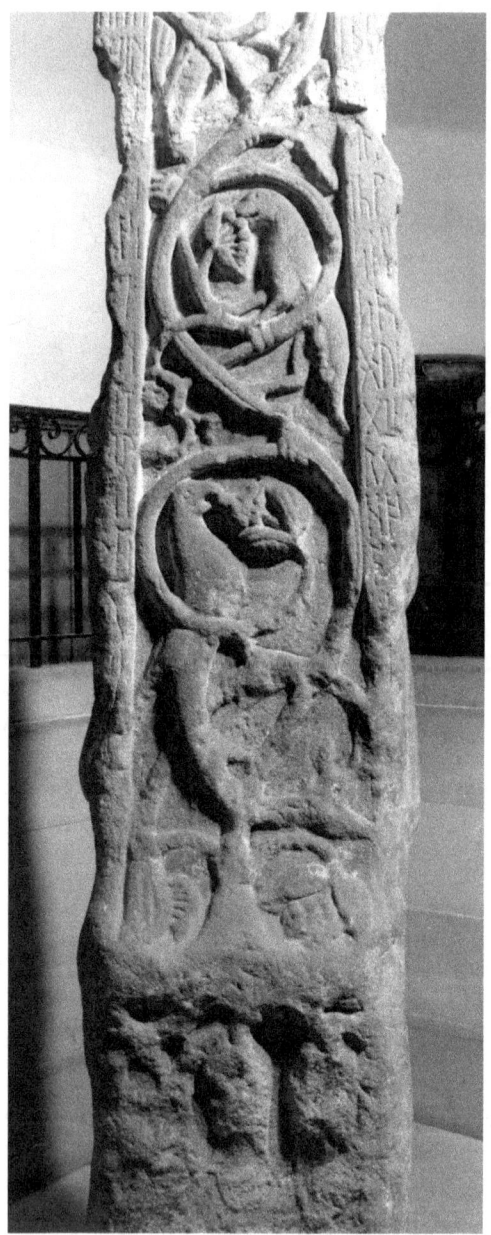

FIG. 39 a and b. RUTHWELL CROSS, VINESCROLL AND RUNIC INSCRIPTION

as a sign of the 'limited Latinity of the parochial clergy';[3] however, Thomas Bredehoft has pointed out that most of the 'speaking object' inscriptions that survive are in Old English rather than Latin, regardless of their audience or date.[4] This raises the question of a play between languages and the possibility that the inscription functioned on more than one level. For those who did not know Latin and to whom the inscription might have been read, it would have carried a straightforward biblical reference, and one that was itself a cultural signifier. For those who knew both Latin and exegesis, however, the inscription provided something of a riddle. In the exegetical tradition, Noah's ark was a type of the church, while the Latin word for the rainbow covenant, *arcus*, played with the form of the actual arch into which the inscription is carved. A further metonymic connection could be made between inscription and material, the arch/arc being made of stone, the rock on which the church was built both literally and metaphorically. Similarly complex relationships between languages, word and object or image, and word and audience, are found throughout the art of early medieval England. Moreover, some form of play on the materiality of the object and the voice of the inscription is very much the norm for Anglo-Saxon speaking objects indicating that object (or image) was perceived as the equal of text in the making of meaning.

## RELATIONSHIPS BETWEEN THE VERBAL AND THE VISUAL

Two of the earliest and most frequently studied of Anglo-Saxon monuments are the Ruthwell Cross and the Franks Casket. In terms of size and material they could not be more different from each other. The Ruthwell Cross is a monumental public sculpture. Originally standing at more than five metres high, it was intended to be seen from a distance as well as up close, and it was almost certainly made for a monastic community rather than an individual. The Franks Casket, on the other hand, is a delicate portable object. Arguments vary as to its function, but whether it was made for a private patron or not, it was certainly intended to be read close up, and not by a crowd. The Ruthwell Cross is made of stone while the Franks Casket is made from the bone of a whale and was thus once part of a living being which gives its voice a different sort of resonance from that of the cross.

The Ruthwell Cross is carved with scenes and inscriptions arranged to create an almost symmetrically balanced monument with half of the cross devoted to figural scenes depicting largely biblical subjects, and half

---

[3] Richard Gameson and Fiona Gameson, 'The Anglo-Saxon Inscription at St Mary's Church, Breamore', *ASSAH* 6 (1993), 1–10, at 2.
[4] Thomas A. Bredehoft, 'First-Person Inscriptions and Literacy in Anglo-Saxon England', *ASSAH* 9 (1996), 103–10.

devoted to the vinescroll inhabited by both naturalistic and fantastical birds and beasts. Of the figural scenes, exactly half include women, a gender balance that is unique amongst surviving early Anglo-Saxon monuments. The panels on the west face of the shaft have a eucharistic symbolism,[5] while those on the east face have a baptismal significance; together the two sides also refer to the active and contemplative elements of the monastic life. The inscriptions on the two broad sides are in Latin prose and function like captions, identifying the figures and scenes depicted. They are written in the Roman alphabet, arranged around the individual panels to which they refer, and written in the third person. The two narrow sides are inscribed with an Old English poem written in runes that runs (basically) down the length of the shaft (fig. 39), balancing the upward movement of the vinescroll. The poem is written in the first-person voice of the cross. The monument must be understood then as multilingual and speaking in at least two different voices. This is also quite clearly a monument that demanded the viewer to move around it, to read and to see, to put together its different images, voices and spaces in order to arrive at an understanding of its meaning. It is also a monument that invites all to participate (even as it excludes the non-Christian, the illiterate, and those literate only in other languages). It depicts and contains a community in and through the body of Christ. This may be explanation enough for its balanced inclusion of female figures, although we know so little about the community by and for whom the cross was erected that there may have been more specific reasons now lost to us – a double community, for example.

One of the primary functions of the cross was to invoke a metonymic vision of the Crucifixion arrived at through an understanding of its texts and its images of figures and animals who touch, hold or consume the body of Christ in its multiple forms. The sacramental significance of the cross has been thoroughly detailed in the many publications of Éamonn Ó Carragáin,[6] so I will outline here only the way in which that symbolism relates to its overall programme. The cross bearing the body of Christ in its multiple forms is at the centre of the programme, and from it our vision moves outward in both chronological time and physical space to a set of metonymically related themes and images, before moving back to the image of Christ on the cross. This is every bit as much a shape-shifting vision of the cross as that which appears to the dreamer in the poem *The Dream of the Rood*. We are, no matter where we begin reading the visual programme, confronted by a monumental cross, covered alternately and simultaneously with blood and with the jewel of the body of Christ. As we stand directly beneath the cross and look up, it appears, like the cross

---

[5] In all cases references are to the original orientation of the cross.
[6] See Ó Carragáin, *Ritual and the Rood* and bibliography therein for the extensive literature on the monument.

in *The Dream of the Rood*, to rise up to span the heavens. Reading up the original west face of the shaft, each panel depicts a figure or pair of figures who present Christ to us in alternately literal and symbolic form. Mary holds the body of the infant Christ in the flight into or out of Egypt; Paul and Anthony break bread, the body of Christ present in the eucharist, in the desert; the beasts in the desert cross their paws as they support the adult body of Christ; at the top John the Baptist holds the eternal sacrificial yet triumphant body of the Agnus Dei. In the terminals of the now lost cross head were the four evangelists accompanied by their symbols, and there was possibly a Christological symbol at the centre. The viewer is presented alternately with the living and the eternal Christ, the physical body and its symbolic manifestations, and finally with the evangelists who bore witness to the life and divinity of Christ and who, according to Bede, spoke *veritas historiae* because they were eye-witnesses.[7]

On the original east face of the shaft (fig. 40) we move again from a Marian scene in the lowest panel to one involving John the Baptist at the top. The figures on this side, along with their accompanying inscriptions, are more active in comparison to the more iconic scenes on the west face. At the bottom is the Annunciation with the angel Gabriel just entering the space of the panel as Mary shrinks backwards in humility (fig. 22);[8] in the healing of the man born blind, Christ reaches out towards the eyes of the blind man bringing him to light (or vision); Mary Magdalene washes Christ's feet with her tears and dries them with the hair of her head; and at the top, Elizabeth is reaching

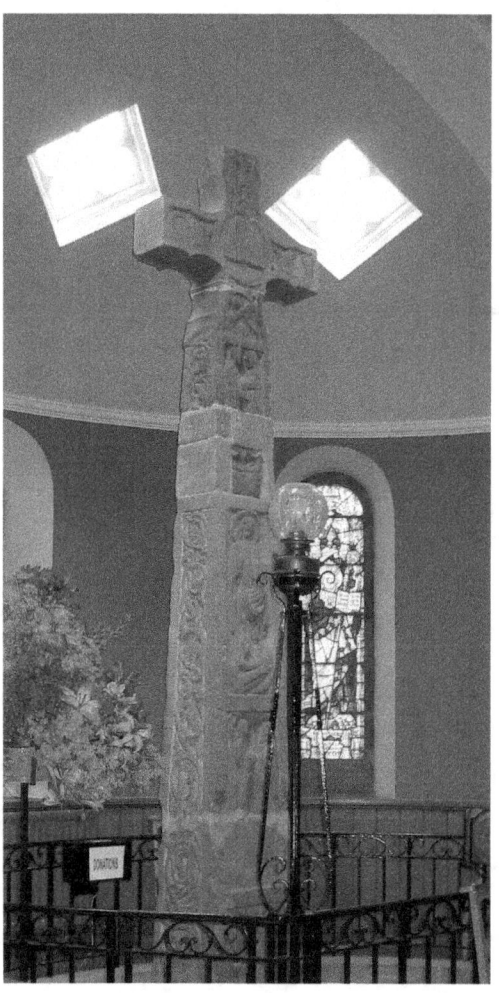

FIG. 40.
RUTHWELL
CROSS,
ORIGINAL
EAST SIDE

---

[7] Bede, *Expositio in Lucam*, ed. D. Hurst, CCSL 120 (Turnhout, 1960), 120.
[8] The Crucifixion carved on the base beneath the Annunciation is a ninth-century addition, and provides a very clumsy image of the event the cross as a whole asks the individual viewer to envisage within his or her own mind.

out to touch Mary's belly. Here the viewer supplies what cannot be seen, the unborn John the Baptist leaping in his mother's pregnant belly as he recognizes the divinity of the unborn Christ. The designer(s) and/or sculptor(s) have organized the iconographic programme so that the pivotal points of the visual narrative, the panels at the top and bottom of each side, involve the same figures: Mary and John the Baptist, a woman and a man, both of whom touch the body of Christ before his birth, during his life and after his death (though admittedly these moments are not all depicted on the cross). In two panels, the Annunciation and the Visitation, the body of Christ is not visually present and must be supplied by the mind's eye of the viewer – its unseen presence is after all key to both episodes. In the other two, the flight into/out of Egypt and John the Baptist with the Agnus Dei, it is not only represented but presented to the viewer.

The Visitation panel has also been turned into a depiction of the sisters Martha and Mary through the addition of the inscription, which reads 'Martha and Mary ... [something]' possibly 'Martha and Mary *merentes dominae*', and has been reconstructed alternatively as 'Martha and Mary worthy women' or 'Martha and Mary mother of the Lord'.[9] Both readings remain problematic, but we must consider the idea that they are deliberately so. If the cross has multiple meanings, and it is beyond question that it does, there is no reason that individual panels could not also carry multiple meanings. If this is indeed the case, the panel would refer to the active and contemplative sides of the monastic life, of which Martha and Mary were the female representations. It would thus provide a balance to the Paul and Anthony panel on the west side. As a Visitation scene, the panel would relate to the liturgical office of Vespers at which the Magnificat, which Mary sings at the Visitation, would have been sung, paralleling the Benedictus sung to John the Baptist at Lauds and the Agnus Dei chant sung at morning mass. There are many other connections one could make between these and other panels on the cross, but the focus in this chapter is on voice, and what is of primary importance about these panels in this context is the way in which they function to integrate the texts and images of the two broad sides of the cross with the bodies and voices of the community.[10]

The inscriptions of the two narrow sides of the shaft (fig. 39) work in a parallel but slightly more complex manner. On the original north side of the shaft the cross speaks as the masculine gallows (galgu):

> [+ond]geredæ hinæ god almeittig·
> þa hewalde on galgu gistiga
> modig f[ore] [allæ] men

---

[9] The surviving inscription reads [-] marþ[a] mar[ia] m...r dominnae c[-].
[10] On the differing voices of the Latin inscriptions of the two broad sides see further Karkov, 'Naming and Renaming'.

> [b]ug ...
> [ahof] ic riicnæ kyninc·
> heafunæs hlafard
> hælda ic ni dorstæ
> [b]ismærædu unket men ba æt[g]ad[re
> i]c [wæs] miþ blodi bist[e]mi[d]
> bi[got][en of] ...[11]

Reconstructed, the verses translate as follows:

> Almighty God stripped himself
> when he wished to mount the gallows,
> brave in the sight of all men.
> I dared not bow.
> I [raised aloft] a powerful king.
> The Lord of heaven
> I dared not tilt.
> Men insulted the pair of us together.
> I was drenched with blood
> [begotten from that man's side].

The emphasis in these verses is on the revelation and display of both Christ and the cross, a verbal parallel to the imagery of the west face.

On the south side of the shaft the cross identifies itself as the rod (a feminine word). This dual or shifting gendering of the cross is something that also occurs in *The Dream of the Rood*, where the rood is converted from a wooden root (the masculine noun stefn) to a tree possessed of voice (the feminine noun stefn).[12] We read:

> [+k]ris[t] wæs on rodi·
> hweþræ þer fusæ fearran kwomu
> æþþilæ til anum ic þæt al bi[h][eald]
> s[aræ] ic w[æ]s· mi[þ] so[r]gu[m] gi[d]rœ[fi]d
> h[n]a[g] ...
> miþ s[t]re[l]um giwundad
> alegdun hiæ [h]inæ limwœrignæ· gistoddu[n
> h]im [æt] [his] [li][c]æs [hea]f[du]m
> [bih]ea[ld]u[n h]i[æ þ]e[r] ...[13]

---

[11] Square brackets indicate letters that have been supplied or restored based on the text of *The Dream of the Rood*. The original runic reads: [runic text]

[12] Sarah Larratt Keefer, "'Either/And' as 'Style' in Anglo-Saxon Christian Poetry', in *Anglo-Saxon Styles*, ed. Karkov and Brown, 179–200.

[13] [runic text]

> The reconstructed translation would be:
> Christ was on the cross.
> But eager ones came hither from afar.
> Noble ones came together. I beheld all that.
> I was terribly afflicted with sorrows.
> I bowed [to the hands of men],
> wounded with arrows.
> They laid him down, limb-weary;
> they stood at the shoulders of the corpse.
> They looked upon the Lord [of heaven].

The coming together of figures, including figures from afar, and the bowing of the sorrowful cross again provide verbal parallels to both the voice of the inscriptions and the actions of the figures on the east face.

The arrangement of both runic inscriptions is identical, running first across the top border, then down the right side, then down the left side. It is an arrangement found at an earlier date on early Christian and Byzantine objects, most notably the cross of Justin II and the miraculous icon of Santa Maria in Trastevere.[14] It is also one that necessitates the reader making the sign of the cross with her or his own eyes. Of equal significance is the fact that in reading we are forced to move our eyes both along and across the vinescroll so that text and ornament merge in our experience of these sides of the cross. The viewer becomes one with the animals nibbling at the bunches of grapes, and one with the cross raising aloft Christ's bleeding body and then lowering of it to the hands of men.

Often studied as almost a separate part of the monument, or even as a discrete poem completely divorced from its sculptural and iconographic context,[15] it is the narrow sides of the cross and the voice of the inscription that set Ruthwell apart from other freestanding stone crosses. It is also the narrow sides with their emotional poem spoken in the first-person voice of the cross that are key to understanding the way in which Ruthwell makes the viewer one with its voice and vision. The poem has a first and a second half, a beginning and an end, so for those who could read it or knew it by heart, it directed movement around the monument. Like many contemporary sculptures, Ruthwell is not self-contained; it requires the physical presence of the viewer for its completion.

To understand exactly how image, voice and the interaction of the viewer with the monument work, we will begin standing before the

---

[14] See Ó Carragáin, *Ritual and the Rood*, 52, 236, 241 (cross of Justin II), 240–1 (Santa Maria in Trastevere icon).

[15] But see Éamonn Ó Carragáin, 'Who Then Read the Ruthwell Poem in the Eighth Century?' in *Aedificia Nova: Studies in Honor of Rosemary Cramp*, ed. Catherine E. Karkov and Helen Damico (Kalamazoo, MI, 2008), 43–75.

original west side.¹⁶ In all four panels carved on this face of the cross we are presented with the body of Christ. The Christ child on his mother's lap, the breaking of the bread (neatly paralleled by the breaking of the poem in two), and the Agnus Dei are all held out for our reception, while in the largest of the panels, the beasts raise aloft and display the body of Christ above their crossed paws. The eucharistic symbolism of these scenes looks forward to the first section of the poem on the monument's north side. It is in this section of the poem that the cross, like the figures on the west face, raises Christ aloft, and it is in this section of the poem that it, along with the viewer as s/he reads the poem, is drenched with blood from the wound in Christ's side. The iconographic conventions of medieval art tell us that the wound in Christ's side was usually in his right side, and that standing to the right of Christ places the reader in the position of Mary (or Ecclesia born from the wound in Christ's side) or perhaps in the position of the spearbearer who was cured of his blindness and converted when Christ's blood fell upon his eyes. We are, in other words, on the side on which we would, no matter with which of these figures we might identify, be drenched with blood were we a participant in the actual Crucifixion. However, the poem asks us to envisage ourselves not only as participants in the Crucifixion but also as the Cross itself. As we read the poem we recite the words 'I dared not bow', 'I raised aloft a powerful king', 'I was drenched with blood'. While we are shown figures holding the body of Christ on the west side of the shaft, it is only here in reciting the poem that we become one of those figures.

The opening verses of the poem effect a transition between the two broad faces of the cross so that, having been drenched with blood and having participated in the eucharist and undergone a baptism of sorts, we then turn to the east face of the shaft, the imagery of which centres on scenes with baptismal significance, but also begins to ask us not only to touch or hold but to internalize the body of Christ. Like the blind man, or like the blind spearbearer, we are brought to light – something that would have been experienced quite literally if the panel were lit by the rays of the rising sun. Like Mary Magdalene we are born sinners and must be brought to penitence. Like both Mary Magdalene and the Virgin Mary we are also humble before God and in awe of the mystery of the incarnation. The panels also look forward to the end of the poem on the south side of the shaft in which, having raised aloft the body of Christ, the *rod* bows down, afflicted with sorrows.

After the triumphant statement 'Christ was on the cross', the central lines of the verses turn to the private internal struggle of the cross. In reading the poem, we, like the cross, are afflicted with sorrows and

---

¹⁶ Other readings are of course possible. One could begin, for example, with the poem on the north side. The overall reading of the cross, however, changes very little, no matter where one begins to read.

wounded by arrows. On the north side we were covered with blood, but on the south side we bleed. Here the poem also tells us 'Ic þæt al biheald' (I beheld all that). The cross witnesses and records and invites us to do so along with it. It places us in the position of John the Evangelist whose role as witness would become so prominent a feature of late Anglo-Saxon Crucifixion scenes.[17]

As long as one is able to decipher and read the inscriptions, the meaning of the words is clear, but the cross speaks in multiple voices and different languages and records its words in different scripts. It remains questionable whether all of these would have been equally clear even to a literate and learned Anglo-Saxon audience. There is also a tension created between languages. The Latin inscriptions written in a third-person impersonal voice identify the scenes and/or name the figures depicted. They are laid out in a relatively straightforward manner and certainly any literate religious man or woman would have had little trouble either reading them or understanding their meaning. The runic poem is much more difficult and complex. Its layout is not straightforward, as noted above, and the characters themselves are smaller and less easy to decipher. Even if we grant that a learned Anglo-Saxon reader would have been able to make out the individual words and verses,[18] it would not have been an easy task, and it certainly would not have been possible for the average literate person. The poem is in the Old English language, the vernacular, the familiar spoken language of the Anglo-Saxons, but it is written in runes, an alphabet less familiar. The poetic voice of the cross thus unites it with its audience at the same time as it declares its difference from it. Runes were considered an archaic script,[19] and their use in manuscripts in particular has been studied for what it reveals of the apparent 'historical interest' of the Anglo-Saxons,[20] but much less consideration has been given to how the use of the runic affects voice. I would argue that the use of runes for Ruthwell's vernacular poem lends the words of the cross both a sense of age or antiquity and a sense of mystery – as if they were an old story recounted by a wise and aged man or woman. This is on one level exactly what they are. The story *is* an old one, one of the earliest foundation stories of the Christian religion and Christian church; and the cross which speaks the story is equally old and most certainly wise. The cross is also relating a mystery, the mystery of Christ's transformation from his human incarnation to his divine resurrected form. It is a mystery that

---

[17] Jennifer O'Reilly, 'St John as a Figure of the Contemplative Life: Text and Image in the Art of the Anglo-Saxon Benedictine Reform', in *St Dunstan: His Life, Times and Cult*, ed. Nigel Ramsay, Margaret Sparks and Tim Tatton-Brown (Woodbridge, 1992), 165–85.
[18] See Ó Carragáin, 'Who then Read the Ruthwell Poem in the Eighth Century?'
[19] R. I. Page, *An Introduction to English Runes* (London, 1973), 16–17.
[20] Ó Carragáin, *Ritual and the Rood*, 44; David N. Parsons, 'Anglo-Saxon Runes in Continental Manuscripts', in *Runische Schriftkultur in kontinental-skandinavischer und – angelsäsischer Wechselbezeihung*, ed. Klaus Düwel (Berlin, 1994), 195–220.

we can understand although it remains hidden beneath the runic lettering and can be fully understood only by those educated in its mysteries. The inscription may also be understood as paralleling the content of the poem in that it presents a riddle that the reader must struggle to unlock as content and meaning are accessible only after script, word order and language have all been deciphered. Finally, the voice of the inscriptions sets Old English in a different relationship to the monument from Latin, and embeds it anachronistically into the chronology of the past, yet here eternally present, moment of the Crucifixion, an event predating the coming of Latin to England with the Roman conquest begun in AD 43. The poem, in effect, Englishes both the biblical event and the cross.

This of course presumes that the audience of the cross was familiar with the language in which it speaks and, while some must surely have been, it is unlikely that all were. The monument was erected by Anglo-Saxons of the Northumbrian church in an area that had previously been British. Would even a literate or learned member of this group have been able to understand its message? Or, for such an audience, would it have been a symbol of aggression, of the imposition of a new colonizing people, language and church? The mere height of the monument would itself have been impressive, if not intimidating.

For those who erected the cross, however, the poem was also an oral performance spoken in the voice of the cross. The monument thus has a voice, an interior from which it speaks its history, and it is in this respect a living thing. Spoken words always suggest a body and a self that are present, even if the written text, especially a text written in the archaic script of the Ruthwell poem, signifies absence, a distant past and perhaps also death.[21] While we cannot be certain that the hole now at the centre of the Annunciation panel is an original feature or that, if it is, it ever held a relic, the interiority of the cross would have been even more forceful if a relic of the True Cross was contained within it. Relics of the True Cross had the ability to turn the cross-reliquaries that contained them into further relics of the Cross, and thus the Cross itself.[22] It would have brought the dead stone to life, adding both potency and the truthfulness of lived experience, as well as an eye-witness account to the poem, uniting the Ruthwell Cross even more closely with the bodies of those who spoke with it as they moved around it. It would also have provided a fitting model for the mystical vision of the Crucifixion that the poem asks the reader to envisage within his or her own speaking self.

A similar sense of an enigmatic voice and text from the past, a combination of visual and verbal reading, something revealed and yet

---

[21] See further Walter Ong, *Orality and Literacy: The Technologizing of the Word* (London and New York, 1982).
[22] Anatole Frolow, *La relique de la vraie croix. Recherches sur le développement d'un culte* (Paris, 1961).

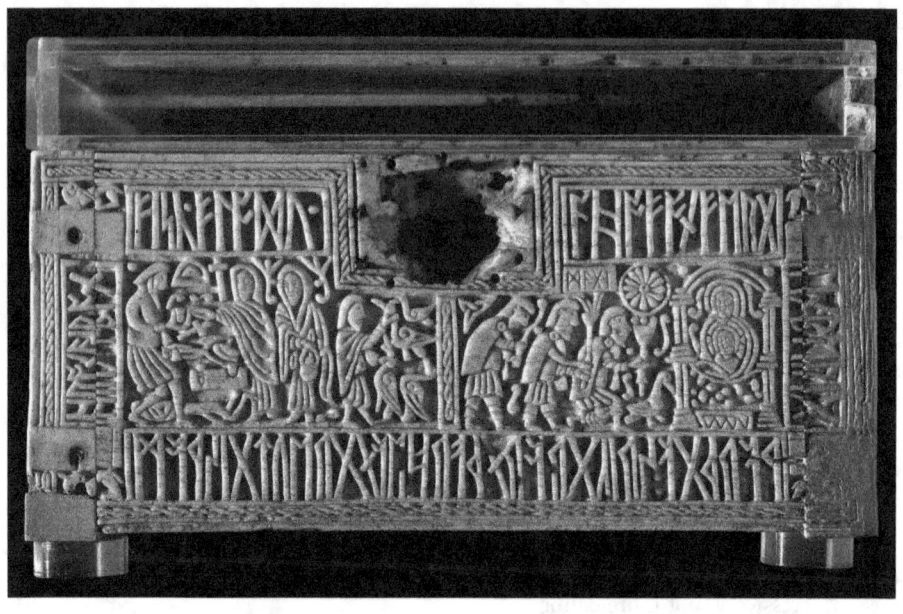

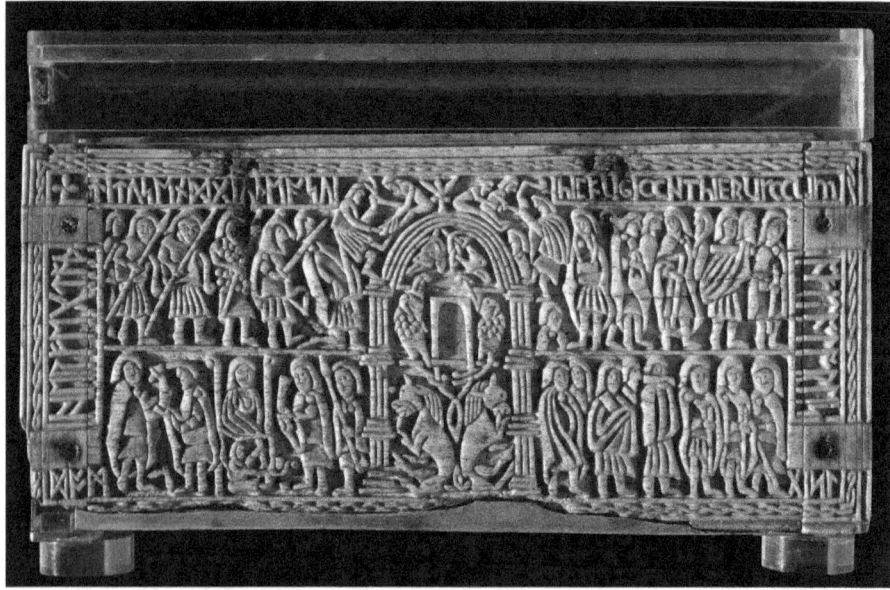

FIG. 41 a and b. FRANKS CASKET, FRONT AND BACK PANELS

concealed, something that hovers between inanimate object and living, being characterizes the Franks Casket (fig. 41), although on the casket all these things are manifested or embedded differently. The Franks Casket is a small (23 x 19 x 13 cm) whalebone box generally believed to have been made in Northumbria, or at least by a Northumbrian craftsman, in the first half of the eighth century.[23] Gaby Waxenberger has recently provided evidence for narrowing the home of the casket (or the person who carved the inscription) to the area of Whitby or Jarrow.[24] The history of the casket is largely unknown. The mention of an ivory box containing relics in documents preserved in the archives at Brioude (Auvergne) suggests that during the Middle Ages it belonged to the church of St Julian the Martyr in Brioude, though of course the evidence is not conclusive.[25] It may have been hidden during the French Revolution, only to be rediscovered in Auzon (Haute-Loire) in the early nineteenth century, but how and when it left England remain a mystery. Its original patron/owner and function are also uncertain. As most of the scenes depicted are secular, the casket is often assumed to have been made for a secular aristocrat, but this is nothing more than an assumption; and because the decoration is so highly literate and learned, the casket is assumed to have been made in a monastic setting, though this too cannot be established with any certainty. While there is little evidence for artistic workshops within secular communities, craftsmen did travel; moreover, attempts to make distinctions between what constitutes the 'monastic' and the 'secular' when it comes to artistic practice and patronage are fraught with difficulties – as the examples of Bishop Wilfrid, abbess Ælfflæd of Whitby, Edith of Wilton and Edith Godwineson make clear. As for its function, the casket was certainly made to contain something, possibly treasure, possibly a book, possibly a relic or relics. In form and design it is quite similar to surviving early Christian reliquaries, even if its imagery is not,[26] but it may also have served multiple functions during its lifetime.

With the exception of the lid, the design of each panel is similar: a narrative scene or scenes surrounded by a lengthy identifying inscription

---

[23] See further Leslie Webster, *The Franks Casket* (London, 2010); Leslie Webster, 'Stylistic Aspects of the Franks Casket', in *The Vikings*, ed. Robert T. Farrell (Chichester, 1982), 20–32; Leslie Webster, 'The Iconographic Programme of the Franks Casket', in *Northumbria's Golden Age*, ed. Jane Hawkes and Susan Mills (Stroud, 1999), 227–46; Ian N. Wood, 'Ripon, Francia and the Franks Casket in the Early Middle Ages', *Northern History* 26 (1990), 1–19; Carol Neuman de Vegvar, 'Reading the Franks Casket: Contexts and Audience', in *Intertexts: Studies in Anglo-Saxon Culture Presented to Paul E. Szarmach*, ed. Blanton and Scheck, 141–59; Richard Abels, 'What Has Weland To Do with Christ? The Franks Casket and the Acculturation of Christianity in Early Anglo-Saxon England', *Speculum* 84.3 (2009), 549–81.
[24] Unpublished paper delivered at the 13th conference of the International Society of Anglo-Saxonists, St John's, Newfoundland, July 2009.
[25] Webster, *The Franks Casket*, 27–9.
[26] On the similarities between the Franks Casket and early Christian reliquaries see Webster, *The Franks Casket*, 31–41.

with additional labels sometimes provided for individual events or figures. The lid has been damaged so that only one panel carved with a battle scene involving a figure labelled 'Ægili' (the Germanic hero Egil) survives, but it is possible that a lengthy inscription was once carved on the missing portions. The inscriptions are in a mixture of Old English and Latin, in Insular and runic (conventional and encoded) scripts, and are carved in a variety of orientations. Like the Ruthwell Cross, this is not an object that can be read passively, and like the cross it presents the reader with a series of visual and verbal stories, some puzzling, that must be deciphered; like the cross, the arrangement of the inscribed passages draws attention to their difficult and puzzling nature.

The scenes on the casket are divided equally so that three are devoted to stories from Germanic legend and three to scenes from the history of Rome and the Roman church. The front of the casket originally carried the lock and would thus have been the focus of attention for anyone locking or unlocking its contents. On the left is a scene from the story of Weland the smith, in which the hamstrung Weland is in the process of making a cup (a container) from the skull of King Nithhad's son before raping his daughter, Beaduhild (who subsequently gives birth to the hero Widia), and flying away. On the right the three magi (labelled ᛗᚫᚷᛁ, 'mægi') present their gifts,[27] including a cup, to the enthroned Virgin and Child. An Old English poetic inscription carved in runes surrounds the two scenes, emphasizing visually that they are meant to be read together. It presents the reader with a prosopopeic text that borrows from the convention of textual riddles, but goes far beyond those riddles in its play with materiality. Assuming that we begin reading at upper left, the inscription states:

> fisc flodu ahof   on fergenberig
> warþ gasric grorn   þær he on greut giswom
> Hronæs ban
>
> (The fish beat up the seas [or rose by means of the sea] onto the mountainous cliff; gasric[28] became sad when he swam aground onto the shingle. Whale's bone.)[29]

Alternatively, one could begin reading up the left side so that 'Whale's bone' comes first, though for anyone looking directly at this side of the casket this seems a less obvious place to begin. The section of the verse referring to the 'king of terror' (or the one strong in life) reads retrograde along the bottom of the panel, clearly emphasizing the reversal

---

[27] This is the only text incised rather than carved in relief on the casket.
[28] 'Gasric' has conventionally been translated as 'king of terror', but Waxenberger has recently proposed that it is the name of the whale, meaning something like 'the one strong in life or power' (unpublished paper delivered at the 13th conference of the International Society of Anglo-Saxonists, St John's, Newfoundland, July 2009).
[29] All translations are based on Page, *An Introduction to English Runes*.

of the whale's fortune, and the words 'whale's bone', not part of the verse inscription, are carved along the left edge of the panel next to the scene of Weland the smith. If Waxenberger is correct in suggesting that 'gasric' is actually the name of the whale, it would mean that the casket itself, like so many of the figures depicted on it, has a named identity, drawing attention to its existence as both historical being and object, a box. The identification of the living material from which the casket is made is thus placed alongside the panel depicting the manufacture of a different type of container from the bone of what was once a living being. It has been proposed that the runes chosen for alliteration in this verse, *f* in the first line and *g* in the second, are significant as the name for the *f* rune was *feoh* (treasure) and that for the *g giefa* (gift),[30] and it might be possible to relate these references to the casket's material as well as its function, as the whalebone is both treasure and a gift from the sea.

The next point of focus would be the lid, which originally held the handle used to carry the casket, and which would have been raised and lowered each time the casket was opened. On the lid, Egil the archer defends a fortified dwelling against attack. Behind him a hooded woman stands beneath an arch with double-headed serpents above her head and beneath her feet. Above Egil's shoulder is his name in runes: ᚨᚷᛁᛚ. The handle was originally fitted at the centre of the panel so that the battle rages around the device used to lift the box or its lid when opening the casket, not just to either side of it. Given this arrangement, it is possible that the battle narrative ought to be interpreted as one of defence of the casket and its contents rather than a literal attack on Egil's dwelling.

The back panel has a scene of the fall of Jerusalem at the hands of the Emperor Titus in AD 70, and a group of figures being taken hostage. The inscription, in a mixture of runic and Roman letters reads 'her fegtaþ titus end giuþeasu. Hic fugiant Hierusalim afitatores' (Here Titus and a Jew [or Jews] fight. Here the inhabitants flee Jerusalem). The inscription changes into the Latin language and Roman alphabet for the first part of the description of the flight of the Jews, and then back into Old English and the runic alphabet for the final word 'inhabitants'. It may be that the change in language and alphabet is intended to draw attention to the mention of the Holy City of Jerusalem[31] and/or its destruction by Rome, signalling the start of a new order.[32] However, the move from Old English

---

[30] See e.g., Wolfgang Krause and Herbert Jankuhn, *Die Runeninschriften im älteren Futhark*, Abhandlungen der Akademie der Wissenschaften in Göttingen, Philologisch-Historische Klasse, 3rd ser. 65 (Göttingen, 1966), 205–6; Alfred Becker, *Franks Casket: zu den Bildern und Inschriften des Runenkästchens von Auzon* (Regensburg, 1973), 98–100; Marijane Osborn, 'The Lid as Conclusion of the Syncretic Theme of the Franks Casket', in *Old English Runes and Their Continental Background*, ed. Alfred Bammesberger, Anglistische Forschungen 217 (Heidelberg, 1991), 249–68, at 252–3.
[31] Hinton, *Gold and Gilt, Pots and Pins*, 100.
[32] Webster, *The Franks Casket*, 38.

to Latin and back again also serves to embed the Latin within the Old English and the Roman within the runic. As was the case with Ruthwell, or with Bede's description of Heavenfield and Gregory's meeting with the Angle boys, the language and alphabets suggest a complex layering of time, voice, geographies and peoples. An event from Rome's history is told in Old English, the words identifying the Jewish city of Jerusalem are written in Latin, but its inhabitants are identified in Old English. Certainly Jewish history disappears here beneath both the Latin and the Roman, just as the city and its temple 'disappeared' into the world of Rome, but what happens to the Jews is more complex. Here *affitatores* is a corrupt form of the Latin *habitatores*, but written in runes, transforming the inhabitants of Jerusalem into a people that is both Roman (language) and 'Anglo-Saxon' or 'Germanic' (alphabet), yet not quite either. The inscription draws attention to transformation or metamorphosis (as did the inscription on the front of the casket, though a transformation of a different sort), and furthers the Anglo-Saxons' self-identification with the Israelites. At lower left the word *dom* (judgement) is carved next to a scene of judgement, and at lower right the word *gisl* (hostage) next to a scene of a figure or figures being led away. A figure seated beneath the throne at left holds out a cup in a gesture reminiscent of that of Weland on the front of the casket.

On the left side of the casket an inscription reading 'romwalus and reumwalus twœgen gbroþær afœddæ hiæ wylif in romæcæstri oþlæ unneg' (Romulus and Remus, two brothers, a she-wolf nourished them in Rome, far from their native land) surrounds a scene of the twins suckled by a she-wolf while a second wolf and four soldiers look on. In this case, the words 'a she-wolf nourished in Rome' are inscribed upside down, so that the viewer/reader must turn the casket to make sense of them, physically interacting with it, as she or he was made to interact with the Ruthwell Cross. The upside-down words draw attention to the city of Rome, but it is possible that their inversion also refers to the darker side of the myth, to the fact that the foundation of the city involved the murder of Remus by Romulus and Romulus's subsequent rape of the Sabine women. In its allusions to murder and rape, the panel would then have connections with the scene of Weland on the front of the casket. (And of course the fact that Romulus and Remus were exiled as infants to hide them from an evil king has parallels with the story of Christ.) There is no cup in this panel, but the twins do drink from the body of the wolf, a living creature, and the upside-down inscription helps to emphasize this aspect of the panel as well.

On the right side of the casket is a mysterious scene believed to derive from Germanic legend. The surrounding inscription is in alliterative verse and encrypted.[33] It reads:

---

[33] See Webster, *The Franks Casket*, 14 for details of the verse's incryption.

Her Hos sitiþ     on harmherga
agl[·] drigiþ     swa hiræ Ertae gisgraf
sarden sorga     and sefa torna

The conventional translation reads: 'Here Hos sits on the sorrow mound; she suffers distress as Ertae had imposed it upon her, a wretched den [?wood] of sorrows and torments of mind.'[34] Waxenberger, however, translates very differently: 'Listen/here, the company presides over the harmful burial place/mound (always). The awesome opponent/ferocious fighter always performs/acts/endures. Anger has left Ertae assigned/decreed by means of the horse distress, the grave of sorrow, and the sad mood.' Although it is brought out particularly acutely in Waxenberger's translation, either reading provides an echo of the inscription on the front of the casket in its tone of sadness and change in fortune, and imagery of death. If Waxenberger's reading is correct, the eternal performance or endurance of the ferocious fighter calls to mind the awesome opponent, the whale, who continues to perform and endure as casket.

Within the panel the words *risci* (rushes or reeds), *wudu* (wood) and *bita* (biter) are inscribed above the horse's back, beneath its feet and in front of its head respectively. While the scene cannot be connected to any known text or story, the creature sitting on the mound at left, its muzzle bound by a serpent, is presumably Hos. Another figure appears to be contained within a burial mound between the horse and the hooded figure with the staff. The cup above the mound, whatever its function in the narrative, provides a link with the two scenes on the front of the casket. The three cloaked figures at right are a mystery.

There are many ways in which the visual narratives of these panels might be understood as fitting together. Scholars have identified themes of life and death, danger and redemption, defence and victory, exile and return, civilization and wilderness, treasure, and evil vs. heroism running throughout them.[35] I have drawn attention to the presence of the cup as container and the body of the she-wolf as container of nourishment because they relate directly to the function, material and main inscription of the casket, and thus the primary concerns of this chapter – voice and materiality. Although not spoken in the first person, the inscription on the front of the Franks Casket draws our attention to the fact that the casket was once a living creature and as such the object itself negotiates the space between the living and the dead, the past and the present, the past of the stories depicted and the here and now of the casket as it was originally used. If it held a relic or a gospel book, the focus it places on living matter would be particularly appropriate as both relics and sacred books – as

---

[34] Unpublished paper delivered at the 13th conference of the International Society of Anglo-Saxonists, St John's, Newfoundland, July 2009.
[35] See above note 23.

well as the words contained within them – were living things, or at least things that existed somewhere in a liminal state between life and death.

Much has been made of the primary inscription's riddling nature, but the real riddle is not in the verses themselves but in the materiality of the casket and its transformation from one type of living creature to another. It was once a whale and, even as a box, it still is. Together with the box itself, the inscription tells the story of that transformation from the lively fish to the sad and stranded whale to bone to box. If it is a riddle, it is perhaps closer to the sort of riddle posed by the Ruthwell Cross, which asks the viewer/reader to put together elements of a story to arrive at a larger truth, than to the textual riddles of Aldhelm or the Exeter Book. As was the case with the Ruthwell poem, the inscription names the object in two different forms (gallows and *rod* at Ruthwell; threatening whale and mastered bone on the casket) and asks the reader to meditate on the movement from the one to the other. If Ruthwell asks the viewer not to name what it is but to consider what its name means,[36] the Franks Casket can be understood as asking the viewer to do the same. The two related but very different scenes on the front of the casket might provide a visual clue that the casket itself has two meanings and two natures. The inscription might also be understood then as functioning as a warning. In the *Physiologus* tradition, which was known to the Anglo-Saxons, the whale was associated with trickery, deceit and terror. While it may have been transformed into a container for something precious, might the way in which the inscription calls our attention to the frightening or powerful nature of the living whale have provided a warning against tampering with the casket and its contents? Bone was living material; might it have embodied the threat of a return to its former nature? If this was the case, then the inscription on the front of the casket, especially if read alongside the battle scene on the lid, takes on a defensive function, protecting the contents of the casket and warning anyone attempting to tamper with them that all might not be as it seems at first glance. On the other hand, the whale was also well known from the biblical story of Jonah and the whale, a typological reference to the Resurrection of Christ. Such a reference would be fitting if the casket was indeed meant to hold a relic or a religious book, both of which were ordinary living material transformed into something eternal and sacred. It would also underscore the nature of a box, which is to reveal as well as conceal, two themes that are also at the heart of the narrative scenes the inscription surrounds. Moreover, both the voice of the inscription and the runic script in which it is carved speak of the past. Runes, as noted above, were an archaic, historicizing form of script, and in providing an eye-witness account of the powerful living whale transformed into a sad and stranded creature, the Old English

---

[36] See further Karkov, 'Naming and Renaming'.

verses speak of the past of the object, as the visual narratives of the casket speak of the historic and heroic pasts of the maker(s) and recipient(s) of the casket, as well as of its contents.

## OBJECT, VOICE AND SELF

Very different in tone and nature are the inscriptions on the Coppergate helmet, the St Ninian's Isle chapes and the Sutton, Isle of Ely, disc brooch (figs. 42–44), each an object made for a particular individual (two of them named) and for use within a secular context. Each also invokes the voice and authority of its owner, albeit in slightly different ways and to differing ends. Thomas Bredehoft has studied the first-person inscriptions on Anglo-Saxon objects in terms of the ways in which they were made accessible through the spoken word within fundamentally textual communities.[37] Most if not all such inscriptions, he believes, were meant to be read aloud so that the object took on the voice of the reader (who did not necessarily have to be the owner of the object). Given the number of such inscriptions that survive,[38] it is beyond doubt that the Anglo-Saxons were quite familiar with speaking objects and knew that their inscriptions said something, but it does not necessarily follow that communal access to the texts via the spoken word was what gave them their efficacy and power. Was it actually necessary for the inscription to be read out loud by someone lending his or her voice to the object? Might the power inherent in the statement of ownership or curse rather have been increased if the object itself was seen as having its own voice, even if the words it 'spoke' might not have been comprehensible to all? A verbal equivalent to the life objects such as the Sutton Hoo regalia took on through the powerful beasts and serpents that crawled across them, but one that granted the object even more of a vestige of subjectivity.

The Coppergate helmet from York (fig. 42) was made in the north of England in the second half of the eighth century. Although not as ornate or well made as the more famous Sutton Hoo helmet or those that were dismantled to form part of the Staffordshire hoard, it is by default a luxury item that would have been made for and worn by an elite warrior, as only the elite could afford armour. The helmet itself is made of iron, with a chain-mail curtain protecting the back of the neck, and copper-alloy fittings which run over the eyebrows and form a cross that runs from nasal to nape and ear to ear. The design shows the influence of both late Roman *Spangelhelmen* and Swedish helmets from Vendel and Valsgärde, Uppland

---

[37] Bredehoft, 'First-Person Inscriptions and Literacy in Anglo-Saxon England'.
[38] Bredehoft lists twenty-four inscriptions: 'First-Person Inscriptions and Literacy in Anglo Saxon England', 104–5.

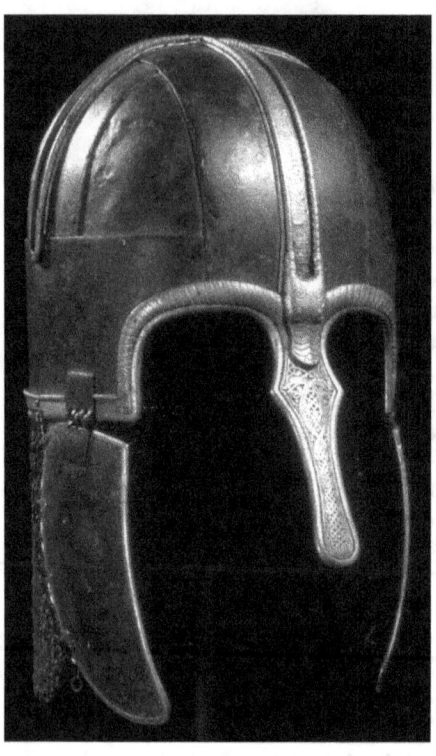

FIG. 42.
COPPERGATE
HELMET

(which are themselves based on the Roman *Spangelhelm*).[39] The decoration is first and foremost apotropaic, its purpose to protect the warrior Oshere for whom it was made. The nasal is protected by two intertwined beasts that grip each other with their forelegs and bite down on each other's lappets. The arches of the eyebrows are formed by two serpents whose toothy heads rest next to the outer corners of the eyes. The band that stretches over the top of the head from nasal to nape begins with a large serpent's head that appears to bite down on the tails of the serpents that cover the eyebrows. Its tail ends in two confronted serpents baring their teeth. As long as these beasts remain intact so, presumably, does the head of the warrior. The imagery of threatening toothy beasts can be paralleled on numerous items from both the Germanic and Insular traditions.[40] The repoussé inscription contained within the body of the serpent offers a protective Christian counterpart to the beast imagery, both in its words and in the sign of the cross formed by it and the secondary inscription. The primary inscription reads retrograde from front to back 'INNOMINE · DNI · NOSTRI · IHV · SCS · SPS · D · ET · OMNIBUS · DECEMUS · AMEN · OSHERE· XPI' (In the name of our Lord Jesus, the Holy Spirit, God and with [or to] all we pray. Amen. Oshere. Christ). The two sections of the crossing band repeat the primary inscription and are also retrograde. From the crown of the head to the left ear the inscription reads 'INNOMINE · DNI · NOSTRI · IHV · SCS · SPS', and from the crown to the right ear 'OMNIBUS · D[ECEMUS] · AMEN · OSHERE'.

The prayer is written in Oshere's voice and requests protection from God presumably during battle. Its doubling was probably intended to increase its ability to protect, both in its repetition, a common device of charms,[41] and in its forming the sign of the cross, a sign associated

---

[39] See further Sonia A. O'Conner's comments in Dominic Tweddle, ed., *The Anglian Helmet from Coppergate*, Archaeology of York: The Small Finds 17/8 (London, 1992), 1082–132.
[40] See further O'Conner in Tweddle, *The Anglian Helmet from Coppergate*, 1132–65, and discussion of the St Ninian's Isle chapes below.
[41] On doubling, repetition and other verbal formulae in charms see Karen L. Jolly, *Popular Religion in Late Anglo-Saxon England: Elf Charms in Context* (Chapel Hill, NC, 1996), 117–68.

historically with protection in battle for figures such as King Oswald (d. 642) and the Emperor Constantine.[42] The doubling of the prayer also mirrors the doubling of the animal ornament, the two creatures contained in the nasal and the doubling of the serpents over the brows and at the end of the primary inscription. The way the plates of the secondary inscription are arranged would require the reader, whether a heavenly reader looking down from above or perhaps the soul of Oshere reading from below, to make the sign of the cross in moving the eyes from front to back then from the centre to the left ear, and finally from the centre to the right ear.

Elizabeth Okasha has identified the closest parallels for the text of the prayer in early Irish liturgical texts, especially the *Gloria in excelsis* in the late seventh-century Antiphonary of Bangor (Milan, Biblioteca Ambrosiana MS C.5, fol. 33r).[43] The inscription is in Anglo-Saxon capitals of the type found in Insular manuscripts of the early eighth century.[44] The letters themselves are neatly formed and consistent, suggesting that the prayer was written out by a scribe before being copied onto the metal strip. The fitting of the inscription so that the prayer is retrograde, however, presents a problem. It has been assumed that this is an error, that the plate was attached to the helmet upside down, that it was the incised rather than the repoussé side that should have been uppermost.[45] This is of course possible, especially if whoever was responsible for the helmet's assembly was unable to read. It is also possible that Oshere himself was either not literate in Latin, and so did not notice the mistake or that it was simply the presence of the cruciform prayer and not its arrangement that mattered. It is also possible, however, that the 'reader' was intended to be the speaker, the soul or spirit of Oshere, rather than any external viewer, even a heavenly one, and that the arrangement suggested a prayer directed from Oshere – it is after all Oshere who is doing the praying in the inscription – to Christ and God during battle. A loose parallel might be provided by the cross-incised panel added to the inner lid of the coffin of St Cuthbert. Admittedly the shape of the cross is the same whether viewed from above or below, but presumably it was added to the inside of the coffin primarily for its protective presence over the body of Cuthbert as it would not have been visible, to human eyes anyway, from outside the coffin.

Okasha also questioned the arrangement of the name of Christ, which places the XPI of Christ at the end of the prayer rather than directly after the IHV of Jesus, wondering whether it was simply a mistake or intentional. Given the formulaic nature of the prayer and the care taken

---

[42] On Constantine and Anglo-Saxon England see especially Wood, 'Constantinian Crosses in Northumbria'.
[43] In Tweddle, *The Anglian Helmet from Coppergate*, 1014.
[44] See further Michelle P. Brown in *The Making of England*, ed. Webster and Backhouse, 60–2.
[45] Okasha in Tweddle, *The Anglian Helmet from Coppergate*, 1013.

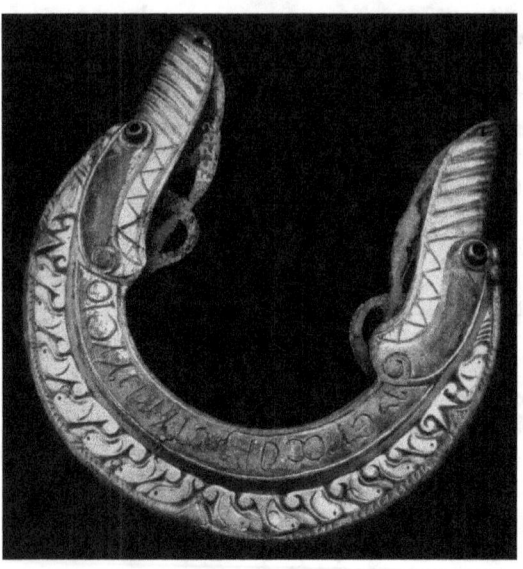

FIG. 43.
ST NINIAN'S
ISLE CHAPE

by the scribe who wrote it out, the latter explanation seems most likely, a way perhaps of suggesting the existence of Christ beyond earthly time and order, as the A text of the Anglo-Saxon Chronicle frames its opening with an invocation of Christ, or Alfred's genealogy is traced back beyond Adam to an origin in Christ[46] or, perhaps, as the cruciform inscription itself would have been set physically between Christ's human descendant Oshere and the eternal Christ who awaited him in heaven. Obviously it is speculative at best to imagine that anything so complex was envisaged, and what may be at work here is a simple protective doubling formula mirroring the doubling of the text of the prayer and of the beasts.

A similar, albeit simpler, doubling is evident on one of a pair of late eighth-century silver-gilt chapes from the St Ninian's Isle hoard (fig. 43). There is some question as to whether the chapes are Anglo-Saxon or Pictish, with most recent opinion identifying them as Pictish;[47] nevertheless, even if Pictish, they show a degree of Anglo-Saxon influence and are of a type with the other objects discussed in this chapter. Indeed, while there is no exact parallel for the chapes, the crest of the Coppergate helmet is frequently cited as providing a close comparison.

A chape is a decorative fitting for a sword scabbard and so, like the York helmet, must be interpreted within the context of battle even if, in the end, they embellished only ceremonial scabbards. While each chape takes the form of a double-headed creature, they are different from each other, and the two sides of each chape are also treated differently. The body of one is decorated with key, zig-zag, spiral and interlace patterns – primarily geometric on one side and zoomorphic on the other – and the beast heads at both ends and on both sides bite on their tongues. The second chape bears an inscription divided between its two sides. On the front the heads of the beasts bite tiny fish, while on the back the teeth are simply clenched. The inscription is in cursive minuscule and reads 'IN

---

[46] D. Dumville and S. Keynes, *The Anglo-Saxon Chronicle A Collaborative Edition*, vol. 3, *MS A*, ed. J. M. Bately (Cambridge, 1986), 45–6.
[47] George Henderson and Isabel Henderson, *The Art of the Picts: Sculpture and Metalwork in Early Medieval Scotland* (New York, 2004), 113; see also Webster and Backhouse, eds., *The Making of England*, 223–4; Susan Youngs, ed., *'The Work of Angels': Masterpieces of Celtic Metalwork, 6th–9th Centuries AD*, ed. (London, 1989), 110.

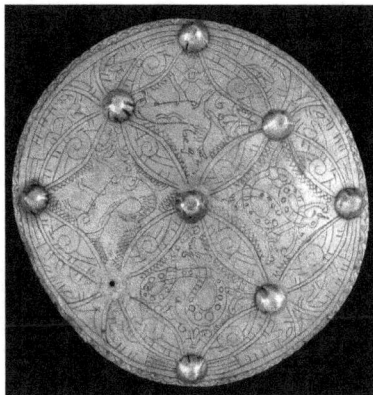 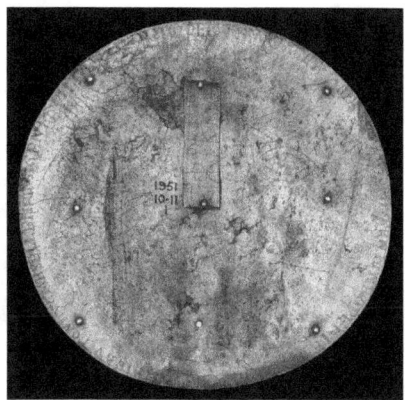

NOMINE DS (front), RES AD FILI SPUS SCIO'. It can be translated as 'In the name of God, property of the son of the Holy Spirit'.

FIG. 44, a and b. SUTTON, ISLE OF ELY, BROOCH

Like the inscription of the York helmet, the words invoke divine protection, but rather than offering a prayer they proclaim ownership in an interesting way. Both the scabbard and presumably the sword it held might be understood as the property of the son of the Holy Spirit along with their bearer. They are the property of Christ and whoever steals or damages the sword, or wounds or kills its owner, goes against God. Yet we might also understand that, as a descendant of Christ, the sword's owner is also a 'son' of the Holy Spirit, a warrior for Christ perhaps, so the formula quite simply proclaims the sword to be his property although also invoking the wrath of God against anyone who might steal it. The division of the inscription might be understood as reflecting its dual function, with the 'In the name of God' suggesting protection for the sword's bearer and the power for or under which he fights, and the 'property of the Holy Spirit' proclaiming ownership and hence a warning against assault on either or both. While the wording and division of the inscription open it out to interesting alternative readings, it is ultimately of a type with the curses and anathema found on other objects and also in manuscripts from across the Anglo-Saxon era. In proclaiming ownership and authority they invoke the power of a self not necessarily present and able to protect his or her possession.

The Sutton, Isle of Ely, disc brooch (fig. 44), an Anglo-Scandinavian object from the first half of the eleventh century, is a more standard example of this type of inscription. The brooch is made of hammered silver and decorated with a pattern of intersecting circles containing zoomorphic and foliate ornament in an Anglo-Saxon version of the Scandinavian Ringerike and Urnes styles.[48] It is of sub-standard workmanship, but also relatively

---

[48] On Scandinavian art styles see David M. Wilson and Ole Klindt-Jensen, *Viking Art* (London, 1966).

large (14.9 x 6.4 centimetres) suggesting that it was made to project some sort of perceived status. There are two inscriptions on the back of the brooch: one, on a strip that once held the pin and catchplate, consists of seven pseudo-runic characters and may have been meant to evoke some sort of magic or protective formula; the main inscription is in verse and inscribed around the rim of the brooch. It is both lengthy and literate and is made up of a single alliterative line followed by two rhyming couplets:

+AEDƷEN ME AGE HYO DRIHTEN
DRIHTEN HINE AƷERIE ÐE ME HIRE ÆTFERIE
BUTON HYO ME SELLE HIRE AGENES ƷILLES

(+Ædwen owns me, may the Lord own her. May the Lord curse him who takes me from her, unless she gives me of her own free will.)

David Hinton has suggested that Ædwen's having felt so strongly about the possible loss of a brooch of such poor quality might be evidence of how 'unprotected' some women might have felt,[49] but the formula used here (a statement of ownership followed by a curse) was a well-known one found in wills and charters of the period, and not just limited to objects or property owned by women.[50] More interesting for present purposes is the fact that the brooch speaks, declaring both that it is owned by Ædwen and that only she has the right to gift it, and calling down a curse on anyone who takes it from her or might later come to own it under suspicious circumstances. Unlike the inscriptions discussed so far, this inscription was not intended to be seen by the public. Unless the brooch was stolen, the inscription would be known and seen only by Ædwen herself. It is possible that the inscription functioned simply to reassure Ædwen that her property was protected;[51] nevertheless, its voice still grants power to the object. The inscription's power as a curse thus relies to a certain extent on her person not being present (otherwise the curse could not have been seen), and to a degree of agency being transferred to the object. It must be understood as having the power to convey threat if the inscription was to be at all effective. The popularity of such curses and warnings in late Anglo-Saxon England implies that there was a widespread acceptance of their efficacy within the culture.

The inscription and voice of the Brussels Reliquary Cross (fig. 45) are rather more complex in language and function. The Brussels Reliquary Cross is most often studied alongside the Ruthwell Cross and *The Dream*

---

[49] Hinton, *Gold and Gilt, Pots and Pins*, 145.
[50] Hinton, *Gold and Gilt, Pots and Pins*, 145; Leslie Webster, 'The Brussels Cross', in *The Golden Age of Anglo-Saxon Art 966–1066*, ed. Janet Backhouse, D. H. Turner and Leslie Webster (London, 1984), 90–92 at 92; Bredehoft, 'First-Person Inscriptions and Literacy in Anglo-Saxon England'.
[51] As suggested by Bredehoft, 'First Person Inscriptions and Literacy in Anglo-Saxon England', 108.

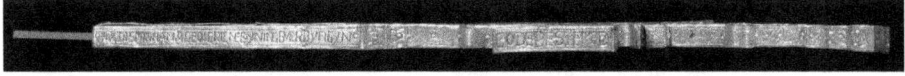

FIG. 45.
THE BRUSSELS
RELIQUARY CROSS

*of the Rood* because its verse inscription includes lines that are also found in the Ruthwell and *Dream* poems, but the Brussels Cross does in fact contain three different types of inscription, setting it apart from both poems and complicating the voices with which it speaks. The date of the cross cannot be established with any certainty, but stylistic, epigraphic and linguistic evidence all point to a date in the early eleventh century.

The decoration that originally covered the front of the cross has been lost, most likely in 1793 when it is documented as having been stripped of its jewels and broken in two by French soldiers under the leadership of Charles François Dumouriez. A secondary inscription on the front of the cross reads:

DIREPTA 7MA/MARTII, PUBLICAE VENERATIONI
RESTITUTA 29NA 7BRIS 1793

(Looted 7 March, restored to public veneration 29 September 1793)

The damage has revealed the relic cavity, a rectangular vertical slot 7 centimetres long, crossed at right angles by a shallower slot about 14 centimetres long, which is said to have once contained a relic of the True Cross.[52] In its original state, the front almost certainly bore a figure of the

---

[52] The wooden core of the cross has sometimes been misidentified as the relic itself, rather than the container for it (William O. Stevens, 'The Cross in the Life and Literature of the Anglo-Saxons', in *The Anglo-Saxon Cross*, ed. Thomas D. Hill and Robert T. Farrell (Hamden, CT, 1977), 1–112 at 16; S. T. R.O. d'Ardenne, 'The Old English Inscription on the Brussels Cross', *English Studies* 21 (1939), 145–64, 271–2, at 145). In 1891 H. Logeman ('L'inscription anglo-saxonne du reliquaire de la Vraie Croix au trésor de l'église des SS. Michel-et-Gudule à Bruxelles', *Mémoires couronnés et autres mémoires de l'Academie Royale de Belgique* 45.8 (1891), 1–31, at 5) described two relic fragments lying one against the other in the relic cavity. A. Hensen ('Het Egmonder Kruis', *Het Gildeboek* 8 (1925), 92–7, at 92) claimed to have measured the actual relic in 1925, giving measurements of 14 cm x 7 cm, and 2 cm x ½ cm, but in 1939, d'Ardenne (145–6) reported that he could not find the relic. According to tradition the Brussels Cross was reputed to contain the largest extant fragment(s) of the True Cross either in the world (Logeman, 5; Hensen, 92), or in the West (d'Ardenne, n. 6). Some scholars have speculated that the relic may have been the fragment of the True Cross sent to King Alfred by Pope Marinus in 883 or 885, as recorded in the Anglo-Saxon Chronicle and Asser's *Life of Alfred*. D'Ardenne (155) believed Alfred's relic to be identical with the relic described by Hincmar as having been thrown in the mud during a riot and rescued by Anglo-Saxon pilgrims in Rome in 864. He also identified it with one of the relics given to Westminster Abbey by Edward the Confessor in a spurious charter of 1066 (S 1043), noting that one relic remained in the abbey until the Dissolution, but that the other vanished; it was this relic, he proposed, that eventually ended up in Brussels (155–6). He noted further (158) that there is a gap in the charter's list of the original owners of the relic between Edgar and Edward, and thought it possible that it was at this time that it passed into the possession of the brothers named in the inscription. Unfortunately, several other houses claimed possession of Alfred's relic. In his history of Glastonbury, William of Malmesbury claims

crucified Christ, quite possibly accompanied by figures of the Virgin and St John the evangelist.

The sides and back of the cross are covered with silver sheeting which is torn in places and missing several fragments. Engraved within gilded roundels on the back of the cross are, at centre, the Agnus Dei carrying a stepped cross and book and facing the inscribed words 'AGNV/SDI' with four zooanthropomorphic book-holding evangelist symbols in the terminals of the cross arms. The inscription '+DRAHMAL MEƷoRHTE' (+Drahmal made me) appears divided symmetrically across the arms of the cross. The use of silver to adorn the cross was a well-established convention going back to the earliest descriptions of the relic preserved in Jerusalem.[53] Ælfric's description of the adorning of the True Cross by the Empress Helena in his homily for the Invention of the Cross accords with both the earlier accounts and the decorative treatment of the Brussels Cross.

> Þa wearð seo cwen micclum gegladod. þæt heo moste ðone maðm on moldan findan. and siððan ðurh tacnum swutelunge oncnawan; Arærde ða cyrcan on ðære cwealmstowe þær seo rod on læg. þam leofan drihtne. and bewand ænne dæl ðære halgan rode mid hwitum seolfre. and hi ðær gesette. and ðone oðerne dæl. lædde to hire suna.[54]

> (Then the queen was much gladdened that she was able to find the treasure in the earth, and afterwards through signs to know its manifestation. Then she raised a church to the dear Lord on the place of execution where the rood lay, and wound one part of the holy rood with white silver, and set it there, and took the other part to her son.)

The primary inscriptions on the Brussels reliquary cross are located on silver sheeting attached to the sides of the cross, and are interspersed with four sections of Ringerike style interlace and scroll decoration stylistically comparable to the decoration on the Sutton, Isle of Ely brooch made in the first half of the eleventh century.[55] The inscription begins on the lower right edge of the cross (as viewed from the back), and reads up the right side of the shaft, across the top, and down the left side.

---

that Glastonbury was given a piece of the relic, although this claim is not supported by other sources. The possible dedication of Shaftesbury Abbey to 'the Holy Cross and St Edward' has been taken to suggest that it too may have owned a piece of the cross (Dorothy Whitelock, *Anglo-Saxon Wills* (Cambridge, 1930), 58–9 and 169–70; Foot, *Veiled Women*, vol. 2, 174–5).

[53] In the early fifth century, for example, the pilgrim Egeria described the relic as encased in silver-gilt: 'loculus argenteus dearatus, in quo est lignum sanctae crucis.' See A. Franceschini and R. Weber, eds, *Itinerarium Egeriae*, CCSL 175 (Turnhout, 1958), 37.

[54] *Ælfric's Catholic Homilies the Second Series*, ed. Malcolm Godden, vol. 1 (Text), EETS ss 5 (Oxford, 1979), 175.

[55] Webster, 'The Brussels Cross', 92.

+ROD IS MIN NAMA GEO IC RICNE CẏNING BÆR
BẏFIGẏNDE BLODE BESTEMED: ÞAS RODE hET ÆÞLMÆR
ⱵẏRICAN 7 AÐELⱵOLD HYS BERoþo[r] CRIstE TO LoFE
FoR ÆLFRICES sAVLE hYRA BERoþoR:

(Cross is my name: once I bore the mighty King, trembling and drenched with blood. This cross Æthelmær, and Æthelwold his brother, ordered to be made for the glory of Christ [and] for the soul of Ælfric their brother.)

Because of the number of individuals named in the inscription it has been especially tempting to try to identify them, though that has proved impossible to date. The language is late West Saxon with one Anglian form (*bestēmed*), and the Æthel- element in the names of the two donors has been taken to indicate an affiliation with the West Saxon royal house,[56] although Æthel- names are far too common for such a connection to be convincing. Cook identified the three brothers as Alfricus, Agelmarus and Agelwardus, three of the six brothers of Eadric Streona mentioned by John of Worcester under the year 1007,[57] but this is linguistically impossible. D'Ardenne, followed by Dickins and Ross, suggested that it might be possible to identify Æthelmær as the son of Æthelwold the chronicler and patron of Ælfric of Eynsham, but did not speculate on the identity of either Æthelwold or their brother, Ælfric.[58] Logeman suggested that the three might have been spiritual rather than biological brothers.[59] The name of the cross's maker, Drahmal, could be either Norse or Continental Germanic.[60]

The inscriptions naming the maker and patrons of the cross both follow well-established formulae. The Drahmal inscription may be compared with that of the Alfred Jewel '+Aelfred mec heht gewyrcan' (Alfred ordered me to be made),[61] a late ninth- or early tenth-century knife from Sittingbourne inscribed on one side '+Sgebereht me ah' (Sigebereht owns me), and on the other '+Biorhtelm me porte' (Biorhtelm made me), or the Ottonian silver Bernward Cross (1007–22) now in the Cathedral and Diocesan Museum, Hildesheim (inv. nr. DS6). The latter bears the inscription 'Bernvvardus presvl fecit hoc' (Bishop Bernward made this) on the upper

---

[56] D'Ardenne, 'The Old English Inscription on the Brussels Cross', 158–9; R. H. M. Dolley, 'The Nummular Brooch from Sulgrave', in *England before the Conquest*, ed. Peter Clemoes and Kathleen Hughes (Cambridge, 1971), 333–49, at 337–8 and 342, at 338.
[57] A. S. Cook, 'The Date of the Old English Inscription on the Brussels Cross', *Modern Language Review* 10 (1915), 157–61 at 157–9. 'Cujus fratres extiterunt Brihtricus, Ælfricus, Goda, Ægelwinus, Ægilwarus, Ægelmerus', John of Worcester, *Florentii Wigorniensis monachi chronicon ex chronicis*, ed. B. Thorpe, 2 vols (London, 1848), vol. 1, 160.
[58] D'Ardenne, 'The Old English Inscription on the Brussels Cross', 159; B. Dickins and A. S. C. Ross, eds., *The Dream of the Rood* (London, 1934), 15.
[59] Logeman, 'L'inscription anglo-saxonne du reliquaire de la Vraie Croix', 17.
[60] Elizabeth Okasha, *A Hand-list of Anglo-Saxon Non-Runic Inscriptions* (Cambridge, 1971), 57, 154.
[61] See below pp. 214–18.

arm of its back. Richard Gameson has compared the primary inscription with that on the front of the Cross of Gisela, Queen of Hungary, made in Regensburg c. 1006: 'Behold the salvation of life through which death died. Wherefore, in beseeching the health of her mother's soul, Queen Gisela ordered this cross to be made. If anyone shall remove this hence, may he be damned with eternal death.'[62] Within Anglo-Saxon England it may also be compared with the inscription on a fragmentary tenth-century cross shaft at Urswick, Lancashire: '+Tunwini setæ æfter Toroʒtredæ bekun æfter his bæurnæ gebidæs þer saulæ (Tunwine raised this cross in memory of his lord [or son] Torhtred. Pray for his soul),[63] or with what can be deciphered of the fragmentary memorial inscription on the Bewcastle Cross: 'Þis sigbecn … gebidaþ þær sawle' (This victory beacon … pray for the soul).

The poetic inscription may also be understood as traditional in so far as it is clearly related to the verses inscribed on the Ruthwell Cross and lines 48–9 of *The Dream of the Rood*. The exact relationship between the three texts, while arousing much speculation, remains uncertain. In 1844, Kemble suggested that *The Dream of the Rood* could have been expanded from an inscription such as that on the Ruthwell Cross (or the Brussels Cross), although ultimately he preferred to see the latter as abbreviated selections from the Vercelli poem,[64] and this has been the conclusion of a number of later scholars.[65] Others have preferred to see the three texts as related in a more indirect way. Dickins and Ross, for example, saw the Brussels inscription as 'reminiscent' of *The Dream of the Rood*,[66] while d'Ardenne suggested that both the Brussels and Ruthwell inscriptions 'draw on phrases common to traditional verse language concerning the Holy Rood, and are doubtless only chance survivors of a body of verse on this subject now lost'.[67] Leslie Webster describes the Brussels inscription as an allusion to *The Dream of the Rood*, but also implies a much closer identification of the Ruthwell and Dream poems, stating that *The Dream of the Rood* is 'known in a manuscript version and from a runic text carved on the eighth-century stone cross at Ruthwell'.[68]

The Brussels Cross is distinctly Anglo-Saxon in its combination of

---

[62] Richard Gameson, *The Role of Art in the Late Anglo-Saxon Church* (Oxford, 1995), 76.
[63] Bailey and Cramp, *Cumberland, Westmorland and Lancashire North-of-the-Sands*, 2, Urswick 1.
[64] J. M. Kemble, 'Additional Observations on the Runic Obelisk at Ruthwell, the Poem of the *Dream of the Holy Rood*, and a Runic Copper Dish Found at Chertsey', *Archaeologia* 30 (1844), 31–46 at 38.
[65] A. S. Cook, 'The Date of the Ruthwell and Bewcastle Crosses', *Transactions of the Connecticut Academy of Arts and Sciences* (1912), 247–9; Cook, 'The Date of the Old English Inscription on the Brussels Cross', 157; Gameson, *Role of Art*, 88.
[66] *The Dream of the Rood*, 18.
[67] D'Ardenne, 'The Old English Inscription on the Brussels Cross', 149; see also Stevens, 'The Cross in the Life and Literature of the Anglo-Saxons', 82.
[68] Webster, 'The Brussels Cross', 91.

visual and verbal imagery, and the two elements must be understood as inseparable parts of its meaning, and of the larger cultural discourse in which it participates. The location of the primary inscription makes it unlikely that it would have been read out publicly, although it would certainly have been known to its literate makers and users, and thus have formed an integral part of their experience of the cross as both a functional reliquary and a devotional object. Both the first-person voice of the poetic inscription, and the way in which the reader/viewer must either turn the cross or move around it to put the various pieces of its meaning together unite it with the Ruthwell monument. Being inscribed on a reliquary of the True Cross, however, the Brussels verses would certainly have taken on a reality that we can only speculate might have been achieved at Ruthwell.

The symbolic programme of the cross began with the now lost imagery covering the relic on its front. We know that the front was originally decorated with precious metal and gems, and it is quite possible that the metalwork sheeting was decorated with foliate scrollwork, perhaps containing fruits and animals. Sections of scrollwork decoration still survive on the silver sheeting around the side of the cross. Variations on this type of decoration cover the fronts of the late eighth-century Rupertus Cross, the *c.* 1000 Victoria and Albert reliquary cross (fig. 26), and, of course, the sides of the Ruthwell Cross. The purpose of such imagery was to convey the idea that the cross was not only a means of death but also the eternal life-giving tree of life, the true vine, and an image of paradise. The gemstones may have included garnets, such as are used on the gold and garnet pectoral cross of St Cuthbert or the Staffordshire hoard folded cross, and/or red or purple glass or stone, as is used on the front of the Rupertus Cross. Objects such as these indicate that the combination of gold and red, the one quite literally seen through the other on the Cuthbert and Staffordshire hoard crosses, was a traditional part of Anglo-Saxon visual culture and not just a part of the visionary imagery of *The Dream of the Rood*. The repeated use of patterns of five insets on the Rupertus Cross, five garnets on the Staffordshire hoard cross, and the four semicircular cells that frame the central circular garnet on the Cuthbert cross, demonstrate that the placement of five gems on the beam of the cross in *The Dream of the Rood* was also a material reality.

It is clear from comparison with other surviving tenth- and eleventh-century altar and reliquary crosses that the front almost certainly bore a figure of the crucified Christ, which would likely have been worked in either ivory or metal. The Victoria and Albert Museum crucifix reliquary, for example, supports an ivory figure of Christ. As noted previously, the relic cavity beneath the corpus contains the remains of a finger, but the inclusion of the word *ligni* (wood) in the fragmentary inscription around the side of the cross suggests that its cedar core might have been considered a relic of the True Cross. An eleventh-century altar or processional cross now in the Nationalmuseet, Copenhagen (D894), has a gilt-copper corpus.

The figure is Scandinavian but the cross appears to be Anglo-Saxon. Literary descriptions indicate that three-dimensional Crucifixion groups are likely to have been more common than surviving evidence indicates. King Æthelstan gave a gold and ivory cross (perhaps a Crucifixion) to Chester-le-Street in 934, while Cnut is said to have placed his crown on a crucifix at Winchester. The *Liber Eliensis* records the presence at Ely of a Crucifixion with life-sized figures of Christ, Mary and John worked in silver.[69] Like the Ely Crucifixion, as noted above, the Brussels Cross may have included flanking figures of the Virgin and St John. Similar, though not freestanding, figures survive in both ivory (St Omer, Musée Sandelin, no. 2822) and metalwork (York, The Yorkshire Museum, 632.47). Alternatively, though admittedly much less likely, the Virgin and John (if present) could have been worked in enamel, like the evangelist symbols on the front of the Victoria and Albert Crucifixion reliquary or, perhaps, like the figures of abbess Matilda and duke Otto at the base of the Matilda Cross in Essen Cathedral, made between 973 and 982.

The Crucifixion with Mary and John is a relatively common theme in both Anglo-Saxon manuscript illumination and architectural sculpture in the tenth and eleventh centuries. In such scenes, Mary and John serve multiple functions. Mary is present as a guarantee of Christ's humanity and as an intercessor. John too is an intercessor, but he is also a witness, the evangelist who saw and wrote about the Crucifixion and the wound in Christ's side, the wound which covered the 'trembling' cross with blood. Mary and John are also mourners whose presence lends testimony to both Christ's life and his death on the cross. If Mary and John were a part of the Brussels Cross, they would have served, in their multiple roles, to help draw the viewer into participation in the Crucifixion. Moreover, like the cross itself, Mary and John were closely connected with Christ's body. Mary had borne and held Christ, while John was the favourite disciple who rested his head on Christ's breast. In handling the cross, as one would have to have done to read the inscriptions around its side, Anglo-Saxon men and women would also have held the body of Christ.

But Mary and John need not have been physically present on or beside the Brussels Cross for the viewer to have made these associations. The inscription itself is placed around the sides of the cross, and its location would have forced anyone reading it automatically to place him or herself in the place of Mary or John alongside the cross – as does the Ruthwell poem. As at Ruthwell the line 'I bore the mighty King, trembling and drenched with blood' is placed on the side that would have been to Christ's right, the side of the wound, and the side on which Mary stands gesturing to the wound in several late Anglo-Saxon Crucifixion scenes. To Christ's left, in the position of John, is the memorial inscription naming

---

[69] E. O. Blake, ed. *Liber Eliensis* (London, 1962), vol. 2, 98, 168.

the three brothers with, on the lower part of the shaft, the words 'for the love of Christ and for the soul of Ælfric their brother'. This part of the inscription not only places the reader in the position of witness to both the Crucifixion and the mourning and devotion of the patrons, but also evokes the love of Christ that John, the most beloved of the disciples, embodied.

Both parts of the inscription form an appropriate transition between the imagery and symbolism of the front and those of the back of the cross. On the front of the cross the suffering of Christ was represented (or at least signified), while on the back we see his victory in the form of the triumphal apocalyptic lamb. On this side is represented the moment of the Last Judgement, at which time Ælfric's soul would be united with Christ, presumably helped along by the devotional act of his brothers. The lamb too is a multivalent symbol, representing simultaneously the sacrifice of Christ and the glory and eternal life that sprang from it. The book that he holds is the Book of Life (Revelation 5:1) and the cross is a symbol of both the sacrifice of the Crucifixion and the triumph of the risen Christ. The ultimate source of the image is Revelation 4 and 5, but there is also a reference to John 1:29 in which John the Baptist exclaims 'Behold, there is the lamb of God that takes away the sin of the world'. The Agnus Dei inscription helps to bring out this second meaning, and would immediately have reminded an Anglo-Saxon audience of the Agnus Dei chant, derived from the words of the Baptist: 'Agnus Dei qui tollit peccata mundi, miserere nobis'. The chant was sung by the clergy and people who took part in the mass as the bread was broken – as Christ's body was broken on the cross. The combination of referents invokes an eternal present in which the sacrificial body of Christ is made present in the bread and wine of the mass, participation in which will help to lead to union with the triumphal Christ. The imagery also relates back to the figures of Mary and John (regardless of whether they were present on the cross) in that it was Mary who bore the lamb[70] and John who was understood to be the author of both Revelation and the gospel that recorded the words of John the Baptist.

## WORD, IMAGE, BOOK

While the Brussels Cross, the Franks Casket and the Ruthwell Cross all display lengthy texts, they are primarily objects that have been given very particular voices that relate closely to their specific functions. Manuscripts, on the other hand, being made of animal skin, living matter, were

---

[70] A prayer in the Arundel Psalter, produced in Winchester c. 1060, describes Mary as the one 'qui genuisti agnum purgantem'. London, BL, Arundel 60, fols. 145r–147v. See Barbara Raw, *Trinity and Incarnation in Anglo-Saxon Art and Thought* (Cambridge, 1997), 162.

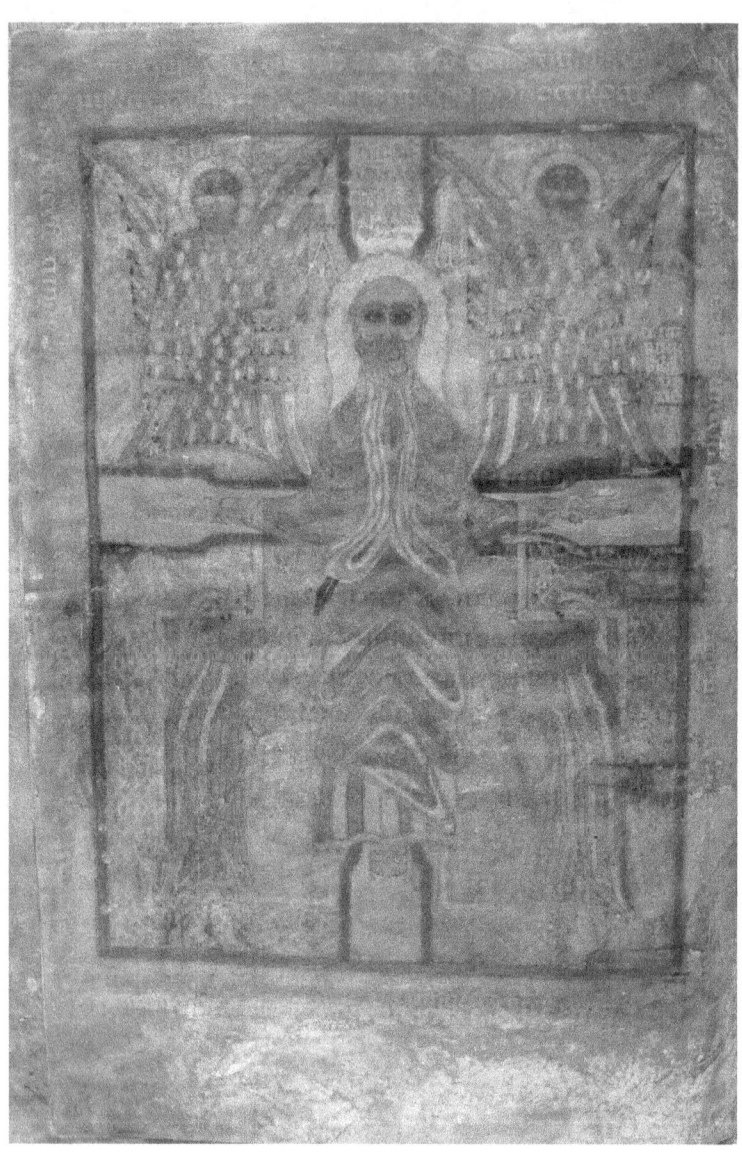

FIG. 46.
DURHAM
GOSPELS,
CRUCIFIXION

acknowledged throughout the medieval period as having life and voice in a way that other objects generally were not. But they also contained words and images that augmented that perception of life, and this is especially true of religious books which carried the living words of Christ and scripture. Manuscripts will be treated in more detail in the following chapter, but there are some ways in which inscriptions gave particular voice to images and books that merit discussion here.

The earliest 'speaking' manuscript image to survive from Anglo-Saxon England is the Crucifixion (fig. 46) on folio 38³ verso of the late seventh- or early eighth-century Durham Gospels (Durham, Cathedral Library, MS A.II.17). The inscriptions that surround the image on all sides compare in their length, complexity and involvement of the reader with those on the Ruthwell Cross and, like the Ruthwell Cross and Franks Casket inscriptions, they ask the reader/viewer to meditate on the meaning of the image before him or her, and on the nature of Christ. The content of the inscriptions has recently been clarified by Jennifer O'Reilly:[71]

> Top: Scito quis et qualis est qui talia cuius titulus cui nulla est inuenta passus p(ro) nobis p(ro)p(ter) hoc culpa.
> Right: Auctorum mortis deicens uitam nostram restituens sit amen conpatiamur.
> Left: Surrexit a mortuis [...] sedet ad dextram d(e)i patris.
> Bottom: Ut nos cum resuscitatos simul et regnare faciat ...
>
> (Know who and what kind he is who suffered such things for us caused by this (and) whose title is 'in whom no sin was found'. Casting down the author of death renewing our life if we suffer along with him. He rose from the dead (and) sits at the right hand of God the Father. So that when we have been restored to life he might make us also to reign with him.)

As at Ruthwell, the inscription requires the viewer to move around the image, albeit this time with the eyes alone, in order to put together its different parts and discern its larger meaning. At Ruthwell, the use of runes made the reader's task that much more difficult, demanding meditation on script, word order and word division. On the Crucifixion page the reader must puzzle out and rearrange the inscription at the top of the page in order to fathom its meaning. Once divided into two parallel clauses it becomes an unambiguous command for the reader to meditate on the two natures of Christ represented visually in the crucified yet living Christ of the miniature: 'Know who and what he is who suffered such things for us. Know who and what he is whose title is "in whom no sin was found."'[72] The Durham Crucifixion page, like the Ruthwell Cross, asks the viewer to participate in the Crucifixion, but it does so slightly differently. At Ruthwell, the image of the Crucifixion itself was kept from the viewer who was asked to envisage it as he or she moved around the cross standing in the place of Mary or John; the Durham Gospel page presents the image, but asks the viewer to identify with and share in the suffering of Christ. Ruthwell also required the reader to meditate on the nature of

---

[71] All transcriptions and translations follow Jennifer O'Reilly, '"Know Who and What He Is": The Context and Inscriptions of the Durham Gospels Crucifixion Image', in *Making and Meaning in Insular Art*, ed. Rachel Moss (Dublin, 2007), 300–16.
[72] See further O'Reilly, '"Know Who and What He Is"', 315–16.

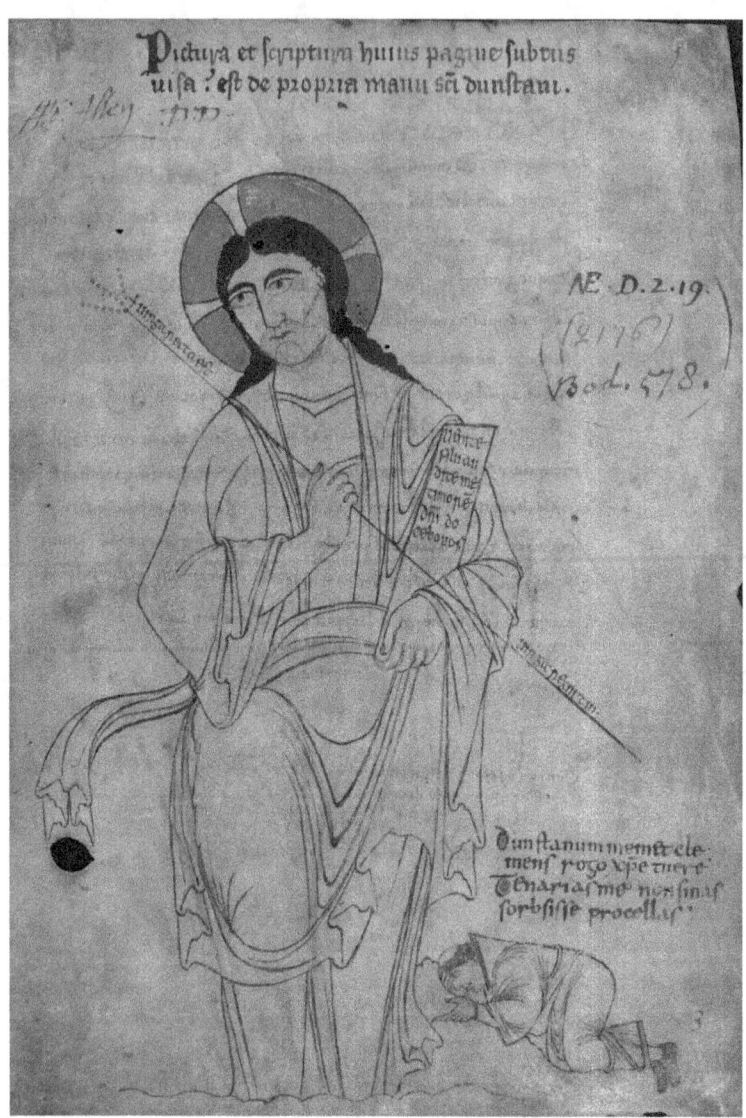

FIG. 47.
PORTRAIT
OF DUNSTAN
WITH CHRIST,
ST DUNSTAN'S
CLASSBOOK.
OXFORD, BODL.
LIB. AUCT. F.4.32,
FOL. 1

the cross, while the Durham page requires meditation on the nature of Christ. Nevertheless, the demands made on the viewer/reader, as well as the miniature's predominantly yellow and red colour scheme, suggestive of gold and blood, indicate that the page ought to be understood, along with the Brussels Reliquary Cross, in terms of the Ruthwell/*Dream of the Rood* tradition.

Just such a personal meditation on Christ is visualized in the tenth-century pictorial frontispiece to St Dunstan's Classbook (Oxford, Bodl.

Lib., MS Auct. F.4.32, fol. 1r), which bears a drawing of Dunstan as a monk prostrate in humility before an imposing figure of Christ (fig. 47). With just a few strokes of the pen the artist has suggested an earthly ground on which Dunstan kneels and above which Christ rises. The way in which Christ's hem overlaps the edge of the hill on which Dunstan kneels has the effect of pushing Christ out at the viewer, suggesting a true visionary experience. The page contains a number of inscriptions, three of which are 'contemporary' with the drawing: the verse distich above the bowed figure of Dunstan, and the words inscribed on the book and above the shaft of the rod held by Christ. Forensic analysis has revealed the chronological layers of text and image on the frontispiece, and has demonstrated that the drawing and inscription on the rod and book came first, and that the inscription above Dunstan and some details of the drawing were added later by a second hand.[73] The inscription above the rod is from Psalm 44.7: '+uirga recta est, uirga regnitiu' ('the sceptre of thy kingdom is a sceptre of uprightness'). The book is inscribed with a line from Psalm 33.12: 'uenite filii audite me timorem domini docebo uos' ('come, children hearken to me: I will teach you the fear of the Lord'). Both texts are closely related to the image of Christ and help to affirm its visual emphasis on a Christ who is both a ruler in heaven and a teacher in this world through the eternal life of Word and word. The phrase from Psalm 44.7, as has been noted,[74] is repeated in the text of the Benedictine Rule, a text that was central to the Benedictine Reform in which Dunstan was actively involved. It thus serves to connect the ideals of the two monastic writers and reformers (Benedict and Dunstan) across the centuries through their shared devotion to Christ and the monastic life – and one might also add their love of books and learning. But the two phrases also relate more specifically to Dunstan as owner and reader of this book. Christ alone is Dunstan's Lord and teacher. This book is a classbook, a commonplace book, a book intimately reflective of Dunstan's own learning. The three sections that would have been part of the manuscript in Dunstan's day include a diverse set of educational texts:[75]

> Section 1 (fols. 1–9): ninth-century Brittany: part of Book 1 of Eutyches's *Ars de verbo* (a Latin grammatical treatise).[76]
> Section 3 (fols. 19–36v): early ninth-century Wales: *Liber Commonei* (the 'Book of Commoneus', also a sort of commonplace book) comprised

---

[73] See Mildred Budny, '"St Dunstan's Classbook" and its Frontispiece: Dunstan's Portrait and Autograph', in *St Dunstan: His Life, Times and Cult*, ed. Ramsay et al., 103–42, at 129–30.
[74] See e.g., Gameson, *Role of Art*, 80.
[75] The present arrangement of the contents is not the original one.
[76] Section 2 (fols. 10–18) is an eleventh-century Anglo-Saxon homily on the finding of the True Cross.

of computistical, alphabetical, exegetical and liturgical texts in Latin and Greek.

Section 4 (fols. 37–47): ninth- to tenth-century Wales: Book 1 of Ovid's *Ars Amatoria*.

In addition to the texts in Latin and Greek there are glosses in Welsh and Breton, and a single tenth-century hand believed to be that of Dunstan himself has made additions to each of the three sections.[77] The same hand is responsible for the distich written above the figure of Dunstan in the drawing, as well as for a distich on the verso of the same folio. The former reads:

> Dunstanum memet clemens rogo spe tuete
> Tenarias me non sinas sorbisse procellas.
>
> (I beg you merciful Christ to watch over me, Dunstan, do not permit the Taenarian storms to overwhelm me.)

The two parts of the distich have their source in very different texts. The first line is based on the prayer of Hrabanus Maurus in the last *Carmen* of *De laudibus sanctae crucis*, while the second has a source in a description of the entrance to the underworld, Taenarum, in Statius's *Thebaid*, II, 32–5.[78] It is echoed in spirit in the distich on the verso of the portrait page, two lines from Eugenius of Toledo's epigram *De bono pacis*:

> Qui cupus infestum semper vitare chelidrum
> Cordis ab affectu pace repelle dolum.
>
> (You who desire always to avoid the hostile fetid serpent, repel deceit from the disposition of the heart of peace.)

Along with the image, the request for protection from hell and damnation in both verses is close in tenor to a number of Anglo-Saxon prayers and other texts, the majority of which are associated with the monastic reform, that request safe passage to heaven for the soul after death.[79]

The inscriptions of the frontispiece have a protective function that corresponds to the imagery but,[80] much like the contents of the manuscript as a whole, they bring together separate texts that have no direct relationship with each other for the edification of the book's owner.

---

[77] See Budny, 'St Dunstan's Classbook', 139–40 for the evidence that the hand is almost certainly that of Dunstan.

[78] Helmut Gneuss, 'Dunstan and Hrabanus Maurus: Zur Hs. Bodleian Auctarium F. 4. 32', *Anglia* 96 (1978), 136–48.

[79] Mary Clayton, 'Delivering the Damned: A Motif in Old English Homiletic Prose', *MÆ* 55 (1986), 92–102; Mary Clayton, *The Cult of the Virgin Mary in Anglo-Saxon England* (Cambridge, 1990), 255; Catherine E. Karkov, 'Judgement and Salvation in the New Minster Liber Vitae', in *Apocryphal Texts and Traditions in Anglo-Saxon England*, ed. Kathryn Powell and Donald Scragg (Cambridge, 2003), 151–63.

[80] Budny ('St Dunstan's Classbook', 135) has described the drawing and distich as echoing depictions of the Harrowing of Hell.

They also function intertextually to make larger thematic and exegetical connections between the texts they quote or make reference to, and to link Dunstan as author to the authors of those texts – most notably Hrabanus Maurus and Benedict. The drawing, with Dunstan prostrate before Christ, makes the connection to Hrabanus even stronger as the *Carmen* from which the first line of the distich is quoted is embedded in an image of Hrabanus prostrate before the cross.

The B text of the *Vita sancti Dunstani* describes Dunstan as having diligently cultivated the art of writing as well as that of drawing or painting (*pingendi*) in his pursuit of knowledge and study of sacred texts.[81] While neither the drawing nor the inscriptions on the book and rod are in Dunstan's own hand, his addition of the distich to the page makes it clear that the image was to be 'read' as a self-portrait. Indeed, as Dunstan added elements of both text and drawing to the page, the final image can be understood as his own work, and the distinction between hands more the concern of modern scholarship and its pursuit of the 'authentic' than of the Anglo-Saxons – or even of much of the premodern world. The inscription written in an archaizing Gothic hand at the top of the page can then be considered quite correct in its assertion that 'Pictura et scriptura huius pagine subtus visa est de propria manu sci dunstani' (The image and writing seen below on this page is by the very hand of Saint Dunstan). The fact that the image is a drawing helps to further the sense of the unity of the page. Both image and inscriptions are made with the same tools, pen and ink, and here are executed in the same colours, and are the result of similar gestures made with the hand.

Outline drawing was an extremely popular form of manuscript illumination in Anglo-Saxon England and its implications for our understanding of the relationship between text and image in the manuscripts in which it is used is worthy of a study in its own right. Much has been made of the influence of the Utrecht Psalter, which arrived in England some time before the year 1000, on the development of drawing as a major art form,[82] but that of earlier Anglo-Saxon manuscripts such as Dunstan's Classbook or the pen and ink initials of early tenth-century manuscripts such as the Tanner Bede (Oxford, Bodleian Library, MS Tanner 10) or the Durham Ritual (Durham Cathedral Library MS A.IV.19) should not be overlooked. The image of Christ king and judge that prefaces a *c.* 1020–30 manuscript of Ælfric's homilies (Cambridge, Trinity College B.15.34, fol. 1; fig. 48) may appear much simpler, albeit neater, than the Dunstan image, but it is in fact equally complex and quite possibly as close

---

[81] 'Hic etiam inter sacra litterarum studia ut in omnibus esset idoneus, artem scribendi ... pariterque pingendi, peritiam diligenter excoluit, atque ut ita dicam omnium rerum utensilium vigil inspector effulsit': W. Stokes, ed., *Memorials of Saint Dunstan, Archbishop of Canterbury* (London, 1874), 20–1.

[82] See e.g., Melanie Holcomb, ed., *Pen and Parchment: Drawing in the Middle Ages* (New Haven, CT, and London, 2009), 10–13.

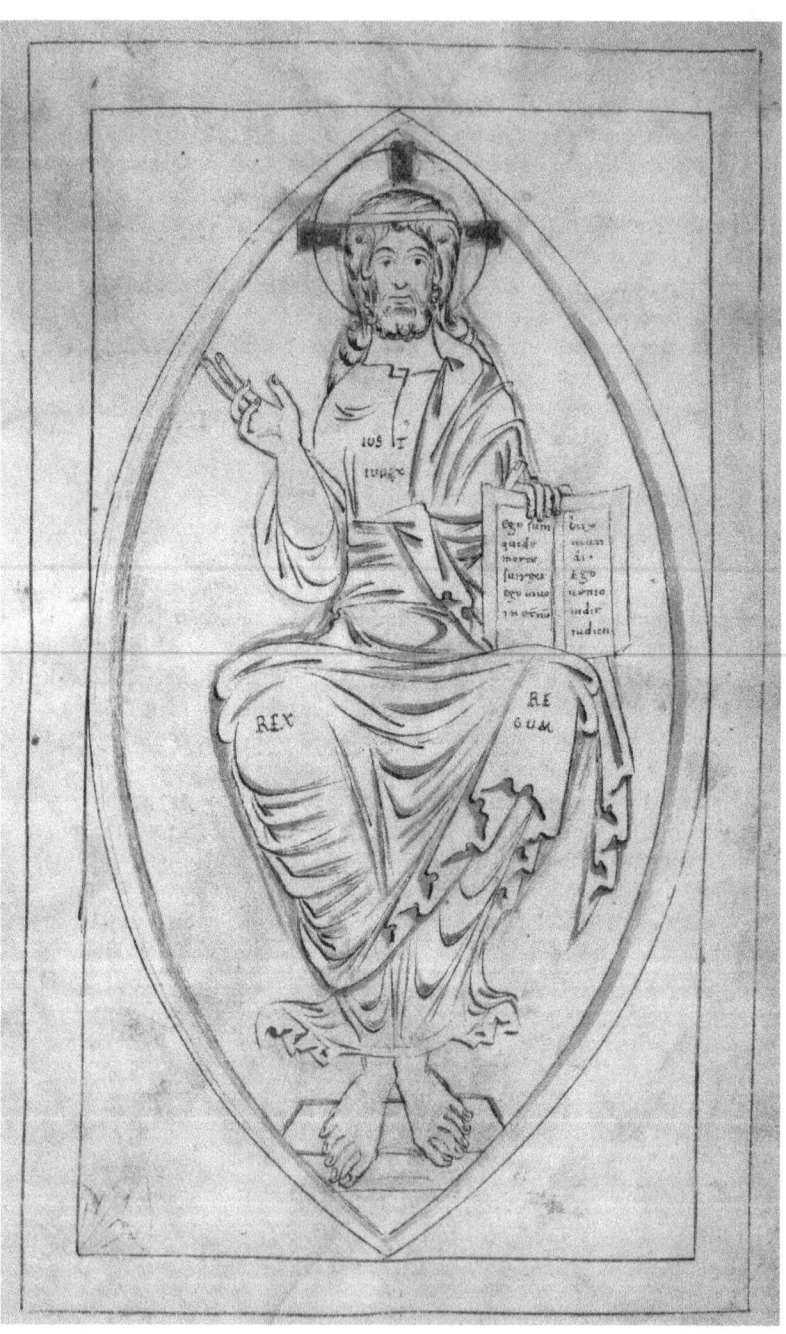

FIG. 48. CHRIST JUDGE. CAMBRIDGE, TRINITY COLLEGE LIBRARY, MS .15.34, FOL. 1

to Ælfric's ideals as the image of Christ was to those of Dunstan (though neither the drawing nor any part of the manuscript is the work of Ælfric's own hand). The manuscript itself is incomplete and now contains twenty-eight of Ælfric's homilies for Easter through to the eleventh Sunday after Pentecost. It has been described as 'the most important single witness to Ælfric's intention to provide a complete series of *Temporale* homilies … throughout the ecclesiastical year'.[83] The drawing shows Christ enthroned in a mandorla and staring straight out at the viewer. On his breast are the words 'iustus iudex' (just judge), a reference to 2 Timothy 4.8, Psalm 7.12 and Isaiah 11.4,[84] and on his knees 'rex regum' (king of kings), a reference to Revelation 17.14 and 19.16.[85] The book that he holds open reads 'Ego sum qui de morte surrexi ego uiuo in et[er]nu[m] lux mundi. Ego uenio in die iudicii' (I am the one that rose from the dead; I live eternally, the light of the world. I come at the day of judgement), a reference in part to John 8.12 and Revelation 1.17–18.[86]

Attempts have been made to connect the content of the drawing with the text of the homilies. The drawing originally faced the homily for Easter Sunday, and Easter was associated with the Second Coming, although Ælfric's homily for the day makes only passing reference to the connection. Kristine Haney and Richard Gameson have suggested that the artist may have been influenced by the earlier Blickling Homilist who, in Blickling Homily 7 'warns that the Last Judgement will occur on Easter Day, and … begins his homily for Easter with a description of God in Judgement'.[87] But, as Gameson himself notes, any connection between the drawing and the Blickling Homilies would be ironic as they represent a tradition that Ælfric hoped his own writings would replace.[88] Rosamond McKitterick suggests alternatively that the drawing may be connected with the theme of the homily for the first Sunday after Pentecost which deals with death, the soul and the Last Judgement,[89] but that homily begins on folio 232 of the manuscript, and the connection with the frontispiece could therefore

---

[83] Simon Keynes, *Anglo-Saxon Manuscripts in Trinity College*, Old English Newsletter Subsidia 18 (1992), 34.
[84] 2 Timothy 4.8: 'there is laid up for me a crown of justice, which the Lord the just judge will render to me in that day.' Psalm 7.12: 'God is a just judge, strong and patient.' Isaiah 11.4: 'But he shall judge the poor with justice, and shall reprove with equity the meek of the earth.'
[85] Revelation 17.14: 'he is the Lord of lords and King of kings.' Revelation 19.16: 'And he hath on his garment and on his thigh written: KING OF KINGS AND LORD OF LORDS.'
[86] John 8.12: 'I am the light of the world. He that followeth me, walketh not in darkness, but shall have the light of life.' Revelation 1.18: 'And alive and was dead, and behold I am living forever and ever.'
[87] Kristine Haney, *The Winchester Psalter: An Iconographic Study* (Leicester, 1986), 58; Gameson, *Role of Art*, 24.
[88] Gameson, *Role of Art*, 24 n. 82.
[89] Rosamond McKitterick, in *The Cambridge Illuminations: Ten Centuries of Book Production in the Medieval West*, ed. Paul Binski and Stella Panayotova (London, 2005), 65.

not be direct. It seems more likely that the meaning was more general. As Barbara Raw notes, the phrase 'just judge' was applied in Psalm 7 to 'the God who protects the virtuous when under attack', and in Isaiah to the God who 'judges the wretched with integrity, and with equity gives a verdict for the poor of the land'.[90] The words on Christ's breast connect the acts of judgement and protection with kingship, while those on the book place both in the context of the Last Judgement. The drawing as a whole thus reminds the viewer that Christ is a judge who protects the poor and provides the faithful with light and with life, although it does not, as Raw implies, suggest that Christ is a judge who is without severity.[91] Throughout his homilies and letters, Ælfric was concerned with the state of England and its people, the justice and judgement of the king and the moral responsibilities of the wealthy, albeit it in a metaphorical rather than direct way. He commented on the cowardice of submitting to the Danes (who he portrayed as aggressive pagan conquerors and harbingers of final judgement), the problem of unfair laws and taxation, and the proper uses of wealth and power.[92] The image of Christ Judge, with its references to kingship, justice and final judgement, was a reminder to the reader that kings too would face severe judgement when they stood before the King, and that the oppressed and the poor would find salvation in heaven. It is, moreover, not just the image of Christ that is given voice; the book he holds also speaks with him. On one level, the speaking book is a sign of the inseparability of Christ from the Word, but on another it is also a sign of the written nature of judgement. All human deeds were recorded in the Book of Judgement that would be opened at the Second Coming, but the book displayed here is also a reminder that human deeds were increasingly subject to the jurisdiction of written texts in the form of laws and charters (as well as that judgement that was written on the body) in the here and now.[93]

Writing, reading and books became increasingly important acts and images in Anglo-Saxon manuscript art, and evangelist portraits provided one of the most multivalent images for scribes and illuminators as, on one level, the images served as portraits of the very activities in which they were themselves engaged. The meaning and roles of the writing evangelists,

---

[90] Raw, *Trinity and Incarnation*, 124–5; see above n. 84.
[91] Raw, *Trinity and Incarnation*, 125–6.
[92] Clare A. Lees, *Tradition and Belief: Religious Writing in Late Anglo-Saxon England* (Minneapolis, 1999), 97–100; J. E. Cross, 'The Ethic of War in Old English', in *England Before the Conquest: Studies Presented to Dorothy Whitelock*, ed. Clemoes and Hughes, 269–82; Malcolm Godden, 'Ælfric's Lives of Saints and the Problem of Miracles', *Leeds Studies in English* n.s. 16 (1985), 83–100, at 89–90, 92–6; Malcolm Godden, 'Money, Power and Morality in Late Anglo-Saxon England', *ASE* 19 (1990), 41–65, esp. 51–65; Mary Clayton, 'Ælfric and Æthelred', in *Essays on Anglo-Saxon and Related Themes in Memory of Lynne Grundy*, ed. Jane Roberts and Janet L. Nelson (London, 2000), 65–88.
[93] See further Katherine O'Brien O'Keeffe, 'Body and Law in Anglo-Saxon England', *ASE* 27 (1998), 209–32; Reynolds, *Anglo-Saxon Deviant Burial Customs*.

the sources and transmission of their texts and their relationship to contemporary Anglo-Saxon author scribes had a long tradition,[94] but they were also spelled out in the famous colophon, something of a verbal portrait, added to folio 259r (the end of John's gospel) of the Lindisfarne Gospels by the scribe/glossator, Aldred, in the tenth century.[95] The colophon, in effect, maps the movement of word and text from God and Christ to the evangelists, and then to their successors, Eadfrith, Eðilwald, Billfrith and Aldred, who in the last line of the colophon establishes a connection between himself and St John. There has been much debate over the source and authenticity of this colophon but, as noted above, the discovery by Jane Roberts of traces of early poetic verse embedded within its opening lines suggests that Aldred was expanding on an earlier colophon, perhaps one contemporaneous with the production of the manuscript.[96] The additional text in the right-hand margin both gives voice to Aldred's written words and physically mediates between the closing of the original eighth-century gospel text and the colophon, suggesting that all parts of the book speak with one voice just as the evangelists, the original gospel authors, and the makers of this gospel book worked to one purpose.

The idea of sacred books being the products of a sort of authorial genealogy became quite widespread in late Anglo-Saxon England, but not all books or 'letters' were made to speak the way that the Lindisfarne Gospels are enjoined to do. Although I will return to the visual aspects of evangelist portraits and authorial genealogy in the next chapter, one manuscript, the Eadwine Psalter merits special attention here as it provides not just a more highly developed version of the speaking letter but also a sort of closure to the Anglo-Saxon tradition. Cambridge Trinity College R.17.1, the Eadwine Psalter, was produced at Christ Church Canterbury in the middle of the twelfth century (ca. 1155–60). It is thus an Anglo-Norman (or Romanesque) manuscript, but it both appropriates Anglo-Saxon, and specifically Christ Church, traditions, and translates them into a new visual language. It is the work of at least ten monastic scribes and six artists.[97] Eadwine, for whom the manuscript is named, may have been one of the scribes; alternatively, he may have been in charge of designing

---

[94] O'Reilly, 'The Library of Scripture'; Catherine E. Karkov, 'Evangelist Portraits and Book Production in Late Anglo-Saxon England', in *Cambridge Illuminations: The Conference Papers*, ed. Stella Panayotova (London, 2007), 55–63; Catherine E. Karkov, 'Writing and Having Written: Word and Image in the Eadwig Gospels', in *Writing and Texts in Anglo-Saxon England*, ed. Alexander R. Rumble (Woodbridge, 2006), 44–61; Cassiodorus, *Cassiodori senatoris Institutiones*, ed. R. A. B. Mynors (Oxford, 1963); Cassiodorus, *Explanation of the Psalms*, ed. and trans. P. G. Walsh, 3 vols (New York, 1990).
[95] See above p. 35.
[96] Roberts, 'Aldred Signs Off'.
[97] See Margaret Gibson, T. A. Heslop and R. Pfaff, eds. *The Eadwine Psalter: Text, Image, and Monastic Culture in Twelfth-Century Canterbury* (London, 1992).

the book or overseeing the project, and some believe he may also have been the manuscript's patron. The linguistic and textual complexity of the psalter is justly famous. It is a *psalterium triplex*, combining the three translations of the text attributed to Jerome, the Gallicanum (the main text), the Romanum and the Hebraicum (both written in smaller script and narrower columns which run parallel down the sides of the page). In addition the manuscript includes interlinear translations into Old English (accompanying the Romanum) and Anglo-Norman French (translating the Hebraicum), the *parva glosatura* or *glossa ordinaria* (a standard gloss or commentary on Psalms 1–150), a series of exegetical prologues, tituli and collects and, of course, the illuminations which might be considered both a visual narrative and a gloss on the written text. The manuscript now begins with a calendar but most likely originally opened with a series of at least four leaves of painted narrative consisting of Old and New Testaments subjects from Exodus to the Acts of the Apostles (now separated from the manuscript and divided between London and New York).[98]

Amongst art historians, the manuscript is perhaps best known for the 'portrait' of the scribe Eadwine on folio 283v (plate 5), without doubt one of the most famous images to survive from twelfth-century England. Yet, while it is one of the best-known pages from the psalter, it has most frequently been studied outside, or as an addendum to, the manuscript in which it is contained. It has been considered, largely on stylistic grounds, to be an addition to the manuscript but this is problematic as it fails to take account of the length of time over which the manuscript may have been produced, and further assumes that all the psalter artists were working in a single style that did not change over time. And if added later, how much later? However, even if a later addition, the portrait provides a fitting point of closure to the manuscript's combined textual and pictorial programme.

That there is a close relationship between word and image in the Eadwine Psalter should not be in any way surprising. The interplay between the words of the psalms and the miniatures that preface them had been established already in the *c.* 800 Utrecht Psalter, one of the primary pictorial sources for Eadwine. In that manuscript (which contains only the Gallicanum), each psalm is preceded by a miniature that, for the most part, provides a literal representation of its words, with the monochrome of the drawings helping to bring out the unity of image and text. That visual relationship is *possibly* compromised somewhat by the addition of colour in the drawings of British Library Harley 603, the earliest of the three 'copies' of Utrecht to be made at Christ Church after the manuscript arrived in England sometime shortly before the year 1000,

---

[98] London, BL, MS Add. 37472(1); London, Victoria and Albert Museum, MS 661; New York, Pierpont Morgan Library M 521 and 724.

but is re-established and indeed strengthened in Eadwine by the addition of colour to the text (in the form of decorated initials), text to some of the illustrations, and the general mise-en-page of the manuscript with its studied balance of the different versions of the psalms and commentaries on them. In Eadwine, the arrangement of the miniatures running across the whole of the page after the prologue but before the psalm proper allows the miniatures to serve as a point of union for the multiple textual translations that follow, the image being equally applicable to each translation. The heteroglossia of the text, in other words, follows from and brings us back to the common language of the image. The process of reading sequentially through the psalter brings us finally to the portrait of Eadwine, from whose pen the majority of the text flowed, and whose image at the end serves as the ultimate sign of the inseparability of word and image in this manuscript. He in turn looks back over the book he has just written, for and by which he will be praised, his figure mirroring and balancing that of the blessed man of Psalm 1 with whose image and textual description the psalter proper began.

The portrait is surrounded by and in dialogue with its inscription in which the scribe speaks to the text (again literally the letter) and the letter responds:

> Scriptor: s[c]riptorum princeps ego. Nec obitura deinceps laus mea nec fama. Quis sim mea littera clama. Littera: Te tua s[c]riptura quem signat picta figura. Predicat Eadwinum fama per secula vivum. Ingenium cuius libri decus indicat huius. Quem tibi seque datum munus dues accipe gratum.
>
> (Scribe: I am the chief of scribes, and neither my praise nor fame shall die; shout out, oh my letter, who I may be. Letter: By its fame your script proclaims you, Eadwine, whom the painted figure represents, alive through the ages, whose genius the beauty of this book demonstrates. Receive, O God, the book and its donor as an acceptable gift.)[99]

The inscription is arranged so that our eyes criss-cross the figure of the writing Eadwine as we read. It begins at the upper left and runs across the top and then down the right-hand border, then goes back up to the top of the left-hand border and runs down, and then across beneath Eadwine's feet – rather similar to the arrangement of the inscription on the Durham Gospels Crucifixion page. The last words written at the bottom of the right-hand border are 'picta figura' (painted figure), and our eyes then have to cross the painted figure itself in order to read the remainder of the inscription. It is possible that the arrangement was intended to suggest further that this is a conversation taking place in the present, or in an eternal present – as the letter proclaims, Eadwine as scribe remains 'alive

---

[99] T. A. Heslop in *The Eadwine Psalter*, ed. Gibson *et al.*, 180. Heslop's translation.

through the ages'. Colour may also have been used to indicate Eadwine as the ultimate source of the words, green having been chosen both as the dominant colour of the scribe and for the words identifying the speakers, *scriptor* and *littera*, the latter word placed level with the book in which Eadwine writes. Eadwine sits copying the psalms (songs of praise), while the letter affirms the praise he will receive though his actions.

Tessa Webber has described the Eadwine Psalter as a monument to the inherited textual and pictorial traditions of Christ Church, but does not explain exactly what she means by 'inherited pictorial traditions'.[100] Is it simply that Eadwine, as Heslop characterized it, is an 'edition' of Utrecht?[101] Clearly the complexity of the manuscript tells us that cannot be the case. Nor should we see it only in the tradition of Utrecht and Harley 603, though it cannot be denied that it references both manuscripts. Certainly that is a part of its purpose, but only a part of it. The expansion of the pictorial programme into the initials, and the emphasis on authorship and the relation between the book, its producers and its users are new and should be understood as part of its scholarly agenda. Like the combination of text and languages, it combines an imported tradition (the basic visual content of the Utrecht derived miniatures) with Anglo-Saxon elements (for example, the use of coloured-outline drawing, the relation between centre and margin),[102] with a new style of illumination to create something that is simultaneously traditional and innovative. The Eadwine portrait is key to this process. It is, as any number of art historians have emphasized, a new type of author portrait, which gives unusual prominence to the work and status of a contemporary named scribe. Eadwine is the prince of scribes, not just a humble labourer for God, and his book shouts out, not just reveals his identity and skills, or greets the reader, as did the Lindisfarne colophon. Yet, as Aldred's colophon portrayed him verbally as a successor to the evangelist authors, Eadwine is represented visually in the guise of a writing evangelist. Webber describes the portrait as unique both in its scale and in its iconography, and there is no doubt that size does set the image apart, nor that technically the iconography is unique; yet the portrait is also indebted to the scribal traditions set forth by Aldred and exemplified most notably by Eadwine's predecessor at Christ Church, Eadwig Basan, whose work will be discussed in the following chapter. Eadwine's inscribed portrait and his psalter might both be said to double the past in the sense that they provide both continuity with the past and its traditions and a statement for a new post-Anglo-Saxon future.

[100] *Cambridge Illuminations*, ed. Binski and Panayotova, cat. no. 25.
[101] *The Eadwine Psalter*, ed. Gibson et al., 48–9.
[102] See below p. 190.

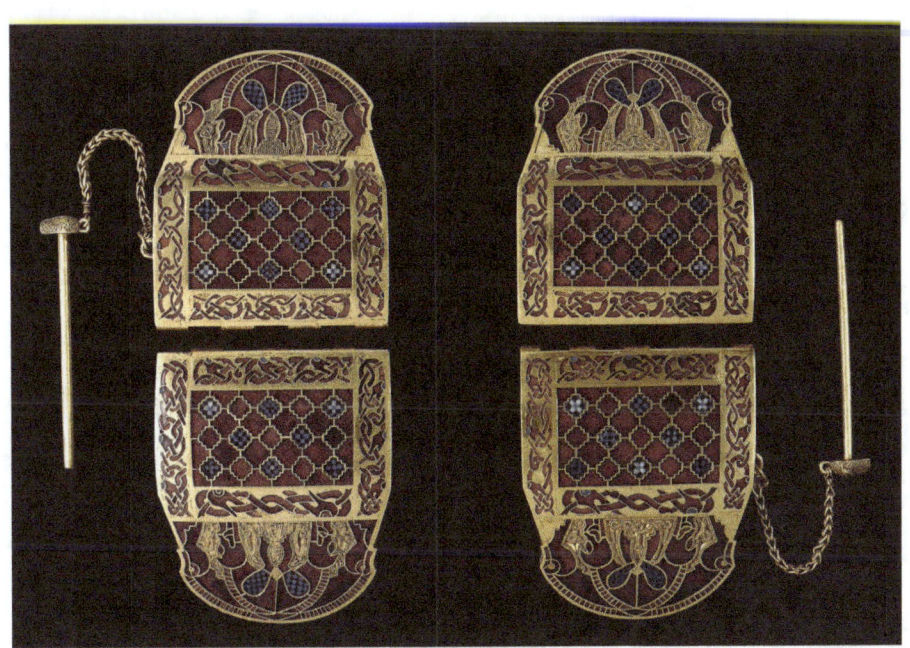

PLATE 1  SHOULDER CLASPS FROM SUTTON HOO MOUND 1.

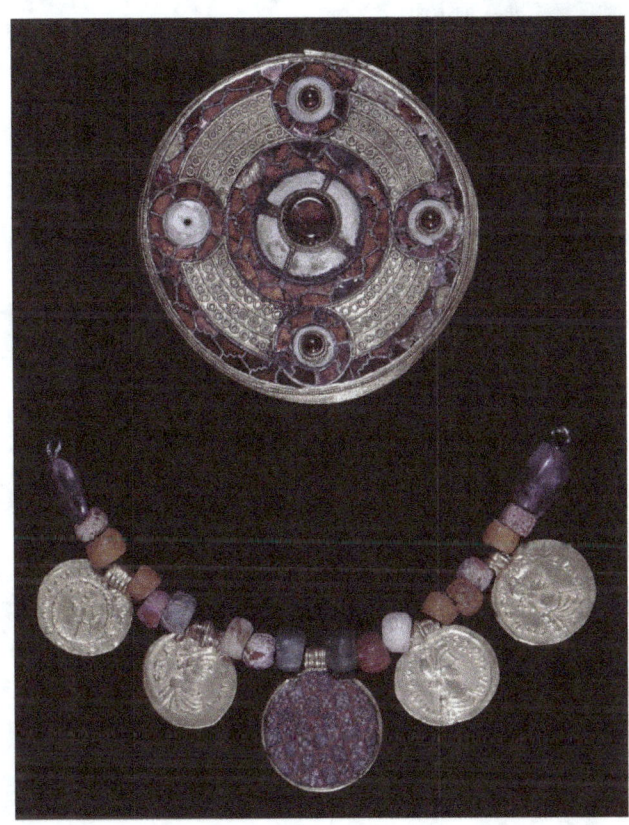

PLATE 2  SARRE BROOCH AND NECKLACE.

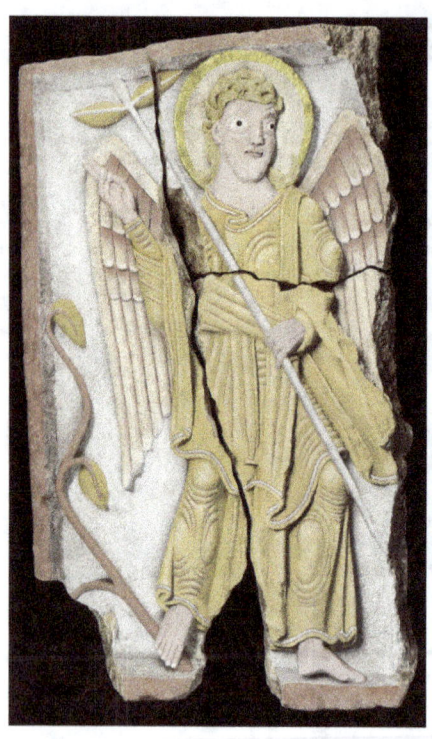

PLATE 3   LICHFIELD ANGEL WITH COLOUR DIGITALLY RESTORED.

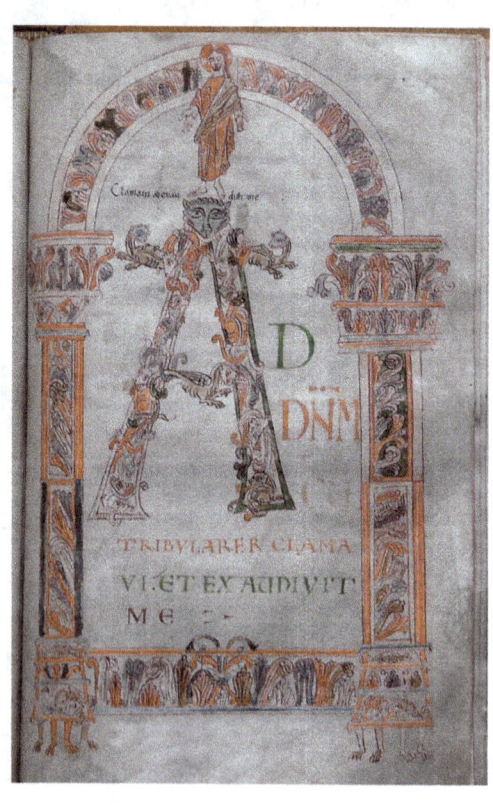

PLATE 4   SALISBURY PSALTER, FOL. 122.

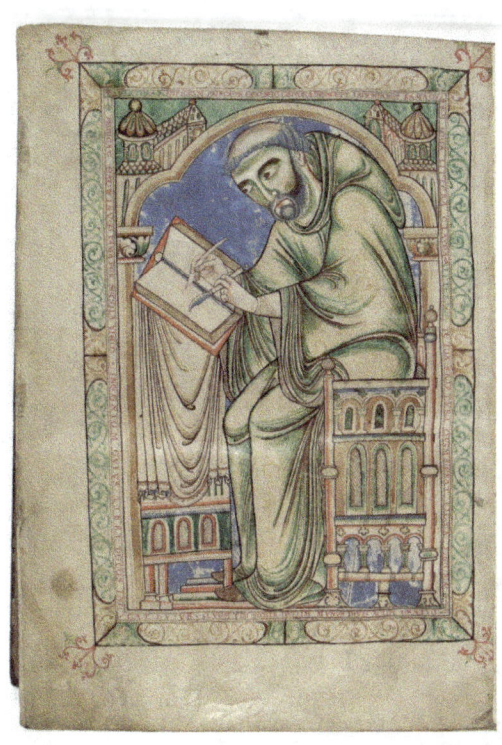

PLATE 5   PORTRAIT OF THE SCRIBE EADWINE, EADWINE PSALTER. CAMBRIDGE, TRINITY COLLEGE LIBRARY, MS R.17.1, FOL. 283V.

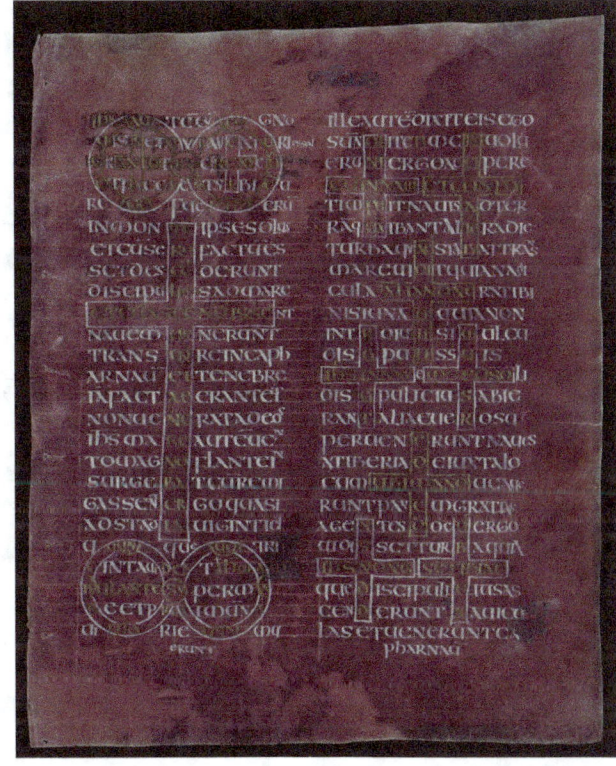

PLATE 6   PAGE WITH CROSSES, STOCKHOLM CODEX AUREUS. STOCKHOLM, ROYAL LIBRARY, MS A.135, FOL. 11.

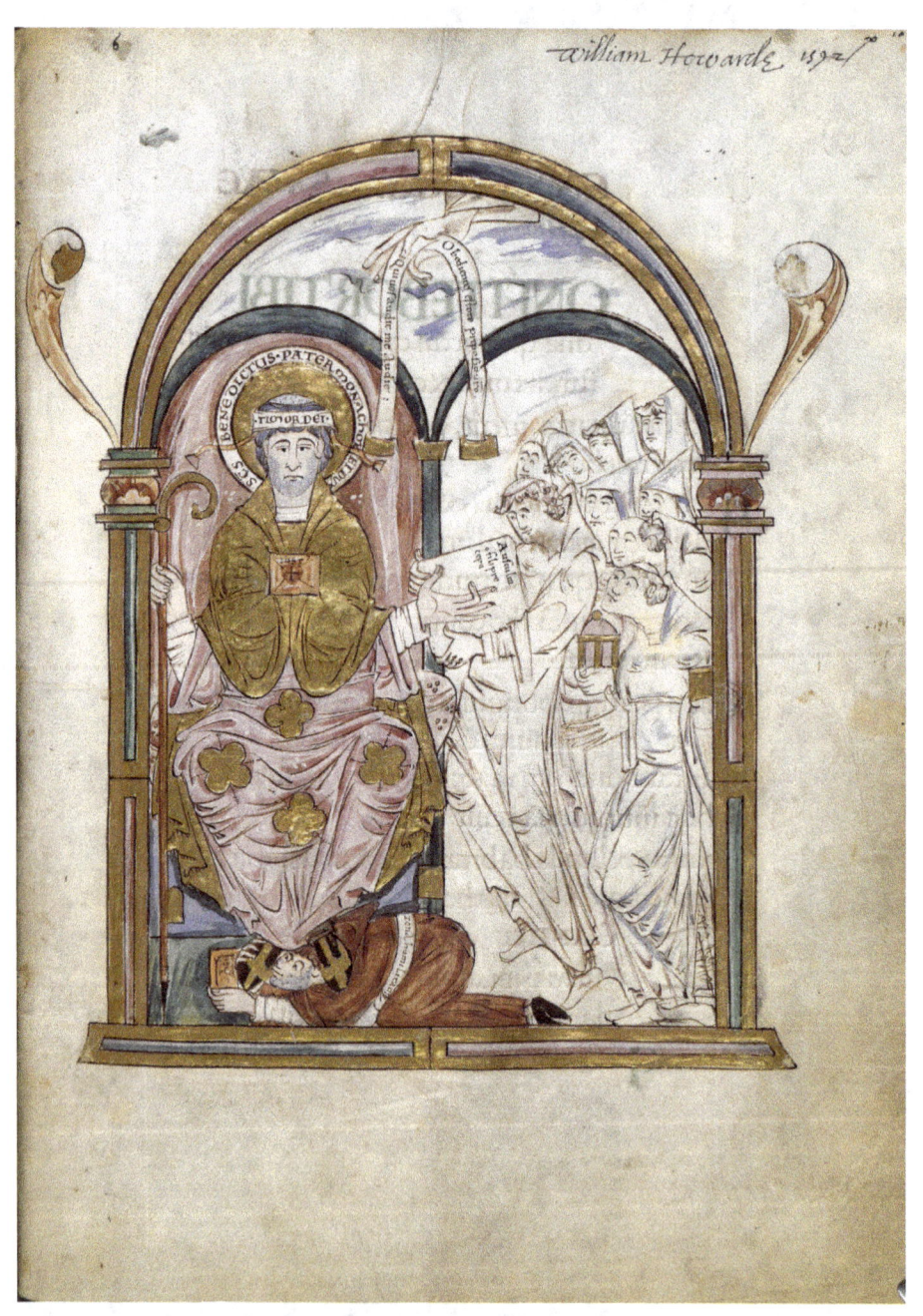

PLATE 7   PORTRAIT OF EADWIG FROM THE EADWIG PSALTER. LONDON, BL, MS ARUNDEL 155, FOL. 133.

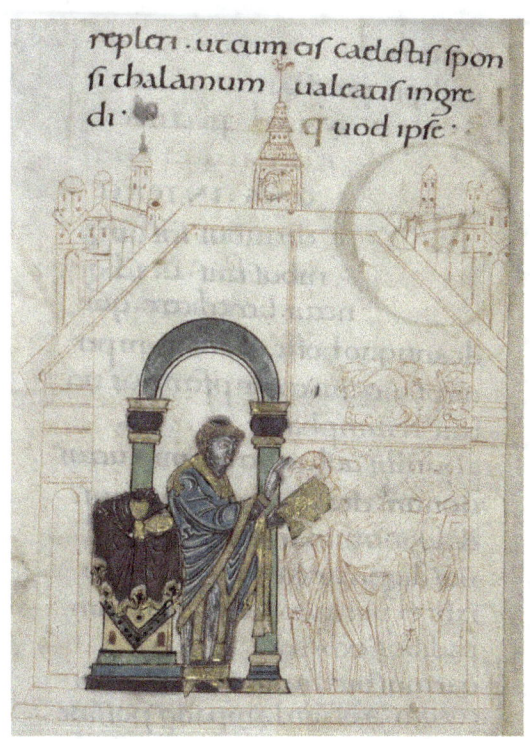

PLATE 8   DEDICATION OF A CHURCH, BENEDICTIONAL OF ÆTHELWOLD. LONDON, BL, MS ADD. 49598, FOL. 118V.

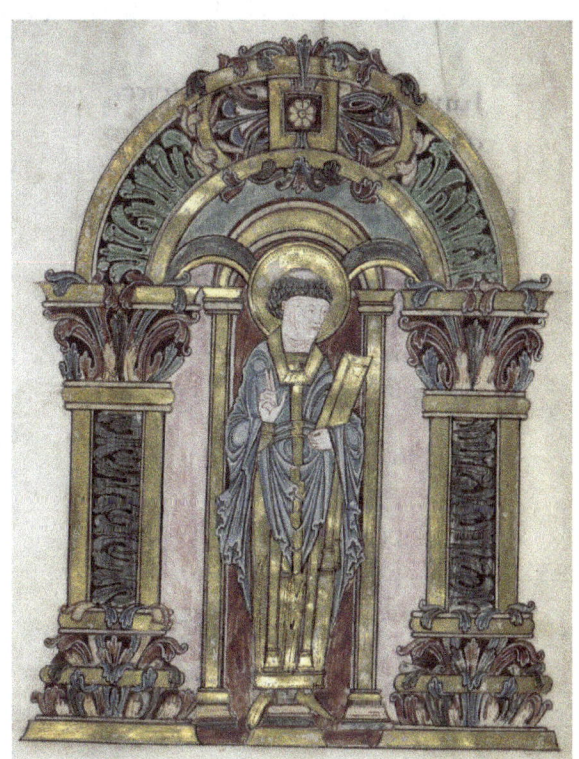

PLATE 9   ST SWITHUN, BENEDICTIONAL OF ÆTHELWOLD. LONDON, BL, MS ADD. 49598, FOL. 90V.

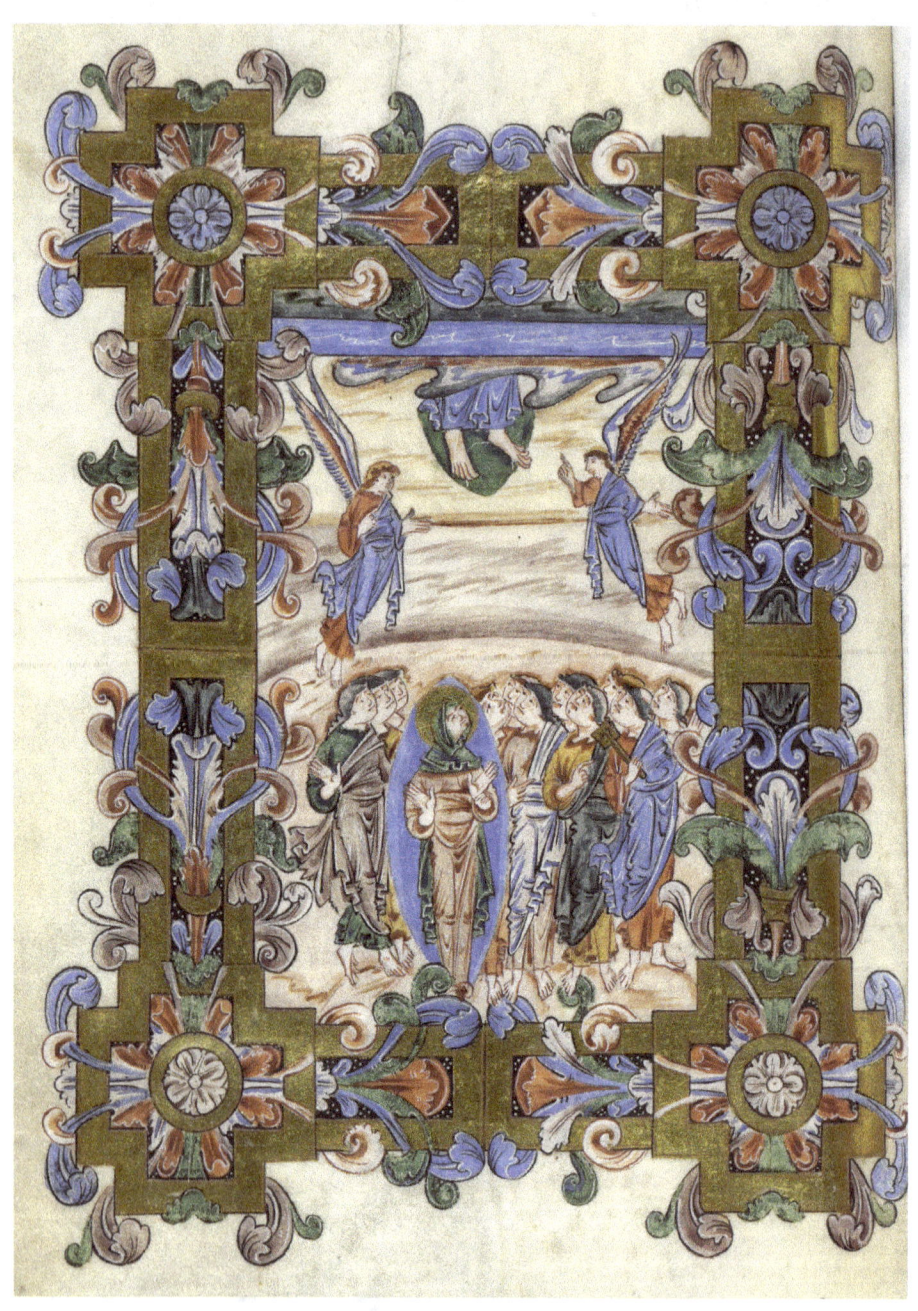

PLATE 10   ASCENSION OF CHRIST, SACRAMENTARY OF ROBERT OF JUMIÈGES. ROUEN, BIBL. MUN. MS Y 6, FOL. 81V.

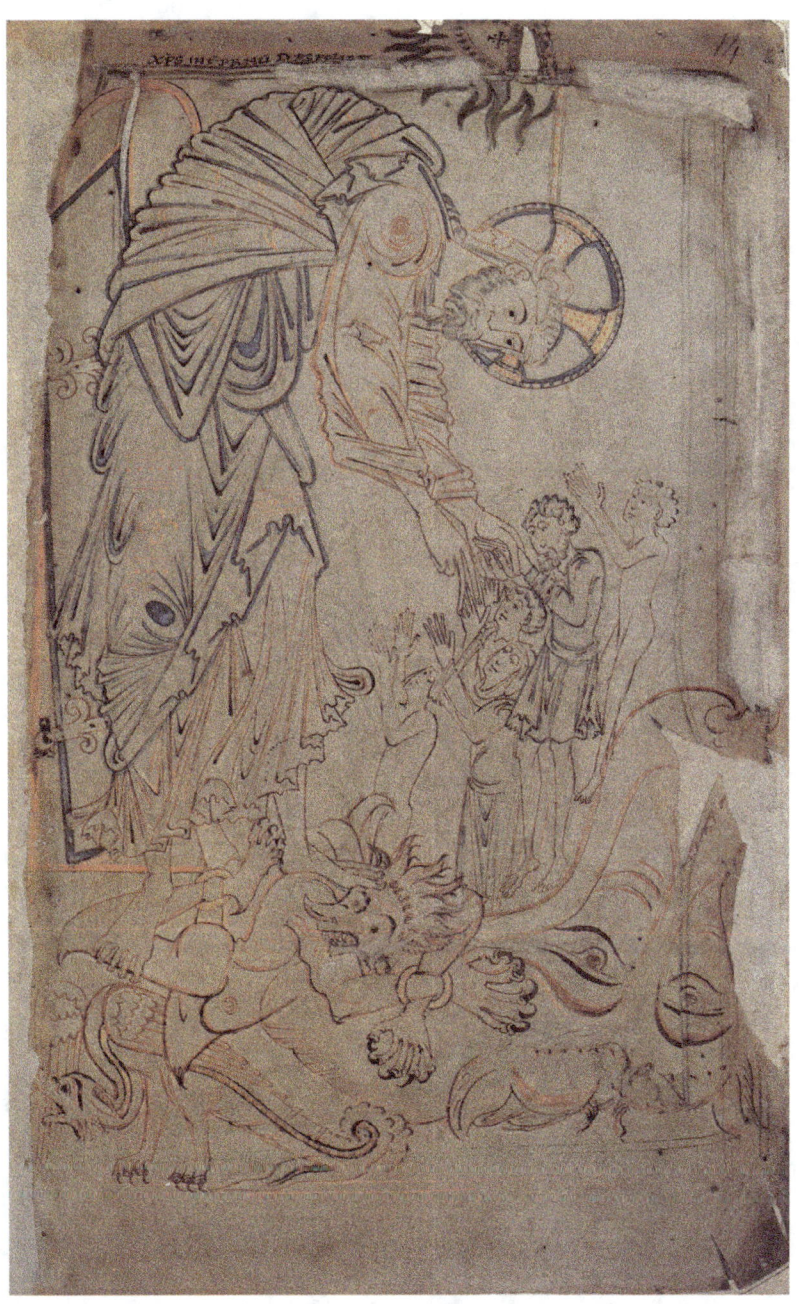

PLATE 11 HARROWING OF HELL, THE TIBERIUS PSALTER. LONDON, BL, MS COTTON TIBERIUS C.VI, FOL. 14.

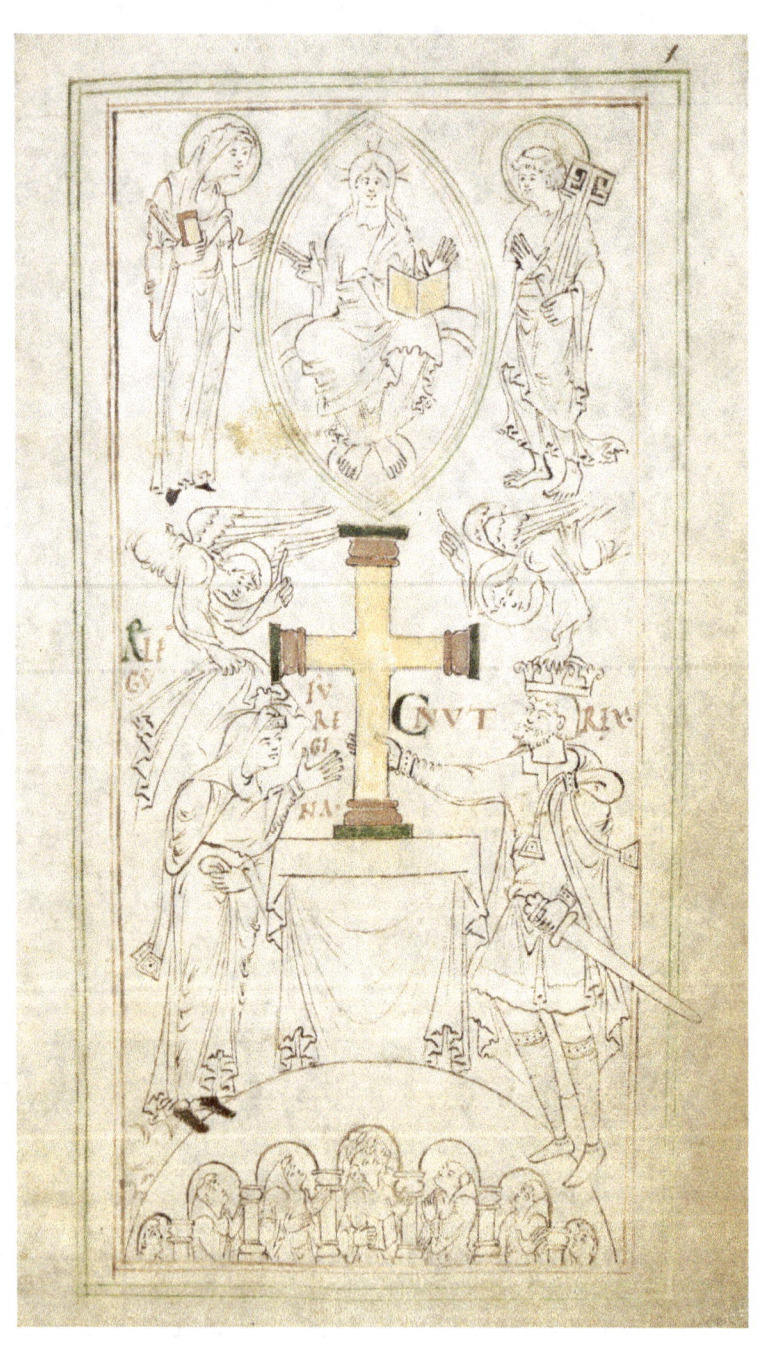

PLATE 12   EMMA AND CNUT PRESENT A CROSS TO THE NEW MINSTER WINCHESTER, NEW MINSTER LIBER VITAE. LONDON, BL, MS STOWE 944, FOL. 6.

# BOOKS, WORDS AND BODIES

5

Books were crucial to the economy of conversion, conflict and expansion within Anglo-Saxon England in a way that no other type of object was. The books brought north with Augustine and his followers were the real tools of the conversion process. Books recorded the history of church and people, and books could be amongst the most prominent players in war, whether as talismans, miracle-workers, spoils or 'hostages' of battle. The Stockholm Codex Aureus (fig. 51; plate 6) was ransomed from the Danes by Ealdorman Ælfred and his wife Werburh in the middle of the ninth century, though perhaps without the precious book cover in which it would originally have been bound. They presented it to Christ Church Canterbury for the good of their souls and that of their daughter.[1] The Lindisfarne Gospels lost its jewelled cover to the Vikings, but it also played an important role in the decision of the Cuthbert community to remain in England rather than fleeing to Ireland in the face of Viking attack.[2] It remained a crucial part of the community's identity, as the addition of the Old English gloss in the tenth century, the 'copying' of elements of its illumination in the late tenth- or early eleventh-century Copenhagen Gospels (fig. 9), and the campaign to have it returned to the north after its exhibition in Newcastle upon Tyne in 1996 demonstrate. King Alfred and his descendants were also quick to pick up on the power of the book in the formation of cultural identity and the promotion of a specific political or religious agenda, as is discussed below. Nicholas Howe has described the Anglo-Saxons as 'writing the map of Anglo-Saxon England',[3] and while he was most concerned with the role of texts, images had an equally important part to play in that process. Most importantly, images allowed for self-identification with the figures, spaces and actions represented, not just for illuminators and scribes, but also for the Anglo-Saxon men and women who read their words and paused over their images.

---

[1] See below p. 188.
[2] See below p. 276.
[3] Howe, *Writing the Map of Anglo-Saxon England*.

Nonne tu ds qui reppulisti nos · & non
egredieris in uirtutib: nostris ·
Da nobis auxilium de tribulatione ·
& uana salus hominis ·
In deo faciemus uirtutem · & ipse ad nihi
lum deducet tribulantes nos · LX
INCIPIT IN YMNIS PSALM DAVID GOV. ECCLE
Exaudi ds deprecationem meam
intende orationi meae ·
A finib: terre ad te clamaui · du anxia
ret ur cor meu in petra exaltasti me ·
Deduxisti me quia factes spes mea turris
fortitudinis a facie inimici ·
In habitabo in tabernaculo tuo in secla ·
pteger in uelamto alarum tuarum ·
Qm tu ds ms exaudisti orationem mea ·
dedisti hereditate timtib: nomen tuum ·
Dies sup dies regis adicies annos ei · usq:
in diem generationis & generationis ·
Permanet in æternu in conspectu dei
misc diam & ueritate ei quis requiret ·
Sic psalmum dicam nomini tuo in sclm scli ·
ut reddam uota mea de die in diem ·

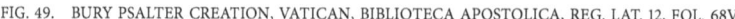

FIG. 49. BURY PSALTER CREATION, VATICAN, BIBLIOTECA APOSTOLICA, REG. LAT. 12, FOL. 68V

## WORD AND IMAGE IN MANUSCRIPT ART

The contributions made by the Anglo-Saxons to the development and design of the book and the style and iconography of manuscript art make the subject of books, their makers and their readers deserving of a chapter in their own right. One of the most important and long-lasting of these contributions was the creation of a complex set of relationships between word and image, none of which could really be classed as the speaking objects discussed in the last chapter, that begin at the level of the letter. All medieval illuminated manuscripts present a unity of word and image in which the two function together convey the message of the book to the reader and guide her or his progress through it. Moreover, because the same materials were used for the creation of both, they have a similar materiality. Letter forms and lines of text, especially in luxury manuscripts, also had an aesthetic appeal.

From its earliest phases, the union of word and image proved a fertile ground for artistic innovation in the Insular and Anglo-Saxon world. Insular manuscripts such as the early seventh-century psalter known as the Cathach of St Columba (or Colum Cille) (Dublin, Royal Irish Academy, s.n.), believed by some to date from Columba's own lifetime and perhaps to be by his own hand,[4] contain initial letters that metamorphose into geometric ornament and animal forms. Similar types of initial occur in Continental manuscripts of the same date, although the letters in the Continental manuscripts tend to take the form of creatures or to contain them rather than transforming from the one to the other. The Insular initials not only bring the letter to life through their visible shape-shifting, but in doing so negate the gap between text and ornament as the letter becomes simultaneously a part of a word to be read and a decorative image with an aesthetic appeal. Words such as 'decoration' and 'ornament' have traditionally carried a negative meaning in art historical scholarship, having been used largely to suggest that something is mere pattern or ornament devoid of meaning, and thus not really serious art, an attitude that goes back to an Orientalist view of art and art history current in the nineteenth century. But it would be a mistake to believe, on the one hand, that ornament *must* carry meaning in order to have a value or, on the other, that all ornament is without meaning.[5] One of the most

---

[4] Columba died in 597. On the date and origin of the manuscript see Martin Werner, 'Three Works on the Book of Kells', *Peritia* 11 (1997), 250–326. For a digital facsimile of the manuscript with discussion see Michael Herity and Aiden Breen, *The Cathach of Colum Cille: An Introduction* (Dublin, 2002). 'Cathach' means 'battler' and the psalter is known to have been carried into battle as a talisman – though perhaps given its living words and nature it might better be understood as an active agent.

[5] See e.g., Irene J. Winter, 'Defining "Aesthetics" for Non-Western Studies: The Case of Ancient Mesopotamia', in *Art History, Aesthetics, Visual Studies*, ed. Michael Ann Holly and Keith Moxey (Williamsburg, MA, 2002), 3–28; Patricia Stirnemann, 'Where Can

famous initials in the Cathach, the Q that begins Psalm 90, for example, transforms from a letter into a spiral and then into a collared beast head carrying a cross on its neck and looking back at the words of the psalm. The protective images of both cross and beast head can be related to the words of the first two verses of the psalm:

> 1. He that dwelleth in the aid of the Most High shall abide under the protection of the God of Jacob.
> 2. He shall say to the Lord: Thou art my protector and my refuge: my God in him I will trust.

On the other hand, it would be difficult if not foolhardy to suggest that the pen flourishes that fill one side of the bowl of the Q were intended to do anything other than balance the composition and add visual interest to the page. The lack of 'iconographic content', however, does not make them any less important a part of either the visual composition or the idea that the decoration of the book reflected the beauty of the words it contained. Similar caution should be applied to interpretation of the famous animals that fill the letters and scamper between the lines of the c. 800 Book of Kells (Dublin, Trinity College Library, MS 58); the fact that some of these creatures are clearly symbolically or thematically related to the passages they accompany should not lead us to assume that this is the case for each and every animal.[6]

The tradition of text as decoration that begins with the Cathach reached its apogee, at least in terms of its spread across the page, in the decorated incipit and chi-rho pages of the great Insular gospel books like the Book of Kells, the Lindisfarne Gospels (fig. 50) or the Stockholm Codex Aureus (fig. 51). In these manuscripts a beautifully balanced integration of words and images fills an entire page, in some instances making it difficult for the reader to make out the letters and words without a certain degree of meditation on their forms. This was certainly intentional, as Cummian, amongst others, stressed that the act of meditation brought revelation, in this case the revelation of the word.[7] The Lindisfarne Gospels and Codex Aureus pages also illustrate another Insular innovation, the use of diminuendo, the process of gradually decreasing the size and

---

We Go from Here? The Study of French Twelfth-Century Manuscripts', in *Romanesque Art and Thought in the Twelfth Century: Essays in Honor of Walter Cahn*, ed. Colum Hourihane (Princeton, NJ, 2008), 82–94. Historically crucial to the debate over the nature of 'ornament' are Alois Riegl, *Problems of Style Foundations for a History of Ornament*, trans. E. Kain (Princeton, NJ, 1992, first published in 1893); Alois Riegl, *The Late Roman Art Industry*, trans. R. Winkes (Rome, 1985, first published in 1901); Alois Riegl, *Historical Grammar of the Visual Arts*, trans. Jacqueline E. Jung (New York, 2004, published posthumously in 1966).

[6] See, for example, the provocative yet problematic reading of these images in Heather Pulliam, *Word and Image in the Book of Kells* (Dublin, 2006).

[7] M. Walsh and D. Ó Cróinín, eds. *Cummian's Letter 'De Controversia Paschali' and the 'De Ratione Computandi'* (Toronto, 1988).

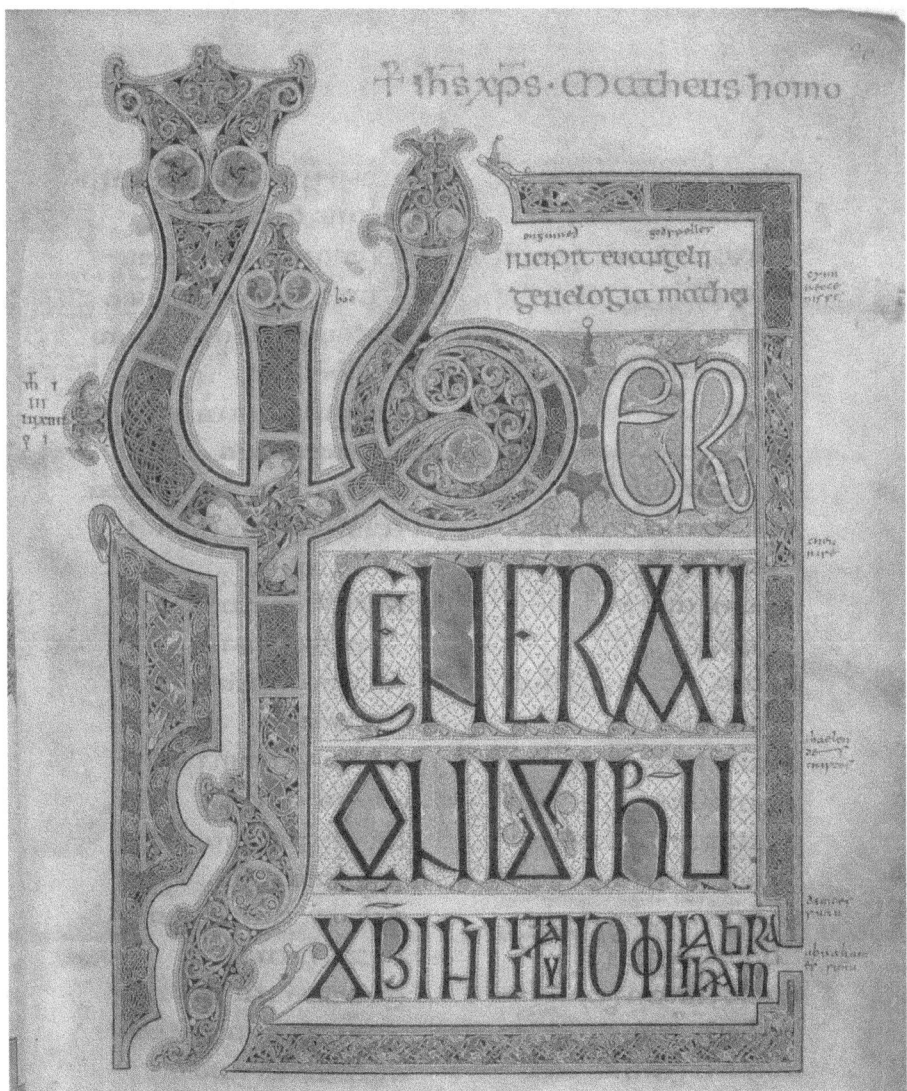

FIG. 50. INCIPIT TO MATTHEW, LINDISFARNE GOSPELS, LONDON, BL, MS COTTON NERO D.IV, FOL. 27

ornamentation of the letters until they merge into the normal script of the text. The use of diminuendo too helped to bridge the division between image and word.

A related development was the historiated initial, one of the best-known and long-lived of the Anglo-Saxon innovations in manuscript art. A historiated initial does not simply contain or take the form of

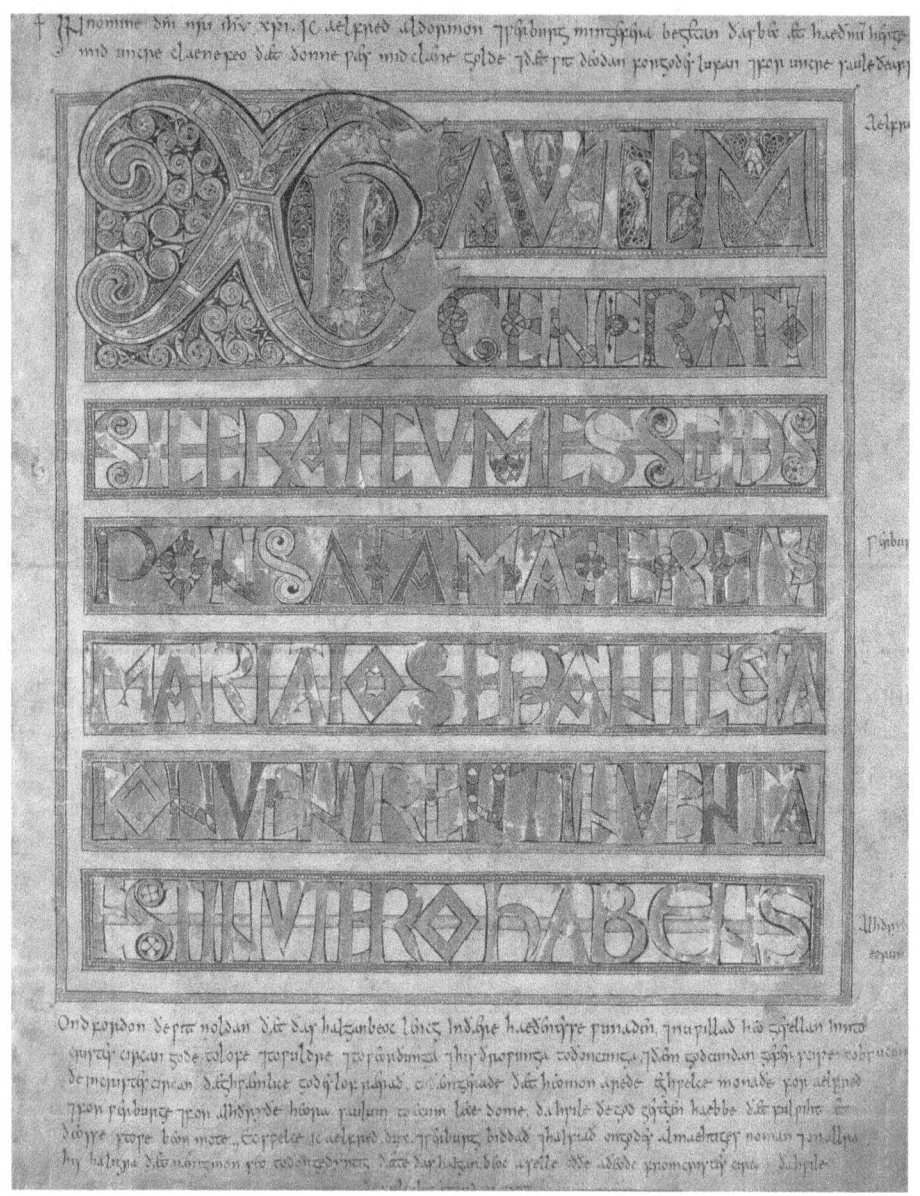

FIG. 51. CHI-RHO PAGE, STOCKHOLM CODEX AUREUS. STOCKHOLM, ROYAL LIBRARY, MS A.135, FOL. 161

an animal or figure, but contains or is part of an abbreviated narrative scene that relates directly to the text in which it is found. The earliest surviving historiated initials occur in the eighth-century St Petersburg copy of Bede's *Historia Ecclesiastica* (St Petersburg, National Library, Q.v.I.18, fol. 26v) and the Vespasian Psalter (London, British Library, Cotton Vespasian A.i, fols. 31r, 53r). In the Bede manuscript, thought to be a product of Wearmouth-Jarrow, the relationship between image and text is straightforward: a portrait of Pope Gregory the Great is contained within the initial that begins Bede's account of the year 605, the year in which Gregory died. Even so, a later hand has mistakenly written Augustinus in Gregory's halo. In the Vespasian Psalter, probably from St Augustine's Canterbury, the relationship is less straightforward. Psalm 26, the psalm of David before he was anointed, is introduced by a large initial D within which a spear-carrying David and Jonathan clasp hands. The image is one of faith and camaraderie in the face of tribulation, in this case David's struggles against Jonathan's father Saul. David rescuing the lamb from the lion is set within the D that begins Psalm 52, a visual metaphor for the relationship between God and humanity on which the psalm centres. In both cases the relationship between the episode depicted and the text of the psalm is not immediately apparent. It is necessary that the reader know the different episodes from the life of David and be able to understand their applicability to the text through the process of *ruminatio*, literally meditating on the deeper meaning of the image/text rather than understanding it simply on the surface level of the letter. The episodes chosen for depiction are so general that they could equally appropriately have prefaced any number of psalms. Both Psalms 26 and 52 are important liturgically, but it may be the fact that both begin with the letter D that led to the choice of these images at these points. Together with the full-page miniature of David playing his harp surrounded by musicians and dancers (now folio 30r, but originally probably a frontispiece), and the now lost initial to Psalm 1, which is believed to have depicted Samuel anointing David, they are also part of the beginning of an illustrated cycle of the life of David within Anglo-Saxon psalters that would ultimately culminate in the pictorial cycle that prefaced the Eadwine Psalter.

By the end of the Anglo-Saxon period historiated initials had become increasingly complex and sophisticated compositions. A prime example is the preface to the Canon of the Mass in the *c.* 1021 Red Book of Darley (CCCC, MS 42, pp. 52 and 53).[8] The historiated initial is the T of 'Te

---

[8] See further Catherine E. Karkov, 'Text and Image in the Red Book of Darley', in *Text and Image: Studies in Anglo-Saxon Literature in Honour of Éamonn Ó Carragáin*, ed. Alistair Minnis and Jane Roberts (Turnhout, 2008), 135–48. For images of the pages discussed see Mildred Budny, *Insular, Anglo-Saxon and Early Anglo-Norman Manuscript Art at Corpus Christi College Cambridge: An Illustrated Catalogue* (Kalamazoo, MI, 1997), cat. no. 44.

igitur' on page 53, but the composition of which it is a part must be understood in the context of the double-page opening. On page 52 the Preface begins with an image of Christ in majesty surrounded by angels with the words of the preface arranged around them. On this page the image is literally part of the text and the whole works to unite the words of the preface with the God to whom they are addressed.[9] The words 'vere dignum et iustum est equum et salutare' are written in small capitals within Christ's mandorla, physically surrounding him with the words of praise that would have been read or sung by the reader. Beginning with the word 'nos', they spread out around the lower bodies of the angels and flow seamlessly into the regular lines of the text written at the bottom of the page. The image of the heavenly Christ on page 52 is balanced by that of the Crucifixion on page 53 where the T of 'Te igitur' forms the cross on which Christ's body is suspended. The depiction of the Crucifixion within the 'Te igitur' had been established early, appearing in both Merovingian and Carolingian manuscripts, but the Red Book of Darley image has a multivalency unmatched in its earlier models. In addition to being part of a paired set of images, the details of the hand of God and the dove of the Holy Spirit that flank Christ's head and the figure of the Virgin who stands to Christ's right turn the crucifixion simultaneously into a depiction of the Trinity with Mary. The blood that flows from the wound in Christ's side towards both Mary and a living shoot from the 'tree-of-life-cross' suggests the birth of Ecclesia,[10] a fitting image with which to begin the Canon of the Mass.

While the historiated initial may be the most obvious manifestation of the Anglo-Saxon focus on the integration of image and text, there are a number of surviving manuscripts in which we see that interest expanding to fill entire pages, indeed entire books. The Stockholm Codex Aureus (Stockholm Royal Library, MS A.135), produced somewhere in Kent in the middle of the eighth century, is one such manuscript. The Codex Aureus is truly imperial in both scale and style. At 395 x 320 millimetres it is one of the largest early medieval manuscripts to survive. Its size, its dimensions and its script have all been understood as an evocation of late antique imperial manuscripts.[11] Its pages alternate between purple stained and plain pages, with the text written in gold, silver and coloured inks, again all clear signs of its allegiance to the traditions of Rome and

---

[9] 'Vere dignum et iustum est, equum et salutare, nos tibi semper, et ubique gratios agere' corrected spellings (It is indeed fitting and right, our duty and our salvation, always and everywhere to give thanks to you).

[10] Ecclesia was born from Christ's side at the moment of the Crucifixion. In England the personification of Ecclesia had been associated with Mary from at least the tenth century. See Clayton, *The Cult of the Virgin Mary in Anglo-Saxon England*, 12, 15, 158, 169, 170, 247–8.

[11] See e.g., Richard Gameson, ed., *St Augustine and the Conversion of England* (Stroud, 1999), 340–3.

Constantinople. But it is not wholly Roman. Style and motif work to unite imperial classicism with Insular traditions in a way that declares the power and glory of the new Anglo-Saxon church. The great purple pages on which crosses of various shapes have been superimposed on the text (plate 6) are frequently described as *carmina figurata* (figured poems), a type of composition most closely associated with Constantine's court poet Publilius Optatianus Porphyrius, but this is not strictly accurate. True *carmina figurata* are forms of acrostic in which the phrases contained within the image (or parts of it) form secondary texts that can be read in their own right in addition to being read as part of the narrative in which they are embedded.[12] In the Stockholm Codex Aureus, however, there are no secondary texts; the cross patterns are simply laid over portions of the gospel text which read only in the normal manner from left to right. The patterns highlight important passages but they do not form separate discrete and readable texts. It may have been enough for the manuscript's makers simply to quote the tradition rather than to adopt it wholesale, or it may have been felt inappropriate to alter the words of the gospel in any way – Porphyrius's *carmina* were his own verse compositions, not biblical texts. This does not mean, however, that the pages were either easy to produce or intended to be 'merely' decorative. The different types of ink used meant that while words of one colour were being added, space had to be left for those to be written in other colours, while on the cross-patterned pages the size and spacing of the letters had to be adapted to fit within the shapes and spaces of the design.[13] Clearly the scribes were working to a complex and exquisitely designed master plan. The cross is a sign of Christ and the Crucifixion (the Word within the word), and the purple a symbol of the blood of Christ as well as of imperial splendour. On the page reproduced in plate 6, the gold cross and saturating purple are seen through and against each other, bringing to mind once again the great visionary cross described in *The Dream of the Rood*.

Debate continues over the exact origins of the Codex Aureus. A letter written by Boniface to Abbess Eadburh of Minster-in-Thanet provides evidence that the nuns of that abbey were practised in the art of writing in gold (chrysography) and may well have had the resources to produce such a splendid luxury book,[14] while Christ Church Canterbury is known to have owned a copy of Porphyrius's *carmina figurata*.[15] Whatever the case,

---

[12] See also Hrabanus Maurus, *In honorem Sanctae Crucis*, ed. M. Perrin, CCCM 100–100A (Turnhout, 1997).
[13] See further Richard Gameson, ed., *The Codex Aureus: An Eighth-Century Gospelbook: Stockholm, Kungliga Bibliotek, A. 135*, 2 vols (Copenhagen, 2002).
[14] *Der Briefe des Heiligen Bonifatius und Lullus*, ed. M. Tangl, MGH epistolae selectae I (Berlin, 1916), no. 35. See also Brown, 'Female Book-Ownership and Production in Anglo-Saxon England'; Michelle P. Brown, ed., *In the Beginning: Bibles before the Year 1000* (Washington, DC, 2006), 184
[15] Gameson, *St Augustine*, 337.

the book was definitely in the library of Christ Church from the middle of the ninth century when Ealdorman Ælfred and his wife Werburh bought the book back from the Vikings and presented it to the monastery. Their act of pious generosity is recorded, appropriately enough, on the chi-rho page of the manuscript (fig. 51).

+In nomine Domini nostri Ihesu Christi. Ic Aelfred aldormon ond Werburg min gefera begetan þas bec æt hæðnum herge mid uncre clæne feo; ðæt ðonne wæs mid clæne golde. Ond ðæt wit deodan for Godes lufan ond for uncre saule ðearf[e], ond for ðon ðe wit noldan ðæt ðas halgan beoc lencg in ðære hæðenesse wunaden, ond nu willað heo gesellan inn to Cristes circan God to lofe ond to wuldre ond to weorðunga, ond his ðrowunga to ðoncunga, ond ðæm godcundan geferscipe to brucen[n]e ðe in Cristes circan dæghwæmlice Godes lof ræraõ; to ðæm gerade ðæt heo mon arede eghwelce monaðe for Aelfred ond for Werburge ond for Alhðryðe, heora saulum to ecum lecedome, ða hwile ðe God gesegen hæbbe ðæt fulwiht æt ðeosse stowe beon mote. Ec swelce ic Aelfred *dux* ond Werburg biddað ond halsiað on Godes almaehtiges noman ond on allra his haligra ðæt nænig mon seo to ðon gedyrstig ðætte ðas halgan beoc aselle oððe aðeode from Cristes circan ða hwile ðe fulwiht [s]t[on]da[n mote].
Aelfre[d]   Werbur[g]   Alhðryð[16]

(+In the name of our Lord Jesus Christ. I Ælfred ealdorman, and Werburg my wife bought this book from the heathen army with our own money; that purchase was made with pure gold. And we did that for the love of God and for the benefit of our souls, and because neither of us wanted these holy writings to remain longer in heathen hands. And now we wish to present them to Christ Church for the love and glory and honour of God, and in thanks for his sufferings, and for the use of the pious Christ Church community which daily glorifies God; in order that they should be read aloud each month for Ælfred and for Werburg and for Alhthryth, for their souls' eternal salvation, as long as God commands that Christians might survive in that place. And further I, Ælfred earl, and Werburg beg and entreat in the name of God almighty and all his saints that no man should be so bold as to give away or take this holy book from Christ Church as long as Christians survive there.
Ælfred   Werburg   Alhthryth their daughter

Their act of piety is thus written in such a way that it surrounds the monogram of Christ, the name of God to whom their entreaty is addressed.

---

[16] Dorothy Whitelock, ed., *Sweet's Anglo-Saxon Reader in Prose and Verse* (Oxford, 1967), 205.

While the cross-patterned pages looked to late antiquity for their models, the chi-rho page is indebted to earlier Insular art. The fact that this section of Matthew's gospel is given special attention at all is an Insular phenomenon following in the tradition of manuscripts like the Lindisfarne Gospels or the Book of Durrow (Dublin, Trinity College Library, MS A.4.5 (57)), and the spiral patterns within or against which the great chi floats should be compared with the designs in those earlier manuscripts. Together with the animal ornament that fills the chi and the spaces between the letters of 'XPI autem', they give this page a dynamism and vivacity that the patterned pages cannot match. As in Lindisfarne, image is used here to bring the text to life. With the exception of the beast-headed arms of the chi, the animal ornament of this page reflects its Southumbrian origins. Here we see complete animals (and one human figure) often symmetrically displayed within the compartments formed by and between the letters of the text, rather than the shape-shifting forms of the animal-letters in the Lindisfarne Gospels or the Cathach of St Columba. But like the letters of those manuscripts, the style and motifs seen here are based on those of metalwork, and are designed to indicate the treasured nature of the word.[17] Along with the copious amount of gold that gives the manuscript its name they also work literally to turn the word into a precious object.

The chi-rho and patterned pages of the Codex Aureus bring imagery into the space of the text, but the Bury Psalter (Vatican, Biblioteca Apostolica Vaticana MS reg lat 12), made sometime between c. 1020 and the mid-eleventh century, takes the opposite approach, exploiting the space of the margin and surrounding the words of the psalms with imagery.[18] The psalter was made for the monastery of Bury St Edmunds either in house or at Christ Church Canterbury.[19] Its style and iconography have been linked with the Harley 603 psalter made at Christ Church, but artists and scribes did travel so the connection is not necessarily a sign

---

[17] The animal ornament in the Book of Cerne is based on a style of metalwork known as the 'Trewhiddle style', named after a silver hoard found at Trewhiddle, Cornwall, in 1774. It is characterized by lively triangular animals confined within self-contained fields. The style quickly became popular across the south of England. In Kent and Mercia it was particularly influential on a group of eighth- and ninth-century manuscripts known as the 'Tiberius group', which includes the Codex Aureus and the Book of Cerne discussed below. On the Trewhiddle style see David M. Wilson and Christopher E. Blunt, 'The Trewhiddle Hoard', *Archaeologia* 98 (1961), 75–122. On the Tiberius group as a whole see Brown, *The Book of Cerne*; Jennifer Morrish, 'An Examination of Literature and Learning in the Ninth Century', unpublished D.Phil dissertation, Oxford University, 1982.
[18] The images are reproduced in full in Thomas H. Ohlgren, *Anglo-Saxon Textual Illustration: Photographs of Sixteen Manuscripts with Descriptions and Index* (Kalamazoo, MI, 1992), no. 3.
[19] The calendar (fols. 7–12) includes Bury feasts highlighted in gold. There is also a prayer to the Virgin and St Edmund on folio 162v, as well as references to the foundation of the community and dedication of its church in the Easter Tables (fols. 16v–19r).

of provenance. The illustrations of the Bury Psalter are a development of the 'literal' psalter illustration tradition exemplified by Harley 603 and the Eadwine Psalter, in which the images literally translate the psalm texts into visual narratives, but for the most part they are far less literal, highlighting particular words or passages from the individual psalms rather than presenting a complete pictorial translation. On folio 22r, for example, in the margin next to Psalm 2, a crowned figure who could be either Christ or David (or both) stands on a hill labelled 'mons syon' and holds a scroll inscribed with verse 6 of the psalm: 'Ego autem constitutum sum rex ab eo super sion, montem sanctum eius praedicans praeceptum eius' ('But I am appointed king by him over Sion his holy mountain, preaching his commandment'). The figure stands frontally starring straight out at the viewer in a way that underscores the importance of his identity and his message. Moreover, in contrast to the arrangement of images in Harley 603 or the Eadwine Psalter which are arranged within the central space of the page preceding the psalms they illustrate, the drawings in the Bury Psalter appear alongside, above, around and even across the words on the page, giving the book a dynamic liveliness unlike anything in the other two manuscripts. A demon on the bottom of folio 24v shoots an arrow across the page and hits a female figure holding a vessel labelled 'vas mortis', an image which is a visually entertaining reference to the psalm's focus on the punishment of sinners. On folio 73v the Ascension of Christ surrounds the text of Psalm 67 in reference to the opening verse of the psalm 'Let God arise', as well as to 67:19 'Thou hast ascended on high'. Mary and the apostles stand in the left and right margins of the page looking and gesturing up towards the ascending Christ, only his feet and the hem of his garment visible at the top of the page. This 'disappearing Christ' type of Ascension is an Anglo-Saxon innovation.[20] A second Anglo-Saxon innovation appears in the margins beside Psalm 60 on folio 68v. As an allusion to the God of time who adds days, years and generations to time (verse 60:7), the Creator is depicted as a head above a circle of Creation (fig. 49).[21] From his mouth issue trumpets and within the circle that forms his body, his hands hold a balance. The sense of movement in the image is quite subtle. The world is just in the process of coming into being by means of both the word, signified by the fiery trumpets, and the tools of measure, the balance. A crowned king kneels beneath the image, one hand raised to his mouth in a gesture that suggests the prayers and songs of praise offered in the psalm. The composition as a whole can thus be understood as a metaphor for the book, also produced through a combination of words and tools, and its function, to be recited or sung. The scribe/artist once again takes his

---

[20] See below p. 234.
[21] Similar images appear in the Tiberius Psalter (London, BL, Cotton Tiberius C.vi, fol. 7v) and London, British Library, Royal I.E.VII, fol. 1v.

place in an authorial genealogy that stretches back to the Word, and the book's readers are the descendants of the Old Testament men and women who first sang the psalms.

The tripartite division of the manuscript was to have been marked by framed initial pages introducing Psalms 1, 51 and 101, but only the first two were completed. Both pick up on the image of Creation and its obvious connection to the creation and reception of the book. At the centre of the enlarged B of Psalm 1 (Beatus vir), is a writing monk most likely intended to be a portrait of the scribe, a predecessor to the portrait of Eadwine (plate 5). If the two birds contained within medallions in the borders of the frame may be identified as doves, they serve to link the writing monk with both David, author of the psalms, and the Holy Spirit which inspires all writers of sacred texts. The initial Q that begins Psalm 51 (Quid gloriaris) contains the enthroned Virgin holding a palm and sceptre with a dragon at her feet. Inscribed above her are the words 'oliva fructifera', referring to the fruitful olive tree of verse 10. Two veiled book-holding women gaze up at her from the roundels of the borders. The inscription and adoring figures help to unite the reader with both word and image by evoking the last two verses of the psalm:

> 10. But I, as a fruitful olive tree in the house of God, have hoped in the mercy of God for ever yea for ever and ever.
>
> 11. I will praise thee for ever, because thou hast done it: and I will wait on thy name, for it is good in the sight of the saints.

The initial that begins Psalm 1 in the Bury Psalter contains an image of the scribe, but in the very late Anglo-Saxon gospel book now in Reims (Bibliothèque Municipale, MS 9), the composition is reversed and the text becomes almost a detail at the centre of the image of evangelist as scribe (fig. 52). Many evangelist portraits include the first words of the appropriate gospel on the page of the book or scroll in or on which they write, but what sets the Reims gospel book apart is that the words are not repeated on the page that follows so that the image literally becomes the incipit of the text. To be sure, with the exception of Matthew, the Reims evangelists are not actually shown in the process of writing, but rather are gesturing or pointing to the openings of their gospels which are written in gold letters on plaques rather than in open books. As Gameson notes, the compositions may owe something to the plaque-holding angels that are part of the often lengthy pictorial introductions in Ottonian liturgical manuscripts,[22] but the integration of word and image is wholly Anglo-Saxon. Image and word appear as simultaneous creations. The rigid lines, stiff poses and very stylized and tame acanthus ornament of the miniatures

---

[22] Gameson, *Role of Art*, 41; see also Robert G. Calkins, *Illuminated Books of the Middle Ages* (Ithaca, NY, 1983), ch. 4.

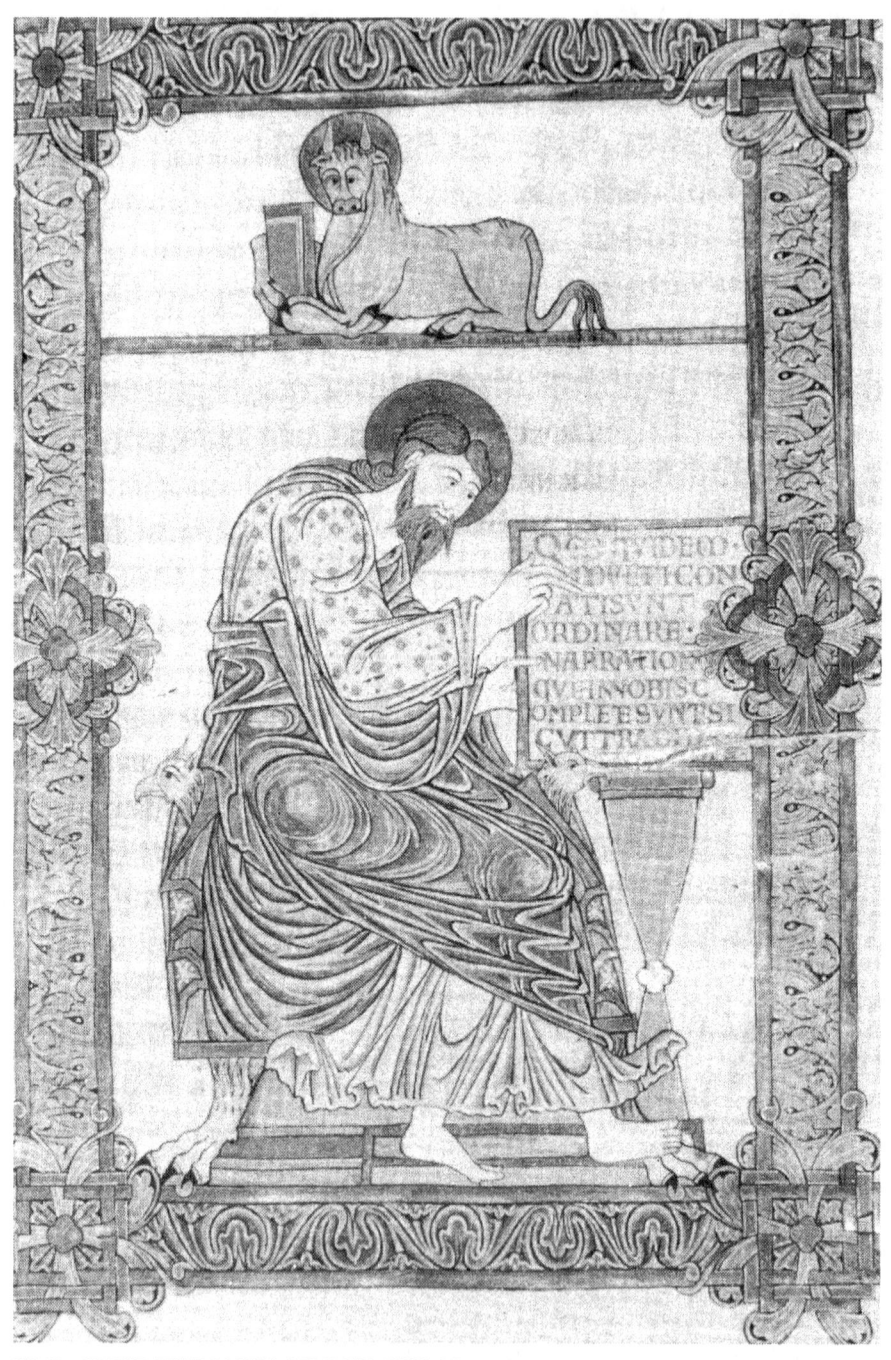

FIG. 52. ST LUKE, REIMS GOSPELS. REIMS, BIBL. MUN., MS 9, FOL. 88

may not be as visually exciting as the dynamic drawings of the Bury Psalter and other manuscripts, but the style does suggest a solemnity and grandeur appropriate to its luxury status. Moreover, the generous amount of gold used in the miniatures creates a flickering play of light across the page and brings the words at its centre to life. The manuscript was donated to St Remi, Reims, by Ealdorman Ælfgar of Mercia in memory of his son Burchard interred at that monastery.

## ANGLO-SAXON EVANGELISTS

Evangelist portraits and other types of author portrait are always images that provide a form of visual exegesis on the production of texts. Anglo-Saxon evangelists, their writings and texts relating to them constitute an important class of manuscript art, functioning in a profoundly intertextual and intervisual way. While most evangelist portraits are contained in gospel books, they also occur in, or have a strong influence on, other types of book – as the discussion of the portrait of the scribe Eadwine in chapter 4 makes clear.

The Book of Cerne is a prayerbook made *c.* 820–40 in Mercia, possibly for Bishop Aedelwald of Lichfield.[23] It contains gospel extracts accompanied by portraits of the four evangelists, but the images introduce texts from the conclusions rather than the beginnings of the gospels.[24] The Cerne evangelist miniatures are unique in depicting the evangelist symbols as full-length figures standing beneath arches surmounted by roundels containing busts of the evangelists (figs. 53, 54), and Michelle Brown has quite reasonably suggested that the innovative compositions might be attributable to the fact that Cerne is not a gospel book, and the designer(s) and artists might have felt less bound by tradition.[25] Inscriptions contained within the miniatures bring out the relationship between evangelist and symbol. Each inscription is divided in two with the first half identifying the evangelist and the second half the evangelist in the form of his symbol. The inscription on the Matthew page reads '+Hic Matheus in humanitate. +Hic Matheus in angelica asspectu videtur' (+Here Matthew appears in human form. +Here Matthew is seen in the aspect of an angel). That surrounding John and his eagle reads '+Hic Johannis in humanitate. +Hic Johannis vertit frontem in aqvilam' (+Here John appears in human form. +Here John changes his likeness to that of an eagle). The inscriptions draw our attention to the transformative relationship between author and symbol, while facial expression and the shape of the haloed heads, as well as colour, visually underscore the fact that author and symbol are identical. While it is far more common for

---

[23] See most especially Brown, *The Book of Cerne*, 178–83.
[24] See Brown, *Book of Cerne*, on the manuscript's contents.
[25] Brown, *Book of Cerne*, 74.

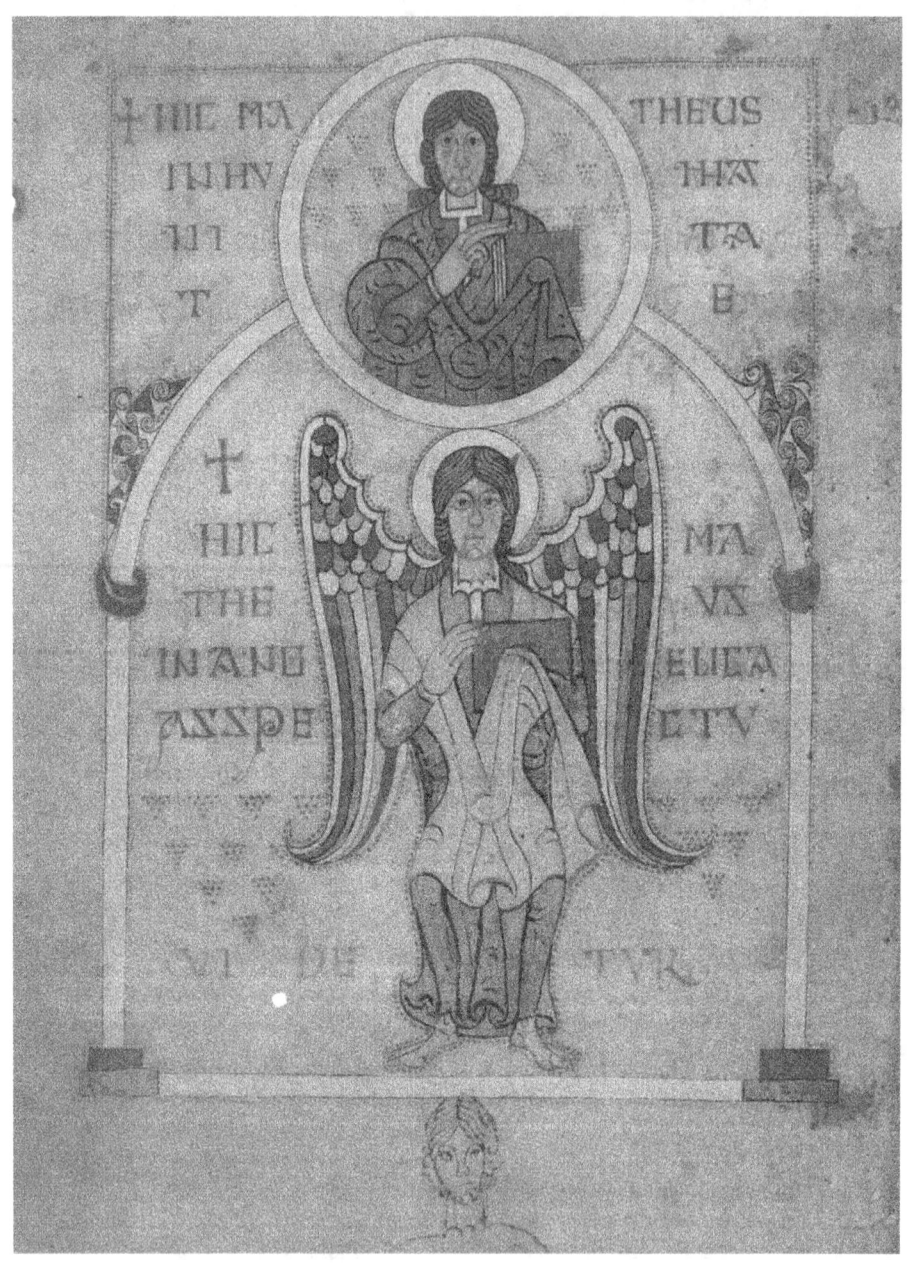

FIG. 53. ST MATTHEW, THE BOOK OF CERNE. CAMBRIDGE, UNIVERSITY LIBRARY, LL.1.10, FOL. 2V

BOOKS, WORDS AND BODIES

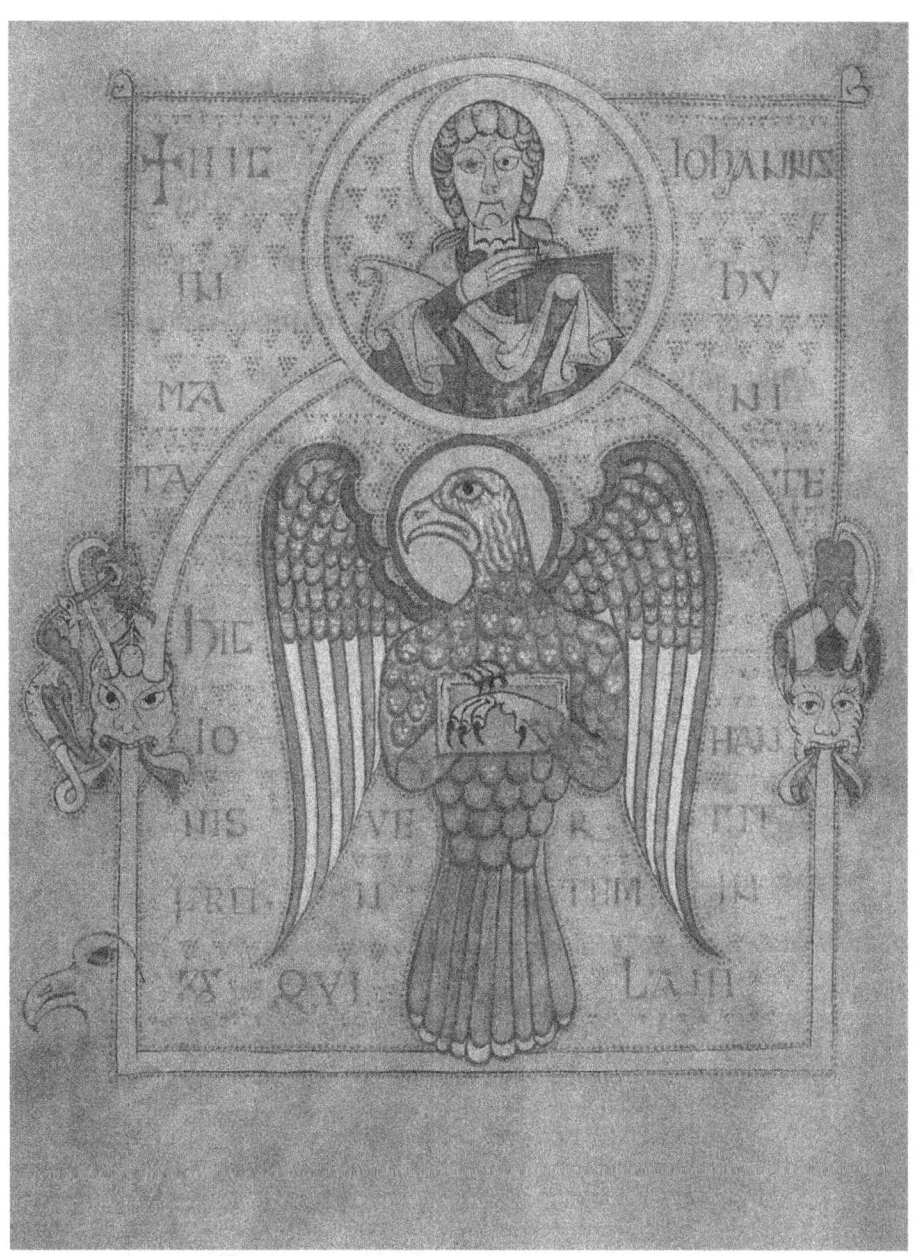

FIG. 54. ST JOHN, THE BOOK OF CERNE, CAMBRIDGE, UNIVERSITY LIBRARY, LL.1.10, FOL. 31V

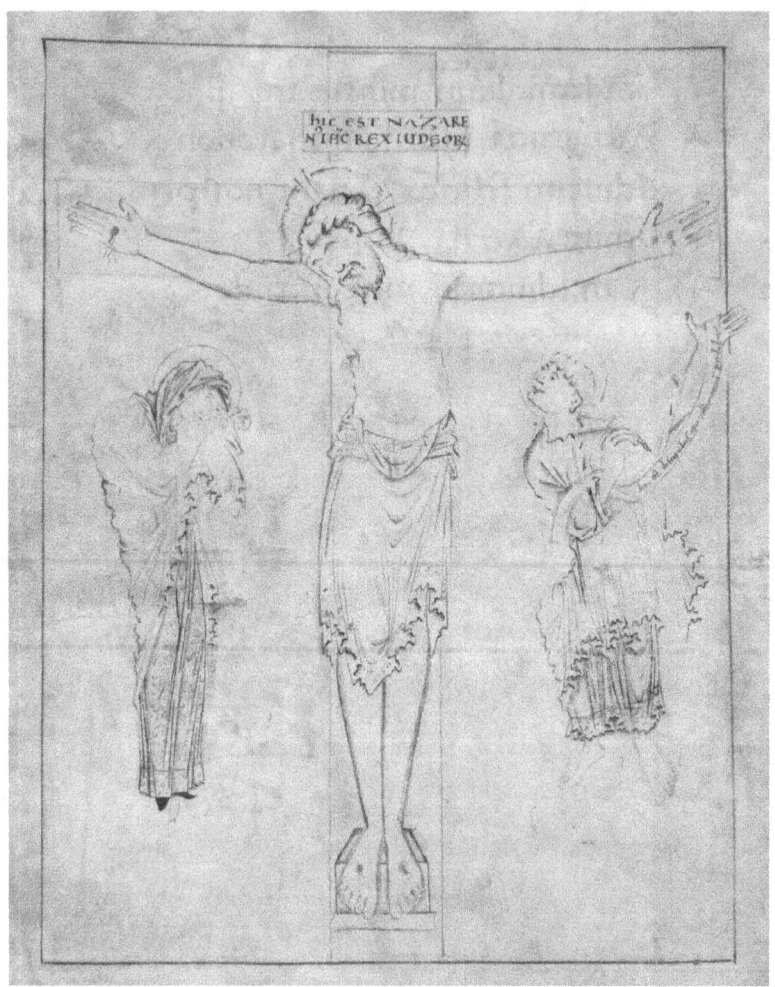

FIG. 55. CRUCIFIXION, THE RAMSEY PSALTER. LONDON, BRITISH LIBRARY, MS HARLEY 2904, FOL. 3V

evangelist portraits to depict the symbol inspiring the writing evangelist (as in the Lindisfarne Gospels portrait of Matthew (fig. 8) in which the evangelist is shown writing beneath his trumpeting symbol), the Cerne composition emphasizes the dual nature of the single figure – no doubt intended as a reference to the dual nature of Christ about whom the four wrote.

The representation of unity and difference is carried through the series of four evangelist portrait pages, demonstrating that the gospels themselves are a unity in four parts, and that the four evangelists speak with one voice, and this is achieved through both text and image. The first part of each of the four inscriptions, the part surrounding the evangelist bust, is identical but the second part differs,[26] and while the basic composition of each page is identical, colour and details of both the frames and figures differ. Moreover, as is usual with evangelist portraits, subtle details help to establish pairings within the group of four. In Cerne the pairing of Matthew with John and Mark with Luke is achieved through the representation of the symbols, with those of Matthew and John depicted frontally and those of Mark and Luke in three-quarter profile. Both Matthew and John witnessed the events about which they wrote, while Mark and Luke did not.[27]

St John held an especially crucial position throughout the Middle Ages because of his importance as a teacher, a witness, and the apostle who was closest to both Christ and God. He alone had, in the words of Alcuin, seen 'the Word in the beginning, God issuing from God, light from light'.[28] The opening words of his gospel were also believed to have special power and were sometimes written on tiny scrolls and worn as amulets. In the Ramsey Psalter (London, BL, MS Harley 2904), produced in Winchester in the last quarter of the tenth century, John appears in his role as eye-witness to the Crucifixion (fig. 55). To the right of Christ, framed by the blood that flows from the wound in his hand and side, stands the Virgin Mary holding her face in her hands in sorrow, her body closed in upon itself in mourning and contemplation. In contrast, John stands on the opposite side of the cross gazing intently up at the dead body of Christ and displaying a scroll on which he has just written the words 'Hic est discipulus qui testimonium perhibit' ('This is the disciple who giveth testimony'). The words are from John 21.24: 'This is the disciple who giveth testimony for these things, and hath written these things and we know that his testimony is true. As with the inscriptions discussed in chapter 4, the words echo those of the evangelist's eye-witness account of the Crucifixion in John 19.35 as well as the Resurrection testimony of John 21.24. 'Physical sight thus becomes a metaphor for spiritual insight',[29] and the sorrow and suffering of the Crucifixion are balanced by the triumph of the Resurrection.

The themes of sin and redemption inherent in the Crucifixion, in which Christ died to redeem the sins of humanity, are taken up in the words of Psalm 1 which the drawing introduces. The connection is emphasized by John's dramatic pose and the hand which sweeps his scroll upwards towards the beginning of the psalm. The image of John as author also

---

[26] The second part of the inscriptions on the Mark and Luke pages read: '+Hic Marcus imaginem tenet leonis' (+Here Mark holds the image of a lion); '+Hic Lucas formam accepit vituli' (+Here Luke takes the nature of a calf).
[27] See further Augustine, *De concensu evangelistarum*, ed. F. Weihrich, CSEL 43 (New York, 1963).
[28] Alcuin, *Commentariorum in Joannem, lib. 1*, PL 304, col. 1045; Bede, *Homilia VII* and *Homilia VIII*, PL 94, cols. 38 and 46.
[29] See further O'Reilly, 'St John as a Figure of the Contemplative Life', 166.

takes the place of the image of David as author and composer of the psalms that had become common in early medieval manuscripts and, in so doing, the idea that the words of the Old Testament are fulfilled in those of the New is visualized. The typological relationship between the two was also made visible in the introduction by Insular and Anglo-Saxon artists of a christological cycle of images to the standard imagery of the life of David.[30]

It is also possible to extend the importance of authorship beyond the manuscript itself. In a sermon for the Assumption, Ælfric took up the image of the writing evangelist, describing the eye-witness record of the Crucifixion made by John as he and Mary stood in sorrow beneath the cross.[31] The Ramsey Psalter image is in many ways a first; it is the first to show the writing evangelist as part of the Crucifixion, it is the first to show the grieving Mary, and it is a drawing of exceptional beauty, having no immediate precedent in Anglo-Saxon art.[32] There are numerous earlier images that are executed in the outline drawing technique, but none that show such a delicacy of style, liveliness of line, or impression of the volume and movement of the figures. T. A. Heslop has drawn particular attention to the way in which the artist used the edge and nib of the pen to vary the strength and width of the lines, demonstrating a true mastery of the art of drawing.[33] The use of colour creates an aesthetically pleasing formal balance and also works symbolically (along with scale) to unite the figures of Mary and John and to distinguish them from the body of Christ. Similarly, the firm outlines of Christ's body contrast with the wavy lines used for the Virgin and St John. At the same time, the artist has suggested John's christomimesis by subtly echoing the curve of Christ's body in that of the writing evangelist. As was the case with the frontispiece to St Dunstan's Classbook (fig. 47), the size of Christ, and the way in which his cross stands in front of the lines delineating the landscape and fills the frame, push his crucified body out towards the viewer as a focus for devotion.

The artist of Harley 2904 worked on at least three other surviving manuscripts: London, BL, MS Harley 2506 (folios 36–44v), a copy of Cicero's *Aratea* along with treatises by Abbo of Fleury; a copy of Gregory's Homilies on Ezekiel (Orléans, Bibliothèque Municipale MS 175); and the Boulogne Gospels (Boulogne, Bibliothèque Municipale MS 11), on which

---

[30] See Kathleen Openshaw, 'Weapons in the Daily Battle: Images of the Conquest of Evil in the Early Medieval Psalter', *Art Bulletin* 75.1 (1993), 17–38.

[31] Raw, *Anglo-Saxon Crucifixion Iconography*, 97–8; Ælfric, *The Homilies of the Anglo-Saxon Church. The First Part, Containing The Sermones Catholici, or Homilies of Ælfric*, ed. and trans. Benjamin Thorpe, 2 vols (London, 1844, 1846), vol. 1, xxx, 438.

[32] The great initial B of Psalm 1 in the same manuscript, with its lush acanthus ornament, golden borders and central beast-head mask, is another innovation that was to have a powerful influence for centuries to come.

[33] T. A. Heslop, 'The Implication of the Utrecht Psalter in English Romanesque Art', in *Romanesque Art and Thought in the Twelfth Century*, ed. Hourihane, 267–89, at 273.

he collaborated with Abbot Otbert (990–1007). The first two manuscripts are attributed to Fleury and the third to Saint-Bertin, suggesting that the artist was an itinerant Anglo-Saxon working both within England and in Continental houses that maintained close connections with their English counterparts.[34]

The third of these manuscripts, the late tenth-century Boulogne Gospels, has the most extensive programme of illumination of any surviving Anglo-Saxon gospel book. It contains sixteen elaborately decorated Canon Tables, a depiction of Christ in majesty, four evangelist portraits, four narrative scenes on each of the gospel incipit pages, and an additional folio depicting the ancestors of Christ between the portrait and incipit pages in Matthew. The extended cycle of imagery that prefaces Matthew's gospel may again show the influence of Ottonian gospel books in which elaborate pictorial and decorated gospel introductions were becoming common.[35] Each of the four sets of images and incipits is different and each provides a different way of presenting the integration of image and text. The Matthew sequence begins on folio 10v where Matthew sits hunched over his gospel book writing at left, his wide open eyes looking towards the figures of David, Abraham, Isaac and Jacob seated in two tiers at the right. On the facing page (folio 11r), twenty-four ancestors of Christ are depicted as half figures standing within a four-tiered arcade. Folio 11v (fig. 56) is divided between a further twelve portraits of Christ's ancestors in the upper half of the page, and the Annunciation and Visitation in the lower half. Folio 12r (fig. 57) is again divided vertically with the Annunciation to the shepherds and Nativity at left and the opening words of the gospel at right. Most of the figures and scenes are accompanied by identifying inscriptions. The way in which Matthew sits writing as he gazes towards the images before him suggests a visualization of the historical events that lie behind his gospel and perhaps also emphasizes his role as witness to the gospel events even though he could not have been witness to the specific episodes depicted. At the same time, the sequence presents the first chapter of Matthew's gospel in an abbreviated pictorial form: 'The book of the generation of Jesus Christ, the son of David, the son of Abraham ... And he knew her not till she brought forth her first born son: and he called his name Jesus.' Here image both precedes and leads us into the text. The two are quite literally bridged on the incipit page itself, where the semicircle containing the choir of angels at the top of the page crosses the space of both, simultaneously directing our attention to the end of the pictorial narrative and the beginning of the written one. The

---

[34] Dunstan had gone into exile in Flanders in 955, only to return to England when he was appointed archbishop of Canterbury in 957, and the relationship between Canterbury and Flemish Benedictine houses remained strong.
[35] See Calkins, *Illuminated Books of the Middle Ages*, ch. 4. Temple (*Anglo-Saxon Manuscripts*, 66) notes specific connections with manuscripts produced in Reichenau, Trier and Fulda.

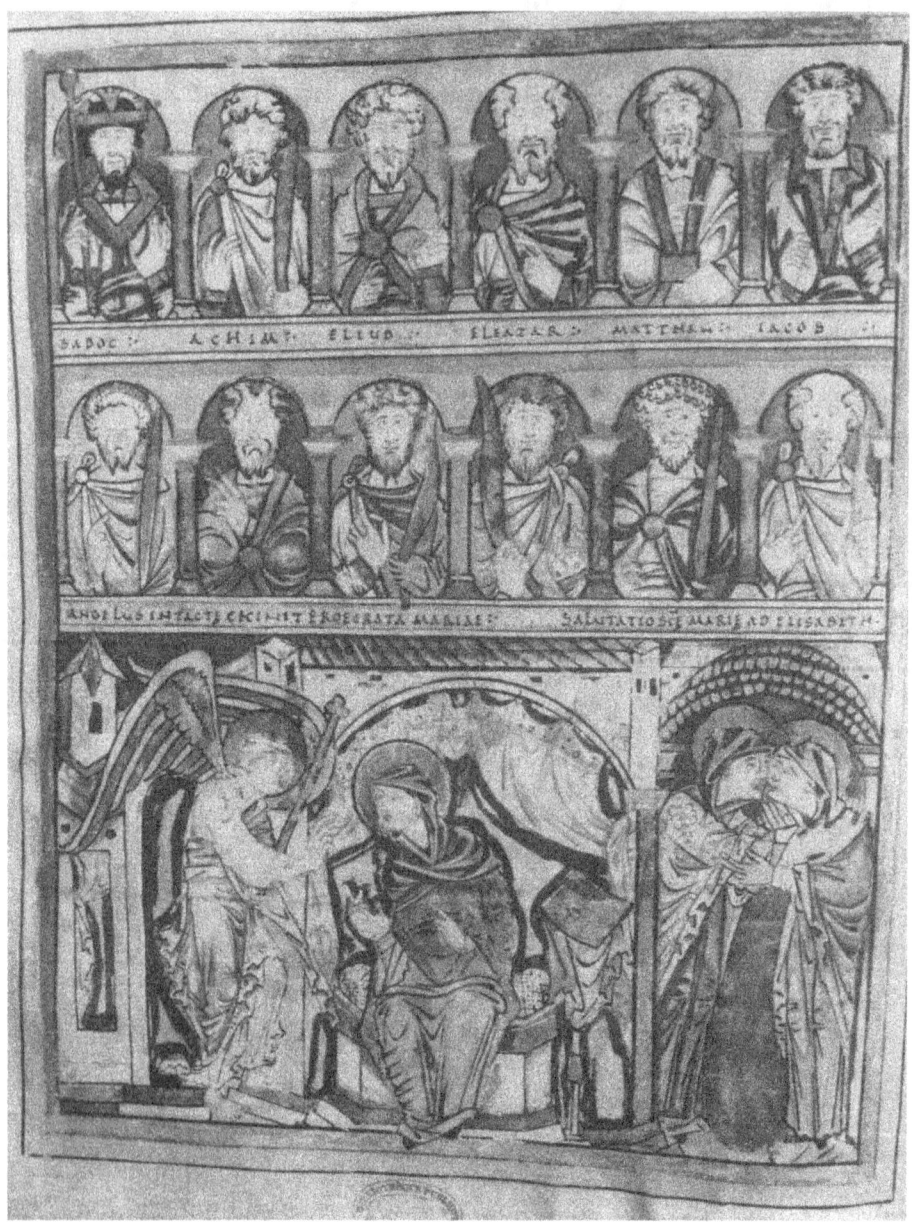

FIG. 56.   ANCESTORS OF CHRIST, BOULOGNE GOSPELS. BOULOGNE, BIBL. MUN. MS 11, FOL. 11V

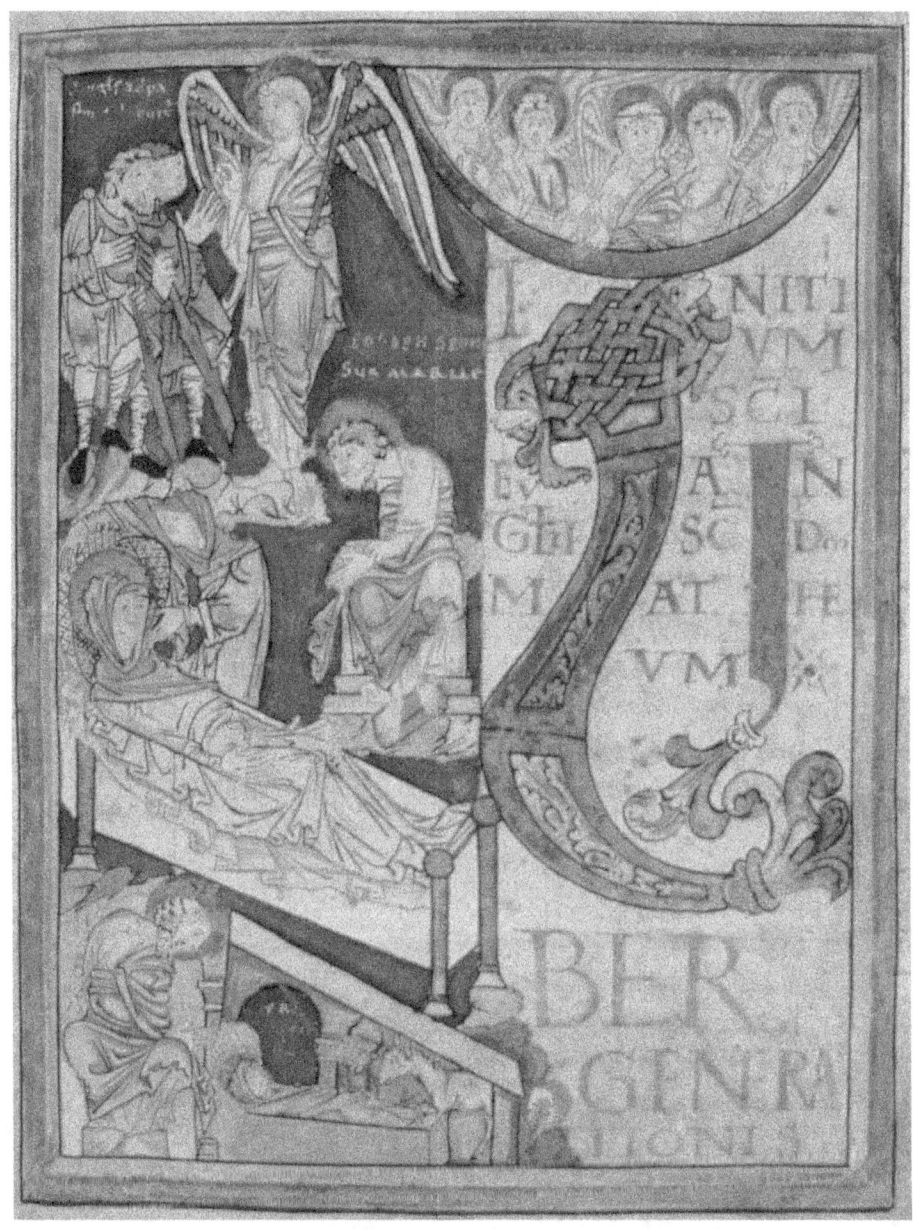

FIG. 57. ANNUNCIATION AND NATIVITY, BOULOGNE GOSPELS. BOULOGNE, BIBL. MUN. MS 11, FOL. 12

opening letter of Matthew's gospel, the L of 'Liber', is also both text and ornament. It is a part of the word 'Liber', but at the same time the beast heads that peer from the interlace at its top draw the viewer's eyes back to the Nativity and the choir of angels, with colour helping to further unite it with the imagery.

Richard Gameson has discussed a slightly different sort of coming together of word and image on the opening pages of John's gospel. Here Christ is enthroned at the centre of the great letter I that fills the middle of the page and begins the gospel text: 'In principio erat verbum et verbum erat ...' ('In the beginning was the word and the word was ...'). It too is both text and image, and the two angels that flank and gesture towards it direct our attention to its status as image and to the identity of Christ as Word. The figures stand against a background containing three different texts, the gospel rubric and incipit proper in the lower two-thirds of the page, and at the top the titulus 'Principium finisque patris verbum deus hic est' (Here is the beginning and the end the Word of God the Father). As Gameson makes clear, 'This placing of an image of Christ ... actually on the first letter of the gospel itself may surely be regarded as a deliberate conflation of word and image to illustrate – to equivalence in fact – the mystical, paradoxical beginning of John's text: "In the beginning was the Word and the Word was with God and the Word was God".[36]

The tenth-century Arenberg Gospels (New York, Pierpont Morgan Library M 869) is also a product of Christ Church Canterbury. The book's programme of illustration consists of a frontispiece with the Crucifixion witnessed by Mary and John, eight pages of Canon Tables decorated with scenes that elaborate on the nature of Christ, and four evangelist portraits, all executed in a combination of colour outline drawing and painting. The evangelists all sit writing within architectural settings derived from architectural details in the Utrecht Psalter (Utrecht, University Library, MS 32), which had been brought to England at some point before the year 1000, and became hugely influential, especially in Canterbury.[37] Above each of the evangelists is his symbol, and in the frames surrounding the symbols are inscribed lines 355–8 of Book 1 of Sedulius's fifth-century *Carmen paschale*. The association of these lines with the four evangelists was known by the sixth century in Italy, and was used in the sixth-century St Augustine's Gospels (CCCC MS 286) believed to have been brought to England during the time of St Augustine. This raises the possibility that the repetition of the lines in the Arenberg Gospels might be a reference back to the origins of Canterbury and the Anglo-Saxon church. As the Eadwine Psalter and the manuscripts associated with Eadwig Basan demonstrate,

---

[36] Gameson, *Role of Art*, 41, see also 132–3.
[37] For the extent of the Utrecht Psalter's influence on later manuscript art see Koert van der Horst, William Noel and W. C. M. Wüstefeld *The Utrecht Psalter in Medieval Art: Picturing the Psalms of David* ('t Goy, 1996).

Christ Church was certainly concerned with its own origins and history and with referring back to them in the many manuscripts its scribes and artists produced; however, the lines were also frequently included in Carolingian evangelist portraits and thus may have been too widespread for so specific a reference to have been either intended or understood.

As is often the case with evangelist portraits, the portrait of John (fig. 58) is treated differently from, and in this case slightly more elaborately than, those of the other three. Matthew, Mark and Luke all write or look down at the books in which they are about to write while John, pen in hand, gazes up towards the hand of God emerging from the upper left.[38] Above him his symbol, the eagle, grasps a rolled scroll in its talons and spreads its wings as if in flight, suggesting that John has already written and that his words are now being taken up to God. The image captures perfectly the words of the inscription: '+more · volans · aquile · verbo · petit · astra · Iohannes' (by means of the flying eagle St John reaches the heavens through the word). Jane Rosenthal has pointed out that 'the medallion encircling the eagle, which is framed in leaves bound at the top like a wreath, transforms the beast of John into a symbol of Christ's victorious ascension',[39] a way of symbolizing John's closeness to Christ as well as his christomimetic nature.[40] The transformation of the eagle as well as the relationship between John and Christ are underscored by the arrangement of the inscription, which places the words *aquile* and *verbo* either side of the medallion in the upper border of the frame, as well as by the similar angle at which both the eagle with its scroll and John with his footstool are depicted. Both figures seem to be rising up to heaven, while none of the other evangelists nor their symbols is depicted at such an angle.[41]

That John's word reaches the kingdom of heaven, as the words of the inscription tell us it does, is suggested subtly by the breaking of the frame and inclusion of a miniature building representing the kingdom of heaven at the top of the page. As is the case with all gospels books, the four

---

[38] By tradition John's gospel was transmitted to him directly from God via the Holy Spirit, while Matthew, Mark and Luke wrote from the words of Christ, Peter and Paul respectively. The tradition is recorded by Aldred in the colophon added to the Lindisfarne Gospels in the tenth century. See Brown, *Lindisfarne Gospels*, 103; and above p. 34.

[39] Jane Rosenthal, 'The Unique Architectural Settings of the Arenberg Evangelists', in *Studien zur Mittelalterliche Kunst 800–1250. Festschrift für Florentine Mütherich zum 70 Geburtstag*, ed. Katharina Bierbrauer et al. (Munich, 1985), 145–56, at 152.

[40] See further Jerome, *Commentarium in Matheum*, ed. D. Hurst and M. Adriaen, CCSL 77 (Turnhout, 1969), 3–4; Augustine, *De consensu evangelistarum*, lib. I, cap. 4, 6–7; Augustine, *In evangelium Johannis*, ed. R. Williams, CCSL 36 (Turnhout, 1990), trac. I, 5, 2–3; Bede, *In Lucae evangelium expositio*, ed. D. Hurst, CCSL 120 (Turnhout, 1960), 8–10; O'Reilly, 'St John as a Figure of the Contemplative Life'; Jeffrey Hamburger, *St John the Divine: The Deified Evangelist in Medieval Art and Theology* (Berkeley, CA, 2002).

[41] All miniatures from the manuscript are reproduced in Ohlgren, *Anglo-Saxon Textual Illustration*.

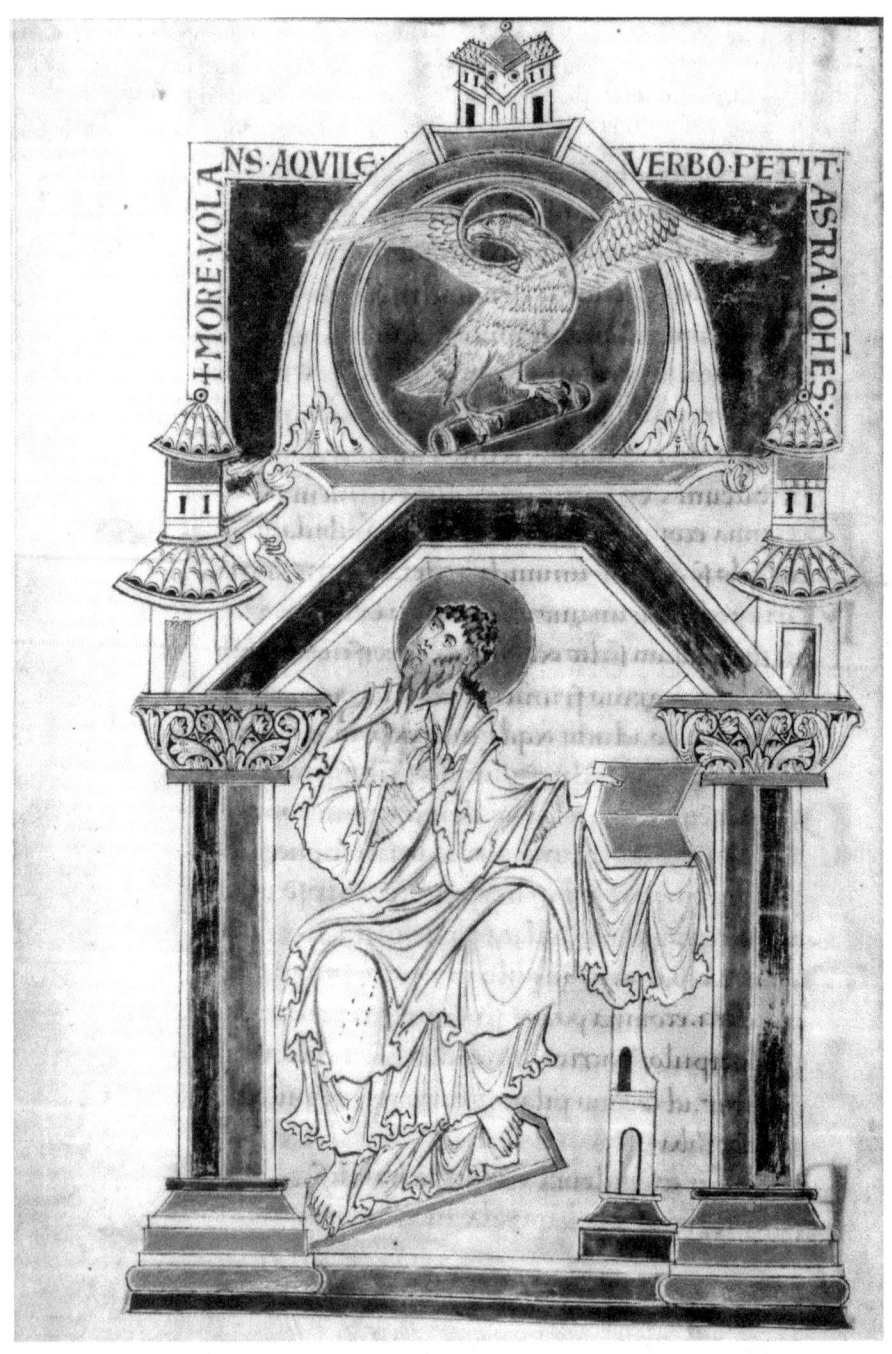

FIG. 58. ST JOHN, ARENBERG GOSPELS. NEW YORK, PIERPONT MORGAN LIBRARY, M. 869, FOL. 126V

evangelist portraits must be understood as a programme of illustration and not just separate images because, while each was the author of a discrete book, the four were understood as speaking with one voice. Read together, the evangelist portraits in the Arenberg Gospels reveal an increasing movement of the symbols with their scrolls and books upwards and out of the space of the miniature. The trapezoidal compartment that Matthew's symbol inhabits is completely contained within the bordered miniature, while the upper curve of the trefoil containing Mark's symbol breaks the lower bar of the border but not the upper one. The pinnacle at the top of the triangular pediment of the lion of Luke curls upward to break the border completely, and finally the medallion of John's eagle not only breaks the frame of the miniature but opens outward at the top towards the miniature kingdom of heaven.

## THE SCRIBE, THE ARTIST AND THE SELF

Whether or not professional lay artists existed in Anglo-Saxon England has been the subject of some speculation. Common sense tells us that they must have done so, especially in the later Anglo-Saxon period, but concrete evidence of their existence has not been forthcoming. We know the names of some artists – the Drahmal who made the Brussels Reliquary Cross and the makers of the Lindisfarne Gospels, for example – and we know that some, like the artist of the Ramsey Psalter, were itinerant and thus perhaps more likely to be professional, but beyond that we enter the realm of speculation. A scribal parallel for the Ramsey Psalter artist is provided by the famous Christ Church Canterbury scribe Eadwig Basan who is known to have been the scribe of the Eadwig Gospels (Hanover, Kestner Museum WMXXIa 36), the Eadwig (or Arundel) Psalter (London, BL, Arundel 155), the Grimbald Gospels (London, BL, Add. 34890), a gospel lectionary now in Florence (Florence, Biblioteca Medicea Laurenziana, Plut. XVII.20), several charters (S 22, 950, 985 and possibly 914), portions of the York Gospels (York Minster, Chapter Library, Add. 1) and two psalters (London, BL, Harley 603 and BL, Cotton Vespasian A.i). It is also believed that Eadwig was the artist of the Eadwig Gospels, the Eadwig Psalter and possibly also the York Gospels.[42] A portrait believed to be a self-portrait of Eadwig survives on folio 133r of the *c.* 1012–23 Eadwig Psalter (plate 7).[43]

---

[42] Karkov, 'Writing and Having Written'; see also Pfaff, 'Eadui Basan: Scriptorum Princeps?'
[43] Richard Gameson suggests alternatively that it is a portrait of the then dean of the monastery: 'The Scribe Speaks? Colophons in Early English Manuscripts', H. M. Chadwick Memorial Lecture 12 (Cambridge, 2002), 27; *Role of Art*, 86. In both the Eadwig Psalter and the Eadwig Gospels the text written on scrolls within the miniatures is in Eadwig's hand, suggesting that even if he was not the artist he worked very closely with the artist in the creation of the images. For this reason the identification of Eadwig as artist-scribe is accepted here.

The miniature shows the enthroned St Benedict presenting his Rule to the Christ Church community, while the prostrate Eadwig kisses his feet and offers him the psalter in return.[44] The combination of techniques and figure styles used for the miniature has received much attention. Benedict is seated in a formal frontal pose befitting his status as both the 'father of monasticism', as the inscription on his halo labels him, and saint. He is depicted in a combination of full colour wash and gold leaf that distinguishes him from the group of monks, depicted in outline drawing, who stand in somewhat exaggerated poses and in profile to the right. A number of devices have been used to bridge the temporal and spiritual gulf that separates Benedict from the Christ Church community: the Rule and the hands of Benedict and the monk who receives it, the scroll held by the hand of God, and the figure of Eadwig all cross the central column that forms the border between the two spaces.

The series of inscriptions within the miniature also work to further the hierarchy of importance established amongst the figures as well as to create a spiritual dialogue between them. One phrase on the scroll held by the hand of God is directed towards Benedict and the other towards the monks, establishing the rule of God as the basis both for the relationship between them and for the teachings of the books they exchange. On the side directed towards Benedict is a phrase from Luke 10.16, 'Qui vos audit, me audit' ('He who hears you hears me'), and on the side towards the monks 'Obedientes estote prepositi u[est]ro' ('be obedient to your superior'). On the open book held by the lead monk are the first words of the prologue to the Rule of Benedict: 'Ausculta, o fili, precepta'. The full opening line of the prologue reads 'Ausculta, o fili, precepta magistri, et inclina aurem cordis' ('Listen carefully, my son, to your master's precepts, and incline the ear of your heart'). Benedict's gesture towards the phrase makes it appear as if he is teaching the monks from the open book, while the prostrate Eadwig beneath his feet literally enacts the order to incline the ear of the heart. Though not written on the open book, these are words that the community would have known by heart, and their literal enactment is a sign that they are an active part of the monks' lived experience and not just empty words on the page. Similarly, Benedict's diadem bears the words 'timor dei' (fear of God), as Richard Gameson has noted, a reference to chapter 7 of the Rule which teaches the monks that 'The first step in humility then is for a man to set the fear of God always before his eyes'. Again, the lesson is embodied by Eadwig himself whose girdle bears the words 'zone of humility'. It is perhaps not because of misplaced pride, but rather because he shows himself obedient to both the words of the Rule and those of God, that Eadwig is depicted, like Benedict, in full colour, and that more of his body is located within the

---

[44] The book is inscribed *lib(er) ps(almorum)*.

space occupied by the saint than that occupied by the monks. The location of the miniature within the manuscript is also important. It is placed at the end of the psalter text, like a 'visual colophon',[45] and before the monastic canticles. It may thus be seen as a pictorial equivalent to the written colophon signed by Eadwig at the end of the Gospel of John in the Eadwig Gospels discussed below.

In his *Institutiones*, Cassiodorus had written about the power of the hand of the scribe, its ability to 'unleash tongues with the fingers' (*digitis lingua aperire*),[46] its power over evil and its service to the law of God:

> Arundine currente verba caelestia describuntur, ut, unde diabolus caput Domini in passione fecit percuti, inde eius calliditas posit extingui. accidit etiam laudibus eorum, quod factum Domini aliquo modo videntu emitari, qui legem suam, licet figuraliter sit dictum omnipotentis digiti operatione conscripsit. multa sunt quidem quae de tam insigni arte referantur, sed sufficit eos dici librarios, qui librae Domini iustitiaeque deserviunt.
>
> (With gliding pen the heavenly words are copied so that the devil's craft, by means of which he caused the head of the Lord to be struck during His passion, may be destroyed. They deserve praise too for seeming in some way to imitate the action of the Lord, who, though it was expressed figuratively, wrote His law with the use of His all-powerful finger. Much indeed is there to be said about such a distinguished art, but it is enough to mention the fact that those men are called scribes who serve zealously the scales of the Lord.)[47]

The Eadwig Psalter image is all about the law of God as it is translated by Benedict and manifested in his Rule, and as that is translated by Eadwig and manifested in this manuscript. The inscribed books and scrolls, and the manner in which they are passed from the hand of God and then from figure to figure, make that abundantly clear. Whether or not the image of Eadwig is in any way a portrait in the modern sense of an image that captures a subject's likeness, it is a portrait of Eadwig's professional identity and thus, in a sense, his 'self'. Eadwig was a monk, a maker of books and, in the latter capacity, a writer whose words mediated between the human and the divine – just as he is portrayed in the psalter miniature.

In the *c.* 1020 Eadwig Gospels, the pictorial programme presents a study of textual production and the power of words and scribes that could literally illustrate the words of Cassiodorus quoted above. It opens with

---

[45] Gameson, *Role of Art*, 86; 'The Scribe Speaks', 26–7.
[46] Cassiodorus, *Institutiones*, ed. Mynors, 75. See also Cassiodorus, *Explanation of the Psalms*, vol. 1, 441.
[47] Cassiodorus, *Institutiones*, ed. Mynors, 75–6; translation: L. W. Jones, ed., *An Introduction to Divine and Human Readings by Cassiodorus Senator* (New York, 1966), 109.

a pair of Canon Tables containing the hand of God holding a compass and scales and an image of Christ logos in their respective tympana that set the context for the human scribal creation that follows within that of divine Creation – the word descending from its source in the Word.[48] The four evangelists are represented not only in the act of writing – very much the norm for Anglo-Saxon evangelist portraits – but as enacting four sequential steps in the process of writing, and the lack of symbols helps to keep the viewer's focus on their very human activity. Matthew is preparing to write. He holds an open book and penknife in one hand and a pen in the other, his tools of scribal creation paralleling those of divine Creation held by the hand of God at the beginning of the manuscript. Mark sharpens his pen, and Luke puts pen to page. John holds out a scroll with the opening words of his gospel for the viewer to read. Beneath his feet is the prostrate figure of the heretic Arius, who holds a scroll inscribed with his denial of the Godhead impaled by the scroll bearing John's words which refute it. The text, written upside down on the scroll held by Arius, reads 'erat tempus quando non erat' ('there was a time when he was not'), while that held by John reads 'In principio erat verbum et verbum erat apud Deum et Deus erat verbum hoc erat in principio' ('In the beginning was the Word and the Word was with God, and the Word was God. The same was in the beginning'). This final miniature again refers back to the opening Canon Tables in which the beginning and the Word are presented simultaneously. There is surely no more subtle and masterful depiction of the power of words or scribes surviving from the early Middle Ages.

Eadwig's colophon, written just after the end of John's gospel, figures him as the successor to the four evangelists. It reads,

> Pro scriptore precem ne temnas fundere pater, Librum istum monachus scripsit EADUUIUS BASAN. Sit illi longa salus. Vale seruus dei .N. et memor esto mei.
>
> (Do not refrain from pouring forth a prayer for the scribe, father, this book was written by the monk Eadwig, surnamed Basan. May he have long-lasting health. Farewell servant of God, N, and remember me.)

The N of the final line may refer to an unnamed patron or it may be a sign of a more general appeal for prayers to any and all future readers. It also serves to align the pious reader with the scribe; both are servants of God whose copying and reading of scripture are signs of their service. As Cassiodorus explained in both his *Institutiones* and his commentary on Psalm 44.2, the Holy Spirit that was present in biblical authors was also present in those who devoutly preserved their words, whether through

---

[48] For a detailed study of the sequence of imagery see Karkov, 'Writing and Having Written'.

translation, or glossing or copying.[49] Eadwig's colophon asks the reader to write him or herself into the process by adding a name to the anonymous N of the colophon.

The evangelists of the Eadwig Gospels had an influence on a number of other gospel books and manuscripts, especially the mid-eleventh-century gospel lectionary now Cambridge, Pembroke College, MS 302. There are similarities in some of the details of style and iconography, especially the golden robes incised in imitation of niello work. More importantly, the evangelists are again depicted without their symbols and seated at their desks in four different activities that are all part of the unified act of writing: Matthew contemplates his open book and dips his pen in an inkwell; Mark sharpens his pen; Luke, his pen behind his ear, bends over the page; John begins to write.[50] The sequence is not as smooth as it is in the Eadwig Gospels, but its meaning is the same. In this manuscript there is no scribal colophon and the identities of scribe and artists are unknown – it is not in fact even clear in which monastery the manuscript was produced – but the function of the book and the role of the reader in the dissemination of its lessons are taken up in anecdotal scenes of reading and listening painted between the arches of the final Canon Tables (figs. 59, 60).[51] On folios 5v–6r a man, whose cowl suggests that he is a monk, reads from an open book, while across the page his student listens intently, one hand raised to his face as if in contemplation of the meaning of the words or lesson. On folio 6v a tonsured monk sits reading to himself from his open book.

Gospel lectionaries were meant to be used for readings aloud during the Mass. They were thus active vehicles of public instruction in ways that other sorts of manuscripts, personal prayerbooks for example, were not. The accounts of Christ's Passion in the first two gospels in Pembroke 302 have been marked to indicate the dialogue of Christ and other characters. It was quite common to mark both gospel books and lectionaries in this way as a means of indicating passages that were meant to be sung aloud, and the different letters marking the text served as graphic indicators of

---

[49] Cassiodorus, *Institutiones*, ed. Mynors, 1.15:11; translation: Jones, *Divine and Human Readings by Cassiodorus*, 109; Cassiodorus, *Explanation of the Psalms*, vol. 1, 441. See further O'Reilly, 'The Library of Scripture'. While there is little evidence that the *Institutiones* circulated in Anglo-Saxon England between the age of Bede and the eleventh century, *In Psalmos* was known and copied throughout the period. See Helmut Gneuss, *Handlist of Anglo-Saxon Manuscripts: a List of Manuscripts and Manuscript Fragments Written or Owned in England up to 1100* (Tempe, AZ, 2001), nos. 77e, 154f, 237 and 822f (*In Psalmos*), and nos. 263, 573, 713 and 185e (*Institutiones*).
[50] See Karkov, 'Evangelist Portraits and Book Production in Late Anglo-Saxon England'.
[51] On the debate over the manuscript's provenance see Karkov, 'Evangelist Portraits and Book Production in Late Anglo-Saxon England'; T. A. Heslop, 'Manuscript Illumination at Worcester c. 1055–1065: The Origins of the Pembroke Lectionary and the Caligula Troper', in *The Cambridge Illuminations: The Conference Papers*, ed. Panayotova, 65–76.

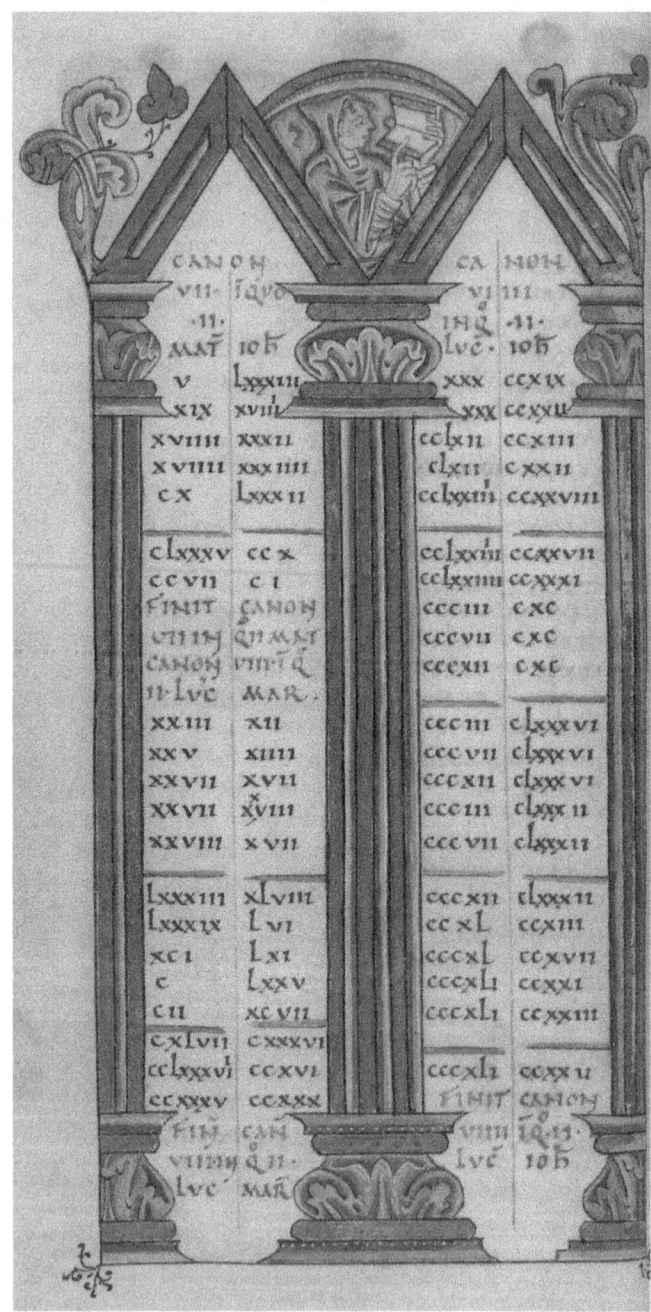

FIG. 59. CANON TABLE, HEREFORD GOSPELS. CAMBRIDGE, PEMBROKE COLLEGE MS 302, FOL. 5V

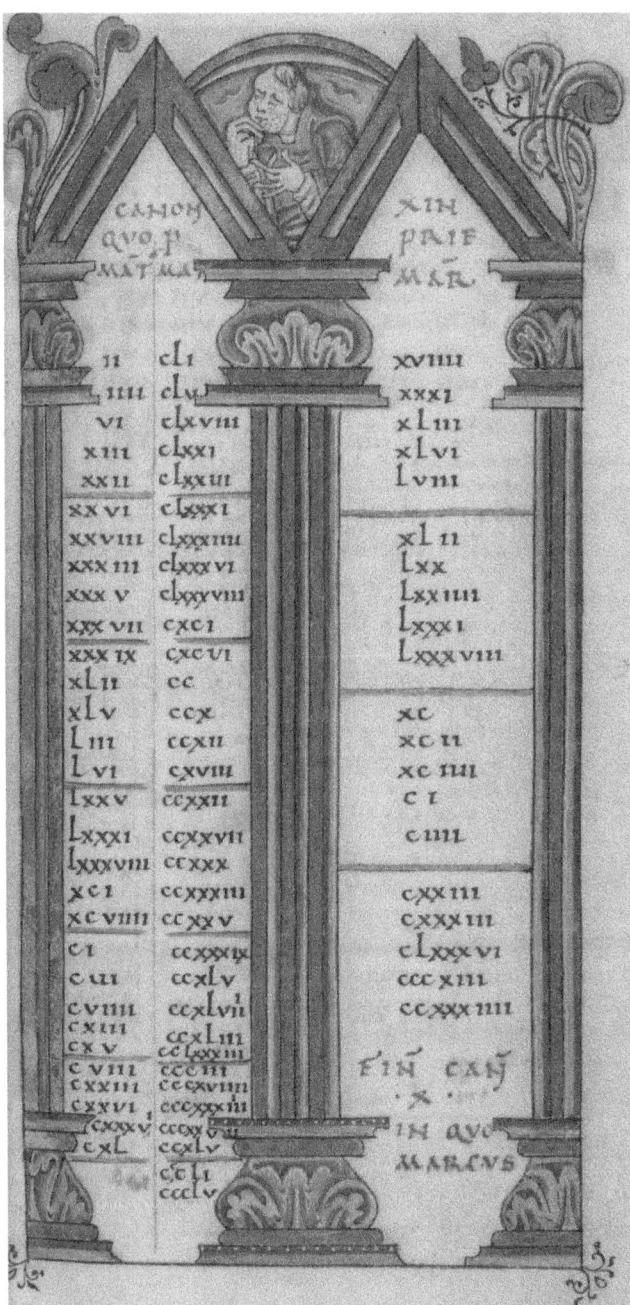

FIG. 60. CANON TABLE, HEREFORD GOSPELS. CAMBRIDGE, PEMBROKE COLLEGE, MS 302, FOL. 6

both different characters and differing tones of voice.[52] In the mid-eleventh century, the date at which Pembroke 302 was produced, the singing would normally have been done by the deacon, who would have modulated his tone to suggest the voices of the different characters. Pembroke 302 could never actually have been used in such a way as only portions of the text have been marked for use, and its lavish decoration suggests that it may have been intended as a display manuscript, or possibly a book for private devotion. Nevertheless, its miniatures construct a narrative of the creation and transmission of books that is absolutely central to Anglo-Saxon culture. The combination of imagery reflects the use and function of books and reading practices in general. Books were instructional whether one was reading quietly alone, instructing students or addressing a larger audience as part of the religious ceremonies of the church. Pembroke 302 is similar to both the frontispiece to the *Regularis Concordia* and the Eadwig Gospels and Psalter discussed above in its focus on the production, dissemination and use of texts. Its series of evangelist portraits provides a (self) portrait of the role of the scribe/illuminator, while the images between the arches of the canon tables provide a point of self-identification for the reader.

## ALFRED, BOOKS AND ANGLO-SAXON IDENTITY

While artists and scribes such as Eadwig Basan recorded or projected their own identity into the books they produced, King Alfred (ruled 871–99) famously used books and language as a way of constructing and consolidating an Anglo-Saxon national identity. He was not the first to do this; Bede's *Historia ecclesiastica*, written for a king, certainly did similar work, and Alfred just as certainly built on the foundations established during the 'golden age' of Bede. If we have Bede to thank for the *gens Anglorum*, it was Alfred who created the Anglo-Saxons with his new title *rex Angulsaxonum*.[53] It is, however, with the rise to power of the West Saxon court under Alfred and his successors that a sustained emphasis on lay literacy and books becomes visible in both the documentary and material records. Alfred's concerns were more with language than with imagery, but they were motivated at least in part by images, the beautiful illuminated opening letters of a book of English poetry held by his

---

[52] See further K. Young, *The Drama of the Medieval Church*, 2 vols (Oxford, 1933); Ursula Lenker, *Die Westsächsische Evangelienversion und die Perikopenordnungen in Angelsächsischen England* (Munich, 1997), 99–100. Lenker notes examples such as t = Christ, s = the Jews, or, c = *celeriter*, t = *tenere* or *trahere*, s = *sursam*.

[53] On the title see Susan Reynolds, 'What Do We Mean by "Anglo-Saxon" and "Anglo-Saxons"?' *Journal of British Studies* 24 (1985), 395–414; David Townsend, 'Cultural Difference and the Meaning of Latinity in Asser's *Life of King Alfred*', in *Cultural Diversity in the British Middle Ages: Archipelago, Island, England*, ed. Jeffrey Jerome Cohen (New York, 2008), 57–73.

mother.⁵⁴ The growth of an Alfredian textual culture not only provided an impetus for the increased variety of manuscripts and objects related to reading and writing throughout the tenth and eleventh centuries, but also laid the foundations for the monastic reform. Alfred's promotion of the English language and an English identity that both incorporated and eclipsed British cultural and linguistic diversity is well rehearsed.⁵⁵ Like the age of Bede, the reign of Alfred is a point of origin, and one that repeats in many ways that former age. There are miracles of literacy (Caedmon and Alfred), attempts to write histories of church and people (the *Historia ecclesiastica* and Alfred's prefaces), battles against the pagans (British and Scandinavian). They are not identical but they do repeat. The extent of Alfred's success can be measured by the way in which the Anglo-Saxons would refer back to the age of Alfred just as Alfred referred back to that of Bede. It also, as Barbara Yorke has noted, became a point of origin for the modern British Empire and its uneasy if insistent Englishness.⁵⁶

Unless it can be shown that a manuscript was made for a particular patron or for use within a specific monastery or court, it is almost impossible to differentiate between books produced for use in the church and those produced for use within secular aristocratic circles. Moreover, books such as the New Minster Liber Vitae (plate 12), which was made by and for the monastic community, still promoted a royal agenda, while manuscripts such as the gospel books of Judith of Flanders or Margaret of Scotland (fig. 77) are likely to have been used primarily within court chapels. What is true for books is equally true for the objects associated with reading and writing. A group of at least six objects has been

---

⁵⁴ 'Cum ergo quodam die mater sua sibi et fratribus suis quendam Saxonicum poematicae artis librum, quem in manu habebat, ostenderet ait: "Quisquis vestrum discere citius istum codicem possit, dabo illi illum." Qua voce, immo divina inspiratione, instinctus <Ælfredus>, et pulchritudine principalis litterae illius libri illectus ... tunc ille statim tollens librum de manu sua, magistrum adiit et legit.'('One day, therefore, when his mother was showing him and his brothers a book of English poetry which she held in her hand, she said: "I shall give this book to whichever one of you can learn it the fastest." Spurred on by these words, or rather by divine inspiration, and attracted by the beauty of the initial word in the book. Alfred ... immediately took the book from her hand, went to his teacher and learnt it). W. H. Stevenson, ed., *Asser's Life of King Alfred* (Oxford, 1904), 20; translation: Keynes and Lapidge, *Alfred the Great*, 75.
⁵⁵ Patrick Wormald, 'Bede, the *Bretwaldas* and the Origins of the *gens Anglorum*', in *Ideal and Reality in Frankish and Anglo-Saxon Society. Studies Presented to J. M. Wallace-Hadrill*, ed. Patrick Wormald, Donald Bullough and Roger Collins (Oxford, 1983), 99–129; Patrick Wormald, 'The Making of England', *History Today* 45.2 (1995), 26–32; Sarah Foot, 'The Making of Angelcynn: English Identity before the Norman Conquest', *Transactions of the Royal Historical Society*, 6th ser., 6 (1996), 25–49; Davis, 'National Writing in the Ninth Century'; Nicole Guenther Dicenza, *The King's English: Strategies of Translation in the Old English Boethius* (Albany, NY, 2005).
⁵⁶ Barbara Yorke, 'Alfredism: The Use and Abuse of King Alfred's Reputation in Later Centuries', in *Alfred the Great*, ed. Reuter, 361–80; Yorke, 'The "Old North" from the Saxon South in Nineteenth-Century Britain'.

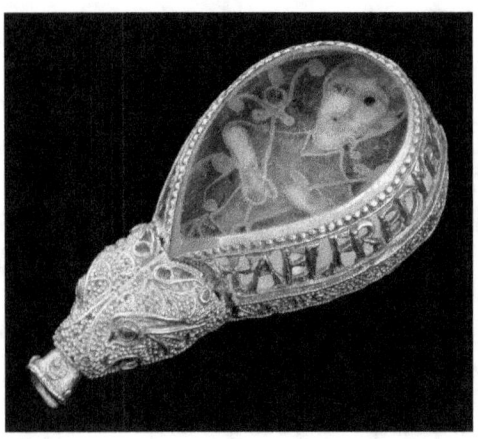

FIG. 61. THE ALFRED JEWEL

identified as *æstels*, generally thought to be book pointers.⁵⁷ In the copy of his translation of the *Regula Pastoralis* intended for Bishop Wærferth of Worcester, Alfred states that in each of the copies of the book he had made for his bishops he included an *æstel* worth 50 *mancuses* of gold, and that no one was to remove the *æstel* from the book.⁵⁸ The two occurrences of the word in the manuscript have been glossed by the Latin *indicatorium* and *festuca* so that a book pointer or marker of some sort seems a reasonable interpretation.⁵⁹ This does not mean, however, that all the objects currently identified as *æstels* must have been part of the group made for and distributed by Alfred, nor that we need necessarily attempt to link them all either iconographically or symbolically, although it may well be significant that four of the six are decorated with cross patterns and include enamel inlays and that two, the Alfred and Warminster Jewels, include a reused piece of crystal.

The Alfred Jewel (fig. 61) is by far the most famous and most elaborate of the *æstels*. Although it cannot be proven definitively that the Jewel is an *æstel*, that it ever accompanied one of Alfred's books, or indeed that it was made at the command of the king,⁶⁰ its find site (North Petherton, four miles from Athelney, Somerset), materials,⁶¹ style and iconography are all in accord with its being the product of Alfred's court. It also has a number of specific connections with ideas and themes central to the *Regula Pastoralis* and its Alfredian translation, as well as with other texts and models of kingship and nation central to Alfred's reign.

---

⁵⁷ In addition to the Alfred Jewel they are: the Minster Lovell Jewel given to the Ashmolean in 1869 and supposedly found in Minster Lovell, Oxfordshire, in 1860; the Bowleaze Cove Jewel found in 1990 in Weymouth, Dorset; the Warminster Jewel found in 1997 at Cley Hill near Warminster, Wiltshire; a 'jewel' found at Bidford-on-Avon, Warwickshire, in 1999; a 'jewel' found at Aughton, South Yorkshire, in 2005. There is also a 'jewel' found in Borg, Norway, in the 1980s which has been connected to the visit of Ohthere (a merchant trading in walrus ivory) to Alfred's court. See David A. Hinton, *The Alfred Jewel and Other Late Anglo-Saxon Metalwork* (Oxford, 2008), 33. Two other possible *æstels* have also come to light (pers. com. David Hinton).
⁵⁸ 'Ond ic bibiode in Godes noman ðæt nan mon ðone æstel from ðære bec ne do, de ða boc from ðæm mynstre.'
⁵⁹ The other most plausible suggestion is that it topped some sort of official staff. See Webster, '*Aedificia Nova*' and Hinton, *The Alfred Jewel*, for discussion.
⁶⁰ The title 'cyning' is not used in the Jewel's inscription: '+ÆLFRED MEC HEHT GEWYRCANA' (+Alfred ordered me to be made).
⁶¹ Although, as David Hinton points out (*The Alfred Jewel*, 13), the workmanship is not outstanding.

Leslie Webster has divided Alfredian artefacts into two groups, 'those which appear to be innovative ... and those which adopt traditional forms, but with new or unusual iconography'.[62] The Alfred Jewel she classifies amongst the former, but this may be somewhat misleading. While the object type, as well as the word *æstel*, does seem to originate in the Alfredian period, the materials and the iconography rely on established traditions. The Jewel, like so much of Anglo-Saxon material and textual culture, incorporates items from the Roman world into a new Anglo-Saxon context. The Jewel features two great imperial references: the refashioned Roman rock crystal and a Carolingian inspired foliate design on its back. The beast-head terminal that would originally have held the pointer, however, is of typically Insular type. Aside from being a highly valued and relatively rare gem for the Anglo-Saxons, rock crystal itself was an inherently powerful material that carried spiritual meaning, being commonly associated with purity, innocence and faith.[63]

Mattthew Kempshall has drawn attention to the fact that, in his Homilies on Ezekiel, Gregory the Great elaborated on the significance of precious stones as symbols of the faith and love of those within the church, and on the significance of cut stone, in particular, as symbolic of those within the church who teach through both their words of instruction and the example of their model lives.[64] Crystal in particular was symbolic of Christ.

> Crystallum ... ex aqua congelascit et robustum fit. Scimus uero quanta sit aquae mobilitas. Corpus autem Redemptoris nostri, quia usque ad mortem passioni subiacuit, aquae simile iuxta aliquid fuit, quia nascendo, crescendo, lassescendo, esuriendo, sitiendo, moriendo, usque ad passionem suam per momenta temporum mobiliter decucurrit ... Sed quia per resurrectionis suae gloriam ex ipsa sua corruptione in incorruptionis uirtutem conualuit, quasi crystalli more ex aqua duruit ... Aqua ergo in crystallum uersa est, quando corruptionis eius infirmitas per resurrectionem suam ad incorruptionis est firmitatem mutata.[65]
>
> (Crystal ... hardens from water and becomes firm. Indeed we know how active water is. The body of our Redeemer was somewhat similar, because it was subject to suffering even unto death; since by being born, by growing, by becoming weary, by being hungry, by being thirsty, by dying, it actively

---

[62] Webster, 'Aedificia Nova', 81.
[63] See Genevra Kornbluth, *Engraved Gems of the Carolingian Empire* (University Park, PA, 1995), 18; Audrey Meaney, *Anglo-Saxon Amulets and Curing Stones*, BAR Brit. Ser. 96 (Oxford, 1981), 90–6.
[64] Matthew Kempshall, 'No Bishop, No King: The Ministerial Ideology of Kingship and Asser's *Res Gestae Aelfredi*', in *Belief and Culture in the Middle Ages*, ed. Richard Gameson and Henrietta Leyser (Oxford, 2001), 106–27, at 127.
[65] Gregory the Great, *Homiliae in Hiezechihelem*, ed. M. Adriaen, CCSL 142 (Turnhout, 1971), 95.

rushed through the moments of time right up to the passion ... Through the glory of [that body's] resurrection, it changed from corruption into the perfection of incorruption, it grew hard just as crystal [hardens] from water ... Water was turned into crystal, since the weakness of corruption was changed into the strength of incorruption through his resurrection.)[66]

Moreover, the association of Christ with crystal was inherent in the Old English word *cristesmæl* or *cristelmæl*, meaning 'cross', and crystal was used for crosses in the early Anglo-Saxon church.[67] Crystal was also a material associated with legal divination and hence the bringing of truth to light in both Francia and Anglo-Saxon England; the openwork setting that carries the inscription allows the translucence and light-reflecting qualities of the Jewel's crystal to appear to best advantage. The same is true of the Warminster Jewel crystal, which is held in place only by narrow beaded wire bands. According to Bede (following Pliny), crystal cut into a hexagonal shape was symbolic of the man wise by divine grace.[68] It is also likely that crystal had a more personal meaning for Alfred as it was one of the ingredients included in the prescription said to have been sent to the king by the Patriarch Elias (878–907) as a cure for his second illness, although the medicinal value of crystal itself stemmed from its mystical association with the elements and with Christ.[69]

Whether symbolic specifically of Christ or symbolic more generally of purity and faith, the meaning and function of the crystal form a perfect complement to the enamelled figure, most frequently identified as a personification of Sight and/or the Wisdom of God. Sight has an ambivalent role in Alfredian prose – it could elevate or betray, leading one forward to the light of God and truth, or backward into sin and perdition, as the story of David and Bathsheba taught.[70] The little figure on the Jewel,

---

[66] Trans. Kornbluth, *Engraved Gems*, 18.
[67] Meaney, *Anglo-Saxon Amulets*, 92.
[68] Bede, *Explanatio Apocalypsis* (*PL* 93, 129–206) III.21. Meaney (*Anglo-Saxon Amulets*, 92) believes that Bede's words apply only to beryl and not rock crystal because of his description of the stone as akin to water illuminated by the sun, but both water and sunlight are elements commonly associated with rock crystal.
[69] See David Pratt, 'The Illnesses of King Alfred the Great', *ASE* 30 (2002), 39–90, at 72; Audrey Meaney, 'Alfred, the Patriarch and the White Stone', *AUMLA: Journal of the Australasian Universities Language and Literature Association* 49 (1978), 65–79. 'The White Stone is good for stitch and flying venom and for all strange mishaps. You must scrape it into water and drink a good deal and scrape a part of the red earth into it; and the stones are all very good to drink from against all unknown things. When fire is struck from the stone it is good against lightning and thunders, and against all kinds of delusions; and if a man has gone astray on his way let him strike a spark before him, he will soon be right. All this Dominus Elias, a patriarch in Jerusalem, ordered to be said to King Alfred' (Meaney, 66).
[70] Paul Kershaw, 'Illness, Power and Prayer in Asser's *Life of King Alfred*', *Early Medieval Europe* 10.2 (2001), 201–24, at 213–18; Allen Frantzen, 'Sodom and Gomorrah in the Prose Works of Alfred's Reign', in *Alfred the Wise*, ed. Jane Roberts, Janet L. Nelson and Malcolm Godden (Cambridge, 1997), 25–33.

with his staring eyes and his protective crystal, might then be meant as a guide on the path forward to wisdom. Indeed, as Matthew Kempshall has noted, there is no reason that the figure could not represent both Sight and the Wisdom of God, particularly as both are central concerns in the text of the *Regula Pastoralis*, and to at least one point at which the Alfredian translation elaborates on the Latin original. The good priest (and by extension all those in pastoral roles) must 'cunne god ond yfel tosceadan' (know how to distinguish good and evil), and must serve the cause of those in his care because of his inner judge.[71] This is necessary because the good priest, judge or ruler is 'to Cristes bisene and to his anlicnesse ðær asset (established as a type and a likeness of Christ).[72] While Gregory describes the good leader as operating as a servant of the divine, Alfred describes him as more than a servant, as a type of Christ.[73] Colour symbolism might further relate specific details of the Jewel to particular lines in the *Regula Pastoralis*,[74] but this is debatable, as similar colours are used in the enamelled plates of the Minster Lovell Jewel which has a very different and non-figural iconography. Even if such precise symbolism was not intended, the pose of the figure can be related with both Sight and judgement.

Given the overall imagery, the colours, and the generally accepted association with the king, the symbolism of the Alfred Jewel and the little figure may reasonably be extended to include Alfred himself,[75] particularly given the typological relationship between the wise ruler and Christ established in the text that the Jewel is thought to have accompanied. It has been suggested that the Jewel might have functioned as a sort of seal,[76] but even if this was not the case it may be understood as a manifestation of all those qualities that Alfred viewed as most necessary for a leader, whether of a kingdom or a church: wisdom, judgement, authority, insight and obedience to earthly and divine law – and hence of the pious people and united nation that the king's policies and written texts were trying to construct. The Jewel also functioned as a pointer towards the way in which the qualities of a good leader were to be attained. If it is indeed an *æstel*, the now missing pointer would have skimmed the surface of

---

[71] H. Sweet, ed., *King Alfred's West Saxon Version of Gregory the Great's Pastoral Care*, EETS o.s. 45, 50 (London, 1871–72), 79.
[72] *King Alfred's West Saxon Version of Gregory the Great's Pastoral Care*, ed. Sweet, 79.
[73] See further Karkov, *Ruler Portraits*, 30–1.
[74] See Karkov, *Ruler Portraits*, 31; Kempshall, 'No Bishop, no King', 125. See also Kitson, 'Lapidary Traditions in Anglo-Saxon England. II: Bede's *Explanatio Apocalypsis* and Related Works'.
[75] See also Anton Scharer, *Herrschaft und Repräsentation: Studien zur Hofkultur König Alfreds des grossen*, Miteilungen des Instituts für Österreichische Geschichtsforschung Ergänzungsband 36 (Munich, 2000), 47–8.
[76] See Karkov, *Ruler Portraits*, 33; Seth Lerer, *Literacy and Power in Anglo-Saxon Literature* (Lincoln, NE, 1991), 84. See also Simon Keynes, *The Diplomas of King Æthelred 'The Unready', 978–1016* (Cambridge, 1980), 136; Kornbluth, *Engraved Gems*, 84.

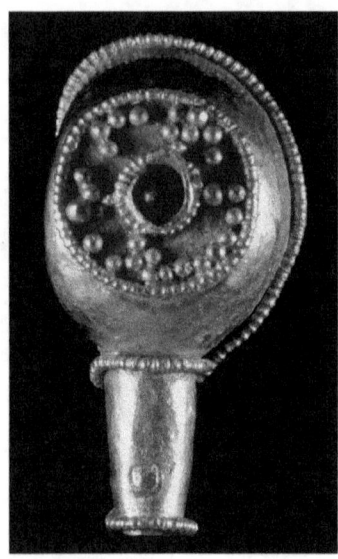

FIG. 62.
THE BOWLEAZE
COVE JEWEL

the page, while the figure beneath the crystal would have stood out as a personification of the eternal wisdom to be gained through a thorough understanding of the text, through seeing and reading properly.

The Bowleaze Cove Jewel (fig. 62) is less costly than the Alfred Jewel and does not have its complex iconography; nevertheless its design may also have been intended to evoke sight and thus reading and wisdom. At its centre is a blue glass bead surrounded by granulation, the blue standing out from its golden setting like an eye; a similar effect is achieved by the Warminster Jewel, which has a central blue glass bead set against a piece of rock crystal.[77] On a deeper level, such symbolism could be connected with the mind's eye and the quest for wisdom that features so prominently in Alfred's writings,[78] even though there is no direct link between either the Bowleaze or Warminster Jewels and the king. Perhaps because there are neither inscriptions nor figural imagery to engage the attention of the viewer, the sense of scrutiny seems even more pronounced, and it is not clear whether it is the viewer or the page that is under scrutiny. It is possible to understand the Bowleaze Cove Jewel as a cipher for both the reader and the act of reading. It mimics the eye of the reader, but it also turns its gaze back at the reader in a way that promotes reflection on what is read and how it is read.

Also associated with books and literacy, but with writing rather than reading, is a mid-eleventh-century ivory box identified as a pen case, now in the British Museum (fig. 63). Like the Alfred Jewel and the Franks Casket (fig. 41), the decoration of the case is related to its function as an object. It was designed to contain, to hold things within it, and across much of its deeply carved surfaces birds, beasts and dragons bite at and devour plants and other beasts. Down one long side of the case dragons attack a rider who attempts to defend himself with a spear, and lions devour a fallen man. The narrower end of the box forms a snarling open-mouthed lion with two crouching beasts within its jaws; on the lid, two small dragons are caught in the mouth of another dragon-like creature whose body takes the form of an inhabited acanthus tree containing paired birds and lions, two pairs of which consume its leaves with wide open mouths.

Hunting is also a central theme on the box. All the creatures are

[77] Webster, 'Aedificia Nova', 87.
[78] David Pratt, 'Persuasion and Invention at the Court of Alfred the Great', in *Court Culture in the Early Middle Ages: The Proceedings of the First Alcuin Conference*, ed. Catherine E. Cubitt (Turnhout, 2003), 189–221.

# BOOKS, WORDS AND BODIES

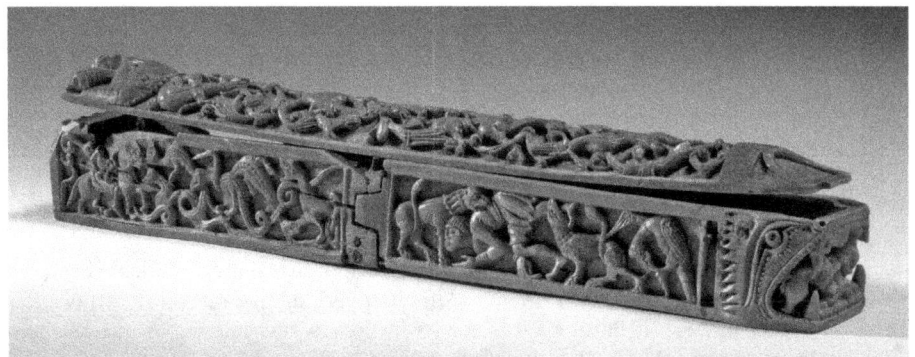

FIG. 63. IVORY PEN BOX

hunting: the dragon of the lid and end and the dragons of the one long side hunt men and beasts. On one end of the other long side archers shoot at birds perched in a tree, and on the other end two men dig at the roots of a second tree while a bird pecks at its branches. If the box is indeed a pen case it would have held quill pens, and the number of birds depicted on its exterior may thus be a sign of its concealed contents. Its imagery can be compared with Riddle 51 from the Exeter Book. The riddle describes four creatures, one of which flies through the air, dives, and is either a warrior leading the way or is led by the writing warrior. The solution to the riddle is believed to be a quill pen and the three fingers that hold it as it moves across the page, is dipped in an inkwell and so forth.

> Ic seah wrætlice wuhte feower
> samed siþian; swearte wæran lastas
> swaþu swiþe blacu. Swift wæs on fore
> fuglum framra; fleag on lyfte
> deaf under yþe. Dreag unstille
> winnende wiga, se him wægas tæcneþ
> ofer fæted gold feower eallum.[79]

(I saw four creatures travelling together marvellously; dark were their paths; their tracks very black. Swift was its movement, more active than birds; it flew in the air, dove under the waves. It worked restlessly, the fighting warrior who pointed to them the way over the decorated gold, four in all.)

More generally, it might be possible to interpret all the scenes of hunting and consuming on the pen case as entertaining references to the pursuit of wisdom, which it was, after all, the job of the reader to do, to hunt for meaning in the text through the process of *ruminatio*, literally consuming words to get at the nourishment of their deeper meaning. The corresponding task of the author or scribe was to present spiritual truths

---

[79] Bernard J. Muir, *The Exeter Anthology of Old English Poetry*, vol. 1 (Exeter, 1994), 325.

in such a way that they were concealed yet attainable, like the contents of the box. In terms of style, the pen case has parallels in numerous late Anglo-Saxon as well as post-Conquest manuscripts. Indeed, its style and imagery would be amongst the most common elements of Anglo-Saxon art to be adopted by the new culture.

## THE BODY IN MANUSCRIPT ART

Tenth- and eleventh-century manuscripts also show a marked change in style from those of the pre-Alfredian period. There is, on the whole, less interest in linear pattern for its own sake, less interest in interlace and abstraction, and more of an interest in narrative, the human figure and secular society. There is also a much more obvious use of style and image to both reference the Anglo-Saxon past and construct particular versions of that past to suit specific personal and political agendas. Certainly, we have seen manipulation of the past before in the history of Anglo-Saxon art and architecture – it was there in the Roman buckle and early churches at Canterbury with which this book began, for example – it is simply that by the tenth century there was more of a known and historicized past to be used, and arguably more of a sense of national identity. It was now possible to look back along with Alfred at an Anglo-Saxon golden age as well as to Alfred's own golden age, to mine them, reproduce them and set them to work. Some of this work centred around words and texts, but some of it also centred around bodies.

It is useful here to repeat Hans Belting's observations on the relationship between images and bodies:

> Images traditionally live from the body's absence, which is either temporary (that is spatial) or, in the case of death, final. This absence does not mean that images revoke absent bodies and make them return. Rather, they replace the body's absence with a different kind of presence. Iconic presence still maintains a body's absence and turns it into what might be called visible absence. Images live from the paradox that they perform the presence of absence and vice-versa.[80]

This is true for all images in that they depend on bodies to produce and perceive them, but it is also true for the body in representation, especially for the iconic body, the body that is a sign for and of both absence and presence. Nowhere is this clearer in Anglo-Saxon art than in the representations of St Swithun and St Æthelthryth in the Benedictional of Æthelwold (London, BL, Add. MS 49598), which both depend for their meaning on the play between the absence and presence of the bodies

---

[80] Belting, 'Image, Medium, Body', 312.

of the saints – both literally and metaphorically – and the absence and presence of the manuscript's patron.

Æthelwold was a great manipulator of image and cult, and Swithun and Æthelthryth are but the most prominent products of his abilities. Swithun was an obscure bishop of Winchester (852–63) about whose life virtually nothing is known. His fame rests entirely on his translation by Æthelwold and the cult that was developed around him subsequent to that. So good was Æthelwold in promoting the cult that Ælfric was able to attribute the lack of a contemporary record of Swithun's life to the carelessness of the community prior to the reform,[81] with no thought that it might not have been deemed especially worthy of record by that community. Swithun's grave is said to have been located to the west of the Old Minster. There is a certain ambiguity in the documentary sources as to whether it was marked by some form of monument prior to the tenth century;[82] nevertheless, its prominence is thought to be one of the reasons for the selection of Swithun as the focus of cult.[83] A second reason may have been the ability of the chosen saint to provide continuity, perhaps even mend the rift between the pre- and post-reform communities through the absent body returned and made present in multiple forms. According to the *Translatio et miracula S. Swithuni*, written by Lantfred, a Frankish member of Æthelwold's Old Minster community, Swithun's first appearance after his death was to a smith in a vision in which the saint ordered him to go to Eadsige, a canon expelled by Æthelwold, and instruct him tell Bishop Æthelwold to exhume St Swithun's remains.[84] This may be no more than just a story, but it was indisputably Æthelwold who began the transformation of the grave-site into a major architectural monument. For the 971 translation of Swithun's relics into the church, a double-apsidal western transept was constructed over the grave, linking the church to St Martin's tower which stood to its west. By the time of its dedication in 980 this had been transformed into a martyrium which took the form of a massive square westwork of Continental inspiration. Within this structure, built over the grave, was a substantial tomb-shrine, which may have housed the silver-gilt reliquary that King Edgar had given to the Old Minster to hold the saint's bones.[85] It seems more likely, however, that the reliquary was located at the east end of the church near the high

---

[81] Ælfric, *Ælfric's Lives of Saints*, ed. W. W. Skeat, EETS o.s. 76, 82, 94, 114, 2 vols (London, 1881–1900), xxi, lines 5–12, pp. 440–3.
[82] See Crook, *The Architectural Setting of the Cult of Saints*, 163.
[83] Lapidge, *The Cult of St Swithun*, 15.
[84] For an edition and translation see Lapidge, *Cult of St Swithun*, 252–333.
[85] It could also be that the reliquary was situated in a chapel on the upper floor of the westwork. In his *Narratio metrica de S. Swithuno*, Wulfstan of Winchester relates that Edgar gave 300 pounds of silver, gold and rubies for the production of the reliquary, and that it was engraved with scenes that included the Passion, Resurrection and Ascension of Christ. Lapidge, *Cult of St Swithun*, 493.

altar, and that the tomb shrine simply marked the spot of the original burial which had also became a site of miracles.[86]

The Old Minster had originally been dedicated to SS Peter and Paul and, much like a latter day Peter, Swithun's body provided the rock on which the expanded church was built. This is precisely how he appears in the Benedictional of Æthelwold (plate 9). Dressed in blue and gold, Swithun stands beneath one arch and in front of another, just as his body had originally rested in the tomb now enshrined beneath the westwork and in front of the western entrance to the nave of the church – the image both memorializing and making present on the pages of the book the body that had been translated to lie before the high altar. Swithun has also, like one of the apostles, become a pillar of the church. His feet rest on a column base slightly lower and larger than those of the columns supporting the archway behind him, indicating that he is indeed standing before it. Two smaller arches spring from the columns of the acanthus filled arches of the border and meet his body at the level of his head. His identification as a column and assimilation to an apostle were also memorialized in the mass commemorating the 971 translation which described him as an 'Olympic column of shining glory, illustrious with miraculous splendour' and likened him to an apostle.[87] The saint looks towards the beginning of the accompanying benediction on the facing page and raises his hand in blessing, as if giving approval to the text, thought to have been composed by Æthelwold himself.

> Deus qui praesentis diei festiuitatem in beati antistitis Suuithuni celebritate uenerabilem sanxisti, tribue nobis tanti patronis interuentu practice uite subsidium ac aeterne theorice lucrum. Amen. Quiqui illum nouissimis ferme mundi temporibus multiplici ac pene ineffabili miraculorum copia ut fidei faculam identidem succenderet sanctissimum manifestare uoluit. Vos uirtutum omnium fecunditate floridos fidei spei caritatisque rore perfusos, in sancto proposito cum bonis operibus perseuerare concedat. Amen. Quo pii suffragatoris doctrina irradiati, et multiplici suffragio corroborati, illi in celesti regione mereamini adiungi, qui hodierna die tripudians caeli secreta penetrauit. Amen.
>
> (O God, Who have blessed the venerable feast of this present day for the celebration of St Swithun, grant us through the intercession of so great a patron assistance in this active life and the bounty of the eternal contemplative life. Amen. And may He Who wished in almost the last days of the world to reveal

---

[86] Wulfstan of Winchester describes the healing of a crippled boy who was thrown into the tomb by his mother shortly after the removal of the relics. Lapidge, *Cult of St Swithun*, 463.

[87] Robert Deshman, *The Benedictional of Æthelwold* (Princeton, NJ, 1995), 138.

him as most holy through an abundant and all but inexpressible supply of miracles so that he should constantly ignite the torch of faith, grant that you may, flourishing in the fertility of all virtues and suffused with the dew of faith, hope, and charity, persevere in the sacred task with good works. Amen. So that, illuminated by the teaching of the merciful supporter and strengthened by his manifold assistance, you may deserve to be joined in the celestial realm with him who on this day joyfully entered the recess of heaven. Amen.)[88]

Image and text work together to suggest that the saint and his patron are mutually supportive of and dependent on each other in a sort of pre-Hegelian version of the master/servant relationship. The text of the translation praises Swithun, while the image of the saint blesses the composition, and it ultimately becomes uncertain who is working in the service of whom. Each promotes and empowers the other, something that is made clear in the Benedictional by the final image (fol. 118v) which accompanies the benediction for a church and shows Æthelwold dressed in the same colours as Swithun standing beneath an arch, one hand raised in blessing and the other holding a golden book (plate 8).

This type of symbiotic relationship cannot be seen to have existed in the case of Æthelwold and Æthelthryth; the bishop was always in clear control, and the saint safely distanced by both history and representation. As I have argued elsewhere, 'desire for and denial of the female body' are at the heart of the history of the virgin queen and abbess Æthelthryth, from the age of Bede through to the end of the Anglo-Saxon era and beyond.[89] The essence of the story as recounted by Bede in Book iv.19–20 of the *Historia ecclesiastica* is well known. Æthelthryth (d. 679) was the daughter of King Anna of East Anglia who maintained her virginity through her marriage to Ealdorman Tondberht of the South Gwyre and, after his death, to King Ecgfrith of Northumbria. She became a nun with the help of Bishop Wilfrid, and ended her life as abbess of Ely. Her ability to maintain her purity through both marriages, along with her ability to deny desire are certainly central to Bede's admiration for her. At the same time, however, narrative, the telling of her story and history, provides a means of possession through which she remains simultaneously concealed and revealed. Narrative, as Susan Stewart articulates, 'both invents and distances its object and thereby inscribes again and again the gap between signifier and signified that is the place of the generation of the symbolic'.[90] Representation, even when non narrative, can do similar work.

---

[88] Translated in Lapidge, *Cult of St Swithun*, 87–8.
[89] Karkov, 'The Body of St Æthelthryth', 398.
[90] Susan Stewart, *On Longing: Narratives of the Miniature, the Gigantic, the Souvenir, the Collection* (Baltimore, MD, 1984), ix.

It is with Bede's account of her burial and translation that Æthelthryth's body enters the symbolic order. Originally interred in a plain wooden coffin in the abbey's cemetery, Æthelthryth's body reappears to make manifest its saintliness sixteen years later at her translation into the church. Because Æthelthryth performed no miracles during her lifetime, and because there were no supernatural signs or visions of her sanctity, the proof had to be written on and through the body itself – its incorruption, its ability to heal itself post mortem, and its perfect fit into the white marble coffin miraculously discovered for the translation. Moreover, Bede's description of the translation ceremony itself never quite reveals the body at its centre. A tent is erected over the grave and the tent surrounded by singing monks and nuns. These layers are penetrated one by one by the doctor, Cynefrith, who attended the abbess during her final illness and who is called upon to provide witness to her sanctity. The entrance to the tent is drawn aside for him, the cloth covering Æthelthryth's face is removed, but the crucial opening into the body, the wound that was a sign of the abbess's mortality and pride, has closed, leaving only the slightest trace of a scar, and has closed itself to the only mortal who had penetrated it.[91]

Æthelthryth remained enclosed within her shrine at Ely from her 695 translation until the tenth century when her body was discovered (*invenit*) by Bishop Æthelwold beside the high altar during his reform of the abbey and reconstruction of its church, *c.* 970. Æthelwold's claim was that it had been lost due to the neglect of the secular canons who controlled the abbey prior to its reform. The account contained in the *Liber Eliensis* does emphasize, however, that the body of the saint remained concealed, and that those who tried to open or see inside the tomb did so at their own peril.

> Corpus autem beatissime virginis regine Æðeldreðe in ecclesia secus altare maius in loco, quo transtulerat illam sancta Seaxburga, invenit venerandus pater Æðwoldus, quam certissime intentatam et inconspectam, non sub terra delitescentem, sed desuper eminentem reliquid. Et quidem hoc illi ad maiorem gloriam accrescit, quod nemo ipsius tumban pandere, nemo inspicere presumpsit. Qui vero illam aliquando intueri temptabant, sicut in miraculis eiusdem legitur, absque mora oculis de capite evulsis miserabiliter interierunt.[92]

(And the venerable father Æthelwold found the body of the most blessed virgin Queen Æthelthryth in the church near the high altar in the place in which St Seaxburh had translated her, and he left her with the greatest certitude unexamined and uninspected, not in concealment beneath the earth but raised

---

[91] On the topos of the wound in the lives of female saints see especially Burrus, 'Macrina's Tattoo'.
[92] Blake, ed., *Liber Eliensis*, 120.

up above it. And indeed it accrued to her greater glory that no one presumed to open her tomb and look inside. Indeed, those who did ever try to look upon her, as one reads in the account of her miracles, perished miserably without delay, their eyes being torn out of their head.)[93]

The discovery was followed by the translation to Ely of the bodies of Æthelthryth's sister Seaxburh, Seaxburh's daughter Eormenhild, Eormenhild's daughter Wærburh, and Wihtburh of Dereham all of whom were said to be incorrupt,[94] and all of whom relied on their relationship to Æthelthryth for their importance. The original translation of Æthelthryth's body was thus repeated and replicated by the elevation and translation of her relatives. Byrhtnoth, Æthelwold's appointee as abbot of Ely, also donated four gem-encrusted gold and silver statues of the virgins to Ely at some point before his death c. 999. They stood in pairs to either side of the high altar.[95] As both works of art and devotional objects the statues made visible the bodies of the four saints concealed within their tombs. They also presented what Dominic Montserrat has described in another context as 'an aesthetic of the surface'.[96] In so doing, they drew attention to the act of concealment and the absent body, replacing it with a precious skin that was intended to symbolize the pure and sacred nature of the relic, but which also signified its transformation into a precious commodity. This is made clear in the *Liber Eliensis* where the language used to describe the plundering of the church by the Normans both foregrounds the precious coverings of the statues and treats their removal as akin to the stripping of the female saintly bodies: 'in deditione magni regis Willelmi excrustate et queque meliora et maiora ecclesie ornamenta ablata solum nuda ligna hactenus valent intueri'[97] ('They were stripped of their covering in the surrender to King William the Great – moreover, all the better and larger ornaments of the church were removed – and it is only as bare wood that they can be seen to this day'[98]).

The Benedictional of Æthelwold was produced in Winchester between 971 and 984, so that it is likely that it predates the golden statues of the virgins. However, its image of Æthelthryth (fig. 64) displays a similar

---

[93] Janet Fairweather, trans., *Liber Eliensis: A History of the Isle of Ely from the Seventh Century to the Twelfth* (Woodbridge, 2005), 144.
[94] There is no record in Bede of Æthelthryth having a sister named Wihtburh, and she is probably an invention of the tenth century. For the lives of Æthelthryth's 'sisters' see Goscelin, *Goscelin of Saint-Bertin. The Hagiography of the Female Saints of Ely*, ed. and trans. Rosalind C. Love (Oxford, 2004).
[95] See Keynes, 'Ely Abbey, 672–1109', for a discussion and reconstruction of what the area around the high altar might have looked like.
[96] Dominic Montserrat, 'Unidentified Human Remains: Mummies and the Erotics of Biography', in *Changing Bodies, Changing Meanings: Studies on the Human Body in Antiquity*, ed. Dominic Montserrat (London, 1998), 162–9, at 166.
[97] Blake, ed., *Liber Eliensis*, 79.
[98] Fairweather, *Liber Eliensis*, 103.

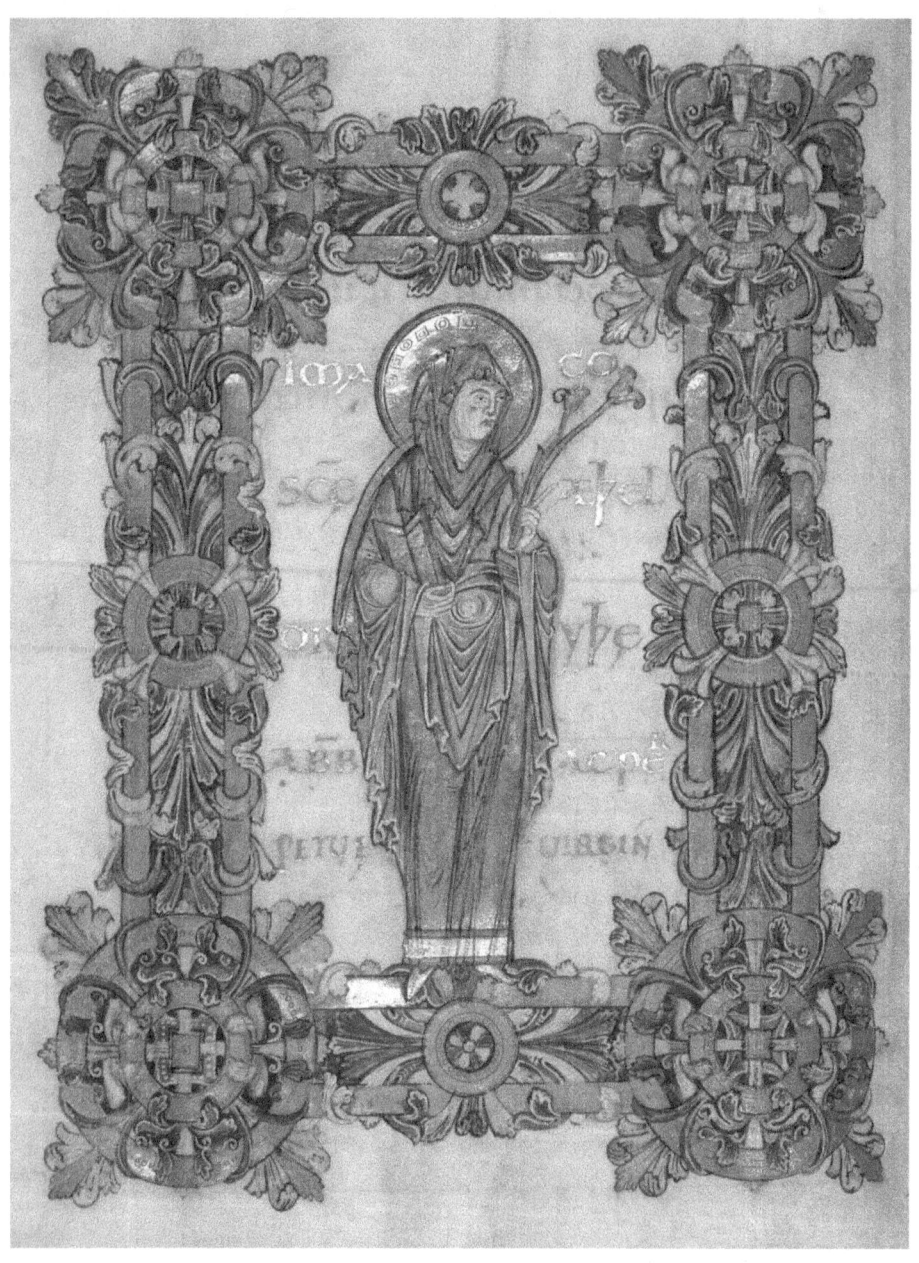

FIG. 64. ST. ÆTHELTHRYTH, BENEDICTIONAL OF ÆTHELWOLD, LONDON, BL, MS ADD. 49598, FOL. 97V

aesthetic and does much the same work. The painted image of the saint is covered in gold and further confined within the golden letters of the inscription and the golden trellis of the frame. The coloured ink wash used for the skin and tunic of the saint, as well as for the acanthus of the frame, add to the richness of the page and to the sense of a build-up of surface ornament. Moreover, the inscription draws attention to the fact that the saint is an image, a representation of an absent body, by identifying her precisely as such. It, and the blessing for Æthelthryth's feast day which begins on the facing page, are, like the blessing for Swithun, believed to have been composed by Æthelwold himself. But here the words serve both to enclose Æthelthryth and to emphasize her subservience to both divine will and the will of Æthelwold as both author and manipulator of her cult. Together inscription and blessing read:

> Imago sanctae Æþeldryþe abbatissa ac perpetue virgin. Omnipotens unus et aeternus deus pater et filius et spiritus sanctus, qui beatae aeðeldryðe animum septiformis gratiae ubertate ita succensum solidauit, ut duorum coniugum thalamis asscita immunis euaderet, castamque sibi piissimus sponsam perpetim adoptaret, uos ab incentiua libidinum concupiscentia muniendo submoueat, et sui amoris igne succendat. Amen. Et qui eius integritatem per imputribile corpus post obitum manifeste designauit, signisque miraculorum ineffabiliter ostendit, uos in sanctis operibus castos fideliter usque ad uitae terminum perseuerare concedat. Amen.
>
> (Image of Saint Æthelthryth abbess and perpetual virgin. May the omnipotent and eternal God, the Father and the Son and the Holy Spirit, who made the will of blessed Æthelthryth steadfast and so ablaze with the bounty of seven-fold grace that, summoned to the marriage beds of two husbands, she avoided them, remaining intact, and was taken as a chaste bride in perpetuity by the most just one, remove you from the burning desire of lust by protecting you, and kindle the fire of his own love. Amen. And may he, who displayed her purity manifestly through her incorruptible body after death, and revealed her ineffably by signs of miracles, allow you to persevere faithfully in holy works, chaste to the end of your life, Amen.)[99]

As has been noted previously, the real seventh-century Æthelthryth was a learned, dynamic and influential woman who over the course of her lifetime occupied every position of power possible for a woman in the early Middle Ages. She was in turn princess, widow, queen, nun and abbess. It is only in the hands of her male biographers and patrons that she disappears beneath the poetic effects of the song Bede wrote in her

---

[99] Translation: Deshman, *The Benedictional of Æthelwold*, 122.

honour, the text of her benediction, and the gilded and jewelled surfaces of Æthelwold's miniature and Byrhtnoth's statue. A similar fate befell her contemporary Hildelith (fl. 700), abbess of Barking Abbey, and her nuns. Hildelith was important enough in her time that a now lost *libellus* of her life was written – on which Bede based his portrait of her in the *Historia ecclesiastica* – and she was in close communication with both Boniface and Aldhelm. Following an exchange of letters the latter composed his prose *De virginitate* for her and her community.[100]

There is no doubt that the purpose of *De virginitate* was to regulate monastic behaviour with respect to the purity and enclosure of the body, but how specifically that regulation was addressed to the female body is debatable. At the time that Aldhelm wrote, Barking was a double house with Hildelith presiding over a community that included both nuns and monks. Presumably they would have had equal access to the books in the monastic library, but would their reading practices have been different? Even if Aldhelm seems to address himself specifically to the nuns in the opening lines of his text, does that mean that only they would have read it, or that he expected only them to read it? There are aspects of the text that complicate the picture. Aldhelm does include male virgins in his list of exempla; he also includes the chaste, those who were married before adopting the religious life; he asks his readers to picture themselves as male athletes, as warriors for Christ, and as fertile bees. Throughout the text, however, it is the female body that predominates, and it is the female body more than the male one that is 'exposed' through Aldhelm's often violent and sexualized metaphors and narrative techniques.[101] Even if the content of *De virginitate* is surprising to the modern reader, and even if the text cannot be read as providing evidence of a 'golden age' of monastic power and independence for Anglo-Saxon women,[102] Aldhelm does address the Barking community in a way that acknowledges their intelligence, literacy and self-control, but this is far from the image of the community provide by the illustration to a copy of *De virginitate* produced at St Augustine's Canterbury in the late tenth century (fig. 65). Even though the image is meant to depict the nuns of Barking, its composition and relation to the text draw more attention to their absence than their presence. As was the case with the image of Æthelthryth, the historical women remain hidden beneath a screen of male authorship.

By the late tenth century *De virginitate* had become an extremely popular instructional text and, in the hands of the reformers, a distinctly gendered one. It is its power to regulate the bodies of women in particular

---

[100] For the text of the prose version see Michael Lapidge and Michael Herren, trans. *Aldhelm: The Prose Works* (Cambridge, 1979), 59–132; for the text of the poetic version see Michael Lapidge and James Rosier, trans. *Aldhelm: The Poetic Works* (Cambridge, 1985), 102–67.
[101] Lees and Overing, 'Before History, Before Difference'.
[102] Lees and Overing, 'Before History, Before Difference', 319, 323.

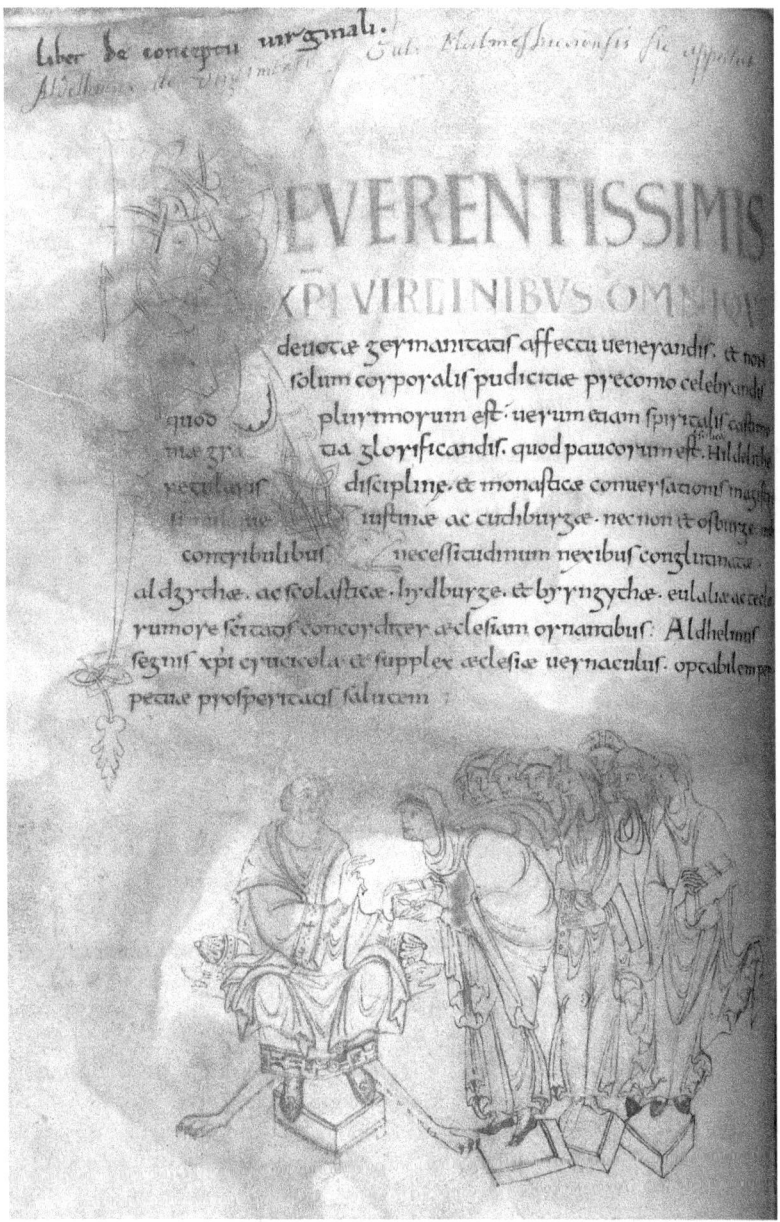

FIG. 65. THE NUNS OF BARKING RECEIVE THEIR BOOK FROM ALDHELM, *DE VIRGINITATE*.
LONDON, LAMBETH PALACE LIBRARY MS 200, FOL. 68V

that comes out in the manuscript's prefatory drawing. In this image, the nuns, presumably led by Hildelith, are shown receiving the book from the author. One of the nuns clasps an additional book, but this is the artist's only concession to the intelligence and literacy with which Aldhelm credited his original readers. Aldhelm himself is depicted as the male voice of wisdom. Seated on a lion-headed throne reminiscent of the throne of Solomon, he holds out the book with one hand and raises the other in a gesture of instruction. The nuns bow in silent gratitude, their windblown clothing and the box-like shapes on which they perch precariously making them seem more like a gaggle of schoolgirls than a group of learned women. Certainly it would be hard to imagine, looking at this picture, that Aldhelm's text was produced at the request of the nuns and followed an exchange of letters. It thus rests uneasily between the prologue and the first chapter of the text, both of which document Aldhelm's high regard for the nuns and their learning.

Nine nuns are depicted in the drawing, possibly an attempt by the artist to represent the ten individuals named in the prologue:

> To the most reverend virgins of Christ, (who are) to be venerated with every affection of devoted brotherhood, and to be celebrated not only for the distinction of their corporeal chastity, which is (the achievement) of many, but also to be glorified on account of (their) spiritual purity, which is (the achievement) of few: Hildelith, teacher of the regular discipline and of the monastic way of life; and likewise Justina and Cuthburg; and Osburg too, related (to me) by family bonds of kinship; Algith and Scholastica, Hidburg and Berngith, Eulalia and Thecla – (to all these nuns) unitedly ornmamenting the Church through the renown of their sanctity, Aldhelm dilatory worshipper of Christ and humble servant of the Church (sends his) best wishes for perpetual prosperity.[103]

The fact that the drawing is both monochrome and unframed assimilates it visually and spatially to the letters of the text, as does the use of minuscule, a script whose curves and flowing nature blend harmoniously with the shapes and pen-strokes of the drawing. Together, script and drawing suggest that Aldhelm is speaking the words written above him, even though the drawing in no way suggests his veneration of the nuns.

The opening lines of the first chapter, on the other hand, are written in formal display capitals and set within a prominent frame, the rigid outlines and wide panels of which serve to separate it from the nuns (who also turn their backs to it) on the facing page. The layout further serves to separate the nuns from their own textual production, which the chapter documents.

---

[103] Lapidge and Winterbottom, *Aldhelm: The Prose Works*, 59.

> Some time ago, while proceeding to an Episcopal convention accompanied by brotherly throngs of associates, I received most pleasurably what had been written by your Grace to my humble self and, with my hands extended to the heavens, I took care joyously to extend immense thanks to Christ on behalf of your welfare. In your writing not only were the ecclesiastical compacts of (your) sworn vows – which you had pledged with a solemn promise – abundantly clear, but also the mellifluous studies of the Holy Scripture was manifest in the extremely subtle sequence of your discourse.[104]

A similar distinction between wise male author/teacher and grateful female pupils, and an even further separation of the nuns from the record of their literacy can be seen in the two miniatures that preface a *c.* 1000 Christ Church Canterbury copy of *De virginitate* (Oxford, Bodleian Library, Bodley 577).[105] In this manuscript the haloed Aldhelm appears on folio 1r alone and enthroned before his writing desk, as if motivated to write solely by his own divine inspiration. On the verso of the page he presents his completed work to a slightly more stable, though no less subservient, group of four nuns.

At the same time that the learning and power of religious women such as Hildelith and her nuns were becoming less visible, the position of the queen and her prominence within the church were becoming more visible, though her role was no less under the control of the male hierarchy of church and state. The tenth-century Benedictine Reform had established the queen as the patron and protector of women's religious houses, and had modelled her in this capacity on the image of the Virgin Mary. In art, a new emphasis on the queenly status of the Virgin Mary helped both to publicize the parallel between the earthly queen and Mary queen of heaven and to promote the agenda of the reformers. The earliest image of the Coronation of Mary occurs on folio 102v of the Benedictional of Æthelwold, and it rapidly provided a model for other manuscripts such as Rouen, Bibliothèque Municipale Y.7, the Benedictional and Pontifical of Archbishop Robert, made at the New Minster, Winchester, *c.* 980 (fig. 66). The focus of the miniature in the Benedictional of Archbishop Robert is, however, rather different from that of the Benedictional of Æthelwold. In the Benedictional of Æthelwold, the bed of the Virgin floats in the middle of the miniature accompanied by three women, two of whom grieve while the third adjusts Mary's pillow. Below them is a scene of the reunion of the apostles led by Peter and Paul, while above them the hand of God, accompanied by four angels, reaches down to present Mary with her crown. The inclusion of the apostles and women follows the narrative of the Transitus quite closely, although the Coronation is not a part of that

---

[104] Lapidge and Herren, *Aldhelm: The Prose Works*, 59.
[105] Temple, *Anglo-Saxon Manuscripts*, no. 57.

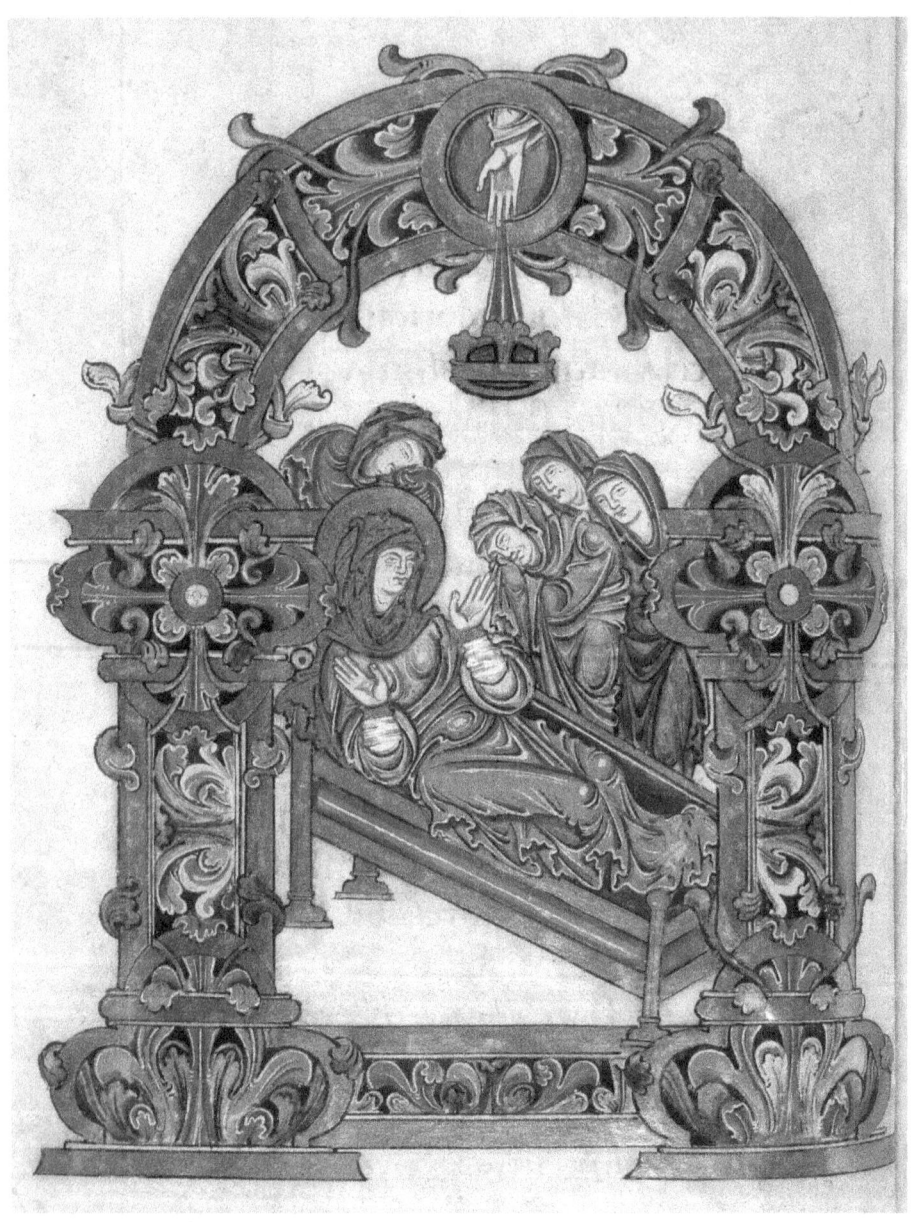

FIG. 66. DEATH AND CORONATION OF THE VIRGIN, BENEDICTIONAL OF ARCHBISHOP ROBERT. ROUEN, BIBL. MUN. MS Y. 7, FOL. 54V

narrative.[106] In the Benedictional of Archbishop Robert, the composition is less crowded and the Virgin herself is given greater prominence. There are no apostles or angels, and even the hand of God is confined within the boundaries of the arched border. Within the central space of the miniature a more earthly Virgin rests on a more clearly delineated bed accompanied by four grieving women. The crown too receives greater prominence, floating against the blank vellum background and thus foregrounding Mary's elevation to queen of heaven. Sadness and joy, the humility of the human Mary and the glory of her heavenly status, are eloquently balanced against each other. Details of the iconography may be interpreted as signifying the status of the Virgin as both bride and mother. It is after her Dormition and assumption into heaven that Mary becomes the bride of Christ and receives her crown, but it is through motherhood, through her bearing of the Christ child, that she is made worthy of her crown. The bed on which she lies, the fact that she is depicted as still alive and the inclusion of the woman at the head of the bed, a detail borrowed from images of the Nativity in which a midwife adjusts Mary's pillow, all allude to representations of the birth of Christ.[107] As Deshman notes, in the Benedictional of Æthelwold miniature of the Dormition the servant behind Mary's head does not cry, a detail that he believes identifies her as the good servant who follows Mary's orders not to cry and continues to serve her faithfully.[108] In the Rouen miniature, however, she does cry, although her two companions merely bow their heads rather than wipe the tears from their eyes. It may be that the artist of the Rouen miniature has moved farther away from the nativity model, perhaps placing a greater emphasis on the emotion and drama of the scene, both of which began to play a much greater role in Anglo-Saxon art after the reform.[109] Whatever the reasons for the simplified composition, however, and whatever Mary's individual merits, it should be remembered that she was queen only because she was the bride of the king.

The new iconography of the Coronation of Mary has been linked to the new role of the Anglo-Saxon queen as patron and protector of monasteries as established in the *Regularis Concordia* and other reform-era texts.[110]

---

[106] See further, Deshman, *The Benedictional of Æthelwold*, 124.
[107] See e.g., folio 15v of the Benedictional of Æthelwold.
[108] Deshman, *The Benedictional of Æthelwold*, 28–31.
[109] See, for example, the late Anglo-Saxon architectural sculptures discussed above pp. 82–85.
[110] 'Conlugique suae Ælfthrithae sanctimonialium mandras ut impauidi more custodies defenderet cautissime praecepit; ut uidelicet mas maribus femina feminis, sine ullo suspicionis scrupulo subueniret' ('And he saw to it that his Queen, Ælfthrith, should be the protectress and fearless guardian of the communities of nuns; so that he himself helping the men and his consort helping the women there should be no cause for any breath of scandal'): Symons, *Regularis Concordia*, 2. See also *Regularis Concordia*, 7; 'Edgar's Establishment of the Monasteries', in *Councils and Synods with Other Documents Relating to the English Church*, ed. Dorothy Whitelock, M. Brett and C. N. L. Brooke, vol. 1 (Oxford, 1981), 150.

While the idea may have been to recreate the queen in the image of Mary, it was not necessarily an empowering act or image, although some queens did deploy it as a way of achieving and maintaining power. Emma, queen to two successive kings of England, seems to have wholeheartedly embraced the image.[111] Certainly the problematic combination of virginity and motherhood, nuptial and royal imagery, with death or dormition made this an ambivalent image for any earthly queen, and in later Romanesque and Gothic art the Dormition and Coronation of Mary would become very separate scenes. What the image does make clear, however, is that the queen's position, like Mary's, was derived solely from her relationship to her husband. Any official power she may have wielded was dependent on marriage, and could be strengthened if she bore a son and heir. Nevertheless, women such as Edgar's queen, Ælfthryth, could and did gain power and influence through their role as monastic patrons. In Ælfthryth's case, her patronage of the monastic reform and founding of a number of religious houses may have led to the church's ignoring whatever role she might have played in the murder of Edward the Martyr in 978. Her actual role, if any, in the murder is debatable but, according to William of Malmesbury, she founded both Wherewell and Amesbury as penance for her part in it. She was also a great patron of Barking.[112]

Another new iconography, that of the 'disappearing Christ' version of the Ascension of Christ, is related thematically and compositionally to the Dormition and Coronation. The earliest surviving version of this type of Ascension is on folio 164v of the Sacramentary of Robert of Jumièges (Rouen, Bibliothèque Municipale MS Y6 (274)) produced c. 1020 (plate 10). The focal point of both the Dormition/Coronation and the Ascension is the undepictable moment of transition from the earthly world of those witnessing the event to heaven, suggested visually by the contrast between what is seen and what remains unseen. In the Coronation of the Virgin, the crown descends from the kingdom of heaven above, which is not represented within the space of the miniature even though it is suggested by the hand of God. In the Ascension of Christ, the feet of Christ remain within the human space of the miniature while the rest of his body has disappeared into the heavenly realm beyond the frame.[113] The spiritual connection between Christ and his mother is furthered in the Sacramentary miniature by the mandorlas that surround both figures. Although she is still alive on earth, the Virgin's mandorla is a sign of her future exalted place in heaven.

Meyer Schapiro identified several possible influences but no one

---

[111] See below p. 269.
[112] William of Malmesbury, *Gesta Pontificum*, ed. Hamilton. See also Marc A. Meyer, 'Women and the Tenth-Century English Monastic Reform', *Revue bénédictine* 87 (1977), 34–61, at 55–61; Foot, *Veiled Women*, vol. 2, 21–5, 27–33, 215–19.
[113] See also the discussion of the same image in the Bury Psalter pp. 189–93 above.

specific source for this type of Ascension. Textually, there are similarities with literary sources such as Cynewulf's poem on the Ascension (also known as *Christ II*), in which Christ's companions watch him disappear through the roof of the temple, and one of the Blickling Homilies in which Christ's power to ascend on his own up into a cloud (rather than the cloud carrying him up) is emphasized.[114] He also notes, however, both that late Anglo-Saxon art in general shows an increasing interest in naturalism and a desire to capture the visual and emotional affect of this moment on the companions who witness the event and that this might have inspired the new iconography.[115] Deshman has argued against any Anglo-Saxon interest in naturalism,[116] but it is emotion and affect that interest me here. Certainly the drama of the scene is enhanced by the exaggerated curls and animated movement of the acanthus ornament that seem about to burst out of the confines of the frame. Colour is also used to good effect to direct the eye around the miniature and help to illuminate its theological content. A brilliant blue unites the figures of Mary and Peter with the heaven into which Christ ascends, a sign of their own future entry into heaven and their respective roles of queen and gatekeeper of the heavenly kingdom. Expressive strokes and lines of colour are also used to define the clouds surrounding Christ's feet and to create the illusionistic background. These stylistic effects have been identified as characteristic of Canterbury manuscripts of the first half of the eleventh century, although there is some disagreement about where the Rouen manuscript was produced.[117] A note on folio 228r records that the manuscript was presented to the abbey of Jumièges by Robert of Jumièges, who was bishop of London from 1044 to 1051 before becoming archbishop of Canterbury in 1051. He fled England in 1052, and it seems most likely that he took the manuscript with him.

Many of the dramatic effects of late Anglo-Saxon art have been linked to the development of liturgical drama that followed the monastic reform, with its attention to individual participation and emotional impact. Drama in terms of pathos, voice and the ability to convey personality, especially the inner turmoil of a character, is also a part of many of the poems that survive in late Anglo-Saxon manuscripts. It is, for example, one of the methods used to relate the four poems of the Junius 11 manuscript (Oxford, Bodleian Library, MS Junius 11) to each other, and it is also

---

[114] Morris, ed., *The Blickling Homilies of the Tenth Century*, 120–1; Meyer Schapiro, 'The Image of the Disappearing Christ: The Ascension in English Art around the Year 1000', in his *Late Antique, Early Christian and Medieval Art: Selected Papers* (New York, 1979), 267–88, at 270, 272, 273.
[115] Schapiro, 'The Image of the Disappearing Christ', 281–5.
[116] Robert Deshman, 'Another Look at the Disappearing Christ: Corporeal and Spiritual Vision in Early Medieval Images', *Art Bulletin* 79 (1997), 518–46.
[117] For a discussion of its attribution to Winchester, Canterbury, Peterborough and Ely see Temple, *Anglo-Saxon Manuscripts*, p. 90.

a feature of the manuscript's unfinished cycle of drawings.[118] The four poems of the Junius manuscript, *Genesis*, *Exodus*, *Daniel* and *Christ and Satan*, are based on biblical texts but depart significantly from the biblical version of events.[119] They are the work of at least five different poets, four scribes and two artists, and show evidence of having been written and rewritten over time until they were brought together to form the Junius manuscript some time around the year 1000, possibly at either Christ Church Canterbury or Winchester. The *Genesis* poem itself is something of a problem. Traditionally scholars have seen a change in the narrative and style of the poem between lines 235 and 851, and have suggested that a separate poem on the same subject (*Genesis B*) was interpolated into the longer text (*Genesis A*) at this point. Certainly there are pages missing from the manuscript after line 235 as the poem jumps from the naming of the rivers of paradise to God's command not to eat the apple; however there is nothing missing and no break in the action after line 851 – the poem moves seamlessly from a description of Adam and Eve's remorse after eating the apple to God's discovery of their actions. *Genesis A* has suffered at the hands of *Genesis B*, which is considered to be the better written and more interesting poem, both in its style and in its dramatic and psychological content. It appeals to the reader's emotions, and that appeal is picked up in a number of the miniatures.

Despite all the difficulties, few today would doubt the general unity of the manuscript which has come to be understood as presenting the reader with an epic of fall and redemption. Retelling and recomposition, for example the rewriting of *Genesis B* into *Genesis A*, is now perceived by many to be integral to the establishment of that unity. At the most general level, the Junius 11 poems are arranged in a basically chronological order, yet the narrative both in and between the poems is non-linear and cyclical – the story moves forward while at the same time circling back on itself, certain episodes are told (and depicted) more than once, but always with variation. This is a form of composition that seems designed to unite the poems by bringing out recurring themes, words and voices, as well as to unite the world of the manuscript's readers with that of their biblical predecessors by making the latter very human. The manuscript has also been punctuated throughout for recitation – in fact it is set apart from the other surviving Anglo-Saxon vernacular poetic codices by the

---

[118] See, Karkov, *Text and Picture in Anglo-Saxon England*; Bernard J. Muir, ed., *MS. Junius 11: The Origins of English Poetry, a Masterpiece of Anglo-Saxon Art*. Bodleian Library Digital Texts 1 (Chicago, 2005) (and bibliography therein). All the images are available at: http://image.ox.ac.uk/show?collection=bodleian&manuscript=msjunius11

[119] For editions of the poems see A. N. Doane, ed., *Genesis A: A New Edition* (Madison, WI, 1978); A. N. Doane, ed., *The Saxon Genesis: An Edition of the West Saxon Genesis B and the Old Saxon 'Vatican Genesis'* (Madison, WI, 1991); Peter J. Lucas, ed., *Exodus* (London, 1977); Robert T. Farrell, ed., *Daniel and Azarias* (London, 1974); Robert E. Finnegan, ed., *Christ and Satan: A Critical Edition* (Waterloo, Ontario, 1977). The translations that follow are my own.

consistency of its punctuation. Voice, then, from the telling and retelling of stories from Creation and the Logos to the Last Judgement, to the compiling and illustrating of the manuscript *c.* 1000, to the reading of the poems at the turn of the first millennium and today, is crucial to any understanding of it as a book.

The drawings comprise one level of retelling, as well as an obvious first level of interpretation: that is to say, the artists did not just copy models or provide literal illustrations but interpreted the textual material in the images. Similarly, just as the text includes different types of voice (such as description, dialogue, gnomic sayings and authorial interventions), the drawings address both text and audience in different ways. The drawing of Enoch on page 60, for example, shows him haloed, holding an open book, and standing on a dragon, although none of these details is mentioned in the text. All three, however, help to identify Enoch as a type of Christ and to establish the relationship of the episode to the Harrowing of Hell and the Last Judgement, New Testament events that are both foreshadowed in verbal and visual motifs throughout the Old Testament poems and recounted at greater length in *Christ and Satan*.

Other images seem designed to capture the flow of the narrative through the active poses and gestures of the figures and/or the general composition of the page. When Satan sends his messenger out from hell to tempt Adam and Eve (fig. 67), the movement of the figures on the page mirrors the narrative action of the poem. The diagonal poses of Satan and his messenger suggest the passage of evil upward from hell into Eden, a movement that is continued in the curves formed by Eve and a serpent and the figures of Adam and Eve on the right. The latter point us to a continuation of the text on the facing page that describes Satan's plans for the temptation of the first couple. Yet other images present the viewer with puzzles or choices, so that we are required to interpret visual signs properly, just as in reading we are required to interpret the words of the poem properly.

During the Temptation, Satan's messenger shifts shape. He takes on the form of the snake before approaching Adam and trying to convince him that he is God's messenger bringing God's command to eat the apple, God being too busy to come himself. Adam refuses to believe him because his words make no sense, but also because he does not look like any angel he has ever seen (þu gelid ne bist / ænegum his engla þe ic ær geseah). The messenger then turns to Eve, telling her that even though Adam has refused to believe that he is an angel from God she must do so as he clearly does not look like a devil (ne eom ic deofle gelic). She eats, is given a vision of heaven, and is thoroughly convinced of the truth of the false words and images. When she then convinces Adam to eat the apple she emphasizes the angelic beauty of the messenger. He shifts from being merely not like a devil to being a perfect angel. There is clearly a difference between the figure Adam sees and the figure Eve sees, and the artist has captured the difference in his depiction of the two separate moments. In the first (p. 24), the messenger has black hair, bare legs, a hooked nose and a bit of drapery that flies out like a tail; he certainly does look nothing like an angel. In the second (p. 28), he is light and slender with covered legs, softer features and even a diadem. Although combining the two different appearances of the messenger into one figure was beyond the capabilities of Anglo-Saxon artists, the attempt here to convey visually the shape-shifting nature of Satan and his servants, the fact that one must look closely and vigilantly to discern the truth behind a seemingly beautiful façade, looks forward to Gothic representations of the Prince of the World, a handsome youth from the front, but a skeleton whose flesh is eaten by snakes and toads when seen from the rear.[120]

Sounds and words, hearing and speaking properly, are as important within the Junius 11 manuscript as seeing and reading properly. There are multiple voices within the poems that speak with differing levels of authority. The voices of the poets are present in the texts of their poems, as each in turn interrupts the action with first-person comments on the source or meaning of words and events. The poet of *Christ and Satan* ends his account of the Doubting of Thomas with a gnomic utterance that echoes the opening words of the *Genesis* poem. In *Christ and Satan* we read:

> Forþon men sceolon    mæla gehwylce
> secgan drihtne þanc    dædum and weorcum,
> þæs ðe he us of hæftum    ham and gelædde
> up to eðle,    þær we agan sceolan
> drihtnes domas,
> and we in wynnum    wunian moton.
> Us is wuldres leoht
> torht ontyned,    þam þe teala þenceð. (lines 549–56)

> (Therefore, each of times men shall say thanks to the Lord with deeds and with works, because he led us out of bondage up to the homeland where we shall possess the glory of the Lord, and we may dwell in joys. The bright glory of the Lord is revealed through those who think rightly.)

And in *Genesis*:

> Us is riht micel    ðæt we rodera weard,
> wereda wuldorcining,    wordum herigen,
> modum lufien!    He is mægna sped,
> heafod ealra    heahgesceafta,
> frea ælmihtig.    Næs him fruma æfre,
> or geworden,    ne nu ende cymþ

---

[120] One of the most famous examples of the image is part of a sculptural group depicting the parable of the Wise and Foolish Virgins at Strasbourg Cathedral.

ecean drihtnes,   ac he bið a rice
over heofenstolas   heagum þrymmum. (lines 1–8)

(It is very right that we praise with words and love in our hearts the guardian of heaven, the head of all high creation, the Lord almighty. There was not for him ever a beginning or source brought about, nor never an end will come to the everlasting Lord, but he will rule over the thrones of heaven with high power.)

*Daniel* begins with the words 'Gefrægn ic Hebreos eadge lifgean / in Hierusalem' ('I learned that the Hebrews live happily in Jerusalem'), while in *Exodus* we read 'þa ic on morgen gefrægn modes rofan / hebban herebyman hludan stefnum' ('then in the morning, I have heard tell, strong in mood they raised up their trumpets with their loud voices', lines 98–9). In Old English poetry, statements such as these lend scholarly authority to the poets' words. The implication is that these are events that have been recorded in books or handed down via oral tradition, and thus have historical truth. In these and similar passages the poets seem to be present as witnesses, and their authoritative statements provide a contrast to the false words and manipulative language of figures such as Satan or his messenger.

The poets also use both sounds and words to make certain passages appealing to both ear and mind. In the opening lines of *Genesis* quoted above, the first sentence is full of soft liquid sounds that are pleasant to the ear. Alliteration and wordplay are important features of Old English poetry in general, and are here used to unite the Creator (*weard*) with the logos (*word*).[121] Further, they establish a connection between divine order and proper speaking, and help to unite the readers of the poem across time and with the moment described (and depicted): 'we ... wordum herigen' (we praise with words).

Order and harmony are balanced in Junius 11 by the threat of destruction and chaos and by dissonance – the fall that balances redemption. The fall of the rebel angels, for example, is both narrated and depicted twice in *Genesis*, and is told for yet a third time in *Christ and Satan*. Each time the story is told differently, and each time we are drawn further into the character and language of Satan. Satan becomes more and more human. The first account is described impartially. Lucifer rebels against God.

Sceop þa and scyrede   scyppend ure
oferhidig cyn   engla of heofnum,
wærleas werod.   Waldend sende
laðwendne here   on langne sið,
geomre gastas;   wæs him gylp forod,

---

[121] Roberta Frank, 'Some Uses of Paronomasia in Old English Scriptural Verse', in *The Poems of MS Junius 11. Basic Readings*, ed. R. M. Liuzza (New York, 2002), 69–98, at 73.

> beot forborsten,   and forbiged þrym,
> wlite gewemmed.   Heo on wrace syððan
> seomodon swearte,   siðe ne þorfton
> hlude hlihhan,   ac heo helltregum
> werige wunodon   and wean cuðon,
> sar and sorge,   susl þrowedon
> þystrum beþeahte,   þearl æfterlean
> þæs þe heo ongunnon   wið gode winnan. (lines 65–77)
>
> (Our Creator then shoved and cut off that presumptuous race of angels from heaven, traitorous troop. The Ruler sent the rebellious army on a long journey, miserable spirits. Their pride was shattered, boasts broken, glory abased, beauty humbled. Thereafter they rested in dark misery, the journey did not give them cause for loud laughter, but they remained weary in hell torments, and knew darkness, sorrow and pain, suffered torment covered in darkness, terrible retribution because they had begun to fight against God.).

Peace is then restored in heaven.

In the second fall of the angels, Lucifer speaks out defiantly against the Lord, lamenting his position as a mere subordinate. He is overheard by God and he and his followers are cast into hell. Their fall is followed this time not by peace but by a lengthy lament in which Satan expresses his grief at losing heaven and at the thought of Adam replacing him in God's favour, and lays out his plan for revenge against Adam and Eve. We are presented now with a psychological portrait of Satan in which he has fallen into a state akin to that of the human, complete with very human motivations and desires. The error (and fallen nature) of Satan's logic and his misuse of language – he speaks out against God, he sends a messenger to talk Adam and Eve into going against God's word – is marked out aurally in the manuscript by metrical differences, harsher fricatives and hard consonants. For example, 'Ac ðoliaþ we nu þrea on helle þæt syndon þystro and hæto, / grymme, grundlease' ('But now we suffer pain in hell, that is darkness and heat, grim, fathomless', lines 389–90).

The drawings also bring us closer to Satan's character and make him and his demons more human. In the image accompanying the first fall (p. 3), the battle in heaven takes precedence over the fall and torment of the angels. Only the lower third of the page is devoted to the fallen angels, and the emphasis is on their falling, or having been cast out, and the transformation of the once beautiful Lucifer into the monstrous Satan. In the second picture (p. 16), the focus is more on the difference and distance between heaven and hell. In heaven all is peace and serenity and no notice is taken of the chaos below, while in hell we now see fire and torment, not just the fall. Both the demons and Satan become more human in appearance, and Satan turns to look back up at heaven, a pose that is in perfect accord with his growing sense of anger and loss. Hell

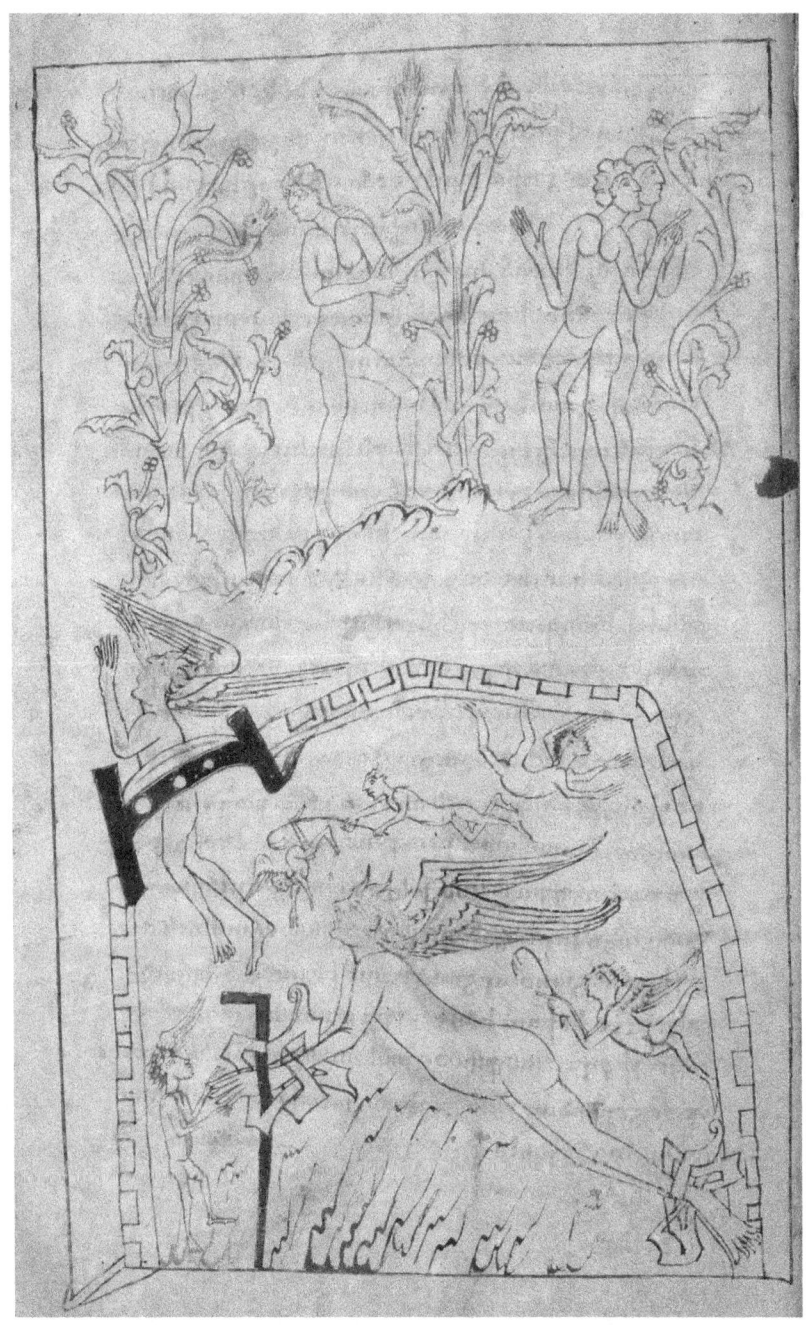

FIG. 67. SATAN SENDS HIS MESSENGER TO TEMPT ADAM AND EVE. OXFORD, BODL. LIB., MS JUNIUS 11, P. 20

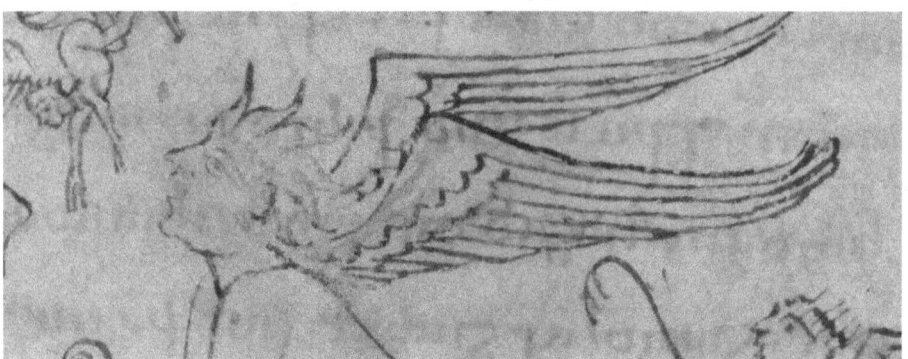

FIG. 68. DETAIL OF SATAN. OXFORD, BODL. LIB., MS JUNIUS 11, P. 20

in both drawings is depicted as a hell mouth, a traditional Insular motif that takes on an added significance because of the flawed speech and evil language that resonate from it. The next time we see Satan, in the drawing depicting the messenger departing from hell on page 20, he has become even more human, with an exquisitely human and expressive face (figs. 67, 68). The mouth of hell has been replaced by a less permeable opening and, although Satan cannot physically leave hell, he can send his thoughts, words and commands back into the world through his messenger and a series of open mouths. Where once he fell into the mouth of hell, it is his mouth now that emits the words that will ultimately leave hell and bring about the fall of Adam and Eve.

Only in *Christ and Satan* does Satan recognize the true hopelessness of his own situation, and his lament becomes a rhythmic chant.

> Eala drihtnes þrym.   Eala duguða helm.
> Eala meotodes miht.   Eala middaneard.
> Eala dæg leohta.   Eala dream godes.
> Eala engla þreat.   Eala upheofen.
> Eala þæt ic eam ealles leas.   Ecan dreames. (lines 164–7)
>
> (Alas the glory of the Lord. Alas the helmet of men. Alas the power of God. Alas earth. Alas the light of day. Alas the joy of God. Alas the troop of angels. Alas the heavens above. Alas that I am completely without eternal joy.)

The poem ends with a reordering of biblical events that places the Temptation of Christ and final vision of Satan in hell *after* the Ascension of Christ. The most generally accepted explanation for this is that the poet (and/or compiler of the manuscript) wished to end with the human. At his Temptation, Christ conquers as man rather than as God, and the episode thus provides a tangible model for emulation by the human reader – we can all overcome temptation, we cannot all ascend on our own to heaven. Moreover, at his Temptation Christ conquers as a reader and knower of scripture, he responds to each temptation with quotations from scripture.[122] Unlike Eve in *Genesis*, he recognizes the error of Satan's language and his logic, and rather than taking the kingdom Satan offers, as does Eve, he casts Satan into hell – another echo of the fall of the angels. It ends, as it began, with paired descriptions of God in heaven and Satan in hell, and it ends by offering the reader a choice of words, actions and fates – and it ends with a cacophonous chorus of demonic voices that underscore the urgency of the choice.

> Hæfdon gewunnon    godes andsacan
> blac bealowes gast,    þæt he on botme stod.
> Þa him þuhte    þæt þanon wære
> to helleduru    hund þusenda
> mila gemearcodes ...
> Ða he gemunde    þæt he on grunde stod.
> Locade leas wiht    geond þæt laðe scræf,
> atol mid egum,    oððæt egsan gryre
> deofla mænego    þonne up astag.
> Wordum in witum    ongunnon þa werigan gastas
> reordian and cweðan:
> 'La, þus beo nu on yfele! Noldæs ær teala!' (lines 717–29)
>
> (God's enemies had won [hell] – the black spirit of evil, so that he [Satan] stood on the bottom. Then it seemed to him that thence to the door of hell was a hundred thousand miles ... Then he remembered that he was standing on the bottom. He looked, the hideous creature, with his eyes across the evil cavern until a terrible torment in many devils rose up. The wretched spirits began to speak in torment and said 'Indeed, be thus now in evil! You would not previously do rightly!')

The openness of the ending positions the reader forever within the cycle of fall and redemption, good and bad reading, true and false interpretation, that will not be completed until the coming of the Last Judgement.

The reason for the repeated retellings of and references to the fall of the angels in the poems of the Junius 11 manuscript remains a subject of speculation and debate. It is curious though that it is a theme that became increasingly popular in the years that saw the return of the Vikings and the conquest of England by Swein and Cnut. The subject is depicted again in the frontispiece to London, British Library, MS Cotton Claudius B.iv, produced in the second quarter of the eleventh century. Perhaps its sudden popularity reflected the general mood of anxiety and fear evident throughout the homilies, sermons and charters of the time. These documents make it clear that both the English church and the country's

---

[122] Ruth Wehlau, 'The Power of Knowledge and the Location of the Reader in *Christ and Satan*', in *The Poems of MS Junius 11*, ed. Liuzza, 287–301, at 293–4.

Christian order were perceived to be under threat. In his *Sermo Lupi ad Anglos*, Wulfstan II, archbishop of York (d. 1023), wrote:

> Leofan men, gecnawað þæt soð is: þeos worold is on ofste, 7 hit nealæcð þam ende, 7 hit is on worolde aa swa leng swa wyrse; 7 swa hit sceal nyde for folces synnan ær Antecristes tocyme yfelian swiðe, and huru hit wyrð þænne egeslic 7 grimlic wide on worolde. Understandað eac georne þæt deofol þas þeode nu fela geara dwelode to swyþe, 7 þæt lytle getreowþa wæron mid mannum, þeah hy wel spæcon, 7 unrihta to fela ricsode on lande.[123]

> (Beloved men, know that which is the truth: this world is in haste, and it nears the end, and it is in this world ever the longer ever the worse; and so it must needs be because of the people's sins until the coming of the Antichrist things quickly grow worse, and indeed it will then become awful and grim widely in the world. Understand well also that the devil has now for very many years led this nation into error, and that there has been little loyalty within men, although they spoke well, and too many injustices reigned in the land.)

If the English had begun as angels at the time of the conversion, they had now been led astray by the devil, just like the fallen angels, and there was certainly a fear that this was a permanent fall from grace. No one expressed that fear better than Wulfstan, who connected the manifold sins of the people with the current crisis, and who voiced his wrath in a way that explicitly connected two moments of conquest: the conquest of Britain by the Anglo-Saxons, and the conquest of England by the Danes.

> An þeodwita wæs on Brytta tidum Gildas hatte. Se awrat be heora misdædum hu hy mid heora synnum swa oferlice swyþe God gegræmedan þæt he let æt nyhstan Engla here heora eard gewinnan 7 Brytta dugeþe fordon mid ealle. And þæt wæs geworden þæs þe he sæde, þurh ricra reaflac 7 þurh gitsunge wohgestreona, ðurh leode unlaga 7 þurh wohdomas, ðurh biscopa asolcennesse 7 þurh lyðre yrhðe Godes bydela þe soþes geswugedan ealles to gelome 7 clumedan mid ceaflum þær hy scoldan clypian. Þurh fulne eac folces gælsan 7 þurh oferfylla 7 mænigfealde synna heora eard hy forworhtan 7 selfe hy forwurdan. Ac utan don swa us þearf is, warnian us be swilcan; 7 soþ is þæt ic secge, wyrsan dæda we witan mid Englum þonne we mid Bryttan ahwar gehyrdan.[124]

> (There was a historian in the time of the Britons called Gildas. He wrote about their misdeeds and how they with their sins

---

[123] Wulfstan, *The Homilies of Wulfstan*, ed. Dorothy Bethurum (Oxford, 1957), 267.
[124] Wulfstan, *The Homilies of Wulfstan*, 274–5.

so very excessively infuriated God that he at last let the army of the English conquer their land and destroy all the troops of the Britons. And that came about just as he said, through robbery by the powerful, and through the coveting of ill-gotten property, through breaking of law by the people, through unjust judgements, through the laziness of the bishops and through the horrible cowardice of the preachers of God, those who swallowed truth entirely too often and mumbled in their jaws when they should have cried out. And also through the foul wantonness of the people and through gluttony and through manifold sins they destroyed their land and they fell themselves. But let us do as is necessary, let such be a warning to us; and what I say is the truth, we know of worse deeds amongst the English than we ever heard of amongst the Britons.)

The devil was now within the nation, and it is probably no coincidence that it was at around the same time that a new subject appeared in Anglo-Saxon art: the Harrowing of Hell. Four representations of the subject survive, two in the Harley Psalter (London, BL, Harley 603, fols. 8 and 71) from the first half of the eleventh century, one on a mid-eleventh-century relief carving now in Bristol Cathedral, and the other in the Tiberius Psalter (London, BL, Cotton Tiberius C.vi; plate 11), believed to have been made at Winchester *c.* 1050 for the private devotional use of a member of the church.[125] It was a very personal book in which the miniatures were meant to offer hope to its owner by encouraging an identification of the very human daily struggle against evil in this world with the struggles and ultimate triumphs of King David and of Christ.[126] The expressive style and active figures of the drawings, as well as the subtle use of colour, all serve to engage the eye and mind, while the focus of each miniature on a single subject encourages contemplation of that subject's deeper meaning. One of the most prominent themes of its pictorial cycle is the dramatic battle between the forces of God and of Satan. In this drawing hell is an amorphous shapeless place that has no distinct boundaries, just as it was represented and described in the Junius 11 manuscript. It is both and yet neither architectural and/nor organic as it can be entered both through the doorway behind the figure of Christ and through the beast-mouth from which Christ is rescuing Adam, Eve and a number of other souls. In contrast to the bound Satan and the human souls that can be confined within hell, Christ is unconfinable and uncontainable. He is much too big to be confined in the space of either the drawing or the page, and has to stoop in order to rescue the tiny humans before him – a pose that also helps

---

[125] The Tiberius Psalter includes eleven decorated initials, two fully painted miniatures, and twenty-four pages of line-drawings. It is the earliest surviving psalter to contain a typological cycle of Old and New Testament miniatures.
[126] See further Openshaw, 'Weapons in the Daily Battle'.

to convey the drama and action of the moment – yet he is still connected to heaven by the yellow band filled with red dots that rises to meet the heavenly starburst at the top of the page. Christ's uncontainability is a sign of his divine nature, but the artist has also managed to convey a sense of his human nature through the suggestion of a physical form beneath the drapery, his calm yet caring expression and his sensitively drawn hands. Christ in this miniature is both a violent warrior who tramples Satan and grips his leg with the claw-like toes of his right foot, and a kind and gentle source of solace as represented in the face and hands that he turns towards the figures he rescues.

The Harrowing of Hell offered the hope of ultimate salvation to those in fear for their souls. The Anglo-Saxon versions of the theme do not include portraits of contemporary rulers, as do some of their Byzantine counterparts,[127] but the viewer was intended to identify with the figures of Adam and Eve, the parents of the human race. The artist has indicated this in the Tiberius C.vi miniature by clothing them while the other souls are shown nude, and by using the same blue ink to delineate their garments that he uses for the robes of Christ. The scene thus holds out the possibility that, even if the Anglo-Saxons had fallen spiritually, morally or literally, they could regain their place in heaven with Christ and his angels through the weapons of prayer and belief offered by the book.

---

[127] Anna D. Kartsonis, *Anastasis: The Making of an Image* (Princeton, NJ, 1986).

# ART AND CONQUEST 6

As I stressed at the beginning of this book, virtually every ethnic or geographic label we could attach to the art produced in the country we now call England is problematic at best. 'Anglo-Saxon' or 'English' have been used throughout as a matter of both convenience and necessity, as to qualify discussion of each and every object or image would make for a long and tedious read. In order to understand the visual language of style and representation, the language through which the art of any period, area or people speaks, it is necessary to establish some parameters. There are styles, subjects and types of monument that do characterize the culture of c. 500 to c. 1100 in the area governed by the Anglo-Saxons, and some of them are unique to that period and that area. However, Anglo-Saxon art never existed in a vacuum, and its emergence and development over the centuries were very much a matter of give and take, a process of Anglo-Saxon artists and patrons working in dialogue with other cultures – the Irish, Scots and Welsh, the Romans, the Normans, the Carolingians and Ottonians, the Scandinavian world, and so forth. Glossed over in the creation of origin legends, whether they are literary or material (as discussed in Chapter 1) is the conquest through which those who come to possess a territory frequently create themselves through a precarious balance of identification with yet distancing from previous inhabitants and/or neighbouring cultures. For the Anglo-Saxons, the ruins of Roman-Britain, displayed concretely in the traces of Romano-British art and architecture that filled the country, became the foundation on which Anglo-Saxon art and architecture were built. The decay of the old culture both signified and justified the need for and the right of the new. The coming of Christianity added a sense of inherent moral and religious primacy manifested in, for example, Bede's and the anonymous author of the Whitby Life of Gregory's accounts of Gregory the Great's encounter with the Anglo-Saxon boys in Rome,[1] or the legend of King Arthur. As Patricia Ingham writes,

---

[1] See above p. 68.

> The nation is always an illusion, a fantasy of wholeness that threatens again and again to fragment from the inside out. Fantasies of national identity teach peoples to desire union; they help inculcate in a populace the apparent 'truth' that unity, regulation, coordination, and wholeness are always better, more satisfying, and more fascinating, than the alternatives. Yet in order to promote desires for national unity, the nation, its core identity, must appear always to have been there, poised to fascinate its people and ready to be desired.[2]

Those of us who study 'national' arts or literatures generally both desire and help to perpetuate these fantasies. In the story of Gregory's meeting with the boys in Rome, the boys are made to stand for an England that is already inherently both united and blessed, and this is played out in the language of the encounter on foreign soil, as it was played out in the landscape of England itself. Rather than being a unified people or nation (Bede's *gens Anglorum*), the Anglo-Saxons were from the start a hybrid people, and their art reflects that hybridity.

The hybridity of early Anglo-Saxon art has already been discussed in the sections of this book that have dealt with the ways in which early Anglo-Saxon art made manifest its claims to its competing Germanic and Roman heritage or identity (whether we understand that heritage or identity as 'real' or constructed), and the ways in which it made visible elements of an 'Insular' culture shared, at least in part, with the inhabitants of Ireland, Scotland and Wales. This chapter will therefore focus on the hybrid forms and political/cultural dialogues that emerged from the English encounter with two groups, the one descended from the other, who were more or less successful in their military and political conquest of the country, but who both ultimately became assimilated into English culture and in so doing transformed its art: the Scandinavians and the Normans.

'The Vikings' were a transnational imaginary constructed by the peoples with whom diverse groups from the countries that are now Denmark, Sweden and Norway came into contact. They might never be said to have conquered England in any lasting political sense, although Scandinavian rulers did at different times govern both various parts of it and, during the reign of Cnut, the country as a whole, but they did have a profound effect on English identity and culture. They were also participants in an important cultural flow amongst the geographical areas bordering the North Sea, arguably from long before the start of the 'Viking Age'.[3] A sustained process of contact, confrontation and assimilation

---

[2] *Sovereign Fantasies: Arthurian Romance and the Making of Britain* (Philadelphia, PA, 2001), 17.

[3] See John Hines, *The Scandinavian Character of Anglian England in the Pre-Viking Period*, BAR Brit. Ser. 124 (Oxford, 1984). For a comparative model see Peregrine Horden and Nicholas Purcell, *The Corrupting Sea: A Study of Mediterranean History* (Oxford, 2000).

began in earnest, however, in June 793 with the first Viking attack on the rich monastery of Lindisfarne, with raids on coastal areas of England continuing into the early ninth century. From in the middle of the ninth century, Scandinavian armies began overwintering in England and the quest for portable wealth that had driven the earlier raids was replaced by the desire for land and political power. York was under Viking control by 867 and the kingdoms of Mercia and East Anglia soon followed suit. In the late ninth century the armies of Wessex, led most famously by King Alfred, began to fight back, eventually gaining dominance over the whole of the country until the reappearance of the Scandinavians in 980 during the reign of Æthelred II. Historians distinguish between a 'First Viking Age' (c. 780–900) and a 'Second Viking Age' (c. 980–1066), but this has limited value for understanding either the cultural flow between England, Denmark and Norway (and the areas further afield with which they were in contact), or the art historical record. It is however useful to bear in mind that it was the first wave of Viking invasions that allowed Alfred and his successors to create such a strong sense of an English identity, both literate and Christian, around which the country could rally and through which Bede's gens Anglorum would be transformed into the Anglo-Saxons. And that process allowed for the creation of a set of cultural binaries that has carried over into modern scholarship: Christian/pagan, literate/illiterate, civilized/barbaric, peaceful/violent. By extension, Viking art was read as pagan, illiterate, barbaric and violent in subject matter and in its technique, which depended in part on the looting and melting down of the arts of Christian peoples, and most especially Christian churches.

Fear and trauma are an intrinsic part of the history of war and conquest, and there is indisputable evidence that the Anglo-Saxons suffered both. There is the well-known legend of St Æbbe the Younger and the nuns of Coldingham who cut off their noses and upper lips to save themselves from rape by the Vikings c. 870, while the harsh justice of the reigns of Æthelred II and Cnut is recorded in their law codes.[4] The terror of divine retribution that fills the *Sermo Lupi* can be related directly to the horror of the Viking conquests of the eleventh century. Naturally people feared not only for themselves but for their wealth and possessions. The burial of hoards is one of the practices associated with such periods of cultural conflict and instability, and for the British Isles the practice is associated particularly with the expansion of the Scandinavian armies across England, though of course there are important hoards from the Roman, sub-Roman and Anglian periods as well. While hoards preserve objects and can thus reveal quite a lot about period and regional styles, dress and the like, they can also tell us a great deal about larger cultural

---

[4] See O'Keeffe, 'Body and Law in Late Anglo-Saxon England'.

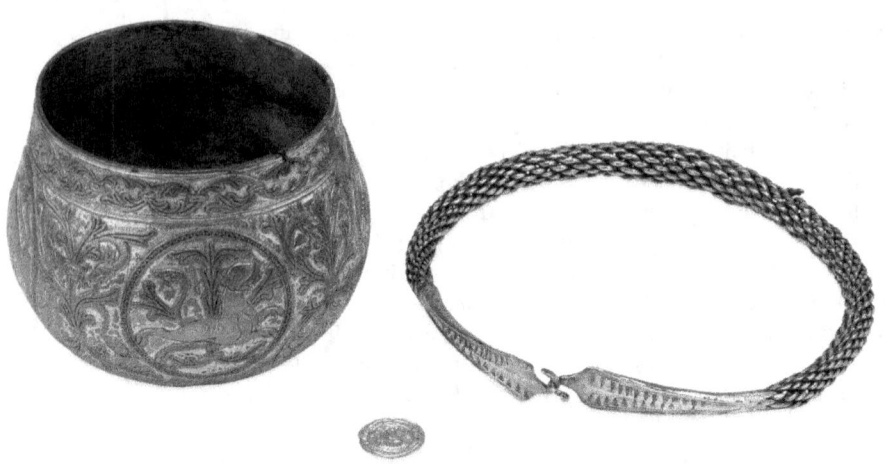

FIG. 69. BOWL FROM THE HALTON MOOR HOARD

concerns. The Vale of York hoard discovered in 2007 has been dated on coin evidence to 927–28. One of the largest Viking hoards ever discovered, it includes 617 coins, sixty-seven pieces of silver, a Carolingian silver-gilt cup made *c.* 900 and a gold arm-ring. The coins include examples from as far afield as Afghanistan, northern Russia, North Africa and Samarkand, and provide some idea of the scale of economic networks in existence at the time. Most of the objects were contained within the Carolingian cup, which was itself already old at the time that the hoard was deposited, suggesting that it, and perhaps other objects in the hoard, were valued heirlooms and not simply objects assembled for their bullion value. The bowl is contemporary with and very similar in style to the silver bowl from the Halton Moor hoard buried *c.* 1027 (fig. 69). Also contained in the Halton Moor hoard were a silver neck-ring, 860 silver pennies and two gold pendants decorated with imagery based on coin designs. The Halton Moor hoard again provides evidence of objects preserved over long periods of time seemingly for their aesthetic value alone, but we might also ask whether the age of objects like the bowl, or perhaps their association with previous owners, their historical value or political significance were also a part of their value. Similarly, with jewellery based on coin designs: were the cultural or political references of the 'original' preserved, or were they simply a fashionable form of jewellery? It is undeniable that jewellery conveyed wealth, status and personal or social identity, but it is only the most elaborate pieces, such as the Fuller brooch, or the royal rings discussed in chapter 3, that are generally seen as carrying complex political meaning. Regardless of the meaning of the individual objects in a hoard, the burial of the hoard itself provides fascinating evidence of what a person wished or was able to conceal at a time of great stress. If the idea was to return and reclaim the hoard when the danger had passed, then intact hoards become indexes of the scale of the trauma and devastation.

The Pentney brooches (fig. 70) are part of a hoard buried near Pentney, Norfolk, at some point in the first third of the ninth century. The six brooches consist of two pairs and two singletons and may have been the product of a single craftsman or workshop. All six are beautifully designed and executed in the 'Trewhiddle style', named for the eponymous hoard discovered in Trewhiddle, Cornwall in 1774, and no two are exactly alike. The use of silver, or gilt-silver, for the set reflects the decline in gold supplies that had occurred over the preceding century, but it also provided metalsmiths with a new aesthetic that exploited the light/dark contrast of silver and niello as well as the light and dark patterns of silver openwork to full effect. Like the Vale of York hoard, the brooches are thought to have been buried during the Viking raids, in this case the raids on East Anglia, but whether that is the case or not, they are likely to reflect an increased taste for ostentatious display that Alcuin, for example, blamed for the Viking incursions. The Viking 'crisis' may in turn have caused people to revert to investment in personal display as a means of boosting success and self-confidence, a form of denial that serves simply to highlight the chaos of the period.[5] Such wealth was portable, easily moved or hidden in times of crisis, but just as easily lost to invading armies or future generations.

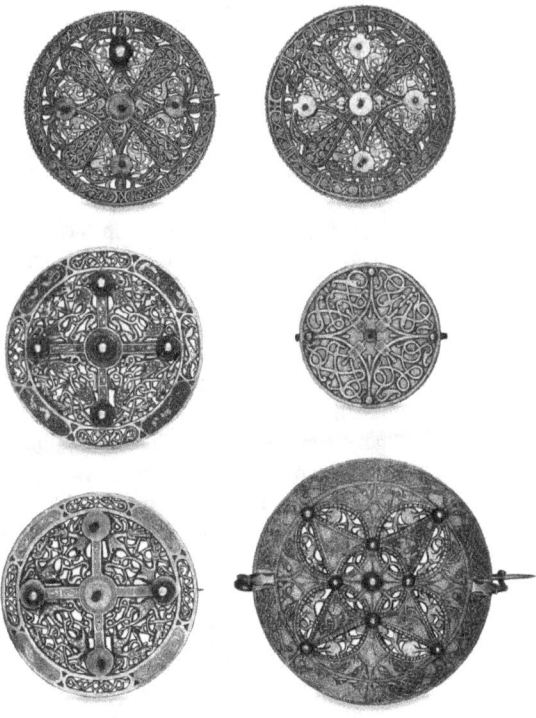

FIG. 70. PENTNEY BROOCHES

The location of hoards was largely dependent on landscape. Both victims and aggressors buried their treasure in places that were hidden but also locatable from features in the landscape – whether natural or manmade – should the person who buried the hoard return. The point was above all that the owner was supposed to be able to find the treasure again once the danger had passed. Scholars frequently attempt to relate individual hoards to specific historical events, especially battles, but hoards are also signs of an intimate and immediate relationship between the person or

---

5   Hinton *Gold and Gilt, Pots and Pins*, 114.

persons who buried the hoard and a landscape that it is now impossible to either know or recreate. Once settled, the Scandinavian invaders had a permanent and profound impact on the landscape in much more public ways, especially in the north of the country, where the evidence of place names and land ownership reveal an enduring cultural hybridity. Anglo-Scandinavian sculpture in Mercia, Yorkshire and Northumbria was and is a part of this landscape and reflects the area's cultural hybridity.

Art historical scholarship has added yet another division between the Anglo-Saxons and the Scandinavians: the Anglo-Saxons were masters of the art of monumental stone sculpture and the Scandinavians were not – a scenario that echoes uncannily the earlier portrayal of the Anglo-Saxons as themselves needing instruction in stone carving and stone architecture from Roman and Continental masters. The initial conflict between Anglo-Saxon and Scandinavian sculptural traditions (or lack thereof) rapidly gave way to what has been described as a culture of syncretism in which Christian and pagan imagery could exist side by side, with the pagan assimilated into the dominant Christian culture.

Scandinavia, however, was not without a tradition of monumental sculpture. The Gotland stones and the large number of rune stones that survive across Scandinavia provide evidence for a tradition of incised and decorated stone monuments which in certain areas predate the Anglo-Saxon tradition. It is true that no works of high-relief sculpture or sculpture in the round survive in stone in any of the Scandinavian countries prior to the Viking age. Nor do surviving stones reveal an interest in the rendering of naturalistic space or depth on the part of the carvers, and these differences in style and technique locate these monuments outside the already dominant classical tradition. However, stone sculpture became very much an Anglo-Scandinavian medium as the Scandinavian settlers transformed the Anglian tradition in terms of style, monument type and the sheer scale of production.[6] 'What is most striking about Anglo-Scandinavian Mercia and Northumbria', Richard Bailey writes, 'is the tremendous explosion of sculptural activity in the tenth century. Compared with the earlier Anglian period of the eighth and ninth centuries, the number of sites involved in sculptural production goes up by a factor of five.'[7] In specific regions such as Cheshire the contrast is even more pronounced.[8] For the Scandinavians, as for the Anglo-Saxons, sculpture was a tool of the elite, but it was the secular rather than the ecclesiastical elite that came to dominate the production and display of

---

[6] See especially Richard N. Bailey, *Viking Age Sculpture in Northern England* (London, 1980); Bailey, *England's Earliest Sculptors*, ch. 5; James T. Lang, 'The Hogback: A Viking Colonial Monument', in *ASSAH* 3, ed. Sonia Chadwick Hawkes, James Campbell and David Brown (Oxford, 1984), 85–176.

[7] Bailey, *England's Earliest Sculptors*, 79.

[8] See Richard N. Bailey, *Cheshire and Lancashire*, CASSS 9 (Oxford, 2011).

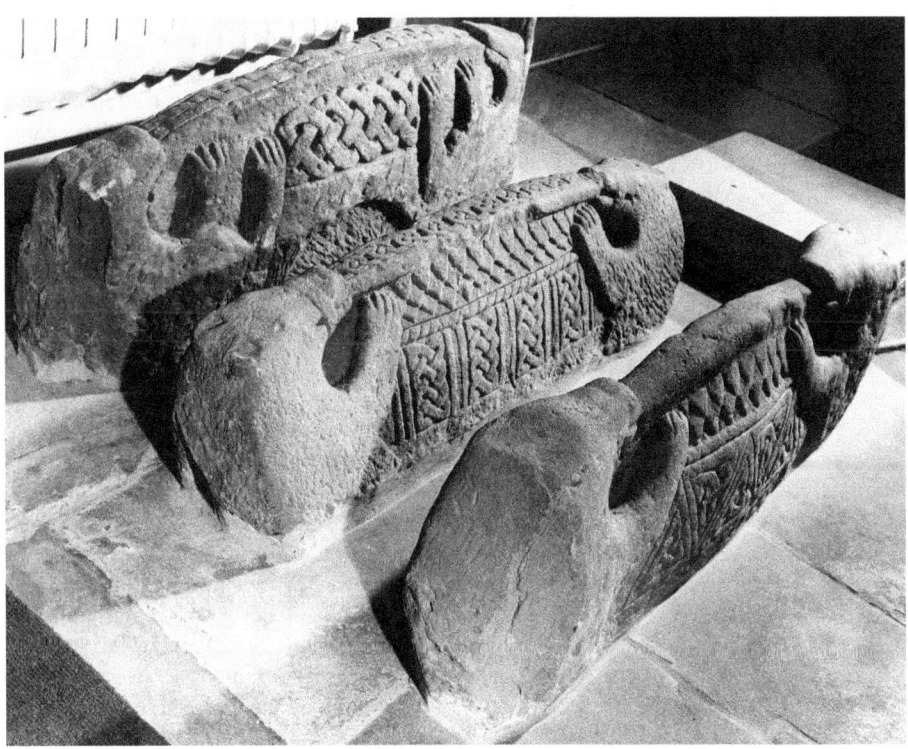

FIG. 71. THREE OF THE BROMPTON HOGBACKS

Anglo-Scandinavian stone sculpture. As in the Scandinavian homelands, the majority of this sculpture took the form of commemorative or memorial monuments, but in terms of monument type, as well as style and iconography, we find an original and innovative combination of Anglo-Saxon and Scandinavian traditions.

One of the most characteristic forms of Anglo-Scandinavian sculpture is the hogback (fig. 71), a funerary or memorial monument found predominantly, though not exclusively, across the north of England. The hogback has been described as a 'Viking colonial monument',[9] but this is inaccurate. It is in fact a postcolonial monument, a hybrid form developed out of the meeting of Scandinavian, Anglo-Saxon and early Christian artistic traditions rather than simply an art form of a colonial culture. As Richard Bailey has aptly put it, both archaeological and documentary sources from the north of England provide evidence of a 'rapid mutual adjustment between the English and the Scandinavians'.[10] But we might also think of this relationship in terms of language, the visual language of form and style perhaps reflecting the negotiation between spoken

[9] Lang, 'The Hogback'.
[10] Bailey, *Viking Age Sculpture*, 96.

languages that must have existed in the north of England at this time. It is possible to see the Brompton hogbacks as negotiating between the languages of three separate traditions. The shape of the monument is based on that of Scandinavian houses, but it is also a translation into stone of the house-shaped shrines with their gable end-beasts that the Vikings encountered (and looted) across Europe. In England, there was already a practice of deeply carved stone monuments based on these same shrines, as evidenced by works such as the Hedda Stone in Peterborough Cathedral, or the shrine of St Chad,[11] though surviving examples lack the end beasts. The motifs and scenes carved on the roof and sides of the hogbacks, as well as their layout, also reveal a merging of Insular and Scandinavian traditions. On the Brompton hogbacks illustrated in fig. 71, for example, the naturalistic bears and panelled arrangement of the interlace ornament are both in the Insular tradition. The preference for geometric ornament is found in earlier Scandinavian art in all media, although the knotted patterns seen on the upper and middle hogbacks are derived from Anglian art. If the bears carry specific meaning it has never been identified satisfactorily. Indeed, Bailey describes their origins as 'one of the great puzzles of Viking art'.[12] The way in which the Brompton animals grip the stone might suggest some sort of protective function, but the fact that some are muzzled might indicate a threat kept in check. Other hogbacks, the Warrior's Tomb at Gosforth, for example, are decorated with zoomorphic and looped ornament in the Scandinavian Jelling style. On one of its long sides, the Warrior's Tomb bears a possibly secular procession of warriors, a type of scene that does not occur in England before the Anglo-Scandinavian period. Its companion, the Saint's Tomb, has a crucified Christ carved at both ends.[13] The similarity of the hogbacks at individual sites or within particular local groupings has led to the identification of a number of workshops. At Brompton, the remains of eleven hogbacks were discovered in the foundations of the chancel of the church when the church was rebuilt in the nineteenth century. They take a range of different forms and are decorated with a variety of patterns and motifs, but all are the product of a single workshop working in a particularly innovative plastic style.[14] It is probable that the middle and lowest of the hogbacks pictured are the work of the same sculptor, and it has been suggested that the cruder style yet similar decoration of the upper hogback might identify it as 'a copy made after the demise of the more expert atelier'.[15] Although individual workshops and hands can be recognized, we have no way of knowing much about the artists themselves. From the number

[11] See above p. 79.
[12] Bailey, *Viking Age Sculpture*, 97.
[13] See Bailey and Cramp, *Cumberland, Westmorland and Lancashire North-of-the-Sands*, 105–8.
[14] Lang, *Northern Yorkshire*, 74.
[15] Lang, *Northern Yorkshire*, 72.

and distribution of monuments produced it seems likely that workshops comprised professional artists, and from the range of secular, mythological and Christian scenes and symbols depicted, that they were under lay control. It also seems likely that they would have included both Anglo-Saxon and Anglo-Scandinavian craftsmen as the latter would have needed some initial training in design and technique.

Despite the increasing secularity of sculpture in tenth- and eleventh-century England, most of the sites at which Anglo-Scandinavian sculpture is found are in fact established church sites – like Brompton and Gosforth – and include traditionally Christian Anglo-Saxon monument types such as freestanding stone crosses. These too the Scandinavian settlers adopted to suit their own tastes and requirements. The Gosforth Cross (fig. 72) is the most famous and perhaps the most eclectic of these. It is an exceptional monument by any standards, rising to nearly five metres in height and carved from a single piece of stone. Like the Brompton hogbacks, its form, style and imagery reveal an original combination of Anglian, Insular and Scandinavian elements. The standing stone cross is an Anglian type of monument, but the ringed cross head is an Insular feature that is found on crosses in Ireland and Scotland though not in pre-Viking England. The abstract, zoomorphic and figural carvings are, with the exception of the Crucifixion, from the Scandinavian tradition, though at Gosforth both Christian and Scandinavian scenes have been reinterpreted to present a dialogic understanding of the balance established between doom and salvation, the death of one order and the birth of another, features that have led to its being seen as emblematic of the assimilation of the Scandinavian settlers and the birth of a new hybrid culture. The traditional view is that the Scandinavian settlers were assimilated into Anglo-Saxon Christian culture, and eventually they were, although it has been suggested that it might be more appropriate

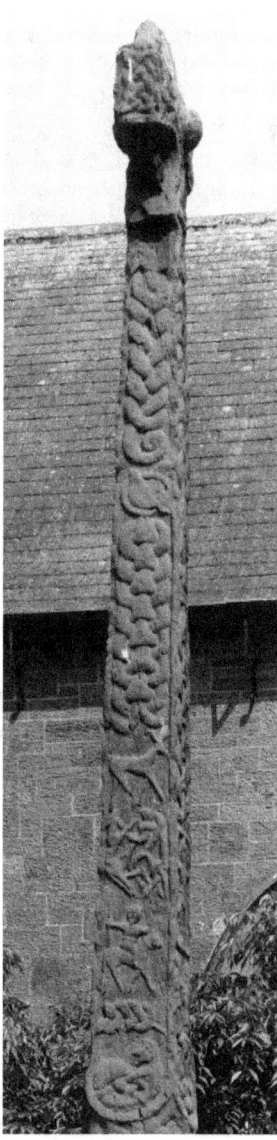

FIG. 72. THE GOSFORTH CROSS

to identify a preceding phase in which Christianity was assimilated into the world view of the Norse.[16]

The layout of the carving, with the figures and motifs distributed up and down the sides of the shaft rather than confined within panels, is taken from early Scandinavian art such as the Gotland stones or the carvings on the wooden objects from the Oseberg ship burial. However, the fact that this arrangement demands the participation of the viewer, forcing him or her to create meaning by putting the separate scenes and motifs together to form larger narratives or symbolic associations, may put the Gosforth Cross in the tradition of such Anglian monuments as the Ruthwell Cross, although it is certainly possible to question whether there are iconographic narratives at Gosforth.[17] The lower part of the Gosforth shaft is circular and partially decorated with an all-over pattern of ring-chain ornament. Above the ring-chain the shaft becomes rectangular in section with the figural scenes and naturalistic animal motifs on three of the four sides sandwiched between the ring-chain of the lower shaft and the biting beasts whose bodies are formed from variations on the ring-chain pattern. On the fourth side a section of knotwork is placed between the lower shaft and two spearbearing horsemen, one depicted right side up and the other upside down. The only clearly Christian scene on the cross is the Crucifixion carved on its east side, but it is an unusual version of the Crucifixion. Christ is not shown on the cross but standing in a cruciform pose with his arms stretched out to overlap the moulding of the panel that contains him, a composition borrowed from Irish metalwork. Below the figure of Christ are the spearbearer, Longinus, and a female carrying a drinking horn (or horn-shaped object). Richard Bailey has argued that the woman is Mary Magdalene carrying her alabastron rather than Ecclesia,[18] but an identification with Ecclesia should not be ruled out entirely.[19] The figure can be paralleled in the drinking-horn-carrying Valkyrie of the Gotland stones and an image of Ecclesia would be appropriate to both the apparently syncretic message of the cross and to the spiritual triumph and creation of a new order signified by the Crucifixion. Below the Crucifixion is a double-headed serpent, a traditional way of representing hell and/or the defeat of evil. Above the Crucifixion, and separated from it by a section of 'Borre-style' ring-chain, is a scene that has been identified as the god Viðarr who broke the jaws of the wolf that had killed his father Oðinn and survived Ragnarǫk. It may provide a Norse mythological parallel for both the triumph of good and the defeat of evil inherent in the Crucifixion

---

[16] David Stocker, 'Irregularities in the Distribution of Stone Monuments', in *Cultures in Contact: Scandinavian Settlement in England in the Ninth and Tenth Centuries*, ed. Dawn M. Hadley and Julian D. Richards (Turnhout, 2000), 179–212, at 194.
[17] Bailey, *England's Earliest Sculptors*, 87.
[18] Bailey, *Viking Age Sculpture*, 130; Bailey, *England's Earliest Sculptors*, 89; Bailey and Cramp, *Cumberland, Westmorland and Lancashire North-of-the-Sands*, 102.
[19] Knut Berg, 'The Gosforth Cross', *JWCI* 21 (1958), 27–43.

scene. The spearbearing figure also provides a link between the figural scenes on the four sides of the shaft: on the east face, both Longinus and Viðarr hold spears, each of the other three faces includes one or two mounted warriors with spears, and there is a man holding both a spear and a drinking horn on the west face of the cross.

All three of the remaining sides of the shaft are carved with scenes that may be from or related to the story of Ragnarǫk. On the west face of the shaft, approximately level with the Crucifixion, is the god Heimdallr holding a spear and the horn with which he will announce the final battle. At the bottom of the panel, separated from Heimdallr by one of the spearbearing horsemen, is his enemy Loki, shown bound beneath the serpent with his wife, Sigyn, attempting to catch the serpent's venom in a bowl. If the woman with the vessel on the east face of the shaft is interpreted as Ecclesia carrying a vessel with which to catch the blood of Christ, Sigyn with her bowl of venom provides an inversion of the motif, but one which also announces the coming of a new order, as it is with Loki's escape from his bonds that the final battle of the gods begins. The imagery of the south face of the shaft (fig. 72) has never been explained with any certainty. The mounted warrior could be Oðinn on his horse but, if so, are the other horsemen on the cross also to be understood as Oðinn? The fettered wolf has been identified by some as Garm,[20] whose freedom and howling would signal the beginning of Ragnarǫk. It is possible that the hart or deer at the top of the panel is a symbol of baptism or rebirth, and that the creature at the bottom of the panel is meant to signify hell and/or the world serpent. It may also be that the whole panel is intended to be a depiction of the hunt of the soul (with the hart signifying the soul) although such an interpretation would perhaps fit less comfortably with the rest of the imagery on the cross.

It is also possible that the imagery carried less specific references to Scandinavian and Christian myths or stories, and that the typological relationship between the images that modern scholars eager for narrative resolution and closure read in the cross was much more ambivalent. There are images at Gosforth, like the multiple warriors, that resist iconographic interpretation, and the layout of the ornament is not conducive to any typological reading. The bulk of the decoration on the Gosforth Cross, however, is neither figural nor narrative, at least not obviously so. It consists primarily of knots and ring-chains, and forces us again to confront the question of whether or not such patterns – and they are generally dismissed as patterns – carried meaning. Is it significant, for example, that while the ring-chain patterns have been linked to motifs found in metalwork at Borre (Vestfold, Norway), they are in fact very

---

[20] See further Bailey and Cramp, *Cumberland, Westmorland and Lancashire North-of-the-Sands*, 102.

different?[21] Is this a way of expressing continuity with the past in the creation of something new and different – the coming once again of a new type of order and authority? If these ring-chains are not like those found in the art of the Scandinavian homelands, they are also not like earlier Anglo-Saxon interlace and knotwork. Unlike the interlace designs of the Bewcastle Cross, for example, which are all confined within panels and thus lead the viewer visually to contemplate and unravel each separate pattern (fig. 21), at Gosforth the beast-headed sections of knots and links seem to surge up and down the shaft and across its internal landscape,[22] perhaps as a way of suggesting the drama of the final battle. The patterns might also have evoked an association with armour, with the cross thus becoming a protected and protective weapon in the battle. Whatever the case, the sense of motion and drama they convey is continued in the unusual cross head with its interwoven mouldings.

For all the drama and violence of its imagery, however, Gosforth remains emblematic, at least in the scholarship, of a harmonious and creative Anglo-Scandinavian hybrid culture. Yet within the Christian kingdom of the cross there is a narrative imbalance. The Crucifixion is one small panel in a series of carvings given over to scenes of battle and conflict. Moreover, as noted above, the Crucifixion is all wrong. Christ is not on the cross,[23] the female figure is on the wrong side, and both attendant figures are cut off from the body of Christ by the moulding that surrounds him. I am not arguing that the Gosforth Cross does not have Christian content, or that it is not, on one level, a Christian monument, but simply that it may have more nuanced and shifting meanings reflective of its status as a material statement of hierarchies of power – religious, political, cultural. Moreover, it is part of a larger landscape filled by the end of the Anglo-Scandinavian period with similar statements. Gosforth alone had at least four crosses and two hogbacks. Monumental stone sculpture had become not only an Anglo-Scandinavian medium, but one that mapped the postcolonial landscape of the north of England at the end of the tenth and into the eleventh century. Even more clearly than at Brompton, there are multiple voices and multiple languages evident at Gosforth. Do they reflect a comfortable syncretism of the Anglo-Saxon and the Scandinavian? Or do they rather reflect the postcolonial moment of Anglo-Scandinavian

---

[21] See Bailey, *Viking Age Sculpture*, pl. 7 and fig. 60. On the styles of Scandinavian art see Wilson and Klindt-Jensen, *Viking Art*.

[22] There is in fact a balance between motion up and down the shaft: on the two main faces the motion is both up and down, leading the eye in two directions at once, while the motion on one of the narrow sides is up (the side with the wolf and hart) and on the other it is down.

[23] While it might be argued that the monument itself is the cross of the Crucifixion, its location on the lower part of the shaft beneath scenes from Scandinavian mythology is problematic.

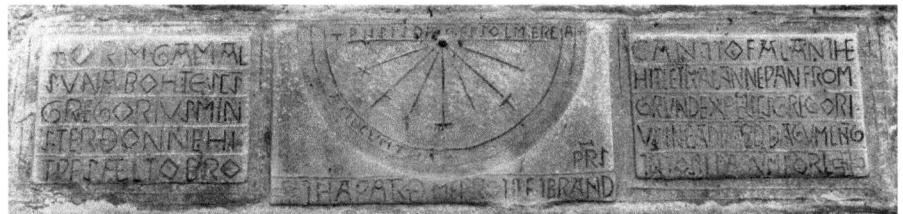

FIG. 73. THE KIRKDALE SUNDIAL

England, the awkward, violent and frequently unresolved tension between languages that exists in any colonial or diasporic situation.[24]

While discussion of the Brompton hogbacks and Gosforth Cross has focused on issues of hybridity as they relate to monument type, style and visual language, the reuse or appropriation of site is also an important feature of Anglo-Scandinavian England, just as it was with the arrival of the Anglo-Saxons. John Blair has noted that assemblages of Anglian and Anglo-Scandinavian sculpture survive at churches in Ryedale and the Vale of Pickering (Lastingham, Kirkdale, Stonegrave, Kirkbymoorside, Hovingham and Middleton), and that the continuity and reuse of site for which they provide evidence might be characteristic of Yorkshire as a whole.[25] Kirkdale, the site of a wealthy pre-Viking church, is especially important, not only for its assemblage of sculpture (the remains of six ninth- to tenth-century crosses, two eighth- or ninth-century grave-slabs, part of a hogback, and an eleventh-century sundial),[26] but also for its clear documentation of lay patronage and the language of its inscriptions. The inscribed sundial at Kirkdale (fig. 73) commemorates the rebuilding of the church of St Gregory c. 1060. The sundial is divided into three sections with the dial itself placed between the two panels bearing the main inscription, and with shorter inscriptions included beneath and around the dial. All inscriptions are in Old English and inscribed in Latin capitals. The main inscription reads:

> +Orm Gamalsuna bohte scs Gregorius minster ðonne hit pes æl tobrocan 7 tofalan 7 he hit let macan nepan rom grunde chr[ist]e 7 scs Gregorius in Eadpard dagum cing 7 (i)n Tosti dagum eorl+
>
> (+Orm Gamalsuna bought St Gregory's minster when it was completely broken and fallen down, and he had it rebuilt from the ground [for] Christ and St Gregory in the days of King Edward and in the reign of Earl Tostig+)

---

[24] On the specific relationship between Old English and Old Norse see Matthew Townend, *Language and History in Viking Age England: Linguistic Relations between Speakers of Old Norse and Old English* (Turnhout, 2002).
[25] Blair, *The Church in Anglo-Saxon Society*, 314–15.
[26] See Lang, *York and Eastern Yorkshire*, 158–66.

As Tostig was earl between 1055 and 1065, the rebuilding and inscription can be fairly precisely dated. Orm was not a member of the upper echelons of the Anglo-Scandinavian aristocracy in the area, so the sundial and rebuilding are also valuable evidence for the increasing participation of the minor aristocracy in public patronage. The clumsy arrangement of the inscription and some of its constituent words and letters might be attributable to the inability of such patrons to employ the most skilled carvers, though they could equally well be due to a lack of highly skilled carvers in the area at the time of the rebuilding. The church itself, though modest in scale, seems to have been architecturally innovative,[27] and the sundial itself is quite fine. The inscriptions on the panel that bears the dial relate to its makers and its function. The inscription at the bottom of the panel reads '+7 Haparð me proh(te) 7 Brand prs (+and Hawarð made me and Brand the priest); and that around the dial reads '+þisis d(æg)es solmerca + æt ilcum tide +' (+this is the day's sun-marker at every hour, or this is the mark of the sun for each hour).[28]

The language of the inscription is as important as the reuse of the site for what it has to tell us about the postcolonial culture of the area. While written in English and in Latin lettering, its form is not classical, and its features include weakening of unstressed vowels, a loss of distinction in endings, and problems with grammatical gender, all of which 'could be the effect of a strong Norse admixture in the local population, as evidenced by the Norse names in the inscription',[29] although they could equally well be the result of an internal metamorphosis of the language. Similarly, '*solmerca* can either be taken as a hybrid Old Norse and Old English word meaning "something which marks (the position of) the sun", or an Old Norse loanword meaning "the mark of the sun."'[30] However we wish to interpret the individual words, the hybridity of the language at Kirkdale provides an interesting comparison with the bybridity of style and subject matter, the visual language, evident at both Brompton and Gosforth. There is an awkwardness here that creates some ambiguity in meaning. We cannot be certain whether *solmerca* is an Old Norse word or a new word that is partly Old Norse and partly Old English, and the one meaning is not the same as the other. Moreover, how conscious would Orm and his contemporaries have been of the ambiguities and differences in meaning this admixture of languages created? Similarly, in putting together the different pictorial and decorative elements of the Gosforth Cross, how conscious would patrons and carvers have been of all the subtleties in reading that modern scholarship, 'fluent' in both its languages, allows? For the moment, these must remain open questions.

[27] Blair, *The Church in Anglo-Saxon Society*, 358.
[28] Lang, *York and Eastern Yorkshire*, 165, citing R. Page.
[29] Lang, *York and Eastern Yorkshire*, 166.
[30] Lang, *York and Eastern Yorkshire*, 166, quoting R. Page.

The trauma and violence of the period also had its impact on monuments associated with areas that had remained more firmly connected to Anglo-Saxon traditions. Scenes of battle and hunting as well as apocalyptic imagery began to appear with increasing regularity in artwork produced by both the Anglo-Saxons and the Anglo-Scandinavians during the tenth century. At Gosforth, the majority of the figural scenes have to do with Ragnarǫk, but on a series of four cross heads now preserved in the Monks' Dormitory at Durham Cathedral, a new interest in the Apocalypse and Revelation is evident.[31] The origins of the cross heads and the larger meanings of the monuments from which they came are lost to us as they were discovered in 1891 as fragments in the foundations of the Norman chapter house. They had been reused by the Normans as rubble in the rebuilding of Durham Cathedral, perhaps the most politically important church in the north of England, and their destruction and burial thus documents yet another postcolonial moment in their history and that of the area. The fragment illustrated here (fig. 74) is the finest of the three cross heads, which all share what seems to be a complex yet ambiguous set of images. On one side of all three is a scene generally believed to represent a baptism (ordination has also been suggested) at the centre of the cross head, with ecclesiastical figures looking on in the cross arms. On the other side is a version of the Crucifixion which, in the example illustrated, is represented in a form that allows it to be read simultaneously in apocalyptic terms. At the centre is the Agnus Dei, its body superimposed on a cross in a symbolic Crucifixion. Beneath the lamb's front right foot is the sealed book that will be opened at the Last Judgement. The circular object in front of the lamb may be an image of the host.[32] Above the lamb is a winged figure flanked by two heads and, in the cross arms, two large winged creatures who appear to be bound, along with a variety of smaller creatures. The compositions in the cross arms are both crowded and confusing. It is possible that they represent the forces of hell, although it is also possible that they are, along with the winged human figure in the upper arm, meant to represent three of the

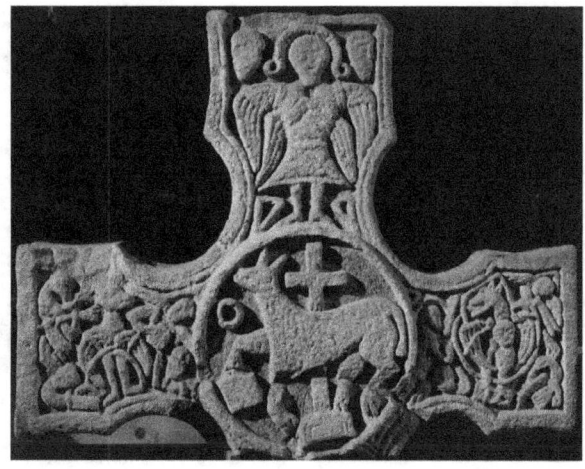

FIG. 74. CROSS HEAD, DURHAM CATHEDRAL

---

[31] Cramp, *County Durham and Northumberland*, 68–72.
[32] Bailey, *Viking Age Sculpture*, 171.

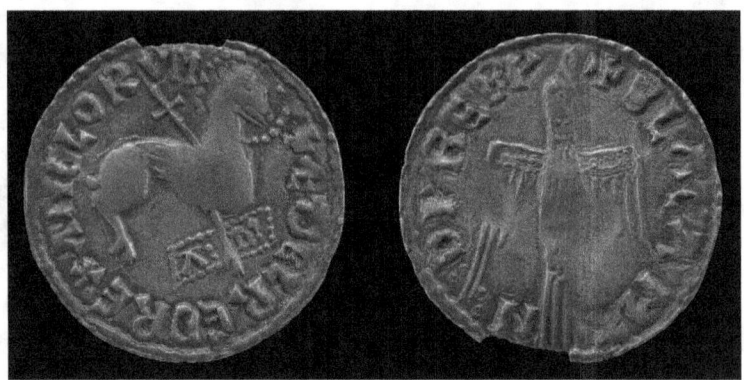

FIG. 75. AGNUS DEI PENNY

four symbols of the evangelists.[33] If they are the evangelist symbols they are highly unusual, to say the least. Richard Bailey has suggested that the composition as a whole is a visualization of Revelation 4: 6–8 by an artist who 'exceeded ... [his] competence', with the beasts in the cross arms a somewhat confused rendering of the four living creatures with wings full of eyes and the elders that surround the lamb and the throne.[34] This is possible, and some of the figures do appear to be prostrate (the man in the lower left corner of the left arm, for example), perhaps a reference to Rev 5:8: 'And when he had opened the book, the four living creatures, the four and twenty ancients fell down before the lamb, having every one of them harps, and golden vials full of odours, which are the prayers of the saints.' Other figures, however, seem to be trapped and struggling to break free from their bonds, for example the man in the upper right section of the arm. This combination of poses and the central scene with its striding lamb and closed book are more suggestive of a darker message in which the audience of the sculpture, like the figures in the cross arms, is located within the events of the last days, yet left hanging in the balance and awaiting the opening of the book and final judgement. The monks of the Cuthbert community had established themselves at Durham in 955, and it would be tempting to associate such seemingly theologically rich works with them, however, there were other churches in the area, so any such connections must remain in the realm of hypothesis. Moreover, the lack of iconographic and compositional clarity might be seen as militating against the production of the sculpture at such a comparatively wealthy and learned centre.

Fear and uncertainty were, however, felt at the highest levels. Similar and related apocalyptic motifs are found in art of all media in the tenth and

---

[33] The fourth, now lost, would have been below.
[34] Bailey, *Viking Age Sculpture*, p. 171.

eleventh centuries,³⁵ as well as in homilies and hagiography, most notably the writings of Ælfric and Wulfstan II of York, especially the latter's *Sermo Lupi* of 1014.³⁶ One of the finest and most subtle artistic versions of the theme is to be found on the very rare series of Agnus Dei pennies issued by Æthelred II in 1009 (fig. 75). The coinage has been connected specifically with the arrival of Thorkell the Tall's army at Sandwich in August 1009, and the stringent programme of prayer, almsgiving and fasting set out in the law code VII Æthelred drafted by Archbishop Wulfstan and issued at Bath that same month.³⁷ The spectacle must have been impressive, with barefoot congregations processing through the countryside led by priests bearing relics and calling upon God for deliverance, prostrate communities of monks singing psalms and everyone reciting psalters. The Agnus Dei pennies may be understood as conveying a similar call for divine assistance in visual form, and hence convey a more hopeful message than the Durham cross heads may have carried.³⁸ On the obverse is the lamb of God with a cross staff and a book inscribed with the alpha and omega, and on the reverse the dove of the Holy Spirit soaring upwards towards heaven. There is nothing about the Durham sculptures that suggests any such movement upwards. The symbolism of the coins is to some degree straightforward. The lamb represents both Christ as sacrificial innocent, 'the lamb of God, which taketh away the sin of the world' (John 1.29), and Christ as the conqueror of evil in the lamb of Revelation 21. The dove too is a symbol of peace and innocence but also of the divine inspiration that could bring spiritual victory. The political message of the coins is thus quite clear. Yet, as Simon Keynes has pointed out, the series seems to have had a particularly broad appeal across both Anglo-Saxon and Scandinavian cultures. It was imitated in both Scandinavian and Hiberno-Norse coinage and many of the coins have been pierced suggesting that they were worn as jewellery or amulets.³⁹ If the original message was a call for peace and deliverance it seems likely to have been a call that was shared by people on both sides. Similar motifs, possibly inspired by the coinage, appear on jewellery of the period such as the Sulgrave brooch, with its lamb, and the

---

[35] See especially Leslie Webster, 'Apocalypse Then: Anglo-Saxon Ivory Carving in the Tenth and Eleventh Centuries', in *Aedificia Nova: Studies in Honor of Rosemary Cramp*, ed. Karkov and Damico, 226–53.
[36] See above p. 244.
[37] See Simon Keynes, 'An Abbot, an Archbishop, and the Viking Raids of 1006–7 and 1009–12', *ASE* 36 (2007), 151–220, at 179–89; Whitelock *et al.*, *Councils and Synods with other Documents Relating to the English Church*, 379–82.
[38] On the pennies see Mark Blackburn and Simon Keynes, 'Three New *Agnus Dei* Pennies of King Æthelred the Unready', *ASE* 39 (2011); Dolley, 'The Nummular Brooch from Sulgrave'; Keynes, 'An Abbot, an Archbishop, and the Viking Raids', 190–201. Only twenty coins have been discovered to date, with only three having been found in England.
[39] Keynes, 'An Abbot, an Archbishop, and the Viking Raids', 200–1.

Bicester brooch, with its dove.⁴⁰ The Agnus Dei coinage is one of only a handful of issues that break with the standard formula of cross or hand of God and royal bust seen on so much of late Anglo-Saxon coinage, and a reminder of the complex symbolism and artistic quality that coins could exemplify. Its popularity and rapid adoption are also indicative of the extent to which coins could spread imagery and message, and thus of their effectiveness as propaganda.

All hopes for an English victory were of course futile. Thorkell's army continued to raid the county and demand tribute from the English until 1012. In 1013 an army led by Swein Forkbeard, king of Denmark, conquered the country and drove Æthelred and his family into exile in Normandy. Swein died in 1014 and was eventually succeeded by his son Cnut, who was in turn driven into brief exile by the return of Æthelred but came back to claim permanent victory at the battle of Assandun on 18 October 1016. By November of that same year he was king of England. Cnut was simultaneously king of England (1016-35) and king of Denmark (1018-35), as well as an important ruler in a European context.⁴¹ While there is no doubt that he was a Christian king, he was adept at marketing his image to suit the circumstances. To the Danish he was a warrior in true Viking tradition, to the English he projected an image of pious patronage and good Christian rule in the tradition of his Anglo-Saxon predecessors, and across Europe he consolidated his position as ruler of a northern empire by such diplomatic activities as mingling with the court of Emperor Conrad II, the founder of the Salian dynasty, and marrying his daughter, Gunnhild, to Conrad's son Henry in 1036.

Cnut's own marriage alliances were equally strategic to the building of his empire. His first liaison (there is some debate about whether it was or was not a marriage) was with Ælfgifu of Northampton, the daughter of Ealdorman Ælfhelm, which provided him with both a powerbase in England and the support of a prominent Mercian family. The second, his 1017 marriage to Æthelred's widow Emma/Ælfgyfu of Normandy (hereafter Emma), provided continuity with the old regime, a possible means of curtailing any claim to the throne by her two sons with Æthelred, Alfred and Edward, and a connection to the Norman court. The marriage seems to have been successful both personally and politically, and both Emma and Cnut appear to have been devoted to a strategically co-ordinated rule, if not to each other. Art was but one medium through which this was conveyed. The well-known portrait of Emma and Cnut that prefaces the Winchester Liber Vitae of 1031 (London, BL, MS Stowe 949) is a visual statement of the dual image of power and piety they wished to project (plate 12). The cross at the centre is in full colour, immediately catching

---

⁴⁰ Dolley, 'The Nummular Brooch from Sulgrave'; Keynes, 'An Abbot, an Archbishop, and the Viking Raids', 201; Webster 'Apocalypse Then', 240 n. 53.
⁴¹ In 1028 he also claimed rule over Norway and parts of Sweden.

the eye of the viewer and marking the point of intersection of the different spaces into which the miniature is divided. The upper half of the page contains heaven, ruled over by an enthroned Christ flanked by Mary and Peter, figures of queenship and piety, wisdom and judgement respectively. Angels descend from above to unite heaven and earth at the level of the cross arms in a composition that references the portrait of Edgar presenting his charter to Christ in the 965 New Minster Charter (London, BL, Cotton Vespasian A.viii), a book which would have been displayed alongside the Liber Vitae on the altar at Winchester. To Christ's right, Emma receives a veil, and to his left Cnut receives a crown. The monks of the New Minster look on from the arch beneath the feet of the queen and king. One of the primary purposes of the page seems to have been to provide a record of Cnut's gift of a golden altar cross to the abbey in the 1020s, an act which merited the king's inclusion in the book of the community's special dead, but the page does much more than that. It locates the royal couple in a space that is both of and above this world, represented by the monks in their architectural setting and the eternal space of heaven respectively. This is fitting for a book whose purpose was to aid those who had either been or were patrons, friends or members of the community to a blessed afterlife in heaven. In a sense Emma and Cnut, though still very much alive at the time the drawing was made, lead the group as it is their names and images with which it opens, although the procession of figures led by angels on the following page moves in a different direction.

The Liber Vitae drawing also establishes a multifaceted identity for both the king and queen in which all their royal attributes take on a double meaning. Cnut is represented as pious – his hand on the cross would convey that much even if we knew nothing of the donation. The sword indicates that he is a strong military ruler, and this aspect of his nature is highlighted by the way in which it breaks the lines of the frame.[42] His imperial pretensions are signified above all by the prominent arched crown, which resembles that worn by the Ottonian and Salian emperors.[43] While perhaps not obvious to the modern viewer, an Anglo-Saxon audience might also have been reminded of the crown, or crowns, that Cnut is said to have donated to various churches, including the New Minster.[44] The pose of the angel above Cnut's head, with one hand firmly grasping the crown and the other pointing upwards towards Christ, is

---

[42] Cnut's military power is a preeminent part of his portrayal in Scandinavian literature. See Roberta Frank, 'King Cnut in the Verse of his Skalds', in *The Reign of Cnut*, ed. A. R. Rumble (London, 1994), 106–24.

[43] See Karkov, *Ruler Portraits*, 137; J. Deer, 'Kaiser Otto der Grosse und die Reichskrone', in *Beitrage zur Kunstgeschichte und Arkëologie des Frümittelalter* (Cologne, 1962), 261–77; M. Schulze-Dörlamm, *Die Kaiserkrone Konrads II: eine archäologische Untersuchung zu Alter und Herkunft der Reichskrone* (Sigmaringen, 1991).

[44] Karkov, *Ruler Portraits*, 126; Henry of Huntingdon, *Historia Anglorum (History of the English People)*, ed. D. Greenway (Oxford, 1996), 368–9; Heslop, 'The Production of *de luxe* Manuscripts and the Patronage of King Cnut and Queen Emma', 187.

certainly meant to suggest that the crown was not just an emblem of earthly power but also a sign of heavenly reward. No matter how pious Cnut was and/or how pious the monks of the New Minster wished to present him as being, his half of the image is all about power.[45] The crown and the sword are symbols of kingship and Cnut's firm grasp of the prominent sword is indicative above all of his military strength. The cross too may be interpreted as a weapon, as the promotion of the king's good Christian image was one of the ways in which he maintained his rule over the English people, and the way he is shown with one hand on the cross and the other on his sword, underscores this fact. Above Cnut, Peter hold his keys, a symbol both of judgement in general and of his position as gatekeeper of heaven but, in the scene of Last Judgement that follows, he wields them as a weapon just as the king would wield his sword.

The figure of the queen is more unusual (and hence more problematic and more interesting) and more prominent in the composition – indeed, its prominence is what makes it so unusual. The overall composition of the page is based on the double ruler portraits of Byzantine and Ottonian art,[46] but in all earlier surviving royal portraits the queen stands to Christ's left, not in the position of honour to his right. Visually, Emma's black slippers, no doubt included to match those of the Virgin who stands above her, serve to draw the viewer's attention to the figure of the queen. The reasons for her prominence may be many and varied. In part she may have been placed to Christ's right because that is where Mary stands, and one purpose of the page is to establish a relationship between the heavenly and earthly courts and thus the sacral side of earthly power. The relationship between Mary and the Anglo-Saxon queen was an important part of reform ideology in Winchester and remained strong long after the reform period itself. However, it should be noted that while Mary stands to Christ's right in Byzantine art, the Byzantine empress does not. Emma was also a patron of the New Minster in her own right. Her gift of the 'Greek shrine' with its various relics is recorded in the list of relics inserted before the portrait (now folio 58v) in the mid-eleventh century,[47] and it

---

[45] On Cnut as violent conqueror see Elaine Treharne, *The Politics of the English, 1000–1200* (forthcoming), chs. 1 and 2.

[46] See, for example, the *c.* 982–3 Ottonian ivory depicting Christ crowning Otto II and Theophanu now in the Cluny Museum (http://www.musee-moyenage.fr/ang/pages/page_id17997_ull2.htm).

[47] See Jones, 'Emma's Greek *Scrine*'. The shrine contained: 'Þæt is of Sancte Iohanne baptisita .7 of montem Sion .7 of ðæm stane þe se rod stod on uppan ðe ure dryhten onðropode .7 of þære binnan ðe ure dryhten onlæg .7 of mensa domini .7 of þare gyrde þe Moyses hæfde ofer þa readan sæ .7 of þare dune monte caluarie .7 sepulchrum domini .7 of lignum domini .7 of sanctę Andreę apostolę .7 of sanctę Pancrate .7 of Melchisedech .7 of sancte Uedeste .7 of sancte Ypolite .7 of sancte Pelai .7 of sancte Cyriace .7 sancte Martines toð .7 of sancte Remei .7 sancte Hilarii .7 sance Ceaddan toð .7 of sancte Firmine .7 of Cosme 7 Damiane .7 of sancte Gaugerice .7 of sancte Georige .7 manna domini .7 of ures dryhtenes reafe .7 sancte Tremori .7 sancte Bricii .7 of sancte Maximiane .7 sancte Cyllias earm .7 sancte Ualentinus heafod .7 of sancte Desideri.' (That

is possible that her patronage was greater or of longer standing than that of Cnut. It is also conceivable, especially in light of the later portrait of Emma in the *Encomium Emmae* discussed below, that her prominence, and prominent association with Mary were of her own making, built on the traditions begun during the reform at Winchester. The combination of the veil she receives from the angel and the diadem already on her head also keeps the focus on Emma's twin attributes of Marian piety and queenliness. But as with the image of Cnut, her attributes and her association with Mary are not just signs of her piety, they are also the signs of and tools by which she achieved and held power on earth. The veil was a multifaceted symbol and could signify not only piety, Mary and the spiritual rewards of heaven, it was also a symbol of marriage. Similarly, the book that Mary holds is both a symbol of her wisdom and a weapon that Emma would use on her own behalf on earth. Its importance as well as its double status are emphasized by the fact that it is picked out in red and yellow like the cross. It was above all by deploying books as a means of creating a particular image of queenship in which she was, like Mary, the wife and mother of kings, that Emma attempted to maintain her power.

The power of the queen was of course limited by the conventions of the day. Emma could not rule in her own right, she could only take part in governing the kingdom through marriage to the king and through becoming the legitimate mother of *æthelings*. However, in Emma's case the role of wife and mother took on a national significance that it does not seem to have had for any previous queen. It is clear from the textual accounts of Emma and Cnut's marriage that, despite her Norman birth, Emma represented Englishness in that she represented a legitimate link to the rule of the English land and people for Cnut. Whether it was to placate her sons or those still loyal to Æthelred, to locate himself within the established Anglo-Saxon royal genealogies, or all of those things, Cnut's marriage to Emma was a metaphor for his claim to the land, and it is certainly possible that her pivotal position between dynasties, between land and king, and between the church and the court had an influence on her position on the page.

One feature of the drawing that has not perhaps received as much attention as it deserves is the role of the inscription in the larger meaning of the miniature. It is not simply a label of the status of the queen and king

---

is of John the Baptist and of Mount Sion, and of the stone on which the cross stood on which our Lord suffered, and of the manger in which our Lord lay, and of our Lord's table, and of the staff that Moses had over the Red Sea, and of the hill of Mount Calvary, and of our Lord's sepulchre, and of the wood of the Lord, and of St Andrew the apostle, and of St Pancratius, and of Melchisedek, and of St Valentine, and of St Yppolitus, and of St Pelagia, and of St Cyriacus, and of St Martin's tooth, and of St Remigius, and of St Hilarius, and of St Cead's tooth, and of St Firminius, and of Saints Cosmos and Damian, and of St Gaugericus, and of St George, and of the manna of our Lord, and of St Cyllias's arm, and of St Valentine's head, and of St Desiderius.)

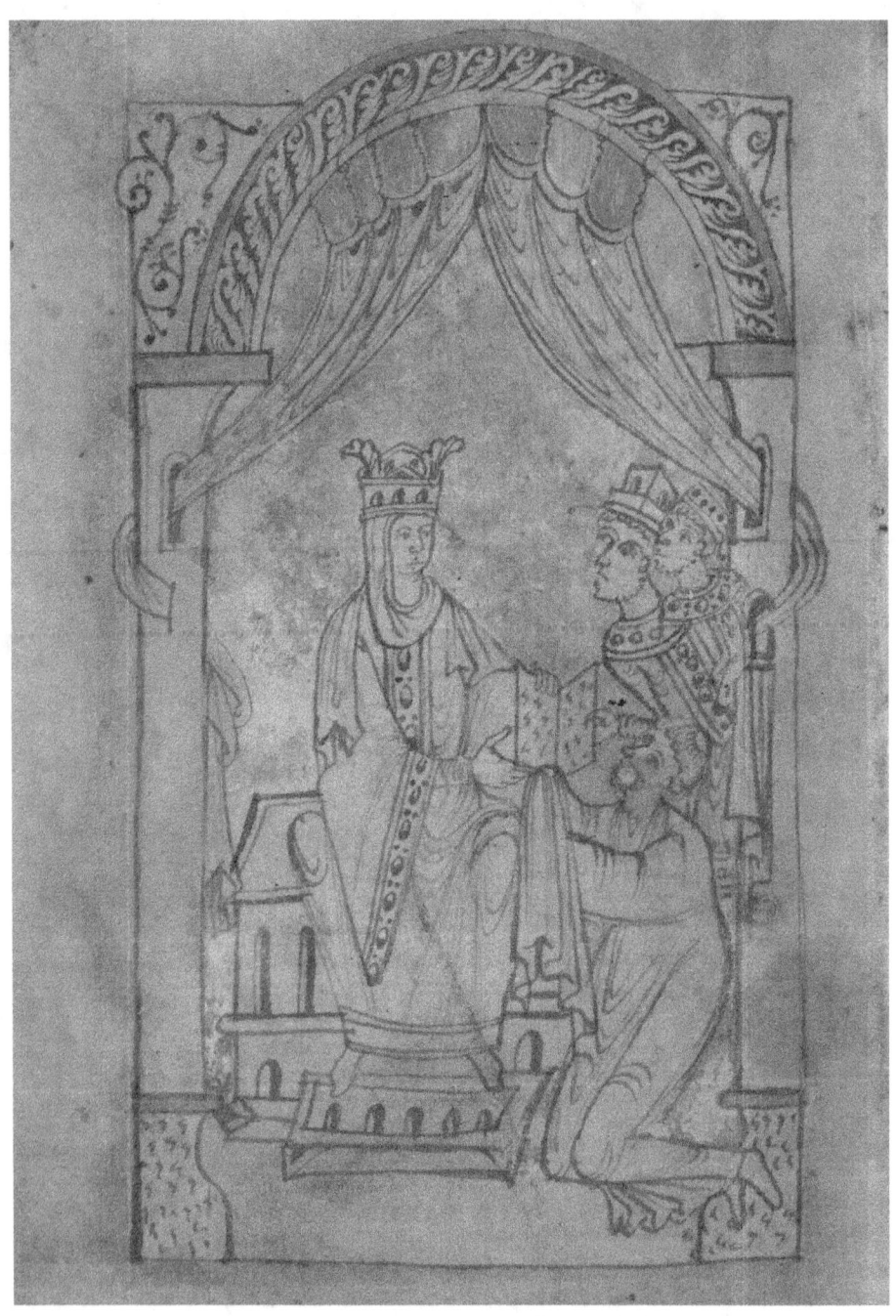

FIG. 76. EMMA ENTHRONED, *ENCOMIUM EMMAE*. LONDON, BL, MS ADD. 33241, FOL. 1V

within it. Both Emma and Cnut were foreign rulers, and their dynastic fit and acceptance by various factions of the Anglo-Saxon church and state had been (and would continue to be) a matter of comment. The inscription in the Liber Vitae 'Englishes' both, and in so doing reinforces a certain postcolonial hybridity. Emma appears under the English name she either took or was given at the time of her marriage to Æthelred II in 1002, a name that was chosen to convey precisely that sense of Englishness and link with dynastic traditions discussed above. As a king, Cnut would not have adopted a new name, but his name too appears here unsurprisingly in its English form (Cnut rather than Knútr or Cnuto). The titles of both queen and king however are in Latin, the universal language of the church elite. Whatever the reasons for the choice of names, spellings and, one could add, scripts, the inscription serves to remind the reader of the multilingual and hybrid world that the Anglo-Saxon court must have been at the time. Emma had been raised in a multilingual court in Normandy. Her Danish mother, Gunnor, and her sisters had been given Frankish names although there is no evidence that they used them in the way that Emma clearly used her English name. Her mother is also believed to have been an important informant for Dudo of Saint-Quentin's *De moribus et acti primorum Normanniae Ducum*, a collection of historic tales composed for the court of Emma's father. The multiple Old English, Latin and Old Norse sources that document Cnut's reign indicate that he too was adept at the manipulation of language and reader, even if he may not have been literate in all the languages themselves.[48] The placing of the names and images of Emma and Cnut at the head of this particular book, a book that records the names of the multiple groups of men and women remembered by the New Minster community, also serves to figure them as rulers over a section of their kingdom that transcended temporal boundaries as their historical rule transcended geographic and linguistic ones.

Emma's identification with both England and the Virgin Mary is even stronger in the dedication portrait that prefaces the *Encomium Emmae* (London, BL, Add. 33241), written for Emma in 1041–42 somewhere in northern France, Flanders or even England itself by a monk from the monastery of Saint-Bertin (fig. 76). As has been noted many times, the frontispiece corresponds closely with the image of Emma and her two sons created in the text, especially the original ending of the text, which paints a verbal portrait of the peaceful co-rule of Emma, Harthacnut and Edward that is totally at odds with the historical reality of the situation. In the portrait Emma appears enthroned, receiving her book from the scribe/encomiast, while Edward and Harthacnut look on, in a composition that

---

[48] See Matthew Townend, 'Knútr and the Cult of St Óláfr: Poetry and Patronage in Eleventh-Century Norway and England', *Viking and Medieval Scandinavia* 1 (2005), 251–79; Matthew Townend, 'Contextualizing the Knútsdrápur: Skaldic Praise-Poetry at the Court of Cnut', *ASE* 30 (2001), 145–79.

is clearly based on the Adoration of the Magi.[49] The position of the book, placed squarely in the space that would be occupied by the Christ child in an Adoration scene, suggests that it is her true son, which in one sense it is as it presents a reinvention of the story of her marriage to Cnut and their joint rule designed specifically to produce an image of Emma as a beloved leader of both people and sons. This is a rather different identification of the book with the body than was the case in the manuscripts of Edgar's reign, but a related phenomenon nonetheless. The text also famously describes her as a virgin (*virgo*) at the time of her marriage to Cnut despite the fact that she had two sons from her previous marriage, Edward and Alfred, in a move that seems at the very least designed to gloss over the fact of their existence.

> Inuenta est uero haec imperialis sponsa in confinitate Gallane et praecipue in Normandensi regio ne stirpe et opibus ditissima, sed tamen pulcritudinis et prudentiae deleotamine omnium eius temporum mulierum praestantissima, utpote regina famosa ... Sed abenegat illa, se unquam Cnutonis sponsam fieri, nisi illi: iusiurando affirmaret, quod numquam alterius coniugis filium post se regnare faceret nisi eius ... Placuit ergo regi uerbum uirginis, et iusiurando facto uirgini placuit uoluntus regis.
>
> (The imperial bride was, in fact, found within the bounds of Gaul, and to be precise in the Norman area, a lady of the greatest nobility and wealth, but yet the most distinguished woman of her time for delightful beauty and wisdom, inasmuch as she was a famous queen ... But she refused ever to become the bride of Cnut, unless he would affirm to her by oath that he would never set up the son of any wife other than herself to rule after him ... Accordingly the king found what the virgin said acceptable and when the oath had been taken, the virgin found what the king said acceptable.)[50]

The text also resolutely refuses to name Æthelred II, so that within this book Alfred and Edward remain without earthly father, the progeny instead of the book and its words. This recasting of Emma, widow and mother, as Emma, virgin bride, looks forward precociously to much later royal practice, as exemplified by the case of Elizabeth Woodville, a widow with two children who was married to Edward IV in 1464 in an elaborate ceremony during part of which she played the role of the Virgin Mary,[51]

---

[49] Karkov, *Ruler Portraits*, 153; C. E. Karkov, 'Emma: Image and Ideology', in *Early Medieval Studies in Memory of Patrick Wormald*, ed. Baxter, Karkov, Nelson and Pelteret, 509–20.

[50] Campbell and Keynes, *Encomium Emmae*, 32. Translation based on this edition.

[51] J. L. Chamberlayn, 'Crowns and Virgins: Queenmaking during the Wars of the Roses', in *Young Medieval Women*, ed. K. J. Lewis, N. J. Menuge and K. M. Phillips (Stroud, 1999), 47–68.

though Elizabeth's use of the image was certainly without the ruthlessness of Emma's.

The drawing is more overt in associating Emma with England itself than was the Liber Vitae miniature. In this portrait Emma is enthroned and crowned as a ruler in her own right. Moreover, the crown that she wears is based on the architectural crowns of the personifications of cities and other territories as depicted in Roman, early Christian and Byzantine art.[52] It is so unusual within the context of Anglo-Saxon or Norman art of the period that one can only imagine that it was deliberately chosen for its specific connections with those images of sovereign territory. We know from the documentary sources (the *Encomium* amongst them) that Cnut and other early medieval kings chose their partners for their associations with particular geographic areas as well as particular dynasties – Ælfgifu of Northampton with Mercia, for example – so it is beyond doubt that queens, along with other noblewomen, would have made similar associations. Art-historically, however, Emma's image sets a model that would be followed for centuries to come.

The image of Emma as mother with the book as her son is also apt because the *Encomium* seems to have set a precedent for literate queens to use the book as a means of achieving or maintaining position and power and of telling their own stories or versions of history. Such women may well have existed in England prior to the eleventh century, but it is only beginning with Emma that the manuscript evidence survives. Edith Godwineson, Emma's daughter-in-law, followed her example by commissioning the *Vita Edwardi*, an account of her marriage to Edward the Confessor that is modelled closely on the *Encomium*, and that takes up its image of virginity in the casting of Edith and Edward as willing participants in a chaste marriage; Edith appears in the pose of a mourning Mary in the scene of Edward's deathbed in the Bayeux Tapestry. The *Vita* also claims that, like Emma, Edith was multilingual, able to speak, if not read, the languages of Gaul, Denmark and Ireland as if they were her mother tongue.[53] Judith of Flanders, whose numerous gospel books were mentioned above,[54] was Emma's grand-niece and, during her first marriage to Earl Tostig, Edith's sister-in-law. Through her second marriage to Welf of Bavaria she became mother-in-law to the highly literate and politically influential Countess Matilda of Tuscany. Margaret of Scotland (c. 1045–93), famed for her love of books and reading, was the granddaughter of Æthelred II (through his first wife, also named Ælfgifu) and may have been placed under Edith's protection when her father, Edward the Exile,

---

[52] See e.g., the heads of two Genius or Tutela figures from Carlisle in Coulston and Phillips, ed. *Corpus signorum imperii romani*, nos. 472 and 473, pp. 156–7, pl. 107.
[53] Barlow, *The Life of King Edward who Rests at Westminster*, rev. edn, 22.
[54] P. 213.

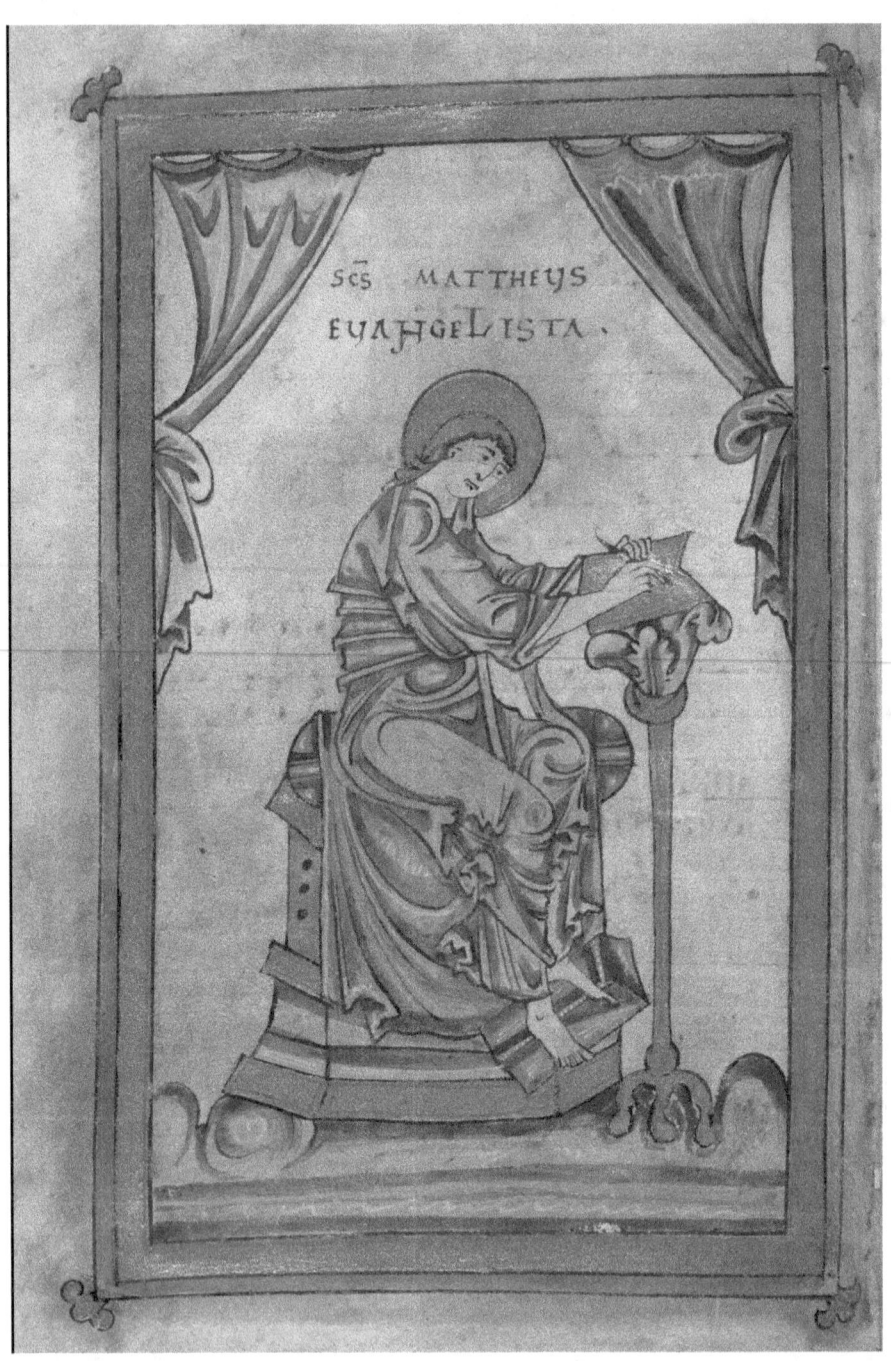

FIG. 77. ST MATTHEW, ST MARGARET'S GOSPEL. OXFORD, BODL. LIB., MS LAT. LITURG. F.5, FOL. 3V

died shortly after returning to England from Hungary with his family in 1057.

Margaret married King Malcolm III 'Canmore' of Scotland in 1070. Her Life, written in the period 1104–7 for her daughter Edith-Matilda, queen of Henry I of England, portrays her as a model of learning, humility, piety and queenliness. Her political connections with England and the house of Wessex are equally present and no doubt central both to her own marriage alliance and that of her daughter. Her authority is also made to extend back to Roman-Britain. In the Life she is compared to the Empress Helena and thus figured as the mother of a new dynasty, as well as a leader of religious conversion and church reform – as was Bertha, the first Christian queen of Kent.[55] Oxford, Bodleian Library, MS Lat. Lit. F5, the so-called St Margaret Gospels, is believed to have been one of her personal and most favoured books (fig. 77). It is a portable manuscript that is actually a hybrid of a gospel book, lectionary and prayerbook. Like a lectionary it contains gospel extracts rather than the full texts of the gospels, but they are in the order in which they occur in the gospels rather than in their liturgical order as they would be in a lectionary. It also contains the incipits to and passion narratives from all four gospels. Richard Gameson has compared its contents with those of the books of Nunnaminster and Cerne,[56] which is interesting in light of the connection of Nunnaminster and the Tiberius group of manuscripts to which it belongs with female ownership and literacy.[57]

Although Bodleian Lat. Lit. F.5 has become known as the St Margaret Gospels, we cannot really be sure that it was her book. The manuscript has been dated to the period 1030–70, the period before Margaret became queen. It is possible that it was produced for her while she was in England, perhaps at Wilton where she may have been educated, where both Edith Godwineson and Margaret's great-great-aunt Edith of Wilton had been educated, and where her daughter Edith-Matilda would be educated. It is not the grandest of books and certainly cannot compare with other royal manuscripts, or even the several gospel books of Judith of Flanders, so such a scenario is conceivable. Alternatively, she may have acquired it second hand (as King Æthelstan had acquired some of his best-known manuscripts), she may have inherited it, or it may have been given to her as a gift. Stylistically it is entirely Anglo-Saxon and its miniatures of the four evangelists are best compared with those in the Eadwig Gospels (Hanover, Kestner Museum WMXXIa 36). It is true that folio 21 contains a poem recording the loss and recovery of the book:

---

[55] The Life is translated in Lois L. Huneycutt, *Matilda of Scotland: A Study in Medieval Queenship* (Woodbridge, 2003), 161–78. The comparison to Helena is on p. 169.
[56] Richard Gameson, 'The Gospels of Margaret of Scotland and the Literacy of an Eleventh-Century Queen', in *Women and the Book: Assessing the Visual Evidence*, ed. Jane H. M. Taylor and Lesley Smith (London, 1997), 149–71, at 152.
[57] Brown, 'Female Book-Ownership and Production in Anglo-Saxon England'.

Christe tibi semper grates persoluimus omnes
Tempore qui nostro nobis miracula pandis;
Hunc librum quidam inter se iurare uolentes;
Sumpserunt nudum sine tegmine nonque ligatum
Presbyter accipiens ponit sinuamine uestis.
Flumine transmisso codex est mersus in amnem;
Portitor ignorat librum penetrasse profundum;
Sed miles quidam cernens post multa momenta;
Tollere iam uoluit librum de flumine mersum
Sed titubat subito librum dum uidet apertum;
Credens quod codex ex toto perditus esset;
At tamen inmittens undis corpus cum uertice summo;
Hoc euangelium profert de gurgite apertum;
O uirtus clara cunctis, O gloria magna;
Inuiolatus enim codex permansit ubique;
Exceptis foliis binis que cernis utrinque;
In quibus ex undis paret contractio quedam;
Que testantur opus Christi pro codice sancto;
Hoc opus ut nobis maius mirabile constet
De medio libri pannum lini abtulit unda;
Saluati semper sint rex reginaque sancta;
Quorum codex erat nuper saluatus ab undis.
Gloria magna Deo, librum qui saluat eundem.

(O Christ, we will always give thanks to you who make miracles known to us in our own time. Certain folk who wanted to swear an oath among themselves, Took up this book, bare without a wrapper and not fastened. A priest took it and placed it in the fold of his robe. As he crossed the river, the codex plunged into the torrent. The bearer was unaware that the book had sunk to the depths. Much later, however, a certain soldier caught sight of it. Straightaway he wanted to raise the submerged book out of the river; but when he saw that the book was open, suddenly he hesitated believing that the codex would be utterly ruined. Nevertheless, he hurled himself head first into the waves and bore the open gospel book out from the whirlpool. What virtue clear to all, what great glory! For the codex survived entirely undamaged except for the two folios which you see at either end in which some cockling from the water is apparent which proclaim the work of Christ on behalf of the sacred codex. In order that this work should be manifested to us as even more miraculous, the water washed away the sheet of linen from the middle of the book. May the king and holy queen be safe for ever whose codex was recently saved from the waves. All glory be to God who saved the book in question!)[58]

---

[58] Gameson, 'The Gospels of Margaret of Scotland', 165–6.

The poem does not mention Margaret by name, but the events it describes are in accord with those described by Turgot in the Life of Margaret:

> She had a Gospel Book, thoroughly covered with gems and gold, in which images of the four evangelists were embellished with paint mixed with gold, and indeed, throughout each capital letter glowed reddish with gold. This book she had always loved more dearly than the others in which she studied and read. Once, while this book was being transported, it happened that she crossed over through a ford in a river. The person carrying the book continued to ride along, unconcerned because he had no idea that the book had been dropped. Indeed, it was a long time later, when he wished to bring out the book, that he realized for the first time that it was not there. For a long time the book was sought, but it was not found.
>
> At length, the book was found, lying open at the bottom of a deep river, and its pages were being swept back and forth continuously by the rapid motion of the water. There had been some silk protective cloths that covered the golden letters to prevent them from being worn away by continuous contact with the facing pages, but the cloths had been swept away by the force of the river. Who would think that the book would be worth anything any longer? Who would believe even one letter would still appear in it? But without a doubt, it was drawn up from the middle of the river intact, uncorrupt, and undamaged, so much so that it scarcely seemed to have been touched by the water! The pages remained as white as before, and everything was intact, and the forms of the letters remained just as they had been. The only damage was to the final leaves, where some signs of moisture could just barely be seen. At once, the book was brought back to the queen, and the miracle was related to her, and she returned thanks to Christ, and from then on the queen loved the book even more than she had before.[59]

The similarity of the two accounts has led to the assumption that the book must have been Margaret's,[60] but this is in fact far from certain. The book shows no signs of water damage (though that is of course the miracle), and the two accounts differ in significant details: in Turgot's version there is no oath, the queen is present on the journey, there is no accidental discovery by a soldier, and a number of silk protective cloths rather than just a single piece of linen are said to have been lost from the book. Moreover, Margaret is known to have been devoted to St Cuthbert and was a great benefactor of Durham Cathedral. She donated both a cross

---

[59] Huneycutt, *Matilda of Scotland*, 175.
[60] Gameson ('The Gospels of Margaret of Scotland', 149), for example, states that it 'proves' the book to be hers.

and a gospel book to the community, and they in turn obtained relics of her hair and teeth after her death. It is possible then that the miracle was invented, or perhaps augmented, to correspond with a similar miracle in which Cuthbert's book, thought to be the Lindisfarne Gospels (figs. 7, 8, 50), was thrown into the sea when a ship carrying the Lindisfarne community and the relics of St Cuthbert to Ireland was overwhelmed by a storm, as recorded in the *Libellus de Exordio atque Procursu istius hoc est Dunhelmensis Ecclesie*, attributed to Symeon of Durham.[61] There is, of course, the problem of date; the inscription in 'Margaret's book' has been dated on palaeographic grounds to the late eleventh century – presumably before her death in 1093, if it was indeed her book – while Symeon was writing between 1104 and 1109. The miracle, however, deals with events of 875, the year in which the monks left Lindisfarne because of the Vikings, and should therefore, if true, have been known at an earlier date. Dating a text on palaeographic grounds is as subjective and difficult as is dating an image on stylistic grounds, so it may also be that the inscription should not be so precisely dated. Moreover, Margaret's Life was written at exactly the same time that Symeon was writing, while Turgot was prior of Durham and before he became bishop of St Andrews in 1109.

Nicholas Howe has illuminated the ways in which the story of Exodus became part of the origin legend of the Anglo-Saxons, as well as the ways in which that legend was retold, reworked and reaffirmed in the stories of later journeys over water throughout the Anglo-Saxon period.[62] The stories of both Cuthbert's and Margaret's books may well be two such retellings – indeed the plagues of Exodus 4:9 and 7:17 are cited in the account of Cuthbert's miracle.[63] Both stories are told in the context of originary moments: the rebuilding of Durham Cathedral and its passage from an Anglo-Saxon to an Anglo-Norman monument in the case of Cuthbert, and the return of the house of Wessex from its exile overseas in the case of Margaret. Margaret herself made two journeys, the first to England from Hungary and the second from England to Scotland, before her daughter Edith-Matilda returned to the throne of England at her marriage to Henry I in 1100. It would have been at or shortly after the time of Matilda's marriage that the Life of Margaret would have been commissioned. The family's place in the Durham community's memory, and memory of Anglo-Saxon history, is affirmed in the bond of confraternity between them recorded in the Durham Liber Vitae:

> Hec est c(on)uentio qua(m) c(on)uent(us) S(an)c(t)i Cuthberti MALCOLMO regi Scottor(um) (et) MARGARITE regine, filiisq(ue) eor(um) (et) filiab(us) se p(er)petuo seruare promisit.

---

[61] Symeon of Durham, *Libellus de Exordio atque Procursu istius hoc est Dunhelmensis Ecclesie*, ed. and trans. David Rollason (Oxford, 2000), 112–21.
[62] Howe, *Migration and Mythmaking in Anglo-Saxon England*.
[63] Symeon of Durham, *Libellus de Exordio*, 114–15.

Scilic(et) ut p(ro) rege (et) regina du(m) uiuunt un(us) cotidie
paup(er) nutriat(ur), (et) duo ite(m) paup(er)es in cena d(omi)
ni ad co(m)mune mandatu(m) p(ro) eis habeant(ur), (et) una
collecta ad letanias (et) ad missa(s) habeat(ur). Sed utru(m)q(ue)
in hac (et) p(ost) hanc uita(m) ta(m) illi qua(m) filii (et) filie
eor(um) participes sint om(n)ium que fiunt ad seruitiu(m) D(e)
i in monast(er)io S(an)c(t)i Cuthberti, missaru(m) uidelic(et),
psalmor(um), elemosinaru(m), uigiliaru(m), orationu(m) (et)
q(u)icq(u)id e(st) hui(us)modi. Singularit(er) u(er)o pro rege (et)
regina a die obit(us) sui in c(on)uentu triginta plenaria officia
mortuor(um), (et) totide(m) U(er)ba mea fiant. Vn(us)q(u)
isq(ue) aut(em) sacerdos triginta missas. Ceteror(um) un(us)
q(u)isq(ue) .x. psalt(er)ia cantent. Anniuersariusq(ue) eor(um)
festiue sic(ut) Regis Ethelstani singulis annis celebret(ur).[64]

(This is the covenant which the convent of Saint Cuthbert has promised to Malcolm, king of the Scots, and to Queen Margaret, and to their sons and daughters, to keep for ever. Namely that, on behalf of the king and queen, while they are alive, one poor man shall be nourished daily, and likewise two poor men shall be maintained for them on Thursday in Holy Week at the common Maundy, and a collect said at the litanies and at mass. Further, that they both, in this life and after, they and their sons and daughters, shall be partakers in all things that be to the service of God in the monastery of St Cuthbert, that is to say in masses, in psalms and alms, in vigils and prayers and in all things that are of this kind. And for the king and the queen individually, from the day of their death there shall be thirty full offices of the dead in the convent, and *Verba mea* shall be done every day, and each priest shall sing thirty masses and each of the rest ten psalters; and their anniversary shall be celebrated as an annual festival like that of King Athelstan.)[65]

Margaret's identification with England and Englishness (and by extension that of her husband) was layered in a way that transcended time and history. She was a new Helena, she was a daughter of King Alfred and the house of Wessex, like King Æthelstan she was celebrated by the most important religious community in the north of England, and she was related in miracles and sanctity to the great national saint Cuthbert.

Cuthbert's story was itself undergoing multiple retellings in the late eleventh and early twelfth centuries. The post-Conquest, postcolonial

---

[64] David Rollason and Lynda Rollason, eds., *The Durham Liber Vitae*, London, British Library, MS Cotton Domitian A.VII (London, 2007), vol. 1, 155–6.
[65] G. W. S. Barrow, 'The Kings of Scotland and Durham', in *Anglo-Norman Durham*, ed. David Rollason, Margaret Harvey and Michael Prestwich (Woodbridge, 1994), 311–23, at 314; see also Valerie Wall, 'Malcolm III and the Foundation of Durham Cathedral', in ibid., 325–37, esp. 333.

Cuthbert was very different from the Cuthbert about whom Bede and the author of the anonymous Life of Cuthbert wrote. That Cuthbert was a gentle pastoral figure. That Cuthbert, especially in the anonymous Life, was a friend to important abbesses and had significant interaction with communities of religious women. The post-Conquest Cuthbert was a much harsher and more judgemental saint who would not tolerate any disobedience, especially that of women. Symeon relates that

> In nullum autem pene ecclesiarum, quas confessor beatus siue ante siue nunc, in tempore fuge uel post, sui sacri corporis presentia illustrauit, ulla usque hodie feminis esse constat intrandi licentia ... Que consuetudo usque hodie diligenter obseruatur, in tantum ut nisi metus hostilis uel concrematio loci compellat, nec in cimiteria quidem ipsarum ecclesiarum ubi ad tempus corpus eius requieuerat, mulieribus introire liceat.
>
> (It remains the case even today that women are not given permission to enter virtually any of the churches which the blessed confessor has sanctified with the presence of his sacred body either now or formerly, in the time of his flight or afterwards ... This custom [of excluding women from his church] is still meticulously observed today, to such an extent that women are not given permission to enter the cemeteries of those churches where his body rested for a time, unless they are forced to seek refuge there, either from fear of enemy attack, or because the place where they are living has been burned down.)[66]

However, Symeon is careful to locate the beginnings of this new attitude in the Anglo-Saxon past, namely Cuthbert's dismay at the dissolute ways of the nuns of Coldingham as recounted by Bede in book iv.25 of the *Historia ecclesiastica*.[67] This new Cuthbert was a hybrid: part Anglo-Norman tool for enforcing control of the north, part rallying point for a new Cuthbert community eager to retain some links with Anglo-Saxon ways. The movement of Cuthbert's relics from Lindisfarne to Chester-le-Street and eventually to Durham had expanded his territory to cover an area many times larger than that under the control of other saints and their communities, and both saint and community were unwilling to relinquish full control of their land and power. This is played out in the expanded versions of Cuthbert's Life that were produced after the Conquest. At the heart of these lives, with their narrative cycles of illustrations, is a message of obedience to the saint, no matter what the reader's ethnic or political identity. Oxford, University College, MS 165 is believed to have been

---

[66] Symeon of Durham, *Libellus de Exordio*, 104–5, 108–9.
[67] Symeon's work takes as its basis, indeed appropriates verbatim, large sections of the *Historia ecclesiastica*.

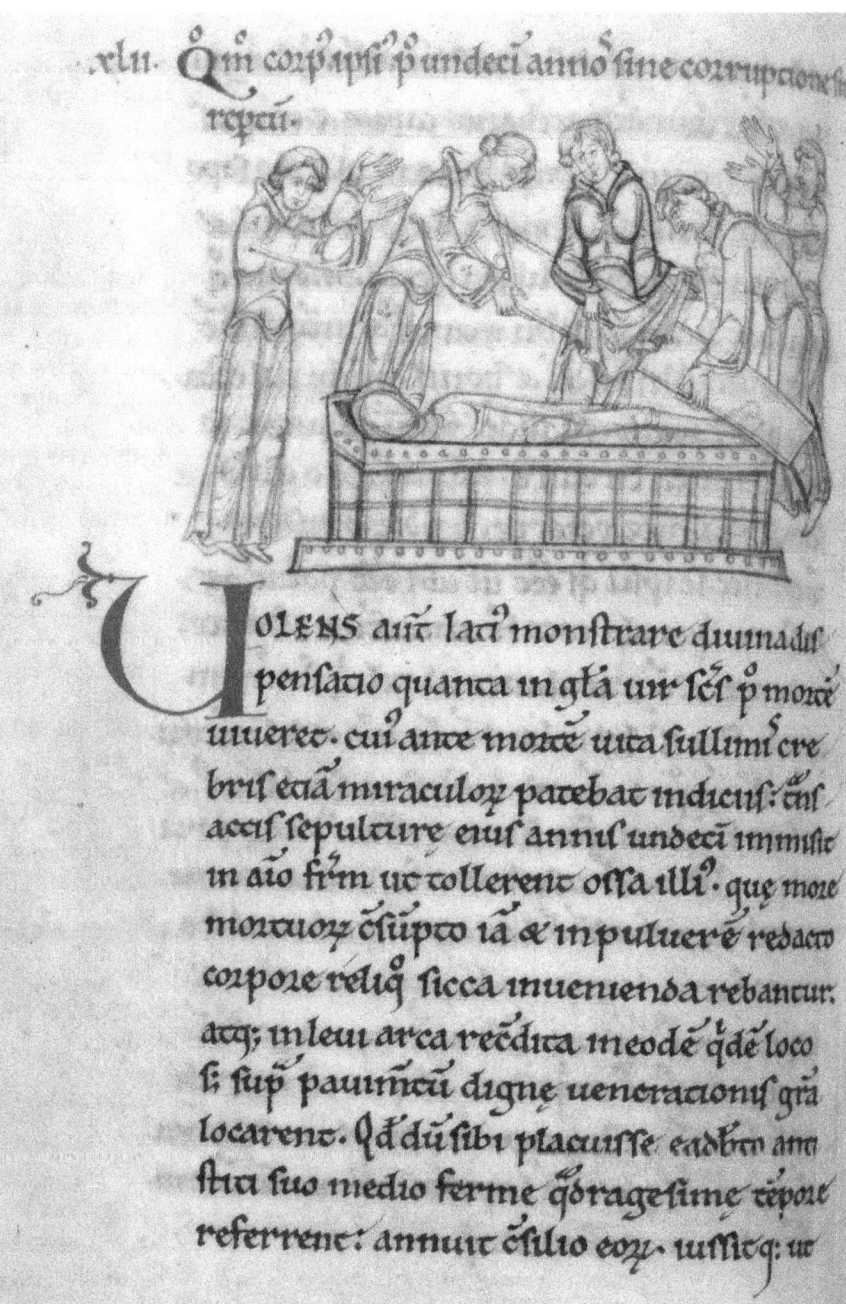

FIG. 78. DISCOVERY OF CUTHBERT'S INCORRUPT BODY, LIFE OF CUTHBERT. OXFORD, UNIVERSITY COLLEGE MS 165, P. 118

produced at Durham Cathedral Priory *c.* 1100–20 (fig. 78),[68] making it roughly contemporary with the works discussed above. The first forty-six chapters of the Life are based on Bede's Life of the saint and events from the *Historia ecclesiastica*. The final seven consist of miracles credited to the saint from the reign of Alfred to 1080. Kauffmann notes that 'It may be assumed that these miracles were collected soon after 1083, when the community of Benedictine monks was installed at Durham by Bishop William of St Calais, and certainly before 1104, the date of the translation of the relics, a key event which is not included in the text.'[69] These final seven chapters all deal with miracles related to the obedience of kings (chapter 49, in which Alfred is rewarded by Cuthbert) or the saint's preservation of his land and power in the wake of Scandinavian, Scottish or Norman aggression, including the story of the flight of the monks and the loss of the gospel book (chapter 50). It also includes a miracle that is yet another reworking of the Exodus/migration myth, in which the monks fleeing William the Conqueror in 1069 return to Lindisfarne with the body of St Cuthbert, arriving with dry feet despite having crossed to Holy Island at high tide.

Central to each of the chapters in the manuscript, as well as to the drawings that preface them, is the body of St Cuthbert. The drawing illustrated is from the last of the chapters taken from Bede's life of St Cuthbert, in which the monks find the body of the saint incorrupt after eleven years in the grave, an event that would be repeated multiple times including the translation of 1104. It was in that year that Cuthbert's body was moved to its new resting place behind the high altar of the still incomplete cathedral. In preparation for the ceremony the monks opened the coffin and found the body in an incorrupt state looking as if asleep and giving off sweet smells. Doubt of the miracle was expressed by one of the assembled abbots, but it was publically confirmed by the abbot of Sées.

> Involuta explicans vestimenta circa venerandum caput, utraque illud manu cunctis aspicientibus paululum erexit, et in diversas reflectendo partes integra omnibus juncturis colli compage reliquo id corpori cobaerere invenit. Deinde, manu admota, firmius aurem trahens et retrahens, et post hoc alias quoque corporis partes manu perscrutante explorans, solidum nervis et ossibus, cum carnis mollitie repperit corpus. Id etiam per caput tenendo concutiens, adeo in sublime erexit, ut in habitaculo suse quietis pene sedere visum fuerit …[70]

---

[68] The origin of the manuscript is not certain, but it has been attributed to Durham on stylistic and palaeographic grounds as well as its subject matter.

[69] C. M. Kaufmann, *Romanesque Manuscripts 1066–1190* (London, 1975), 67.

[70] *Symeonis Dunelmensis Opera et Collectanea*, ed. I. Hodgson-Hinde, Surtees Society (London, 1868), 196.

(Unfolding the vestments around the venerable head, he raised [the head] a little in both hands for all who were looking on, and by bending it in different directions found it to be connected with all joints of the neck to the rest of the skeleton of the body. Then, probing, more firmly pulling and tugging the ear, and examining other parts of the body with his probing hand, he found the body solid in sinews and bones with the softness of the flesh. Also shaking it by holding the head, he raised it up so that it was seen almost to sit in its abode of quiet ...)[71]

Many saints' bodies were described as incorrupt, but Cuthbert proved his superiority by remaining flexible, and the abbot's seemingly strange shaking and probing of the body serve to prove this point. His importance is also demonstrated by the additional relics of the bones of St Aidan and the head of St Oswald that the monks found within the coffin. Cuthbert really did appear to be suspended between life and death and even within the grave he had his community. The coffin was resealed, placed within a new coffin and carried into the cathedral with great ceremony before being placed in its new marble shrine. Incorruptibility is crucial to the story as it means that Cuthbert's body physically helps to negotiate the movement from Anglo-Saxon to Anglo-Norman by literally existing as both an Anglo-Saxon and an Anglo-Norman body. The same point is made subtly in the style of the Oxford manuscript's miniatures, which combine Anglo-Saxon dynamic line-drawing with a new Anglo-Norman sense of volume and solidity, and more overtly in the manuscript's refusal to show Cuthbert's burial. He is shown on his deathbed and he is shown during translation, but there is no burial.[72] The incorrupt body, along with the written authority of the *Libellus*, provided the new Durham community with an affirmation of their status as rightful keepers of the church and shrine and as heirs to the original Cuthbert community and its holdings.[73]

The determination of the Durham community to create a corporate postcolonial identity is revealed in the hybrid Anglo-Saxon/Anglo-Norman character of virtually everything they produced in the late eleventh and early twelfth centuries, from the Durham *Libellus* and Liber Vitae to the architecture of the cathedral (fig. 79) and the relics it contained. Contemporary with the cathedral and the historical and liturgical texts written for it is the poem *Durham*, which Heather Blurton has recently suggested ought to be read not as a text transitional between

---

[71] For translation and discussion see, C. F. Battiscombe, ed. *The Relics of St Cuthbert* (Oxford, 1956), 105–6; Barbara Abou-El-Haj, 'Saint Cuthbert: The Post-Conquest Appropriation of Anglo-Saxon Cult', in *Holy Men and Holy Women: Old English Prose Saints' Lives and Their Contexts*, ed. Paul E. Szarmach (Albany, NY, 1996), 177–206, at 192.
[72] A point made by Abou-El-Haj, 'Saint Cuthbert', 184–9.
[73] See further, Meryl Foster, 'Custodians of St Cuthbert: The Durham Monks' Views of their Predecessors, 1083–c. 1200', in *Anglo-Norman Durham*, ed. Rollason *et al.*, 53–65.

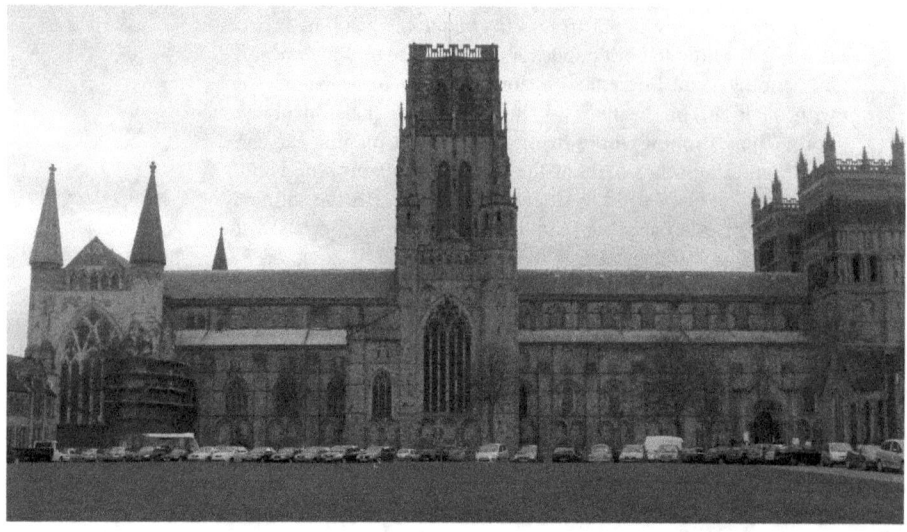

FIG. 79. DURHAM CATHEDRAL

Old and Middle English but as a postcolonial text working to address the tensions that existed between the competing power structures of church and state, which complicates any attempt to view the period as simply about competing Anglo-Saxon and Anglo-Norman identities.⁷⁴ The poem has been dated to the years 1104–9, and is generally believed to have been composed to commemorate the 1104 translation of Cuthbert's relics into the cathedral.⁷⁵ The poem too effects a movement into the cathedral as it moves the reader in from the surrounding river and enclosing woodland to the city and the relics contained within the minster:

> Is ðeos burch breome    geond Breotenrice
> steppa gestaðolad,    stanas ymbutan
> wundrum gewæxen.    Weor ymbeornad,
> ea yðum stronge,    and ðer inne wunað
> feola fisca kyn    on floda gemonge.
> And ðær gewexen is    wudafæstern micel;
> wuniad in ðem wycum    wilda deor monige,
> in deope dalum    deora ungerim.
> Is in ðere byri eac    bearnum gecyðed
> ðe arfesta    eadig Cudberch

---

⁷⁴ Heather Blurton, '*Reliquia*: Writing Relics in Anglo-Norman Durham', in *Cultural Diversity in the British Middle Ages*, ed. Cohen, 39–56. One caveat is that Blurton fails to understand the ways in which the original Anglo-Norman cathedral would have done some of the same work.
⁷⁵ See Seth Lerer, 'Old English and Its Afterlife', in *The Cambridge History of Medieval Literature*, ed. David Wallace (Cambridge, 1999), 7–34, at 8; Christopher Cannon, 'Between the Old and the Middle of English', *New Medieval Literature* 7 (2005), 203–21, at 214.

and ðes clene   cyninges heafud,
Osuualdes, Engla leo,    and Aidan bsicop,
Eadberch and Eadfirð    æðele geferes.
Is ðer inne midd heom    Æðelwold biscop
and breoma bocera Beda,    and Boisil abbot,
ðe clene Cudberte   on gecheðe
lerde lustum,   and he his lara wel genom.
Eardiæð æt ðem eadige in in ðem minstre
unarimede    reliquia,
ðær monia wundrum gewurðað    ðæs ðe writ seggeð,
midd ene drihnes wer    domes bideð.

(This city is famous throughout Britain, steeply founded, the stones around it wondrously grown. The Wear runs around it, the river strong in waves, and there in it dwell many kinds of fish in the mingling of the water. And there has also grown up a secure enclosing woods; in that place dwell many wild animals, countless animals in the deep dales. There is also in the city, as it is known to men, the righteous blessed Cuthbert and the head of the pure king – Oswald, lion of the English – and Bishop Aidan, Eadbert and Eadfrith, the noble companions. Inside with them is Bishop Æthelwold and the famous scholar Bede, and Abbot Boisil, who vigorously taught the pure Cuthbert in his youth, and he [i.e., Cuthbert] learned his lessons well. Along with the blessed one, there remain in the minster countless relics where many miracles occur, as it is said in writing, awaiting the Judgement with the man of God.)[76]

As Blurton argues, rather than being nostalgic for the past, the poem acts as 'a reliquary for the past', though whether it is in fact a 'more appropriate shrine' than the cathedral itself is questionable.[77] Blurton's focus is on the work of language and composition in the poem, and she sees its use of both the English language and Anglo-Saxon metric and alliterative forms as a deliberate appropriation of that past to bolster the community's claims to property and ownership, rather than as some form of political or cultural nostalgia.[78] But the poem is equally important for its deliberate layering of time and writing of place. As Nicholas Howe stresses, its opening reference to *geond Breotenrice*, 'evokes the historical period when the British held the island between the departure of the Romans and the arrival of the Angles, Saxons, and Jutes'.[79] It reaches back to the very origins of England itself, embedding the city of Durham in a precolonial past which suggests that before the arrival of the Anglo-

---

[76] Text and translation are taken from Blurton, '*Reliquia*', 40–1.
[77] Blurton, '*Reliquia*', 42, 45.
[78] See Blurton, '*Reliquia*', 45–9.
[79] Howe, *Writing the Map of Anglo-Saxon England*, 226.

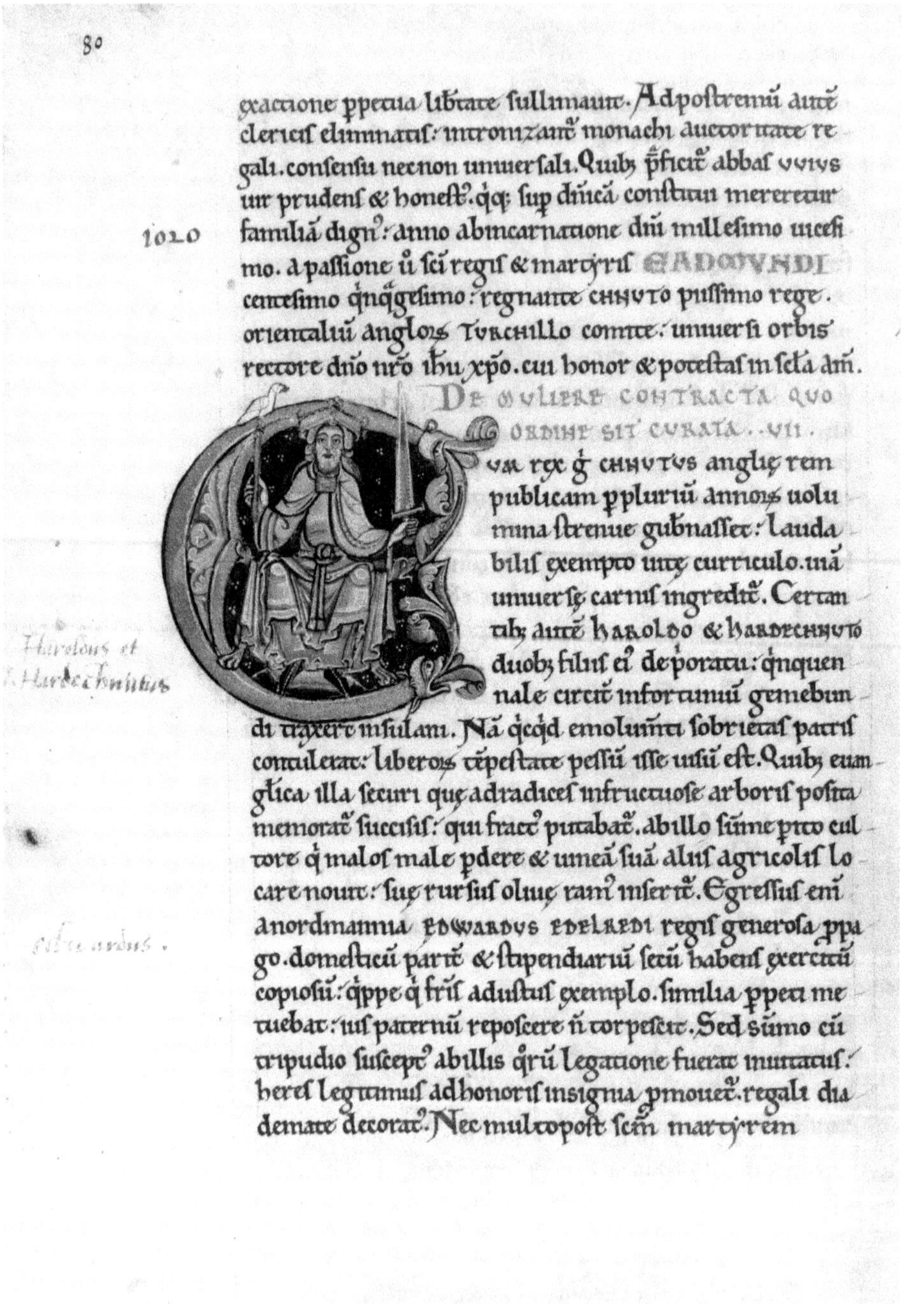

exactione ppetua libtate sullimauit. Ad postremu aute
clericis eliminatis: intronizant monachi auctoritate re
gali consensu necnon uniuersali. Quib; pficit abbas vvivs
uir prudens & honest. qq; sup dnica constitui mereretur
familia digñ: anno ab incarnatione dñi millesimo uicesi
mo. a passione u sci regis & martyris EADOVNDI
centesimo qnqgesimo: regnante CNVTO piissimo rege.
orientaliu anglo2 TVRCHILLO comite. uniuersi orbis
rectore dño nro ihu xpo. cui honor & potestas in scla am.

DE MVLIERE CONTRACTA QVO
ORDINE SIT CVRATA ..VII.

VM REX q CNVTVS angliç rem
publicam p plurium anno2 uolu
mina strenue gubnasset: lauda
bili exempto uitç curriculo. ma
uniuersç carnis ingredet. Certan
tib; aute HAROLDO & HARDECHNVTO
duob; filiis eu deportatis: qnquen
nale circit infortuniu gemebun
di traxert insulam. Nā qcqd emolumti sobrietas patris
contulerat: liberos tempestate pessu isse usui est. Quib; eum
glica illa securi quç ad radices infructuose arboris posita
memorat' successis: qui fruct' putabat. a illo sūme p tō cul
tore q malos male p dere & uineā suā aliis agricolis lo
care nouit: sup rursus oliuç ramū inserit'. Egressus eni
a nordmannia EDWARDVS EDELREDI regis generosa ppa
go. domesticu parte & stipendiariu secu habens exercitu
copiosu: qppe q fris adustus exemplo. similia p peti me
tuebat: ius paternu reposcere ñ torpescit. Sed sūmo cū
tripudio suscept' a b illis qrū legatione fuerat inuitatus:
heres legitimus ad honoris insignia p mouet'. regali dia
demate decorat'. Nec multo post scm martyrem

FIG. 80. CNUT ENTHRONED, LIFE AND MIRACLES OF EDMUND. NEW YORK, PIERPONT MORGAN LIBRARY, M 736, FOL. 41V

Saxons Durham was always already present, as Heavenfield was already a sacred place before Oswald's Christian victory. The poet also uses the present tense in the list of the names of the saints resting within the city to suggest that it *is* these men, not just their long dead bones, that reside here, in the same way that the refusal to depict Cuthbert's burial in the Oxford manuscript, or the flexibility of his body at the 1104 translation, suggests a body more 'alive' than those of most other saints.

While the sustained effort of the Durham community to proclaim the power and possessions of its saint may be unusual, other monasteries also used art and hagiography to establish their own connections with an Anglo-Saxon past and to protect their property in the Anglo-Norman present. One of the best-known examples of such a ploy is New York, Pierpont Morgan Library M736, produced at Bury St Edmunds c. 1130 (fig. 80). The manuscript contains the *Miraculi Sancti Edmundi Regis et Martyris* which has been attributed to Osbert of Clare but is based on a set of writings compiled by Herman the archdeacon c. 1100; the *Passio Sancti Edmundi* by Abbo of Fleury of c. 998; and lessons and hymns for the office of St Edmund. Barbara Abou-El-Haj has demonstrated the way in which the manuscript's description and illustration of miracles performed by the saint in the Anglo-Scandinavian past are deployed as weapons against theft, corruption and unfair taxation in the Anglo Norman present.[80] The success of the endeavour is demonstrated by the fact that Bury St Edmunds, one of the most important Anglo-Saxon monasteries, retained its status and was one of the wealthiest, most powerful and most politically connected abbeys up until the time of its dissolution. The manuscript is known especially for its gruesome depiction of the deaths of a group of thieves who had attempted to steal treasures from the church (fol. 19v) and of the saint killing King Swein with a spear because of his demand for tribute from the abbey (fol. 21v), as well as for the primacy of the series of full-page narrative miniatures over the text.[81] But in this case the manuscript is also about proper kingship from a monastic perspective. The point made over and over is that Edmund was both a pious king and a major monastic patron. He was not, however, a great military leader, which is rather ironic as his banner was later carried into battle by the English. Like the author of *Durham*, the manuscript reaches back into the past to link the twelfth-century abbey with the origins of England. The first two of the thirty-two miniatures that precede the text depict the arrival of the Angles, Saxons and Jutes, and their defeat of the Britons.

---

[80] Barbara Abou-El-Haj, 'Bury St Edmunds Abbey between 1070 and 1124: A History of Property, Privilege and Monastic Art Production', *Art History* 6 (1983), 1–30; see also Cynthia Hahn, '*Peregrinatio et Natio*: The Illustrated Life of Edmund, King and Martyr', *Gesta* 30.2 (1991), 119–39.
[81] On this aspect of the manuscript see Cynthia Hahn, *Pictured on the Heart: Narrative Effect in Pictorial Lives of Saints from the Tenth through Thirteenth Centuries* (Berkeley, CA, 2001), 216–17, 237–46.

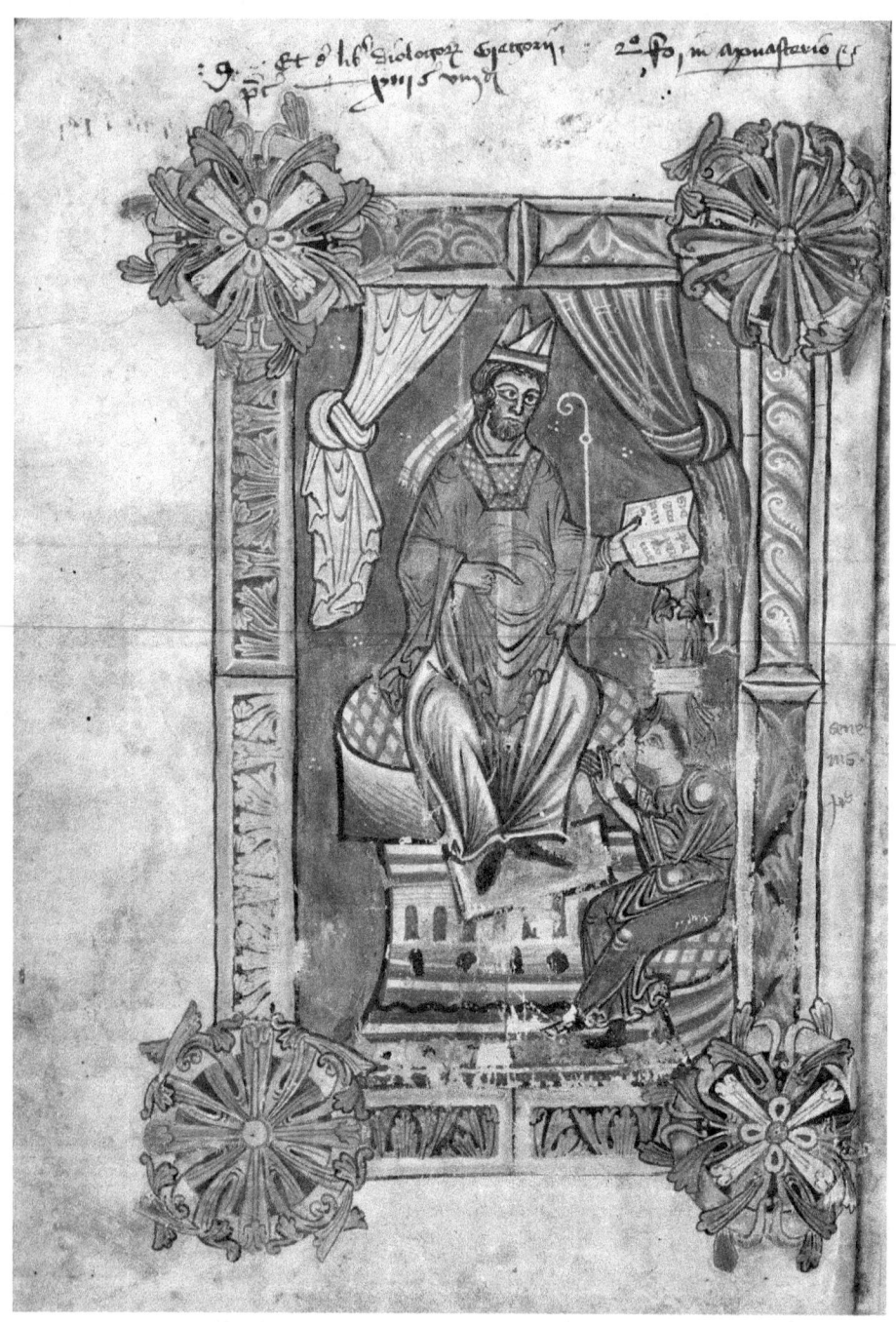

FIG. 81. GREGORY THE GREAT, DIALOGUES OF GREGORY. OXFORD, BODL. LIB., MS TANNER 3, FOL. 1

The images then jump several hundred years in time to the crowning of Edmund as king of East Anglia, his struggles against the Danes, his death in 864 and subsequent miracles, one of the most important of which is the killing of Swein. The 'miracle' is witnessed by Swein's son Cnut, who goes on to become a benefactor of the abbey. The message that a violent conqueror can become a peaceable and pious king is strengthened by the symbols of the two facets of his kingship that he holds in this portrait, the sword in his left hand and the dove-capped sceptre in his right, images of war, peace and authority that recall the New Minster Liber Vitae portrait.

## DIALOGUES OF TIME AND PLACE

The beginnings of Anglo-Saxon England, as it conceived of itself as a Christian nation, have their origins in the era of Gregory the Great in words, in language and in land. It was Gregory whose dialogue with the Anglo-Saxon boys in the market in Rome began the story of the conversion that was to prevail in England over that of the Irish Columban church. It was Gregory whose dialogue imbued the Anglo-Saxons with an inherent goodness and spirituality that combined potently with their vision of themselves as a chosen people. It was the English boys and their meeting with Gregory that set in motion a series of journeys between Rome and England, England and Rome that would bind the two together both spiritually and politically in an ongoing dialogue. It is fitting then that we turn here at the end of this book to one of the last images of Gregory to survive from Anglo-Saxon England (fig. 81), or perhaps one of the first to survive from Anglo-Norman England, the frontispiece to the Bodleian Library Tanner 3 copy of the Dialogues of Gregory the Great. The miniature shows Gregory and Petrus in dialogue, appropriately enough, with the imposing figure of Gregory looming large over his tiny interlocutor, as his shadow had loomed large over England for half a millennium at the time that the image was made in the second half of the eleventh century, probably at Worcester. What is particularly interesting about this image of Gregory, however, is the extent to which it has been retouched and redrawn by a later hand. Many manuscripts, the Junius 11 manuscript, for example, contain later doodles, sculptures such as the Nunburnholme Cross are recarved so that entirely new scenes are created,[82] miniatures are sometimes augmented with additional lines or colours; but it seems that the artist who retouched this miniature did not want to simply doodle, copy, touch up the occasional line, or even change the image into a new scene. Rather it seems that he wanted to create a palimpsest in which the older image is created anew but in a

[82] Martin Foys, 'New Media and the Nunburnholme Cross', in *Cross and Cruciform in the Anglo-Saxon World: Studies to Honor the Memory of Timothy Reuter*, ed. Sarah Larratt Keefer, Karen L. Jolly and Catherine E. Karkov (Morgantown, WV, 2010), 340–68.

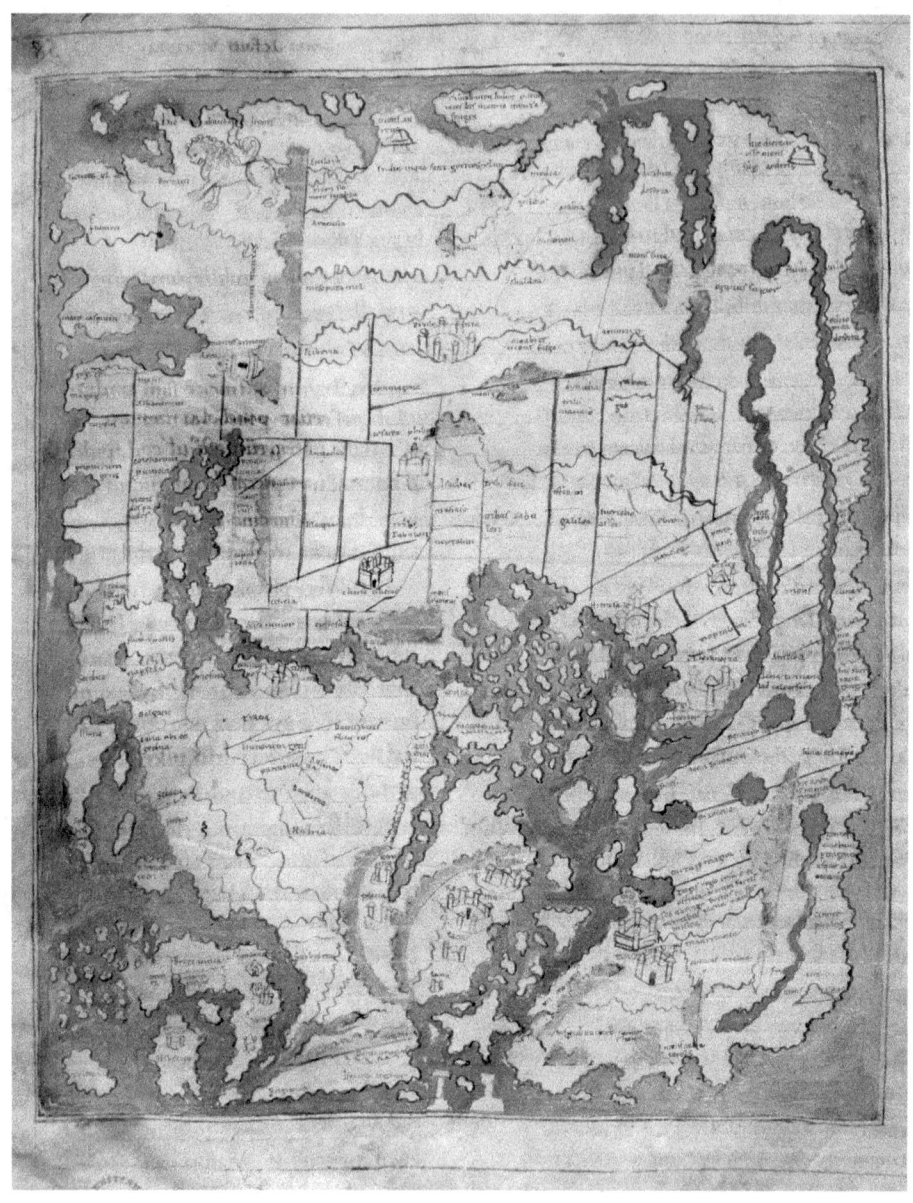

FIG. 82. COTTON MAPPAMUNDI. LONDON, BL, MS COTTON TIBERIUS B.V, FOL. 56V

slightly different style, with the original remaining visible beneath the later trace. Lines have been hardened, colours brightened and decorative details embellished, but Gregory remains a recognizably Anglo-Saxon figure at the centre. In its tracing and retracing, the movement of this second hand creates a collision of worlds. The drawing becomes akin to an act of historical remembering, a sort of drawing in and of time that binds the present of the redrawing back to the moment of the original drawing's creation, and beyond that to the time and figure of Gregory himself. It is also possible to perceive the act of redrawing as akin to the act of *ruminatio*, a way of getting at the deeper meaning of the image as the hand and eye move carefully over its surface details. Intentionally or not, it provides an artistic parallel for the model of authorship or reading elucidated by Cassiodorus, a visual genealogy of artistic rather than textual production that in itself takes the viewer back to the early days of Anglo-Saxon England and the Anglo-Saxon church and refiguring Gregory as a typically Anglo-Saxon author. However, in its tracing of the original the second hand also introduces a certain ambivalence. Tracing is an act of possession in that it is a means of making someone else's image one's own, of mastering it. In mapping the lines and contours of the original artist's work, the second artist both attempts to master the composition and to remake it as his own. At the same time, the hand of the second artist is following, conforming to the compositional and stylistic foundations laid by the first artist. Even as it rewrites Gregory for a new era, it embeds that era within an earlier order.

The style of the original drawing in the Tanner 3 frontispiece is similar to that of a very different image of time and place, and a very different type of mapping, the mid-eleventh-century Cotton Tiberius B.v mappamundi (fig. 82). While the Tiberius B.v image is literally a map in a way that the drawing of Gregory is not, they are both attempts at possession through the artistic process. The drawing of the lines, images and names that form the map is itself a mapping process in its attempts to define and possess a pre-existing territory. The Tiberius mappamundi may be a map of a different order, but it is just as much about the relationship of eleventh-century England to its past and to stories of its past. Although famous for its fair approximation of the shape of England, the map is not geographically accurate, but geographical accuracy was not its goal. Rather it is a depiction, a representation of a particular way of viewing the relationship between England and the larger geographic and temporal world. It is an image, just like all the other images discussed in this book and, like many of them, it includes words that help the viewer to understand the purpose of the image. England, as in the poem *Durham*, is labelled Britannia, a name that immediately suggests its historic British and Roman roots. Certain contemporary cities on the map have been labelled: London and Winchester, the twin capitals of England, Armagh in Ireland, Rome, Jerusalem, Constantinople. These cities, like others on the map, all have a twin political and religious significance; they are all the habitations of both kings and saints. But the map also connects these present places with the biblical past, with the resting place of Noah's Ark, with Babylon, Chaldea and important sites from Exodus such as Mount Sinai, the Red Sea (shown parted on the map), and the River Nile,[83] as well as with fabulous places and peoples such as the land in which many lions are found and the Griffon people. It is not alone in including these locations: other surviving mappamundi include the wondrous races and give special attention to biblical sites, itineraries and especially Mosaic material.[84] Like other maps, the Tiberius map is heavily reliant on Orosius. Without doubt, however, the representation of this material here would have had special meaning to the Anglo-Saxons, and the way in which geography is visualized in the Tiberius map does set it apart. Unlike other such maps, however, this places neither Rome nor Jerusalem at its centre; its centre, as Martin Foys has noted, is in fact empty space,[85] a privileging perhaps of the space between cities and cultures rather than of any one city or culture itself. It may perhaps be significant that the empty space lies between Jerusalem and Tarsus, home of Archbishop Theodore of Canterbury, renowned for his biblical exegesis as well as for his teachings on astronomy and computus,[86] interests clearly shared by the patron of this manuscript.[87] At the top of the map is not Paradise, but an earthly paradise, the island of Taprobane which, according to the inscription, reaps the fruit of the earth twice a year.[88] The map's combination of names and places invites the viewer to contemplate the origins of the Anglo-Saxon world, but it also, as Nicholas Howe reminds us, is an image of elsewhere in a manuscript that he labelled a 'Book of Elsewhere'.[89] Together with other items contained in the manuscript – lists, itineraries, calendars, the *Wonders of the East* – it locates Britannia/England as a place at once familiar and foreign in a world that is at once familiar and foreign.[90] One could add that the map does this quite literally by echoing the shape of England in the shape of Asia and the Holy Land. Their borders have similar, though not identical contours. London and Winchester are

---

[83] See Foys, *Virtually Anglo-Saxon*, 125–6 for detailed images and descriptions.
[84] Foys, *Virtually Anglo-Saxon*, 225 n. 66.
[85] Foys, *Virtually Anglo-Saxon*, 141.
[86] On Theodore see Bernard Bischoff and Michael Lapidge, *Biblical Commentaries from the Canterbury School of Theodore and Hadrian* (Cambridge, 1994); Michael Lapidge, ed., *Archbishop Theodore* (Cambridge, 1995).
[87] The manuscript also includes a calendar, computistical texts and tables, Cicero's *Aratea*, and the Marvels of the East. For a complete list of its contents see Patrick McGurk et al., eds., *An Eleventh-Century Miscellany: British Library Cotton Tiberius B.V, Part I*, EEMF 21 (Copenhagen, 1983).
[88] For identification of many of the places and peoples as well as translation of some of the inscriptions see http://bob.drew.edu/mappaemundi/mapEditor.swf
[89] Howe, *Writing the Map of Anglo-Saxon England*, 151–94, at 154.
[90] In fact Howe describes the manuscript as a narrative *mappamundi*: *Writing the Map of Anglo-Saxon England*, 194.

located at approximately the same point in the curve of the island as is Jerusalem in the curve of the Holy Land. This visual strategy might then be related to the textual strategy of 'similarity and difference' exemplified by the lists of popes, bishops, kings, emperors and abbots which writes, for example, the archbishops of Canterbury into the ecclesiastical genealogies of Jerusalem, Rome, Alexandria and Antioch.[91] The map, in effect, not only produces many Englands but does so in a way that embeds England in shape, name, history and experience in many times and many places. It reaches out from the marginal yet central, tiny but expansive island at the lower left, to possess the very empires and centres from which it had been colonized historically, intellectually and spiritually. Both ideologically and visually it redraws and rewrites the world in relation to England just as Anglo-Saxon art had, from its very beginnings, remade the past in terms of the present. In so doing it represents, perhaps more clearly than any other single image, the central role of representation in the formation of an England, an English history and an English cultural identity.

---

[91] Howe, *Writing the Map of Anglo-Saxon England*, 161–6. Howe notes that this same strategy can be seen in other of the manuscript's contents.

# BIBLIOGRAPHY

Abels, Richard. 'What Has Weland To Do with Christ? The Franks Casket and the Acculturation of Christianity in Early Anglo-Saxon England.' *Speculum* 84.3 (2009), 549–81.

Åberg, N. *The Anglo-Saxons in England during the Early Centuries after the Invasion*. Uppsala, 1926.

Abou-El-Haj, Barbara. 'Bury St Emunds Abbey between 1070 and 1124: A History of Property, Privilege and Monastic Art Production.' *Art History* 6 (1983), 1–30.

—— 'Saint Cuthbert: The Post-Conquest Appropriation of Anglo-Saxon Cult.' In *Holy Men and Holy Women: Old English Prose Saints' Lives and Their Contexts*, ed. Paul E. Szarmach. Albany, NY, 1996, 177–206.

Ælfric. *Ælfric's Catholic Homilies: The Second Series*, ed. Malcolm Godden, vol. 1 (text), EETS s.s. 5. Oxford, 1979.

—— *Ælfric's Lives of Saints*, ed. W. W. Skeat. EETS o.s. 76, 82, 94, 114, 2 vols. London, 1881–1900.

—— *The Homilies of the Anglo-Saxon Church. The First Part, Containing The Sermones Catholici, or Homilies of Ælfric*, ed. and trans. Benjamin Thorpe. 2 vols. London, 1844, 1846.

Agamben, Giorgio. *Infancy and History: On the Destruction of Experience*. London, 1993.

Alcuin. *Commentariorum in Joannem, lib. 1*. PL 304.

Alexander, J. J. G. 'The Benedictional of St Æthelwold and Anglo-Saxon Illumination in the Reform Period.' In *Tenth Century Studies: Essays in the Commemoration of the Millennium of the Council of Winchester and Regularis Concordia*, ed. David Parsons. London and Chichester, 1975, 169–83.

Anlezark, Daniel. *Water and Fire: The Myth of the Flood in Anglo-Saxon England*. Manchester, 2006.

Arnold, Bettina, and Nancy Wicker, eds. *Gender and the Archaeology of Death*. Walnut Creek, CA, 2001.

Arrhenius, B. *Merovingian Garnet Jewellery: Emergence and Social Implications*. Stockholm, 1985.

Augustine. *De concensu evangelistarum*, ed. F. Weihrich. CSEL 43. New York, 1963.
—— *Confessions*, trans. R. S. Pine-Coffin. Harmondsworth, 1961.
—— *In evangelium Johannis*, ed. R. Williams. CCSL 36. Turnhout, 1990.
Avent, R. *Anglo-Saxon Inlaid Disc and Composite Brooches*. BAR Brit. Ser. 11, 2 vols., Oxford, 1975.
Backhouse, Janet, D. H. Turner and Leslie Webster, eds. *The Golden Age of Anglo-Saxon Art 966–1066*. London, 1984.
Bailey, Richard N. *Viking Age Sculpture in Northern England*. London, 1980.
—— 'St Wilfrid, Ripon and Hexham.' In *Studies in Insular Art and Archaeology*, ed. Catherine E. Karkov and Robert T. Farrell. Oxford, OH, 1991, 3–25.
—— 'Sutton Hoo and Seventh-Century Art.' In *Sutton Hoo: Fifty Years After*, ed. Robert T. Farrell and Carol Neuman de Vegvar. Oxford, OH, 1992, 31–41.
—— *England's Earliest Sculptors*. Toronto, 1996.
—— *Cheshire and Lancashire*. CASSS 9. Oxford, 2011.
Bailey, Richard N., and Rosemary Cramp. *Cumberland, Westmorland and Lancashire North-of-the-Sands*, CASSS 2. Oxford, 1988.
Barlow, Frank. *The Life of King Edward who Rests at Westminster, Attributed to a Monk of Saint-Bertin*. London, 1962.
—— *Edward the Confessor*. Berkeley, CA, 1970.
—— ed. *The Life of King Edward who Rests at Westminster, Attributed to a Monk of Saint-Bertin*, rev. edn. Oxford, 1992.
Barrow, G. W. S. 'The Kings of Scotland and Durham.' In *Anglo-Norman Durham*, ed. David Rollason, Margaret Harvey and Michael Prestwich. Woodbridge, 1994, 311–23.
Barthes, Roland. *S/Z*. London, 1974.
Battiscombe, C. F., ed. *The Relics of St Cuthbert*. Oxford, 1956.
Becker, Alfred. *Franks Casket: zu den Bildern und Inschriften des Runenkästchens von Auzon*. Regensburg, 1973.
Beckett, Katharine Scarfe. *Anglo-Saxon Perceptions of the Islamic World*. Cambridge, 2003.
Bede. *Bedae Presbyteri Expositio Apocalypseos*, ed. R. Gryson. CCSL 121A. Turnhout, 2001.
—— *Bede: The Reckoning of Time*, ed. and trans. Faith Wallis. Liverpool, 1999.
—— *Explanatio Apocalypsis*. PL 93, 129–206.
—— *Homilia VII* and *Homilia VIII*. PL 94.
—— *In Lucae evangelium expositio*, ed. D. Hurst. CCSL 120. Turnhout, 1960.
—— *Expositio in Lucam*, ed. D. Hurst, CCSL 120. Turnhout, 1960.
—— *Venerabilis Baedae opera historica*, ed. Charles Plummer, vol. 1. Oxford, 1986.
Bedingfield, M. Bradford. *The Dramatic Liturgy of the Late Anglo-Saxon Church*. Woodbridge, 2002.
Belting, Hans. *Bild und Kult: eine Geschichte des Bildes vor dem Zeitalter der Kunst*. Munich 1990. Trans. by Edmund Jephcott as *Likeness and Presence: A History of the Image before Art*. Chicago, 1994.

—— 'Image, Medium, Body: A New Approach to Iconology.' *Critical Inquiry* 31.2 (2005), 302-19.
Berg, Knut. 'The Gosforth Cross.' *JWCI* 21 (1958), 27-43.
Bhabha, Homi K. *Nation and Narration*. London, 1990.
—— 'The Third Space: Interview with Homi K. Bhabha.' In *Identity: Community, Culture, Difference*, ed. Jonathan Rutherford (London, 1990), 207-21.
—— 'The World and the Home.' *Social Text* 10.31-32 (1992), 141-53.
—— *The Location of Culture*. London, 1994.
Biddle, Martin. '*Felix Urbs Winthonia*: Winchester in the Age of Monastic Reform.' In *Tenth Century Studies: Essays in the Commemoration of the Millennium of the Council of Winchester and Regularis Concordia*, ed. David Parsons. London and Chichester, 1975, 123-44.
Biddle, Martin, and Birthe Kjølbye-Biddle. 'The Repton Stone.' *ASE* 14 (1985), 233-92.
Binski, Paul, and Stella Panayotova, eds. *The Cambridge Illuminations: Ten Centuries of Book Production in the Medieval West*. London, 2005.
Bischoff, Bernard, and Michael Lapidge. *Biblical Commentaries from the Canterbury School of Theodore and Hadrian*. Cambridge, 1994.
Bishop, T. A. M. 'The Copenhagen Gospel Book.' *Nordisk Tidsckrift for Bok-och Biblioteksväsen* 54 (1967), 33-41.
Blackburn, Mark, and Simon Keynes. 'A Corpus of the Cross-and-Lozenge and Related Coinages of Alfred, Ceolwulf II and Archbishop Æthelred.' In *Kings, Currency and Alliances*, ed. Mark Blackburn and David N. Dumville. Woodbridge, 1998, 125-50.
—— 'Three New *Agnus Dei* Pennies of King Æthelred the Unready.' *ASE* 39 (2011), forthcoming.
Blair, John. 'Anglo-Saxon Minsters: A Topographical Review.' In *Pastoral Care before the Parish*, ed. John Blair and Richard Sharpe. Leicester, 1992, 226-66.
—— *The Church in Anglo-Saxon Society*. Oxford, 2005.
Blake, E. O., ed. *Liber Eliensis*. London, 1962.
Blunt, C. E. 'The Coinage of Offa.' In *Anglo-Saxon Coins: Studies Presented to F. M. Stenton on the Occasion of his 80th Birthday*, ed. R. H. M. Dolley. London, 1961, 39-62.
Blunt, C. E., B. H. I. H. Stewart and C. S. S. Lyon. *Coinage in Tenth-Century England from Edward the Elder to Edgar's Reform*. Oxford, 1989.
Blurton, Heather. '*Reliquia*: Writing Relics in Anglo-Norman Durham.' In *Cultural Diversity in the British Middle Ages: Archipelago, Island, England*, ed. Jeffrey Jerome Cohen. New York, 2008, 39-56.
Boniface. *Der Briefe des Heiligen Bonifatius und Lullus*, ed. M. Tangl. MGH epistolae selectae I. Berlin, 1916.
Bradley, R. 'Time Regained: The Creation of Continuity.' *JBAA* 140-1 (1987-88), 1-17.
Brand, J. *The History and Antiquities ... of Newcastle upon Tyne*, vol. 2. London, 1789.

Bredehoft, Thomas A. 'First-Person Inscriptions and Literacy in Anglo-Saxon England.' *ASSAH* 9 (1996), 103–10.

Broderick, Herbert R., III. 'Meta-textuality, Sexuality and Intervisuality in MS Junius 11.' *Word and Image* 25.4 (2009), 384–401.

Brooks, Nicholas. 'Canterbury, Rome and the Construction of English Identity.' In *Early Medieval Rome and the Christian West: Essays in Honour of Donald Bullough*, ed. Julia M. H. Smith. Leiden, 2000, 221–47.

Brown, Michelle P. *The Book of Cerne: Prayer, Patronage and Power in Ninth-Century England*. London, 1996.

—— *In the Beginning Was the Word: Books and Faith in the Age of Bede*, Jarrow Lecture. Jarrow, 2000.

—— 'Female Book Ownership and Production in Anglo-Saxon England: The Evidence of the Ninth-Century Prayerbooks.' In *Lexis and Texts in Early English: Studies Presented to Jane Roberts*, ed. Christian J. Kay and Louise M. Sylvester. Amsterdam, 2001, 45–67.

—— *The Lindisfarne Gospels: Society, Spirituality and the Scribe*. London, 2003.

—— ed. *In the Beginning: Bibles before the Year 1000*. Washington, DC, 2006.

—— 'The Lichfield Angel: Lichfield as a Centre of Insular Art.' *JBAA* 160.1 (2007), 8–19.

Bruce-Mitford, Rupert. *The Art of the Codex Amiatinus*. Jarrow Lecture. Jarrow, 1967.

—— *The Sutton Hoo Ship Burial*, 3 vols. London, 1978–83.

Budny, Mildred. '"St Dunstan's Classbook" and Its Frontispiece: Dunstan's Portrait and Autograph.' In *St Dunstan: His Life, Times and Cult*, ed. Nigel Ramsay, Margaret Sparks and Tim Tatton-Brown. Woodbridge, 1992, 103–42.

—— *Insular, Anglo-Saxon and Early Anglo-Norman Manuscript Art at Corpus Christi College, Cambridge: An Illustrated Catalogue*. Kalamazoo, MI, 1997.

Burrus, Virginia. 'Macrina's Tattoo.' *JMEMS* 33.3 (2003), 403–17. (Also published in *The Cultural Turn in Late Ancient Studies: Gender, Asceticism, and Hagiography*, ed. Dale B. Martin and Patricia Cox Miller. Durham, NC, 2005, 103–17.)

Calkins, Robert G. *Illuminated Books of the Middle Ages*. Ithaca, NY, 1983.

Cambridge, Eric. 'Archaeology and the Cult of St Oswald in Pre-Conquest Northumbria.' In *Oswald: Northumbrian King to European Saint*, ed. Clare Stancliffe and Eric Cambridge. Stamford, 1995, 128–63.

—— 'The Architecture of the Augustine Mission.' In *St Augustine and the Conversion of England*, ed. Richard Gameson. Stroud, 1999, 202–36.

Campbell, Alistair, and Simon Keynes, eds. *Encomium Emmae Reginae*. Cambridge, 1998.

Cannon, Christopher. 'Between the Old and the Middle of English.' *New Medieval Literature* 7 (2005), 203–21.

Carver, Martin. *Sutton Hoo: A Seventh-Century Burial Ground and Its Context*. London, 2005.

Cassiodorus. *Cassiodori senatoris Institutiones*, ed. R. A. B. Mynors. Oxford, 1963.

—— *Explanation of the Psalms*, ed. and trans. P. G. Walsh. 3 vols. New York, 1990.
Chamberlayn, J. L. 'Crowns and Virgins: Queenmaking during the Wars of the Roses.' In *Young Medieval Women*, ed. K. J. Lewis, N. J. Menuge and K. M. Phillips. Stroud, 1999, 47–68.
Chambers, Iain. *Migrancy, Culture, Identity*. London, 1994.
Chazelle, Celia. 'Christ and the Vision of God: The Biblical Diagrams of the Codex Amiatinus.' In *The Mind's Eye: Art and Theological Argument in the Middle Ages*, ed. Jeffrey Hamburger and Anne-Marie Bouché. Princeton, NJ, 2006, 84–111.
Clayton, Mary. 'Delivering the Damned: A Motif in Old English Homiletic Prose.' *MÆ* 55 (1986), 92–102.
—— *The Cult of the Virgin Mary in Anglo-Saxon England*. Cambridge, 1990.
—— 'Ælfric and Æthelred.' In *Essays on Anglo-Saxon and Related Themes in Memory of Lynne Grundy*, ed. Jane Roberts and Janet L. Nelson. London, 2000, 65–88.
Coatsworth, Elizabeth, and Michael Pindar, *The Art of the Anglo-Saxon Goldsmith*. Woodbridge, 2002.
Cohen, Adam. *The Uta Codex: Art, Philosophy, and Reform in Eleventh-Century Germany*. University Park, PA, 2000.
Colgrave, Bertram, ed. *The Earliest Life of Gregory the Great*. Cambridge, 1985.
Connolly, Seán, ed. *Bede: On the Temple*. Liverpool, 1995.
Cook, A. S. 'The Date of the Ruthwell and Bewcastle Crosses.' *Transactions of the Connecticut Academy of Arts and Sciences* (1912), 247–9.
—— 'The Date of the Old English Inscription on the Brussels Cross.' *Modern Language Review* 10 (1915), 157–61.
Coulston, J. C., and E. J. Phillips. *Corpus signorum imperii romani*, vol. 1, fasc. 6. Oxford, 1988.
Cramp, Rosemary. 'Early Northumbrian Sculpture at Hexham.' In *St Wilfrid at Hexham*, ed. D. P. Kirby. Newcastle, 1974, 115–40.
—— 'Monastic Sites.' In *The Archaeology of Anglo-Saxon England*, ed. David M. Wilson. London, 1976, 201–52, 453–57.
—— *County Durham and Northumberland*, CASSS 1. Oxford, 1984.
—— *Wearmouth and Jarrow Monastic Sites*, vol. 1. Swindon, 2005.
—— *South-West England*, CASSS 7. Oxford, 2006.
—— *Wearmouth and Jarrow Monastic Sites*, vol. 2. Swindon, 2006.
Crawford, Sally. 'Votive Deposition, Religion and the Anglo-Saxon Furnished Burial Ritual.' *World Archaeology* 36 (2004), 87–102.
Crook, John. 'King Edgar's Reliquary of St Swithun.' *ASE* 21 (1992), 177–202.
—— *The Architectural Setting of the Cult of Saints in the Early Christian West c. 300–c. 1200*. Oxford, 2000.
Cross, J. E. 'The Ethic of War in Old English.' In *England Before the Conquest: Studies Presented to Dorothy Whitelock*, ed. Peter Clemoes and Kathleen Hughes. Cambridge, 1971, 269–82.
d'Ardenne, S. T. R. O. 'The Old English Inscription on the Brussels Cross.' *English Studies* 21 (1939), 145–64, 271–2.

Davis, Kathleen. 'National Writing in the Ninth Century: A Reminder for Postcolonial Thinking about the North.' *JMEMS* 28.3 (1998), 61–37.
—— *Periodization and Sovereignty: How Ideas of Feudalism and Secularization Govern the Politics of Time*. Philadelphia, PA, 2008.
Deer, J. 'Kaiser Otto der Grosse und die Reichskrone.' In *Beitrage zur Kunstgeschichte und Arkëologie des Frümittelalter*. Cologne, 1962, 261–77.
Degregorio, Scott. 'Bede's *In Ezram et Neemiam* and the Reform of the Northumbrian Church.' *Speculum* 79.1 (2004), 1–25.
Derrida, Jacques. 'Living On: Borderlines.' In *Deconstruction and Criticism*, ed. L. H. Bloom *et al.* New York, 1979.
Deshman, Robert. '*Benedictus Monarcha et Monachus*: Early Medieval Ruler Theology and the Anglo-Saxon Reform.' *FS* 22 (1988), 204–40.
—— *The Benedictional of Æthelwold*, Princeton, NJ, 1995.
—— 'Another Look at the Disappearing Christ: Corporeal and Spiritual Vision in Early Medieval Images.' *Art Bulletin* 79 (1997), 518–46.
Dicenza, Nicole Guenther. *The King's English: Strategies of Translation in the Old English Boethius*. Albany, NY, 2005.
Dickins, B., and A. S. C. Ross, eds. *The Dream of the Rood*. London, 1934.
Didi-Huberman, Georges. *Devant l'image: Questions posées aux fins d'une histoire de l'art*. Paris, 1990.
—— *Devant le temps: Histoire de l'art et anachronisme des images*. Paris, 2000.
—— *Confronting Images: Questioning the Ends of a Certain History of Art*, trans. John Goodman. University Park, PA, 2005.
Didi-Huberman, Georges, *et al.*, eds. *Relire Panofsky*. Paris 2008.
Doane, A. N., ed. *Genesis A: A New Edition*. Madison, WI, 1978.
—— ed. *The Saxon Genesis: An Edition of the West Saxon Genesis B and the Old Saxon 'Vatican Genesis'*. Madison, WI, 1991.
Dodwell, C. R. *Anglo-Saxon Art: A New Perspective*. Manchester, 1982.
Dodwell, Natasha, Sam Lucy and Jess Tipper. 'Anglo-Saxons on the Cambridge Backs: The Criminology Site Settlement and King's College Hostel Cemetery.' *Proceedings of the Cambridge Antiquaries Society* 93 (2004), 95–124.
Dolley, R. H. M. 'The Nummular Brooch from Sulgrave.' In *England before the Conquest*, ed. Peter Clemoes and Kathleen Hughes. Cambridge, 1971, 333–49.
Dolley, R. H. M., and C. E. Blunt. 'The Chronology of the Coins of Alfred the Great.' In *Anglo-Saxon Coins: Studies Presented to F. M. Stenton*, ed. R. H. M. Dolly. London, 1961, 77–94.
Dumville, D., and S. Keynes *The Anglo-Saxon Chronicle A Collaborative Edition*, vol. 3, *MS A*, ed. J. M. Bately. Cambridge, 1986.
Eastmond, A., and Liz James, eds. *Icon and Word: The Power of Images in Byzantium*. Aldershot, 2003.
Eaton, Tim. *Plundering the Past: Roman Stonework in Medieval Britain*. Stroud, 2000.
Eggleton, Lara. 'Crumbling Empires, Nostalgia and the Politics of Ornament in Islamic Spain.' Unpublished paper delivered at the International Medieval Congress, Leeds, July 2009.

Fairless, Kenneth J. 'Three Religious Cults from the Northern Frontier Region.' In *Between and Beyond the Walls: Essays on the Prehistory and History of North Britain in Honour of George Joby*, ed. Roger Miket and Colin Burgess. Edinburgh, 1984, 228–35.

Fairweather, Janet, trans. *Liber Eliensis: A History of the Isle of Ely from the Seventh Century to the Twelfth*. Woodbridge, 2005.

Farr, Carol A. 'Questioning the Monuments: Approaches to Anglo-Saxon Sculpture through Gender Studies.' In *The Archaeology of Anglo-Saxon England: Basic Readings*, ed. Catherine E. Karkov. Albany, NY, 1999, 375–402.

—— 'Style in Late Anglo-Saxon England: Questions of Learning and Education.' In *Anglo-Saxon Styles*, ed. Catherine E. Karkov and George Hardin Brown. Albany, NY, 2003, 117–20.

Farrell, Robert T., ed. *Daniel and Azarias*. London, 1974.

Felix. *Felix's Life of Saint Guthlac*, ed. Bertram Colgrave. Cambridge, 1956.

Fernie, Eric. *The Architecture of the Anglo-Saxons*. London, 1983.

—— 'Edward the Confessor's Westminster Abbey.' In *Edward the Confessor: The Man and the Legend*, ed. Richard Mortimer. Woodbridge, 2009, 139–15.

Finnegan, Robert E., ed. *Christ and Satan: A Critical Edition*. Waterloo, Ontario, 1977.

Flood, Finbarr B. *Objects of Translation: Material Culture and Medieval 'Hindu–Muslim' Encounter*. Princeton, NJ, 2009.

Foot, Sarah. 'The Making of *Angelcynn*: English Identity before the Norman Conquest.' *Transactions of the Royal Historical Society*, 6th ser., 6 (1996), 25–49.

—— *Veiled Women: Female Religious Communities in England, 871–1066*. 2 vols. Aldershot, 2000.

Foster, Meryl. 'Custodians of St Cuthbert: The Durham Monks' Views of their Predecessors, 1083–c. 1200.' In *Anglo-Norman Durham*, ed. David Rollason, Margaret Harvey and Michael Prestwich. Woodbridge, 1994, 53–65.

Fouracre, Paul, and Richard Gerberding. *Late Merovingian France: History and Hagiography 640–720*. Manchester, 1996.

Foys, Martin K. *Virtually Anglo-Saxon: Old Media, New Media, and Early Medieval Studies in the Late Age of Print*. Gainesville, FL, 2007.

—— 'New Media and the Nunburnholme Cross.' In *Cross and Cruciform in the Anglo-Saxon World: Studies to Honor the Memory of Timothy Reuter*, ed. Sarah Larratt Keefer, Karen L. Jolly and Catherine E. Karkov. Morgantown, WV, 2010, 340–68.

Franceschini, A., and R. Weber, eds. *Itinerarium Egeriae*. CCSL 175. Turnhout, 1958, 37.

Frank, Roberta. '*Beowulf* and Sutton Hoo: The Odd Couple.' In *Voyage to the Other World: The Legacy of Sutton Hoo*, ed. Calvin B. Kendall and Peter S. Wells. Minneapolis, 1992, 47–64.

—— 'King Cnut in the Verse of his Skalds.' In *The Reign of Cnut*, ed. A. R. Rumble. London, 1994, 106–24.

—— 'Some Uses of Paronomasia in Old English Scriptural Verse.' In *The

*Poems of MS Junius 11: Basic Readings*, ed. R. M. Liuzza. New York, 2002, 69–98. (Originally published in *Speculum* 47.2 (1972), 207–26.)

—— 'The Boar on the Helmet.' In *Aedificia Nova: Studies in Honor of Rosemary Cramp*, ed. Catherine E. Karkov and Helen Damico. Kalamazoo, MI, 2008, 76–88.

Frantzen, Allen. 'Sodom and Gomorrah in the Prose Works of Alfred's Reign.' In *Alfred the Wise*, ed. Jane Roberts, Janet L. Nelson and Malcolm Godden. Cambridge, 1997, 25–33.

Freud, Sigmund. 'The "Uncanny".' In *The Standard Edition of the Complete Psychological Works of Sigmund Freud*, ed. James Strachey, vol. 17: *An Infantile Neurosis and Other Works*. London, 2001, 219–56.

Frolow, Anatole. *La relique de la vraie croix: Recherches sur le développement d'un culte*. Paris, 1961.

Gameson, Richard. 'English Manuscript Art in the Mid-Eleventh Century: The Decorative Tradition.' *Antiquaries Journal* 71 (1991), 64–122.

—— *The Role of Art in the Late Anglo-Saxon Church*. Oxford, 1995.

—— 'The Gospels of Margaret of Scotland and the Literacy of an Eleventh-Century Queen.' In *Women and the Book: Assessing the Visual Evidence*, ed. Jane H. M. Taylor and Lesley Smith. London, 1997, 149–71.

—— ed. *St Augustine and the Conversion of England*. Stroud, 1999.

—— ed. *The Codex Aureus: An Eighth-Century Gospelbook: Stockholm, Kungliga Bibliotek, A. 135*, 2 vols. Copenhagen, 2002.

—— 'The Scribe Speaks? Colophons in Early English Manuscripts.' H. M. Chadwick Memorial Lecture 12. Cambridge, 2002.

Gameson, Richard, and Fiona Gameson. 'The Anglo-Saxon Inscription at St Mary's Church, Breamore.' *ASSAH* 6 (1993), 1–10.

Gannon, Anna. *The Iconography of Early Anglo-Saxon Coinage*. Oxford, 2003.

Geake, H. *The Use of Grave Goods in Conversion-Period England, c. 600–c. 850*. BAR Brit. Ser. 261. Oxford, 1997.

—— 'Invisible Kingdoms: The Use of Grave-goods in Seventh-Century England.' *ASSAH* 10 (1999), 203–15.

Gem, R. D. H. 'The Romanesque Rebuilding of Westminster Abbey.' In *Proceedings of the Battle Conference on Anglo-Norman Studies, III, 1980*, ed. R. Allen Brown. Woodbridge, 1981, 33–60.

—— 'Towards an Iconography of Anglo-Saxon Architecture.' *JWCI* 46 (1983), 1–18.

—— 'Documentary References to Anglo-Saxon Painted Architecture.' In *Early Medieval Wall Painting and Painted Sculpture in England*, ed. S. Cather, D. Park and P. Williamson, BAR Brit. Ser. 216. Oxford, 1990, 1–16.

—— 'Reconstructions of St Augustine's Abbey, Canterbury, in the Anglo-Saxon Period.' In *St Dunstan: His Life, Times and Cult*, ed. Nigel Ramsay, Margaret Sparks and Tim Tatton-Brown. Woodbridge, 1992, 57–73.

Gem, R. D. H., and Pamela Tudor-Craig. 'A Winchester School Wall Painting at Nether Wallop, Hampshire.' *ASE* 9 (1981), 71–110.

Gibson, Margaret, T. A. Heslop and R. Pfaff, eds. *The Eadwine Psalter: Text, Image, and Monastic Culture in Twelfth-Century Canterbury*. London, 1992.

Gittos, Helen. 'Sacred Space in Anglo-Saxon England: Liturgy, Architecture and Place.' Unpublished D.Phil thesis, Oxford University, 2002.
Gneuss, Helmut. 'Dunstan and Hrabanus Maurus: Zur Hs. Bodleian Auctarium F. 4. 32.' *Anglia* 96 (1978), 136–48.
—— *Handlist of Anglo-Saxon Manuscripts: A List of Manuscripts and Manuscript Fragments Written or Owned in England up to 1100*. Tempe, AZ, 2001.
Godden, Malcolm. 'Ælfric's Lives of Saints and the Problem of Miracles.' *Leeds Studies in English* n.s. 16 (1985), 83–100.
—— 'Money, Power and Morality in Late Anglo-Saxon England.' *ASE* 19 (1990), 41–65.
Goscelin. *Goscelin of Saint-Bertin. The Hagiography of the Female Saints of Ely*, ed. and trans. Rosalind C. Love. Oxford, 2004.
Gregory of Tours. *The History of the Franks*, trans Lewis Thorpe. Harmondsworth, 1974.
Gregory the Great. *Homiliae in Hiezechihelem*, ed. M. Adriaen. CCSL 142. Turnhout, 1971.
Grierson, P. 'The Canterbury (St Martin's) Hoard of Frankish and Anglo-Saxon Coin Ornaments.' *British Numismatic Journal* 27 (1952–4), 39–51.
Grierson, P., and Mark Blackburn. *The Early Middle Ages (5th–10th centuries), Medieval European Coinage, with a Catalogue of the Coins in the Fitzwilliam Museum, Cambridge*, 1. Cambridge, 1986.
Günzel, Beate, ed. *Ælfwine's Prayerbook*. London, 1993.
Gutmann, Joseph, ed., *The Temple of Solomon: Archaeological Fact and Medieval Tradition in Christian, Islamic and Jewish Art*. Missoula, MT, 1976.
Hadley, Dawn. 'Equality, Humility and Non-materialism? Christianity and Anglo-Saxon Burial Practices.' *Archaeological Review from Cambridge* 17 (2000), 149–78.
Hahn, Cynthia. '*Peregrinatio et Natio*: The Illustrated Life of Edmund, King and Martyr.' *Gesta* 30.2 (1991), 119–39.
—— *Pictured on the Heart: Narrative Effect in Pictorial Lives of Saints from the Tenth through Thirteenth Centuries*. Berkeley, CA, 2001.
Hall, Thomas N. 'Prophetic Vision in *The Dream of the Rood*.' In *Poetry, Place and Gender: Studies in Medieval Culture in Honor of Helen Damico*, ed. Catherine E. Karkov. Kalamazoo, MI, 2009, 60–74.
Hamburger, Jeffrey. *St John the Divine: The Deified Evangelist in Medieval Art and Theology*. Berkeley, CA, 2002.
Hamerow, Helena. *Mucking*, vol. 2: *The Anglo-Saxon Settlement*. London, 1993.
Haney, Kristine. *The Winchester Psalter: An Iconographic Study*. Leicester, 1986.
Harrison, R. M. *A Temple for Byzantium: The Discovery and Excavation of Anicia Juliana's Palace Church in Istanbul*. London, 1989.
Hawkes, Jane. 'Mary and the Cycle of Resurrection: The Iconography of the Hovingham Panel.' In *The Age of Migrating Ideas*, ed. R. Michael Spearman and John Higgitt. Edinburgh, 1993, 254–60.
—— 'The Wirksworth Slab: An Iconography of *Humilitas*.' *Peritia* 9 (1995), 246–89.
—— 'Symbolic Lives: The Visual Evidence.' In *The Anglo-Saxons from the*

*Migration Period to the Eighth Century: An Ethnographic Perspective*, ed. John Hines. Woodbridge, 1997, 311–38.

—— 'Iuxta Morem Romanorum: Stone and Sculpture in Anglo-Saxon England.' In *Anglo-Saxon Styles*, ed. Catherine E. Karkov and George Hardin Brown. Albany, NY, 2003, 69–99.

Henderson, George, and Isabel Henderson. *The Art of the Picts: Sculpture and Metalwork in Early Medieval Scotland*. New York, 2004.

Henig, Martin. *The Art of Roman Britain*. London, 1995.

—— 'Murum civitatis, et fontem in ea a Romanis mire olim constructum: The Arts of Rome in Carlisle and the Civitatis of the Carvetti and Their Influence.' In *Carlisle and Cumbria: Roman and Medieval Architecture, Art and Archaeology*, ed. Mike McCarthy and David Weston, *JBAA* 27. Leeds, 2004, 11–28.

—— 'Remaining Roman in Britain AD 300–700: The Evidence of Portable Art.' In *Debating Late Antiquity in Britain AD 300–700*, ed. Rob Collins and James Gerrard. BAR Brit. Ser. 365. Oxford, 2004, 13–23.

Henry of Huntingdon. *Historia Anglorum (History of the English People)*, ed. D. Greenway. Oxford, 1996.

Hensen, A. 'Het Egmonder Kruis.' *Het Gildeboek* 8 (1925), 92–7.

Herity, Michael, and Aiden Breen. *The Cathach of Colum Cille: An Introduction*. Dublin, 2002.

Heslop, T. A. 'The Production of *de luxe* Manuscripts and the Patronage of King Cnut and Queen Emma.' *ASE* 19 (1990), 151–95.

—— 'Manuscript Illumination at Worcester *c*. 1055–1065: The Origins of the Pembroke Lectionary and the Caligula Troper.' In *The Cambridge Illuminations: The Conference Papers*, ed. Stella Panayotova. London, 2007, 65–76.

—— 'The Implication of the Utrecht Psalter in English Romanesque Art.' In *Romanesque Art and Thought in the Twelfth Century: Essays in Honor of Walter Cahn*, ed. Colum Hourihane. Princeton, NJ, 2008, 267–89.

Hicks, Carola. *Animals in Early Medieval Art*. Edinburgh, 1993.

Hill, Joyce. 'Rending the Garment and Reading by the Rood: *Regularis Concordia* Rituals for Men and Women.' In *The Liturgy of the Late Anglo-Saxon Church*, ed. Helen Gittos and M. Bradford Bedingfield. Woodbridge, 2005, 53–64.

Hill, Peter. *Whithorn and St Ninian: The Excavation of a Monastic Town 1984–91*. Stroud, 1997.

Hines, John. *The Scandinavian Character of Anglian England in the Pre-Viking Period*. BAR Brit. Ser. 124. Oxford, 1984.

—— 'No Place Like Home? The Anglo-Saxon Social Landscape from Within and Without.' In *Anglo-Saxon England and the Continent*, ed. Hans Sauer and Jo Story. Anglo-Saxon Studies 3.Tempe, AZ, forthcoming.

Hinton, David A. *Gold and Gilt, Pots and Pins: Possessions and People in Medieval Britain*. Oxford, 2005.

—— *The Alfred Jewel and Other Late Anglo-Saxon Metalwork*. Oxford, 2008.

Holcomb, Melanie, ed. *Pen and Parchment: Drawing in the Middle Ages*. New Haven, CT, and London, 2009.

Hollis, Stephanie, and W. R. Barnes. *Writing the Wilton Women: Goscelin's Legend of Edith and the Liber confortatorius*. Turnhout, 2004.
Holly, Michael Ann. *Panofsky and the Foundations of Art History*. Ithaca, NY, 1984.
Hope-Taylor, Brian. *Yeavering: An Anglo-British Centre of Early Northumbria*. London, 1977.
Horden, Peregrine, and Nicholas Purcell, *The Corrupting Sea: A Study of Mediterranean History*. Oxford, 2000.
Howe, Nicholas. *Migration and Mythmaking in Anglo-Saxon England*. New Haven, CT, 1989.
—— 'Anglo-Saxon England and the Postcolonial Void.' In *Postcolonial Approaches to the European Middle Ages: Translating Cultures*, ed. Ananya Jahanara Kabir and Deanne Williams. Cambridge, 2005, 25–47.
—— *Writing the Map of Anglo-Saxon England: Essays in Cultural Geography*. New Haven, CT, 2008.
Hrabanus Maurus. *In honorem Sanctae Crucis*, ed. M. Perrin, CCCM 100–100A. Turnhout, 1997.
Huneycutt, Lois L. *Matilda of Scotland: A Study in Medieval Queenship*. Woodbridge, 2003.
Ingham, Patricia. *Sovereign Fantasies: Arthurian Romance and the Making of Britain*. Philadelphia, PA, 2001.
James, M. R. 'Two Lives of Ethelbert, King and Martyr.' *EHR* 32 (1917), 214–44.
Jenkins, F. 'Preliminary Report on Excavations at the Church of St Pancras, Canterbury.' *Canterbury Archaeology* (1975–6), 4–5.
Jerome. *Commentarium in Matheum*, ed. D. Hurst and M. Adriaen. CCSL 77. Turnhout, 1969.
Jewell, Richard. 'Classicism of Southumbrian Sculpture.' In *Mercia: An Anglo-Saxon Kingdom in Europe*, ed. Michelle P. Brown and Carol A. Farr. Leicester, 2001, 246–82.
John of Worcester. *Florentii Wigorniensis monachi chronicon ex chronicis*, ed. B. Thorpe, 2 vols. London, 1848.
Jolly, Karen L. *Popular Religion in Late Anglo-Saxon England: Elf Charms in Context*. Chapel Hill, NC, 1996.
Jolly, Karen L., Sarah Larratt Keefer and Catherine E. Karkov, eds. *The Sign of the Cross in Anglo-Saxon England*. Morgantown, WV, 2007.
Jones, L. W., ed. *An Introduction to Divine and Human Readings by Cassiodorus Senator*. New York, 1966.
Jones, Lynn. 'Emma's Greek *Scrine*.' In *Early Medieval Studies in Memory of Patrick Wormald*, ed. Stephen Baxter, Catherine E. Karkov, Janet L. Nelson and David Pelteret. Aldershot, 2009, 499–507.
Jones, T., ed. *Brut y Tywysogion of the Chronicle of the Princes, Red Book of Hengest Versim*. Cardiff, 1955.
Kabir, Ananya Jahanara, and Deanne Williams, eds. *Postcolonial Approaches to the European Middle Ages: Translating Cultures*. Cambridge, 2005.
Kantorowicz, Ernst. *The King's Two Bodies: A Study in Medieval Political Theology*. Princeton, NJ, 1997.
Karkov, Catherine E. 'The Decoration of Early Wooden Architecture in Ireland

and Northumbria.' In *Studies in Insular Art and Archaeology*, ed. Catherine E. Karkov and Robert T. Farrell. Oxford, OH, 1991, 27-48.

—— 'Æthelflæd's Exceptional Coins?' *Old English Newsletter* 28.3 (1996), 41.

—— 'Whitby, Jarrow and the Commemoration of Death.' In *Northumbria's Golden Age*, ed. Jane Hawkes and Susan Mills. Stroud, 1999, 126-35.

—— 'The Anglo-Saxon Genesis: Text, Illustration and Audience.' In *The Old English Hexateuch: Aspects and Approaches*, ed. Benjamin C. Withers and Rebecca Barnhouse. Kalamzoo, MI, 2000, 187-223.

—— *Text and Picture in Anglo-Saxon England: Narrative Strategies in the Junius 11 Manuscript*. Cambridge, 2001.

—— 'The Body of St Æthelthryth: Desire, Conversion and Reform in Anglo-Saxon England.' In *The Cross Goes North: Processes of Conversion in Northern Europe AD 300-1300*, ed. Martin Carver. York, 2003, 397-411.

—— 'Judgement and Salvation in the New Minster Liber Vitae.' In *Apocryphal Texts and Traditions in Anglo-Saxon England*, ed. Kathryn Powell and Donald Scragg. Cambridge, 2003, 151-63.

—— 'Naming and Renaming: The Inscription of Gender in Anglo-Saxon England.' In *Theorizing Anglo-Saxon Stone Sculpture*, ed. Catherine E. Karkov and Fred Orton. Morgantown, WV, 2003, 31-64.

—— *The Ruler Portraits of Anglo-Saxon England*. Woodbridge, 2004.

—— 'Writing and Having Written: Word and Image in the Eadwig Gospels.' In *Writing and Texts in Anglo-Saxon England*, ed. Alexander R. Rumble. Woodbridge, 2006, 44-61.

—— 'Evangelist Portraits and Book Production in Late Anglo-Saxon England.' In *Cambridge Illuminations: The Conference Papers*, ed. Stella Panayotova. London, 2007, 55-63.

—— 'The Frontispiece to the New Minster Charter and the King's Two Bodies.' In *Edgar, King of the English 959-975: New Interpretations*, ed. Donald Scragg. Woodbridge, 2008, 224-41.

—— 'Pictured in the Heart: The Ediths at Wilton.' In *Intertexts: Studies in Anglo-Saxon Culture Presented to Paul E. Szarmach*, ed. Virginia Blanton and Helene Scheck. Tempe, AZ, 2008, 273-85.

—— 'Text and Image in the Red Book of Darley.' In *Text and Image: Studies in Anglo-Saxon Literature in Honour of Éamonn Ó Carragáin*, ed. Alistair Minnis and Jane Roberts. Turnhout, 2008, 135-48.

—— 'Emma: Image and Ideology.' In *Early Medieval Studies in Memory of Patrick Wormald*, ed. Stephen Baxter, Catherine E. Karkov, Janet L. Nelson and David Pelteret. Aldershot, 2009, 509-20.

—— 'Calendar Illustration in Anglo-Saxon England: Realities and Fictions of the Anglo-Saxon Landscape.' In *The Landscape of Anglo-Saxon England*, ed. Nicholas Higham. Woodbridge, 2010.

—— *Between Languages/Between Styles: The Afterlife of Images and the Origins of England*, forthcoming.

Karkov, Catherine E., and George Hardin Brown, eds. *Anglo-Saxon Styles*. Albany, NY, 2003.

Karkov, Catherine E., Karen L. Jolly and Sarah Larratt Keefer, eds. *The Place of the Cross in Anglo-Saxon England*. Woodbridge, 2006.

Kartsonis, Anna D. *Anastasis: The Making of an Image*. Princeton, NJ, 1986.
Kaufmann, C. M. *Romanesque Manuscripts 1066–1190*. London, 1975.
Keefer, Sarah Larratt. '"Either/And" as "Style" in Anglo-Saxon Christian Poetry.' In *Anglo-Saxon Styles*, ed. Catherine E. Karkov and George Hardin Brown. Albany, NY, 2003, 179–200.
Keefer, Sarah Larratt, Catherine E. Karkov and Karen L. Jolly, eds. *Cross and Cruciform in the Anglo-Saxon World: Studies to Honor the Memory of Timothy Reuter*. Morgantown, WV, 2010.
Kemble, J. M. 'Additional Observations on the Runic Obelisk at Ruthwell, the Poem of the *Dream of the Holy Rood*, and a Runic Copper Dish Found at Chertsey.' *Archaeologia* 30 (1844), 31–46.
Kempshall, Matthew. 'No Bishop, No King: The Ministerial Ideology of Kingship and Asser's *Res Gestae Aelfredi*.' In *Belief and Culture in the Middle Ages*, ed. Richard Gameson and Henrietta Leyser. Oxford, 2001, 106–27.
Kershaw, Paul. 'Illness, Power and Prayer in Asser's *Life of King Alfred*.' *Early Medieval Europe* 10.2 (2001), 201–24.
Kessler, Herbert L. 'Evil Eye(ing) Romanesque Art as a Shield of Faith.' In *Romanesque Art and Thought in the Twelfth Century*, ed Colum Hourihane. Princeton, NJ, 2008, 107–35.
Keynes, Simon. *The Diplomas of King Æthelred 'The Unready', 978–1016*. Cambridge, 1980.
—— *Anglo-Saxon Manuscripts in Trinity College*. Old English Newsletter Subsidia 18 (1992), 000–00.
—— ed. *The Liber Vitae of the New Minster and Hyde Abbey, Winchester: British Library Stowe 944: Together with Leaves from British Library Cotton Vespasian A. VIII and British Library Cotton Titus D. XXVII*. Copenhagen, 1996.
—— 'King Alfred and the Mercians.' In *Kings, Currency and Alliances*, ed. Mark Blackburn and David N. Dumville. Woodbridge, 1998, 1–45.
—— 'Ely Abbey 672–1109.' In *A History of Ely Cathedral*, ed. P. Meadows and Nigel Ramsay. Woodbridge, 2003, 3–58.
—— 'An Abbot, an Archbishop, and the Viking Raids of 1006–7 and 1009–12.' *ASE* 36 (2007), 151–220.
Keynes, Simon, and Michael Lapidge, eds. *Alfred the Great: Asser's Life of King Alfred and Other Contemporary Sources*. Harmondsworth, 1983.
King, Michael, 'Besette swinlicum: Sources for the Iconography of the Sutton Hoo Shoulder-clasps.' In *The Anglo-Saxons in Their World*, ed. Gale Owen-Crocker (forthcoming).
Kitson, Peter. 'Lapidary Traditions in Anglo-Saxon England I: The Background: The Old English Lapidary.' *ASE* 7 (1978), 9–60.
—— 'Lapidary Traditions in Anglo-Saxon England II: Bede's *Expositio Apocalypseos* and Related Works.' *ASE* 12 (1983), 72–123.
Kitzinger, Ernst. 'Interlace and Icons: Form and Function in Early Insular Art.' In *The Age of Migrating Ideas: Early Medieval Art in Northern Britain and Ireland*, ed. R. Michael Spearman and John Higgitt. Edinburgh, 1993.
Kjølbye-Biddle, Birthe. 'Old Minster, St Swithun's Day 1093.' In *Winchester*

*Cathedral: Nine Hundred Years, 1093–1993*, ed. John Crook. Chichester, 1993, 13–20.

Klingender, F. *Animals in Art and Thought to the End of the Middle Ages*. London, 1971.

Kornbluth, Genevra. *Engraved Gems of the Carolingian Empire*. University Park, PA, 1995.

Krause, Wolfgang, and Herbert Jankuhn. *Die Runeninschriften im älteren Futhark*. Abhandlungen der Akademie der Wissenschaften in Göttingen, Philologisch-Historische Klasse, 3rd ser. 65. Göttingen, 1966.

Lang, James T. 'The Hogback: A Viking Colonial Monument.' In *ASSAH* 3, ed. Sonia Chadwick Hawkes, James Campbell and David Brown. Oxford, 1984, 85–176.

—— *York and Eastern Yorkshire*, CASSS 3. Oxford, 1991.

—— *Northern Yorkshire*, CASSS 6. Oxford, 2001.

Lapidge, Michael, ed. *The Cult of St Swithun*, Winchester Studies 4/2. Oxford, 2003.

—— ed. *Archbishop Theodore*. Cambridge, 1995.

Lapidge, Michael, and James Rosier, trans. *Aldhelm: The Poetic Works*. Cambridge, 1985.

Lapidge, Michael, and Michael Herren, trans. *Aldhelm: The Prose Works*. Cambridge, 1979.

—— eds. *The Life of St Æthelwold*. Oxford, 1981.

Leahy, Kevin, and Roger Bland. *The Staffordshire Hoard*. London, 2009.

Lees, Clare A. *Tradition and Belief: Religious Writing in Late Anglo-Saxon England*. Minneapolis, 1999.

Lees, Clare A., and Gillian R. Overing. 'Before History, Before Difference: Bodies, Metaphor, and the Church in Anglo-Saxon England.' *Yale Journal of Criticism* 11.2 (1998), 315–34.

Lenker, Ursula. *Die Westsächsische Evangelienversion und die Perikopenordnungen in Angelsächsischen England*. Munich, 1997.

Lerer, Seth. *Literacy and Power in Anglo-Saxon Literature*. Lincoln, NE, 1991.

—— 'Old English and Its Afterlife.' In *The Cambridge History of Medieval Literature*, ed. David Wallace. Cambridge, 1999, 7–34.

—— '"On fagne flor": The Postcolonial *Beowulf* and Heorot.' In *Postcolonial Approaches to the European Middle Ages: Translating Cultures*, ed. Ananya Jahanara Kabir and Deanne Williams. Cambridge, 2005, 77–102.

Levinson, Wilhelm. 'The Inscription on the Jarrow Cross.' *Archaeologia Aeliana* 21 (1943), 121–6.

Logeman, H. 'L'inscription anglo-saxonne du reliquaire de la Vraie Croix au trésor de l'église des SS. Michel-et-Gudule à Bruxelles.' *Mémoires couronnés et autres mémoires de l'Academie Royale de Belgique* 45.8 (1891), 1–31.

Lucas, Peter J., ed. *Exodus*. London, 1977.

Lucy, Sam. *The Anglo-Saxon Way of Death*. Stroud, 2000.

Mac Airt, S., and G. Mac Niocaill, eds. *The Annals of Ulster (to AD 1131)*. Dublin, 1983.

McGurk, Patrick, with Jane Rosenthal. 'The Anglo-Saxon Gospel Books of

Judith, Countess of Flanders: Their Text, Make-up and Function.' *ASE* 24 (1995), 251–308.
McGurk, Patrick, *et al.*, eds. *An Eleventh-Century Miscellany: British Library Cotton Tiberius B.V, Part I*. EEMF 21. Copenhagen, 1983.
McKitterick, Rosamond. 'The Diffusion of Insular Culture in Neustria between 650 and 850: The Implications of the Manuscript Evidence.' In *La Neustrie*, ed. H. Atsma and K.-F. Werner. Sigmaringen, 1989, 395–432.
McNamara, Jo Ann, and John E. Halborg, with E. Gordon Whatley, eds. *Sainted Women of the Dark Ages*. Durham, NC, 1992.
Maguire, Henry. *The Icons of their Bodies: Saints and Their Images in Byzantium*. Princeton, NJ, 1996.
Marsden, Richard. 'Job in His Place: The Ezra Miniature in the Codex Amiatinus.' *Scriptorium* 49.1 (1995), 3–15.
Mason, Emma. *Westminster Abbey and Its People, c. 1050–c. 1216*. Woodbridge, 1996.
Mayr-Harting, Henry. *Ottonian Book Illumination: An Historical Survey*, 2 vols. London and New York, 1991.
Meaney, Audrey. 'Alfred, the Patriarch and the White Stone.' *AUMLA: Journal of the Australasian Universities Language and Literature Association* 49 (1978), 65–79.
—— *Anglo-Saxon Amulets and Curing Stones*. BAR Brit. Ser. 96. Oxford, 1981.
Mehan, Uppinder, and David Townsend. '"Nation" and the Gaze of the Other in Eighth-Century Northumbria.' *Comparative Literature* 53.1 (2001), 1–26.
Meyer, Marc A. 'Women and the Tenth-Century English Monastic Reform.' *Revue bénédictine* 87 (1977), 34–61.
Meyvaert, Paul. 'The Date of Bede's *In Ezram* and His Image of Ezra in the Codex Amiatinus.' *Speculum* 80.4 (2005), 1087–1133.
Miller, Sean, ed. *Charters of the New Minster, Winchester*. Anglo-Saxon Charters IX. London, 2001.
Mitchell, John. 'The High Cross and Monastic Strategies in Eighth-Century Northumbria.' In *New Offerings, Ancient Treasures: Studies in Medieval Art for George Henderson*, ed. Paul Binski and William Noel. Stroud, 2001, 88–114.
Montserrat, Dominic. 'Unidentified Human Remains: Mummies and the Erotics of Biography.' In *Changing Bodies, Changing Meanings: Studies on the Human Body in Antiquity*, ed. Dominic Montserrat. London, 1998, 162–9.
Morris, R., ed. *The Blickling Homilies of the Tenth Century*, EETS 58, 63, 73. London, 1980.
Morris, Richard. *Churches in the Landscape*. London, 1989.
Morrish, Jennifer. 'An Examination of Literature and Learning in the Ninth Century.' Unpublished D.Phil dissertation, Oxford University, 1982.
Mortimer, Richard. 'Edward the Confessor: The Man and the Legend.' In *Edward the Confessor: The Man and the Legend*, ed. Richard Mortimer. Woodbridge, 2009, 1–40.
Morton, C., and H. Muntz, eds. *The Carmen de Hastingae Proelio of Guy, Bishop of Amiens*. Oxford, 1972.

Muir, Bernard J. *The Exeter Anthology of Old English Poetry*, 2 vols. Exeter, 1994.
—— ed. *MS. Junius 11: The Origins of English Poetry, a Masterpiece of Anglo-Saxon Art*. Bodleian Library Digital Texts 1. Chicago, 2005.
Museum of London Archaeology Service. *The Prittlewell Prince: The Discovery of a Rich Anglo-Saxon Burial in Essex*. London, 2004.
Mütherich, F. 'Zur Datierung des Aachener ottonischen Evangeliars.' *Aachener Kunstblätter* 32 (1966), 66–9.
Nees, Lawrence. 'Reading Aldred's Colophon for the Lindisfarne Gospels.' *Speculum* 78 (2003), 333–77.
Nelson, Janet L. 'Queens as Jezebels: The Careers of Brunhild and Balthild in Merovingian History.' In *Medieval Women: Essays Presented to Rosalind Hill*, ed. D. Baker. Oxford, 1978, 31–77.
—— '"A King across the Sea": Alfred the Great in a Continental Perspective.' *Transactions of the Royal Historical Society* 5th ser., 36 (1986), 45–68.
—— 'Gendering Courts in the Early Medieval West.' In *Gender in the Early Medieval World East and West, 300–900*, ed. Leslie Brubaker and Julia M. H. Smith. Cambridge, 2004, 185–97.
Neuman de Vegvar, Carol. 'Reading the Franks Casket: Contexts and Audience.' In *Intertexts: Studies in Anglo-Saxon Culture Presented to Paul E. Szarmach*, ed. Virginia Blanton and Helene Scheck, Tempe, AZ, 2008, 141–59.
Niles, John D., and Marijane Osborn, eds. *Beowulf and Lejre*. Tempe, AZ, 2007.
Noble, Thomas F. X. *Images, Iconoclasm, and the Carolingians*. Philadelphia, PA, 2009.
O'Brien O'Keeffe, Katherine. 'Body and Law in Anglo-Saxon England.' *ASE* 27 (1998), 209–232.
——, ed. *The Anglo-Saxon Chronicle. A Collaborative Edition*, vol. 5: MS C. Cambridge, 2001.
Ó Carragáin, Éamonn. 'A Liturgical Interpretation of the Bewcastle Cross.' In *Medieval Literature and Antiquities: Studies in Honour of Basil Cottle*, ed. Myra Stokes and T. L. Burton. Cambridge, 1987, 15–42.
—— *The City of Rome and the World of Bede*. Jarrow Lecture. Jarrow, 1994.
—— *Ritual and the Rood: Liturgical Images and the Old English Poems of the Dream of the Rood Tradition*. London, 2005.
—— 'Who Then Read the Ruthwell Poem in the Eighth Century?' In *Aedificia Nova: Studies in Honor of Rosemary Cramp*, ed. Catherine E. Karkov and Helen Damico. Kalamazoo, MI, 2008, 43–75.
Ohlgren, Thomas H. *Anglo-Saxon Textual Illustration: Photographs of Sixteen Manuscripts with Descriptions and Index*. Kalamazoo, MI, 1992.
Okasha, Elizabeth. *A Hand-list of Anglo-Saxon Non-runic Inscriptions*. Cambridge, 1971.
—— 'Memorial Stones or Grave-Stones?' In *The Christian Tradition in Anglo-Saxon England: Approaches to Current Scholarship and Teaching*, ed. Paul Cavill. Woodbridge, 2004, 841–6.

Ong, Walter. *Orality and Literacy: The Technologizing of the Word.* London and New York, 1982.
Openshaw, Kathleen. 'Weapons in the Daily Battle: Images of the Conquest of Evil in the Early Medieval Psalter.' *Art Bulletin* 75.1 (1993), 17–38.
O'Reilly, Jennifer. 'St John as a Figure of the Contemplative Life: Text and Image in the Art of the Anglo-Saxon Benedictine Reform.' In *St Dunstan: His Life, Times and Cult,* ed. Nigel Ramsay, Margaret Sparks and Tim Tatton-Brown. Woodbridge, 1992, 165–85.
—— 'The Library of Scripture: Views from the Vivarium and Wearmouth-Jarrow.' In *New Offerings, Ancient Treasures: Essays in Medieval Art for George Henderson,* ed. Paul Binski and William G. Noel. Stroud, 2001, 3–39.
—— '"Know Who and What He Is": The Context and Inscriptions of the Durham Gospels Crucifixion Image.' In *Making and Meaning in Insular Art,* ed. Rachel Moss. Dublin, 2007, 300–16.
Orton, Fred, and Ian Wood with Clare A. Lees. *Fragments of History: Rethinking the Ruthwell and Bewcastle Monuments.* Manchester, 2007.
Osborn, Marijane. 'The Lid as Conclusion of the Syncretic Theme of the Franks Casket.' In *Old English Runes and their Continental Background,* ed. Alfred Bammesberger, Anglistische Forschungen 217. Heidelberg, 1991, 249–68.
Page, R. I. *An Introduction to English Runes.* London, 1973.
Parkes, Malcolm. *The Scriptorium of Wearmouth-Jarrow.* Jarrow Lecture. Jarrow, 1982.
Parsons, David N. 'Anglo-Saxon Runes in Continental Manuscripts.' In *Runische Schriftkultur in kontinental-skandinavischer und -angelsäsischer Wechselbezeihung,* ed. Klaus Düwel. Berlin, 1994, 195–220.
Pfaff, Richard W. 'Eadui Basan: Scriptorum Princeps?' In *England in the Eleventh Century: Proceedings of the 1990 Harlaxton Symposium,* ed. Carola Hicks. Stamford, 1992, 267–83.
Phillips, E. J. *Corpus signorum imperii romani,* vol. 1, fascicle 1. Oxford, 1977.
Pratt, David. 'The Illnesses of King Alfred the Great.' *ASE* 30 (2002), 39–90.
—— 'Persuasion and Invention at the Court of Alfred the Great.' In *Court Culture in the Early Middle Ages: The Proceedings of the First Alcuin Conference,* ed. Catherine E. Cubitt. Turnhout, 2003, 189–221.
—— *The Political Thought of King Alfred the Great.* Cambridge, 2007.
Prescott, Andrew. *The Benedictional of St Æthelwold: A Masterpiece of Anglo-Saxon Art.* London, 2002.
Pulliam, Heather. *Word and Image in the Book of Kells.* Dublin, 2006.
Raw, Barbara C. 'The *Dream of the Rood* and Its Connections with Early Christian Art.' *MÆ* 39 (1970), 239–56.
—— *Anglo-Saxon Crucifixion Iconography and the Art of the Monastic Revival.* Cambridge, 1990.
—— *Trinity and Incarnation in Anglo-Saxon Art and Thought.* Cambridge, 1997.
*Representations* 106 (2009).
Reynolds, Andrew. *Anglo-Saxon Deviant Burial Customs.* Oxford, 2009.

Reynolds, Susan. 'What Do We Mean by "Anglo-Saxon" and "Anglo-Saxons"?' *Journal of British Studies* 24 (1985), 395–414.
Riegl, Alois. *The Late Roman Art Industry*, trans. R. Winkes. Rome, 1985.
—— *Problems of Style Foundations for a History of Ornament*, trans. E. Kain. Princeton, NJ, 1992.
—— *Historical Grammar of the Visual Arts*, trans. Jacqueline E. Jung. New York, 2004.
Roach-Smith, C. 'Merovingian Coins, etc. Discovered at St Martin's, near Canterbury.' *Numismatic Chronicle* 7 (1845), 187–91.
Roberts, Jane. 'Aldred Signs Off from Glossing the Lindisfarne Gospels.' In *Writing and Texts in Anglo-Saxon England*, ed. Alexander R. Rumble. Woodbridge, 2006, 28–43.
Rodwell, Warwick. 'New Glimpses of Edward the Confessor's Abbey at Westminster.' In *Edward the Confessor: The Man and the Legend*, ed. Richard Mortimer. Woodbridge, 2009, 151–67.
Rodwell, Warwick, Jane Hawkes, Emily Howe and Rosemary Cramp. 'The Lichfield Angel: A Spectacular Anglo-Saxon Painted Sculpture.' *Antiquaries Journal* 88 (2008), 48–108.
Rollason, David, and Lynda Rollason, eds. *The Durham Liber Vitae, London, British Library, MS Cotton Domitian A.VII*, vol. 1. London, 2007.
Rosenthal, Jane. 'The Unique Architectural Settings of the Arenberg Evangelists.' In *Studien zur Mittelalterliche Kunst 800–1250: Festschrift für Florentine Mütherich zum 70 Geburtstag*, ed. Katharina Bierbrauer et al. Munich, 1985, 145–56.
—— 'An Unprecedented Image of Love and Devotion: The Crucifixion in Judith of Flanders's Gospel Book.' In *Tributes to Lucy Freeman Sandler*, ed. K.-A. Smith and C. Krinsky. Turnhout and London, 2008, 21–36.
Rosenthal, Jane, with Patrick McGurk. 'Author, Symbol and Word: The Inspired Evangelists in Judith of Flanders's Anglo-Saxon Gospel Books.' In *Tributes to Jonathan J. G. Alexander*, ed. Susan l'Engle and Gerald B. Guest. Turnhout and London, 2006, 185–202.
Rumble, Alexander R. *Property and Piety in Early Medieval Winchester: Documents Relating to the Topography of the Anglo-Saxon and Norman City and Its Minsters*. Winchester Studies 4.iii. Oxford, 2002.
Rydén, Thomas. *Det anglosaxiska köpenhamnsevangeliariet, Det Kongelige Bibliotek Gl. Kongl. Saml. 10 2o*. Lund, 2001.
Said, Edward. *Reflections on Exile and Other Literary and Cultural Essays*. London, 2000.
Salin, Bernhard. *Die altgermanische Thierornamentik*. Stockholm, 1904.
Schapiro, Meyer. 'The Image of the Disappearing Christ: The Ascension in English Art around the Year 1000.' In his *Late Antique, Early Christian and Medieval Art: Selected Papers*. New York, 1979, 267–88. (Originally published in *Gazette des Beaux-Arts* ser. 6 (March 1943), 135–52.)
—— *Theory and Philosophy of Art: Style, Artist, and Society*. New York, 1994.
Scharer, Anton. *Herrschaft und Repräsentation: Studien zur Hofkultur König Alfreds des grossen*. Miteilungen des Instituts für Österreichische Geschichtsforschung Ergänzungsband 36. Munich, 2000.

Schulze-Dörlamm, M. *Die Kaiserkrone Konrads II: eine archäologische Untersuchung zu Alter und Herkunft der Reichskrone*. Sigmaringen, 1991.
Scull, Christopher. 'Post-Roman Phase 1 at Yeavering: A Reconstruction.' *Medieval Archaeology* 35 (1991), 51–63.
Sharp, Sheila. 'Æthelberht, King and Martyr: The Development of a Legend.' In *Æthelbald and Offa: Two Eighth-Century Kings of Mercia*, ed. David Hill and Margaret Worthington, BAR Brit. Ser. 383. Oxford, 2005, 59–63.
Speake, George. *Anglo-Saxon Animal Art and its Germanic Background*. Oxford, 1980.
Stafford, Pauline. 'Political Women in Mercia: Eighth to Early Tenth Century.' In *Mercia: An Anglo-Saxon Kingdom in Europe*, ed. Michelle P. Brown and Carol A. Farr. Leicester, 2001, 35–49.
Stephen. *The Life of Wilfrid by Eddius Stephanus*, ed. Bertram Colgrave. Cambridge, 1927.
Stevens, William O. 'The Cross in the Life and Literature of the Anglo-Saxons.' In *The Anglo-Saxon Cross*, ed. Thomas D. Hill and Robert T. Farrell. Hamden, CT, 1977, 1–112.
Stevenson, J., ed. *Chronicon Monasterii Abingdon*, vol. 1 of *Rerum Britannicarum Mediiævi Scriptores or Chronicles and Memorials of Great Britain and Ireland*. London, 1858.
Stevenson, W. H., ed. *Asser's Life of King Alfred*. Oxford, 1904.
Stewart, Susan. *On Longing: Narratives of the Miniature, the Gigantic, the Souvenir, the Collection*. Baltimore, MD, 1984.
Stirnemann, Patricia. 'Where Can We Go from Here? The Study of French Twelfth-Century Manuscripts.' In *Romanesque Art and Thought in the Twelfth Century: Essays in Honor of Walter Cahn*, ed. Colum Hourihane. Princeton, NJ, 2008, 82–94.
Stocker, David. 'Rubbish Recycled: A Study of the Re-use of Stone in Lincolnshire.' In *Stone Quarrying and Building in England AD 43–1525*, ed. David Parsons. London, 1990, 83–101.
—— 'Irregularities in the Distribution of Stone Monuments.' In *Cultures in Contact: Scandinavian Settlement in England in the Ninth and Tenth Centuries*, ed. Dawn M. Hadley and Julian D. Richards. Turnhout, 2000, 179–212.
Stokes, W., ed. *Memorials of Saint Dunstan, Archbishop of Canterbury*. London, 1874, 20–21.
Story, Joanna. *Carolingian Connections: Anglo-Saxon England and Carolingian France, c. 750–870*. Aldershot, 2003.
Stroud, Daphne. 'The Provenance of the Shaftesbury Psalter.' *Library*, 6 ser. 1 (1979), 225–35.
Swan, Mary, and Elaine M. Treharne, eds. *Rewriting Old English in the Twelfth Century* (Cambridge, 2000).
Swanton, Michael J. 'Bishop Acca and the Cross at Hexham.' *Archaeologia Aeliana*, ser. 4, 48 (1970), 157–68.
—— ed. *The Dream of the Rood*, rev. edn. Exeter, 1987.
Sweet, H., ed. *King Alfred's West Saxon Version of Gregory the Great's Pastoral Care*. EETS o.s. 45, 50. London, 1871–72.

Symeon of Durham. *Libellus de Exordio atque Procursu istius hoc est Dunhlmensis Ecclesie*, ed. and trans. David Rollason. Oxford, 2000.
—— *Symeonis Dunelmensis Opera et Collectanea*, ed. I. Hodgson-Hinde. Surtees Society. London, 1868.
Symons, T., ed. *Regularis Concordia Anglicae Nationis Monachorum Sanctimonialiumque*. New York, 1953.
Taylor, Harold M., and Joan Taylor. *Anglo-Saxon Architecture*, 3 vols. Cambridge, 1965.
Temple, Elżbieta. *Anglo-Saxon Manuscripts 900–1066*. London, 1976.
Thacker, Alan. 'Kings, Saints and Monasteries in Pre-Viking Mercia.' *Midland History* 10 (1985), 1–25.
—— '*Membra Disjecta*: The Division of the Body and the Diffusion of the Cult.' In *Oswald: Northumbrian King to European Saint*, ed. Clare Stancliffe and Eric Cambridge. Stamford, 1995, 97–127.
Townend, Matthew. 'Contextualizing the Knútsdrápur: Skaldic Praise-Poetry at the Court of Cnut.' *ASE* 30 (2001), 145–79.
—— *Language and History in Viking Age England: Linguistic Relations between Speakers of Old Norse and Old English*. Turnhout, 2002.
—— Knútr and the Cult of St Óláfr: Poetry and Patronage in Eleventh-Century Norway and England.' *Viking and Medieval Scandinavia* 1 (2005), 251–79.
Townsend, David. 'Cultural Difference and the Meaning of Latinity in Asser's *Life of King Alfred*.' In *Cultural Diversity in the British Middle Ages: Archipelago, Island, England*, ed. Jeffrey Jerome Cohen. New York, 2008, 57–73.
Treharne, Elaine M. *The Politics of the English, 1000–1200*. Forthcoming.
Trevedi, Harish, and Susan Bassnett, eds. *Post-Colonial Translation: Theory and Practice*. London, 1999.
Turner, D. H. 'The Copenhagen Gospels.' In *The Golden Age of Anglo-Saxon Art 966–1066*, ed. Janet Backhouse, D. H. Turner and Leslie Webster. London, 1984, 68.
Tweddle, Dominic, ed. *The Anglian Helmet from Coppergate*. Archaeology of York: The Small Finds 17/8. London, 1992.
Tweddle, Dominic, Martin Biddle and Birthe Kjølbye-Biddle. *South-East England*, CASSS 4. Oxford, 1995.
van der Horst, Koert, William Noel and W. C. M. Wüstefeld. *The Utrecht Psalter in Medieval Art: Picturing the Psalms of David*.'t Goy, 1996.
Wainwright, F. T. 'Æthelflæd, Lady of the Mercians.' In *Scandinavian England: Collected Papers of F. T. Wainwright*, ed. H. P. R. Finberg. Chichester, 1975, 305–24.
Wall, Valerie. 'Malcolm III and the Foundation of Durham Cathedral.' In *Anglo-Norman Durham*, ed. David Rollason, Margaret Harvey and Michael Prestwich. Woodbridge, 1994, 425–37.
Walsh, M., and D. Ó Cróinín, eds. *Cummian's Letter 'De Controversia Paschali' and the 'De Ratione Computandi.'* Toronto, 1988.
Warburg, Aby. *The Renewal of Pagan Antiquity*, ed. Kurt W. Forster, trans David Britt. Los Angeles, 1999.

Warren, G. F., and H. A. Wilson, eds. *The Benedictional of St Æthelwold, Bishop of Winchester 963–984*. Oxford, 1910.
Webster, Leslie. 'Stylistic Aspects of the Franks Casket.' In *The Vikings*, ed. Robert T. Farrell. Chichester, 1982, 20–32.
—— 'The Brussels Cross.' In *The Golden Age of Anglo-Saxon Art 966–1066*, ed. Janet Backhouse, D. H. Turner and Leslie Webster London, 1984, 90–92.
—— 'The Iconographic Programme of the Franks Casket.' In *Northumbria's Golden Age*, ed. Jane Hawkes and Susan Mills. Stroud, 1999, 227–46.
—— '*Aedificia Nova*: Treasures of Alfred's Reign.' In *Alfred the Great*, ed. Timothy Reuter. Aldershot, 2003, 79–103.
—— 'Encrypted Visions: Style and Sense in the Anglo-Saxon Minor Arts AD 400–900.' In *Anglo-Saxon Styles*, ed. Catherine E. Karkov and George Hardin Brown. Albany, NY, 2003, 11–30.
—— 'Apocalypse Then: Anglo-Saxon Ivory Carving in the Tenth and Eleventh Centuries.' In *Aedificia Nova: Studies in Honor of Rosemary Cramp*, ed. Catherine E. Karkov and Helen Damico, Kalamazoo, MI, 2008, 226–53.
—— *The Franks Casket*. London, 2010.
Webster, Leslie, and Janet Backhouse, eds. *The Making of England: Anglo-Saxon Art and Culture AD 600–900*. London, 1991.
Wehlau, Ruth. 'The Power of Knowledge and the Location of the Reader in *Christ and Satan*.' In *The Poems of MS Junius 11*, ed. R. M. Liuzza. New York, 2002, 287–301. (Originally published in *JEGP* 97 (1998), 1–12.)
Werner, Martin. 'Three Works on the Book of Kells.' *Peritia* 11 (1997), 250–326.
Whitelock, Dorothy. *Anglo-Saxon Wills*. Cambridge, 1930.
—— ed. *Sweet's Anglo-Saxon Reader in Prose and Verse*. Oxford, 1967.
Whitelock, Dorothy, M. Brett and C. N. L. Brooke, eds. *Councils and Synods with Other Documents Relating to the English Church*, vol. 1. Oxford, 1981.
Wicker, Nancy L. *Goldsmiths, Patrons and Women: Typology, Chronology and the Social Life of Medieval Scandinavian Jewelry*. Forthcoming.
William of Malmesbury. *Gesta Pontificum Anglorum*, ed. N. E. S. A. Hamilton. London, 1870.
—— *De Gestis Regum Anglorum*, ed. W. Stubbs, 2 vols. Rolls Series. London, 1887–89.
Williams, Gareth. 'Mercian Coinage and Authority.' In *Mercia: An Anglo-Saxon Kingdom in Europe*, ed. Michelle P. Brown and Carol A. Farr. Leicester, 2001, 211–28.
Williams, Howard. 'Death Warmed Up: The Agency of Bodies and Bones in Early Anglo-Saxon Cremation Rites.' *Journal of Material Culture* 9 (2004), 263–91.
—— *Death and Memory in Early Medieval Britain*. Cambridge, 2006.
Williams ab Ithal, J., ed. *Annales Cambriae*. London, 1860.
Wilmart, A., ed. 'La Légende de Ste Édith en prose et vers par le moine Goscelin.' *Analecta Bollandiana* 56 (1938), 5–101 and 265–307.
Wilson, David. *Anglo-Saxon Paganism*. London, 1992.
Wilson, David M. *Anglo-Saxon Art from the Seventh Century to the Norman Conquest*. London, 1984.

Wilson, David M., and Christopher E. Blunt. 'The Trewhiddle Hoard.' *Archaeologia* 98 (1961), 75–122.

Wilson, David M., and Ole Klindt-Jensen, *Viking Art*. London, 1966.

Winter, Irene J. 'Defining "Aesthetics" for Non-Western Studies: The Case of Ancient Mesopotamia.' In *Art History, Aesthetics, Visual Studies*, ed. Michael Ann Holly and Keith Moxey. Williamsburg, MA, 2002, 3–28.

Withers, Benjamin. 'Interaction of Word and Image in Anglo-Saxon Art, II: Scrolls and Codex in the Frontispiece to the *Regularis Concordia*.' *Old English Newsletter* 31.1 (1997), 38–40.

Wood, Ian N. 'Ripon, Francia and the Franks Casket in the Early Middle Ages.' *Northern History* 26 (1990), 1–19.

—— 'The Franks and Sutton Hoo.' In *People and Places in Northern Europe, 500–1600: Essays in Honour of Peter Hayes Sawyer*, ed. Ian N. Wood and Niels Lund. Woodbridge, 1991.

—— *The Most Holy Abbot Ceolfrid*, Jarrow Lecture. Jarrow, 1995.

—— 'Constantinian Crosses in Northumbria.' In *The Place of the Cross in Anglo-Saxon England*, ed. Catherine E. Karkov, Sarah Larratt Keefer and Karen L. Jolly Woodbridge, 2006, 3–13.

Wormald, Patrick. 'Bede, the *Bretwaldas* and the Origins of the *gens Anglorum*.' In *Ideal and Reality in Frankish and Anglo-Saxon Society. Studies Presented to J. M. Wallace-Hadrill*, ed. Patrick Wormald, Donald Bullough and Roger Collins. Oxford, 1983, 99–129.

—— 'Æthelwold and his Continental Counterparts: Contact, Comparison, Contrast.' In *Bishop Æthelwold: His Career and Influence*, ed. Barbara Yorke. Woodbridge, 1988, 13–42.

—— 'The Making of England.' *History Today* 45.2 (1995), 26–32.

—— *Legal Culture in the Early Medieval West: Law as Text, Image and Experience*. London, 1999.

Wright, Michael, and Kathleen Loncar. 'Vita of Edith.' In *Writing the Wilton Women: Goscelin's Legend of Edith and Liber confortatorius*, ed. Stephanie Hollis *et al*. Turnhout, 2004, 23–67.

—— '*Translatio* of Edith.' In *Writing the Wilton Women: Goscelin's Legend of Edith and Liber confortatorius*, ed. Stephanie Hollis *et al*. Turnhout, 2004., 69–71, 89–90.

Wulfstan, *The Homilies of Wulfstan*, ed. Dorothy Bethurum. Oxford, 1957.

Yorke, Barbara. 'Alfredism: The Use and Abuse of King Alfred's Reputation in Later Centuries.' In *Alfred the Great*, ed. Timothy Reuter. Aldershot, 2003, 361–80.

—— 'The "Old North" from the Saxon South in Nineteenth-Century Britain.' In *Anglo-Saxons and the North: Essays Reflecting the Theme of the Tenth Meeting of the International Society of Anglo-Saxonists in Helsinki, August 2001*, ed. Matti Kilpio, Leena Kahlas-Tarkka, Jane Roberts and Olga Timofeeva. Tempe, AZ, 2009, 131–49.

Young, K. *The Drama of the Medieval Church*. 2 vols. Oxford, 1933.

Youngs, Susan, ed. '*The Work of Angels*': *Masterpieces of Celtic Metalwork, 6th–9th Centuries* AD. London, 1989.

# INDEX

Aachen 47, 112
Abbo of Fleury 198
   *Passio Sancti Edmundi* 285
Abou-El-Haj, Barbara 285
Abraham 199
Acca's Cross 65-6
Adam 133, 156, 236, 237, 240, 242, 245, 246
Adoration of the Magi 148, 270
Æbbe the Younger, saint 249
Ælfflæd, abbess of Whitby 90, 147
Ælfgar, ealdorman of Mercia 193
Ælfgifu, first wife of Æthelred II 271
Ælfgifu of Northampton 264, 271
Ælfhelm, ealdorman of Northampton 264
Ælfred, ealdorman of Surry 179, 188
Ælfric of Eynsham 161, 171-4, 221, 263
   Homily for the Invention of the True Cross 160
   Sermon for the Assumption 198
Ælfthryth, queen of the English 109, 234
Ælfweard of Wessex 115
Ælfwine, dean of New Minster, Winchester 133
Ælfwyn of Mercia 129
Ælle, king of Deira 101
*æstels* 213-18
Æthelbald, king of Mercia 102-3
Æthelberht, king of Kent 15, 16, 17, 20, 101
Æthelberht of East Anglia 106, 107
Æthelburh, queen of Northumbria 101, 134
Æthelflæd, lady of the Mercians 127-9
Æthelred, ealdorman of Mercia 128
Æthelred II, king 116, 249, 263-4, 267, 269, 271
Æthelstan, king 128, 164, 273, 277
Æthelswith, queen of Mercia, ring of 125-6, 250

Æthelthryth, queen and saint 58, 89, 99, 129, 220, 221, 223-8
Æthelweard of Wessex 115
Æthelwold, bishop of Winchester 46 n11, 88-9, 99, 109-12, 221-8
Æthelwold, chronicler 161
Æthelwulf, king of Wessex, ring of 125-6, 250
Aedelwald, bishop of Lichfield 193
Aelfgiva, saint 131
Afghanistan 250
Africa 250
Agatho, pope 66
Agnus Dei 71, 87, 125, 126, 139, 140, 143, 160, 165, 261-2, 263-4
   chant 140, 165
Aidan, bishop of Lindisfarne 43, 44, 281
Alcuin of York 197, 251
Aldfrith, king of Northumbria 67
Aldhelm 228-31
   *De virginitate* 228-31
   Riddles 152
Aldred, priest and glossator 9, 33-6, 38, 21, 175, 178, 203 n38
Alexandria 291
Alfred, ætheling 264, 270
Alfred, king 14, 109, 113, 114, 131, 134, 156, 159 n 52, 179, 212-18, 220, 249, 277, 280
   coinage of 107-8
   Jewel 130, 161, 213-18
   translation of the *Regula Pastoralis* 108, 214
Alhambra 72
Al-Mansur, Abbasid caliph 105
altar/processional crosses 98, 102, 158-65, 265
Amesbury 131, 234
amulets 197, 263
Angles 5, 11, 14, 283, 285

Anglo-Norman England 1, 9, 248, 261, 271–89
Anglo-Saxon Chronicle (see also Mercian Register) 156, 159 n52
Anglo-Scandinavian England 1, 3, 9, 157, 248–69, 285
Anicia Juliana, princess 46
animal ornament 5, 11, 12, 23, 25, 27, 38, 48, 49, 98, 153, 154, 155, 156, 157, 181–2, 189, 219, 255, 256, 258
  Style 1 23
  Style II 23–4
Anna, king of East Anglia 223
Annunciation 79, 80–2, 139, 140, 145, 199
Annunciation to the shepherds 199
Anthony, saint 139, 140
Antioch 291
Apocalypse 47, 261
apostles 29, 47, 92, 190, 231
Arabic 105–6
architecture 7, 13, 14–20, 43–61, 88–9, 112–13, 115–22, 221–3
Arius, heretic 208
Arles 27
Armagh 289
Arnulf Ciborium 88
Assandun, battle of 264
Asser, monk, bishop of Sherborne 131
  Life of Alfred 159 n52
Athelney 214
Augustine, archbishop of Canterbury, saint 15, 16, 17, 18, 19, 20, 179, 185, 202
Augustine of Hippo, saint 78
  Confessions 77–8
Autun, St Lazare 83
Auzon, France 147

Babylon 290
Bailey, Richard N. 63, 83, 101, 253, 254, 256, 262
Baldhild, queen of Neustria and Burgundy 123
  relics of 124
  seal ring 123–4
  Vita Sanctae Balthildis 123
Bamburgh Castle 43, 44, 67, 96
baptism 20, 85, 100, 104, 143, 257, 261
baptismal fonts 85
Barking Abbey 90, 93, 228–31, 234
Barthes, Roland 42
Bath 109
Bathsheba 216
Bayeux Tapestry 13, 134, 271

Beaduhild, daughter of King Nithhad 148
Bede 17, 20, 44, 45, 53, 66, 67, 68, 76, 79, 82, 91, 100, 103, 139, 150, 213, 216, 227, 247–8, 249, 278, 280
  De Templo 55
  Expositio Apocalypseos 32
  Historia Abbatum 52
  Historia Ecclesiastica 96, 185, 212, 223, 224, 227–8, 278, 280
  Letter to Ecgberht 69
  The Reckoning of Time 73–4
Bede's World, Jarrow 52
Belting, Hans 7, 8, 9, 78, 220
Benedict, saint 49, 110, 113, 169, 171, 206, 207
Benedict Biscop, abbot of Wearmouth 8, 44–5, 46, 48, 52, 58, 61
Benedictine reform 83, 84, 85, 88–9, 109–15, 116, 169, 170, 213, 221, 231, 233–4, 235, 267
Benedictine Rule 169, 206, 207
Benedictus 140
Benno of Trier 132
Berhtwald, archbishop of Canterbury 67
Bernward Cross 161
Bertha, queen of Kent 15, 17, 18, 101, 134, 273
bestiary 85
Bewastle, Cumbria 43, 69
Bewcastle Cross 13, 69–79, 86, 92, 94, 95, 162, 258
Bhabha, Homi K. 4
Bible, Old Testament
  Exodus 4, 39, 135, 176, 276, 290
  Genesis 135
  Isaiah 11 173
  Numbers 102
  Psalm 1 191, 197
  Psalm 2 190
  Psalm 7 173, 174
  Psalm 26 185
  Psalm 44 169
  Psalm 51 191
  Psalm 52 185
  Psalm 67 102, 190
  Psalm 90 182
  Psalm 104 98
  Psalm 109 130–1
  Psalm 151 131
New Testament
  2 Timothy 173
  Acts of the Apostles 176
  John 202
  John 1 165, 263

John 19 197
John 21 197
Luke 10 206
Matthew 189, 202
Revelation 261
Revelation 1 173
Revelation 4 262
Revelation 5 165, 262
Revelation 17 173
Revelation 19 173
Revelation 21 263
Bicester brooch 264
Biddle, Martin 112
Billfrith, anchorite of Lindisfarne 36, 175
Birdoswald 75
Bischofshofn, Austria 66
Blair, John 61, 259
Blickling Homilies 32, 173, 235
Blurton, Heather 281, 283
boars 23, 24, 25, 26
book covers 38, 98, 102, 107, 179
book pointers (see æstels)
Borre Style 4, 256, 257
Bowleaze Cove Jewel 214 n57, 218
bracteates 27
Bradford-on-Avon 83
Brandon 97–9
Breamore, St Mary's 83, 135
Bredehoft, Thomas 137, 153
Breedon-on-the-Hill 62, 80–1, 82, 83, 84
Brioude, St Julian the Martyr 147
Bristol Harrowing of Hell 245
Britain (*Breotenrice*) 26, 101, 145, 244, 283, 289
British Empire 213
Brompton hogbacks 253–4, 255, 258, 259, 260
Brown, Michelle 36, 39, 41, 80, 193
Brussels Cross 158–65, 168, 205
Burchard, son of ealdorman Ælfgar of Mercia 193
Burgred, king of Mercia 125
burial (see also cemeteries) 17, 20, 21, 26, 90–5, 99, 101
Bury St Edmunds 189, 285
Byrhtnoth, abbot of Ely 89, 225, 228
Byzantium 7, 18, 66, 105, 106, 142, 246, 266, 271

Cædmon, poet 96
calendars 97, 131, 132, 176, 189 n19, 290
Cambridge 18
Canon Tables 199, 202, 208, 209–12
Canterbury 14–19, 43, 53 n33, 99, 101, 126, 202, 235, 290
Christ Church 17 n13, 38 n81, 109, 113–14, 175, 178, 179, 187, 188, 202, 203, 205, 206, 220, 231, 236
Church of the Four Crowned Martyrs 18
St Augustine's abbey 17, 185, 228
St Martins 15–16, 17, 18
St Mary 18
St Pancras 18
SS Peter and Paul 17–18, 45
St Saviour 17
Canticle of Habbakuk 49 n20
*carmina figurata* 187
Carolingian art 2, 7, 18, 47, 104, 125, 186, 203, 215, 250
Cassiodorus 39, 208, 289
*Institutiones* 207–8
catacombs 59–61
Celtic Britain 2, 22, 26
cemeteries (see also burial) 21, 26, 51, 58, 90, 97, 101, 113, 224
Cenwalh, king of Wessex 114
Ceolfrid, abbot of Jarrow 39, 52, 58
*Vita Ceolfridi* 52
Ceolwulf, king of Mercia 108
Ceolwulf, king of Northumbria 96
Chad, saint 79, 81–2, 85, 254
Chaldea 290
Charlemagne 104, 125
Court school of 125
Charles the Bald, emperor 125
charters 7, 69, 126, 131, 158, 174, 243
Ismere charter 103
New Minster Charter (see manuscripts, London, BL, Cotton Vespasian A.viii)
S 22 205
S 365 115
S 914 205
S 950 205
S 985 205
S 1043 159 n52
S 1443 115
Chelles 124
Cheshire 252
Chester 109, 128–9
Chester-le-Street 33, 164, 278
Chlothar II, king of Neustria and Burgundy 27
Christ 31, 37 n78, 41, 48, 71, 78, 79, 83, 84, 87, 92, 103, 112, 114, 116, 117, 124, 133, 140–3, 150, 155, 156, 157, 168–9, 175, 188, 190, 196, 202, 203, 215–17, 233, 245, 254, 263, 265
Ascension of 86, 190, 234–5, 242
Baptism of 86
Crucifixion 27, 29, 32 n64, 72, 81,

83, 86–7, 89, 103, 138, 139 n8, 143, 144, 145, 160, 163, 164, 165, 166–8, 177, 186, 187, 196–8, 202, 255, 256–8, 261
  Entry into Jerusalem 86
  flanked by beasts 12, 49 n20
  flight into/out of Egypt 139, 140
  Harrowing of Hell 170 n80, 237, 245–6
  healing the man born blind 139, 143
  in Majesty 86, 172, 186, 199
  Logos 42, 84, 174, 191, 202, 208
  Nativity 85, 199, 202, 233
  over the beasts 95, 132, 139, 143
  Passion 209
  Resurrection 153
  Temptation of 237, 242–3
Cicero, *Aratea* 198
Cividale 63
Clonmacnoise, Ireland 50
clothworking 97
Clovis II, king of the Franks 123
Cnut, king 3, 116, 117, 118, 122, 127, 130, 164, 243, 248, 249, 264–7, 269, 270, 271, 284, 287
Cocidius 75
Codex Grandior 39, 52
coins 16, 26, 27, 28, 102, 104–8, 109, 118, 124, 126–9, 250, 262–4
Coldingham 249, 278
Columba, saint 181
Columban church 43, 287
Conrad II, emperor 264
Constantine, emperor 12, 16, 58, 66, 107, 128, 155, 187
Constantinople 16, 80, 187, 289
  St Polyeuktos 46
Cook, A. S. 161
Coppergate helmet 153–6, 157
Corbie 123
Corbridge 61, 62, 63, 103
Cornwall 5
courts 16, 44, 86, 99–122
Corvey 112
craft-working 97
Cramp, Rosemary 54, 85
cremation 90–1
Crook, John 60
Cross of Gisela 162
cross of Justin II 142
crowns 118, 124, 231, 233, 234, 265, 266, 271
Crucifixion (see Christ, Crucifixion)
crypts 59–61
crystal 214, 215–16, 217, 218
Cummian 182

Curbior 124
curses 153, 157, 158
Cuthbert, saint 37 n78, 67, 90, 91, 155, 275, 276, 277–81, 285
  coffin of 8, 84, 90, 91–2, 155, 281
  community 4, 33, 36, 42, 179, 262, 276, 278
  gospels 53
  Lives of 278–81
  pectoral cross 163
  stole 126
Cynefrith, doctor 224
Cynethryth, queen of Mercia 126–7
Cynewulf, poet 235

D'Ardenne, John 161, 162
Damascus, Great Mosque 66
Daniel in the lions' den 12
David, Old Testament king 105 n22, 185, 190, 191, 198, 199, 216, 245
Davis, Kathleen 2, 76
Deerhurst 85
Denis, saint 132
Derby 128
Derrida, Jacques 10
Desborough necklace 98–9
Deshman, Robert 113, 233, 234
diadems 27, 103, 105, 107, 109, 124, 127, 206, 238, 267
Dickins, Bruce 161, 162
Dodwell, C. R. 6, 7, 8
Doubting of Thomas 238
dove of the Holy Spirit 186, 191, 262, 263
Drahmal, maker of the Brussels Cross 160, 161, 205
drawing 88, 109–114, 168–74, 189–93, 196–8, 202, 206, 229–31, 236–43, 245–6, 281
Dudo of Saint-Quentin, *De moribus et acti primorum Normanniae Ducem* 269
Dumouriez, Charles François 159
Dunstan, archbishop of Canterbury, saint 109–11, 117, 168–71, 173
  *Vita sancti Dunstani* 171
Durham 92, 262, 276, 278, 281–3, 285
  Cathedral 261, 275, 276, 280, 281–3
  cross-heads 261–3

Eadbald, king of Kent 18 n19
Eadbert, bishop of Lindisfarne 91
Eadburh, abbess of Minster-in-Thanet 187
Eadfrið, bishop of Lindisfarne 36, 175
Eadric Streona 161

Eadwig Basan, scribe 114, 178, 202, 205–9, 212
Eadwine, scribe 175–8, 191, 193, 202
Ealhswith, queen of Wessex 108, 114, 115, 128 n108, 213
Eaton, Tim 17
Ecclesia 143, 186, 256, 257
Ecgberht, bishop of York 69
Ecgberht, king of Wessex 108
Ecgfrith, king of Northumbria 44, 223
Edgar, king 109–14, 117, 129, 159 n52, 221, 234, 265, 270
Edith Godwineson 118–22, 131, 134, 147, 271, 273
Edith of Wilton 99, 129, 131, 132, 147, 273
Edith-Matilda, queen of England 273, 276
Edmund, king and martyr 285, 287
Edmund king of Wessex 115
Edward the Confessor, king 96, 117–22, 131, 134, 159 n52, 264, 269, 270, 271
  *Vita Edwardi* 117–21, 122, 134, 271
Edward the Elder, king 109, 114, 115, 126, 127–9
Edward the Exile 271, 273
Edward the Martyr, king 131, 234
Edwin, king of Northumbria 100–1, 104
Egeria, pilgrim 160 n53
Egil, Germanic hero 148, 149
Elias, patriarch 216
Elizabeth, mother of John the Baptist 139
Ely 89, 164, 223–5, 235 n117
  Ely virgins 89, 225
embroidery (see also Bayeux Tapestry) 124, 126
Emma, queen (Ælfgifu/Emma) 3, 86, 116–17, 118, 122, 127, 134, 234 264–71
  *Enconium Emmae* 118, 122, 267–71
enamel 23, 36, 86–7, 164, 216, 217
Enoch, Old Testament prophet 237
Eosterwine, abbot of Wearmouth 46 n12
Erhard, saint 88
Essen 164
Eðilwald, bishop of Lindisfarne 36, 175
Eugenius of Toledo, *De bono pacis* 170
Eusebius 58
Eutyches, *Ars de verbo* 169
evangelists 36, 66 n71, 87, 92, 116, 138, 160, 174, 175, 262
evangelist portraits 9, 36–41, 174, 178, 191, 193–205, 208, 209, 212, 272, 273
Eve 133, 236, 237, 240, 242, 243, 246
Exeter Book 152, 219

exile 3, 4, 13, 16, 44, 52, 150, 151, 264, 276
Ezra, Old Testament scribe 38, 39, 41

fall of the rebel angels 4, 239–40, 243, 244
Fanum Cocidii 69, 75–6
Farne Island 43, 91
filigree 24, 27, 87
Fleury 199
Flixborough 97
Foys, Martin 290
Fragmentary Annals of Ireland 128
Franks Casket 25, 137, 146–53, 165, 167, 218
French Revolution 147
Freud, Sigmund 4
Frithestan, bishop of Winchester 126
Fuller brooch 250
futhorc 98

Gabriel, angel 82, 139
gallows 140, 152
Gameson, Richard 113, 135, 162, 173, 191, 202, 206, 273
Gannon, Anna 127
garnets 23, 24, 25, 26, 27, 29, 32, 98, 99, 163
Glastonbury 115, 159 n52
  pyramids 103
Godgyða, nun 131
Godwine, earl 131
Godwine seal 130–1
gold glasses 124
Golgotha 66
Goscelin of Saint-Bertin 18, 130
  *Life of Edith of Wilton* 130, 132
Gosforth Cross 255–8, 259, 260, 261
  Saint' Tomb 254
  Warrior's Tomb 254
Gotland stones 252, 256
grave markers 49, 57, 71, 93, 103, 259
Gregory of Tours 15
Gregory the Great, pope 16, 20, 52, 101, 134, 150, 185, 217, 247, 287, 289
  *Dialogues* 286, 287
  *Homilies on Ezekiel* 198, 215–16
  *Moralia in Job* 53
  *Regula Pastoralis* 217
Gunnhild, daughter of Cnut 264
Gunnor of Normandy 269
Guthlac, saint 103, 104
Gytha, wife of Earl Godwine 131

Hackness 44, 68, 79, 93–5
Hadrian's Wall 61, 69, 75, 76

halls/houses 100, 254
Halton Moor hoard 250-2
hand of God 84, 186, 203, 206, 207, 208, 231, 233, 234, 264
Haney, Kristine 173
Harthacnut, king 122, 269
Hartlepool 50, 57, 93
Hatfield Chase, battle of 101
Heavenfield 150, 285
  battle of 58, 61, 66, 67, 68
Hedda stone 79, 254
Hegel, Georg Wilhelm Friedrich 223
Heimdallr 257
Helena, empress 16, 160, 273, 277
hell 103, 104, 170, 240, 242, 243, 256, 257, 261
helmets 101, 153-6
Henry I, king of England 273
Henry III, emperor 264
Heraclius, emperor 27, 29
Hermann, archdeacon of Bury St Edmunds 285
Heslop, T. A. 178, 198
Hexham 3, 57, 58-68, 69, 98, 101, 103, 104
Hild, abbess of Whitby 99
Hildelith, abbess of Barking 90, 228-31
hill-forts 100
Hincmar of Reims 159 n52
Hinton, David 98, 104, 130, 158
historiated initials 183, 185-6
hogbacks 253-4, 258
Hovingham 259
  slab 81
Howe, Nicholas 2, 179, 276, 283, 290
Hrabanus Maurus, *De laudibus sanctae crucis* 170, 171
Hungary 273, 276
hybridity 3, 5, 6, 52, 68, 76, 101, 248, 252, 252, 255, 258, 259-60, 269, 278, 281

iconoclasm 7, 65
iconography 8-9, 72, 78, 182
icons 8, 45, 47-8, 79, 142
India 72
Ingham, Patricia 247
Inglesham, St John the Baptist 84-5
interlace 5, 57, 72-9, 94, 156, 254, 258
  knotwork 256, 257
  ring-chain 256, 257, 258
Iona 43
Ireland/Irish 3, 5, 6, 11, 57, 179, 248, 276
Isaac 199
Islamic art 106
Israelites 150

Iurminburg, queen of Northumbria 99
ivory carving 86-7, 106-7, 130-31, 163-4, 218-20

Jacob 199
Jelling style 254
Jerome, saint 39
Jerusalem 66, 149, 150, 160, 289, 290, 291
  Dome of the Rock 66
  Heavenly 66, 71
  Holy Sepulchre 66
jewellery 11-13, 22, 23-30, 32, 96 123-6, 250-1, 263-4
  arm-rings 250
  brooches 26-27, 28, 29, 32, 38, 153, 157-8, 251, 263-4
  buckles 11-13, 14, 21, 23 n40, 220
  girdles 124
  necklaces 26, 27-8, 98-9, 250
  pendants 16, 26, 27, 28-9, 32, 250
  pins 98
  rings 123-26, 250
  strap ends 98
John, of Worcester 161
John, saint 36, 98, 144, 160, 164, 165, 167, 174, 197-8, 202, 203-5, 208, 209
John the Baptist 71, 79, 130, 140, 165
Jonah and the whale 152
Jonathan, Old Testament son of King Saul 185
Jouarre 123
Judith, queen of Wessex 125
Judith of Flanders 134, 213, 271, 273
Jumièges 121, 123, 235
Jupiter column 76
Jutes 5, 14, 283, 285

Kantorowicz, Ernst 112
Kaufmann, C. M. 280
Kemble, J. M. 162
Kempsall, Matthew 215, 217
Kent 17, 18, 27, 45, 58, 108, 186, 273
Keynes, Simon 263
King, Michael 25, 125
Kirkbymoorside 259
Kirkdale, St Gregory's 259-60
Kitzinger, Ernst 72
Kjølbye-Biddle, Birthe 112
knives 161
labours of the month 97
Lang, James 95
Langford 83
language 3, 14, 94, 135, 137-8, 144, 149-50, 176, 213, 240, 242-3, 253-4, 258-60, 271, 282-3
  Latin 14, 33, 68, 145, 150, 269

Old English 5, 14, 33, 68, 144, 145, 150, 161, 259-60
Old Norse 259-60
Lantfred, *Translatio et miracula S. Swithuni* 221
Larling panel 106-7
Last Judgement 81, 83, 84, 85, 165, 173, 174, 237, 243, 261, 266
Lastingham 259
Lauds 140
laws 174, 249 263
lay artists 205, 255
Le Puy-en-Velay, Notre Dame 106
Lejre, Denmark 20
Lerer, Seth 13
Lerins 45
Levison, Wilhelm 58
*Liber Eliensis* 164, 224-5
*Liber Commonei* 169-70
Lichfield angel 79-81, 82, 83, 84, 85, plate 3
Lindisfarne (see also Cuthbert community) 18, 33, 43, 44, 50, 53 n33, 57, 67, 69, 79, 91, 93, 94, 249, 276, 278, 280
literacy 97, 130, 134, 144, 145, 155, 158, 212, 213, 269, 271, 273
Little Billing 85
liturgical drama 85, 235
liturgical processions 43, 52, 102, 263
liturgical vessels 45, 52, 88
Liudhard, bishop 15, 17
Liudhard metalet 16
Logeman, H. 161
Loki 257
London (see also Westminster) 114, 117, 289, 290
   Aldermanbury 117
   St Paul's 117
Longinus, spearbearer 143, 256, 257
Lorraine 132
Lorsch 47
Louis the Pious, king of the Franks 110
Luke, saint 197, 203, 205, 208, 209
Luxeuil 123

Magnificat 140
Mainz 121
Malcolm III (Canmore), king of Scotland 273, 277
manuscripts 11, 29, 33-42, 72, 79, 80, 84, 88-9, 109-17, 125, 131-4, 164, 179-246, 264-91
   Aachen, Cathedral Treasury, Aachen Gospels 112
   Boulogne, Bibliothèque Municipale, MS 11 (Boulogne Gospels) 198-202
   Cambridge, Corpus Christi College, MS 42 (Red Book of Darley) 185-6
   Cambridge, Corpus Christi College MS 286 (St Augustine's Gospels) 202
   Cambridge, Pembroke College MS 302 209-12
   Cambridge, Trinity College, B.15.34 (Homilies of Ælfric) 171-4
   Cambridge, Trinity College, R.17.1 (Eadwine Psalter) 175-8, 185, 190, 191, plate 5
   Cambridge, University Library, MS Ll.I.10 (Book of Cerne) 80, 189 n17, 193-7, 273
   Copenhagen, Royal Library, Gl. Kgl. Sml 10, 2° (Copenhagen Gospels) 38-42, 179
   Dublin, Royal Irish Academy, s.n. (Cathach of St Columba) 102, 181-2, 189
   Dublin, Trinity College Library, MS 58 (Book of Kells) 42 n89, 102
   Dublin, Trinity College Library, MS A.4.5 (57) (Book of Durrow) 189
   Durham, Cathedral Library, MS A.II.17 (Durham Gospels) 166-8, 177
   Durham, Cathedral Library, MS A.IV.19 (Durham Ritual) 171
   Florence, Biblioteca Medicea Laurenziana, Amiatino 1 (Codex Amiatinus) 3, 38-42, 46, 52, 53
   Florence, Biblioteca Medicea Laurenziana Plut. XVII. 20 205
   Hanover, Kestner Museum WMXXIa 36 (Eadwig Gospels) 205, 207, 209, 212, 273
   Lichfield, Cathedral Library, Lichfield Gospels 80
   London, BL, Additional 49598 (Benedictional of Æthelwold) 7, 88-9, 129, 130, 220-8, 231, 233, plates 8-9
   London, BL, Arundel 155 (Arundel or Eadwig Psalter) 113-14, 165 n70, 205, 207-8, 212, plate 7
   London, BL, Cotton Claudius B.iv (Old English Hexateuch) 243
   London, BL, Cotton Domition A.vii (Durham Liber Vitae) 276-7, 281
   London, BL, Cotton Nero D.iv (Lindisfarne Gospels) 3, 5, 9, 13,

29, 30, 33–42, 92, 175, 178, 179, 182, 183, 189, 196, 203 n38, 205, 276
London, BL, Cotton Tiberius A.iii 109–114
London, BL, Cotton Tiberius B.v 288–91
London, BL, Cotton Tiberius C.vi (Tiberius Psalter) 190 n21, 245–6, plate 11
London, BL, Cotton Titus D.xxvii, xxvi (Ælfwine's Prayerbook) 133
London, BL, Cotton Vespasian A.i (Vespasian Psalter) 185, 205
London, BL, Cotton Vespasian A.viii (New Minster Charter) 109, 112, 115 n61, 117, 130, 265
London, BL, Harley 603 (Harley Psalter) 176, 178, 189, 190, 205, 245
London, BL, Harley 2506 198
London, BL, Harley 2904 (Ramsey Psalter) 87, 196, 197–8, 205
London, BL, Harley 2956 (Book of Nunnaminster) 114–5, 273
London, BL, Loan MS 74 (Stonyhurst or Cuthbert Gospels) 53
London, BL, Royal I.E.VII 190 n21
London, BL, Stowe 944 (New Minster Liber Vitae) 117, 122, 129, 213, 264–7, 269, 271, 287, plate 12
London, Lambeth Palace Library, MS 200 (De virginitate) 228–31
Milan, Biblioteca Ambrosiana MS C.5 (Antiphonary of Bangor) 155
Munich, Bavarian State Library, Clm 13601 (Uta Codex) 88
New York, Pierpont Morgan Library, M 736 (Life and Miracles of Edmund) 284–5, 287
New York, Pierpont Morgan Library M 869 (Arenberg Gospels) 202–5
Orléans, Bibliothèque Municipale, MS 175 198
Oxford, Bodleian Library, Auct. F.4.32 (St Dunstan's Classbook) 168–71, 198
Oxford, Bodleian Library, Bodley 577 (De virginitate) 231
Oxford, Bodleian Library, Junius 11 133, 134, 235–43, 287
Oxford, Bodleian Library, Lat. Liturg. F.5 (St Margaret's Gospels) 272–5
Oxford, Bodleian Library, Tanner 3 (Dialogues of Gregory the Great) 286–9

Oxford, Bodleian Library, Tanner 10 (Tanner Bede) 171
Oxford, University College, MS 165 (Life of Cuthbert) 278–81, 285
Paris, BN, lat. 8850 (Gospels of Saint-Medard of Soissons) 125
Paris, BN, n.a. lat. 1203 (Godescalc Evangelistry) 125
Reims, Bibliothèque Municipale, MS 9 191–3
Rouen, Bibliothèque Municipale Y.6 (Sacramentary of Robert of Jumièges) 234–5, plate 10
Rouen, Bibliothèque Municipale Y.7 (Benedictional and Pontifical of Archbishop Robert) 231–3
St Petersburg, National Library, Q.v.I.18 185
Salisbury, Cathedral Library, MS 150 (Shaftesbury Psalter) 131–4, plate 4
Stockholm, Royal Library, MS A.135 (Codex Aureus) 179, 182, 186–9, plate 6
Utrecht, University Library, MS 32 (Utrecht Psalter) 171, 176, 177, 202
Vatican, Biblioteca Apostolica, Reg. Lat. 12 (Bury Psalter) 180, 189–91, 193, 234 n113
York Minster, Chapter Library, Add. 1 (York Gospels) 205
mappamuni 288–91
Margaret, queen of Scotland 134, 213, 271–7
Marinus, pope 159 n52
Mark, saint 197, 203, 205, 208, 209
Marseilles 27
Martha and Mary of Bethany 140
Martin of Tours, saint 15, 16
Marvels of the East (see Wonders of the East)
Mary Magdalene 139, 143, 256
Matilda, abbess of Essen 164
Matilda, countess of Tuscany 271
Matthew, saint 37, 92 196, 197, 199, 203, 205, 208, 209
Maurice Tiberius, emperor 17
McKitterick, Rosamond 173
Mehan, Uppinder 67, 68
Melbury Bubb 85
memory 20, 21, 113, 122
Mercia 58, 80, 102–6, 126–9, 193, 249, 252, 264, 271
Mercian Register 128
Merovingian art 22, 186
Michael, archangel 82, 116

Middleton 259
millefiori glass 23, 24, 25, 26
Milvian Bridge, battle of 58
mimicry 3, 105, 106
Minster Lovell Jewell 214 n57, 217
miracles 67, 79, 90, 213, 222-3, 274-5, 276, 277, 280, 285, 287
missionaries 16
Moissac 49
Monastic reform (see Benedictine reform)
Montserrat, Dominic 225
mosaics 66
Moses 37 n78
Mount Sinai 290
Mucking, Essex 11-13, 14, 23 n40
Murrell Hill tombstone 71

name stones 50, 57, 93, 94
Nether Wallop 83
Newcastle upon Tyne 179
Nicaea, first council of 66
Nicene Creed 65, 66
Nidd, Synod of 67
Nile River 290
Nithhad, king 148
Noah 135, 137, 290
Norman Conquest 5, 11, 280
Normandy 122, 267, 269, 271
Northumbria 39, 44-69, 76, 145, 252
Nunburnholme Cross 9, 287

Ó Carragáin, Éamonn 138
Offa, East Saxon sub-king 117
Offa, king of Mercia 104-6, 108, 126-7
ogham 94
Ohthere, merchant 214 n57
Okasha, Elizabeth 93, 155
*opus signinum* 16
orbs 118
ordination 261
O'Reilly, Jennifer 167
Orientalism 181
Origen 39
origin myths 39, 135, 276, 283, 287
Orm Gamalsuna 259-60
Orosius 290
Orton, Fred 74
Osbert of Clare, *Miraculi Sancti Edmundi Regis et Martyris* 285
Oseberg ship burial 256
Osred, king of Northumbria 67
Oswald, king and saint 44, 58, 66, 67, 68, 91, 155, 281, 285
Oswiu, king of Northumbria 45
Otbert, abbot of Saint-Bertin 199

Oðinn 256, 257
Otto, duke 164
Otto III, emperor 112
Ottonian art 12, 88, 161, 164, 266
Ovid, *Ars Amatoria* 170

paganism 20, 21, 22
Paris 18
 St Denis 123
Paul, saint 231
Paul, saint and hermit 139, 140
Paulinus, archbishop of York 100
pen cases 218-20
Pentney brooches 251
Peter, saint 48, 93, 117, 231, 235, 265, 266
Peterborough 38 n81, 79, 235 n117
*Physiologus* 152
Picts 11, 156
pilgrimage 52, 59, 61, 67, 104, 118, 159 n52
pilgrimage churches 49, 83
Pliny 216
poetry, Old English 7, 13, 148, 152, 235-43, 274
 *Beowulf* 13, 20
 *Christ II* 235
 *Christ and Satan* 236, 237, 238-9, 242-3
 *Daniel* 236, 239
 *The Dream of the Rood* 31-32, 138, 141, 158-9, 162, 168, 187
 *Durham* 281-3, 289
 Exeter Book Riddles 152, 219
 *Exodus* 236, 239
 *Genesis* 133, 236, 238-9
 *Maxims II* 7, 19
 *The Ruin* 7, 19
 Ruthwell Cross poem 138, 140-5, 152, 158-9, 162, 164, 165-78
 Latin 170-1
Poitiers 63
postcolonial theory 2-4
Postwick, 123
Potterne 85
prayer 43, 47, 52, 76, 85, 95, 112, 115, 131, 133, 154-6, 157, 170, 190, 246
Prince of the World 238
Prittlewell 21-2, 26, 28, 102
Publilius Optatianus Porphyrius 187
purses 12, 102

Quoit-brooch style 11, 23 n40

Rædwald, king of East Anglia 20, 21
Ragnarǫk 256-7
rape of the Sabine women 150

Ravenna 18, 66
Raw, Barbara 116, 174
Reculver 19
Red Sea 290
Regensburg 162
*Regularis Concordia* 109–14, 212, 233
Reims, St Remi 193
relics 45, 60, 79, 82, 86, 87, 92, 119, 124, 132, 145, 147, 151, 152, 159, 163, 225, 263, 276, 278, 281, 282
reliquaries 48, 79, 85–8, 92, 99, 107, 119, 145, 147, 158–65, 163, 221–2, 283
Repton, St Wystan 103
Repton Stone 102
riddles 25, 38, 42, 70, 137, 145, 148, 152, 219
Ringerike style 157, 160
Ripon 59
Robert, abbot of Jumièges 122 n83, 235
Roberts, Jane 35, 174
Rochester 19
Romano-Britain 1, 3, 4, 5, 11, 12, 13, 15, 18, 19, 61–5, 68, 69, 75–6, 100, 101, 109, 247, 249, 273, 289
Rome 2, 16, 17, 18, 19, 22, 45, 47, 52, 57, 58, 59, 61, 65, 66, 80, 105, 106, 107, 118, 148, 149, 186, 287, 289, 290, 291
  Old St Peters 45, 60
  S. Maria in Trastevere 142
  S. Pudenziana 66
  St John Lateran (St Saviour's) 17, 66
Romulus and Remus 106–7, 150
Rosenthal, Jane 203
Ross, A. S. C. 161, 162
Rothbury 62
round-barrows 100
Rufinus 58
Rumble, Alexander 115
runes 36, 50, 92, 93–4, 98, 138, 141–2, 144, 148, 149, 150, 151, 152, 158
rune stones 252
Rupertus Cross 66, 163
Russia 250
Ruthwell Cross 13, 25, 80–1, 82, 84, 86, 92, 94, 95, 136–45, 148, 150, 152, 158, 162, 163, 165, 167, 256

S. Juan de Baños 63, 106 n24
St Andrews, Scotland 276
St Ninian's Isle hoard 156
  chapes 153, 156–7
saddles 102
Sæbert, king of Essex 20, 21
Saint-Bertin 269
Samarkand 250
Samuel, Old Testament prophet 185

Sandwich 263
Sarre brooch and necklace 26–8, 29, 32, 38, plate 2
Satan 237–46
Saul, Old Testament king 185
Saxons 5, 11, 14, 283, 285
Scandinavia 3, 22, 27, 164, 252, 256, 258, 263
sceptres 118, 287
Schapiro, Meyer 234–5
Scotland 5, 109, 248, 276, 280
sculpture 43, 48–51, 56–8, 61–6, 68, 79–85, 91–5, 102–4, 116, 137–45, 162, 164, 245, 252–62
seals 118, 123–4, 125, 129–31, 217
Seaxburh, abbess of Ely 224, 225
Sedulius, *Carmen paschale* 202
sermons 243–5
settlements 11, 52, 97–9, 100
Shaftesbury 131, 160 n52
Sherborne 114, 131
shields 102
shrines 79–81, 85, 90, 93, 98, 107, 126, 254, 281
Sight 216, 217
Sigyn, wife of Loki 257
Sitric, king of York 129
Sittingbourne 161
Solomon 230
Snape 21
Spearhavoc, abbot of Abingdon 118 n74
Speyer 121
Spong Hill 90
Staffordshire hoard 11, 26, 99, 101–2, 124 n92, 153
  folded cross 163
stained glass 48, 56
Stanwix 80–1
Statius, *Thebiad* 170
Stephen of Ripon 58, 59, 61
Stewart, Susan 223
stone circles 100
stone masons 15, 52
Stonegrave 259
Strasbourg Cathedral 238 n120
Stroud, Daphne 131, 132
styli 97
Sulcard, *De Constructione Westmonasterii* 118
Sulgrave brooch 263
sundials 73, 74, 76, 77, 84, 259–60
Sussex 58
Sutton Hoo 11, 12, 20–7, 28, 49, 99, 101, 102, 153
  hanging bowls 21–3, 24
  helmet 153

shoulder-clasps 23–27, 29, 125, plate 1
Sutton, Isle of Ely, brooch 153, 157–8, 160
Swein, king 243, 264, 285, 287
Swithun, saint 88–9, 90, 115, 220–3, 227
swords 118, 157, 265, 266, 287
  pommels 101
  scabbard chapes 153, 156–7
Symeon of Durham 65
  *Libellus de Exordio atque Procursu istius hoc est Dunhelmensis* 276, 278, 281

Taprobane 290
Tarsus 290
Temple of Solomon 45–6, 55
Thacker, Alan 67
theatres 100
Theodore, archbishop of Canterbury 45, 290
Thorkell the Tall 263, 264
Thorney 38 n81, 46 n11
thrones 118, 230
Titus, emperor 149
Tondberht, ealdorman of the South Gwyre 223
Tostig, earl 134, 260, 271
Tours 15
Townsend, David 67, 68
translation 3, 33, 177
Trewhiddle hoard 251
  style 189 n17, 251
Trinity 116, 130, 186
True Cross 29, 67, 86, 87, 145, 159–65
Turgot, Life of Margaret of Scotland 273, 275, 276
tweezers 98

uncanny 4, 13, 52, 53, 61
Urnes style 157
Urswick 162
Uttoxeter Casket 86, 87

Vale of York hoard 250, 251
Valsgärde, Sweden 153
veils 265, 267
Vendel, Sweden 153
Vercelli Book 31
Vespers 140
Victoria and Albert Museum, reliquary cross 163, 164
victory figures 80–1
Vienne 45
Vikings (see also Anglo-Scandinavian England, Scandinavia) 5, 11, 33, 117,
128–9, 174, 179, 188, 243, 248–9, 251–4, 263–4, 276, 280, 287
vinescroll 57, 61–6, 68, 72, 98, 138, 142
Virgin Mary 46, 81, 82, 116, 129, 134, 139, 140, 143, 150, 164, 165, 167, 186, 190, 191, 197–8, 202, 231, 234, 235, 265, 266, 267, 269, 270, 271
  and Child 42 n89, 84, 89, 92, 148, 270
  Coronation of 231–4
  Dormition of 232–4
  virginity 89, 270, 271
  visions 142, 145, 237
  Visitation 140, 199
Viðarr 256, 257

Wærferth, bishop of Worcester 214
Wales 5, 14, 109, 248
wall painting 83
Wallingford 130
Wallis, Faith 74
walrus ivory 130–1, 214 n57
Warburg, Aby 80–1
Warminster Jewel 215 n57, 216, 218
Waxenburger, Gaby 147, 149, 151
weapons 101–2, 153
Wearmouth Jarrow 3, 8, 18, 38, 39, 44–5, 50, 53, 61, 69, 79, 104, 185
  Jarrow 45 n5, 49, 52, 53–8, 59, 62–5
  Wearmouth 46–53, 55, 56, 58, 69
Webber, Tessa 178
Webster, Leslie 125, 162, 215
Weland the Smith 148, 149, 150
Welf of Bavaria 271
Wells 85
Werburh, wife of eldorman Ælfred of Surry 179, 188
Wessex 107–8, 114–17, 125–6, 249, 273, 276, 277
Westminster, Abbey 96, 117–22, 159 n52
  palace 117
westworks 88, 112–13, 115–16, 221–2
whalebone 106–7, 137, 147–53
Wherewell 234
Whitby 44, 50 n22, 57, 68, 69, 79, 90, 92, 147
  Life of Gregory 247
  Synod of 43, 50
Widia, Germanic hero 148
Wigstan, saint 103, 104
Wilfrid, bishop of York 45, 58–61, 65, 66, 67, 68, 99, 103, 147, 223
William of Jumièges, Chronicle of 118
William of Malmesbury 59, 61, 159 n52, 234

William of St Calais, bishop of Durham 280
William the Conqueror 280
wills 7, 158
Wilson, David M. 6, 8
Wilton 122, 130, 131, 132, 273
   pendant 28–29
Winchester 83, 84, 96, 109, 112, 114, 197, 221, 235 n117, 236, 247, 265, 289, 290
   New Minster 86, 109, 114, 115–17, 116, 117, 122, 129, 133, 231, 265, 266
   Nunnaminster 114
   Old Minster 88–9, 112–13, 114, 115–16, 221–3
   bishop's palace 116
   royal palace 113, 114
   Queen Emma's house 116–17
Winterbourne Steepleton 83, 84, 85
Wirksworth slab 81
Wisdom of God 216, 217
Wise and Foolish Virgins 238 n120
Witham bowl 23 n40

*Wonders of the East* 290
wondrous races 290
Wood, Ian 45, 55
woodcarving 86, 92
Woodville, Elizabeth 270
Worcester 287
workshops 58, 100, 147, 251, 254–5
Wuffingas 106
Wulfstan of Winchester, *Narratio metrica de S. Swithuno* 221 n85, 222 n86
Wulfstan II, archbishop of York 244, 263
   *Sermo Lupi ad Anglos* 244–5, 249, 263
Wulfthryth, abbess of Wilton 132

Yeavering 19, 96, 99–101, 102, 104
York 129, 153, 249
Yorke, Barbara 213
Yorkshire 252, 259

**Already Published**

*The Art of Anglo-Saxon England*
Catherine E. Karkov

*English Medieval Misericords: The Margins of Meaning*
Paul Hardwick

*English Medieval Shrines*
John Crook

*Thresholds of Medieval Visual Culture: Liminal Spaces*
Edited by Elina Gertsman and Jill Stevenson

*The Marvellous and the Monstrous in the Sculpture
of Twelfth-Century Europe*
Kirk Ambrose

*Early Medieval Stone Monuments: Materiality, Biography, Landscape*
Edited by Howard Williams, Joanne Kirton and Meggen Gondek

*The Royal Abbey of Reading*
Ron Baxter

www.ingramcontent.com/pod-product-compliance
Lightning Source LLC
Chambersburg PA
CBHW071017240526
45469CB00006BD/1956